Lonely Planet Publications
Melbourne | Oakland | London

Becca Blond &
Aaron Anderson

Washington, DC

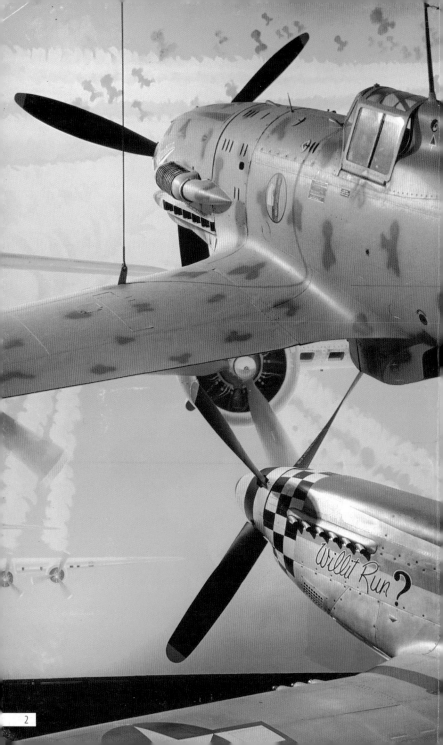

Introducing Washington, DC

'Life, Liberty and the pursuit of a chicken in every pothole…' When it comes to eulogizing the capital of a free world, we think our slogan fits. As powerful as it is dysfunctional, as rich as it is poor, as shabby as it is chic, in a way DC is the American dream. But if there's one lesson the world's toughest superpower learned in the 21st century, it's the American dream doesn't always live up to its promises. Perhaps nowhere is this more obvious than the capital city, with its numerous potholes and lack of chickens to fill them.

DC, like the political parties shaping her, is a city with spilt personalities: one light-hearted, the other darker.

There's the globetrotting, sexy vixen – all feminine marble curves, with a head of grassy green parks, mighty Potomac vistas and inky pools for eyes – laughing with the handsome Senator over Cosmopolitans at the Georgetown bar. The daughter of democracy, the purveyor of liberty and justice, she's an intoxicating heartbreaker heady with power and glitz – be warned you may get so high inhaling her raw energy you'll be empowered to fix the world. In fact, even the most jaded of Washingtonians admit a sense of awe upon seeing the presidential motorcade of black sedans awash in the lights and thunder of police escorts, screaming down Pennsylvania Ave between Capitol Hill and the White House.

But as much as she's a success, DC is also a hard knock. Dig beneath the vixen's shiny marble surface and you'll find a grittier core – boarded up buildings, graffiti filled walls, crack pipes and poor people. In this part of the city, the federal government and its machinery are merely backdrops to life, not the primetime drama. This is the city where people – ordinary and extraordinary – live, work and play.

In DC, minorities are the majority. Sixty percent of them are Black, the highest percentage in the country, and the city thumps to a vibrant African American beat. Despite this diverse population, DC is also one of the most segregated towns in America, with the 39% White population living (and playing) almost exclusively in the smallest and ritziest quadrant, Northwest. Twenty percent of the population falls below the poverty line (and most of this segment is Black) – 8% above the national average.

In a city with the second-highest per capita income in the country, this makes for one pretty messed-up economic disparity.

1 *Washington Monument (p73) viewed from the Tidal Basin promenade* **2** *Vietnam Veterans Memorial (p72)* **3** *African American Civil War Memorial (p113)*

previous pages (left) *World War II fighter planes, National Air & Space Museum (p66)* **(right)** *Street musician near DuPont Circle (p100)*

ndow display, Georgetown
0) **2** *Shake Your Booty*
store (p219), Adams-
gan **3** *Chess players,*
ont Circle (p100)

5

1 *Ben's Chili Bowl (p161), U Street* 2 *Felix (p176), Adams Morgan* 3 *Polly's Café (p17? U Street*

...ndo Del Sol Visual Arts
...re (p101), Dupont Circle
...ki (p189), Adams-Morgan
...adam's Organ (p184),
...ms-Morgan

...owing page *Pandas,*
...onal Zoological Park
...9)

Contents

Published by Lonely Planet Publications Pty Ltd
ABN 36 005 607 983

Australia Head Office, Locked Bag 1, Footscray,
Victoria 3011, ☎ 03 8379 8000, fax 03 8379 8111,
talk2us@lonelyplanet.com.au

USA 150 Linden St, Oakland, CA 94607,
☎ 510 893 8555, toll free 800 275 8555,
fax 510 893 8572, info@lonelyplanet.com

UK 72–82 Rosebery Ave, Clerkenwell, London,
EC1R 4RW, ☎ 020 7841 9000, fax 020 7841 9001,
go@lonelyplanet.co.uk

The Authors

Becca Blond

Becca grew up in Cabin John, MD. She's almost sure she visited every museum and monument in DC before the age of 10 (her mother was a ruthless tour guide). After graduating from Colorado College, she took a job as the city government reporter at the *Manassas Journal Messenger*, and spent much of the year becoming intimately acquainted with DC's excellent nightlife.

Becca returned to Colorado's Rocky Mountains and did a stint reporting for the *Colorado Springs Gazette* and the *Denver Post*, before she began covering the world for Lonely Planet. In the last four years she has authored nearly two-dozen titles, covering everywhere from Latvia to South Africa, Thailand to Tahiti and large chunks of the USA, including the Washington, DC section of *USA on a Shoestring*.

When not on the road, Becca lives in Boulder, CO, with her fiancée Aaron (with whom she co-authored this book) and their bulldog Duke.

BECCA'S TOP DC DAY

It's a gorgeous Saturday in October. Aaron and I are meandering around Georgetown's (p80) shady, cobbled streets. We are heading for M Street, to shop at the stylish boutiques housed in the equally stylish historic brick buildings. After about 45 minutes Aaron insists on lunch. I take him to Sequoia (p150) for an al fresco feast overlooking the Potomac riverfront.

Aaron gets to pick the afternoon activity. The air is crisp and fresh, so he chooses biking. We work off our Maryland crab cake sandwich (a regional specialty) with a bike ride north along the C&O Canal Towpath (p82). With the Potomac on one side and the canal on the other, it really is the perfect autumn ride. We follow the path all the way up to Great Falls National Park (p245), where we pause to watch the kayakers playing in the water. After our excursion, we head into Bethesda for dinner at my all time favorite DC restaurant, the Rio Grande Café (p167). It has the best fajitas ever. Afterwards it's time to hit the town. We go to Adams-Morgan (p103) first for a few Mojitos on the sidewalk at the Rumba Café (p161). Once we've loosened up a bit we head a few doors down to Madam's Organ (p184), for some dancing. Later on, we meet up with friends on U Street (p104) for some serious booty shaking, then end with champagne in a dimly lit velvet-roped lounge off Connecticut Ave in Dupont Circle (p100), late night central for the glam, the gay and the gorgeous.

Aaron Anderson

Born in Memphis, TN, Aaron caught the travel bug following a year backpacking through Europe. After returning to the States, Aaron worked as a professional microbrewer, in Tennessee, New Orleans and finally, Boulder, CO, his current home. This is Aaron's third Lonely Planet gig – he worked on *Western Europe* and *Europe on a Shoestring*.

PHOTOGRAPHER
Dan Herrick

Dan Herrick got his start in photography on a six-month trip through Europe before attending university. Since then he's covered the spectrum of stories, from the Chiapas uprising in Mexico to movie premieres at home in New York City. In Washington, DC he interacted with great people. Climbers at Carderock offered him a hand. An old taxi driver gave an informal tour of Shaw. Jazz musicians shared the lowdown on their favorite clubs and venues. The ethnic food eateries in Adams-Morgan were top notch.

City Life

City Life

WASHINGTON, DC, TODAY

Washington, DC, has always served as the nation's soapbox, but we'd argue it's also the nation's soap opera (just substitute congressmen, the CIA and the Prez, interns, newspaper reporters and TV anchors for actors). The plot in DC changes daily, and like the national deficit there's no limit on what can and does happen.

Chaotic, restless, international, diplomatic, enigmatic, power hungry, eccentric, philanthropic, helpless, poor, ethnic, opinionated, gay – the adjectives describing Washington, DC, and its residents go on and on. But the place (like all good soap opera plotlines) just isn't that easily defined.

Washington, DC, is a city where the egos are big and coolness is determined by how close you are to POTUS (that would be the President of the United States for those not familiar with the lingo). This is probably the only city in the world where Anderson Cooper and the guys from CNN receive the same kind of puppy-dog adulation as the Jolie-Pitts.

DC is a cacophony of sounds, a place where hometown go-go music blaring from the bum's duct-taped boombox on a street corner in shabby chic Adams-Morgan gets mixed with the seductive sizzle of an Argentine tango resonating from a nearby club, and is harmonized with an argument between a Peruvian man and his Irish–Puerto Rican girlfriend in rapid-fire Spanish.

DC is the smell of slow roasting pork, engine exhaust and human sweat on a hot August night on slightly edgy 14th St in the Shaw. It's a bar where a 20–something mixed-race crowd is gathering for drinks and a chat about gentrification and whether or not it's bad or good. It is the struggling single mother in the housing project deep in the heart of Anacostia, worrying about how to pay this month's electricity bill, and whether her son will stay straight and finish high school or join the gang hustling China white on her front stoop.

Washington is also glamorous and fun. She is expensively decorated lounges and exclusive nightclubs in Dupont Circle, where the city's young, hot and gay gather to discuss politics, progress and maybe a little sex over gourmet tapas and French champagne. She is million-dollar brownstone homes in Georgetown, where the city's wheelers and dealers broker power in their masterfully decorated dining rooms, while their couture-clad wives discuss Botox over Chianti across the hall.

Over on Capitol Hill, she serves politics, not olives, with her happy-hour martinis. Home turf of the Hillies (folks who work on Capitol Hill), in this 'hood she is divey bars where staffers exchange business cards and flirtatious gestures. These (often) young and (sometimes) naïve press secretaries and lobbyists, congressional aids, Senate staffers and interns hail from all across America, and bring with them a diverse pool of regional idiosyncrasies. No matter their background, they all seem united by a common dream of doing something big and making *the* difference.

It seems that Washington is always immersed in some scandal or another, and Washingtonians can be gossip addicts – it can be as sexy as power (another problem when it comes to local addictions…) The city also has a bit of a rebellious streak (it did knowingly elect a man charged with possession of crack-cocaine, Marion Barry, back into the mayoral office)

LOWDOWN

Population 582,049

Time zone Eastern Standard Time (GMT minus five hours)

3-star room Around $150

Coffee $3

Essential drink Martini ($10)

Metro fare $1.20 – $3.90

and residents are known for speaking their minds. Politics take the forefront in much cocktail party chatter, especially in the months leading up to the presidential election.

These are exciting times for Washington, DC. The nation as a whole is experiencing a period of restlessness and an overall dissatisfaction with the current administration. The continuing death toll in Iraq, trouble in the Middle East and the ongoing terrorist threat since September 11, 2001 is forcing Americans to question their needs and who can meet them. At the micro level, these national questions also become DC's questions, and Washingtonians are fired up and talking about everything from George W Bush's super low approval ratings in 2006 to immigration reform, the battle for the Supreme Court, whether abortion should remain legal and is the federal government taking on too much of a Big Brother role? But the biggest question of all seems to be: are the Democrats going to make a comeback in '08? And if so, is Hillary going to win?

Here's the deal. In DC, a good election fight is tantamount to kick ass make-up sex and the whole mood of the city becomes amped in the months preceding a presidential bid. After the November election there's a bit of a lull as everyone waits for the lame duck president to actually leave. Come January it's party time again. An inaugural ball is the DC version of the Academy Awards, except Washingtonians would tell you it's cooler (their big party only happens once every four years, thank you very much). If you can score a seat to one of the balls, you can play out that whole childhood Cinderella/Prince Charming childhood fantasy.

DC experienced a flourish of a patriotic renaissance following the September 11 terrorist attacks. American flags flew in suburban yards and showed up on bumper stickers and car windows. Although the region has always been patriotic – DC is the birthplace of democracy, Maryland the home of the Star-Spangled Banner, Virginia has churned out many US presidents – the events of September 11 saw a rekindling of an 'I'm proud to be an American' mentality deeper than party lines. Today evidence of this patriotism lingers, but it's slowly losing momentum as war deaths continue. These days there are as many antiwar slogans as *I Support My Troops* stickers on car bumpers.

Although ethnically diverse, traditionally Washington, DC, is one of the most segregated cities in the country. However, on our last visit (after being away for a few years) we noticed refreshing changes. Although some had always embraced the city's global culture, the phenomena has gone mainstream. White yuppies flood bars once almost exclusively the domain of Black professionals, and everyone is feeling the beat of Africa, Asia and Latin America. DC, it seems, just can't get enough of salsa music, woven tapestries, Mediterranean meze and mint Mojitos. The immigrant community has risen to the occasion and opened bistros, bodegas, spice shops, foreign bookstores and world-music clubs.

Washington, DC, is constantly reinventing itself, which isn't always the best policy. Downtown – once a network of desolate streets and edgy clubs set in empty warehouses – is the star of DC's gentrification line, especially in the area just north of Chinatown near National Public Radio. Shaw – once crippled by racial tension and riots – is now a destination for African heritage tours. Five years ago it was considered risky to own a townhouse east of the capital, today the Capitol Hill neighborhood in Southeast is one of the city's more popular. And Brookland – an Upper Northeast 'hood until recently unknown to many DC residents – is suddenly the city's hottest real-estate market. Then there's the new baseball stadium being built in the heart of Southeast DC, along the Anacostia River, that will replace the current ballpark at RFK Stadium. The $600 million–plus park is set to open in April 2008.

While most Washingtonians are thrilled at the prospect of being able, once again, to root on a hometown team, the location of the Washington Nationals stadium is a lot more controversial (and a contentious point in the November 2006 mayoral election). Touted by some as a developmental savior of the neighborhood, it's thought of by many others as just another victory for gentrification.

Revitalization doesn't come without a price. So while it means hip restaurants and clubs along with valuable community services, renovation of buildings and influx of new residents, it also means increasing property values and rising rents. In a city where more than 20% of its residents live below the poverty line, this is a big deal. Although its purveyors' intentions may have been good, ultimately gentrification boils down to forcing out less affluent, longtime residents who can no longer afford to stay. In DC, this conflict invariably comes down to race: well-to-do whites are scooping up property in places like Shaw and Logan Circle, while poorer Blacks are being pushed further and further away. It's a bit of a vicious cycle, revitalization, especially in a city that already has a problem with segregation. Banishing poorer, usually minority residents, to outer suburbs only creates a wider chasm between the classes.

It's not a problem with an easy solution. The neighborhoods really are looking terrific. In Downtown the streets are bursting with restaurants, theatres and galleries, capped by the huge convention center. Shaw is just a few years behind. Its development is unique, however: the 'New U' remembers its days as Black Broadway and is drawing on that history. (Okay, we're going off on a bit of a tangent here, but we thought you would want to know: U St is hands down the hottest place to hear live music in DC today. It has long been the site of cutting-edge rock venues like the 9:30 Club, p183, and Black Cat, p183. But now you can also hear jazz and the infectious local style, go-go, in the same historic clubs where Duke Ellington and Pearl Bailey played. DC's music scene is about the rediscovery and rebirth of its roots – blending blues and jazz and go-go with modern urban sounds like hip-hop and house.)

Meanwhile, Downtown and on the National Mall the federal government recently completed its own revitalization program with the renovation and major reopenings of old museums (National Museum of American Art and National Portrait Gallery) and the opening of new ones (National Museum of the American Indian). The sparkling, nearly new National WWII Memorial glorifies national unity.

INFAMOUS INLAWS, REBELLIOUS CHILDREN, EMBARRASSING SIBLINGS – SHOCKING PRESIDENTIAL FAMILY CONFESSIONS

Washington media loves to dig up the dirt on the Commander-in-Chief's kin, which the public eats up faster than George W Bush can choke on a pretzel. Below are a few favorite gems.

- The Bush Twins – Poor George W, not only is he the laughing stock of the world, his daughters also have a rebellious streak. In May 2001, the then 19-year-old twins, Barbara and Jenna, were accused by police in Austin, TX, of underage drinking at a Mexican restaurant. Police accused Barbara of being a minor in possession of alcohol and funniest of all, Jenna was accused of trying to use a fake ID to buy booze (how she thought she could pull that kind of anonymity off is beyond us). Charges were dismissed after both girls did community service and paid fines, and Barbara attended alcohol counseling. It wasn't Jenna's first run in with the law – she had previously been charged with underage drinking. Drinking scandals seem to run in the family. Bush kept news of his own 1976 arrest for drunken driving in Maine under the radar until the story broke just days before the 2000 presidential election. Bush stopped drinking on his 40th birthday, in 1986.
- Bill Clinton's Bro – President Clinton's half-brother Roger was a convicted felon. In 1985, Roger spent time in prison for selling cocaine. (But was pardoned by Bill in 2001). Bill Clinton kind of stole his half-brother's thunder, however, when his own marital indiscretions and fondness for Oval Office blowjobs became the scandal du jour and nearly cost him his job.
- The Bush Seniors – Like father, like son. It is no wonder George W Bush is famous for his awkward phrases. He probably learned it from his parents. During the 1984 presidential campaign, sharp-tongued Barbara Bush famously called democratic vice presidential nominee Geraldine Ferraro a word that 'rhymes with rich.' Her husband upped the ante – in the 1988 presidential race, a microphone picked up George HW Bush describing his half-Mexican grandchildren (by son Jeb and daughter-in-law, Columbia) to President Reagan as 'the little brown ones.'
- The Reagan Kids – All four of President Ronald Reagan's kids liked to publicly disagree and openly feud with their father. Michael criticized his stepmother's (Nancy Reagan's) parenting. Maureen opposed her father on gun control and abortion. Ron dropped out of Yale, joined the Joffrey Ballet and danced in his underwear on *Saturday Night Live*. No one could top Patti, however, who posed nude for *Playboy*, and who wrote a memoir, *The Way I See It*, that portrayed both her parents in a negative light.
- Boozy Billy Carter – Billy Carter, brother of President Jimmy Carter, was known as a troublemaker in 1970s' Washington. A colorful southern fellow with a penchant for beer drinking, the guy liked the beverage so much he created his own label – Billy Beer. It flopped.

CITY CALENDAR

Washington's calendar is jam-packed with events, some of the highlights being the Cherry Blossom Festival and the Smithsonian Folklife Festival. The city also gets fired up for the nation's birthday, celebrating Independence Day with free concerts and fireworks.

On national holidays, banks, schools, government offices and some attractions close; transportation runs on a Sunday schedule. For additional events information, contact the Washington, DC Convention & Tourism Co (☎ 202-789-7000; www.washington .org).

JANUARY

Winter is mild, with temperatures usually in the 30s. Every four years (or eight if the US people are forgiving), it's the ultimate social-political event in Washington, DC: Inauguration Day.

FEBRUARY

For Black History Month the Smithsonian museums organize an incredible educational program. For more information call ☎ 202-357-4574.

CHINESE NEW YEAR

Chinatown lights up with dancing and firecrackers. A giant dragon leads a parade through the downtown streets.

MARCH

Spring arrives (temperatures range from 40°F to 55°F); prepare yourself for festival and parade season. The Cherry Blossom Festival takes place in late March or early April.

ST PATRICK'S DAY

☎ 202-637-2474; www.dcstpatsparade.com
On March 17, DC's Irish and wannabes whoop it up at a parade down Constitution Ave.

SMITHSONIAN KITE FESTIVAL

☎ 202-357-2700; www.kitefestival.org
On the last Saturday of March, the skies near the Washington Monument come alive with colors.

NATIONAL CHERRY BLOSSOM FESTIVAL

☎ 202-728-1137; www.nationalcherryblossom festival.org
This two-week arts and culture fest celebrates the blooming of DC's cherry trees and culminates in a parade extravaganza.

CHERRY BLOSSOM 10-MILE RUN

☎ 301-320-3350; www.cherryblossom.org
Thousands of racers run around the Tidal Basin and along the Potomac for cash prizes (or just for fun).

APRIL

Weather goes from fine to fabulous (temperatures between 50°F and 66°F), making April one of the loveliest months in DC. Easter Sunday usually occurs in April.

WHITE HOUSE EASTER EGG ROLL

www.whitehouse.gov/easter; 1600 Pennsylvania Ave
On the Monday after Easter, kids aged three to six are invited to the South Lawn for stories, games and colorful characters (besides your typical politicians).

SMITHSONIAN CRAFT SHOW

☎ 202-357-4000; www.si.edu/craftshow; 401 F St NW, National Building Museum
In mid-April, leading American potters, furniture makers, metalsmiths, glass, paper and textile artists, and jewelry creators display and sell their work.

SHAKESPEARE'S BIRTHDAY

☎ 202-544-4600; www.folger.edu; 201 E Capitol St
On April 23, the Folger Shakespeare Library & Theatre (p87) celebrates the Bard's birthday with jugglers and jesters, music, song and dance.

FILMFEST DC

☎ 202-724-6578; www.filmfestdc.org
Shown at venues around the city, this festival features cutting-edge films by national and international directors. It is held over 10 days at the end of the month.

MAY

May in DC is truly delightful: temperatures range from 60°F to 75°F, and tourist season swings into high gear. Memorial Day, the last Monday of the month, honors the war dead and marks the start of summer.

GAY BLACK PRIDE
☎ 202-667-8188
The nation's largest annual Gay Black Pride celebration takes place on Memorial Day weekend and draws participants from across the country.

ROLLING THUNDER RIDE FOR FREEDOM
☎ 908-369-5439; www.rollingthunder1.com
The Harley Davidson contingent of Vietnam vets commemorates Memorial Day with a ride on the National Mall to draw attention to the POWs and MIAs who were left behind.

JUNE
Things heat up, as temperatures climb into the 70s and 80s. Summer tourist season is in full swing – arrive early and be prepared to stand in line.

CAPITAL PRIDE
☎ 202-797-3510; www.capitalpride.org
DC's version of the international gay pride holiday draws thousands of marchers to the Mall; many bars and clubs host special events.

LAWYERS HAVE HEART 10KM RACE
☎ 703-914-3710-; www.runlhh.org
Lawyers help the American Heart Association raise money by running a 10km loop around Georgetown's Washington Harbour. The race, which is also popular with

non-barrister types, attracts about 4000 runners each year and has raised more than $3.7 million. It is held in early June.

SMITHSONIAN FOLKLIFE FESTIVAL
☎ 202-275-1119; www.folklife.si.edu
For 10 days before Independence Day, this extravaganza celebrates international and US cultures on the Mall lawns in front of the **Smithsonian Castle** (p68).

JULY & AUGUST
Hot town summer in the city. Expect temperatures in the 80s and drippy, sweaty humidity. Congress shuts down and locals retreat to the beach.

INDEPENDENCE DAY
July 4 commemorates the adoption of the Declaration of Independence in 1776. Huge crowds gather on the National Mall to watch fireworks, listen to free concerts and picnic in the sunshine. The Declaration is read from the National Archives' steps.

SEPTEMBER
Life returns to DC after Labor Day (the first Monday in September), the unofficial end of summer. From mid-September to mid-October, cultural events occur in honor of Hispanic Heritage Month.

DC BLUES FESTIVAL
☎ 301-926-1336; www.dcblues.org
In late August or early September, the all-volunteer DC Blues Society sponsors a free, day long festival of top local blues acts at Rock Creek Park's **Carter Barron Amphitheater** (p192).

ADAMS MORGAN FESTIVAL
www.adamsmorganday.org
DC's biggest neighborhood festival takes over 18th St NW on the weekend after Labor Day with live music, vendors and food stalls.

OCTOBER
Autumn brings colorful leaves and wonderful weather for outdoor activities. Look for temperatures ranging from 60°F to 70°F and clear blue skies.

FIVE QUIRKY DC EXPERIENCES

When you're tired of looking at stoic monuments or relic-stuffed museums, then check out the other side of DC. The city is a gold mine for things from the slightly offbeat to the downright bizarre.

- Check out the **Squished Penny Museum** (☎ 202-986-5644; www.squishedpenny.com; Northwest Washington; admission by appointment only), which has an unusual collection of – you heard it – squished pennies, coins, and other ephemera from around the world. Exhibited in the owners' living room, it gives new meaning to the term *common cents*.
- See the famous **Exorcist Stairs** (3600 Prospect St NW, Georgetown) from *The Exorcist*, which gave many people nightmares in the '70s. The steps in the film are at the end of M Street in Georgetown, across from the Key Bridge.
- The stuffed body of Owney, the unofficial postal mascot, rests behind glass at the **National Postal Museum** (☎ 202-633-9849; cnr 1st & Massachusetts Ave NE). Adopted by the postal service in 1888, the dog 'worked' as a mail carrier until 1897 when he died from a mysterious gunshot wound.
- Ever wonder what the world's largest hairball looks like? Wishes do come true at the **National Museum of Health and Medicine** (☎ 202-782-2200; cnr 6900 Georgia Ave & Elder St NW; admission free; 10am-5:30pm). There's a fascinating, oddball display that includes pieces of Abraham Lincoln's skull and a touchable human stomach.
- In Anacostia on V St the world's largest chair towers over Martin Luther King Dr; at 19ft of pure mahogany, no one is sure how it got there.

MARINE CORPS MARATHON

☎ 703-784-2225; www.marinemarathon.com
Known as the people's marathon, this popular road race starts and ends at the Iwo Jima Memorial on the last Sunday in October.

HIGH HEEL DRAG RACE

On October 31, Halloween is celebrated unofficially, including the fiercely competitive High Heel Drag Race, when Dupont Circle's highest heels and craziest costumes race down 17th St.

NOVEMBER & DECEMBER

Holiday season swings into gear. Weather is chilly (40°F to 50°F) and tourism declines (read: prices drop). DC takes on a festive air leading up to Christmas.

KENNEDY CENTER HOLIDAY CELEBRATION

☎ 202-467-4600; www.kennedy-center.org
During the month of December, the Kennedy Center sponsors free music events and activities.

NATIONAL CHRISTMAS TREE & MENORAH LIGHTING

On the second Thursday in December, the president does the honors on the **Ellipse** (p76), the expansive park on the south side of the White House.

CULTURE

IDENTITY

Washington is a city constantly in motion, its demographics changing with the four- or eight-year tides of presidential elections. Each new administration brings with it a new cast of characters from across the country. This leaves permanent Washingtonians – the lawyers, doctors, lobbyists, economists, newspaper reporters and rank-and-file government workers who don't move with each administration – stuck in a transitional, sometimes irritating (having to adjust to an influx of virgin Beltway drivers), situation for a few months. All in all DC is a company town, the company being the federal government. About a third of DC workers are employed by the government, in either federal or city bureaucracies.

Beginning in the 1960s, when there were about 764,000 Washingtonians, the city population began to flow outward into the suburbs seeking to escape the capital's increasing crime rates and failing infrastructure. Today, Washington is a relatively small city, with a

17

AFRICAN AMERICAN WASHINGTON, DC

Washington has always been a 'chocolate city'.

Even back in 1800, during the first session of Congress, it was a heavily African American town: slaves and free Blacks composed 29% of the population. Free Blacks also took up residence in the port of Georgetown, priming the neighborhood for the emergence of a vibrant African American community that worked alongside and socialized with the city's slaves.

In 1800 more than half of the nation's 700,000 slaves lived in Maryland and Virginia. The capital of America's slave trade at that time, Washington contained slave markets and holding pens. Slavers conducted a highly profitable business buying slaves locally and selling them to Southern plantations.

The city's slave population declined throughout the 19th century, while the number of free Blacks migrating to the city rose. One of the century's most influential Black leaders was Frederick Douglass, born on a Maryland plantation in 1818. He helped form the Underground Railroad and raised two regiments of Black soldiers to fight for the Union when the civil war broke out. After the war, Douglass went to Washington to lend his support to the 13th, 14th and 15th Constitutional Amendments, which abolished slavery, granted citizenship to former slaves and guaranteed citizens the right to vote. He later became US marshal for Washington and the US minister to Haiti (the country's first Black ambassador).

In 1867 the country's first African American higher education facility, Howard University, was founded to educate Black residents; by this time, Blacks comprised nearly half the population.

Washington's seemingly post-war progressive attitude towards Blacks deteriorated in the early 20th century when the city adopted racial segregation policies like the rest of the South. The 'progressive' Wilson administration reinforced discrimination by refusing to hire Black federal employees and insisting on segregated government offices. In 1925, the Ku Klux Klan marched on the Mall.

Nonetheless, Washington was a Black cultural capital in the early 20th century. Shaw and LeDroit Park, near Howard University, sheltered a lively Black-owned business district, and Black theater and music flourished along U St NW, nurturing such great minds as Alain Locke and Langston Hughes. Southern Blacks continued to move to the city in search of better economic opportunities. Between 1920 and 1930 Washington's Black population jumped 20%. Citywide segregation eased somewhat with the New Deal (which brought new Black federal workers to the capital) and WWII (which brought lots more).

Later DC was a hub for the civil rights movement. Local Black churches provided gathering places and support networks for participants in the movement (just as they had served as stops on the Underground Railroad years before). When Martin Luther King was assassinated in 1968, the city exploded in protest and violence – a 'revolution' that DC is still recovering from.

Today African Americans represent about 60% of the population, one of the highest percentages in the country. While the city does have a healthy middle– to– upper class population of African Americans, 20% of its population falls below the poverty line and most of this segment is Black. To make things worse, poorer Blacks are being forced out of traditionally affordable housing in the rougher neighborhoods as government and private housing are razed to make way for gentrification (see p12). The racial and economic divide has defined city politics and social relations for decades. Sadly, White and Black Washingtonians do not often mix socially or professionally. These tensions are exacerbated by DC's odd political situation. Congress (mostly White and conservative) controls the budget of DC (mostly Black and liberal), although most Congress members don't even live in the city.

population of about 582,049 people. But the metropolitan area, including the Virginia and Maryland suburbs, is home to more than 6 million people. Three-quarters of metropolitan DC's employed population now works in the suburbs. Even some of the bigger federal agencies have gone suburban – as they grew, they simply ran out of DC real estate.

Quite recently, the outflow has slowed, as good economic times have enabled Washington to revitalize downtown neighborhoods. While widely welcomed, this gentrification also increases racial tensions. Affluent, primarily White home buyers have moved into Downtown, Shaw and Adams-Morgan during recent years, pushing less affluent Black renters further east.

African Americans represent about 55% of the population, one of the highest percentages of Blacks in the country (see the boxed text on above). Other ethnic groups include growing numbers of Asians (2.7%) and Latinos (7.9%). Despite this diverse population, DC is one of the most segregated cities in the country: the 39% of the population that is white lives almost exclusively in Northwest DC.

Since the 1970s, masses of Salvadorans and Jamaicans have transformed segments of DC into modern barrios. More recently, African and Asian immigrants have arrived in lesser numbers. These ethnic groups do not mix particularly well – not with each other and not with pre-existing Black and White populations. Although it is no longer the 'murder capital' of the country, homicide rates remain high, with a major crime spike in summer 2006. Many of these deaths are attributed to ethnic gang warfare, especially among Latino groups.

Outside the African American community, DC is a secular town – the business of government doesn't exactly lend itself to spiritual contemplation. However, the capital is also an international town so most of the world's faiths are represented, including an influential Jewish population, Muslims, Hindus, Mormons, Buddhists and Baha'is.

DC is also a gay-friendly city, with the majority of gay and lesbians living in the classy, and envied, Dupont Circle neighborhood. DC has its own gay and lesbian newspaper, the *Blade*, and it's common to see same-sex couples holding hands walking down the street.

LIFESTYLE

DC is a fun-loving town that knows how to party. Young, vibrant and cosmopolitan, the air radiates an exotic sauciness, especially in summer when temperatures soar and college interns – 70,000 plus – filter in for a taste of power. 'Work hard, play hard' seems to be the motto of the young and restless. And when the sun sinks low over the Potomac, seemingly straight-laced congressional aids, lobbyists and lawyers trade Capitol Hill deal brokering for dingy bars and happy-hour Martinis (although the talk at the table can stay political well into the night), then shift into overdrive at one of DC's many nightclubs.

The metropolitan DC area is the home of the nation's political class, with the US political system retaining the spoils of office: thousands of politically appointed positions in the civil service. Each change of administration means a turnover in these positions, bringing newcomers to town. Once out of office, these politicos tend to stick around, taking temporary refuge at think tanks and policy institutes, working their contacts and biding their time until electoral fortunes change. The political class can often be observed in the early evening at their preferred Hill hangouts and downtown digs.

The federal government attracts one of the nation's best-educated populations. Thirty-nine percent of the population has a bachelor's degree (compared to 24% nationally) and almost 19% has an advanced degree – the highest rate in the country. Education translates into purposefulness on the job. These people are serious about their work, whatever it may be. Not as obsessed as a Wall Street banker (after all, federal employees and contractors are not likely to be getting paid for more than 40 hours of work a week), but dedicated nonetheless.

With a high population of foreign-born residents (more than 13%), international influences are ubiquitous – from ethnic cuisine to world music and foreign films. Most Washingtonians recognize the vast cultural resources at their disposal, but are apt to not take regular advantage of them. Ask any local the last time they visited the Smithsonian and the answer will inevitably be when an out-of-town guest was visiting. Which means only that residents have their own thing going on, whether it be training for the Marine Corps Marathon (p17) or volunteering as a docent at the Octagon (p79), or singing in the St Augustine (p102) gospel choir.

FASHION

DC has long been a suit-and-tie kind of town, and visitors are often stunned by the number of well-coiffed men and women (from young to old) packing into dark and dingy dives where the smell of smoke and grease is thick for happy-hour cocktails. It's also a fashionable town, and just because the bar looks better suited to work boots and jeans, you're likely to see lots of Blahnik heels, Chanel suits and Louis Vuitton carryalls. For the minority of Washingtonians who can afford it, fashion is an important component of life. Status symbols like expensive cars and even more expensive mansions are the norm in the quiet,

YOU KNOW YOU'RE FROM WASHINGTON, DC IF....

- You say you live in DC when talking to outsiders, even though you really reside in Maryland or Virginia, because it's easier... if someone from the metro area asks where you live, however, you always state the state (people actually living in the city consider themselves a different breed than suburbanites, rather snobby eh?).
- You get excited when you see celebrities at restaurants, but your idea of a celebrity is Hillary Clinton, Donald (Rumsfeld, not Trump), Condi or the ever-elusive Dick Cheney (take bonus bragging rights if you discover his 'secure, undisclosed location.')
- Your idea of a good night on the town includes a knock-down-drag-out battle of the brains on whether Hillary will run (and win) in 2008.
- You wear a suit to happy hour and spend most of your time 'networking', ie trying to get the people you work for a meeting with the senator they work for.
- You think potholes the size of small elephants and exploding manhole covers are normal.
- You know the Pentagon is really in Virginia but don't bother to correct anyone because it's just too hard to explain.
- You think it's perfectly normal to have to take a different route due to terrorism-related road closures.
- You have the color-coded terror warning system memorized and flinch when F-15 fighter jets whiz by your house at midnight.
- You know when three helicopters fly overhead the president is in the sky, if there's only two it's someone less important.
- You know not to head to the grocery store when the local weatherman predicts even a flurry of snow because it will be packed with frantic residents stocking up on essentials for the 'giant blizzard.' The blizzard will inevitably turn out to be less than an inch of wet snow that will barely stick to the grass, let alone the pavement; however, the next day all schools will be shut (or at least on a delay) and the city will be paralyzed.
- You know that sometimes when it rains a lot the entire federal government shuts down – DC has a tendency to flood, one of the problems with building the capital of the free world on top a giant swamp.
- When tourists ask if Chevy Chase is named after the actor and you are able to answer, 'No.'
- You never call I-495 anything other than the Beltway and you would never be caught dead referring to National Airport as Reagan National.
- You always get lost on Dupont Circle.
- You are pretty damn sure there has been construction and detours (and those giant potholes) on the same stretch of pavement for a decade now and you've never seen anyone doing anything about it.
- When you say you're heading to the Mall you don't mean you're going shopping.
- You actually spend 45 minutes driving 3 miles down Wisconsin Ave to get to work and don't think twice about it.
- You flat out refuse to take your visiting friend to Adams-Morgan on a Saturday night because 'parking is impossible.'
- You know what POTUS means (President of the United States) and if you have a meeting with the man you'll be the toast of the town (at least for a few hours).

elegant, old-money neighborhoods scattered throughout Northwest and the neighboring Virginia suburb McLean (quite a few Supreme Court Justices live on the same quiet street in McLean, just spitting distance from the CIA, which is also in the neighborhood. We suppose it's a good choice if you're looking for protection). Maryland's ritziest zip code, Potomac 20854, has houses so big they are nothing short of embarrassingly ostentatious.

For the fabulous and rich, anything goes fashion-wise as long as it shows up in next season's *Vogue*. For the fabulous and broke, vintage shops selling anything designer are hot. Most of Washington wears a suit to work. In the African American community, dress ranges from haute couture to street wear, with baggy pants and expensive sneakers still dominating the male fashion trend.

While DC is a designer-conscious city, it doesn't boast the same clusters of designer shopping streets you would find in places like New York or San Francisco. You'll have to hit the malls to find your Louis Vuitton.

FOOD

DC's culinary choices match its population, ie they represent every state in the nation and just about every country on the planet. Downtown DC, Capitol Hill and the White House area are packed with upscale venues catering to the capital-city jet set – steakhouses, seafood and more exotic fare done up for the modern American palette. Adams-Morgan, Dupont Circle and Georgetown have their fair share of swank restaurants, as well as hole-in-the-wall eateries hawking spicy falafel and cheesy pizza until all hours of the night. This is the best place outside of East Africa to sample Ethiopian cuisine. For a truly authentic international eating experience, venture into Shaw or Mount Pleasant for roti with the Jamaicans or *pupusas* (corn meal pastries stuffed with meat or cheese) with the Salvadorans. If you are coming from the Western United States or Texas, you will likely be surprised by the lack of true Mexican restaurants – DC's food is mostly from Central and South America.

SPORTS

America loves its football, and in DC that means the celebrated Washington Redskins. In recent years, the 'Skins have not lived up to their glory days of the 1980s, when they won two Super Bowls, but they still inspire face-painting, beer-guzzling fans and sell out every game.

The DC National Basketball Association (NBA) team, the Washington Wizards, recently generated a lot of publicity when Michael Jordan bought into the team's ownership, then came out of retirement to play. He could not reverse the Wizards' fortunes, however, and he left DC under bad circumstances in 2003. The women's (WNBA) and college (NCAA) basketball-league teams maintain loyal followings among their audiences (pre-teen girls and Georgetown students respectively), but neither the Mystic nor the Hoyas have had much success on the courts in recent years either.

The Washington Capitals – dubbed the Caps – are the National Hockey League (NHL) team that recently acquired Czech phenomenon Jaromir Jagr. DC United has enjoyed modest major-league soccer success; sadly, the Women's United Soccer League champion, Washington Freedom, would not have the chance to defend their title, as the league folded for lack of funding in 2003.

Baseball is in a renaissance in Washington, DC, right now. The city recently acquired its own major-league baseball team, the Washington Nationals – previously DC was stuck rooting for the Baltimore-based Orioles. The city is in the process of constructing them a new stadium in a controversial Southeast location (it's another one of those gentrification packages DC seems so fond of this millennium).

For information on obtaining tickets to all sports events, see p198.

MEDIA

The media in DC really means only one thing: the *Washington Post*. Widely read and widely respected, the local daily is considered among the nation's top newspapers. Its competitor, the *Washington Times*, is owned by the Unification Church and provides an unsurprising, more conservative perspective. However, many are saying these days the *Post* seems more conservative than ever. The national newspaper *USA Today* is based across the Potomac in Arlington, VA. Several TV programs are also based in DC, including the PBS *News Hour* with longtime host Jim Lehrer, CNN's *Larry King Live* and all of the major networks' Sunday morning news programs.

The *Post*, of course, is famed for its role in the uncovering of the Watergate scandal in the early 1970s. Budding reporters Bob Woodward and Carl Bernstein traced a break in at the Watergate Hotel to the top ranks of the White House administration. Then editor and local legend Ben Bradlee took a risk in supporting the investigation and publishing the stories. The discoveries eventually forced the resignation of President Richard Nixon.

Also based in DC is National Public Radio (NPR), the most respected commercial, non-profit free radio network in the nation. Popular shows include *Morning Edition*, *All Things Considered* and *The Diane Rehm Show*. NPR's offices are in the heart of the Downtown redevelopment project.

As the news capital of the free world (and home to thousands of reporters from all over the US, not to mention the world), Washington media is dominated by the big boys; however, smaller independent voices, both digital and print, help energize the scene. For many

DC DECODER

Beltway bandits Consultants who clean up on high-priced government contracts.

Camp intern The city in summertime when young students flood in for stints on the Hill, federal agencies and think tanks.

Cave dweller Old-money Washingtonians, many of whom can trace their ancestry in the city back to pre–Civil War days.

DC, the District What locals call the place (never 'Washington, DC' – who has the time?).

Eye St I St (to avoid confusion with 1st St).

GS Government service level; a professional caste system. The higher the number (eg GS-1 vs GS-15), the higher the salary and prestige.

Hill rat Lifer congressional staffers; named for the book *Hill Rat* by John Jackley.

Langley Often synonymous with 'CIA'; Langley, Virginia is that agency's home.

Potus Secret Service shorthand for President of the United States.

'Skins! Redskins (DC's football team). Generally bellowed.

reporters, getting to report in DC is like getting to Mecca. Positions at bigger papers and especially TV stations are coveted. As a result there are some very good reporters working for the smaller outlets, biding their time until they break the story of a lifetime and move on to greener pastures, so it's not unheard of for the little guy to grab the big scoop here. The *Drudge Report*, an online publication, is a perfect example. They broke the Monica Lewinsky story in the late 1990s.

Washington, DC, has some excellent sources of independent media. The **City Paper** *(www. washingtoncitypaper.com)* keeps an alternative but informed eye on local politics and trends. Another valuable source for local and national events is the **DC Independent Media Center** (www.dc.indymedia.org). Smaller rags filled with juicy Hill gossip include the **Hill** (www. hillnews.com) and **Roll Call** *(www.rollcall.com)*.

To get the scoop on Washington political gossip and humor head to **Wonkette: The DC Gossip** (www.wonkette.com), which also has links to local blogs (Washingtonienne – see p42 – was outed here). You can also catch up on DC celebrity sightings – Sam Donaldson waiting for a cab, the Bush twins downing shots at an unhip bar. Don't worry if you've never heard of some of the names before, some of these folks are *only* famous in Washington – this is a city where CNN anchors are kind of akin to rock stars.

If you're looking for some mind-numbingly funny, but decidedly left-wing political cartoon humor, check out www.markfiore.com. The artist, whose work has appeared in newspapers across the country (and who is a former staff cartoonist for the *San Jose Mercury News*), does hilarious, yet thought-provoking, weekly animated skits in which many jokes are at George W Bush's expense.

LANGUAGE

DC's English is as varied as the city itself. You'll hear plenty of accents and slang from New York, the Midwest, Southern USA and California among the residents of this transient US city, as well as the urban dialect of its African American neighborhoods. Diplomatic and immigrant communities add pockets of multilingualism to the city – you'll hear more Spanish than English in Mount Pleasant and lots of Amharic in Adams-Morgan's African restaurants; Vietnamese is the lingua franca in suburban Virginia's 'Little Saigon.'

Washington, DC, bureaucrats – who seem to spend their days crafting acronyms, abbreviations and neologisms – make their own peculiar contributions to DC's language. It is only in Washington that you will hear acronym-laden constructions like, 'If HR 3401 passes, everyone under GS-10 at HUD and HHS will be SOL' and bureaucratic phraseologies like 'non-means-tested entitlement,' 'soft money' and 'what the meaning of *is* is.'

EDUCATION

Washington is a major college town, home to private schools like Georgetown, George Washington, American, Howard and Catholic universities, along with public universities like University of District of Columbia (UDC) and the massive University of Maryland in nearby College Park, MD. The presence of so many students infuses the city with a diversified, youthful presence easily observed throughout the city. Each of the major schools is different – Georgetown is known for producing the nation's future leaders, especially in the realm of international relations and politics, Howard attracts the African American cream-of-the-crop from around the country, while George Washington has a well-respected medical school.

In 1999 the Clinton administration introduced legislation that allows Washington, DC, residents to attend any public university (if admitted) in the United States at state tuition rates.

ECONOMY & COSTS

The greater Washington area is the third-largest regional economy in the United States, with a gross regional product of nearly $246.8 billion in 2005. While the federal government is the main story in DC, thriving private-sector industries include information technology, bioscience, international business, professional services and tourism. The federal government provides fuel for all of these industries. In the 1990s, the high-tech industry in particular benefited from government spending, and sprouted up – seemingly overnight – in northern Virginia along the Dulles corridor.

Washington, DC, is an expensive place to live and to visit. Once in Washington, the bulk of your travel expenses will be for accommodation. Although fancy hotels in Washington can cost as much as you are willing to pay, it is possible – taking advantage of discounted web rates – to stay in a central, four-star hotel for $150 to $200. Midrange hotels run from $120 to $350, while the hostels in DC cost around $30 for a bed. Eating in DC is also not cheap. Three sit-down meals per day, including one at an upscale restaurant, will easily cost $80 per person. Forgoing drinks or grabbing a meal at a less-expensive venue trims that estimate to $50. At best, self-catering and cheap eats make it possible to eat for about $20 per day.

Keep in mind that Washington offers many opportunities to save money. With free federal sites, museums, concerts and festivals, it's entirely possible to find yourself fully entertained – day and night – without paying a dime. The Smithsonian museums are always free, and galleries like the Phillips Collection and the Corcoran Gallery of Art have reduced entry or free admission on certain days of the week. Happy hours offer excellent value for eating and drinking, and many upscale restaurants have fixed-plate and pre-theater menus that are good value.

HOW MUCH?

Bicycle rental (three hours) $20

Cab fare Downtown from Ronald Reagan Washington National Airport $15

Cappuccino $4

Concert ticket at the 9:30 Club $30

Guinness $6

Movie ticket $9

One-bedroom apartment (one month) $1500

Parking garage (one hour) $6

Washington Post 50c

GOVERNMENT & POLITICS

According to the Constitution, the nation's capital would be exclusively administered by the US Congress. More than 200 hundred years later, Congress has yet to give up this power. Despite the emergence of Washington, DC, as a major metropolitan center, it is an

23

anomalous political entity that functions more like a colony than a state. The grievance of 'taxation without representation,' which sparked the American Revolution, remains unaddressed for Washington residents. In fact, it has recently reappeared as a slogan on some DC license plates.

From the late 19th century, an appointed three-man commission managed city affairs and residents were denied voting rights. The call for Home Rule was first heard early in the 20th century, but it was not until 1964 that DC residents voted in a presidential election for the first time. In 1968, President Johnson replaced the commission system with a mayor and city council. Finally, the Home Rule Act went into effect in 1974, granting limited autonomy, including the right to vote for mayor.

Washingtonians are still denied representation at the federal level, despite having a larger population than Wyoming. In the 1990s, the issue of DC statehood was advanced to redress this situation. The Clinton administration supported the initiative, which was voted down by the House of Representatives. Washington is an overwhelmingly Democratic town and Republicans have little incentive to bring their votes into the political mix.

In March 2000, a federal court panel ruled that Washingtonians have no legal right to a vote in Congress, dealing a severe setback to community leaders and home-rule activists. Mayor Williams summed up the city's disappointment: 'Over the last 200 years, residents of the District of Columbia have fought in nine wars and paid billions of dollars in federal taxes. Yet in our nation's capital – the epicenter of democracy – we lack the most fundamental right of all: the right to vote.'

Taxation remains a chronic source of tension for cash-strapped DC. Two-thirds of the income earned in DC is not taxable by DC because suburbanite earn it (and paid income tax in their home state, not DC).

ENVIRONMENT

THE LAND

DC stands at a pivotal place upon the fall line, the exact point where the coastal plain intersects with the higher, rockier piedmont plateau. Most of Downtown and Southeast DC lie on the delta formed by the joining of the Potomac River and its smaller tributary, the Anacostia River. The federal city was sited here precisely because of this geographic anomaly: it is the last navigable point on the Potomac, which city founders deemed important for trade. Just north of here at Great Falls, the river tangles itself in a series of cliffs and crags, impeding the progress of ships.

In the city, the high ground defined by the fall line proved an attractive setting for the mansions of Washington's wealthy residents – it runs through Georgetown and traces the course of Kalorama Rd. The southern, monumental part of Washington around the Mall is coastal lowland smoothed out by the seasonal flooding of the Potomac and Anacostia Rivers. To control flooding in the 19th century, developers created landfills like West Potomac Park and dredged the Washington Channel.

Washington, DC, is a small city with wide sidewalks and few highways, making it an ideal city for walking.

GREEN DC

Today Washington, DC, is a uniquely green city. Hundreds of acres of protected parks and wetlands make a good home for urban wildlife, including small woodland creatures and aquatic animals like raccoons, turtles, salamanders, beavers, white-tailed deer, weasels, muskrats, foxes and opossums. Olmstead's 2000-acre Rock Creek Park is a particularly attractive habitat. Cardinals, pileated woodpeckers and wood thrushes also flit around here.

The mixed woodlands of DC parks are fetching in springtime, when forsythia, fruit trees – especially cherries and crab apples – and wildflowers (violets, bluebells, wild orchids, chicory and trilliums) burst into a pale-pastel rainbow of blooms. Also native to the city, sometimes in near-virgin stands, are tulip poplars, red-and-white oaks, sycamore, elm, willow, dogwood, beech, hickory and pine.

The waterways and wetlands surrounding the city attract waterfowl and other feathered friends. Hundreds of bald eagles and ospreys nest along the Potomac south of Washington and along the Patuxent River to the east. Kenilworth Gardens, in Northeast DC, is thick with wading great blue herons, red-winged blackbirds and bitterns. In 2000, Mayor Anthony Williams announced a major riverfront redevelopment and cleanup effort that will, hopefully, spur revitalization of the Anacostia as a natural and recreational resource.

URBAN PLANNING & DEVELOPMENT

Since the 1970s, DC's population has declined, as residents have moved up and out to burgeoning suburbia (see Identity, p17). DC's outlying areas are some of the fastest growing in the nation; suburban sprawl and the accompanying automobile dependence have resulted in traffic problems and air pollution. In recent years, the local government responded with innovative transportation solutions: expanding the Metrorail, adding and enforcing designated lanes for High Occupancy Vehicles (HOVs), and allowing bicycles on trains and buses are all ways of encouraging commuters to leave their car keys at home.

ON THE HORIZON

The winds of change are blowing in America's capital. Depending on your direction, the city is either at the height of a cultural renaissance or in the middle of some heavy-duty (and perhaps unnecessary) cosmetic surgery. In truth, Washington is pumping copious quantities of cash into preserving its past while frantically building its future. History is in these days, and DC is crazy about museums. So far $1.5 billion has been spent renovating old and constructing new museums and monuments. While some of the projects are purely about aesthetics, others are being conceived with duel purposes – preserving the arts and sparking urban renewal.

New initiatives like the National's stadium (at the intersection of Potomac Ave and 1st St SE) are purposely being constructed in poor neighborhoods in hopes of jump-starting depressed economies. City planners have no reason to question this gentrification model; it's worked here in the past. The construction of the MCI Center and consequent revitalization of the Downtown is a textbook example. Those skeptical of gentrification's benefits, however, worry about trickle-down effects on local residents who will be unable to afford the sky-high rent that comes with living in an edgy-hot 'hood.

DC isn't concentrating revitalization efforts solely on low-income areas. On Pennsylvania Ave, in a posh district now dubbed the Penn Quarter, a six-story glass structure is going up. The new home of the privately funded **Newseum** (see p95 for more), dedicated to the achievements of news people across the globe, this is one of the city's multi-purpose ventures set to open in 2007. The museum will only occupy about 40% of the 555,000-sq-foot building. The rest of the space will be turned into offices, shops and condominiums in an effort to spearhead neighborhood revival. The $100-million National Children's Museum (replacing the now closed Capital Children's Museum) being constructed at L'Enfant Plaza is another such initiative. Set to open in 2009 it is being envisioned as a family-friendly attraction with exhibits and programs catering to young audiences from around the globe.

On the aesthetic front, the Corcoran Gallery of Art is building a new wing. An undulating metal $120-million Frank Gehry designed creation. And funding has been approved for the Smithsonian Institution National Museum of African American History and Culture at a sight adjacent to the Washington Monument and across the street from the National Museum of American History. A timeframe for construction has not been confirmed, as the museum is currently in initial development and fundraising stages. When completed, the museum will house important documents, artifacts and recordings that bring alive the vibrant cultural contributions African Americans have made to their country over the last 400 years. On the Mall, one of DC's most popular museums, the **National Museum of American History** (p67) is getting a multi-million dollar facelift and set to reopen in 2008, while the **National Portrait Gallery** (p96) just finished its renovation and is looking gorgeous.

The economic upswing in the 1990s sparked investment in Washington neighborhoods, especially Downtown. Projects such as the MCI Center (a huge arena that hosts major sporting events and big-name rock concerts) and the Convention Center are the backbone of the ongoing revitalization in the area. New additions like the National Museum of the American Indian and the National WWII Memorial promise to continue to draw visitors to the Mall. Since September 11, 2001, local government has placed more importance on security concerns when developing public works projects.

Political City ▪

This Political City *Adam Karlin*

Politics and Washington, DC, are more than peanut butter and jelly or milk and cookies. Think more along the lines of 'water' and 'livable planet': the two simply don't exist without each other. Bureaucracy, compromise, republicanism, democracy, and checks and balances are all concepts that influence DC in ways that run far deeper than job climate and social scene. Take location: the American capitol was built on a swamp to satisfy regional politics. Northerners and Southerners agreed, it may have been a malarial swamp, but it was *centrally* malarial. The grid and wagon-wheel layout of the city also draws from the idea of a well-ordered, easily navigable Republic (gotta love the irony that the design conceals America's Escher-like bureaucratic apparatus). In short, to embrace this town, you have to breathe its air, and that's politics: from smoke and dagger backrooms to the massed voice of protest and everything in between.

MOVERS, SHAKERS, LIFERS, PLAYERS

DC, unlike so many other world capitals, is rarely boring, and it owes its excitement to its population. This isn't sleepy Canberra or baffling Brasília; this is the capital of the free world, and it likes to recruit top talent. Yes, there're grey bureaucrats, but in the USA you'd be hard pressed to find a greater concentration of young, motivated individuals, all clawing up the career ladder.

Start at the bottom of the totem pole with pages, high-school students nominated by their congressmen and senators to hand-deliver important documents. Next comes interns: these overworked, underpaid (if paid at all) youngsters can be menial coffee-grabbers or influential speechwriters, and often wear both hats at once. They're also notorious party people, with women sometimes (and chauvinistically) referred to as 'skinterns' for their sometimes skimpy business outfits and occasional Lewinsky-esque dalliances.

Lucky interns become staff, which often means the same job with marginally better pay. Official staff positions may run from policy research ('So what does privatizing social security entail?') to press spokesperson ('The senator doesn't necessarily advocate closing down nursing homes') to letter writing ('Senator Crookshanks is sorry to hear your grandmother's retirement community has been closed…').

By their 30s, political peons have either burned out, earned senior staff roles, or been selected as potential elective material and primed for office in home constituencies. Or they become lobbyists. Lobbyists are (often very highly) paid advocates for a particular cause, and someone who has survived a decade of DC is often well-positioned (and cynical) enough to join their ranks.

So do these hard-driving, highly opinionated, often politically at-odds types get along outside of the office? When they do catch a break, the answer is often: yes. Although some politicos believe in no fraternizing with the enemy, the fact of the matter is Americans have a genius for compromise, and you can't compromise with people you hate. It's not all lovey-dovey, but it's not unheard of for a Republican research analyst to grab a beer, catch a Washington Nationals' baseball game, and even split an apartment with a Democratic Senate staffer.

The jobs described aren't limited to congressional offices either. DC headquarters think tanks, NGOs, lobbying firms, the World Bank and embassies – to name a few. All kinds of Type A intelligentsia roll through here: students at some of the best universities in America; activists campaigning out of their central headquarters; and foreign diplomats, young and old, navigating the power networks of their own countries.

UNDERSTANDING AMERICAN POLITICS

Everyone knows Americans do things differently – spelling, measuring, sports – and the democratic process is no exception. Now some may sneer, 'What democratic process?' and start comparing American presidents to fascist dictators, but the fact is this is the longest-running Republic in the world. On top of that, while the American system was unique in its inception, it has been emulated by governments across the globe (notably in Latin America and Eastern Europe). But the difference runs way beyond organization to philosophy. Whereas many governments exist to protect their citizens, the American model focuses on protecting citizens' *rights* – at least it's supposed to.

SEPARATION OF POWERS

Some may ask, 'What's the difference?' The best answer probably comes from journalist HL Mencken, who summed up many Americans' feeling towards a nanny state: 'The urge to save humanity is almost always a false face for the urge to rule it.' Americans are by and large paranoid of their government. The entire country was founded by anti-authoritarian colonists, while the Civil War was fought over how much power Washington, DC, could exert over the states (among other reasons). Obsessed with keeping government in check, the founding fathers devised a system that disperses power through three branches, all with the ability to smack each other down.

You can visit those branches starting on Capitol Hill, where the legislative branch, better known as Congress, convenes. Put simply, Congress writes laws. There are two bodies assigned this task: the House of Representatives, where 438 congressmen and women are split proportionally by state population (Wyoming gets one, California 53), and the Senate. The latter seats 100 senators: two for each state – a way of giving smaller states equal footing with the more populous ones. Congress not only writes laws, it can also impeach the president, determine the jurisdictional limits of courts and vote out its own members.

Behind the Capitol dome is the Supreme Court, whose 12 justices are appointed by the president to life terms. The court's job is to determine how true to the constitution laws are. Arguably the weakest branch, it has shown muscle in recent years in cases like Hamdan vs Rumsfeld, where a majority Republican-appointed court ruled that special military commissions created by the president since September 11, 2001 were unconstitutional.

A little ways down Pennsylvania Ave sits the White House, where the president heads the executive branch. Unlike a prime minister, the president is both head of state and head of government, and possesses the power to veto (override) Congress' bills, pardon criminals, and appoint a cabinet, judges and ambassadors. But the position isn't quite as powerful as some might think. Many media analysts argue that in a short-attention-span world, it's just easier for everyone to understand a one-person office versus a 538-seat Congress – and assume the former holds the reigns of power.

George W Bush has unabashedly pushed for an 'Imperial Presidency,' an over-muscled executive branch that can lord it over the rest of the American government. Yet despite wiretaps, military commissions and far-right appointees, he has as of this writing only used the veto twice in six years. Instead, Bush relies on loopholes like signature statements, documents that exempt the executive branch from following everyone else's rules (like not torturing war-on-terror detainees). Still, the fact is a stubborn Congress can make a president's life hell. Even in post–September 11 America, the push for greater executive power has upset the separation of powers Americans hold dear, and the president has paid for his hubris with 40% approval ratings.

Finally, while the powers are separated, they are not isolated from each another. The founding fathers figured that each branch's ability to check its partners would generate a healthy tension. This uneasy equality makes compromise a necessity for movement on the issues, and is the true bedrock of American politics.

THE ELECTORAL COLLEGE

In the 2000 presidential election, Al Gore polled 51,003,926 votes to George W Bush's 50,460,110. Bush won the election.

About that whole democracy thing…

Americans vote most of their leaders into office, but not the president (in a similar vein, under a parliament voters elect a party that then selects the prime minister). Instead, they vote for electors: 538 individuals who make up the semi-shadowy Electoral College. It is

DEMS VIEW OF REPUBS, REPUBS VIEW OF DEMS:

The ideologies of America's two major political parties are remarkably close. They diverge a little, mainly over how much government should spend on social services and 'moral' issues like abortion (but what issues aren't moral?). That said, if you bought half the rhetoric spouted in party literature, you'd think they were different species.

A Democrat's ideal ugly Republican is a gun-toting, union-busting, seal-clubbing, insensitive redneck who somehow made his way onto Wall St. He's an odd mix of ill-gotten wealth and provincial lowbrow, a casually racist NASCAR (National Association for Stock Car Auto Racing) fan who shoots first and demands the right to do so with bigger guns, asks for small government in business and big government in the bedroom (with bans on birth control and gay sex), and hides behind the cross and the flag when criticism comes his way.

The Republican bogey is a granola-eating, tree-hugging, draft-dodging lesbian walking out of an abortion clinic (stereotypes don't have to make sense). She responds to the problems of the day by throwing money at inefficient government programs and then demands more taxes. She rails against guns, yet condones what they consider baby-killing. She demands cultural sensitivity in one breath, but wants to deface all public displays of the Ten Commandments.

In the end, each party sees the other as fiscally irresponsible and culturally bankrupt. Let's face it: George W Bush is most Democrats' nightmare given form, and Hillary Clinton terrifies Republicans, which goes some way towards explaining how divided the American electorate is.

the college and its electors who actually pick the president every four years. Although a candidate's name appears in voting booths, individual votes go to the electors, whose votes are supposed to reflect the will of the public.

Every four years candidates push for the magic number of electors – 270 – that gives them over half the votes needed for victory. The states, plus Washington, DC, get as many electors as they have senators and representatives. California tops the list with 55, and Wyoming bottoms out at three. The game is winner-takes-all: when a party wins a state, it get every one of the electoral votes.

Here's how the system works. Let's say it's election day in a state inhabited by 100 people, represented by 10 electors. Come game day, 60 people vote for candidate Smith (or more accurately, for his electors), and 40 for candidate Brown. Although the votes split 6:4, Smith's party takes them all and comes 10 electoral votes closer to victory.

The system was founded for several reasons. First, direct democracy was pretty much considered mob rule in the 1700s; electors were supposed to mollify the base instincts of the people. In addition, the college is supposed to guarantee geographically fair elections. If candidates focused on the popular vote, rather than the states, campaigns (and their promises) would largely be directed at big cities on the coasts. Because every state gets two electors to complement their senators, even the small ones can command election attention.

The counter argument is: 'So what?' Politics are not as regional as they once were, and the concerns of the coasts often overlap those of the heartland. There are also questions of how democratic the college is. Technically, electors can vote how they want, although none have recently gone against their constituents' will. Plus, is it fair for Wyoming, with a population of 510,000 and three electoral votes, to have parity with Montana – population 935,000, and same number of electors?

One recommendation, which sounds like winning the Golden Snitch in quidditch, is to keep the Electoral College but give the popular vote-winner 100 electoral votes, essentially guaranteeing their victory. However, attempts to reform the system are notoriously failure prone.

To learn more about the college (and the debate), check the Federal Election Commission website (www.fec.gov).

THE MEDIA AND WASHINGTON

Washington is a club for the powerful, and reporters have to be able to shake hands with the bouncer and schmooze the hostess to get inside. But once let into the halls of power, are journalists here objective enough to do their jobs?

Yes and no. The Washington, DC, press corps has been criticized in the past for not checking up on the weapons of mass destruction claims that justified the 2003 invasion of Iraq. However, if the media abandoned its post as watchdog at that time, the public was hardly receptive when critical articles actually ran. The *Washington Post*, to name just one example, ran a front-page story during the war's run-up detailing multiple visits Donald Rumsfeld made to Saddam Hussein during the 1980s Iraq-Iran conflict. But a prevailing spirit of jingoism meant the story slipped by, ignored by an audience pumped on patriotism.

DC reporters are mainly guilty of focusing their energy on spontaneous scandals – Monica Lewinsky's relationship with Bill Clinton, and the drinking exploits of George W Bush's twin daughters, Barbara and Jenna, for example – instead of long-term investigations. The latter are costly, difficult to conduct and don't always glean newsworthy stories. The Bush administration is also infamous for shutting out reporters it doesn't approve of, which is a serious threat for journalists whose jobs rely on accessibility. Then again, access isn't everything: The guys who broke Watergate, the scandal that brought down President Richard Nixon, were young metro reporters completely removed from the insider scene.

One supposed remedy to inside-the-Beltway back-slapping are bloggers, citizen journalists independent of the 'mainstream media.' But the feisty blogger, more often than not, just regurgitates the day's news and adds opinionated spin. When they do break a story, it is often by picking up on inaccuracies that slip past editors, or because they have access to the same sources cultivated by reporters – thus making them as 'insider' as the competition.

WASHINGTON'S SITES OF SCANDAL, SEDUCTION & SKULDUGGERY

Washington media loves a good scandal (and some argue spends too much time trying to sniff one out). We offer here only a brief primer on some of the city's best-known scandal sites.

- Scandal Central: Watergate – Towering over the Potomac banks, this chi-chi apartment-hotel complex has lent its name to decades of political crime. It all started when Committee to Re-Elect the President (CREEP) operatives were found here, trying to bug Democratic National Committee headquarters. Thus was launched Woodward and Bernstein's investigation, which would eventually topple Nixon.
- Swimming for It: Tidal Basin – In 1974, Wilbur Mills, 65-year-old Arkansas representative and chairman of the House Ways & Means Committee, was stopped for speeding, whereupon his companion – 38-year-old stripper Fanne Foxe, known as the 'Argentine Firecracker' – leapt into the Basin to escape. Unfortunately for Mills' political career, a TV cameraman was there to film the fun.
- What's Your Position, Congressman?: Capitol Steps – John Jenrette was a little-known South Carolina representative until he embroiled himself in the bribery scandal (dubbed Abscam after Abdul Enterprises Ltd, the faux company set up by the FBI to offer money to members of Congress in return for political favors). Jenrette's troubles were compounded when his ex-wife Rita revealed in *Playboy* that she and her erstwhile husband used to slip out during dull late-night congressional sessions for an alfresco quickie on the Capitol's hallowed marble steps. (And that's not all.)
- Smoking Gun: Vista Hotel – It was in room No 727 that former DC mayor Marion Barry uttered his timeless quote: '…set up…bitch set me up!' when the FBI caught him taking a friendly puff of crack cocaine in the company of ex-model (and police informant) Hazel 'Rasheeda' Moore. The widely broadcast FBI video of his toke horrified a city lacerated by crack violence, but didn't stop it from re-electing Barry in 1994. (The Vista has since changed its name to the Wyndham Washington Hotel.)
- Suicidal Tendencies: Fort Marcy Park – The body of Vince Foster, Deputy Counsel to President Clinton and Hillary Clinton, was found in this remote Mclean, Virginia, park in 1993. Foster was dead from a bullet shot to the head. Investigations by both the Park Police and the FBI determined that the death was a suicide, but conspiracy theories abounded in right-wing rags.
- Stool Pigeon Sushi: Pentagon City Food Court – It was by the sushi bar that Monica Lewinsky awaited Linda Tripp, her lunch date (and betrayer) who led Ken Starr's agents down the mall escalators to snag her up for questioning in the nearby Ritz-Carlton Hotel. Who knew a food court could provide such a media fiesta?

LOBBYISTS

In March 2006, Jack Abramoff was sentenced to five years in prison on fraud and corruption charges. It was the culmination of a series of investigations that revealed the Bush fundraiser had defrauded American Indian tribes of millions of dollars in casino revenue, later used to slip politicians into his pocket. The truth tore apart the 'K Street Project,' a firm of right-wing, special-interest groups that had been trying, since 1994, to buy Republicans into top government leadership roles.

Abramoff was a lobbyist, that breed of political entrepreneur that makes a living advocating for special interests. This isn't Europe, where causes form their own party and seek power through a parliamentary coalition. America favors enterprise, and agenda-pushers here, left and right, directly thrust their message onto elected officials.

Lobbying is traditionally dated to the late 19th century, but took off as a vital component of American politics during the money-minded 1980s. Most politicos see lobbyists as a necessary evil, and while it's the rare politician who admits to being influenced by them, everyone understands their importance: lobbyists are the go-betweens in a city built on client-patron relationships. For better or worse, they have become a vital rung on DC's power ladder.

Foreign governments and tree-huggers, gun nuts and industrialists; every group gets its say here through the work of well-paid and connected advocates. Lobbying ranks, largely based on K Street (to the point that the two terms are synonymous), are swelled by those who know how to navigate the complex social webs of the capital; some watchdogs estimate as many as 40% of former congressman rejoin the private sector as lobbyists.

Wining, dining, vacation packages and the art of giving all of the above without violating campaign contribution laws is a delicate dance. In the wake of the Abramoff scandal, reforms have been passed. The latest keep congressmen and women from becoming lobbyists for two years after they leave office, require quarterly electronic finance disclosures from lobbying firms, and keep lobbyists off the floor of Congress. On the other hand, the act didn't provide what many watchdog groups have been agitating for: an in-house ethics commission to oversee the profession.

MALL OF JUSTICE

Washington, DC, is not just the center of government, it is also the center of demonstration. What the Capitol is to conventional politics, the National Mall is to protest politics. The Mall has provided a forum for people who feel that they or their issue has been shut out by the establishment. Peace-loving war veterans, long-skirted suffragettes, civil rights activists, shrouded white supremacists, tractor-driving farmers and million-mom marchers have staged political pageants on the Mall. Following are great moments in American protest politics:

- Bonus Army (1932) – WWI veterans, left unemployed by the Great Depression, petitioned the government for an early payment of promised bonuses for their wartime service. As many as 10,000 vets settled in for an extended protest, pitching tents on the Mall and Capitol lawn. President Hoover dispatched Douglas MacArthur to evict the 'Bonus Army.' In a liberal display of force, the veterans were routed and their campsites razed.
- 'I Have a Dream' (1963) – The Civil Rights movement was the most successful protest movement, effectively employing boycotts and demonstrations. Reverend Martin Luther King's stirring speech, delivered from the steps of the Lincoln Memorial to 200,000 supporters, remains a high point in the historic struggle for racial equality.
- Anti-War Protests (1971) – The Vietnam War aroused some of the most notable episodes of protest politics. In April 1971, an estimated 500,000 Vietnam veterans and students gathered on the Mall to oppose continued hostilities. Several thousand arrests were made.
- AIDS Memorial Quilt (1996) – Lesbian and gay activists drew more than 300,000 supporters in a show of solidarity for equal rights under the law and to display the ever-growing AIDS quilt, which covered the entire eastern flank of the Mall from the Capitol to the Washington Monument.
- Million Mom March (2000) – A half-million people convened on the Mall on Mother's Day, to draw attention to hand-gun violence and to influence Congress in passing stricter gun-ownership laws.
- Bring Them Home Now Tour (2005) – At least 100,000 protestors demanded the withdrawal of American soldiers from Iraq. They were met with 400 counter-protestors who support a continued American presence. Both sides are led by families who have lost loved ones in the war.

POLITICALSPEAK 101

Here's an example of how heavily politics influences local culture: a DC classic-rock station, 94.7, calls after-work gridlock 'the five o'clock filibuster.' With that in mind, here's a primer on other head-scratching political terms you may hear thrown about:

- Filibuster – The art of delaying the passage of a bill by talking it to death; now used to refer to any sort of painful wait. Longest ever: Strom Thurmond's 24-hour, 18-minute rant to block the (successful) passage of the 1957 Civil Rights Act.
- Gerrymander – When elected officials redraw electoral boundaries for their own benefit, named for the weird, salamander-like shape of a replotted Massachusetts district created by Elbridge Gerry in 1812.
- Pork barrel – Hitching funding (often for dams, roads and airports) to a popular bill that has no relation to the funded projects. For instance: Millions of dollars for new bridges tacked onto a bill that deals with lobbying reform.
- -gate – Any kind of scandal, named for the Watergate hotel, the nexus of the events that led to Richard Nixon's resignation in 1974. Other examples include: Monicagate (for Monica Lewinsky, the intern whose novel use of cigars earned her a 'favored' place in the Oval Office) and Katrinagate (the mismanagement that crippled the emergency response to Hurricane Katrina in 2005).
- Soccer mom/NASCAR dad – Quintessential American voters. The soccer mom is a middle-to upper-class, suburban or ex-urban mom with a cell phone, an SUV and kids to pick up after school. She's a moderate voter, and considered a major source of Bill Clinton's electoral victory. NASCAR dads are working class, uber-patriotic, averse to gay marriage and immigrants, and named for the racing association they love to watch. Considered a backbone of the Republican Party.
- Compassionate conservatism – An oxymoron (joke!). A philosophy and slogan often espoused by George W Bush. The idea that limited government spending and low taxes creates a prosperous society, which inherently helps its own and avoids wasteful federal programs (like welfare and health care, as liberals are quick to point out).
- Red state/blue state – A term for the American political divide (see Dems View of Repubs, Repubs View of Dems, p30) that references the electoral map display used by news services during national elections. In the image, the blue, liberal states dominate the Northeast and the West Coast, while the South and the Heartland are firmly Republican red.
- Neoconservatism – This school of thought calls for more spending on government programs than old-school Repubs are comfortable with, civil equality for minorities and the vigorous promotion of democracy abroad. Sometimes, as recent events have shown, through military means. The idea: America is powerful, America is good, our way of life can't be beat, and if we give oppressed people freedom, they will become our allies.
- Spin/Flack – Ways of throwing the press off politicians. Professional flacks, or spokespersons, 'spin' events and issues to their advantage. Take the abortion debate: 'Pro-choice' activists become 'anti-life' to the 'pro-life' movement, whose opponents deem them 'anti-choice.'
- Stumping – Bringing politics to the people; when candidates on the campaign trail speak at local town halls, schools and fairs to gain face recognition with voters. This most traditional of American campaign tactics has been subverted by internet campaigning via blogs, direct-mailing campaigns to homes and, of course, since the 1960s, TV.

DEMOCRACY IN ACTION

One of the great paradoxes of American politics is how simultaneously accessible and shut off the system is. Visitors can walk into congressional hearings dressed in jeans and a T-shirt and address their elected representatives, in public, with barely any security screening at all. Mass protests have rocked the foundations of government and seared themselves on the national psyche forever. Yet most of the decisions that influence American government are made between small groups of well-connected policy wonks, lobbyists and special interests who are mainly concerned with perpetuating their own organizations.

Americans believe changing the system requires going to DC and coming face to face with their elected officials (there's even a cinematic subgenre devoted to the idea, from *Mr Smith Goes to Washington* to *Legally Blonde 2*). On a grand scale, the equation is partly true. Large protests, often held on the National Mall (opposite), can shift public perception a few points towards a particular cause. But smaller delegations usually require lots of money and clout to affect change.

It's maddening, but the surface of the process is surprisingly open to travelers. Check www.house.gov and www.senate.gov to get the schedules for congressional committee hearings (call ahead to the numbers provided, as some meetings are closed to the public). Passes for Capitol tours and public viewings of Congress are doled out on a first-come, first-served basis starting at 9am on weekdays, at a kiosk on the southwest corner of the Capitol grounds (1st St and Independent Ave SW); go to www.aoc.gov/cc/visit/index.cfm for more details.

Commonwealth visitors may be surprised at how courteous politicians here are in formal, public debate. The decorum is especially strange considering how highly Americans prize informality, but a lot of stock is placed on addressing officials as 'The respected gentleman,' and 'My respected colleague from [insert state here].' That entire system received a brutal (and amusing) shock in May 2005, when Scottish MP George Galloway was called in front of a Senate committee that was investigating possible ties he may have had with Saddam Hussein during the UN oil-for-food scandal. In a performance that dropped jaws and caused snickers across Capitol Hill, Galloway came out swinging, British parliament style, stunning interrogator Senator Norm Coleman into silence with a long, angry monologue about American hypocrisy.

THE SECOND REPUBLICAN REVOLUTION

That soft thud you heard on November 7, 2006, was the Republican Party getting its butt painfully kicked out of a congressional majority. Since 1994, the Grand Old Party had almost continually dominated the legislative branch of American government. During their reign, the Republicans defeated Bill Clinton's health-care reform, successfully blocked the barest whiff of legalized gay marriage, invaded Afghanistan and Iraq, and presided over towering heights of government spending.

Hardly sounds like the Reagan-era, small-government conservatism of the 1980s, but why run a small government if you control it? An almost imperial hubris infected Republicans in the '90s and 'noughties,' an era when officials cheerfully bought out lobbyists and enlisted them to write legislation (with some shady holiday junkets thrown in on the side). But every party ends, and last call came for the Repubs on the heels of corruption investigations into House Majority leader Tom DeLay, his subsequent resignation, the increasing unpopularity of Iraq, the ineffectual federal response to Hurricane Katrina, and a Democrat's dream of a scandal: Mark Foley, Florida congressman and social conservative, accused of sending sexually explicit emails to young male pages.

The 2006 mid-term elections re-ushered the Democrats into control of Congress, but it should be noted the Dems ran fairly conservative candidates against at-risk Republicans. The direction Democrats take now remains to be seen. Will they play toward the center or, like the Republicans did in their 1994 mid-term revolution, energize their base and bump American politics a few points left?

Arts

Arts

Washington is the showcase of American arts, home to such prestigious venues as the National Gallery and the Kennedy Center. The National Symphony Orchestra and the National Theatre embody everything their titles imply: top-notch music and theater to represent the nation. The result is that Washington's arts scene – where it is most visible and most acclaimed – is national rather than local in scope.

It is a blessing for local culture vultures, for sure. Access to the nation's (and the world's) top artists and musicians is reserved for residents of only a few cities; DC is among them because it was deemed appropriate for a political capital.

Often overlooked, however, is another arts scene – a scene representative of DC and not necessarily the USA. It is edgier, blacker, more organic and more experimental. It is colored by the experiences of the city's African American and immigrant populations, lending diversity and ethnicity. It dances around the edges of the more conservative national scene and discreetly tests its boundaries. The Arena Stage, the Corcoran Gallery and the Dance Place are examples of the innovative, experimental venues that draw on local talent and themes in their productions. Loads of smaller art galleries and community theaters around the city are the backbone of this vibrant arts scene.

PAINTING & VISUAL ARTS

Visual arts in DC has three faces: the vast holdings of the National Gallery of Art (p66) and the Smithsonian Institution (p65); the private collections and special exhibits at the Corcoran Gallery of Art (p75) and the Phillips Collection (p102); and the wealth of small commercial galleries supporting local, national and international artists.

The first hardly needs an explanation. The National Gallery of Art comprises two buildings filled with paintings, sculpture, photography and decorative arts from the Middle Ages to the present. The Smithsonian Institution operates the Freer Gallery, the Hirshhorn Museum & Sculpture Garden, the National Museum of African Art, the National Museum of American Art, the National Portrait Gallery (p96), the Renwick Gallery (p77) and the Sackler Gallery (p64) – an impressive collection to be sure. From ancient handicrafts to modern sculpture, the spectrum of the works at these national museums is truly mind boggling.

The Corcoran and the Phillips are private museums that were built from the collections of philanthropic art lovers. The Corcoran Gallery has a renowned collection of 20th-century American prints, photography and painting. The Phillips Collection holds impressionist and modern masterpieces from both Europe and America. Both museums host special exhibits to lure visitors off the National Mall and into their decked-out halls.

The city has been pumping tons of money into the arts lately. Over the last decade $1.5 billion has been spent renovating or constructing new museums and memorials. Especially pertinent to art lovers was the six-year $283-million superb renovation of the old Patent Office Building, home to the National Museum of American Art and the National Portrait Gallery. Aside from the two museums, the building is now home to a unique conservation facility with floor-to-ceiling glass windows that allow visitors to view art conservators at work.

The Corcoran Gallery is also expanding. It's building a $120-million new wing made from undulating steel, designed by acclaimed architect Frank Gehry.

ART GALLERIES

Less known, but no less important, DC is riddled with grassroots art galleries (see p191 for more). Many are owned or operated by the artists themselves. This scene has blossomed since the 1990s, fuelled by DC's reinvigorated neighborhoods and increasingly cosmopolitan population. It is no longer a given that a talented artist will flee to New York to make it big. Some names to look out for on the DC art scene include Colby Caldwell, Steve Cushner, Sam Gilliam, Ryan Hackett, Jae Ko and Nancy Sansom Reynolds. DC can boast bona fide art districts in Dupont Circle and Downtown. The Old Torpedo Factory (p126) in Old Town Alexandria is also an incredible conglomeration of creative minds. These are the places to see the face of DC art at its most pure.

LITERATURE

Washington's literary legacy is, not surprisingly, deeply entwined with American political history. The city's best-known early literature consists of writings and books that hammered out the machinery of American democracy. From Thomas Jefferson's *Notes on the State of Virginia* to James Madison's *The Federalist Papers* and Abraham Lincoln's historic speeches and proclamations, this literature fascinates modern readers – not only because it is the cornerstone of the US political system, but because of the grace and beauty of its prose. Skill with the pen is, alas, no longer a notable characteristic of US presidents.

Apart from politicians' writings, 19th-century Washington literature was created primarily by authors and journalists who resided here only temporarily, drawn to DC by circumstance, professional obligation or wanderlust. Walt Whitman's *The Wound Dresser* and *Specimen Days* and Louisa May Alcott's *Hospital Sketches* were based upon the authors' harrowing experiences as Civil War nurses at Washington's hospitals. Mark Twain had an ill-starred (and short) career as a senator's speechwriter, memorialized in *Washington in 1868*.

Frederick Douglass (1818–95), the abolitionist, editor, memoirist and former slave, is perhaps Washington's most revered writer. His seminal antislavery works *The Life & Times of Frederick Douglass* and *My Bondage & My Freedom* were written in DC, where Douglass lived on Capitol Hill and in Anacostia.

Henry Adams (1838–1918), grandson of President John Adams, often invited DC's literati to salons at his mansion on Lafayette Sq, which became the literary center of the day. His brilliant *Democracy* was the forerunner of many political-scandal novels of the 20th century. His later autobiography, *The Education of Henry Adams*, provides a fascinating insider's account of Washington high society during this period.

In the early 20th century, another salon often took place across town at 15th and S Sts in Shaw. Artists and writers often gathered here, at poet Georgia Douglas Johnson's home, which became the center of the Harlem Renaissance in DC. Her guests included African American poets Langston Hughes and Paul Dunbar.

Another member of this circle was Jean Toomer, author of the subtle, sad *Cane*. Not a novel in the traditional sense, Toomer's seminal work is part poetry, part prose and part play. The book – while lacking a continuous plot or defined characters – is among the strongest representations of Harlem Renaissance literature.

In DC, the Harlem Renaissance is sometimes called the New Negro movement, named after the famous volume by Howard University professor Alain Locke. *The New Negro* – the bible of the Renaissance – is a collection of essays, poems and stories written by Locke and his colleagues. The writing is energetic and subversive; as a snapshot of the Renaissance and the African American experience it is invaluable.

Throughout the 20th century, Washington literature remained a deeply political beast, defined by works such as Carl Bernstein and Bob Woodward's *All the President's Men* and John Kennedy's *Profiles in Courage*. Perhaps the most eloquent poem about DC is Robert Lowell's *July in Washington*, written about the poet's participation in a 1968 political protest.

Many more purely literary writers have appeared on the scene, too. The contemporary writer who is best able to capture the streets and sounds and sights of DC in his writing is Edward Jones. His National Book Award nominee *Lost in the City* is an incredible collection of 14 stories set in inner-city DC in the 1960s and 1970s. Each recounts a tale of an individual facing the complexity of city life in a strangely hopeful way. The portrayal of the city – like the characters themselves – is real and raw.

George Pelecanos is another talented writer whose crime novels show the hard, fast streets of DC that most visitors never see. Filled with sex, drugs and rock 'n' roll, he shows off his intimate knowledge of the city street scene and latest pop culture. (The 'soundtracks' are among the highlights of reading the books.) Pelecanos has written 16 such novels with interwoven themes and characters, but *Hell to Pay* and *Right to Rain* are considered his best.

Marita Golden is a modern African American writer whose novels about contemporary African American families dealing with betrayal, loss, growth and reconciliation have attracted a loyal following. *The Edge of Heaven* is set in DC, where an accomplished 20-year-old student confronts her confusion about reuniting with her parents upon her mother's release from four years in prison.

Paul Kafka-Gibbons addresses the touchy subject of marriage in his second novel, *Dupont Circle*. From the title (and setting), you might guess the subject is gay marriage, but the novel does not exclude anyone. Intertwining plots revolve around three couples – only one is gay but all three are untraditional – who deal with the expectations and realities of being in a relationship. Kafka-Gibbons won the Los Angeles Times Book Prize for his first novel *Love <Enter>* (which does not take place in DC), but this second novel has not been as well received.

Native Washingtonian Gore Vidal often aims his satirical pen at his hometown, that is, Washington, DC. His six-volume series of historical novels about the American past includes *Washington, DC,* an insightful examination of the period from the New Deal to the McCarthy era from the perspective of the capital. *The Smithsonian Institution* is a fantastical historical account of a 13-year-old boy who travels through time to save the world. Readers who can throw all caution to the wind and follow Vidal without skepticism will enjoy the weird and wonderful ride.

Advise & Consent is Allen Drury's fictional account of Alger Hiss' nomination as Secretary of State under Franklin D Roosevelt. The novel brilliantly portrays the conflicting personal and political motivations of his characters – a real revelation of what goes on inside the US Senate.

On a less elevated note, DC has also inspired thousands of potboilers. A representative is the work of Tom Clancy, northern Virginia resident and creator of innumerable right-wing thrillers that sometimes feature Washington's apocalyptic destruction (see *Debt of Honor* and *Executive Orders* for much President-and-Congress offing).

For a fine profile of the contemporary Washington literary scene, check out David Cutler's *Literary Washington: A Complete Guide to the Literary Life in the Nation's Capital.*

WASHINGTON DC IN LITERATURE

- *The Washingtonienne* by Jessica Cutler (2005). The only slightly fictionalized account of a senatorial aide who sleeps her way around the Hill for money, keeps a blog, gets caught and becomes the city's scandal du jour – a juicy beach read.
- *Sammy's Hill* by Kristin Gore (2005). A story of life and love on Capitol Hill. Told through the eyes of 26-year-old Samantha Joyce, a self-deprecating health-care policy advisor to an Ohio senator. Gore, aside from being Al Gore's daughter, is best known for her comedic writing on hits like *Saturday Night Live* and received good reviews for her first fictional attempt. *Sammy's Hill* is an easy, yet witty, well-written read.
- *American Tabloid* by James Ellroy (1994). One of our favorite historical fiction reads ever, this epic tells one version of the Camelot years and the conspiracy to end all conspiracies – the assassination of JFK. It manages to work the Mafia, rogue CIA agents, ruthless Cubans, J Edgar Hoover, Howard Hughes, drugs, and a couple of cops and FBI guys into one crazy story. DC is one of its many backdrops.
- *Advise & Consent* by Allen Drury (1981). A compelling fictional account of personalities and politics in the US Senate.
- *The Dream Keeper and Other Poems* by Langston Hughes (1996). A collection of poignant poems written especially for kids.
- *Hits Below the Beltway* by Dave Barry (2002). Not exactly literature, but still a hilarious account of history and politics by one of America's best-loved columnists.
- *Lost in the City* by Edward Jones (2003). Evocative short stories about people and places in DC.

DC has also been the setting for chick lit in the past years – even Al Gore's daughter, Kristin Gore, penned a novel, *Sammy's Hill*. The most popular book of this genre, however, has to be Jessica Cutler's *Washingtonienne*, which is an only slightly fictionalized tell-all about her Capitol Hill sexual liaisons. Cutler, who was fired from Senator Mike DeWine's (R-Ohio) office after the online blog she kept for friends about 'the presidential appointee who gives her cash after each tryst' exploded into the city's scandal of the month. Her book has since been optioned for a TV miniseries (see p42).

MUSIC

Only in the capital can national orchestras coexist with rebellious punk, all under the rubric of the local music scene. That military marches and soulful go-go both reached their peaks under the watchful eye (and attentive ear) of DC fans is tribute to the city's electric – if eclectic – music scene.

In the early 20th century, segregation of entertainment venues meant that Black Washington had to create its own arts scene – so it created one far more vibrant than anything White Washington could boast. Jazz, big band and swing flourished at clubs and theaters around DC and particularly in the Shaw district. Greats such as Duke Ellington (p40), Pearl Bailey, Shirley Horne, Johnny Hodges and Ben Webster all got their start in the clubs of U St NW. Today this district is reviving as new clubs and theaters open in the historic buildings in the area. After 30 years of neglect, the renowned Bohemian Caverns (p184) now hosts local soul-jazz music. But other venues in the area – like the Black Cat (p183) and the 9:30 Club (p183) – are now DC's premier venues for modern rock, blues and hip-hop. Shaw is not a re-creation of a historical fantasy: it is an organic area, shaped not only by its history but also by modern musical movements.

The scene at these venues is varied, but not particularly unique to DC. The exception – where DC really stands out musically – is where it builds on its local roots in go-go and punk. Go-go is an infectiously rhythmic dance music combining elements of funk, rap, soul and Latin percussion, which stomped onto the city scene in the 1970s (p187). These days, go-go soul blends with hip-hop and reggae's rhythm – everybody dance now! Clubs playing 1980s dance and lounges with mellow house and trance are equally popular.

DC's hardcore take on punk, as embodied by such bands as Fugazi and Dag Nasty, combined super-fast guitar with a socially conscious mindset and flourished at venues in the 1990s. Arlington-based Dischord Records, one of the country's most successful small labels, grew out of the punk scene and remains a fierce promoter of local bands. Check out *Banned in DC*, a photo book by Cynthia Connolly that documents the Washington punk scene of the 1970s and 1980s. While punk is no longer the musical force it once was, its influence on grunge and other modern genres is undeniable. Local bands such as Dismemberment Plan and Dog Fashion Disco are carrying the post-punk torch in DC.

YOUR WASHINGTON DC PLAYLIST

Every city has a soundtrack, and DC is no exception. However, there is a noticeable lack of songs about the city – no one seems to leave their heart in Washington. The following playlist is a mixture of songs about DC and songs by Washington artists.

- 'It Don't Mean a Thing (If it Ain't got that Swing)' by Duke Ellington
- 'Banned in DC' by Bad Brains
- 'Are You My Woman?' by the Chi-Lites
- 'Do Right' by Jimmie's Chicken Shack
- 'Waiting Room' by Fugazi
- 'Idiot Wind' by Bob Dylan
- 'We the People' by Chuck Jones
- 'Rock Creek Park' by The Blackbyrds
- 'Don't Worry about the Government' by Talking Heads
- 'Chocolate City' by Parliament
- '(Don't go back to) Rockville' by R.E.M.
- 'Killing Me Softly with His Song' by Roberta Flack
- 'Washington Bullets' by The Clash
- 'I'm Just a Bill' by School House Rock
- 'Run Joe' by Chuck Jones
- 'Bustin' Loose' by Chuck Jones
- '1 Thing' by Amerie
- 'Radio King Orchestra' by Radio King Orchestra
- 'The Way It Is' by Bruce Hornsby
- 'Red Dirt Girl' by Emmylou Harris
- 'He Thinks He'll Keep Her' by Mary Chapin Carpenter

Showing off its southern roots, DC has spawned some folk and country stars of its own, too, including Emmylou Harris, Mary Chapin Carpenter and John Fahey (who named his seminal folk record label Takoma for Takoma Park, his boyhood home). Folksy keyboardist Bruce Hornsby is a native of nearby Williamsburg, VA.

Popular African American R&B and soul artist Roberta Flack was raised in Arlington, VA. Before establishing her music career, she was the first Black student teacher in an all-White school in posh Chevy Chase, Maryland. She was discovered at a respected Capitol Hill jazz club, Mr Henry's, where the owners eventually constructed her an elaborate stage.

In the alternative rock area, nationally known acts include Jimmie's Chicken Shack, which got its start playing at the now venerated WHFStival (p182).

PERFORMING ARTS

The capital's most visible musicians are the big boys – those from the weighty cultural landmarks like the National Symphony Orchestra (NSO; p194) and the Washington Opera (p194). For the most part, they are not doing anything new. At the NSO, directed by Leonard Slatkin, classical means classical. Placido Domingo directs the Washington Opera. Repertoire and productions tend to air on the traditional side but are technically sound – highlighted by special occasions when Domingo conducts or sings. Diva Denyce Graves, graduate of the local Duke Ellington School of Performing Arts, occasionally graces its stage and thrills her hometown audiences.

A national orchestra of sorts is the Marine Corps Marching Band, based at the Marine Barracks (p91) in Southeast DC. Back in the late 19th century, military marching-band music reached its apotheosis (such as it was) in the work of John Philip Sousa, who directed the Marine Corps Marching Band for many years (and was born and buried nearby). In this era of amped-up patriotism, this genre remains alive and well: the band still performs his work today.

A great resource for information about the contemporary local music scene is the **DC Music Network** (www.dcmusicnet.com).

THE DUKE

'My road runs from Ward's Place to my grandmother's at Twentieth and R, to Seatan Street, around to 8th Street, back up to T Street, through LeDroit Park to Sherman Avenue,' wrote DC's most famous musical son, jazz immortal Edward Kennedy 'Duke' Ellington (1899-1974), describing his childhood in Washington's Shaw district. In the segregated DC of the early 20th century, Shaw hosted one of the country's finest black arts scenes – drawing famed actors, musicians and singers to perform at venues like the Howard Theatre and Bohemian Caverns (p184) – so the Duke took root in rich soil.

As a tot, Ellington purportedly first tackled the keyboard under the tutelage of a teacher by the name of Mrs Clinkscales. He honed his chops by listening to local ragtime pianists like Doc Perry, Louis Thomas and Louis Brown at Frank Holliday's T St poolroom. His first composition, written at 16, was the 'Soda Fountain Rag'; next came 'What You Gonna Do When the Bed Breaks Down?' The handsome, suave young Duke played hops and cabarets all over black Washington before decamping for New York in 1923.

There, Ellington started out as a Harlem stride pianist, performing at Barron's and the Hollywood Club; but he soon moved to the famed Cotton Club, where he matured into an innovative bandleader, composer and arranger. He collaborated with innumerable artists – including Louis Armstrong and Ella Fitzgerald – but his most celebrated collaboration was with composer/arranger Billy Strayhorn, who gave the Ellington Orchestra its theme, 'Take the "A" Train,' in 1941. Strayhorn worked with Duke throughout his life, collaborating on later works like *Such Sweet Thunder* (1957) and *The Far East Suite* (1964).

Ellington's big-band compositions, with their infectious melodies, harmonic sophistication and ever-present swing, made him one of the 20th-century's most revered American composers and his ability to craft arrangements highlighting the singular talents of his musicians made him the foremost bandleader of his time. His huge volume of work – more than 1500 pieces – is preserved in its entirety at the Smithsonian Institution in his old hometown.

For more on the Duke, check out his witty memoir *Music Is My Mistress*, which details his DC childhood and later accomplishments.

THEATER & COMEDY

Political comedy and theater are certainly a fixture of the DC arts scene. The Ford's Theatre (p94) – site of Lincoln's assassination – holds its place in history by presenting traditional, Americana-themed productions. If you're looking for comedy, then head to the Ronald Reagan Building and International Trade Center downtown to catch a performance by the capital's foremost comedy troupe, the Capitol Steps Political Satire (p194). The group cuts up exclusively with biting satire of the goings-on in the White House and on Capitol Hill.

Such theatrical ventures certainly have their place in the nation's capital. There is more, however, to theater in DC. Most Broadway shows will eventually find their way to the National Theatre (p193) or the Kennedy Center (p192). The Arena Stage (p192), home to one of the country's oldest troupes, was the first theater outside of New York to win a Tony and continues to stage diverse productions by new playwrights. Over the course of 25 years, smaller companies like Studio Theatre (p192) have established a strong presence. For almost as long, the Source Theatre (p192) has hosted the Annual Washington Theater Festival, a platform for new plays, workshops and the insanely popular 10-Minute Play Competition. The Folger Shakespeare Library & Theatre (p192) gives new perspective to the Bard. The edgy Woolly Mammoth Theatre Co (p192) and the multicultural Gala Hispanic Theatre (p192) have moved to larger theaters.

What's exciting on the DC theater scene is the proliferation of brand-new companies and community theaters, stepping into the empty spaces that their predecessors have left behind. Acting guilds and theater groups are popping up on every stage in Shaw, Dupont Circle and Capitol Hill, pressing the limits of what theater can do. For example, heritage-based companies, such as Asian Stories in America (p192) and Theater J (p192), are highlighting the works of various ethnic groups. And the District of Columbia Arts Center (DCAC; p192) hosts the innovative Playback, where the audience provides stories to fuel the plot on stage.

CINEMA & TV

Hollywood directors can't resist the black limousines, white marble, counterintelligence subterfuges and political scandal that official Washington embodies. But local film buffs offer up two complaints about all this attention. First, unofficial Washington – the real place where real people live – might as well be Waikiki; few films are set anywhere other than Capitol Hill and it's a rare movie character that does not live in Georgetown (unless they live in the White House). Second, even the movies about official Washington fail to capture how the personalities and politics really work. Then again, since when does Hollywood capture how anything *really* works?

Hollywood's favorite theme for a Washington movie is the political naïf who stumbles into combat with corrupt capital-veterans. Such is the story in the preeminent Washington film *Mr Smith goes to Washington,* in which Jimmy Stewart and his troop of 'Boy Rangers' defeat big, bad government and preserve democracy for the rest of the country. This theme reappears in the 1950 hit *Born Yesterday*, as well as the less lauded but still funny *Dave, Legally Blonde 2* and *Being There.*

For sheer ridiculousness on this same subject we loved the smartness hidden behind the oft-black humor in both *Bullworth* (Warren Beatty and Halle Berry) and *Head of State* (Chris Rock).

Another popular theme for DC-based cinema is the total destruction of the nation's capital by aliens (perhaps some wishful thinking on the part of the West Coast). The best of this genre is *The Day the Earth Stood Still*, both for its underlying pacifist message and its off-Mall DC scenes. Adaptations of this theme include the Cold War–era *Earth vs Flying Saucers* and the Will Smith vehicle *Independence Day.*

DC is a popular setting for political thrillers – action-adventure fans might enjoy *In the Line of Fire* (Clint Eastwood as a savvy secret-service agent protecting the president), *Patriot Games* (Harrison Ford as a tough CIA agent battling Irish terrorists), and *No Way Out* (Kevin Costner as a Navy officer outracing Russian spies). All of them are entertaining, especially the scenes of DC's famous sites.

41

SEX AND DC

Here's the scoop, Sarah Jessica Parker is developing Jessica Cutler's steamy tell-all novel, *The Washingtonienne*, into a half-hour comedy for HBO. Are you thinking what we're thinking: *Sex and the City* goes to Washington? Swapping the Senate cafeteria and the decidedly less cool Saki for NYC's Raw and Bed? Maybe. The show was still in development stages in 2006 so it's really too soon to tell, although we can say there are no plans for Parker to star in it (she will executive produce).

Cutler became famous after DC's Wonkette blog published excerpts from her online diary of real-life sexcapades with six different men, some of whom paid her for sex. She was fired from her job working for Senator Mike DeWine (R-Ohio) as a result.

At the time, Cutler expressed disbelief that anyone even cared.

'If I were sleeping with a Congressman, maybe, but I'm a nobody, and the people I'm writing about are nobodies,' she told the *Washington Post*.

Within a year, however, she had a book published and shortly afterwards Parker's Pretty Matches production company optioned the TV rights to the book.

And what does Cutler think of the project? She's stoked.

'Free heroin for anyone who tunes in,' Cutler told the media about why you'll get addicted.

'Kidding,' she added. 'People can't stop watching a train wreck... She's trying to fake it until she makes it, and whenever you're somewhere not for the right reasons hilarity can only ensue.'

We guess you'll have to tune in to find out.

A twist on this action-packed genre goes like this: unwitting but wise hero discovers a dangerous state secret and so must outwit intelligence forces to save the day. In *The Pelican Brief*, law student Julia Roberts discovers the conspiracy behind the death of two Supreme Court justices, resulting in a whirlwind flight from and fight against the FBI. Most of this film – based on the John Grisham novel – takes place in New Orleans, but there are a few shots of Georgetown. Essentially the same storyline is played out in *Enemy of the State*, except lawyer Will Smith takes on the ultra-mysterious National Security Agency right here in the capital. Both of these entertaining films have suspense-filled plots and well-developed characters, even if the themes are trite.

For a lighter look at intelligence, *The Man with One Red Shoe* is a silly, spoofy story of an unsuspecting musician (Tom Hanks) who is mistaken for a CIA mole. It's good for some laughs and some glimpses of the city. Theodore Flicker's 1967 *The President's Analyst* (James Coburn) has become a political cult classic. The leading man plays the president's psychiatrist who gets into all sorts of trouble with various spies and thugs who are trying to find out what he knows.

The finest satire of the Cold War has to be Stanley Kubrick's 1964 *Dr. Strangelove*. Based at the Pentagon, the plot revolves around a power-mad general who brings the world to the brink of annihilation because he fears a Communist takeover of his 'precious bodily fluids.'

Real-life intrigue has been the subject of more than one DC film. *All the President's Men* is based on Carl Bernstein and Bob Woodward's first-hand account of their uncovering of the Watergate scandal (a young Robert Redford and Dustin Hoffman are brilliant as the reporters.) This film's only disappointment is that it does not take the insiders' account to its completion, but concludes – anticlimactically – with the 1973 *Post* headlines recounting the end of the story.

In 2005, George Clooney directed and starred in the highly praised *Good Night, and Good Luck*. Shot in black and white, it is a stark account of how CBS reporter Edward R Murrow and his producer Fred W Friendly exposed and helped bring down one of the most controversial American senators, Joseph McCarthy.

The only movies where the politician is a good guy are those depicting the US president: *Air Force One, The American President, Primary Colors, Thirteen Days* – all entertaining but idealistic portraits of the Chief Executive facing various crises. A variation on this theme is *Wag the Dog*, a hilarious parody of presidential-election spin: a presidential advisor (Robert De Niro) hires a Hollywood producer (Dustin Hoffman) to 'produce' a war in order to distract voters from an unfolding sex scandal. This marriage of Hollywood and Washington results in the cleverest satire of national politics to date.

Arguably the best – most realistic, most captivating – Washington movie is Otto Preminger's *Advise & Consent*, based on Allen Drury's novel by the same name. For its portrayal of our political system at work, complete with personalities and processes, this film is a must-see. Interesting tidbit: the DC scenes include the first in Hollywood history that were shot in a gay bar.

In 2004, controversial left-wing filmmaker Michael Moore released *Fahrenheit 9/11*, a documentary slamming the Bush administration, in particular, its handling of September 11 and the Iraq War. Much of it is filmed in DC. It won top prize at the Cannes Film Festival and went on to become the most successful documentary in history – it opened first in a select few cinemas nationwide, but seats sold so quickly the movie was released in most major cinemas across the country.

Only a select few films set in Washington, DC, are not about politics. The horrific highlight is undoubtedly *The Exorcist*, the cult horror flick set in Georgetown. The creepy long staircase in the movie – descending from Prospect St to M St in reality – has become known as the Exorcist Stairs (p80). Another classic Georgetown movie is the 1980s Brat Pack flick *St Elmo's Fire*. Demi Moore and Judd Nelson's characters are supposed to be Georgetown graduates, but the college campus is actually the University of Maryland in College Park (although there is the key scene shot in the popular Georgetown bar the Third Edition, p190). For its excellent acting and suspense-filled storyline (and not a few shots of the nation's capital at its finest), *A Few Good Men* is an excellent Washington, DC, movie.

Slam, a 1998 docu-drama, is one of the most powerful DC movies we've seen. It tells the story of Ray Joshua, a gifted young (and jobless) MC trapped in a war-zone DC housing project known as Dodge City. Ray copes with the despair and poverty of his neighborhood by creating haunting poetry.

DC ON FILM

- *Advise & Consent* (Otto Preminger, 1962) A lengthy, but intelligent, inside-the-Capitol story of the interplay of personalities and politics set during Henry Fonda's Secretary-of-State nominations. Gen-X'ers might not get it too much.
- *All the President's Men* (Alan Jpakula, 1976) The suspenseful rendition of Woodward and Bernstein uncovering the Watergate scandal. Enough suspense to keep men and women of multiple generations in their seats.
- *American President* (Rob Reiner, 1965) Tear jerking chick-flick romantic comedy starring Michael Douglas as the Commander-in-Chief and Annette Benning as a tough girl lobbyist and his love interest.
- *Fahrenheit 9/11* (Michael Moore, 2004) This documentary slams the Bush administration, and the way it handled both September 11 and the Iraq War. There's no question the film is super left wing, but most of its points, while often offered out of context, are factually correct.
- *Good Night, and Good Luck* (George Clooney, 2005) Shot in black and white, this is an intense account of how CBS reporter Edward R Murrow and producer Fred W Friendly helped take down controversial senator Joseph McCarthy.
- *Head of State* (Chris Rock, 2003) Chris Rock stars as a lowly DC alderman (similar to a city-council member) whose status is drastically elevated when the Democratic Party nominates him to run in the place of its candidate killed in a plane crash. It's whip smart and dark, and somehow manages to give a picture of just how messed up America's electoral system can be.
- *Mr Smith Goes to Washington* (Frank Capra, 1939) Jimmy Stewart saves the day on Capitol Hill in this well-loved classic where honesty and courage triumph over greed and fear.
- *The President's Analyst* (Theodore Flicker, 1967) James Coburn stars as the president's shrink in this political comedy from the creator of *Barney Miller*. It's garnered a cult following. Coburn knows too much, or so the president's enemies think, and the psychiatrist ends up battling a motley assortment of thugs and spies who are trying to decipher his boss' secrets.
- *Wag the Dog* (Barry Levinson, 1997) A side-busting comparison of making movies and saving elections. Depending on your political affiliation it will either remind you of Clinton or Bush. Either way, it's pretty damn funny in a sort of sick and twisted film-noir way. The humor is probably too deep for kids.

Film fans that want the lowdown on every movie ever shot in DC should read *DC Goes to the Movies* by Jean K Rosales and Michael R Jobe.

Portrayals of DC on TV range from national capital to murder capital. One of the best recent efforts was the Sundance Channel's 2006 six-part docu-reality miniseries entitled *The Hill*. The show, which follows congressman Robert Wexler (D-FL) and his staff, on and off the Capitol Hill, plays like a cross between *CNN* and MTV's *Laguna Beach*.

The semi-popular Geena Davis vehicle, *Commander in Chief,* is modeled after the now off-the-air (but once wildly popular) *The West Wing*. The first few seasons of *The West Wing*, which starred Martin Sheen as the beneficent, liberal president ('the best president we've ever had,' fans claimed), when Alan Sorkin was still writing for the show, were truly brilliant and are well worth renting on DVD.

The District, which had a four-year run from 2000 to 2004 (now available on DVD), is about the other side of DC – the dangerous, crime-ridden streets that are far (symbolically if not geographically) from the White House. Craig Nelson plays the chief of police, who uses unconventional means to fight crime in the capital. The drama is inspired by the real-life experiences of one of its creators, New York Deputy Police Commissioner Jack Maple.

ARCHITECTURE

Washington's architecture and city design are the products of its founding fathers and city planners who intended to construct a capital city befitting a powerful nation. The early architecture of Washington, DC, was shaped by two influences: Pierre Charles L'Enfant's 1791 city plan (p51), and the infant nation's desire to prove to European powers that its capital possessed political and artistic sophistication rivaling the ancient, majestic cities of the Continent.

The L'Enfant Plan imposed a street grid marked by diagonal avenues, roundabouts and grand vistas. He had in mind the magisterial boulevards of Europe. To highlight the primacy of the city's political buildings, he intended that no building would rise higher than the Capitol. This rule rescued DC from the windy, dark, skyscraper-filled fate of most modern American cities.

In an effort to rival European cities, Washington's early architects – many of them self-taught 'gentlemen architects' – depended heavily upon the Classic Revival and Romantic Revival styles, with their borrowed Ionian columns and marble facades (witness the **Capitol**, p84, and Ford's Theatre, p192). Federal-style row houses dominated contemporary domestic architecture and still line the streets of Capitol Hill and Georgetown.

Other fine examples from the Federal period are the Sewall-Belmont house (p88) and the uniquely shaped Octagon Museum (p79). The colonnaded Treasury Building (p78), built by Robert Mills in the mid-19th century, represented the first major divergence from the L'Enfant Plan, as it blocked the visual line between the White House and the Capitol. Mills also designed the stark, simple Washington Monument (p73), another architectural anomaly (and not only because it is 555ft high, taller than the Capitol). Later, other styles would soften the lines of the cityscape, with creations like the French-inspired Renwick Gallery (p77), designed by James Renwick.

At the turn of the 20th century, the McMillan Plan revived many elements of the L'Enfant Plan. It restored public spaces downtown, lent formal lines to the Mall and Capitol grounds, and added more classically inspired buildings, such as the beaux-arts Union Station (p89). During this period, John Russell Pope built the Scottish Rite Masonic Temple, which was modeled after the mausoleum at Halicarnassus, as well as the National Archives (p95).

Classicism came to a screaming halt during and after WWII, when war workers flooded the city. Temporary offices were thrown onto the Mall and new materials developed during wartime enabled the construction of huge homogenous office blocks. Slum clearance after the war – particularly in Southwest DC – meant the wholesale loss of old neighborhoods in favor of modernist boxes, such as the monolithic government agencies that currently dominate the ironically named L'Enfant Plaza.

Washington architecture today is of uncertain identity. Many new buildings, particularly those downtown, pay homage to their classical neighbors while striving toward a sleeker, postmodern monumentalism.

A handful of world-renowned architects have left examples of their work in the city. The National Gallery of Art (p66) is a perfect example. Franklin Delano Roosevelt opened the original building, designed by John Russell Pope, in March 1941. Now called the West Building, Pope's symmetrical, Neoclassical gallery overwhelms the eye at first glimpse (approach it from the Mall for the more powerful experience). Two wings lacking external windows stretch for 400ft on either side of the main floor's massive central rotunda, which has a sky-high dome supported by 24 black ionic columns. In the center are vaulted corridors leading off to each wing, which end with an internal skylight and fountain and plant-speckled garden court.

The East Building of the gallery is perhaps even more spectacular. Designed in 1978 by famed architect IM Pei, the ethereal structure is all straight modern lines that create a triangular shape. The building design was initially difficult to conceive, as Pei was given a strange shaped block of land between 3rd and 4th Sts. He solved the problem by making only the marble walls permanent. The rest of the internal structure can be shaped at will, according to the size of various temporary exhibitions. The design is striking, resembling the Louvre in Paris, with pyramidal skylights rising out of the ground (look up from the ground floor of the museum, you'll see a glassed-in waterfall).

Other famous buildings include Mies van der Rohe's Martin Luther King Jr Memorial Library (p89) and Eero Saarinen's Washington Dulles International Airport (p263). Plans are underway for the Corcoran Gallery of Art (p75) to expand with a fantastic addition designed by Frank Gehry. Gehry is famed for his work on Bilbao's Guggenheim museum.

Sometimes appalling and sometimes awesome, the architecture of this unique city tells much about American political ideals and their occasionally awkward application to reality. The National Mall of today is a perfect example. The western half of the Mall is a straightforward place, a graceful mix of sleek modern creations and Neoclassical marble temples disguised as memorials. The eastern side is an entirely different story, a mishmash of sometimes awesome and sometimes appalling architecture.

It's undergoing a huge renovation, but for now the 1964 National Museum of American History (p67) is possibly the Mall's ugliest piece of architecture – a giant concrete box with huge projecting panels on its facade. The Neoclassical National Museum of Natural History (p67), c. 1911, is much less of an eyesore. Appealing marble arches and columns add character.

One of the most appealing museums on the Mall is the newish National Museum of the American Indian (p68). Designed by Canadian architect Douglas Cardina, it is a curving, almost undulating glass-and-stone building with brown earthy hues and a terraced facade. It sort of brings the Southwest to Washington and successfully updates ancient Indian architectural creations.

The American Indian Museum's neighbor, the National Air and Space Museum (p66) is much less pleasing to look at. It's an unremarkable 700ft-long squat marble spread.

The Hirshhorn Museum (p65) further south along the Mall is a concrete cylindrical creation rising on 15ft stilts above a sculpture-thick plaza. The 1974 Gordon Bunshaft building has been called everything from a spaceship to a doughnut.

TOP FIVE DC BEAUX-ARTS BUILDINGS

Senator McMillan's Plan (1901-02) picked up where L'Enfant's became largely unrealized by reconstructing the face of the nation's monumental core in the beaux-arts style suitable of a powerful nation. Here are some of the best examples of this eclectic French-inspired style that is so DC.

- City Museum of Washington, DC (p97) – Formerly the DC Public Library.
- Corcoran Gallery of Art (p75) – Described by Frank Lloyd Wright as "the best designed building in Washington, DC," fittingly, it is the city's first museum of art.
- Meridian International Center (p104) – A limestone chateau by John Russell Pope.
- Embassy of Romania – Designed by the same firm that gave us DC's Carnegie Institute and the Manhattan Bridge in New York.
- Union Station (p89) – The archetypical example of the neoclassical beauty and grandeur of beaux-arts during the age of railroads.

Arts

ARCHITECTURE

The Smithsonian Institution Building (p68), locally known as the Castle, is our favorite building on the Mall. Dating from 1855, it was designed by James Renwick and features striking Gothic towers and battlements.

Between the Castle and the Hirshhorn Museum one stumbles across the 1881 Arts and Industries Building, which is in need of a little TLC these days (see p64). It was the second public construction on the Mall and has a Victorian energy about it, with a jaunty pattern of polychromatic brick and tile.

The National Museum of African Art (p67) and the Arthur M Sackler Gallery (p64) are modern designs, conjured up by the same Boston architectural firm and opened in 1987. The two, made from embroidered, granite-and-limestone cubes, are connected via an underground walkway. Dating from 1923, Charles A. Platt's Freer Gallery of Art (p64) is an Italianate palazzo constructed with granite and marble, and linked to the Sackler Gallery by an underground passageway.

History

History

THE RECENT PAST
THOSE WERE THE DAYS

With the congressional oversights and crack-rock smoking of the 1990s put to rest, Anthony Williams took his oath as the fourth elected mayor of the capital city in 1999, 25 years after Home Rule commenced. This was the Washington, DC (and by extension, America), of the late Clinton administration, when the economy was growing robustly, the world was at relative peace, the dot.com revolution was still in ascendance and the biggest fear folks had was whether or not the Y2K bug would shut off all the computers. At the same time, Washington's image and respectability were making a comeback. Mayor Williams restored fiscal accountability to District agencies and balanced the city's budget. Under Williams' leadership, the District rebounded and achieved significant improvements in cash management, budget execution and revenue collections. One of the main tenets of this new vision was to create a friendlier government, one that listens to its citizens. Priorities include improving education, public safety and opportunity for all residents.

The turn of the 21st century brought a new administration to the White House. In 2001, George W Bush became the 43rd president of the United States following the most talked about (not to mention highly controversial) national election in modern times. (In 2004, Bush would win himself a second term as president in a slightly less-contested race.)

The Clintons vacated the White House for a less-prominent home on Whitehaven St in Georgetown. George and Laura Bush, along with hundreds of political appointees and hopefuls, settled into new digs in the capital. As a practical (political) joke, staff members of the Clinton White House removed the letter 'W' from all of the computer keyboards in the White House offices.

Many view the waning days of 1999, leading up to the global fireworks of the turn of the millennium, as a strongly optimistic time. They capped a decade that had a wholly different tone from the current one, with the city moving into the future despite trepidations about what this new 'new world order' would translate into – not just for DC, but also the planet.

What a difference a handful of years can make. By late 2006, the country's optimism had all but washed away. More than three years after President George W Bush declared the end of official combat in Iraq, the war was still raging out of control. Reports of military and Iraqi civilian deaths were such a normal part of the evening newscasts that they went unregistered in many Americans minds. Political tensions in Washington, DC, were at an all time high, as was distrust of the current administration. In November 2006, many Americans dissatisfied with sitting back and watching their country go to hell, went to the polls en masse to vote for change. The under-30 voter turnout was estimated at two million more than 2002. The Republican Party lost control of both the House and Senate for the first time in 12 years, heralding a new era and a much-needed change of direction.

Americans who voted for change are cautiously optimistic again, hoping that a majority Democratic Senate will push the United States' foreign policies and domestic agendas back into line, resulting in realistic policies and involvement concerning foreign affairs and caps on government spending.

TIMELINE	1608	1791-2
	Captain John Smith sails up the Potomac and makes contact with the Piscataway Indians	The site for the new federal capital is chosen and initial stone of the Executive Mansion (later named the White House) laid

FAVORITE BOOKS ON DC HISTORY

- *The Birth of the Nation: A Portrait of the American People on the Eve of Independence*, Arthur Schlesinger (1968) Colonial life vividly portrayed.
- *On this Spot: Pinpointing the Past in Washington, DC*, Paul Dickson and Douglas Evelyn (1992) Pinpoints the spots and shows photos where historic events took place.
- *Black Georgetown Remembered: A History of Its Black Community from the Founding of 'The Town of George' in 1751 to the Present Day*, Kathleen M Lesko, Valerie Babb and Carroll R Gibbs (1991) From Indian village to bustling tobacco port to slave town to colonial town, this great narrative tells the story of Georgetown from the very beginning.
- *State of Denial: Bush at War, Part III*, Bob Woodward (2006) A peeling back of the varnish; indictment of perhaps the most controversial presidential wartime decisions in contemporary history.
- *Washington Goes to War*, David Brinkley (1996) An agreeable book about the changes that WWII wrought upon DC as thousands of newcomers flooded into town to fill government jobs.
- *The 911 Report: A Graphic Adaptation*, Sid Jacobson and Ernie Colon (2006) A compelling avant-garde cartoon illustration recounting the controversial history of the fateful day and following weeks that rocked the country's self-assuredness indefinitely.

GOING BUSH

The 2000 presidential election went off with a history-making glitch. On election night, November 7, the media prematurely declared the winner twice, based on exit-poll speculations, before finally concluding that the Florida race outcome was too close to call. It would eventually take a month before the election was officially certified. Numerous court challenges and recounts proceeded after Al Gore lost to George W Bush, despite winning the popular vote. Florida's 25 electoral votes went to Bush after the final recount showed him having squeaked by with a razor-thin margin of 537 votes, thereby defeating Democratic candidate Al Gore. Following the election, recounts by various US news media organizations disclosed Bush would have won if specific recounting methods had been used but that Gore would have been declared president if a thorough statewide recount had been held.

In an ironic twist of fate, Gore as vice president, and thus president of the senate, had to ratify the findings of the Electoral College that Bush indeed had won the election. When each state's vote was read, Gore had to declare he acknowledged its validity. In a show of support, Black Democrats voiced their opposition to Bush's win to both Gore and Congress. Ultimately, Gore gave up, grew a beard and proceeded into political obscurity until 2006 when he popped up in media gossip circles again with the release of his new environmental blockbuster documentary, *An Inconvenient Truth*.

LIFE DURING WARTIME

On September 11, 2001, 30 minutes after the attack on New York's World Trade Center, a plane departing Washington Dulles International Airport bound for Los Angeles was hijacked and redirected toward Washington. Speculation was that the hijackers' primary objective was the White House, but they opted for a more exposed target. The plane crashed into the Pentagon's west side, penetrating the building's third ring. Sixty-six passengers and crew, as well as 125 Pentagon personnel, were killed in the suicide attack.

Like most Americans, Washingtonians had no living memory of war on their territory. The shock of terrorism deeply scarred the nation's public psyche.

In the wake of the hijackers' exploits, prominent media and political figures received lethal doses of anthrax in the mail. Several congressional staffers were infected and two

1800	1814
Congress convenes in the new capital for the first time	An attack by British troops devastates the fledgling capital

DC postal workers died. Though unsolved, the anthrax mailings were eventually attributed to a domestic source.

Over a three-week period in the autumn of 2002, area residents were once again terrorized by unseen assailants. A pair of serial snipers went on a shooting spree in the Washington suburbs; 10 people were dead and thousands badly frightened before the snipers were finally apprehended by police.

The city has been palpably changed by these tragedies. From increasing security measures to declining tourism, the effects of the terrorist attack are evident throughout the capital. The FBI has discontinued its popular tour indefinitely, while metal detectors and baggage screening for entrance to museums is commonplace. The jitters over security measures are not completely absent in the consciousness of area residents. Still, often enough, some crazy person tries to get close enough to the White House to fire off a shot at the president, which of course only leads to more paranoia and limitations. Yet no matter how deep the wound that was inflicted in 2001, Washington, DC, has seen – and survived – worse. So the cogs of the capital machine continue to grind, forcing the wheels of the government to spin. The local and federal city carries on.

On May 1, 2003, George W Bush landed via fighter jet, donning a flight suit, on the deck of the USS *Abraham Lincoln,* and declared 'one victory' in the war on terrorism and an end to combat operations in Iraq. The statement, announced with a huge starred-and-striped banner boasting 'mission accomplished' in the background, was intended to serve as the symbolic end to the war. However, history has proven otherwise.

Three years after 'mission accomplished', the US remains embroiled in the Iraq conflict, and Bush's approval ratings have seen a further slide amid worldwide protests. Even the most die-hard, one-time war supporters are questioning the government's motives, lack of disclosure regarding the staggering funds used getting the country into this quagmire and a seemingly nonexistent exit strategy. Costs are running roughly $200 million a day and the amount spent on four years of war in Iraq and Afghanistan is approaching $300 billion. Some say that short blips, like a bumper sticker, can better convey general sentiment because of the practical simplicity of one-liners. In this case it would be the one that has been showing up on vehicles all over the country since 2003 – 'Iraq is Arabic for Vietnam.'

Critics claim the Bush administration has turned a one-time financial surplus in the budget (from the Clinton years) into the largest national debt America has ever experienced. Bush's approval ratings saw a dramatic drop due to the war in Iraq.

This drop in approval ratings probably caused the beating the Republican Party took nationwide in the 2006 mid-term elections. The country proved it was fed up with the Bush administration, especially how it was handling the war, and democrats took control of the House and the Senate for the first time in 12 years. The political shake-up also led to the confirmation of Nancy Pelosi (D-CA), the first female speaker of the house in US history. Just one day after the election, Secretary of State Donald Rumsfeld resigned as defense secretary. Democrats (and even some Republicans) had been calling for his resignation for months prior to the election, but Bush stood fast by his longtime friend. Even after Rumsfeld announced his resignation, during the ensuing press conference, Bush still praised Rumsfeld's service.

Iran and North Korea are both hot topics in DC these days. At the time of research, North Korea had supposedly tested a nuclear weapon with limited success and Iran was pursuing a nuclear agenda. The president of Iran wished to debate George W Bush, but the US president turned down the invitation and continued to push Iran to abandon its nuclear ambitions, despite Iran's claims that its nuclear program is for peaceful energy purposes only.

The country is now gearing up for the 2008 presidential election (for more on the city's mood, see p12) and the USA has caught political fever. It's anticipated that the Democrats will put forth a major fight for the Oval Office. Hillary Clinton's name is on

1862	1864
The District outlaws slavery in the capital and one year later the Emancipation Proclamation frees all slaves	The Battle of Fort Stevens – the only battle fought on capital soil – is won by the Union

the lips of many as a possible Democratic nominee, while Republicans are speculating that John McCain (who ran against Bush in 2000 for the Republican nomination) will be his party's choice.

FROM THE BEGINNING

EARLY SETTLEMENT

Before the first European colonists sailed up from Chesapeake Bay, Native Americans, primarily the Piscataway tribe of the Algonquian language group, made their home near the confluence of the Potomac and Anacostia Rivers. As many as 10,000 Piscataway inhabited the region, living a sustainable hunter/gatherer/trader lifestyle when the explorers arrived. The first recorded White contact with the Piscataway was in 1608 by the English Captain John Smith, who set out from Jamestown colony to explore the upper Potomac.

Relations with the peaceful Piscataway were amicable at first, but soon turned ruinous for the Native Americans. Vulnerable to European sicknesses, many Native Americans succumbed and their numbers were reduced by half within 25 years. In mid-century, the Piscataway suffered further losses from entanglements in the Indian Wars between the English and the more hostile Susquehannock and Powhatan tribes. By 1700, the few remaining Piscataway migrated out of the region to Iroquois territory in Pennsylvania and New York.

The first European settlers in the region were traders and fur trappers, who plied the woodlands beyond the Allegheny Mountains, often working with local Algonquin Indians. English and Scots-Irish settlers followed, turning the forests into farmland. With the founding of Maryland, soul-saving Jesuits arrived to convert the locals.

By the late 1600s, expansive agricultural estates lined both sides of the Potomac. These tidewater planters became a colonial aristocracy, dominating regional affairs. Their most lucrative crop was the precious sotweed – tobacco – which was tended by African indentured servants and slaves. The river ports of Alexandria and Georgetown became famous for their prosperous commercial centers.

REVOLUTIONARY RESULTS

In the 1770s, growing hostilities between Britain and the fledgling colonies (that were now calling themselves states) led the colonies to draft the Declaration of Independence, formally severing ties with Britain. In 1775, the Continental Congress issued a declaration outlining the colonists' reasons for fighting the British. Perhaps the most empowering section of the declaration stated that Americans were 'resolved to die free men rather than live as slaves.' Also, as a prelude to impending armed conflict, Congress established America's first navy, then appointed a clandestine panel to seek assistance from European nations in the struggle for independence. A year later, the American revolutionaries got the necessary foreign support for which they had hoped. It was a welcome relief because Britain's King George III released a royal decree revoking the American colonies' right to trade and commerce as from March 1776. But in December, Congress learnt that France would lend support and King Louis XVI gave $1 million in arms and munitions. Spain then also promised support. In 1778, American and French representatives signed the Treaty of Amity & Commerce and a Treaty of Alliance in which France officially recognized the United States. France soon became the major provider of supplies to George Washington's army. A decade after the war for independence began, the British Parliament sanctioned the king to negotiate peace with the United States.

1867	1901
Howard University is founded as an institute of higher education for the growing black population	The McMillan Plan initiates a makeover of the capital

WASHINGTON IN THE AGE OF DEMOCRACY

To most visitors in the first half of the 19th century, the city was more a desolate provincial outpost than a dynamic urban center. Washington may have been the seat of federal government, but the states were the real players in political power and economic wealth. Governor Morris, a prominent New Yorker, acidly observed: 'We only need here houses, kitchens, scholarly men, amiable women and a few other trifles, to possess a perfect city.'

The city's rough-hewn appearance was, at least partially, intended. Thomas Jefferson disliked formal displays of power and privilege, and dispensed with the ceremonial pomp of the Washington and Adams presidencies. He was known to greet foreign dignitaries in his slippers. Another champion of the common man, President Andrew Jackson celebrated his inauguration with a raucous open-house party, at which inebriated guests made off with White House furnishings. This sort of official humility tempered – to some extent – the aristocratic pretensions of Washington high society.

Following the Revolutionary War, the fledgling US Congress launched a search for a permanent home. The Constitution, ratified in 1788, specified that a federal territory, no greater than 10 sq miles, should be established for the nation's capital. The newly inaugurated President George Washington chose the site on the Potomac. It was strategically suitable for commerce and river traffic, and politically pleasing to both Northern and Southern concerns. Maryland and Virginia agreed to cede land to the new capital.

Over beers at Suter's tavern in Georgetown, Washington persuaded local landowners to sell their holdings to the government for $66 an acre. In March 1791 the African American mathematician Benjamin Banneker and surveyor Andrew Ellicott mapped out a diamond-shaped territory that spanned the Potomac and Anacostia Rivers. Its four corners were at the cardinal points of the compass, and it embraced the river ports of Georgetown and Alexandria (the latter eventually returned to Virginia). Pierre Charles L'Enfant, a French officer in the Revolutionary War, sketched plans for a grandiose European-style capital of monumental buildings and majestic boulevards. It was named the 'Territory of Columbia' (to honor Christopher Columbus), but residents began calling it the city of Washington.

But L'Enfant's showcase capital went unfinished. The French major was a diva, quarrelling with city commissioners, running afoul of local politicians and knocking down people's houses while they were out of town. In 1792, Washington fired his planner. Meanwhile, land speculators grabbed prized properties, and buildings sprang up haphazardly along mucky lanes. In 1793, construction began on the President's House and the Capitol, the geographic center points of the city. In 1800, John Adams became the first president to occupy the still uncompleted mansion. His wife Abigail hung the family's laundry in the East Room. The city remained a half-built, sparsely populated work in progress.

WAR OF 1812: WASHINGTON BURNS

In the early 19th century, the young nation had yet to become a formidable force in world affairs. US merchants and seamen were regularly bullied on the high seas by the British Navy. Responding to congressional hawks, President James Madison declared war in 1812. In retaliation for the razing of York (Toronto) by US troops, the British assaulted Washington. Work was barely complete on the Capitol in August 1814, when redcoats sailed up the Patuxent River and burned it to the ground. The victorious British embarked on a night of looting and arson. When it was over, most of the city's public buildings had been torched. President and Dolley Madison fled to the Virginia suburbs, with the Declaration of Independence and Constitution in hand.

Although the British were expelled and the city rebuilt, Washington was slow to recover. A congressional initiative to abandon the dispirited capital was lost by just nine votes.

1916-19	1941-44
WWI attracts thousands of people to Washington for the administration of the war	The expanding federal government and its wartime bureaucracy lead to another population boom

SLAVERY IN THE FEDERAL CITY

When Congress first convened in Washington in 1800, the city had about 14,000 residents. It was even then a heavily African American populated town: slaves and free Blacks composed 29% of the population. Free Blacks lived in the port of Georgetown, where a vibrant African American community emerged. They worked alongside and socialized with the city's slaves.

Since its introduction in Jamestown colony in 1619, slave labor had become an essential part of the regional tobacco economy. In 1800, more than half of the nation's 700,000 slaves lived in Maryland and Virginia. The capital of America's slave trade at that time, Washington, DC, contained slave markets and holding pens. Slavers conducted a highly profitable business buying slaves locally in DC and selling them to Southern plantations.

The city's slave population steadily declined throughout the 19th century, while the number of free Blacks rose. They migrated to the city, establishing their own churches and schools.

Washington, DC, became a front line in the intensifying conflict between the North and South over slavery. The city was a strategic stop on the clandestine Underground Railroad, shuttling fugitive slaves to freedom in the northern states. The abolitionist movement fueled further racial tensions. In 1835, the Snow Riots erupted as White mobs set loose on Black Washingtonians. When the rampage subsided, legislation was passed restricting the economic rights of the city's free Blacks. At last, Congress outlawed the slave trade in Washington in 1850; the District Emancipation Act abolished slavery outright in 1862.

FROM SLAVE TO STATESMAN: FREDERICK DOUGLASS

Born Frederick Augustus Washington Bailey in 1818 on a slave plantation along Maryland's Eastern Shore, Frederick Douglass is remembered as one of the country's most influential and outstanding black 19th-century leaders.

In 1838, at 20 years old, he escaped wretched treatment at the hands of Maryland planters and established himself as a freeman in New Bedford, Massachusetts, eventually working for abolitionist William Lloyd Garrison's antislavery paper, the *Liberator*. His years as a slave had led Douglass to a profound personal truth: 'Men are whipped oftenist who are whipped easiest.' After his escape, he took his new last name from a character in the Sir Walter Scott book, *The Lady of the Lake*. Largely self-educated, Douglass had a natural gift for eloquence. In 1841, he won the admiration of New England abolitionists with an impromptu speech at an antislavery convention, introducing himself as 'a recent graduate from the institution of slavery,' with his 'diploma' (ie whip marks on his back). The Massachusetts Anti-Slavery Society hired Douglass, and he traveled the free states as an energetic spokesman for abolition and the Underground Railroad.

Douglass' effectiveness so angered proslavery forces that his supporters urged him to flee to England to escape seizure and punishment under the Fugitive Slave Law. He followed their advice and kept lecturing in England until admirers contributed enough money ($710.96) to enable him to purchase his freedom and return home in 1847.

Douglass then became the self-proclaimed 'station master and conductor' of the Underground Railroad in Rochester, New York, working with other famed abolitionists like Harriet Tubman and John Brown. In 1860, Douglass campaigned for Abraham Lincoln, and when the Civil War broke out, helped raise two regiments of black soldiers – the Massachusetts 54th and 55th – to fight for the Union.

After the war, Douglass went to Washington to lend his support to the 13th, 14th and 15th Constitutional Amendments, which abolished slavery, granted citizenship to former slaves and guaranteed citizens the right to vote. He later became US marshal for Washington and the US minister to Haiti (the country's first black ambassador).

In 1895, Douglass died at his Anacostia home, Cedar Hill, now the Frederick Douglass National Historic Site (p90). His funeral was held at DC's historic Metropolitan AME Church, 1518 M St NW, where one speaker mourned him in words that illustrated what Douglass had meant to black Washington: 'Howl, fir tree, for the Cedar of Lebanon has fallen.'

1963	1968
Martin Luther King Jr leads the civil rights march on the National Mall	Martin Luther King Jr is assassinated in Memphis; Washington, DC, erupts in riotous violence

A HOUSE DIVIDED: CIVIL WAR & RECONSTRUCTION

The 1860 election of Abraham Lincoln meant that the office of president would no longer protect Southern interests in the increasingly irreconcilable rift over slavery. Rather than abide by the electoral outcome, Southern secessionists opted to exit the Union, igniting a four-year fratricidal clash. A prized target, Washington was often near the frontlines of fighting. A ring of earthwork forts was hastily erected around the city to protect it from attack. Washington saw only one battle on its soil: Confederate General Jubal Early's unsuccessful attack on Fort Stevens in northern DC, in July 1864. Washingtonians lived in constant anxiety, however, as bloody battles raged nearby at Antietam, Gettysburg and Manassas.

Washington experienced an influx of soldiers, volunteers, civil servants and ex-slaves. Within three months of hostilities starting, over 50,000 enlistees descended on the capital to join the Army of the Potomac. The city served as an important rearguard position for troop encampments and supply operations.

Only five days after Confederate General Robert E Lee surrendered to Union General Ulysses S Grant at Appomattox, Lincoln was assassinated in downtown Washington at Ford's Theatre (p192).

The Civil War had a lasting impact on the city. The war strengthened the power of the federal government, marking the first efforts to conscript young men into military service and to collect income tax from private households. Warfare brought new bureaucracies, workers and buildings to the capital. Between the war's start and end, the city's population nearly doubled to more than 130,000. Howard University was founded in 1867 to educate Black residents; by this time, Blacks comprised nearly half the population.

The capital economy was bolstered by a postwar boom. Although in many ways a Southern city, Washington was already part of the commercial networks of the north. The B&O Railroad connected the city via Baltimore to the industry of the northeast; while the Chesapeake and Ohio Canal opened a waterway to the agriculture of the Midwest. In 1871, President Ulysses S Grant appointed a Board of Public Works to upgrade the urban infrastructure and improve living conditions. The board was led by Alexander Shepherd, who energetically took on the assignment. He paved streets, put in sewers, installed gaslights, planted trees, filled in swamps and carved out parklands. But he also ran over budget by $20 million or so, and was sacked by Congress, who reclaimed responsibility for city affairs. 'Boss' Shepherd was the closest thing that DC would have to self-government for 100 years.

TURN OF THE AMERICAN CENTURY

As the 1900s began, the US asserted itself on the world stage, competing with Europe to extend its influence overseas. With the Spanish-American War and Theodore Roosevelt's presidency, the US had entered the Age of Empire.

In 1900, Senator James McMillan of Michigan formed an all-star city-planning commission to make over the capital, whose population now surpassed a quarter-million. The McMillan Plan effectively revived L'Enfant's vision of a resplendent city on par with Europe's best. The plan proposed grand public buildings in the beaux-arts style (p45), which reconnected the city to its neoclassical republican roots, but with an eclectic flair. It was impressive, orderly and upper class. The plan entailed an extensive beautification project. It removed the scrubby trees and coal-fired locomotives that belched black smoke from the National Mall, and created the expansive lawn and reflecting pools that exist today.

The Mall became a showcase of the symbols of American ambition and power: monumental tributes to the founding fathers; the enshrinement of the Declaration of Independence and Constitution in a Greek temple; and the majestic Memorial Bridge leading to

1973	1974
Washington, DC, is granted the right to Home Rule	President Nixon resigns under the threat of impeachment stemming from the Watergate scandal

Arlington National Cemetery, hallowed ground of the nation's fallen warriors. Washington had become the nation's civic center, infused with the spirit of history, heroes and myths. The imagery was embraced by the country's budding political class.

The plan improved living conditions for middle-class public servants and professionals. New 'suburbs,' such as Woodley Park and Mount Pleasant, offered better-off residents a respite from the hot inner city, and electric trolleys crisscrossed the streets. Of course, the daily life of many Washingtonians was less promising. Impoverished slums like Murder Bay and Swamppoodle stood near government buildings, and about 20,000 poor Blacks still dwelled in dirty alleyways.

WAR, DEPRESSION, MORE WAR

Two world wars and one Great Depression changed forever the place of Washington in American society. These events hastened a concentration of power in the federal government in general and the executive branch in particular. National security and social welfare became the high-growth sectors of public administration. City life transformed from Southern quaintness into cosmopolitan clamor.

WWI witnessed a surge of immigration. The administration of war had an unquenchable thirst for clerks, soldiers, nurses and other military support staff. By war's end, the city's population was over half a million. This phenomenon recurred in WWII, when the city's population topped a million. A burgeoning organizational infrastructure supported the new national security state. The US Army's city-based civilian employee roll grew from 7000 to 41,000 in the first year of the war. The world's largest office building, the Pentagon, was hastily built across the river to house them all.

In response to the Great Depression, Franklin Roosevelt's New Deal extended the reach of the federal government into the economy. Federal regulators acquired greater power to intervene in business and financial affairs. Dozens of relief agencies were created to administer the social guarantees of the nascent welfare state. In Washington, New Deal work projects included tree planting on the Mall and finishing public buildings, such as the Supreme Court.

THE COLD WAR

The Cold War was without doubt the dominant political reality of the post WWII 20th century. The United States' very public ego battle with the USSR was not fought face to face, but through the use of proxy clients. Korea, Vietnam, Cambodia, Mozambique and Afghanistan were all pawns in the geopolitical, economic and ideological battle. Red fever swept the US. Communists were devils, and the domino theory (if one country turns red the next one will follow until a whole continent topples like a set of dominoes) was coffee table-conversation for many. People built special underground shelters (stocked with canned food and bottled water) to safeguard their families in the event of a nuclear war.

During the 40-plus years known as the Cold War, everything became a race. There was the arms race: Who could build the most intercontinental ballistic missiles fastest? There was the space race: Who could put a man on the moon first? Score one for the USA – Neil Armstrong took the first steps on July 20, 1969.

The Cuban Missile Crisis, which took place over 12 days in October 1962, brought the United States and the Soviet Union to the brink of nuclear war, and many believe that without John F Kennedy's brilliant diplomacy it would have. The president resisted using force to make Soviet President Nikita Khrushchev dismantle the nuclear weapons he had deployed in Cuba (a little too close to US soil to be ignored). Instead, he chose a nonviolent blockade that allowed the Soviet leader to withdraw the missiles without losing face.

1976	1990
Metrorail opens to serve the growing suburban community	In the '90s scandal *du jour*, Mayor Marion Barry is arrested for possession of cocaine

During the Cold War, many covert battles were waged on foreign soil. Perhaps the most famous was the Iran-Contra affair in the 1980s during Ronald Reagan's tenure as president. Folks in his administration, along with the CIA, secretly and illegally sold arms to Iran, a US enemy, and then used the proceeds to finance the Contras, an anti-communist guerilla army in Nicaragua.

The Cold War furthered the concentration of political power in Washington-based bureaucracies. It attracted new breeds of policy specialists – macro-economists, international experts and social engineers. They comprised a better-educated and more prosperous middle class. This trend continued unabated until the Reagan presidency. Even then, the foundations of 'big government' proved too firm to undermine. Candidate Reagan vowed to abolish the Commerce Department once elected. Not only did the bureaucracy survive his tenure, but it constructed a fabulous new office building, ironically named for the 40th president.

SEGREGATION & THE CIVIL RIGHTS MOVEMENT

In the early 20th century, Washington adopted racial segregation policies, like those of the South. Its business establishments and public spaces became, in practice if not in law, 'Whites only.' The 'progressive' Woodrow Wilson administration reinforced discrimination by refusing to hire Black federal employees and insisting on segregated government offices. In 1925, the Ku Klux Klan marched on the Mall.

FROM JACKIE O TO JUST SAY NO

An exhibit on First Lady inaugural gowns has been a longtime Smithsonian favorite, but the role of First Lady has changed in recent years. First ladies are now better known for their social causes than their ceremonial costumes.

From the outset, first ladies served principally as the nation's chief hostess. America's first First Lady, Martha Washington, likened this role to a 'state prisoner.' Cultured Abigail Adams did her best to preside over formal dinners, but privately hated living in a 'wilderness.' Among the founding mothers, vivacious Dolley Madison impressed as hostess par excellence.

In the early 20th century, influenced by the women's movement, the role of First Lady began to move beyond reception halls. Nellie Taft was involved in the capital beautification project and suggested the planting of the cherry trees around the tidal basin. Edith Bolling Wilson secretly performed some of her husband's presidential duties when he was stricken by illness. But it was Eleanor Roosevelt who truly transformed the part. She was a tireless campaigner for her husband and a heartfelt spokesperson for the underprivileged.

Few first ladies have captivated the public as did the graceful Jackie Kennedy, who used her position to patronize the arts. Betty Ford spoke out on a number of issues once taboo for a First Lady, like breast cancer and drug abuse. Rosalyn Carter participated in cabinet meetings. Nancy Reagan implored the masses to 'Just Say No' (to drug use), while Barbara Bush promoted literacy.

Hillary Clinton extended the political role of First Lady broader still. Not satisfied by simply being a president's wife, this practicing lawyer with a charismatic personality to match her husband's, made health-care reform her pet project. When her husband's terms finished, Hillary was not content to drift off into First Lady oblivion. Instead she ran for the US Senate as a Democrat from New York, and won a seat in 2000. At the time of research she was busy preparing to run for a second term. Also in 2006, Hillary was generating lots of buzz around the cocktail circuit and morning talk shows about a 2008 presidential bid. Speculation favors she'll run, but if she does, pundits say the likelihood of her winning a Democratic nomination is rather slim.

Hillary's White House successor, Laura Bush, has returned to the less-controversial model of her mother-in-law as literacy advocate, while at the same time becoming the first-ever president's wife to deliver her husbands weekly radio address. Since 2001, Mrs Bush has focused her attention on publicly exposing the plight of women suffering under repressive regimes such as the Taliban.

1994	1999
After serving six months in prison, Barry is re-elected to a fourth term in office	The Monica Lewinsky scandal breaks; Bill Clinton becomes the first president since Andrew Johnson (in 1868) to be impeached

Nonetheless, Washington was a Black cultural capital in the early 20th century. Shaw and LeDroit Park, near Howard University, sheltered a lively Black-owned business district, and Black theater and music flourished along U St NW. Southern Blacks continued to move to the city in search of better economic opportunities. Between 1920 and 1930, Washington's Black population jumped 20%. Citywide segregation eased somewhat with the New Deal (which brought new Black federal workers to the capital) and WWII (which brought lots more).

In 1939, the DC-based Daughters of the American Revolution barred the Black contralto Marian Anderson from singing at Constitution Hall. At Eleanor Roosevelt's insistence, Anderson instead sang at the Lincoln Memorial before a huge audience – and that iconic moment highlighted a new era of Black-led demonstrations, sit-ins, boycotts and lawsuits. Parks and recreational facilities were legally desegregated in 1954; schools followed soon thereafter. President John F Kennedy appointed the city's first Black federal commissioner in 1961. The Home Rule Act was approved in 1973, giving the city some autonomy from its federal overseers. The 1974 popular election of Walter Washington brought the first Black mayor to office. The capital became one of the most prominent African American-governed cities in the country.

Washington hosted key events in the national civil rights struggle. In 1963, Reverend Martin Luther King Jr led the March on Washington to lobby for passage of the Civil Rights Act. His stirring 'I have a dream' speech, delivered before 200,000 people on the steps of the Lincoln Memorial, was a defining moment of the campaign. The assassination of Reverend King in Memphis in 1968, sent the nation reeling. Race riots gripped the country. DC was no exception. It saw the worst racially motivated conflicts in its history when the city exploded in two nights of riots and arson (centered on 14th and U Sts NW in the Shaw district). Twelve people died and hundreds of mostly Black-owned businesses suffered heavy damage. White residents fled the city en masse, and downtown Washington north of the Mall (especially the Shaw district) faded into decades of economic slump.

The legacy of segregation proved difficult to overcome. For the next quarter-century, White and Black Washington grew further apart. By 1970, the city center's population declined to 750,000, while the wealthier suburbs boomed to nearly three million. When the sleek, federally funded Metrorail system opened in 1976, it bypassed the poorer Black neighborhoods and instead connected the downtown to the White suburbs.

DECAY & DECLINE

By the end of the 1960s no one could ignore the declining situation in Vietnam. The war was taking a giant toll on President Lyndon Johnson's popularity. Americans were growing angry at the rising death tolls and seeming quagmire in Southeast Asia, along with the deteriorating domestic economic situation at home. Demonstrations in Washington were called for, and people took to the street to protest poverty and the Vietnam War.

The political upheaval that began in the 1960s continued unchecked into the next decade. The year 1970 marked the first time DC was granted a nonvoting delegate to the House of Representatives. Three years later the Home Rule Act paved the way for the District's first mayoral election in more than a century.

These were about the only two positives the city experienced that decade. Neighborhoods continued to decay, crack-cocaine hit District streets with a vengeance and housing projects turned into war zones. In fact, by 1980, DC had won the oh-so-lovely tagline of 'Murder Capital of America.'

Jimmy Carter became president in 1977. A 'malaise' marked his tenure. High gas prices, unemployment and inflation climbed to an all-time high. The taking of American hostages in Iran in 1979, an act that Carter had few options for dealing with, was the straw that broke

1999	2000
Washington, DC, elects Anthony Williams as the city's fourth mayor	George W Bush ascends to the presidency despite not winning the popular vote (that went to Al Gore)

the camel's back. In November 1980, he lost his job to Ronald Reagan, a former actor who had once been California governor.

The city's negative trends continued in the 1980s. Elected mayor in 1978, Marion Barry was a veteran of the civil rights struggle. Combative and charismatic, he became a racially polarizing figure in the city.

On January 18, 1990, Barry and companion, ex-model Hazel 'Rasheeda' Moore, were arrested in a narcotics sting at the Vista Hotel. The FBI and DC police arrested the mayor for crack-cocaine possession amid his memorable quote: '…set up…bitch set me up.'

When Barry was re-elected to a fourth term, following a stint in jail, Congress acted to reclaim financial control of the city and end yet another episode in Home Rule.

2001	2006
Planes hijacked by terrorists crash into both towers of the World Trade Center in New York and the Pentagon	Democrats regain control of the Senate and House for the first time in 12 years

Sights ■

Sights

In a way it is Washington, not New York, that best represents the US of A at the micro level. Where better to feel the nation's pulse, see its character and taste its saucy grit than the streets of its capital? From the marble jowls and beaux-arts beauty of Downtown DC to the pimps and hoes pounding the pavement by a swanky new bar in pseudo-tough Shaw, DC dishes up a smorgasbord of neighborhoods as diverse and dynamic as the country itself.

Stay long enough, however, and you'll discover that the 39% of the population that is White lives and plays mostly in the smallest and ritziest quadrant of DC, Northwest. With the exception of jaunts to the Waterfront and Monuments in Southwest, a trip to splashy Capital Hill or ethnic Eastern Market in Southeast, many of Washington's White and rich have never actually set foot outside gentrified DC.

Encompassing vast tracks of the city, DC's lost quadrants are home to desperate, sometimes violent, slums where down-and-out bums loiter near gritty bullet-pocked housing

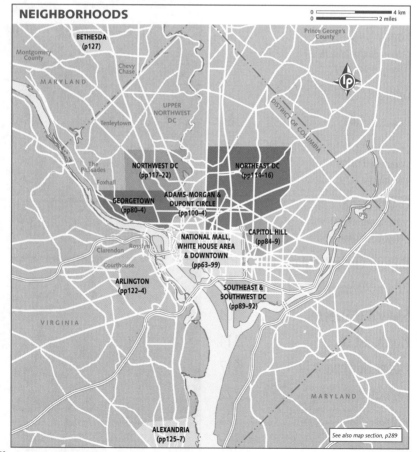

NEIGHBORHOODS

BETHESDA (p127)

Montgomery County

MARYLAND

Chevy Chase

Prince George's County

DISTRICT OF COLUMBIA

UPPER NORTHWEST DC

Tenleytown

The Palisades

Foxhall

NORTHWEST DC (pp117–22)

NORTHEAST DC (pp114–16)

GEORGETOWN (pp80–4)

ADAMS-MORGAN & DUPONT CIRCLE (pp100–4)

Rosslyn

Clarendon

Courthouse

NATIONAL MALL, WHITE HOUSE AREA & DOWNTOWN (pp63–99)

CAPITOL HILL (pp84–9)

ARLINGTON (pp122–4)

SOUTHEAST & SOUTHWEST DC (pp89–92)

VIRGINIA

MARYLAND

ALEXANDRIA (pp125–7)

See also map section, p289

projects, and young gangsters, decked out in the latest ghetto bling and Louis Vuitton, sling dope to end-of-the-liners just hoping to stay high long enough to die.

Dipping into the bowels of the District might sound depressing, but it's also where the majority of Washingtonians live, and it's imperative to understanding the pulse of the city as a whole. That said, please don't go running around Anacostia alone; ask locals about what's safe and what's off-limits.

For the purpose of this guide, we've broken the city into 15 manageable chunks, each defined by geographic factors, but also by activities and atmosphere. We start at the center of it all, the National Mall. Here the museums alone could occupy a visitor for days. Next we move on to the Monuments – we've grouped them together to make your life a bit easier. Then we cruise the surrounding neighborhoods: the revitalized Downtown, packed with restaurants and theaters; the stately White House area and nearby Foggy Bottom; the political heart of Capitol Hill, which surrounds poorer parts of Southeast. Moving further out into the city's vast Northwest and Northeast quadrants, we reach the neighborhoods where local life is liveliest. We make pilgrimages to the Catholic shrines and lush park areas of Northeast DC; explore the unique architecture and history of Georgetown; browse the bookstores and coffee shops of cosmopolitan Dupont Circle and Kalorama; eat ethnic cuisine and bop to world beats in Adams-Morgan; and dive into DC's Black heritage in U Street and the Shaw. City coverage wraps up with Rock Creek Park and the residential streets of Upper Northwest DC. Next we head across the Potomac River to discover Arlington and Alexandria before checking out Bethesda, Maryland's ever-evolving (but always ultrapopular) culinary scene.

ITINERARIES

Two Days

If you've only two days to play with, you don't have time to fool around. Start your Washington DC express tour with breakfast at Jimmy T's (p151) on Capitol Hill. Then wander down to the Mall, admiring the mighty Capitol along the way. Pick a museum on the Mall (p63) or, if the weather is fine, stay outside, enjoy the sunshine and explore the many monuments. Partake of a quintessential DC power lunch at the Old Ebbitt Grill (p145) before heading over to Georgetown for a spot of serious shopping. When you blow your savings, take a walk – head down to the Potomac and walk along the C&O Canal for a while, then double back and have a sunset drink overlooking the river on sleek Sequoia's (p150) patio.

When your stomach starts grumbling, hop in a cab to Adams-Morgan and pop into Rumba Café (p161) for tasty tapas and sumptuous mojitos. All the nightlife you can squeeze into one evening is right here, whether you want to hear some live tunes at **Madam's Organ** (p184) or get your groove on at Heaven & Hell (p188).

On day two you'll want to start in Dupont Circle (p100) and check out the vintage shops and lively galleries before heading south towards the White House (p78). After snapping the requisite photos, spend the rest of the day on the Mall, visiting a few more museums. Don't miss the National Air & Space Museum (p109) – be sure to catch an IMAX flick and touch the moon rock. You'll also need to make sure you check out the Capitol grounds and Washington Monument.

Head to Capitol Hill (p172) to do the Pennsylvania happy hour bar-hopping thing and get a feel for young Washington at its most authentic. Check out the varied nightlife in the Shaw (p183) after dark to listen to everything from African pop to DC hip-hop.

Four Days

Follow the itinerary for two days, then on the third day spend time exploring the Penn Quarter. Visiting the Spy Museum (p94) is mandatory – also check out the newly renovated National Portrait Gallery (p96). Have lunch at one of the restaurants in Chinatown. While in the neighborhood you should also check out the National Archives (p95) to see first-hand the documents that are the foundation of this country. At night catch a show at the National Theatre (p193).

On day four spend the morning at Eastern Market (p87) and find some treasures in the North Hall, as well as at the flea market across the street. Pick up some produce for a picnic feast. Then hop on the Orange Line to Foggy Bottom, rent a bike at Thompson Boat Center (p203) and pedal the Monumental Bike Ride (p134). In the evening, have dinner in Dupont and then head to Ford's Theatre (p94) – where Abraham Lincoln was shot – for a performance.

One Week

Cover the four-day itinerary, adding breathing space where you feel rushed. With a week, you'll have time for a few themed DC days. Check out a couple of our walking tours (p130) – the scandalous one is a personal favorite – or join an organized tour (below). You'll also have time to spend a morning at Mount Vernon (p246) with lunch and an afternoon in Alexandria (p125) exploring Old Town. Just minutes outside DC is fabulous Great Falls National Park (p245), which is definitely worth exploring. You may wish to head further afield to escape urbanity, visiting the Atlantic coast beaches (p257) or Shenandoah National Park (p252) when the weather's nice, or head to Manassas (p247) for an infusion of small-town charm and Civil War history.

ORGANIZED TOURS

DC has more organized tour options than hanging chads in a ballot box. From history to architecture to Black heritage to spies and scandal, there are tours catering to every interest. Likewise for mode of transportation: you can find someone to lead you by boat, bus or bike, or even on your good old-fashioned feet. For a complete list of organized tours of DC, see Cultural Tourism DC (www.culturaltourismdc.org). Here are some of our favorites.

BIKE THE SITES

Map pp292-3

☎ 202-842-BIKE; www.bikethesites.com; 1100 Pennsylvania Ave, Old Post Office Pavilion; adult/child $40/30; ☼ 9am & 1pm; Ⓜ Federal Triangle Knowledgeable guides lead tours of DC's major landmarks, as well as offering more specialized options, such as tours over and under Washington bridges or to Civil War sites. Additional tours vary with the season. The price includes bikes and all necessary equipment.

DC DUCKS

Map p304

☎ 202-966-3825; www.dcducks.com; 50 Massachusetts Ave NE, Union Station; adult/child $32/16; ☼ 10am-4pm Apr-Oct; Ⓜ Union Station In a classic case of defense conversion, amphibious land/water vehicles carry tourists on a waddle around the city streets and a float along the Potomac.

The 90-minute tour departs from Union Station and features visits to the Mall and monuments, as well as the corniest jokes on a city tour.

DC HERITAGE

☎ 202-661-7576; www.culturaltourismdc.org An extensive list of specialized tour options focuses on cultural heritage themes, like Duke Ellington's DC, Civil War history and Old Anacostia.

ODYSSEY CRUISES

Map pp308-9

☎ 888-741-0281; www.odysseycruises.com; 6th & Water Sts, Gangplank Marina; lunch/brunch $41/54, dinner $82-97; ☼ brunch/lunch 11am-1:30pm, dinner 7-10pm Sun-Thu, 8-11pm Fri & Sat; Ⓜ Waterfront Odyssey has the only ship that is designed to fit underneath all of the Potomac's historic bridges; it cruises up past Arlington Cemetery, the Lincoln Memorial, the Kennedy Center and Georgetown.

SPIRIT CRUISES

Map pp308-9

☎ 866-211-3811; www.spiritcruises.com; 6th & Water Sts, Pier 4; Ⓜ Waterfront The *Spirit of Washington* is a huge ship, which hosts lunch, dinner and midnight cruises that sail down the Potomac to Old Town Alexandria. *Spirit* also operates day trips and one-way trips to Mt Vernon (March to November).

TOUR DC

☎ 301-588-8999; www.tourdc.com; group walks $350

At the time of research these excellent tours were limited to pre-arranged group walks (90 minutes in length) while the leader and local travel writer, Mary Kay Ricks, was working on a new book. She planned, however, to return to cheaper (around $15) public walks in the future. When she does, these are great ways to explore DC's neighborhoods, especially Georgetown and Dupont Circle, from another angle. Tours focus on such themes as spies and scandal, Black heritage, the Civil War, the Kennedys, gardens and mansions, and Embassy Row.

TOURMOBILE

☎ 202-554-5100, 888-868-7707; www.tourmobile .com; adult/child $20/10; ⏲ 9:30am-4:30pm; Ⓜ Federal Triangle or Arlington Cemetery

The big boy on the local narrated bus-tour scene, Tourmobile's primary tour runs around the National Mall, Capitol, White House and out to Arlington National Cemetery. You can hop off and reboard free at any of its 25 stops, which is nice for those who aren't able to walk long distances. Tourmobile also does separate tours of Arlington National Cemetery (adult/child $5.25/2.50), Mount Vernon ($7/3.50), and some Black heritage sites ($7/3.50). A twilight tour, See Washington By Night ($20/10), is offered in season.

WASHINGTON WALKS

☎ 202-484-1565; www.washingtonwalks.com; adult/child $10/5

Movie buffs will dig Washington Walks' latest tour: Bus, Camera, Action! Reel Washington. The two-hour jaunt, offered on select Saturdays in August, September and October, takes visitors to the locations used in films like *Mr Smith Goes to Washington*, *The Exorcist*, *All the President's Men*, *No Way Out*, *Broadcast News* and *Independence Day*. Movie buffs who want to get their heart-rate up can join a similar tour offered in partnership with Bike the Sites – it's the same but on two wheels. Other tours include the White House Un-tour (Tuesday to Saturday), plus weekly tours like Haunted Houses and Goodnight Mr Lincoln (great for kids).

NATIONAL MALL

Eating p143; Shopping p207

Welcome to the front yard of America. Stop on by for a Sunday picnic, a game of pick-up or a morning rally. The US throws all its parties – from presidential inaugurations to folk festivals to the 4th of July birthday bash – on its National Mall. And it is here, amid the jumble of museums and monuments lining the green, that Americans memorialize their cultural, scientific and political achievements.

On a day-to-day basis, the Mall hosts sunning tourists, Frisbee-catching dogs, jogging bureaucrats and touting T-shirt salesmen. But this national park is best known for its political gatherings. From suffragettes to victorious soldiers, generations of protesters and celebrants have made the Mall their own. Protesters demonstrated against the Vietnam War during the 1960s; and in 1963, Martin Luther King declared 'I Have a Dream' on the Lincoln Memorial steps. Today gun controllers, Second-Amendment protectors, pro-lifers, pro-choicers, troop supporters and war protesters are as common as tourists on the Mall.

City planner Pierre L'Enfant conceived the Mall as an educational, natural and artistic recourse for DC's residents and tourists. The strange mixture of statuary and buildings offers insight into the ongoing debate over what a national capital – and democracy itself – should be: it's a history lesson in sod and stone.

Although many national monuments are technically part of the Mall, to make your life easier we've grouped these together under a separate heading, Monuments (p68).

TRANSPORTATION

Metro Most sights along the Mall are closest to the Orange Line Smithsonian stop, but if you are headed specifically to the west end, Foggy Bottom-GWU or Farragut West may be closer.

Parking Street parking is not easy but it's not impossible along Constitution and Independence Aves, as well as Jefferson and Madison Drs. Parking becomes legal at 9:30am on weekdays; arrive then or earlier to snag a spot.

Orientation

The National Mall is a 400ft-wide green expanse stretching 3 miles from the Potomac in the west to Capitol Hill in the east. Lined with gravel paths and bordered by tree-shaded avenues (Constitution Ave to the north, Independence Ave to the south), the Mall is fringed by museums and dotted with monuments – for more on these see p68. In this section we focus on the eastern half of the Mall, which is the setting for nine of the museums of the Smithsonian Institution, as well as the National Gallery of Art and the National Sculpture Garden. These massive storehouses of culture line the north and south sides of the green.

ARTHUR M SACKLER GALLERY

Map pp292–3

☎ 202-633-4880; www.asia.si.edu; 1050 Independence Ave SW; admission free; ⊙ 10am-5:30pm, to 8pm Thu Jul & Aug; Ⓜ Smithsonian
Big shot New York research physician, medical publisher and philanthropist Dr Arthur M Sackler had more than a little obsession with the aesthetic Asian art world – over his lifetime he gathered more than 1000 pieces, including centuries-old ceramic, jade and bronze creations. Following his 1987 death he bequeathed these items, along with $4 million to build a gallery to house them, to the Smithsonian.

Although the gallery focuses largely on Sackler's collection, its offerings also include other important gifts like the Vever Collection of Islamic books and contemporary Japanese porcelains.

Exotic rotating exhibits keep things interesting while maintaining the Asian theme. They also help emphasize the visual armchair exploration of faraway places through photographic, textural and artistic masterpieces. Past successes included an exhibit on rural Japanese basket makers and 18th-century Korean art. Don't miss ImaginAsia on the 2nd floor. It is a wonderful interactive exhibit for children aged six to 14. Free lectures, films, gallery talks and tours round out its offerings.

If you have even a passing interest in Asian art and culture this museum is worthy of at least an hour of your time.

FREER GALLERY OF ART

Map pp292–3

☎ 202-633-4880; www.asia.si.edu; 12 St & Jefferson Dr SW; admission free; ⊙ 10am-5:30pm, to 8pm Thu Jul & Aug; Ⓜ Smithsonian
One of the two components of the National Museum of Asian Art (the other half is the Sackler Gallery), the Freer Gallery offers an incredible ensemble of ancient ceramics, Japanese screen paintings, and centuries-old Chinese scrolls. The Freer's Asian art collection (one of the world's finest) was a gift from Charles Lang Freer.

This Detroit industrialist and self-taught connoisseur assembled an incredible collection of ancient ceramics, screen paintings, sculpture and musical instruments from China, Japan, Southeast Asia and the Near East, which are now on display at the Freer Gallery, built in 1923 to house the collection. Freer was also a fan of James McNeill Whistler, whose works appear here too. The museum's famed Peacock Room,

SAVING THE ARTS & INDUSTRIES BUILDING

Once an exquisite Victorian dream of red brick, multicolored tiles and fanciful ironwork, the Arts & Industries Building (Map pp292–3; 900 Jefferson Dr SW) sadly shut its doors in 2004 after years of underuse and neglect. Constructed in 1881 to receive the 1876 Centennial Exposition's collections, the polychrome red, tan, black and blue brick building was placed on the National Heritage Endangered list in 2006. Currently the folks at the Smithsonian say the museum is closed for renovations and will eventually reopen, but no date had been set at time of writing.

Although it was the original home of the Smithsonian, back when it was known as the National Museum, most of the museum's eclectic collection of scientific and industrial artifacts and artworks were later distributed to other Mall museums. But in its heyday the museum hosted excellent ever-changing, but rarely seen, exhibits on history, science and society.

Outside the museum, kids (and quite a few adults) can still enjoy good, old-fashioned fun on the antique carousel. Pick your horse (or lion or tiger) and take her for a spin – literally. It's one of our fondest childhood memories.

AN AMERICAN INSTITUTION

The **Smithsonian Institution** owes its existence to a single mysterious line in the 1826 will of a British chemist who never visited the USA. Should his heir, a nephew, die childless, James Smithson wrote, 'I then bequeath the whole of my property...to the United States of America, to found at Washington, under the name of the Smithsonian Institution, an establishment for the increase & diffusion of knowledge among men.'

Smithson was born in 1765, the illegitimate result of an affair between Elizabeth Macie (a wealthy widow) and the first Duke of Northumberland. After distinguishing himself at Oxford, Smithson had an illustrious career as a chemist and mineralogist: he was best known for his discovery that zinc carbonates are minerals rather than zinc oxides. (A zinc carbonate, smithsonite, is named for him.) He undertook more-fanciful research as well, on such topics as the chemical composition of a woman's teardrop and the ideal method for making coffee. He had no children, and his nephew died heirless, leaving the Smithson fortune in American hands.

Given Smithson's political views – he slammed the British monarchy as a 'contemptible encumbrance' and publicly embraced the infant US democracy's ideals – his $508,318 bequest wasn't much of a surprise to anyone except the US Congress, which promptly looked this gift horse in the mouth. 'Every whippersnapper vagabond...might think it proper to have his name distinguished in the same way,' grumbled Senator William Preston, and Senator John C Calhoun argued that Congress wasn't authorized to accept the money and that it was 'beneath American dignity to accept presents from anyone.' Anti-British sentiment informed some of this debate: the 1814 British torching of Washington remained fresh in many American minds. Finally, in 1846, Congress deigned to accept the gift and used it to build a museum and research center, the seed of today's sprawling Smithsonian.

Smithson is now literally a part of the Smithsonian – his remains lie in a marble bier in the Castle's Crypt Room, just inside the entrance.

The Smithsonian of today is a museum complex with a collection so massive only 1% is on display at any given point. But it is so much more than a collection of museums. It is also a vast research and educational institution that cares for approximately 140 million artworks, scientific specimens, artifacts and other objects. Ten of its 18 DC museums are scattered across the National Mall with the rest found around the city. The organization also operates the National Zoological Park and throws an annual folklife festival on the National Mall each summer. Millions of visitors flock to these attractions each year, along with the year-round offerings of films, lectures, kids' activities and other programs, most free.

The best part about the Smithsonian museums is that there's no entry fee, so you needn't feel guilty about not staying all day. Plus, if you're traveling with the tykes, free admission means you can come and go in accordance with your little one's attention span. Offering visitors everything from American presidential garb to stuffed zebras, these museums are a fabulous shrine to all things American.

Museums are open from 10:30am to 5pm and closed on December 25. Dial ☎ 202-633-1000 for information about the museums.

originally designed by Whistler for a London ship owner, features gilded murals and an elaborate system of wood shelving that displays prized Chinese porcelains – it is well worth exploring.

It's hard to say which is better, the Freer or the Sackler; they kind of complement each other and should be visited in tandem. If you're short on time, you'll just have to dip quickly into a shorter exhibit in each.

HIRSHHORN MUSEUM & SCULPTURE GARDEN Map pp292-3

☎ 202-357-2700; www.hirshhorn.si.edu; 7th St & Independence Ave SW; admission free; ☼ 10am-5:30pm, to 8pm Thu Jul & Aug; Ⓜ L'Enfant Plaza
The Smithsonian's cylindrical modern art museum exhibits an impressive array of 19th- and 20th-century sculpture and canvases in chronological fashion, from modernism's early days to the present day. Highlights include sculpture by Rodin, Brancusi, Calder and Moore, plus canvases by Bacon, Miró, O'Keeffe, Warhol, Stella and Kiefer.

Standout recent additions include Hiroshi Sugimoto's eerie black-and-white gelatin silver print on paper, entitled *World Trade Center*. Although created in 1997, the work has a dark foreshadowing quality to its grainy composition.

Outside and across Jefferson Dr, the sunken Sculpture Garden is a beautifully landscaped setting with a rich collection of works, like Rodin's *The Burghers of Calais*. The sculpture garden is a great place to go on a date (a favorite with young local lovers) – wander past twisted pieces of iron and kiss behind the groomed green bushes. Seriously, it's romantic.

The Hirshhorn hosts a wide range of tours, lectures and workshops, including some fabulous events for kids. On Thursday and Saturday, the **Improv Art Room** invites kids to create their own works of art.

NATIONAL AIR & SPACE MUSEUM

Map pp292-3

☎ 202-357-2700; www.nasm.si.edu; 4th St & Independence Ave SW; admission free, IMAX or planetarium adult $8.50, senior & child $7;
☾ 10am-5:30pm, tours 10:15am & 1pm;
Ⓜ L'Enfant Plaza

We Washingtonians never tire of this DC favorite, no matter how many times we drag our visiting friends and relatives through its giant plate-glass doors. With real nuclear missiles, the Apollo 11 command module and an actual chunk of the lunar rock, who could resist? Touching the moon should be your first mission: line up and rub your fingers across the well-worn surface. Be sure to make a wish; we've heard they often come true… The cavernous halls fill quickly (every year eight million people fly through here), but the place never feels too crowded. Maybe it's because the ceilings are so high that you can string airplanes from them – the Wright Brothers' 1903 *Flyer* (which made the world's first successful airplane) and Charles Lindbergh's *Spirit of St Louis* (the first nonstop solo transatlantic flight) are both here.

There are 23 different galleries presenting the history of aviation and space exploration via interactive displays and historic artifacts. We'd recommend walking through the DC-7 cockpit, checking out the WWII permanent exhibit and taking the controls on the flight stimulator ride. The Wright Brothers exhibit, opened in 2003 to honor the landmark's 100th anniversary, documents in rich detail how humans learned to fly.

Whatever you do, don't miss the astronauts' ice cream (around $3), which can be purchased in the museum gift shop, and the **Lockheed Martin IMAX Theater**, which offers a rotating list of films shown throughout the day. *To Fly*, the grizzled granddaddy of in-your-face IMAX films, still plays here daily, along with newer offerings.

Alternative shows at the **Albert Einstein Planetarium** send viewers hurtling through

space on tours of the universe. All of these shows sell out (especially the IMAX), so buy your tickets as soon as you arrive at the museum.

The museum has a second exhibition facility, **Steven F Udvar-Hazy Center** (www.nasm.si.edu/museum/udvarhazy), at Washington Dulles International Airport. Visitors can wander across suspended walkways and airborne bridges to get a close-up view of hundreds of fighter planes, space ships and other flying machines suspended from the 10-story ceiling. Of the 200 aircraft and 135 spacecraft, highlights include the SR-71 Blackbird (the fastest jet in the world), and space shuttle *Enterprise*. Many engines, rockets, satellites, helicopters and experimental flying machines are on display for the first time. Visitors can also observe ongoing preservation work in the restoration hangar, or hang out in the observation tower and watch the planes take off and land at Dulles airport. A shuttle bus transports guests from the Air & Space Museum on the Mall to the Dulles airport facility four times per day (adult/child return $15/13).

Together the two sites comprise the world's largest collection of aviation and space artifacts, which we think is pretty damn cool.

NATIONAL GALLERY OF ART

Map pp292-3

☎ 202-737-4215; www.nga.gov; 4th St & Constitution Ave NW; admission free; ☾ 10am-5pm Mon-Sat, 11am-6pm Sun; Ⓜ Archives-Navy Memorial

This author has fond memories of getting lost amid the National Gallery of Art's exotic treasures as a kid. She'll never forget the way it felt to stand tiny next to Alexander Calder's massive childlike mobile. Made from cutouts of the brightest primary colors and set in a four-story atrium, it generally knocks the breath out of everyone who sees it.

Affiliated with but not a part of the Smithsonian, the National Gallery needs two buildings (connected by an underground tunnel) to house its massive collections (more than 110,000 objects) of painting, sculpture and decorative arts from the Middle Ages to the present. It also houses scores of touring exhibitions that go on display here. Kids love the walking escalator that traverses the two buildings (and conveniently empties into the airy cafeteria where you can let the wind from the air-conditioning vent blow out your skirt while you press your nose against the giant sheet of glass looking out onto a cascading waterfall). The place has the whole underground Louvre pyramid thing going on.

The original neoclassical building, known as the **West Building**, exhibits primarily European works, from the Middle Ages to the early 20th century, including pieces by El Greco, Monet and Cézanne. Don't miss the room full of Renoirs, including the famous *Girl with a Hoop*, an 1881 portrait Renoir was commissioned to paint of nine-year-old Marie Goujon. The National Gallery is also the only gallery in America displaying a da Vinci painting *(Ginevra di' Benci)*. Interactive computers in the Micro Gallery allow visitors to design their own tour.

Across 4th St NW, the angular **East Building**, designed by IM Pei, is where you'll find the Calder mobile along with other abstract and modern works. Smaller upstairs galleries hold special exhibits and permanent items like Picasso's *Family of Saltimbanques*. A small Matisse cutouts gallery on the 3rd floor opens for limited hours.

NATIONAL MUSEUM OF AFRICAN ART
Map pp292-3

☎ 202-357-4600; www.nmafa.si.edu; 950 Independence Ave SW; admission free; ☼ 10am-5:30pm, to 8pm Thu Jul & Aug; Ⓜ Smithsonian
Enter the museum's ground level pavilion through the Asian moon gates and geometric flower beds of the beautiful **Enid A Haupt Memorial Garden**. Take note of the African rhythms around you. Then descend into the dim underground exhibit space, connected by tunnel to the Sackler and the Freer. Devoted to ancient and modern sub-Saharan African art, the peaceful galleries display masks, textiles, ceramics, ritual objects and other examples of the visual traditions of a continent of 900 distinct cultures. It comprises the country's foremost collection of traditional work. You can't see it all, but don't miss the eight Hot Spots highlighted at the information desk. We like the small collection of highly accomplished creations from

the Kingdom of Benin. The works all relate to the rule of the Oba, or king, of the Edo-speaking people who lived in what is now Nigeria. Some of the pieces date back as far as the 15th century. Keep an eye out for the copper-alloy heads, made from sophisticated wax casts. The most intriguing is the defeated enemy. You can tell he's not Edo by the four raised scars over each eye (the other heads only have three).

NATIONAL MUSEUM OF AMERICAN HISTORY
Map pp292-3

☎ 202-357-2700; www.americanhistory.si.edu; 14th St & Constitution Ave NW; admission free; ☼ 10am-5:30pm; Ⓜ Federal Triangle
This museum is about to get a major overhaul – it closed its doors in September 2006 for two years of renovations. This is a good thing and a bad thing. On the upside, when it reopens it will feature snazzy upgrades such as a better viewing area for the Star-Spangled Banner (in the past it could get a bit chaotic when crowded). On the downside, for the present, venerated historic touchstones like the original American flag along with kitschy icons such Dorothy's ruby slippers, the original Kermit the Frog and Fonzie's *(Happy Days)* jacket will be out of reach. When the place opens its doors again, however, you can bet the museum will be back to celebrating US culture in full force. To keep up to date on the renovation, check out the museum's website.

NATIONAL MUSEUM OF NATURAL HISTORY
Map pp292-3

☎ 202-357-2700; www.mnh.si.edu; 10th St & Constitution Ave NW; admission free, IMAX adult $8.50, senior & child $7; ☼ 10am-5:30pm, to 7:30pm Jun-Aug, tours 10:30am & 1:30pm; Ⓜ Federal Triangle
Welcoming more than nine million guests each year, this is one of the world's most visited museums – and it just keeps getting better with two new exhibits added in the last five years. The excellent **Hall of Mammals** demonstrates how mammals have evolved by adapting to changing environments, while the sometimes raw and bitter-tasting **African Voices** captures the dynamism, diversity and influence of Africa's people scattered across the globe.

67

The exhibits at this museum get up in your face; they are so interactive visitors actually feel the rainstorm on the savannah and see what the hunting jaguar is stalking. The old favorites are also still here: the fossilized bones of the gargantuan T-Rex; the glittering 45-carat Hope Diamond; and live tarantula feedings at the insect zoo. The Discovery Room contains hands-on science exhibits that enable children to examine – up close and personal – shells, bones, geodes, costumes and more stuff that they are not normally allowed to touch.

The Johnson IMAX Theater shows nature extravaganzas like *Bugs! in 3D* daily. Movies sell out so buy tickets as soon as you arrive, or online in advance. A fun Friday night adventure – for kids and adults – is to visit the IMAX Jazz Café.

NATIONAL MUSEUM OF THE AMERICAN INDIAN

Map pp292-3

☎ 202-287-2020; www.americanindian.si.edu; 4th St & Independence Ave SW; ⏰ 10am-5:30pm, to 7:30pm Jun-Aug; Ⓜ Smithsonian

The Smithsonian's latest addition (opened in September 2004) tells the story of the American Indian in a format not often employed by mainstream museums, with mixed results. The idea, to use native communities' authentic voices and own interpretations of events to debunk stereotypes, is imaginative but unfortunately comes across as a little dry and too texty to hold the casual sightseer's attention for too long.

The intent is right, however. Planned in the mid-1990s, the museum took nine years to curate and makes an effort to recognize and honor the many Native American tribes, including the Sioux, Navajo, Cherokee and Pueblo, who lived on American soil well before the White man showed up. The collection, which consists of nearly a million objects reaching back thousands of years, comes from Canada and Mexico as well as the United States.

Also on the upside, the museum is a joy to look at. The snazzy modern shape of rounded lines and bright colors is constructed from native materials. Check out the shelves in the two gift shops (packed with great stocking stuffers) – in places

they are inlaid with purple and white tiles hewn from quahog shells by the Wampanoag tribe of Martha's Vineyard. Set on a 4.5-acre plot, with almost three of these acres exquisite gardens, the place has a Zen-like quality that feels in tune with nature.

NATIONAL SCULPTURE GARDEN

Map pp292-3

www.nga.gov/feature/sculptgarden/splash.htm; 9th St & Constitution Ave NW; admission free; ⏰ 10am-5pm Mon-Sat, 11am-6pm Sun, to 8pm Fri Jun-Aug; Ⓜ Archives-Navy Memorial

This is Washington's Central Park, sure to bring out the romantic in even the most cynical of lovers. Take a date (or perhaps just a friend for a walk and a spot of gossip). The National Gallery of Art's delightful 6-acre garden is studded with whimsical sculptures like Roy Lichtenstein's *House*, a giant Claes Oldenburg typewriter eraser and Louise Bourgeois' leggy *Spider*. They are scattered around a fountain – a most welcome place to dip your feet in summer. From November to March the garden's central fountain becomes the quaint Ice Rink (adult/child $8/6; ⏰ 10am-10pm). Skate rental is available.

SMITHSONIAN CASTLE

Map pp292-3

☎ 202-357-2700; www.smithsonian.org; 1000 Jefferson Dr SW; admission free; ⏰ 9am-4pm Mon-Sat; Ⓜ Smithsonian

James Renwick designed this turreted, red-sandstone fairytale creation in 1855. Today the Castle houses the Smithsonian Visitors Center. This informative first stop on the Mall is a source for an orientation film, multilingual touch-screen displays and free guides and maps, such as the excellent *Exploring African American Heritage at the Smithsonian* pamphlet.

MONUMENTS

The national monuments on the Mall are America's most treasured history lesson, the physical embodiment of everything that's patriotic (and iconic) about the USA. From giggling schoolchildren to grandparents celebrating golden wedding anniversaries, millions make the pilgrimage to these massive mounds of marble each year. They come to comprehend the meaning behind the land of the free and the home of the brave (and all the sacrifices the fight for the American idea of democracy entailed). They come to pay tribute to the country's founding fathers, fallen heroes and most influential statesmen. They come to marvel at the simple beauty of the Washington Monument set against a sublime spring backdrop of flowering pink cherry trees, to smile at their sparkling mirror-image in the larger-than-life Reflecting Pool, to search for names of lost relatives etched into the sobering jet-black marble walls at the Vietnam Veterans Memorial.

When the Vietnam Veterans Memorial opened in 1982 it generated huge controversy. But its popularity sparked a monument binge. Overkill, critics claim: the excess of monuments detracts from the significance of any one structure. But no matter what the pundits say, no one can deny that all the marble, columns, fountains and lawns make the western half of the National Mall completely breathtaking and awe-inspiring.

Orientation

The majority of Washington's monuments and memorials are clustered on the western half of the National Mall. The Washington Monument marks the eastern boundary, and makes a good starting point. With the exception of the Washington Monument, most of the monuments and memorials are not near Metro stops and parking is horrendous, so you'll need to either join a tour or put on your walking shoes – it's about one mile from the Washington Monument to

the cluster of memorials to its west. Other memorials and monuments are found in nearby Arlington (p122).

CONSTITUTION GARDENS
Map pp292-3

☼ dawn-dusk; Ⓜ Smithsonian

Originally planned to be a Rivoli-style amusement park, Constitution Gardens – really just a grove of trees – is a shady place for a stroll. In its midst, a small kidney-shaped pool is punctuated by a tiny island holding the Signers' Memorial, a plaza honoring those who signed the Declaration of Independence. At the northeast corner of the gardens an intriguing, aged stone cottage is a remnant of the days when the Washington City Canal flowed through this area. The 1835 C&O Canal Gatehouse was the lock-keepers' house for the lock that transferred boats from the City Canal onto the C&O Canal (p82), which begins in Georgetown.

DISTRICT OF COLUMBIA WAR MEMORIAL Map pp292-3
West Potomac Park off Independence Ave; ☼ 24hr

Near the Korean War Memorial, this small monument commemorates local soldiers killed in WWI. This circular temple, set amid a grove, is a nice place to escape Mall crowds. Dedicated by President Herbert Hoover on November 11, 1931 (Armistice Day), this is the only local District memorial on the Mall.

Preserved in a corner of the 47ft-tall circular domed temple, supported by 12 Doric 22ft-high marble columns, are the names of the 26,000 Washingtonians who served in the war. Look at the base for the names of the 499 DC soldiers killed in action.

FRANKLIN DELANO ROOSEVELT MEMORIAL Map pp306-7
☎ 202-426-6841; www.nps.gov/fdrm; Memorial Park; ☼ 8am-midnight; Ⓜ Smithsonian

When locals are giving guests the requisite DC memorial tour, they save the FDR memorial until after dark. Not only is the combination of light and water more powerful at night, the place is void of crowds.

FDR didn't want a grand memorial. In fact, when asked about a more traditional memorial, he reportedly responded: 'If any memorial is erected to me, I should like it to consist of a block about the size of this desk and placed in front of the Archives Building. I want it plain, without any ornamentation, with the simple carving 'In Memory of.' This request was honored in 1965, when a small, stone slab was placed at the corner of 9th St and Pennsylvania Ave NW. Though overshadowed by the tribute on the Tidal Basin, the first FDR memorial– the one that remembers FDR the way he wanted – still stands at its designated spot (see Map pp292–3).

Despite the former president's wishes, planners later felt that the memorial stone slab wasn't grand enough, so this second (and grand), 7.5-acre memorial opened in 1997. On the Tidal Basin's west bank, the fabulously landscaped area is composed of four red-granite 'rooms' that narrate FDR's presidency through statuary and inscriptions, punctuated with cascades and peaceful alcoves. The unique memorial tells the story of the 32nd president, rather than simply displaying a single monumental image.

GEORGE MASON MEMORIAL

Map pp306-7

☎ 202-426-6841; www.nps.gov/gemm; Ohio Dr SW; ⏱ 8am-midnight; Ⓜ Smithsonian

This little oasis of flowers and fountains honors the famed statesman and author of the Commonwealth of Virginia Declaration of Rights (a forerunner to the US Bill of Rights). A bronze sculpture of Mason sits in a lovely setting, amid his wise words against slavery and in support of human rights.

KOREAN WAR VETERANS MEMORIAL

Map pp292-3

☎ 202-426-6841; www.nps.gov/kowa; ⏱ 8am-midnight; Ⓜ Foggy Bottom-GWU

Dedicated in 1995, this memorial depicts a troop of 19 heavily cloaked soldiers on night patrol in the rice paddies. The larger-than-life-size statues are shown mid-stride, realistically exhausted and anxious. The striking setting is enhanced by a granite wall and Pool of Remembrance along with fiber-optic lighting for night viewing. It's a poignant reminder of America's forgotten war.

LINCOLN MEMORIAL

Map pp292-3

☎ 202-426-6841; www.nps.gov/linc; ⏱ 9.30am-midnight; Ⓜ Foggy Bottom-GWU

Here's a local secret: if you're ever stuck in a thunderstorm while wandering around the Mall, make a dash for the Lincoln Memorial. Thunder seems to rumble like clockwork nearly every 4th of July, and everyone in the know takes shelter under the marble dome, crouching near the foot of the enormous chair in which a gigantic Lincoln holds court.

In a stunning location, the Lincoln Memorial is a favorite location spot for Hollywood blockbusters. In the early morning hours Owen Wilson and Vince Vaughn discussed girls on the memorial steps in the *Wedding Crashers;* Reese Witherspoon's Elle Woods sought Lincoln's advice in *Legally Blonde 2;* and many a romantic kiss has been shot on the marble steps at sunset.

The monument perfectly balances the long axis of the Mall, and is a counterpoint to the Capitol at the eastern end. The 2000ft **Reflecting Pool** stretches in front, its shallow, duck-speckled waters reflecting both the Lincoln and Washington Memorials. Designed by Henry Bacon to resemble a Doric temple, the memorial's 36 columns represent the 36 states in Lincoln's union. Within, the seated statue of Lincoln, sculpted by Daniel Chester French, is framed by the carved text of the Gettysburg Address and Lincoln's Second Inaugural.

Since its completion in 1922 the memorial to the author of the Emancipation Proclamation has also been a symbol of the Civil Rights movement. Dr Robert Moten, president of historically Black Tuskegee Institute, was invited to speak at the memorial's dedication, yet officials sat him in a segregated section of the audience, sparking protests by outraged African Americans.

In 1939 Black contralto Marian Anderson, barred from the Daughters of the American Revolution's Constitution Hall, sang from the memorial's steps; the historic 1963 March on Washington reached its zenith here when Martin Luther King, Jr delivered his 'I Have a Dream' speech. An engraving of his famed words now marks the spot where MLK stood.

NATIONAL WORLD WAR II MEMORIAL Map pp292-3

☎ 800-639-4992; www.wwiimemorial.com; Ⓜ Smithsonian

DC's newest memorial is particularly moving at dusk, when the American flags are lowered and the mixture of white lights illuminating marble pillars and fountains, reflecting in inky pools, creates a picture that's as haunting as it is beautiful.

Dedicated on Memorial Day (May 29) 2004, the memorial emphasizes the unprecedented unity of the nation during WWII, in hopes of inspiring such nationalism in post-WWII generations while honoring the 16 million Americans who served in the armed forces during the war, the 400,000 who died and the many millions more who helped the war effort at home, collecting scrap metal and tending victory gardens.

Constructed around the old Rainbow Pool, at the eastern end of the Reflecting Pool, the memorial is appropriately placed between the Washington Monument and the Lincoln Memorial. Its plaza is anchored by dual arches, symbolizing the victory in both the Atlantic and Pacific theaters, and surrounded by 56 granite pillars, one for each state and territory, plus the District of Columbia. The Freedom Wall somberly sparkles with 4000 hand-sculpted gold stars, one for every 100 Americans who lost their lives between 1941 and 1945 (the stars are replicas of those worn by mothers who lost their sons in the war). Today, you'll often see widows and families placing flowers or fading black-and-white photos of handsome young men at the foot of the wall, in remembrance of lost loved ones.

The memorial serves as more than just a nostalgic experience. The website is home to the WWII Registry and Messaging Center, where vets can reconnect on electronic post boards and search for lost friends over the registry.

THOMAS JEFFERSON MEMORIAL

Map pp306-7

☎ 202-426-6841; www.nps.gov/thje; ☽ 8am-midnight; Ⓜ Smithsonian

Set on the south bank of the Tidal Basin amid the cherry trees (check it out in late March or early April when the blossoms

NATIONAL CHERRY BLOSSOM FESTIVAL

A fluttering gauze scarf of the palest pink encircles the Tidal Basin, at the west end of the National Mall, each spring in late March or early April, as 1300 Japanese cherry trees explode into bloom.

In 1912, the Japanese government presented the forerunners of these trees to President Taft as a goodwill gift. They are mostly of the Yoshino variety, whose blooms are nearly pure white, but a handful of pink-blooming Akebono trees add a shimmer of dawn-like rose to the scene.

Washingtonians immediately adopted the trees as a symbol of their city. When the Tidal Basin was chosen as the site of the Thomas Jefferson Memorial, protesters even chained themselves to trees to prevent their removal. During WWII, the trees were occasionally vandalized, but they thrived anyway. In 1965 the Japanese government provided the US with 3800 more trees, which were planted along the Mall and near the Washington Monument. Later-blooming Kwanzan cherry trees were planted in East Potomac Park.

The city's biggest annual festival, the **National Cherry Blossom Festival** (☎ 202-728-1137; www .nationalcherryblossomfestival.org), is timed to co-incide with the trees' blossoming. However, because the blossoming time is somewhat unpredictable, and because Washington's quirky spring weather sometimes pelts the blossoms off the trees with icy rain and wind, the festival doesn't always get its flowers. Nonetheless, the parades, speeches, parties and cultural events draw thousands of tourists and mark the official start of warm weather for Washington.

are blazing pink), this memorial honors the third US president, political philosopher, drafter of the Declaration of Independence and founder of the University of Virginia – Thomas Jefferson. Designed by John Russell Pope to resemble Jefferson's library at the university, the rounded, domed monument was initially derided by critics as 'the Jefferson Muffin.' Inside is a 19ft bronze likeness, and excerpts from Jefferson's writings are etched into the walls.

TIDAL BASIN Map pp306-7

☎ 202-484-0206; ☽ 8am-dusk; Ⓜ Smithsonian

Beloved for the magnificent Yoshino cherry trees that ring it, the Tidal Basin attracts joggers, strollers and picnickers to its shady banks. The orchard was a gift from

Japan in 1912; since then, every year in late March or early April the banks shimmer with pale pink blossoms.

The enchanting **National Cherry Blossom Festival** (p15) celebrates this event – the first two weeks of April draw 100,000 visitors to DC for the festivities, which culminate in a big parade.

The amoeba-shaped Tidal Basin actually serves a practical purpose as well as being aesthetically pleasing: it flushes the adjacent Washington Channel. At high tide, river waters fill the basin through gates under the Inlet Bridge; at low tide, gates under the Outlet Bridge open and water streams into the channel.

To experience DC's fabulous vistas from another angle, head out onto the water. Visit the **Tidal Basin Boathouse** (☎ 202-479-2426; 1501 Maine Ave SW; boat rental $8-16; ☽ 10am-7pm mid-Mar–mid-Oct) and rent out a paddleboat. You wouldn't think it, but spinning around the basin in a paddleboat for an hour can burn quite a few calories (and can really tire out the kids). Make sure you bring the camera; there are great views, of the Jefferson Memorial in particular, from the water.

UNITED STATES BOTANIC GARDEN

Map pp292-3

☎ 202-225-8333; www.usbg.gov; 100 Maryland Ave SW; admission free; ☽ 10am-5pm; Ⓜ Capitol South
Resembling London's Crystal Palace, this iron-and-glass greenhouse provides a beautiful setting for displays of exotic and local plants. It is not technically part of the Smithsonian Institution, but it is located at the eastern end of the Mall alongside the Smithsonian museums. Highlights of the garden include cycad trees that produce 50lb cones, and the mammoth and smelly Titan Arum. Behind the conservatory, across Independence Ave, you'll find the grand **Bartholdi Fountain**.

VIETNAM VETERANS MEMORIAL

Map pp292-3

☎ 202-426-6841; www.nps.gov/vive;
☽ 8am-midnight; Ⓜ Foggy Bottom-GWU
Even the profound WWII cenotaph cannot diminish the tear-jerking quality of this somber arrow of black stone at Washington, DC's most emotional memorial. Since its 1982 dedication, the Vietnam Veterans

Memorial has been an American pilgrimage site – it is a quiet place to remember the soldiers killed or missing in one of America's least popular wars (the current Iraq War is right up there unpopularity-wise these days). Originally conceived to reconcile a divided nation, the memorial was designed by a 21-year-old Yale architecture student, Maya Lin. The two walls of polished Indian granite meet in a 10ft apex. The walls are inscribed with the names of the 58,209 soldiers killed in the Vietnam War, arranged chronologically by date of death. The Vietnam Veterans Memorial is an eloquent inversion of the Mall's other monuments: rather than a pale, ornate structure reaching skyward, it is dark, austere and burrows into the earth, symbolizing the war's wound to the national psyche.

Paper indices at both ends help you locate individual names. The most moving remembrances are notes, medals and mementos left by survivors, families and friends; some of these are collected by park rangers and displayed at the **National Museum of American History** (p67).

In 1984 opponents of Maya Lin's design insisted that a more traditional (and far less interesting) sculpture of soldiers be added nearby. Also nearby is the tree-ringed **Women in Vietnam Memorial** depicting female soldiers aiding a fallen man. Veterans dedicated to finding lost POWs have set up permanent camps around the monument, passing out pamphlets and Congressional petitions to search for soldiers still missing three decades after the war's end.

WASHINGTON DC MARTIN LUTHER KING JR MEMORIAL

Map pp292-3

www.mlkmemorial.org; Ⓜ Smithsonian
Ground breaking started in the fall of 2006 for this new memorial, which honors America's most influential Civil Rights leader. The memorial is being built on the Tidal Basin, near the Jefferson and FDR Memorials, and will convey themes of democracy, justice and hope – all cornerstones of MLK's teachings. The design includes a crescent-shaped wall with sermon inscriptions etched onto its stone surface. The centerpiece of the memorial will be a Stone of Hope, featuring a 30ft-tall likeness of Dr King. The memorial is expected to open in 2008.

WASHINGTON, DC FOR CHILDREN

DC is the best city in the country to bring the kids. Not only is the place one giant history lesson, it is also filled with fun for tots, including regular exhibits and special events. Here's a list of highlights if you have young ones in tow.

Hirshhorn Museum & Sculpture Garden (p65) Young at Art programs introduce children to artistic study; the regularly scheduled Improv Art classes give kids the chance to make their own artworks.

International Spy Museum (p94) Kids can eavesdrop on bugged conversations and crawl through imitation air ducts.

National Academy of Sciences (p77) Let your kids climb into Einstein's lap and look out at the universe. It's a quiet leafy spot perfect for a picnic and spontaneous science lesson.

National Air & Space Museum (p63) A guaranteed kiddy favorite – those who dream of being a pilot or an astronaut can test their skills.

National Geographic Explorers Hall (p99) Interactive exhibits on natural history, dinosaurs, weather, animals and space exploration.

National Museum of Natural History (p67) The number one museum for kids, complete with dinosaurs, diamonds and the new Mammal Hall.

National Sculpture Garden & Ice Rink (p68) Kids will delight in the surreal statues and refreshing fountain.

National Zoological Park (p119) An obvious first stop for monkey-lovers and snake-spotters.

Rock Creek Park Nature Center & Planetarium (p121) Hands-on ecological displays, kids' nature hikes and planetarium shows.

Washington Dolls' House & Toy Museum (p120) A marvelous collection of Victorian dolls' houses and toys.

Washington National Cathedral (p120 Saturday family programs let kids hear stories and create gargoyles or stained-glass windows to take home.

WASHINGTON MONUMENT

Map pp292-3

☎ 202-619-7222; www.nps.gov/wamo; Constitution Ave & 15th St; admission free, reservations $2; 🕙 9am-5pm, tickets available from 8am; Ⓜ Smithsonian

Strangely, this pale, quite phallic, obelisk needling the sky near the Mall's west end was originally conceived as an equestrian statue to honor George Washington, the country's first president. We guess it grew a little big for its britches. At 555ft the monument is not only the tallest building in DC (by federal law no structure can reach above it), it is also the tallest masonry structure in the world!

Construction began in 1848 but a lack of funds during the Civil War kept building in a quagmire and the 90,854-ton brick and marble structure was not completed until 1888. The original marble was drawn from Maryland, but the source dried up about a third of the way through construction and contractors had to turn to Massachusetts for marble. If you look closely there is a visible delineation in color where the old and new marble meet.

Inside the monument, an elevator quickly whisks you to an observation landing deck which, at 500ft, offers truly spectacular views of the city and surrounds. Most visitors agree that the panoramic green and marble vista of Washington and her rivers is well worth any wait to reach the observation deck. In the days before September 11, 2001 it was possible to descend the 897 steps rather than taking the elevator – the shaft's interior is decorated with inscribed stones. Believe it or not, when the monument first opened the elevator was not considered safe for women so, while men got to ride in style to the top, women had to make the trek on foot! Talk about gender equality. Due to security concerns it is no longer possible for visitors to take the stairs.

Same-day tickets for a timed entrance to the monument are available at the **ticket kiosk** on the monument grounds. Distribution starts at 8am; make sure you arrive early – tickets for the monument are limited. Alternatively, you can reserve your tickets for a small fee by calling in advance. Food, drink and large bags are prohibited.

Sights

MONUMENTS

WHITE HOUSE AREA & FOGGY BOTTOM

Eating p144; Shopping p209; Sleeping p225

If you've never been to Washington before, wait until dark to visit this neighborhood. When the sun has set (and the rush hour traffic cleared) hail a cab outside the Capitol and drive down Pennsylvania Ave toward the White House. It's an awesome sight with a déjà vu flavor. The wide boulevard lined with leafy trees and stately buildings, smeared red and white with the lights of passing cars, the expansive green of the ellipse to your left, the shining white marble monolith glowing against an inky pink sky on your right – this is the classic Washington set-up shot played on a thousand silver screens across the world.

You'll need to return in the morning, of course, to explore this famous (rather fun) neighborhood in more depth. At first look, the most recognized address in America (that would be 1600 Pennsylvania Ave NW) is strikingly accessible. The mansion is set so close to the road you can almost peek in the windows to see what Dubya or his successor is up to. If you wait around, it seems he might come out the front door to say howdy.

When you step back, however, the majesty of the scene becomes apparent. Forbidding iron gates surround the White House grounds. The Old Executive Office Building and the Treasury Building, on either side of the mansion, are giant-sized and lavishly trimmed. The South Lawn is a wide, green sea separating the president and the people. All around are gargantuan office buildings housing federal agencies and international organizations; stretches of park studded with marble statues; and views of the Capitol or the Washington Monument. Take it all in: this neighborhood – with its grand architecture and symbolic layout and sweeping views – is befitting of the residency of the most powerful leader of the Western world.

Besides the president and his family, not many people live around here. The fancy mansions around Lafayette Sq now house museums, hotels and private clubs, not residents. Thousands of white-collars fill these office buildings each day and keep the US Government ticking. They may hit one of the local pubs for a drink after work, but then they retire to more residential areas like Georgetown or Dupont Circle, or check into a room at a nearby hotel, or hop on the Metro out to the suburbs. These streets are remarkably quiet at night.

By day, however, they bustle with bureaucrats and diplomats, tourists and lobbyists. Helicopters roar above, transporting important people to important places. In-line skaters and street hockey players take advantage of the car-free zone in front of the White House. Lafayette Sq fills up with poster-toting ideologues, chess-playing pensioners and lunch-munching White House staffers (all this goes on and the homeless guy doesn't even wake up).

Orientation

Pennsylvania Ave cuts across Northwest DC on a diagonal from the Capitol to the White House. These homes of two of the branches of the government balance on either end of the axis, in a visual metaphor for the power balance between the executive and legislative. Pennsylvania Ave continues on its northwestern trajectory into Georgetown, but not without a major detour (where there is no access for cars) around the president's home.

The White House area and Foggy Bottom comprise a square (in shape as well as attitude) bounded by the blue Potomac River in the west and the green National Mall. These two natural strips of color at the neighborhood's border, however, are a contrast to its interior. Straight streets and grey blocks of office buildings dominate this little piece of the city, lending it a much more urban character than other parts of DC.

The exception is the White House, set back on lush lawns and flanked by leafy, green Lafayette Sq to the north and the huge Ellipse to the south. Together with the ornate Old Executive Office Building and the colossal Treasury Building, which are on either side of the White House on Pennsylvania Ave, these landmarks comprise the southeast corner of the neighborhood.

For our purposes, the northern boundary of the neighborhood is L St NW, although K St NW – one block south – is a busier, more prominent thoroughfare.

Further west, the confluence of K St, 23rd St, Pennsylvania Ave and New Hampshire Ave forms Washington Circle. Known as Foggy Bottom, the area's nickname probably derives from the district's original inhabitants (a gasworks, brewery, cement factory and other smog-producing industries); modern wits, however, say the name describes the bureaucratic hot air arising from the area's numerous federal agencies.

The campus of George Washington University (GWU) dominates these blocks south of Washington Circle, but you might not recognize it: the urban campus blends right into the surrounding city with no iron gates or green quad to define it. South of GWU, anchoring the west end of the neighborhood, the Kennedy Center and the Watergate rise over the banks of the Potomac.

WHITE HOUSE AREA

BLAIR & LEE HOUSES

Map pp292-3

1653 Pennsylvania Ave NW; ☿ closed to public; Ⓜ Farragut West

The 1824 Blair House has been the official presidential guesthouse since 1942, when Eleanor Roosevelt got sick of tripping over dignitaries in her White House. A plaque on the front fence commemorates the bodyguard killed here while protecting President Truman from a 1950 assassination attempt by Puerto Rican pro-independence terrorists.

The neighboring 1858 Lee House was built by the famous general's family. Here scion Robert E Lee declined command of the Union Army when the Civil War erupted.

CORCORAN GALLERY OF ART

Map pp292-3

☎ 202-639-1700; www.corcoran.org; 500 17th St NW; adult/student/senior/family $5/1/3/8, free Mon & 5pm Thu; ☿ 10am-5pm Wed-Mon, to 9pm Thu; Ⓜ Farragut West

In a beautiful 1897 beaux-arts building overlooking the Ellipse, the Corcoran exhibits American and European masterworks, with an emphasis on 19th- and early-20th-century American artists. Special exhibits often focus on particular artists or historical themes, such as Lichtenstein's sculptures and drawings, or the art of the Harlem Renaissance. The Corcoran is particularly known for its surveys of historic and modern photography. It also houses the College of Art & Design and mounts intriguing exhibits of its students' work.

Café des Artistes, in the 1st floor atrium, is an elegant restaurant serving light lunch fare. A weekly Sunday gospel brunch features area singers, and jazz musicians play Thursday evenings.

Behind the Corcoran, on E St NW between 18th and 20th Sts NW, pretty Rawlins Park is named for President US Grant's Secretary of War. With goldfish in its little pond and blooming magnolias in spring and summer, it's among downtown DC's most charming oases.

In 2006, after years of setbacks, the Corcoran finally commissioned famed Spanish Guggenheim architect Frank Gehry to construct a stunning third wing. When completed in 2009 it is expected to house sculptures on the north side of the building.

DECATUR HOUSE Map pp292-3

☎ 202-842-0920; www.decaturhouse.org; 748 Jackson Place NW, visitor entrance 1610 H St NW; admission by donation; ☿ 10am-5pm Tue-Sat, to 8pm Thu, noon-4pm Sun; Ⓜ Farragut West

Designed in 1818 by Benjamin Latrobe for the War of 1812 naval hero Stephen Decatur, the Decatur House sits at Lafayette Sq's northwest corner. Decatur is best remembered for his skills fighting Barbary pirates – sadly these same skills came to little use a year after he moved into his new home, when he got himself killed in a duel. A tour shows you the house's austere architectural charms, and details the lives of not only its famous tenants – including Martin Van Buren and Henry Clay – but also the slaves who waited upon them.

DEPARTMENT OF THE INTERIOR MUSEUM Map pp292-3

☎ 202-208-4743; www.doi.gov/museum /interiormuseum/mission.htm; 1849 C St NW; admission free; ⏱ 8:30am-4:30pm Mon-Fri, 1-4pm 3rd Sat of month; M Farragut West

Responsible for managing the US's natural resources, the Department of the Interior operates this small but excellent museum to educate the public about its current goals and programs. It includes landscape art, Indian artifacts and historical photos of Indian life, as well as exhibits on wildlife and resource management. Reserve in advance for guided tours of the building itself, which contains 25 tremendous New Deal murals from the 1930s and 1940s. Show a photo ID to enter.

ELLIPSE Map pp292-3

Constitution Ave btwn 15th & 17th Sts NW

The expansive park on the south side of the White House is known as the Ellipse, named for the elliptical road circling the interior. The park is studded with a random collection of monuments, such as the Zero Milestone (the marker for highway distances all across the country) and the Second Division Memorial. But the more important function of the Ellipse is to host sporting events, parades and festivals – ranging from the lighting of the national Christmas tree, to military drill performances, to Lance Armstrong's final ride.

FEDERAL RESERVE

Map pp292-3

☎ 202-452-3149; www.federalreserve.gov; 20th St NW btwn C St & Constitution Ave; admission free; ⏱ tours by reservation; M Farragut West

'The Fed' conjures up strong images of high-powered executives and bureaucrats crafting the economic ebbs and flows of the country. Unfortunately, you won't see too much of that on this tour, which focuses on the architecture of the Eccles Building that houses the Fed. It does feature a film, The Fed Today, and a visit to the Board Room. The tour is recommended for adults only; kids under college age will likely get bored at the Board.

Visitors can also view the Fed's art collection, parts of which are displayed in the atrium of the Eccles Building. The permanent collection is a survey of American art dating from the 1830s to the present. The Board also presents rotating thematic exhibitions of borrowed art on varied themes, such as currency design. A recent exhibit, Complexity, showcased work by artists employing a variety of media to explore complex systems like traffic, the weather and the stock market.

HAY-ADAMS HOTEL

Map pp292-3

☎ 202-638-6600; www.hayadams.com; cnr H & 16th Sts; M Farragut West

Sweeping arches and elegant columns are trademarks of this awesome Renaissance-revival building. Across from the Decatur House, the hotel is a DC landmark as far as politicking goes. This is where Henry Kissinger lunched regularly and Oliver North did much of his Iran-Contra fundraising inside its walls. The Clintons stayed the night during Bill's first inauguration. If you want to stay, see p226.

LAFAYETTE SQUARE

Map pp292-3

Pennsylvania Ave btwn 15th & 17th Sts NW

The land north of 1600 Pennsylvania was originally deeded as part of the White House grounds. However, in 1804 President Thomas Jefferson decided to divide the plot and give half back to the public in the form of a park, now known as Lafayette Sq. A statue of Andrew Jackson astride a horse holds court in the center of the park, while the statues anchoring the four corners are all foreign-born Revolutionary leaders. A visit to the park is a lesson in a less remembered aspect of history, the non-American freedom fighters who helped ensure George Washington had a presidency to preside over in the first place.

In the southeast corner check out the likeness of the Marquis de Lafayette, a Revolutionary War general by the age of 19! Although Lafayette was branded a traitor in his native France following the war, when he returned to the infant America in 1824 he was lauded with various honors, including this park. A more bizarre creation is found in the park's northeast corner. Here lies a memorial to Tadeusz Kosciusko, a Polish freedom fighter and prominent engineer in Washington's army. The sculpture features the general towering over an angry imperial eagle killing a snake atop a globe. The inscription at the base is one of DC's most brazen. Taken from Scottish poet Thomas Campbell, it reads: 'And Freedom shrieked as Kosciusko fell!'

NATIONAL ACADEMY OF SCIENCES
Map pp292-3

☎ 202-334-2436; www.nationalacademies.org /nas/arts.nsf; 2101 Constitution Ave NW; admission free; ☽ 9am-5pm Mon-Fri; Ⓜ Foggy Bottom-GWU

The academy advises the government on scientific and technical issues, and also hosts scientific and art exhibitions, concerts and symposiums. Recent exhibits have included Under Antarctic Ice, featuring incredible photographs of this harsh but breathtakingly beautiful environment, and An Intimate View of Flowers (self-explanatory). Concerts are often held on Sunday afternoons.

The nicely landscaped grounds along Constitution Ave feature DC's most huggable monument: the Albert Einstein statue. The larger-than-life, sandal-shod, chubby bronze reclines on a bench, and little kids crawl all over him. He's elevated on a 'star map' pedestal that depicts the heavens that his theories reshaped for humanity.

OLD EXECUTIVE OFFICE BUILDING
Map pp292-3

www.whitehouse.gov/history/eeobtour; 17th St NW & Pennsylvania Ave; ☽ closed to public; Ⓜ Farragut West

Truman called it 'the greatest monstrosity in America;' Hoover griped that it was an 'architectural orgy.' Yet the ornate Old Executive Office Building (or Eisenhower Executive Office Building, as it is officially known) delights most visitors today. It was designed by Alfred Mullet in the 1870s to house State, War and Navy Department staff. His design was roundly blasted, and poor old Mullet killed himself two years after its completion. Today it houses White House staff. The OEOB is no longer open to the public for tours, but the website's virtual tour offers a glimpse of some of the rooms.

ORGANIZATION OF AMERICAN STATES & ART MUSEUM OF THE AMERICAS Map pp292-3

☎ 202-458-6016; www.oas.org; 201 18th St NW; admission free; ☽ 10am-5pm Tue-Sun; Ⓜ Farragut West

A sort of forerunner to the UN, the OAS is an international organization founded in 1890 to promote cooperation among North and South American nations. Its main building at 17th St and Constitution Ave is a marble palazzo surrounded by the sculpture-studded Aztec Gardens. In the small building behind it, the OAS operates the Art Museum of the Americas, featuring an incredible collection of art that spans the 20th century and the Western Hemisphere. Works represent southern interpretations of constructivism and surrealism, as well as more recent pieces of geometric and pop art.

RENWICK GALLERY
Map pp292-3

☎ 202-357-2700; www.americanart.si.edu; 17th St & Pennsylvania Ave NW; admission free; ☽ 10am-5:30pm; Ⓜ Farragut West

The Smithsonian's Renwick invites you up the stairs of its regal 1859 mansion and then startles you with wild pieces of artistic whimsy. This is the national crafts museum, displaying woodwork, ceramics, sculpture, metalwork and furniture. But 'crafts' doesn't really describe these pieces – they're wonderfully creative artworks. The many playful pieces make it a wonderful place to introduce kids to art. They especially love Larry Fuentes' *Game Fish*, a sailfish trophy meticulously adorned with beads, buttons, tiles, dominoes, yo-yos etc. Grown-ups like the Grand Salon and Octagon Room, recently restored in the grand gilded-age styles of the 1870s and 1880s.

ST JOHN'S CHURCH
Map pp292-3

☎ 202-347-8766; 1525 H St NW; ☽ 9am-3pm, service 12:10pm, Sun services 8am, 9am & 11am; Ⓜ McPherson Sq

A small, butter-colored building, St John's isn't DC's most imposing church, but it is one of its most charming. St John's is the 'Church of the Presidents' – every president since Madison has attended its services at

VISITING THE WHITE HOUSE

Although it's not impossible to visit the White House, security concerns in a post–September 11 world make it a hell of a lot harder (you used to be able to line up early in the morning and take a group tour). If you are determined (and a US citizen or resident), however, get together a group of 10 or more and request a tour through your congressional representative. If you don't have a full group, it's best to try anyway, as sometimes two parties can be combined. Requests may be granted six months in advance and are confirmed approximately one month prior (prepare for a background check to be run).

If you make it, the self-guided tours are offered between 7:30am and 12:30pm Tuesday through Sunday and are scheduled on a first come, first served basis. Tours are free. For the most current info, call the 24-hour line ☎ 202-456-7041.

least once. Designed in 1815 by Capitol architect Benjamin Henry Latrobe, the church reserves a pew (No 54, purchased by Madison) for presidential families. Lyndon Johnson prayed here on the first morning of his presidency, after JFK was killed.

TREASURY BUILDING
Map pp292-3

☎ 202-622-2200; www.treasury.gov; 1500 Pennsylvania Ave NW; ☼ closed to public; Ⓜ McPherson Sq

The 1836 Greek-revival colossus (each of its 30 columns –36ft high – was carved from a single granite block) is decorated as befits a treasury, with golden eagles, ornate balustrades and a two-story Cash Room, constructed with eight types of marble. US currency was printed in the basement from 1863 to 1880. This building no longer prints any money, but it is often confused with the present 'money factory,' the Bureau of Printing & Engraving, south of the Mall. Unfortunately tours of the building have been suspended, but the website offers a virtual tour under Education.

WHITE HOUSE Map pp292-3

☎ 202-456-7041; www.whitehouse.gov; 1600 Pennsylvania Ave NW; ☼ closed to public; Ⓜ Farragut West

Every US president since John Adams has lived in this 132-room mansion at America's most famous address. Its stature has grown through the years: no longer a mere residence, it's now the central icon of the American presidency.

The Presidential Palace – as it was once known – has changed a great deal over history (and with its changing residents). It was not originally white, for example. After the British burned the building in the War of 1812, it was restored and painted. It was Teddy Roosevelt that later gave official sanction to the executive mansion's popular name.

An overhaul in 1950 gutted almost the entire interior, and Jacqueline Kennedy's extensive redecoration campaign in the 1960s replaced the previous hodgepodge with more tasteful furnishings. Presidents have customized the property over time: Grant put in a personal zoo; FDR, a pool; Truman a balcony, Bush a horseshoe-throwing lane and Clinton a jogging track. Some residents never leave: it's said that Eleanor Roosevelt and Harry Truman both sighted Lincoln's ghost in Abe's old study.

Back before Herbert Hoover's era, presidents used to open the doors at noon each day to shake visitors' hands. Alas, no longer. Daily tours of the White House have been suspended since September 11, 2001 (although Laura Bush conducts a video tour at the White House Visitors Center). The White House grounds are occasionally opened for special events, however, such as **Tee-ball on the South Lawn** and the **Easter Egg Roll**, held every Easter Monday for kids aged three to six.

Concerns for the safety of the President make the White House off-limits to the public these days unless you organize a group tourleft. We know it's not nearly as good as the real thing, but you can still get a feel for what the inside of the White House looks like by visiting the official website. Here, in the Life of the White House section, President George W Bush, Laura Bush, Vice President Cheney and other administration heavyweights narrate video tours of famous rooms including the Oval Office and Roosevelt Room. The video presentations are actually quite interesting and filled with little White House trivia nuggets. For example, Bush talks about how each president designs his own Oval Office rug and how the presidential seal in the middle of the room was altered after WWII by President Harry Truman to represent America as a nation at peace, not war – ironic commentary coming from Bush's mouth.

In lieu of touring the actual White House itself, visitors can browse exhibits, watch historic reenactments and take a video tour of the White House at the **Visitors Center** (☎ 202-208-1631; www.nps.gov/whho; 1450 Pennsylvania Ave NW; admission free; ⏰ 7:30am-4pm; Ⓜ McPherson Sq) in the Malcolm Baldrige Hall in the Department of Commerce building. It's obviously not the same as seeing the real deal first-hand, but the Visitors Center does provide an overview of the history of the White House, as well as fun anecdotes about the presidential families (and pets!) who have graced its halls. Each month, the visitors center also puts on free performances in which actors recreate the lives of presidents and patriots.

FOGGY BOTTOM

GEORGE WASHINGTON UNIVERSITY
Map pp292-3
☎ 202-994-6602; www.gwu.edu; 801 22nd St NW; admission free; ⏰ 9am-5pm Mon-Fri, 10am-3pm Sat, closed May-Jul; Ⓜ Foggy Bottom-GWU
George Washington was so hell-bent on starting a university he left money in his will to endow a school of higher learning. His wish came true in 1821, when an Act of Congress founded Baptist College, the precursor to today's George Washington University. The school has played an important role in the city's gentrification process, buying up town houses and building new structures on such a scale that it has become the city's second biggest landowner after the federal government! Like Georgetown, George Washington has its share of famous alumni– J Edgar Hoover, Jacqueline Kennedy Onassis, Colin Powell.

The school is spread over several blocks between F, 20th and 24th streets and Pennsylvania Ave in Foggy Bottom. The best bit of the campus is University Yard, between G and H and 20th and 21st Sts – Colonial-revival buildings flank a green park bedecked with red roses and a statue of – who else? – Washington. If you're interested in checking out the school itself, the Academic Center has campus maps and occasional student-led historical walking tours around the area.

KENNEDY CENTER
Map pp292-3
John F Kennedy Center for the Performing Arts; ☎ 202-467-4600, 800-444-1324; www.kennedy-center.org; 2700 F St NW; ⏰ 10am-midnight, tours 10am-5pm Mon-Fri, 10am-1pm Sat & Sun; Ⓜ Foggy Bottom-GWU (free shuttle 9:45am-midnight Mon-Sat, noon-8pm Sun)
Overlooking the Potomac, the Kennedy Center was dedicated in 1964 as a 'living memorial' to JFK. The center's theaters, concert hall, opera house and cinema almost single-handedly reversed Washington's former reputation as a cultural desert. (The site had previously housed the Christian Heurich Brewery, makers of Senate-brand beer until 1956.)

Offering lovely river views from the terrace (or from the Roof Terrace Restaurant), the Kennedy Center is a great place to have a drink. Guided tours depart from the gift shop and showcase the main theaters, as well as the impressive Hall of States, which features the flags of states hung in the order they entered the Union, and the Hall of Nations, which features flags of nations recognized by the US. But the best way to see the center is at one of the many festivals, films or concerts held here year-round. The **Millennium Stage** hosts a varied and exciting program of free concerts every day at 6pm. See Entertainment for more information (p192).

OCTAGON MUSEUM
Map pp292-3
☎ 202-638-3105; www.theoctagon.org; 1799 New York Ave NW; pre-arranged group tours $5; ⏰ tours by arrangement; Ⓜ Farragut West
Designed by William Thornton (the Capitol's first architect) in 1800, this is a symmetrically winged Federal structure designed to fit an odd triangular lot. Behind it, the American Institute of Architects' (AIA) large modern offices wrap around the little house like a protective older brother. Knowledgeable docents show you the Octagon's hidden doorways, twin staircases and period furniture. Upstairs galleries host exhibits on architecture and design; downstairs exhibits explain the careful archaeological work required to restore this and other old houses.

At the time of research the museum was only open for pre-arranged group tours, but there were plans to reopen the museum on a daily basis in the future – check the website for the latest.

ST MARY'S EPISCOPAL CHURCH
Map pp292-3

☎ 202-333-3985; 730 23rd St NW;
Ⓜ Foggy Bottom-GWU
Built in 1887, St Mary's was home to the first Black Episcopal congregation in DC. James Renwick, designer of the **Smithsonian Castle**, created the beautiful red-brick building especially for the congregation.

STATE DEPARTMENT
Map pp292-3

US Department of State; ☎ 202-647-3241;
www.state.gov; 22nd & C Sts NW; admission free;
⏲ tours by reservation 9:30am, 10:30am & 2:45pm
Mon-Fri; Ⓜ Foggy Bottom-GWU
The State Dept is a forbidding, well-guarded edifice, but you can tour its grand Diplomatic Reception Rooms, where Cabinet members and the Secretary of State entertain visiting potentates amid ornate 18th-century American antiques. Call at least a month beforehand to reserve a tour spot, and bring photo ID; no kids under 12 are admitted.

WATERGATE COMPLEX
Map pp292-3

☎ 202-965-2300; www.watergatehotel.com; 2650 Virginia Ave NW; Ⓜ Foggy Bottom-GWU
The riverfront Watergate complex is a posh private community encompassing apartments, designer boutiques and a deluxe hotel. Its curious name derives from a never-realized 1930s' plan to build a ceremonial water gate in the Potomac, a stairway onto which visiting dignitaries could disembark. Now its name is synonymous with American political scandal: in 1972 a break-in at Democratic National Committee headquarters here was linked to CREEP – the Committee to Re-elect the President – leading to the unprecedented resignation of the sitting president, Richard Nixon. With the Watergate's undulating facade and dragon-tooth balconies, it's among DC's most recognizable landmarks. The upscale restaurant **Jeffrey's at the Watergate** (p146) is a romantic dinner-date destination with a lovely view of the Potomac.

GEORGETOWN
Eating p147; Shopping p210; Sleeping p228
Georgetown is Washington's cheerleader. Bubbly, beautiful, brainy and only a little bit mean (when it comes to your wallet,

---

CONGRESS – IT'S JUST LIKE COLLEGE

For every senator living the good life in a million-dollar Georgetown town house, there's another public servant living like a college kid in a shabby studio with all the comforts of a dorm room.

Members of Congress make $165,200 per year, which may not be enough for representatives to maintain two households. The Constitution stipulates senators and congressmen maintain a voting address in their district, while the amount of time they spend in Washington means they'll also need a place to crash in DC (which happens to be the 11th most expensive real-estate market in the US: the median house price is $425,500).

What does this translate to? Lawmakers are coming up with creative ways to save money on rent in the capital. Representative Jim Marshall, a Georgia Democrat, saves pennies by sleeping on an air mattress in his office. Congressional newbies, and brothers, Senator Ken Salazar and Representative John Salazar, both Colorado Democrats, are bunking together for the first time since growing up poor in south-central Colorado (they used to sleep five brothers to a bed). This time each guy has his own room.

Even if you own one of those fancy row houses, it doesn't mean you're sleeping alone. Many legislators lessen costs by renting rooms to colleagues. California Democrat (it always seems to be the Democrats) George Miller rents space to three colleagues, Senators Charles Schumer of New York and Richard Durbin of Illinois and Representative William Delahunt of Massachusetts (all the men are fellow Democrats). Delahunt and Schumer sleep on cots in the living room, while Durbin gets one of the two bedrooms.

'We spend a lot of time talking politics into the night,' Miller told *Bloomberg News* in August 2006. 'It's cheap and it works.' In the same interview Miller sang Durbin's praises as a rat catcher, something the senator has had to do at least once.

that is), the neighborhood is synonymous with elite education, high-dollar real estate, sublime shopping and lots and lots of old money. Georgetown University, a Jesuit school known for churning out future world leaders (Bill Clinton is an alumnus) and basketball players, is here. And many of Washington's blue-blood gentry – 2006 presidential loser John Kerry and his wife Teresa own a $4.7-million brownstone here, so does former Secretary of State Madeline Albricht – choose to set up shop along the neighborhood's quiet tree-lined cobblestone streets.

Isolated both geographically and historically, Georgetown has long maintained a unique identity in DC. The town of George was a bustling trading port long before the federal city was established; it was annexed by the District of Columbia only in 1871. Even today, just a few avenues traverse the valleys of Rock Creek Park, leaving Georgetown physically cut off from the rest of the city. Frankly, the neighborhood's wealthy residents like it that way. When DC built the Metro in the 1980s, local residents vetoed a Georgetown stop, condemning future generations of visitors to shuttle buses and the endless pursuit of parking.

Lack of transportation does not keep out the crowds, however. Nor do high rents deter shop owners and restaurateurs, whose trendy ventures are busting out all over this place. Like it or not, Georgetown cannot stop development. It is not limited to retail, either: older industrial buildings are being converted not only into shopping malls, but also into hotels, office complexes and upscale housing.

It wouldn't seem that wealthy bankers and lawyers would mix well with bargain-hunting, beer-pounding college students, but Georgetown embraces these contrasts. Some of DC's fanciest restaurants and cheapest eats are found here; stately mansions sit alongside dilapidated student row houses. In fact its poor college students are a rather driven breed: they may be taking bong hits in their dorm room on weekends, but they are also acing organic chemistry and international relations classes not tailored for stoners. In a nutshell these are the kids who are going to be living in those ritzy brownstones in 10 years.

The bars and boutiques draw swarms of students and suburbanites on week-

TRANSPORTATION

Metro The Georgetown community resisted having the Metro in its midst, so the neighborhood is not easily accessible by public transit. The closest stop is Foggy Bottom-GWU, from where a 50c shuttle bus (25c with Metrorail transfer) leaves every 10 minutes during the hours of Metro operation. Route 1 runs down K St NW and up Wisconsin Ave to R St NW before turning around. Route 2 runs all the way down M St NW and crosses the Francis Scott Key Bridge to the Rosslyn Metro station.

Bus Any of the number 30 buses (32, 34, 36) travel down Wisconsin Ave from Tenleytown and up M St NW to Washington Circle.

Parking Street parking can be near impossible, especially on weekend evenings. Look for spots on O, P or Q Sts NW between 29th and 31st. The garage beneath Georgetown Park mall is accessible from Wisconsin Ave.

ends. But Georgetown's real treasures are tucked away from the hubbub of Wisconsin Ave and M St NW. Wander the cobblestone streets – lined with flowering arbors and Federal architecture – and soak up a little antebellum charm. Check out the famous Exorcist Stairs at the end of M Street, across from Key Bridge. Head down to the bustling waterfront, for which the National Park Service recently announced $15 million in funds to build a new riverside park, and take a stroll along the Potomac before heading for a sundowner at one of the European-style open-air cafés lining the river. Georgetown is also home of some of DC's best shopping – boasting everything from designer clothing boutiques, furniture galleries, secondhand jean stores, outdoor clothing shops and lots of chain retailers. See p210 for more on maxing out the credit card.

Orientation

Quaint, historic Georgetown is wedged in between Rock Creek Park, Georgetown University and the Potomac River. Only a few streets connect Georgetown to the rest of the city, adding to the neighborhood's unique flavor. Georgetown's commercial heart is the intersection of M St NW and Wisconsin Ave: both streets are walled with ethnic eateries, trendy boutiques,

FUELED BY MULE

When construction on the C&O (Chesapeake & Ohio) Canal began in 1828, American prosperity depended on its water-ways. Thousands of miles of canals provided a means of transportation and trade throughout the growing country. The C&O would join the Chesapeake Bay and the Ohio River, fulfilling a longtime dream to connect the Potomac River basin to the coastal plain. Unfortunately, by the time the project was complete in 1850, the C&O Canal was already obsolete, rendered out of date by the almighty railroad.

Nonetheless, the canal remained in operation for 74 years. Mules trudged along the towpath – originally 12ft wide – pulling boats containing cargo of all types. A series of 74 lift locks raised the boats about 605ft over the course of the 185 miles between Georgetown and Cumberland. The slow boat was not particularly profitable, however, especially as it was vulnerable to weather. After several devastating floods, the canal finally closed in 1924.

Today, cyclists and boaters benefit from the canal, now a national park. But you can still experience the canal the old-fashioned way aboard the *Canal Clipper* or the *Georgetown*. Mules pull these barges full of passengers on one-hour journeys along the canal. The historical program includes rangers in period dress and a working lock that raises and lowers the boat 8ft. Barges leave from the visitors center two or three times a day, Wednesday through Sunday from May to October. Fares are adult/child/senior $8/5/6. This is a fabulous activity for children.

cramped bookstores and happening bars. Further south, the C&O Canal – which used to act as a road – runs east to west between M St and the river.

The walled campus of Georgetown University occupies the southwest corner of the neighborhood. University buildings and row houses populated by students are found on many of the surrounding streets. These same streets also boast some of DC's loveliest homes and gardens.

The grid is at its most effective here: it's impossible to get lost. M through T Sts NW run east–west; and numbered streets from 27th to 37th NW run north–south. Aside from a few streets, the grid is disrupted only by Wisconsin Ave, which cuts across the middle from north to south.

C&O CANAL & TOWPATH
Map p299
www.nps.gov/choh; btwn M St & Potomac River; 🚌 Georgetown shuttle from Foggy Bottom-GWU Metro

On a hot summer day, do as locals do and head to the Chesapeake & Ohio Canal and its towpath for a day of hiking, biking or canoeing.

From its Georgetown start, the historic C&O Canal runs 185 miles upriver to Cumberland, in western Maryland. The towpath alongside, originally for the mules that towed the boats, is now a DC favorite for hikers and bikers looking for an easy escape from the urban jungle. There's just something soothing about walking along the sandy towpath with the tranquil, sometimes smelly, inky green canal on one side and the mighty brown rush of the Potomac on the other. There are many spots to get off the path and venture down to the river – some spots are all rocks and rapids, others calm and sandy holes perfect for a quick dip (beware, the Potomac can have a very strong current, though). It's also cool to explore the C&O by canoe. For more on that and renting bicycles, see p199.

Within Georgetown's central zone, the canal runs parallel to M St a few blocks south. Crisscrossed by walkways and bridges, it is lined on either side with old warehouses and factory buildings that have been renovated into upscale retail and entertainment complexes. Stop by the **C&O Canal Visitors Center** (☎ 202-653-5190; 1057 Thomas Jefferson St; ☼ 10am-4pm Apr-Oct, weekends only Nov-Mar) to learn about ranger-led walks and canal boat rides.

One of the best bits of the canal in Georgetown is the few blocks between Thomas Jefferson and 31st Sts. Here artesian houses that date from the mid-19th-century building boom have been lovingly restored, turned into shops, offices and homes, and line the streets along the canal.

DUMBARTON HOUSE
Map pp300-1
☎ 202-337-2288; www.dumbartonhouse.org; 2715 Q St NW; adult/student incl tour $5/free; ☼ 10am-2pm Tue-Sat, hourly tours 10:15am-1:15pm; 🚌 Georgetown shuttle from Foggy Bottom-GWU Metro

Often confused with Dumbarton Oaks, Dumbarton House is a modest Federal historic house, which was constructed by a wealthy family in 1798. It is now run by the Colonial Dames of America. The genteel but gently witty tours focus not only on the house – chockablock with antique china, silver, furnishings, rugs, gowns and books – but also on quaint Federal customs, like passing round the chamber pot after formal dinners so gentlemen could have a group pee.

DUMBARTON OAKS Map pp300-1

☎ 202-339-6401; www.doaks.org; 1703 32nd St NW; admission to collection free, gardens adult $5, senior & child $3; ☺ 2-5pm Tue-Sun; ☐ Georgetown shuttle from Foggy Bottom-GWU Metro

This 19th-century mansion houses a fine art museum and research libraries, and is set in 16 acres of terraced gardens (enter the gardens through R St gate). Paths wind down toward Rock Creek amid boxwood and wisteria; 19 pools and fountains add coolness; and banks of cherries, crab apples and forsythias explode with color in spring. Although the gardens are popular, they hold many nooks and corners that let you find your own quiet bower. The museum features renowned Byzantine and pre-Columbian collections. The main house's music room has an intricately painted beamed ceiling and El Greco's *The Visitation*. It was here, in 1944, that the agreement to create the UN was forged.

AFRICAN AMERICAN GEORGETOWN

Three sites recall the history of Georgetown's 19th-century free black community, who lived in an area known as Herring Hill. Founded in 1816, **Mt Zion United Methodist Church** (Map pp292–3; ☎ 202-234-0148; 1334 29th St NW) is DC's oldest black congregation. Its original site, on 27th St NW, was a stop on the Underground Railroad.

Nearby, at **Mt Zion Cemetery** (Map pp296–7; 2700 Q St NW) and the adjacent **Female Union Band Cemetery** (Map pp296–7; behind 2515-2531 Q St NW) are the overgrown headstones of many free black residents. The church hid escaping slaves in a vault here. You can reach the cemeteries from Wisconsin Ave by heading east on Q St NW and turning left at the path just before 2531 Q St NW.

EXORCIST STAIRS

Map p299

3600 Prospect St NW; ☐ Georgetown shuttle from Rosslyn Metro

Movie buffs may recognize the setting of 1973's shockfest *The Exorcist*: two of little Regan's hapless victims met their fates at the vertiginous Exorcist Stairs. Unsuperstitious Washingtonians use them as an exercise tool – run up the supersteep stairs and you'll get what we're talking about. If you're having trouble locating the steps, look for the Exxon Station on M St almost directly across from Key Bridge and they are right next door, hidden in an appropriately dark and creepy corner.

GEORGETOWN UNIVERSITY

Map p299

☎ 202-687-6538; www.georgetown.edu; 37th & O Sts NW; ☐ Georgetown shuttle from Rosslyn Metro

Founded in 1789, America's first Roman Catholic university was originally directed by the country's first Black Jesuit, Father Patrick Healy. Today, about 12,000 students pursue degrees here and give the neighborhood much of its energetic vibe. Notable Hoyas (derived from the Latin *hoya saxa*, 'what rocks') alumni include both Clintons. Georgetown's handsome, shaded campus retains some original 18th- and 19th-century buildings. At the east gate, the imposing, Flemish-style 1879 **Healy Building** is impressive with its tall clock tower. Lovely **Dalghren Chapel** and its quiet courtyard are hidden behind. It's easy to wander around the attractive grounds – enter through the east gate.

GEORGETOWN WATERFRONT

Map p299

K St & Potomac River, NW; ☐ Georgetown shuttle from Rosslyn Metro

The Georgetown Waterfront is a favorite with couples on first dates, singles hoping to hook up, families out for an evening stroll and yuppies and bling-clad rappers showing off their big yachts twinkling in the Potomac. South of the C&O Canal, K St fronts the Potomac River and the area between it and the water has become known as the Georgetown Waterfront, home to parkland, retail space, lofts and restaurants. The riverside Washington Harbor (look for it east of 31st St) is a modern complex of towers set around a circular terraced plaza filled with fountains (they light up like rainbows at night). Here you'll find loads of restaurants and alfresco bars. The waterfront on either side has been earmarked by the National Park Service to be turned into Georgetown Waterfront Park, a $15-million project still in the planning phase.

KREEGER MUSEUM
Map pp290-1

☎ 202-328-3552; www.kreegermuseum.org; 2401 Foxhall Rd NW; admission $8; ✆ tours by reservation 10:30am & 1:30pm Tue-Fri, without reservation 10am-4pm Sat; 🚐 Georgetown shuttle from Rosslyn Metro

One of DC's more obscure attractions, this little known museum is tucked away in the hills northwest of Georgetown, and houses a fantastic collection of 20th-century modernist art. The museum shows off its impressive collection – Monet, Renoir, Picasso and Mark Rothko are all represented – on 90-minute, reservation only tours and through Saturday open houses. The museum rotates its exhibits, with something different showing all the time, so you're just as likely to get African art and Mayan artifacts as Edvard Munch's dark expressionism.

OAK HILL CEMETERY
Map pp300-1

☎ 202-337-2835; 30th & R Sts NW; ✆ 10am-4pm Mon-Fri; 🚐 Georgetown shuttle from Foggy Bottom-GWU Metro

This 24-acre, obelisk-studded cemetery contains winding walks and 19th-century gravestones set into the hillsides of Rock Creek. James Renwick designed the lovely gatehouse and the wee gneiss chapel, both c 1850.

OLD STONE HOUSE
Map p299

☎ 202-426-6851; www.nps.gov/rocr /oldstonehouse; 3051 M St; admission free; ✆ noon-5pm Wed-Sun; 🚐 Georgetown shuttle from Foggy Bottom-GWU Metro

Sitting incongruously in the midst of the Georgetown shopping drag is DC's oldest surviving building. Built in 1765 as a one-room house, it's since been a

boardinghouse, tavern, brothel and shop. It was almost demolished in the 1950s, but a persistent (albeit false) rumor that L'Enfant used it as a workshop while designing DC saved it for posterity. The Park Service now maintains it as an example of 18th-century life, exhibiting some of the original architectural features and furniture. The small garden is a peaceful place to recover from too much walking.

TUDOR PLACE
Map pp300-1

☎ 202-965-0400; www.tudorplace.org; 1644 31st St NW; house tour adult/child/student/senior $6/2/3/5, self-guided garden tour $2; ✆ 10am-3pm Tue-Sat, noon-4pm Sun; 🚐 Georgetown shuttle from Foggy Bottom-GWU Metro

This 1816 neoclassical mansion was owned by Thomas Peter, a landowner and tobacco merchant, and his wife Martha Custis Peter, granddaughter of Martha Washington. The urban estate stayed in the prominent Peter family until opened to the public in 1984, so it preserves pieces of the family's, as well as the country's, history. Today the mansion functions as a small museum, and features furnishings and artwork from Mount Vernon. Its 5 acres are beautifully landscaped with gardens, fountains, walkways and orchards.

CAPITOL HILL
Eating p151; Shopping p213; Sleeping p229

If Adams-Morgan is the soul of DC, then surely Capitol Hill is its heart. Synonymous with political dealing and power wheeling, this is the geographic and legislative center of the city. The turbulent air reeks of testosterone, is driven by winds of

TRANSPORTATION

Metro The Union Station Metro stop is on the Red Line. For destinations on the south side of the Capitol, use Capitol South or Eastern Market, both on the Orange and Blue Lines.

Parking Street parking is possible on the residential streets of Capitol Hill. There is also a parking garage at Union Station, which offers two hours free if you validate your ticket at one of the shops inside.

ambition and is heavy with the weight of goals not yet attained. Hillies – as residents are affectionately known – exude a contagious energy. Absorb as much as you can while wandering these streets, overhearing gossipy staffers exchanging news and idealistic interns debating views. Politics excite passion, which is what makes Capitol Hill a uniquely passionate place.

Everyone has a dream on the Hill. In the hallowed marble halls of the Capitol there's a senator daydreaming about a presidential bid and a journalist sniffing out a story worthy of a Pulitzer. At the boisterous dive bar down the street there's a lowly congressional staffer (with an official-looking identification tag to prove it) placing his business card in the palm of the senator's press secretary, hoping to snag a more prestigious gig. But he's being distracted by the lobbyist slurping Miller Lite one barstool over. The girl in the suit with the Southern drawl is talking his ear off, trying to sell his people on her people's big issue. Outside the heavy brown wooden door, there's a down-and-out bum panhandling change from the well-dressed patrons. He's dreaming of moving off the streets and into one of those refurbished brownstones he sees sitting so pretty down the quiet tree-lined avenue.

Away from the frenetic pulse of the Capitol, the neighborhood's mood mellows. The further east you travel, the more laid-back and less politically charged attitudes become. Many transient Hillies live here, but so do old-timer Washingtonians, low-income minorities and young yuppie families. They might meet for lunch at Jimmy T's and actually *not* discuss the upcoming election.

Union Station, north of the Capitol, greets a steady flow of local and out-of-town commuters in a marble entrance hall fit for a king – think sweeping marble archways, gold-trimmed ceilings and polished marble floors. Not only is the 1907 beaux-arts building a travel gateway, it's also a destination of its own, chock full of shops, restaurants and a Cineplex.

Blocks from the Hill, Eastern Market adds a bohemian element to the otherwise conventional atmosphere and attracts artists, furniture-refinishers and farmers selling their merchandise.

Take some time to wander the neighborhood's brick sidewalks, checking out iron gates and historic architecture: Federal, Greek-revival, Empire-style and Victorian row houses line every street on the Hill. As recently as the 1980s, much of Capitol Hill and Southeast DC was off-limits, a wasteland of crumbling mansions and crime-ridden streets. Now the area has been revitalized and reenergized. Stately homes are repaired to their original condition, children and dogs frolic in the parks, and neighbors meet for coffee along 8th St.

Orientation

The Capitol building presides over its namesake neighborhood from its west end. Lush green lawns and the obligatory House and Senate office buildings to the north and south surround the building. The wide-open plaza north of the Capitol allows an unbroken view of the magnificent beaux-arts Union Station. The Supreme Court, the three Library of Congress buildings and the Folger Shakespeare Library & Theater are immediately east of the Capitol.

From this Hill hub, E Capitol St runs east through the residential neighborhood of Lincoln Park and terminates at the Armory and RFK Stadium. Constitution and Independence Aves do the same to the north and south, respectively. And Pennsylvania Ave juts out to the southeast on a diagonal and heads across the Anacostia River. Outside of the Capitol building itself, most of the neighborhood's activity is clustered up around Union Station and down along Pennsylvania Ave. Eastern Market is on 7th St SE, just south of Independence Ave. Otherwise, the streets are relatively quiet, characterized by architectural gems, parks and glimpses of the Capitol dome. The residential part of Capitol Hill can be tricky to navigate, as different streets in close proximity can have the same letter, depending on whether they are north or south of E Capitol St (ie A St NE is just two blocks north of A St SE). Pay attention to the directional (NE or SE) to avoid confusion.

CAPITOL Map p304

☎ 202-225-6827; www.aoc.gov; admission free; ⏱ 9am-4:30pm; Ⓜ Capitol South

It's definitely a toss-up deciding Washington's most iconic image – the Capitol or the White House. We're going to have to put

WATCHING CONGRESS

To watch floor action when Congress is in session is to see history in the making. It's easy to obtain a pass to the galleries. US citizens: call or visit your senator's or representative's office (Capitol switchboard ☎ 202-224-3121). Foreign visitors: request passes from the House or Senate appointment desks on the Capitol's 1st floor.

Committee hearings are often more interesting than open sessions, and some are open to the public. Before your visit, check the *Post*'s 'Today in Congress' listing for details of current hearings and votes, or check www.house.gov and www.senate.gov.

US citizens can also request appointments with their senators and representatives by calling or writing, as early as three months beforehand.

on the Team Capitol jersey – there's just nothing quite like the sight of the towering 285ft cast-iron dome topped by the bronze Statue of Freedom, ornate fountains and marble Roman pillars set on sweeping lawns and flowering gardens that just screams this is DC.

The political center of the US government and geographic center of DC itself, the Capitol sits atop a high hill overlooking the National Mall and the wide avenues flaring out to the city beyond. It houses the legislative branch of Congress and is home to the Senate and the House of Representatives. The House has 435 members, and the size of a state's population determines how many representatives it gets in the House. Representatives are elected to serve two-year terms. There are 200 members of the slightly more prestigious Senate – two for each state. Senators serve six-year terms.

Pierre L'Enfant chose this site for the Capitol in his original city plans of 1791, describing it as 'a pedestal waiting for a monument.' Construction of the Capitol began in 1793, as George Washington laid the cornerstone, anointing it with wine and oil in Masonic style. The story does not continue so smoothly, however. Midway through construction, in 1814, the British marched into DC and burnt the fledgling Capitol to the ground. The dispiriting destruction tempted people to abandon the DC experiment altogether, but the government finally rebuilt it. In 1855 the iron dome (weighing nine million pounds) was designed, replac-

ing a smaller one; the House and Senate wings were added in 1857. Everyone breathed a sigh of relief when the final touch, the 19ft Freedom sculpture, was placed atop the dome in 1863.

Inside the grand halls and ornate chambers you really get a feel for the power-playing side of DC – the historical vibe is so strong it can be intoxicating. The centerpiece of the Capitol is the magnificent Rotunda (the area under the dome). A Constantino Brumidi frieze around the rim replays more than 400 years of American history. Look up into the eye of the dome for the *Apotheosis of Washington*, an allegorical fresco by the same artist. Other eye-catching creations include enormous oil paintings by John Trumbull, depicting scenes from the American Revolution.

The House of Representatives meets in the south wing, the Senate in the north wing. When either body is in session, a flag is raised above the appropriate wing. (Appropriately, the House office buildings – Rayburn, Longworth and Cannon – are on Independence Ave south of the Capitol; Senate buildings – Hart, Dirksen and Russell – are on Constitution Ave to the north.)

The Capitol closed for a few months following September 11, 2001 – it was suspected, along with the White House, to be the target for Flight 93 before it crashed in Pennsylvania. The US government made the decision to reopen the people's house to the people shortly after this, however, with extra security measures in place – you can no longer just wander in and check out the rotunda. The building is accessible by guided tours, conducted between 9am and 4:30pm Monday through Saturday.

Visitors must obtain free tickets for tours on a first-come, first-served basis, at the **Capitol Guide Service kiosk** located along the curving sidewalk southwest of the Capitol (near the intersection of 1st St SW and Independence Ave). Ticket distribution begins at 9am daily. Oversized backpacks and bags are forbidden in the Capitol, as are bottles, cans or any liquids. Tours visit the dramatic Rotunda (with a view of the dome from the inside), Statuary Hall and the old Supreme Court chamber. Docents are knowledgeable. The tour ends downstairs in the Crypt, which has some exhibits on the Capitol's history.

Construction on the United States Capitol Visitor Center has taken longer than expected – original estimates had the project completing in 2005 – but unforeseen development hurdles have pushed the anticipated opening date to spring 2007. It will provide tourists with a variety of amenities, including an exhibition gallery, cafeteria and gift shops. Oh, and next time it starts to rain you can seek shelter from the storm here as well (the website proclaims it will 'provide visitors shelter from the unpredictable DC weather').

CAPITOL GROUNDS Map p304

The Capitol's sweeping lawns owe their charm to famed landscape architect Frederick Law Olmsted, who also designed New York City's Central Park. During the Civil War, soldiers had camped in Capitol halls and stomped around its lawns. In 1874, spring cleaning was in order: Olmsted added lush greenery and majestic terraces, creating an elegant landscape that gave rise to over 4000 trees from all 50 states and many countries: look for labels on the trunks. Northwest of the Capitol is the charming 1879 **grotto**, a redbrick hexagon with black-iron gates and an interior well.

At the base of Capitol Hill, the **Capitol Reflecting Pool** (Map pp292–3) echoes the larger, rectangular Reflecting Pool at the other end of the Mall. This pool actually caps the I-395 freeway, which dips under the Mall here. The ornate **Ulysses S Grant Monument** (Map pp292–3) dominates its eastern side, showing the general in horseback action.

EASTERN MARKET Map p304

☎ 202-546-2698; www.easternmarket.net; 7th St & N Carolina Ave SE; ☻ 10am-6pm Tue-Fri, 8am-4pm Sat & Sun; Ⓜ Eastern Market

Eastern Market bursts into full bloom on weekends when craftspeople, food vendors and a flea market spill over the sidewalks outside the market. Washingtonians have been flocking to this bohemian delight for decades now in search of free-trade crafts, attic antiques, fresh flowers and seafood. The place is an ethnic smorgasbord and the heart of the Capitol Hill community. Built in 1873, it is the last of the 19th-century covered markets that once supplied most of DC's food. South Hall has food stands, bakeries, flower

stands and delis. North Hall is an arts center where craftspeople sell handmade wares. For specifics on food, see p151.

FOLGER SHAKESPEARE LIBRARY & THEATRE Map p304

☎ 202-544-4600; www.folger.edu; 201 E Capitol St; admission free; ☻ 10am-4pm Mon-Sat, tours 11am; Ⓜ Capitol South

The world's largest collection of the bard's works, including seven First Folios, is housed at the Folger Library: its **Great Hall** exhibits Shakespearean artifacts and other rare Renaissance manuscripts. Most of the rarities are housed in the library's reading rooms, closed to all but scholars, except on Shakespeare's birthday (April 23). You can peek electronically via the multimedia computers in the **Shakespeare Gallery**, however. The gorgeous **Elizabethan Theatre** replicates a theater of Shakespeare's time. With its woodcarvings and sky canopy, the castle is an intimate setting for plays, readings and performances, including the stellar annual PEN/Faulkner readings. East of the building is the **Elizabethan Garden**, full of flowers and herbs that were cultivated during Shakespeare's time.

LIBRARY OF CONGRESS

Map p304

☎ 202-707-5000; www.loc.gov; admission free; ☻ 10am-5pm Mon-Sat; Ⓜ Capitol South

The world's largest library, housed in three different buildings (Adams Bldg, 2nd St & Independence Ave SE; Jefferson Bldg, 1st & E Capitol Sts SE; Madison Bldg, 1st St SE between Independence Ave & C St SE) contains approximately 120 million items, including 22 million books, plus manuscripts, maps, photographs, films and prints. But don't expect to see many books when you visit: most of them are shelved on more than 500 miles of closed library stacks in the three library buildings. Touring the Library of Congress is nonetheless fascinating. In the historic 1897 Jefferson Building you can wander around the spectacular Great Hall, ornate with stained glass and marble, and scope out the three-story Main Reading Room. (Who can get any work done in here?) The visitors center shows a brief film, and there are guided tours. On the 1st floor, American Treasures displays historical documents ranging from

Alexander Graham Bell's lab book entry to clips of Groucho Marx on the *Johnny Carson Show*. Both the Jefferson and the Madison Buildings house exhibits, including cool pop-culture in the Bob Hope Gallery of American Entertainment.

Anyone over the age of 18 carrying photo ID can use the library, and more than a million people do so each year. The **Main Reading Room** is in the Jefferson building, but it is just one of 22 reading rooms. To find what you're looking for check out the info desks and touch-screen computers scattered about the Jefferson and Madison buildings. The Library of Congress is a research library, meaning you can't check the books out, but you can read away inside its confines.

The **National Digital Library** is an online service that allows you to access papers, maps and musical scores in machine-readable format (the desks in the Main Reading Room are wired for laptops). Other tasty morsels available online include major exhibitions, prints, photographs, political speeches and films.

The Madison Building also hosts concerts, and screens classic films in the **Mary Pickford Theater** (p196).

LINCOLN PARK

Map p304

E Capitol St btwn 11th & 13th Sts SE

Lincoln Park is the lively center of Capitol Hill's east end. Freed Black slaves raised the funds to erect the 1876 **Emancipation Memorial**, which portrays the snapping of slavery's chains as Lincoln proffers the Emancipation Proclamation. The **Mary McLeod Bethune Memorial**, DC's first statue of a Black woman, honors the educator and founder of the National Council of Negro Women. Near the park, at 14th and E Capitol Sts, the **Car Barn** (Map pp290–1; now private housing) was DC's 19th-century trolley turnaround. South of here on 11th St SE, an 1860s builder constructed the lovely **Philadelphia Row** (Map p304; 124–54 11th St SE) for his homesick Philly-born wife.

NATIONAL POSTAL MUSEUM

Map p304

☎ 202-357-2991; www.postalmuseum.si.edu; 2 Massachusetts Ave NE; admission free; 🕓 10am-5:30pm; Ⓜ Union Station

This place is cool. In the National Capitol Post Office Building, just west of Union Station, the newest Smithsonian museum features kid-friendly exhibits on postal history from the Pony Express to modern times. Also here are antique mail planes, beautiful old stamps, Cliff Clavin's postal carrier uniform (from the TV sitcom *Cheers)* and great special exhibits of old letters (from soldiers, pioneers and others).

SEWALL-BELMONT HOUSE

Map p304

☎ 202-546-1210; www.sewallbelmont.org; 144 Constitution Ave NE; admission by donation; 🕓 11am-3pm Tue-Fri, noon-4pm Sat; Ⓜ Union Station or Capitol South

This historic home is a feminist landmark: it has been the home base of the National Woman's Party since 1929, and for 43 years it was the residence of the party's legendary founder, suffragette Alice Paul. Paul spearheaded efforts to gain the vote for women – enshrined in the 19th Amendment – and wrote the Equal Rights Amendment. Docents show you historical exhibits, portraits, sculpture and a library that celebrates feminist heroines.

SUPREME COURT

Map p304

☎ 202-479-3030; www.supremecourtus.gov; 1 1st St NE; admission free; 🕓 9am-4:30pm Mon-Fri; Ⓜ Capitol South

The Supreme Court of the United States convenes in an imposing 1935 all-marble building designed by Cass Gilbert. The seated figures in front of the building represent the female Contemplation of Justice and the male Guardian of Law; panels on the 13,000lb bronze front doors depict the history of jurisprudence. The interior grand corridor and Great Hall are no less impressive. Downstairs is an exhibit on the history of the court and a striking statue of John Marshall, fourth Chief Justice.

On days when court's not in session you can hear lectures about the Supreme Court in the courtroom (and check out its lofty architecture). When court is in session, try to hear an oral argument. Queues form out front starting at 8am: choose the appropriate one depending on whether you wish to sit through the entire argument or observe the court in session for a few minutes. Justices hear arguments at 10am Monday to Wednesday for two weeks every month from October to April. The release of orders and opinions, open to the public, takes place in May and June. Check the *Post*'s Supreme Court Calendar listing or the Supreme Court website for case details.

UNION STATION

Map p304

☎ 202-289-1908; www.unionstationdc.com; 50 Massachusetts Ave NE; ⊗ 10am-9pm Mon-Sat, noon-6pm Sun; Ⓜ Union Station

Unlike any shopping experience in the country, except perhaps Vegas, this larger-than-life 1907 beaux-arts creation is also Washington's most impressive gateway. The depot was beautifully restored in 1988 (after years of neglect), and transformed into a contemporary city center and transit hub. Besides Amtrak connections to destinations throughout the East, it has a cinema, food court (one of the best in the city) and 200,000 sq ft of shops (including some unique boutiques: check out p213 for more on retail therapy).

Wandering around the huge main hall, the Grand Concourse, is a humbling experience. The cavernous room is patterned after the Roman Baths of Diocletian (although shields are strategically placed across the waists of the unusually modest legionnaire statues) and is almost too much to take in – be sure to sit on one of the marble benches for a few minutes and just absorb (it's amazing how small the people look next to the sweeping, golden domed ceilings). In the station's east wing is the old Presidential Waiting Room (now B Smith's), where dignitaries and celebrities once alighted when they traveled to DC.

The station's exterior offers vistas of the Capitol and avenues radiating south toward the Mall. Just south along Louisiana Ave NW you'll find **Union Station Plaza**, a grassy park with a large fountain cascade, and the **Taft Memorial Carillon**, whose bells ring every quarter-hour.

SOUTHEAST & SOUTHWEST DC

Eating p153

In the Southeast quadrant, hope collides with despair. It's a gritty wasteland of low-rent tenements pockmarked by bullet holes and colored with graffiti. A place where

TRANSPORTATION

Metro Eastern Market, on the Orange and Blue Lines, is on Pennsylvania Ave. Navy Yard, on the Green Line, is at the west end of the Navy Yard. To reach the National Bureau of Engraving & Printing, the United States Holocaust Memorial Museum or any of the attractions around the Tidal Basin, the nearest Metro stop is Smithsonian. Use the Waterfront-SEU Metro stop to visit the marina area.

Parking Free parking is available on-site at the Anacostia Museum and at the Frederick Douglass National Historic Site. Parking for the Marine Barracks is available in the lot at 1201 M St SE. There is also a parking garage at the Navy Yard – enter through the gate at 11th & O Sts SE. Free parking is available at the north end of East Potomac Park, underneath the bridges. If you wish you go to Hains Point, there is parking further south along Ohio Dr, although it tends to fill up on weekends.

the dive bars are really dives, serving rum chasers with their pints of sorrow. And the new playground for local kids comes neatly secured by chain-link fences and heavy locks. It is home to down-and-out drunks and single mothers from broken families; to religious grandparents whose greatest wish is seeing their grandchild make it out of the slum alive. Washington's forgotten corner is a starting ground for impoverished but ambitious immigrants opening small shops and little restaurants to get enough cash to get the hell out of Dodge. And it is an ending point for crack addicts living out their last years in squalid housing projects.

Southeast DC is a place that always seems on the verge of becoming something, yet is incapable of actually getting there. For decades urban do-gooders have spoken of gentrification, of cleaning up the streets, bringing business back to areas whose names most Washingtonians have only heard in the news – connected with another homicide. So far revitalization hasn't exactly happened, but with the development of the Nationals stadium, there's a pretty good chance it will eventually start. Whether the outcome of this gentrification will be positive or negative, however, will take years to determine. For now Southeast DC (with the exception of the gentrified bits around the Hill and select attractions) remains a hard-knock place.

Sights

SOUTHEAST & SOUTHWEST DC

In comparison, the Waterfront area of Southwest DC is a textbook example – both good and bad – of urban renewal. In response to economic decline in the first half of the century, the city launched in Southwest DC one of its most sweeping gentrification projects. The effort destroyed most of the historic Federal architecture and displaced many of the poor, mostly Black residents. The cement office blocks and apartment complexes that went up created the modern – but soulless – residential neighborhood that is here today.

On the upside, IM Pei's Waterfront Mall (Map pp308–9), covering the 1100 block of 6th St, is a sleek apartment/commercial complex that epitomizes contemporary Southwest DC. It's brought money into the local economy, and a diverse crowd throngs to its channel-front restaurants for a breezy cocktail or seafood and crab feast. Other highlights include the cherry-tree-trimmed Tidal Basin and wide-open East Potomac Park.

Orientation

Pennsylvania Ave and Southeast Fwy both run northwest to southeast across the Southeast quadrant. For our purposes, Southeast DC refers to the area south of Pennsylvania Ave and north of the Anacostia River, and bounded by S Capitol St on the west side. The Southeast is an especially disruptive freeway completely severing any continuity between the neighborhoods on either side of the highway. North of the freeway, the 8th St corridor between Pennsylvania Ave and G St SE is bursting with development; just south of G St SE are the tidy Marine Barracks. By contrast, the southern tip of the Southeast quadrant, tucked in between the Southeast Fwy and the Anacostia River, is desolate and depressed. The Washington Navy Yard is a well-maintained and heavily guarded oasis in the midst of it.

Anacostia refers to the small piece of Washington DC that is southeast of the Anacostia River. Hwy I-295 – known as the Anacostia Fwy in the south and as Kenilworth Ave further north – cuts across the neighborhood and parallels the river. Anacostia Park occupies much of the riverfront property to the north, while a huge US Naval Station dominates the southern embankment. Southeast of I-295, Anacostia is a confusing mishmash of run-down houses, shops with iron bars on their windows and the odd museum or historic spot. Visitors should not be paranoid, but this isn't a neighborhood for a stroll. You are better off driving or taking public transport to the sights here.

Southwest DC – DC's smallest quadrant – is a triangle-shaped area south of Independence Ave (and the National Mall) and west of S Capitol St. The eastern and southern boundaries are the Potomac and Anacostia Rivers respectively.

The Federal Rectangle area just south of the Mall is home to several gigantic federal agencies, such as the US Department of Agriculture, as well as the United States Holocaust Memorial Museum and the National Bureau of Printing & Engraving. The rest of the quadrant is mostly residential, save the riverfront marina area on the Washington Channel and the naval base further south. A finger of land known as East Potomac Park, or Hains Point, stretches south from the Tidal Basin and forms a peninsula between the Washington Channel and the Potomac River.

SOUTHEAST DC
ANACOSTIA MUSEUM
Map pp290-1

☎ 202-287-3306; www.si.edu/anacostia; 1901 Fort Pl SE; admission free; ☷ 10am-5pm; ☐ W1 or W2 from Anacostia Metro

Originally a neighborhood gathering place, the Anacostia Museum expanded into a regional heritage center celebrating Black history and culture in DC and the mid-Atlantic states; it is now operated by the Smithsonian Institution and is known as the Anacostia Museum & Center for African American History & Culture. Rotating exhibits focus on themes such as the transatlantic slave trade, the earliest free Black communities in the New World, and art, photography and sculpture by Black artists. The museum usually has full calendars of free concerts, films and workshops during Black History Month (February).

FREDERICK DOUGLASS NATIONAL HISTORIC SITE Map pp290-1
☎ 202-426-5961; www.nps.gov/frdo; 1411 W St SE; admission free; ☷ 9am-4pm, to 5pm Jun-Aug; ☐ B2 or B4 from Anacostia Metro

This rather bulky title refers to Cedar Hill, the great abolitionist's Anacostia home, which is maintained by the National Park Service as a museum honoring Frederick Douglass' life and work. Diplomat, author and former slave, Douglass lived here from 1877 until his death in 1895. The house still contains most of his original furnishings, down to his wire-rim eyeglasses on his roll-top desk. Hourly tours are entertaining and informative, touching on Douglass' 5-mile walk to work on Capitol Hill, his authorship of the *Narrative of the Life of Frederick Douglass* and his impressive five-figure salary. The hilltop home has a commanding view of DC. Start at the visitors center embedded in the foot of the hill, where you can see a short biographical film.

MARINE BARRACKS

Map pp308-9

☎ 202-433-6060; www.mbw.usmc.mil; 8th & I St SE; ☺ parade 8:45pm Fri; Ⓜ Eastern Market
The 'Eighth and Eye Marines' are on largely ceremonial duty at the nation's oldest Marine Corps post. Most famously, this post is home to the Marine Corps Band, once headed by John Philip Sousa, king of the military march, who was born nearby at 636 G St SE. On Friday evenings in summer you can watch a two-hour ceremonial drill parade featuring the band, the drum and bugle corps, the silent drill team and the mascot bulldog. Call weeks in advance for reservations or show up for general admission at 8pm.

MARINE CORPS MUSEUM

Map pp308-9

☎ 202-433-3840; www.usmcmuseum.org; Washington Navy Yard Bldg 58; admission free; ☺ 10am-4pm Mon-Fri; Ⓜ Navy Yard
This small museum within the Navy Yard (enter from 11th St SE) recently underwent a renovation and traces the history of the Marine Corps since its inception in 1775. The exhibit's attempt to personalize the history with profiles of individuals is interesting, but it's not necessarily interactive or eye-catching. A special exhibit honors the 50th anniversary of the Korean War. There are other war artifacts, such as the flag raised by marines over Iwo Jima in WWII.

SOUTHWEST DC

BENJAMIN BANNEKER PARK

Map pp308-9

10th & G Sts SW
This park honors Benjamin Banneker, a free Black, self-taught astronomer and mathematician. Banneker and another man, Andrew Ellicot, were hired by George Washington in 1791 to help lay out the 10-sq-mile plot that would define the District by using celestial calculations. Pierre L'Enfant then designed the city with Banneker and Ellicot's settings. It's a grassy circular spot near the Waterfront. You'll need to drive there.

EAST POTOMAC PARK

Map pp308-9

Ohio Dr SW
Local residents flock to this waterside park for biking, running, fishing, golfing and picnicking. Though only a short distance from the National Mall, it is undiscovered by tourists, lending it an unassuming, neighborhood feel. A 5-mile paved trail – great for biking or in-line skating – runs around the park's circumference, paralleling Ohio Dr. The center of the park is the East Potomac Park Golf Course (p203). At the park's southern tip, known as Hains Point, an eerie and unexpected sculpture, the Awakening, portrays a giant emerging from the earth. Kids love climbing around on this thing, as well as in the nearby playground.

The park sits on a finger of land, which extends southward from the Tidal Basin into the Potomac River. On foot, you can access the park by following trails that lead from the Thomas Jefferson Memorial (Map pp306–7) under the bridges. You'll need to drive there; you can park on the shoulder of Ohio Dr. For more on other DC monuments, check out p68.

NATIONAL BUREAU OF ENGRAVING & PRINTING Map pp292-3

☎ 202-874-3019; www.bep.treas.gov; 14th & C Sts SW; admission free; ☺ visitors center 8:30am-3pm; tours 8am-2pm Mon-Fri, & 3:30-7pm Jun-Aug; Ⓜ Smithsonian
If money does not grow on trees, where does it come from? You can see for yourself at the National Bureau of Engraving

& Printing, where all US paper currency is designed, engraved and printed. Forty-minute guided tours demonstrate how $700 million a day is churned out, and show exhibits on counterfeiting and un-usual bills. Seeing gobs of green makes it a big thrill with the kids. Line up at the **NBEP ticket kiosk** (Raoul Wallenberg Pl) for tickets; arrive early, as only a limited number are distributed. You can receive up to five tickets for entrance at a designated time on the same day.

TITANIC MEMORIAL
Map pp308-9
Waterside Park; M Waterfront-SEU
Near the Waterfront's south end, Water-side Park contains this memorial to honor the men who sacrificed their lives to save the women and children aboard the sink-ing ship. Just south is **Fort Lesley J McNair**, an army post established in 1791 and burned by the British in 1814. The Lincoln-assassination conspirators were hung at McNair in 1865; it now houses the National Defense University and National War College (closed to the public).

UNITED STATES HOLOCAUST MEMORIAL MUSEUM
Map pp292-3
☎ 202-488-0400; www.ushmm.org; 100 Raoul Wallenberg Pl SW; admission free; ☽ 10am-5:30pm, to 7.50pm Tue Apr-Aug; M Smithsonian
The somber, soaring Holocaust Mu-seum is unlike any other DC museum. In remembering the millions murdered by the Nazis, it is brutal, direct and impassioned. Its exhibits leave many visitors in tears and few unmoved. James Ingo Freed designed the extraordinary building in 1993 and its stark facade and steel-and-glass interior echo the death camps themselves.

Apart from the permanent exhibits, the candlelit Hall of Remembrance is a sanctuary for quiet reflection; the Wexner Learning Center offers text archives, photo-graphs, films and oral testimony available on touch-screen computers. If you have young children in tow, avoid the perma-nent exhibits, which are very graphic; instead, opt for Remember the Children, a gentler kids' installation, on the 1st floor.

Same-day passes (up to four per per-son) to view the permanent exhibit are available at the pass desk on the 1st floor. The passes allow entrance at a designated time (arrive early because they do run out). Alternatively, for a surcharge, tickets are available in advance at www.tickets.com or ☎ 800-400-9373.

WATERSIDE PARK
Map pp308-9
M Waterfront-SEU
A few historic homes – curiosities in this neighborhood – survived the 1950s urban clearance. The **Law House** (1252 6th St SW) is a Federal-style row house that was built by one of the first DC land speculators in 1796. From the same period, the **Wheat Row houses** (1313–1321 4th St SW, south of N St SW) have human-scale brick facades that add warmth to the neighborhood.

DOWNTOWN
Eating p154; Shopping p214; Sleeping p231
Downtown is the flagship product in DC's gentrification line. Only a few decades ago a listless, crime-ridden neighborhood of inter-est solely to government workers, working immigrants and squatters, today it's a shiny happy place where people of all classes and colors live, work and play along the most powerful stretch of pavement in America.

Pennsylvania Ave forms a straight line between the US and the Capitol, linking

TRANSPORTATION

Metro Every Metro line passes through Down-town, and they all intersect each other around here. McPherson Sq (Blue or Orange Line) is in the neighborhood's northwestern corner, border-ing the White House district. Mt Vernon Sq/7th St-Convention Center (Green or Yellow Line) is on the northern border with the Shaw district. On the southern border in the Penn Quarter, Federal Triangle (Orange, Blue) and National Archives-Navy Memorial (Orange, Blue, Yellow, Green) are just north of the National Mall. Metro Center (Red, Orange, Blue) and Chinatown-Gallery Place (Red, Yellow, Green) are in the middle of it all.

Parking Street parking is near impossible around here; use the **PMI parking garage** (727 6th St NW, between F & G Sts; 1325 G St NW).

the legislative and executive headquarters. The Penn Quarter – as this power corridor is known – grew out of a need to support and cater to one or both of these institutions. Although its original purpose in still evident in the grand luxury hotels and huge federal buildings lining the wide avenue, Downtown is no longer just a place to work and visit. It's a place to live. Museums, department stores, dance clubs, and loads and loads of restaurants keep life interesting. If DC can claim a theater or art district, they are both here. Indeed, this is the most urban part of DC, perhaps the only place with 'bright lights, big city' in the air.

Also in the air: the aromas of General Tsao and Kung Pao. The streets around 7th and H Sts NW – the colorful Friendship Arch marks the spot – have been the heart of DC's Chinese community since the turn of the century. Chinese restaurants, pharmacies and laundries crowd these streets; spicy smells and Chinese characters add an ethic element to downtown DC.

As noted earlier, this lively downtown is a recent development. Like urban areas throughout the country, DC suffered after WWII when residents left the city in droves for the American dream in the suburbs. Despite the federal government's presence just a few blocks away, property values in this area plunged, businesses closed and there was little reason to go downtown.

Improved economic times in the 1990s allowed the DC government to dump serious money into resuscitating the downtown area, and efforts are paying off. The MCI Center – home to DC's professional basketball and hockey teams – opened in the early 1990s, bringing sports fans and concertgoers in droves. Business types congregate at the vast new convention center north of Mt Vernon Sq. Unfortunately, all this construction has threatened the cohesiveness of Chinatown, but the dwindling community has rallied to preserve its cultural heritage (and this is still the best place to come for Chinese food). As if there is not enough going on, local officials and businesses are dreaming up new ways to lure people downtown outside of working hours: 'art crawl' gallery tours led by local artists; open-air concerts on Pennsylvania Ave; or a hip-hop happening nightclub in the courtyard of a federal building.

The country's National Aquarium is Downtown but it is not impressive enough for you to waste money on the entrance fee. If you want to see fish, head to Baltimore's much cooler aquarium (see p250). You'll also find the massive, neo-brutalism concrete Federal Bureau of Investigation building here, at the corner of 10th St and Pennsylvania Ave. In the years before September 11, 2001 it was a major DC tourist attraction – lines formed around the block to check out the spy exhibit. For now, you'll have to be satisfied with a virtual tour at www.fbi.gov/aboutus/tour/tour.htm. The National Press Club (14th & F Sts) is also here. It's a cool building to stroll around, but you'll need to be (or be accompanied by) a member of the working press, with ID to prove it, to attend any of the events or visit the top-floor bar (yes, they are exclusive here and proud of it). The free taco bar is a huge hit among DC's news crowd. If you can find a journalist friend who's a member (or if you happen to be a working member of the press), visit the bar for Friday happy hour, when it's packed with young and old reporters looking to network, both professionally and personally.

Orientation

Downtown is a portmanteau name loosely applied to the area in the Northwest quadrant that is north of the National Mall and east of the White House (for our purposes, between 1st and 14th Sts NW and Constitution Ave and L St NW). This area is commonly divided into two labels, Old Downtown (comprising the area north of the National Mall, including the Penn Quarter, Federal Triangle and Chinatown) and New Downtown (the area north of Foggy Bottom buttressing Dupont Circle and bordered roughly by Massachusetts, New Hampshire, Pennsylvania and New York Aves).

Immediately north of the Mall, Pennsylvania Ave stretches from the Capitol and heads northwest toward the White House. This stretch, known as the Penn Quarter, is filled with snazzy restaurants, bureaucratic buildings and tourist spillover from the Mall. As an extreme example of a bureaucratic building, the massive, modern Ronald Reagan Building (the second largest federal building) occupies two entire blocks – from 12th St to 14 St NW – along Pennsylvania Ave. This southwestern

Sights

DOWNTOWN

FBI TRIVIA

The FBI was established in 1908 with the motto 'Fidelity, Bravery, Integrity', and early investigative techniques were based on those used by a 19th-century Scottish immigrant named Allan Pinkerton who ran a successful detective agency. The FBI got its name on the nation's radar in the 1920s and 1930s when it started battling gangsters and attempted to enforce Prohibition – both meaty subjects for Hollywood to memorialize forever.

Today the agency operates under the umbrella of Homeland Security (it received loads of negative scrutiny and became the butt of many a late-night comedian's joke following September 11–related bungles). Its 10,000 agents are charged mainly with protecting the country on the domestic front from terrorist threats, although it still pursues more traditional tasks like arresting drug traffickers and other shady underworld characters.

corner of the neighborhood is sometimes called Federal Triangle, after the Metro stop here. Metro Center is a few blocks north.

Downtown's main drag – 7th St NW – runs from the National Archives and Navy Memorial in the south, north to Mt Vernon Sq and beyond to the new City Museum of Washington and the vast new Washington Convention Center complex. Chinatown is at the very center of it all. These days, Chinatown is perhaps more aptly described as MCI-town, as the mammoth sports arena sits in the middle of it; the arena's opening has fueled the revitalization of the area.

East of Chinatown is Judiciary Sq. The square itself is lovely, containing the National Law Enforcement Officers Memorial and fronted by the exquisite National Building Museum. The surrounding streets are overwhelmingly concrete – big boxy buildings crowding the sidewalk and blocking the sun.

OLD DOWNTOWN
Penn Quarter
BEAD MUSEUM
Map pp292-3

☎ 202-624-4500; www.beadmuseumdc.org; 400 7th St NW; admission free; ☯ 11am-4pm Wed-Sat, 1-4pm Sun; Ⓜ Archives-Navy Memorial

The Bead Society of Greater Washington operates this museum to showcase the aesthetic and symbolic qualities of beads – one of mankind's earliest and most enduring creative expressions. Exhibits are internationally focused and the society maintains an impressive library on site.

FORD'S THEATRE & PETERSEN HOUSE
Map pp292-3

☎ 202-347-4833; www.nps.gov/foth; 511 10th St NW; admission free; ☯ 9am-5pm (except during rehearsals or matinee performances); Ⓜ Metro Center

On April 14, 1865, John Wilkes Booth, actor and Confederate sympathizer, assassinated Abraham Lincoln, as President and Mrs Lincoln watched *Our American Cousin* in the Presidential Box of Ford's Theatre. The box remains draped with a period flag to this day. The theater is open during the day to wander around on your own or join a tour. Check out the Lincoln Museum in the basement, which maps out the assassination's details and displays related artifacts. See also Entertainment (p192).

After being shot, the unconscious president was carried across the street to die at Petersen House, which is also open for walks through; its tiny, unassuming rooms create a moving personal portrait of the president's slow and tragic death. Another assassination-related site is nearby: Surratt House, now the restaurant Wok & Roll (p154; 604 H St), is where the Lincoln-assassination conspirators met in 1865. Its owner, Mary Surratt, was eventually hanged at Fort McNair for her part.

INTERNATIONAL SPY MUSEUM
Map pp292-3

☎ 202-393-7798, 866-SPYMUSEUM; www.spymuseum.org; 800 F St NW; adult/child $15/13; ☯ 10am-8pm Apr-Oct, 10am-6pm Nov-Mar; Ⓜ Gallery Pl-Chinatown

If you've ever wanted to step into James Bond's shoes and live a glamorous spy life, this is the place to learn the secrets. DC's hottest attraction illustrates high-tech gadgetry, notorious spy cases, secret methods and the not-so-pleasant consequences of being an international person of mystery.

The much-acclaimed museum of espionage opened just in time to fill a void left by the end of FBI tours: spy fans can still get their fill of spy artifacts, anecdotes and interactive displays. All visitors are invited to play the role of a secret agent by adopting a cover at the start of their visit. Throughout the museum, you can try to identify disguises, listen to bugs and spot hidden cameras. Most of the exhibit is historical in nature, focusing on the Cold War in particular (a re-creation of the tunnel under the Berlin Wall is an eerie winner).

Lines form early to get in. Despite being open for years now and charging an entrance fee, the Spy Museum is as popular as ever, especially with kids. We waited dutifully in line and crammed into the elevator and packed exhibit rooms with everyone else. In the end we were impressed by the cool gadgets and interactive displays, but left with a slightly vacant feeling like the place packed more hype than meaty exhibits.

MARTIN LUTHER KING JR MEMORIAL LIBRARY
Map pp292-3

☎ 202-727-1221; www.dclibrary.org/mlk; 901 G St NW; admission free; 9:30am-9pm Mon-Thu, 9am-5pm Fri & Sat, 1-5pm Sun; M Metro Center
DC's main library is in Mies van der Rohe's only Washington building, a low, sleek black-glass structure; peek inside to admire the colorful mural portraying the Civil Rights movement. The MLK Library is an important community and cultural center, sponsoring readings, concerts, films and children's activities. You can also access the internet here.

NATIONAL ARCHIVES
Map pp292-3

☎ 202-510-5400; www.archives.gov; 700 Pennsylvania Ave NW; admission free; 10am-5:30pm Sep-Mar, 10am-7pm Apr-May, 10am-9pm Jun-Aug; M Archives-Navy Memorial
Inside this grand neoclassical building (enter from Constitution Ave NW) is a dimly lit rotunda with the three original documents upon which the US government is based: the Declaration of Independence, Constitution and Bill of Rights. Not to mention the 1297 version of the Magna Carta, courtesy of Texas billionaire (and erstwhile presidential candidate) H Ross Perot. Don't expect to linger over the Big Three – guards make you keep moving – but you can study the Magna Carta and other documents at your leisure.

These precious documents are sealed in airtight, helium-filled cases that sink nightly into an underground vault to protect them from attack or theft. After the ongoing renovation at the National Archives, the exhibit will also include

NEW NEWSEUM

The old Newseum was the coolest museum in DC, so we have great hopes that when it reopens at its swank new facility at one of DC's hottest new corners, 6th St and Pennsylvania Ave NW, it will be just as cool.

The old museum offered a fascinating, hands-on look at how the news is reported, produced, spun and consumed. In one hall, block-long screens flashed a dazzling multimedia visual display of the day's breaking stories (like something straight out of a movie), while the day's front pages from the world's top newspapers were displayed below.

The Newseum is the brainchild and dependent of the Freedom Forum, a nonpartisan international foundation dedicated to preserving a free press.

The 600,000-sq-ft steel-and-glass creation is expected to open in late 2007. Once in operation, it will have six levels of journalism displays to explore, including an interactive newsroom and broadcast studio that will allow visitors to create and tape their own newscasts or write their own stories. Also on the menu are thoughtful exhibits examining journalistic ethics, historic events and the journalists who covered them.

And while journalism often seems like a glamorous career choice, the museum's founders believe in presenting the whole truth without any sugar coating. They do it simply with a memorial dedicated to the more than 1600 journalists who lost their lives covering the world's story.

The museum's on-site restaurant, the Source, is sure to be a hit. Celebrity chef Wolfgang Puck's first East Coast dining venture, it will offer casual fare on the 1st floor and fine dining upstairs, with a menu inspired by Puck's other successful Los Angeles and Las Vegas restaurants.

Public Vaults, to give visitors the feeling of going inside the stacks at the archives, as well as a theater and gift shop.

The archives themselves preserve reams of essential government documents, from the Louisiana Purchase Treaty to the Emancipation Proclamation. Researchers can access documents from 8:45am to 5pm Monday to Saturday; enter from Pennsylvania Ave.

NATIONAL MUSEUM OF AMERICAN ART & NATIONAL PORTRAIT GALLERY

Map pp292-3

☎ 202-275-1500; www.americanart.si.edu; 9th & F Sts NW; admission free; Ⓜ Gallery Pl-Chinatown

These inseparable Smithsonian museums are looking brilliant these days, thanks to a multimillion facelift. They are roommates in the 19th-century US Patent Office building, a neoclassical quadrangle that hosted Lincoln's second inaugural ball and a Civil War hospital. Walt Whitman based *The Wound-Dresser* upon his experiences as a volunteer nurse here ('The hurt and wounded I pacify with soothing hand/I sit by the restless all the dark night…').

The Portrait Gallery's permanent collection contains more than 4000 images of well-known faces from all walks and eras of life, housed in spacious environs. The presidential portraits are particularly notable. Keep an eye out for Gilbert Stuart's famous *Lansdowne* portrait of George Washington and a carefree bust of a first-term Bill Clinton. The sports and performing arts paintings and photographs are also fascinating. We particularly like the painting of the famous Yankees player Mickey Mantle watching teammate Roger Maris hit another home run in the 1961 season.

The Museum of American Art's holdings are the largest collection of American art, colonial to contemporary, in the world. The museum is a bit of a holding facility for the Smithsonian, a place where the institution stores some 38,000-odd pieces of art, from sculpture to photography, folk art, crafts, prints and drawings. It is known especially for its 19th-century collection of American Western art, including nearly 400 pieces by George Catlin, who is known for his haunting portrayals of American Indians living on the Great Plains.

NATIONAL MUSEUM OF WOMEN IN THE ARTS

Map pp292-3

☎ 202-222-7270; www.nmwa.org; 1250 New York Ave NW; adult/child/student/senior $5/free/3/3; Ⓨ 10am-5pm Mon-Sat, noon-5pm Sun; Ⓜ Metro Center

The only American museum exclusively devoted to women's artwork resides in this magnificent Renaissance-revival mansion. Its collection – 2600 works by almost 700 female artists from 28 countries – moves from Renaissance artists like Lavinia Fontana to 20th-century works by Kahlo, O'Keeffe and Frankenthaler. The permanent collection is largely paintings, and mostly portraits at that – not as rich a range as one might hope. But special collections are incredibly varied, ranging from Maria Sibylla Merian's natural history engravings to Native American pottery. Rotating exhibits are also extraordinary, gathering works from around the world and introducing them to a wider audience.

NAVY MEMORIAL & NAVAL HERITAGE CENTER

Map pp292-3

☎ 202-737-2300; www.lonesailor.org; 701 Pennsylvania Ave NW, Market Sq; admission free; Ⓨ 9:30am-5pm Mon-Sat, film noon; Ⓜ Archives-Navy Memorial

The circular plaza is bordered by masts sporting semaphore flags; on its western side a sculpted seaman – the *Lone Sailor* – hunches down in his peacoat as a tribute to sea service. The Naval Heritage Center is on the same grounds and displays artifacts and ship models, and has a meditation room and a Navy Memorial Log. At noon daily its theater screens the gung-ho *At Sea*, which dramatically depicts battle-group maneuvers.

OLD POST OFFICE PAVILION

Map pp292-3

☎ 202-606-8691; www.oldpostofficedc.com; 12th St & Pennsylvania Ave NW; admission free; Ⓨ 9am-7:45pm Mon-Sat, 10am-5:45pm Sun; Ⓜ Federal Triangle

The landmark 1899 Old Post Office Pavilion – nicknamed 'Old Tooth' for its spiky clock tower – is a downtown success story. Threatened with demolition during much of the 20th century, the Romanesque building was restored in 1978 and became a key attraction. Now its beautiful, bunting-draped, 10-story central atrium holds shops, a large food court, a discount-ticket counter and government agencies. The Park Service operates a glass elevator that takes visitors to the 270ft-high **observation deck** for a broad view of downtown and a close-up look at the carillon bells. The free tour starts from the northwest corner of the pavilion's ground floor.

Judiciary Square

CITY MUSEUM OF WASHINGTON, DC
Map pp292-3
☎ 202-785-2068; www.citymuseumdc.org; 800 Mt Vernon Sq; admission/film/combo adult $3/6/8, senior & student $2/5/6; 10am-5pm Tue-Sun, 3rd Thu of month to 9pm; M Mt Vernon Sq/7th St-Convention Center or Gallery Pl-Chinatown
Housed in the historic Carnegie Library at Mt Vernon Sq, this fun interactive museum highlights the local side of DC – the people, events and communities that have shaped the city since its founding. Exhibits explore the growth of specific neighborhoods and ethnic groups, or themes such as cultural identity in sports. An extensive library – which is open to the public – provides access to old photographs, maps and other archives. The DC Historic Preservation Office also operates an archaeology laboratory to work on and display archaeological finds. The film, which is a funny look at the juxtaposition between the federal city and local DC, is a great introduction for kids.

NATIONAL BUILDING MUSEUM
Map pp292-3
☎ 202-272-2448; www.nbm.org; Judiciary Sq, 401 F St NW; admission by donation $5; 10am-5pm Mon-Sat, 11am-5pm Sun, tours 12:30pm, family program 2:30pm Sat & Sun; M Judiciary Sq
Devoted to the architectural arts, this underappreciated museum is appropriately housed in an architectural jewel: the 1887 Old Pension Building. Four stories of ornamented balconies flank the dramatic 316ft-wide atrium. The Corinthian columns are among the largest in the world, rising 75ft high. An inventive system of windows and archways keeps the so-called Great

Hall glimmering in natural light. This space has hosted 16 inaugural balls – from Grover Cleveland's in 1885 to George W's in 2005.

The showy space easily overshadows the exhibits, but they're worthwhile nonetheless – Washington: City and Symbol examines the deeper symbolism of DC architecture; and Tools as Art features highlights from a fun collection donated by John Hechinger, hardware industry pioneer. Check the website for a schedule of rotating exhibits, concerts and family programs.

NATIONAL JAPANESE AMERICAN MEMORIAL
☎ 202-530-0015; Louisiana Ave btwn New Jersey Ave & D St; 24hr
Patriotism of Japanese immigrants to the US during WWII is remembered at this triangular plaza with inscriptions commemorating such sentiment. The centerpiece of the grounds is a statue depicting two cranes bound with barbed wire. It is meant to symbolize the battle to overcome prejudice against Japanese-Americans in the decades following the bombing of Pearl Harbor in 1941.

NATIONAL LAW ENFORCEMENT OFFICERS MEMORIAL
Map pp292-3
☎ 202-737-3400; www.nleomf.com; 605 E St NW; admission free; memorial 24hr, visitors center 9am-5pm Mon-Fri, 10am-5pm Sat, noon-5pm Sun; M Judiciary Sq
The memorial on Judiciary Sq commemorates the 14,500 US police officers killed on duty since 1794. In the style of the Vietnam Veterans Memorial, names of the dead are carved on two marble walls curving around a plaza; new names are added during a moving candlelight vigil each year in May. Peeking over the walls, bronze lion statues protect their sleeping cubs (presumably as law enforcement officers protect us).

The nearby **visitor center** houses several exhibits about the history of the memorial and the law enforcement officers it honors.

Plans are underway for a National Law Enforcement Museum, which will open across from the memorial in 2008.

Chinatown & the Convention Center

CHINATOWN
Map pp292-3

7th & H Sts NW; Ⓜ **Gallery Pl-Chinatown**
The world's largest single-span arch, **Friendship Arch**, was built cooperatively by the Washington city government and its sister city Beijing. It stands as the entrance to and symbol of DC's small Chinatown. Here you will find colorful signs with fancy characters; potent aromas emanating from restaurants; grocery stores; and pharmacies cluttered with exotic-looking fruits and herbs. The Chinese flavor is somewhat diluted by the arrival of the MCI Center and the nearby convention center, but this is still the place to come for dim sum.

MCI CENTER Map pp292-3
☎ **202-628-3200; www.mcicenter.com; 601 F St;** Ⓜ **Gallery Pl-Chinatown**
When the sparkling $200 million, 20,000ft-high MCI Center opened in 1997, the streets surrounding it were considered gritty and a little too mean to take the family there. All that changed within a few months of the stadium opening – sports bars, shops and restaurants opened near it. Aging tenements were torn down, replaced by high-dollar lofts and luxury condominiums. Professional sports returned to the city. The NBA's Washington Wizards and NHL's Capitals both made the center their home turf, and the place also hosts major concerts. Even if there's not an event going on, you can still pop inside to visit shops and restaurants.

NATIONAL PUBLIC RADIO
Map pp292-3

☎ **202-513-3232; www.npr.org; 635 Massachusetts Ave NW; admission free;** ☽ **tours 11am Thu;** Ⓜ **Mt Vernon Sq/7th St-Convention Center**
One of America's favorite radio news outlets, old-fashioned NPR (not too long ago they were still producing newscasts by splicing reels of audio with a razor blade and tape instead of the much more modern, less injury-prone, digital method) offers tours of its fabulous head offices at the corner where Downtown's gentrification district meets Chinatown's chaotic hustle. Visitors see the satellite control center and desks for national, foreign, science and arts news, as well as the studios where shows like *Morning Edition* and *All Things Considered* are recorded.

NEW DOWNTOWN

BETHUNE COUNCIL HOUSE
Map pp292-3

☎ **202-673-2402; www.nps.gov/mamc; 1318 Vermont Ave NW;** ☽ **10am-4:30pm Mon-Sat;** Ⓜ **McPherson Sq**
One of 17 children born to poor parents (both ex-slaves), on a cotton farm in South Carolina in 1875, Mary McLeoad Bethune grew up to become one of country's most well-known African American residents. In 1904 Bethune founded the Daytona Educational and Industrial School for Negro Girls (which was later named Bethune-Cookman College) to train teachers to serve the African American community. In 1935, the National Association for the Advancement of Colored People (NAACP) recognized Bethune with an award for her dedication. Shortly after, President Franklin Roosevelt asked her to serve as his special advisor on minority affairs, and Bethune moved to Washington, DC. She then rose through the political ranks to become the first Black woman to head a federal office.

Her Vermont Ave home, where she lived for seven years, has been transformed into an archive and research center and small museum administered by the National Park Service. Rangers lead you on tours here and show you videotapes about Bethune's life. Exhibits, lectures and workshops on Black history are held here as well.

B'NAI B'RITH KLUTZNICK MUSEUM
Map pp296-7

☎ **202-857-6583; bnaibrith.org; 1640 Rhode Island Ave NW; admission by donation;** ☽ **10am-5pm Sun-Fri, to 3:30pm Fri Dec-Apr;** Ⓜ **Dupont Circle**
One of the country's largest Judaica collections, covering history and culture from antiquity to present, is on the B'nai B'rith building's ground floor. In its quiet rooms are archaeological artifacts, folk art and beautiful ritual objects, including silver Torah crowns, Kiddush cups, menorahs, Passover platters and rarities like a 1556 Torah scroll. Exhibits address subjects

like early Jewish settlement in the US, the Holocaust, and Jews in American history and the arts. The museum's newest exhibit is the National Jewish American Sports Hall of Fame. A tranquil sculpture garden is behind the museum.

K STREET Map pp292-3
Ⓜ Farragut North or Mcpherson Sq
What happened? K Street didn't used to be this cool. When this author was growing up, the place had slightly more oomph to it than visiting the dentist. But these days corporate America's district headquarter street is seriously happening. Heck, George Clooney even chose it as the location for an HBO series by the same name – admittedly we didn't really get the show, but we do get K Street. Once the sole turf of lobbying firms, law firms and political and economic consulting firms, today the place has some of DC's fattest expense account restaurants, and the smell of power is rich. Ten years ago the street was dead after dark, but now, folks aren't heading straight home after a day at the office, they're simply swapping the professional suit for Blahniks and jeans and hitting the new lounge down the street.

During the day, Franklin Sq (between 13th and 14th Sts) is our favorite. It's a large stretch of green open space thick with trees, paths and benches. Check out the Victorian-era red-brick Franklin School keeping watch over the patch. The architecture around McPherson Sq, named for Civil War general James B McPherson who once commanded the Army of Tennessee, is fabulous. Keep an eye out for the 1924 Neoclassical, limestone Investment Building (15th and K). Also noteworthy are the lion's head plaques of the terra-cotta Southern Building (805 11th St), which are meticulously carved and date from 1910.

METROPOLITAN AME CHURCH
Map pp296-7
Metropolitan African Methodist Episcopal Church;
☎ 202-331-1426; 1518 M St NW; ☾ 10am-6pm Mon-Sat; Ⓜ McPherson Sq
Built and paid for in 1886 by former slaves (quite a feat considering its impressive size), the Metropolitan AME Church occupies an imposing red-brick Gothic structure and is one of the city's most handsome, yet striking, churches.

Statesman and orator Frederick Douglass often preached here, and his state funeral was held here in February 1895. On the day of his burial, Black schools closed, crowds packed the exterior to pay respect and flags flew at half-mast. For more on Frederick Douglass, see p53.

NATIONAL GEOGRAPHIC EXPLORERS HALL Map pp296-7
☎ 202-857-7588; www.nationalgeographic.com; 17th & M Sts NW; admission free; ☾ 9am-5pm Mon-Sat, 10am-5pm Sun; Ⓜ Farragut North
This natural science museum at National Geographic Society headquarters can't compete with the Smithsonian's more extensive offerings downtown, but it's is worth a stop if you have kids in tow. They'll enjoy its rotating, hands-on exhibits on exploration, adventure and earth sciences. Recent exhibits have included Shackleton's Antarctic-expedition photography and natural history drawings from *National Geographic* magazine's early years.

The society's year-round series, Live… from National Geographic, at the Gilbert Grosvenor Auditorium (☎ 202-857-7700), located in the National Geographic Society Headquarters next to the Explorers Hall, includes films, concerts and lectures by famed researchers and explorers.

WASHINGTON POST
Map pp292-3
☎ 202-334-7969; www.washingtonpost.com; 1150 15th St NW; admission free; ☾ tours by reservation 10am-3pm Mon; Ⓜ McPherson Sq

TRANSPORTATION

Metro On the Red Line, the Dupont Circle Metro station is at the center of the action. Farragut North is a few blocks south. If you are headed south of the circle, the Orange Line may be more convenient. Use Foggy Bottom-GWU to reach the West End, and Farragut West or McPherson Sq further east.

Parking There is no reason to drive to this neighborhood. If you must, during the day it is possible to find a meter or to park on residential streets for up to two hours. Street parking becomes much more difficult during evening hours. There are some parking garages (20th St & N St NW).

Want to see where Woodward and Bernstein toppled a president? Stop by the *Post*'s headquarters. Its free tours don't reveal much of the paper's operations but do show you the busy newsroom and explain how the paper is printed.

DUPONT CIRCLE & KALORAMA

Eating p156; Shopping p216; Sleeping p232

Shop for political schlock and vintage garb then grab a gourmet latte and head to the spacious park in Dupont Circle. The neighborhood is particularly alluring on a sunny, blue October day when the trees blaze gold and pumpkin. The air is crisp, cool enough to contemplate purchasing the sweater displayed in the plate glass window of a stylish boutique on trendy Connecticut Ave. In the park children and dogs frolic in the grass, young lovers linger over a sandwich and a kiss on a well-worn bench. In a shady corner, a homeless man surveys the sad contents of his shopping cart and takes the first sip of the day's first 40oz swathed in a crinkly paper bag.

Dupont Circle is an eclectic neighborhood as much home to the homeless as it is to the hip. This is a land where world-traveling diplomats and guitar-strumming bohemians, scantily clad gorgeous gays and high-powered pinstripe suits all unite. Arguably the center of the nonfederal universe in DC, this is a land of plush ambassadorial estates and refined galleries, gay bars, secondhand bookstores, vintage shopping and haute cuisine.

Be it high noon or midnight, Dupont Circle bustles around the clock. During the week workers from the area's office buildings descend for a breath of fresh air or a bite to eat; on weekends shoppers browse the trendy boutiques and local farmers market; and every night of the week diners of all dimensions flock to Dupont's lively restaurants and cafés. The area is also known for its art scene, home to numerous galleries, many of which put on first-Friday-of-the-month openings, complete with hors d'oeuvres and sparkling wine. For more on Dupont galleries, see p191.

A spin around the circle itself displays Dupont's heterogeneous character. At its center, Samuel Francis Dupont, rear admiral of the Union Navy, sits amid sunbathers, chess players, dog walkers and lost souls. At the circle's edge are grand remnants of the days when Dupont was a millionaire's ghetto. The private **Sulgrave Club** (Map pp296–7; 1801 Massachusetts Ave NW) has attracted only the highest society to socialize with each other. The **Washington Club** (Map pp296–7; 15 Dupont Circle), another private club, was once the home of Cissy Patterson, who hosted President and Mrs Coolidge (and, consequently, Charles Lindbergh) while the White House was undergoing renovations in 1927. These turn-of-the-century mansions sit alongside commercial buildings that are home to modern-day millionaires, like the dramatic **Euram Building** (Map pp296–7; 21 Dupont Circle). The **Riggs Bank** (Map pp296–7; 1913 Massachusetts Ave NW) does more retail business in foreign currency exchange than any other bank in the city.

Kalorama adjoins Dupont Circle to the northwest. Greek for 'beautiful view,' it was named for an estate built by Jefferson confidante Joel Barlow that dominated this hilly area in the 19th century. Now Kalorama is a sleepy enclave of embassies and the brick-and-stone mansions and deep gardens of DC's ultrarich. This is the neighborhood of DC's storied 'cave dwellers' (old-money residents). Home to presidents from Wilson to Harding, the area is still thick with powerful politicos and ambassadors.

Orientation

Dupont Circle really is a traffic circle where major thoroughfares Massachusetts Ave and Connecticut Ave intersect with New Hampshire Ave and 19th and P Sts NW. All of these streets are crowded with restaurants and cafés, pubs and clubs. The surrounding number and letter streets (roughly 14th through 22nd Sts NW running north to south, and M through U Sts NW running east to west) are mixed residential and commercial areas, boasting some of DC's loveliest quarters and liveliest corners. Buzzing pockets of activity pop up at the intersection of 18th St and Florida Ave NW, 18th St between P and Q Sts NW, and 22nd and M Sts NW.

Northwest of Dupont Circle, foreign embassies pepper Massachusetts Ave, known here as Embassy Row. Sheridan Circle, at its intersection with 22nd and R Sts NW, is the center of Washington's diplomatic community. Southeast of Dupont Circle, Mass Ave is punctuated by lesser-known traffic circles at 16th and N Sts NW (Scott Circle), and at 14th and M Sts NW (Thomas Circle).

For our purposes, the neighborhood is bounded by Rock Creek Park in the west, Kalorama Rd in the north, 14th St in the east and L St in the south. In the northwest corner (bounded by Massachusetts, Connecticut and Florida Aves, and Rock Creek Park) is the quieter but no less elegant Kalorama. The fashionable West End, full of power-lunch restaurants and luxury hotels, is in the southwest corner between New Hampshire Ave and Rock Creek Park.

CATHEDRAL OF ST MATTHEW THE APOSTLE Map pp296-7

☎ 202-347-3215; www.stmatthewscathedral .org; 1725 Rhode Island Ave NW; ☼ tours 2:30pm Sun, Mass 5:30pm Sat, 7am, 8:30am, 10am (Latin), 11:30am, 1pm (Spanish) & 5:30pm Sun; Ⓜ Dupont Circle

The sturdy red-brick exterior doesn't hint at the marvelous mosaics and gilding within this 1889 Catholic cathedral, where JFK was laid in state and his funeral mass was held. Its vast central dome, altars and chapels depict biblical saints and eminent New World personages – from Simón Bolívar to Elizabeth Ann Seton – in stained glass, murals and scintillating Italianate mosaics; almost no surface is left undecorated. Evening's the best time to visit, when flickering candles illuminate the sanctuary, but you can attend Mass on Sunday morning or slip in almost any time to look around.

EMBASSY ROW

Map pp296-7 & Map pp300-1

Massachusetts Ave btwn Observatory & Dupont Circles NW; Ⓜ Dupont Circle

Walk around the world as you cruise down Massachusetts Ave's embassy row. Since embassies are actual foreign soil, this is the only place in America where you can step foot into 50 countries in one day! Spend a few hours trying to figure out which country an embassy represents by its colorful

flag hanging out front or its individual, often nationally flavored, character. The visually stimulating Chancery of the Italian Embassy, completed in 1999, just off Massachusetts on Whitehaven St, is a great example. Its facade is made from stones cut to size in Italy then installed in DC by imported Italian masons!

Many consider the 4-acre British Embassy the queen of the row. Look for it in a fantastic 1928 red-brick mansion with a statue of Winston Churchill out front, with one foot placed on British soil, the other outside the embassy property line, planted in the USA (it's a symbol of his Anglo-American descent and solidarity between the two allies).

FONDO DEL SOL VISUAL ARTS CENTER Map pp296-7

☎ 202-483-2777; www.dkmuseums.com/fondo .html; 2112 R St NW; admission by donation; ☼ 12:30- 5:30pm Tue-Sat; Ⓜ Dupont Circle

This delightful artist-run community museum promotes the Americas' cultural heritage and arts through exhibits of contemporary Latin American artists' work, pre-Columbian artifacts, *santos* (carved wooden saints) and folk art. In late summer the Caribbean Festival features salsa and reggae music.

HEURICH HOUSE

Map pp296-7

☎ 202-429-1894; 1307 New Hampshire Ave NW; admission by donation $5; ☼ tours 12:15pm & 1:15pm Wed; Ⓜ Dupont Circle

Looking very much like a medieval castle, this 31-room mansion was designed by John Granville Myers for local brewer Christian Heurich. The interior is predominantly Renaissance and rococo revival. A period garden park, a refuge for nearby office workers, offers the perfect spot for contemplation or a quiet lunch break.

ISLAMIC CENTER

Map pp300-1

☎ 202-332-8343; 2551 Massachusetts Ave NW; admission free; ☼ 10am-5pm; Ⓜ Dupont Circle

The national mosque for American Muslims is a beautiful though incongruous building in the midst of Embassy Row. Topped with a 160ft minaret, the pale limestone mosque (which faces Mecca)

is so delicately inscribed with Koranic verse that it appears to float above Massachusetts Ave. Inside, the mosque glows with bright floral tiling, thick Persian rugs and gilt-trimmed ceilings detailed with more Koranic verse. You can enter to look around; remove your shoes, and women must bring scarves to cover their hair.

PHILLIPS COLLECTION

Map pp296-7

☎ 202-387-2151; www.phillipscollection.org; 1600 21st St NW; admission to permanent exhibit weekdays free, special exhibits, Artful Evenings & weekends adult/child under 18/student/senior $8/free/6/6; ☽ 10am-5pm Tue-Sat, noon-7pm Sun, Artful Evenings 5-8:30pm Thu; Ⓜ Dupont Circle
Founded in 1921, DC's oldest museum of modern art is famed for its extensive collection of impressionist and postimpressionist pieces. Monet, Degas, Whistler, van Gogh and Klee are all represented, with Renoir's panoramic *Luncheon of the Boating Party* crowning its holdings. The stately brownstone also draws art lovers for its special exhibits, which in recent years have included masterpieces by Marsden Hartley, Georgia O'Keeffe, Alfred Stieglitz and Pierre Auguste Renoir. On Thursdays the gallery hosts Artful Evenings, featuring live jazz and free appetizers.

ST AUGUSTINE CATHOLIC CHURCH

Map pp296-7

☎ 202-265-11470; www.saintaugustine-dc.org; 15th & V Sts NW; ☽ mass noon Sun; Ⓜ U Street-Cardozo
Let the spirit move you at DC's oldest and sweetest-sounding Black Catholic congregation. St Augustine's gospel choir rocks the house every Sunday at noon. The unrivalled show features the 165-member choir, often clad in Kenti cloth, and talented, spirited soloists singing their hearts out. The Mass is long, but it offers a unique glimpse of the role of religion in contemporary African American society, lively music and a little spiritual nourishment.

Founded in 1858, St Augustine's congregation moved to the Gothic-revival building at 15th and V Sts NW in 1961. It was a bold move, as it also marked a merger with an all-White congregation; the joined churches became known as Sts Paul & Augustine. The name reverted to St

TRANSPORTATION

Metro The nearest Metro stations are Red Line's Woodley Park-Zoo/Adams Morgan or Green Line's U Street-Cardozo. From Woodley Park it's a pleasant 20-minute walk over the Duke Ellington Memorial Bridge to the heart of Adams-Morgan. Alternatively, for 35c (with a rail transfer), you can ride the U Link shuttle, which runs from 6pm Sunday to Friday and from 10am on Saturday until the Metro closes. It travels between the Woodley Park and U Street-Cardozo Metro stops via Calvert, 18th and U Sts NW. The schedule is timed to make the last trains leaving from the Woodley Park Metro.

Parking Sometimes it is possible to find street parking on the other residential streets west of Columbia Rd or east of 18th St NW. Otherwise, use the public lot at 18th St & Belmont Rd.

Augustine in 1982, but the congregation continues to welcome members of all races and ethnic groups, especially foot-tapping, hand-clapping sopranos and basses who feel the spirit.

TEXTILE MUSEUM

Map pp296-7

☎ 202-667-0441; www.textilemuseum.org; 2320 S St NW; admission by donation $5; ☽ 10am-5pm Mon-Sat, 1-5pm Sun, tours by reservation 10:15am-3pm Mon-Sat; Ⓜ Dupont Circle
Near the top of the list for DC's best non-Smithsonian museum, this gem is the country's only textile museum, and is as unappreciated as the art itself. In two historic mansions, its cool, dimly lit galleries hold exquisite fabrics and carpets dating from 3000 BC to the present. Accompanying wall commentary explains how the textiles mirror the social, spiritual, economic and aesthetic values of the societies that made them. Founded in 1925, its collection includes rare kimonos, pre-Columbian weaving, American quilts and Ottoman embroidery. (Find the flaw: traditional textile artists, from Islamic carpet makers to Appalachian quilters, weave intentional flaws into their work to avoid mimicking God's perfection.)

Upstairs, the learning center will keep older kids entertained – and learning – for hours. Hands-on (literally!) exhibits demonstrate weaving patterns, dying techniques and more.

WOODROW WILSON HOUSE

Map pp296-7

☎ 202-387-4062; www.woodrowwilsonhouse
.org; 2340 S St NW; adult/senior $6/4; ☽ 10am-
4pm Tue-Sun; Ⓜ Dupont Circle

This Georgian-revival mansion offers guided hour-long tours focusing on the 28th president's life and legacy. Genteel elderly docents discuss highlights of Wilson's career (WWI, the League of Nations) and home, which has been restored to the period of his residence (1921–24). The tour features a lovely garden, a stairwell conservatory, European bronzes, 1920s-era china and Mrs Wilson's elegant dresses, all of which offer a glamorous portrait of Roaring '20s DC society.

ADAMS-MORGAN

Eating p160; Shopping p218; Sleeping p237

Enigmatic Adams-Morgan is the soul of the city. The bohemian love child of a sultry Latino soap star and an eccentric African immigrant, she's a saucy spitfire with a penchant for entertaining. Arrive on 18th St on a sizzling summer night, when the air is laced with strains of Congolese pop and Jamaican reggae, scented with sweat and grease and beer and you'll get a taste for what we're talking about. Pheromones fly faster than drunken revelers tumble out of the salsa clubs and basement dives that line the ethnically diverse, somewhat rough-and-tumble streets. These same cool kids slurp oily slabs of pizza on dirty curbs across from exclusive lounges where bling-toting fashionistas of every color strut in front of velvet ropes, hoping to catch the bouncer's intimidating eye.

Adams-Morgan is a global village, home to immigrants from Latin America, the Caribbean, Africa and Southeast Asia. The result of this international stew is a vibrant, funky neighborhood that seduces the taste buds with strange, exotic flavors and energizes the body with all sorts of sounds.

The neighborhood received its name in 1955 when DC became the first large US city to voluntarily integrate its schools. Its moniker comes from two local elementary schools: historically White Adams and Black Morgan. In the early 20th century Meridian Hill was a very fashionable address. Since then, the streets around Adams-

Morgan have seen their highs and lows, as the population has become more diverse, both ethnically and economically. Today Adams-Morgan is an edgy 'hood that offers residents a lively urban atmosphere at (slightly) reduced rents. The surrounding residential streets are home to upper-middle-class folks with an appreciation for the cosmopolitan. The internationals come out to Adams-Morgan by night to get a taste of home or to get their groove on, but most of them retreat before sunrise to their abodes in Arlington or Tacoma or neighboring Mt Pleasant.

By day the place is quiet, although shops selling ethnic ingredients, world music and imported finery do a brisk business. But nightlife is what's happening here. And nobody can resist the exotic flavors. There is something for everyone: students dancing at Heaven & Hell (p188), gringos learning a few steps of salsa, gay boys enjoying the famed Perry's (p161) drag show, yuppies eating Ethiopian at Meskerem (p160) with their hands…

Adams-Morgan takes the dancing outside in September, when DC's largest neighborhood festival takes place. Musicians, vendors, and foodies come out for Adams Morgan Festival (p16), a weekend-long street fair.

Orientation

Adams-Morgan is a little international hub on Columbia Rd and 18th St NW, just south of their intersection. The long blocks of 18th St between Florida Ave and Columbia Rd are wallpapered with bars, clubs, new and secondhand bookstores, record stores, retro and nouveau clothing boutiques, sidewalk cafés and rooftop restaurants. The surrounding streets are primarily residential and surprisingly quiet. Be careful walking these streets at night, especially east of 18th St, as crime does spill over from the rougher neighborhoods to the north and east.

East of the hub is Meridian Hill, which marks the geological fall line between the rocky piedmont plateau and the softer coastal plain. Meridian Hill Park, which runs along 16th St NW, marks the eastern boundary of the neighborhood. The western boundary is Rock Creek Park and the zoo. Just north is Mt Pleasant, DC's most Latino neighborhood, where Salvadoran

TRANSPORTATION

Metro The nearest Metro stations are Green Line's U Street-Cardozo and Shaw-Howard U.

Parking There is a paid parking lot near the 9:30 Club (p183) at 8th & V Sts NW.

pupuserías (restaurants serving *pupusas*, meat-stuffed pastries) and Central American groceries line the streets.

DISTRICT OF COLUMBIA ARTS CENTER Map pp296-7

☎ 202-462-7833; www.dcartscenter.org; 2438 18th St NW; 🚌 shuttle from Woodley Park-Zoo/Adams Morgan Metro

This grass roots center offers emerging artists a space to showcase their work, from theater to multimedia creations. The 750-sq-ft gallery features rotating visual arts exhibits, while plays and other theatrical productions take place in the 50-seat black box theater. It's worth checking the website to see if anything interesting is going on, as this homegrown initiative introduces you to some wonderful, still obscure artists.

MALCOLM X PARK Map pp296-7

Ⓜ U Street-Cardozo

Unofficially dedicated to Malcolm X, this park scales a hillside from the Shaw neighborhood to Adams-Morgan's upper reaches, and adds much-needed scenery to the area. The park was constructed in the early 20th century, when Meridian Hill was a very fashionable district. Built astraddle the fall line between the piedmont plateau and the Atlantic coastal plain, the park emphasizes its locale with terraced walkways and a waterfall cascade. An eccentric mix of statuary, from Joan of Arc to Dante, enlivens its contoured lawns. It's lovely in springtime, when the dogwoods and azaleas flower, but it isn't safe to visit after dark.

MERIDIAN INTERNATIONAL CENTER Map pp296-7

☎ 202-667-6800; www.meridian.org; 1630 Crescent Pl; admission free; ⏰ 2-5pm Wed-Sun; Ⓜ U Street-Cardozo

Here in the middle of the city, architect John Russell Pope built this French country chateau, complete with a stately walled entrance, charming cobblestone courtyard and decorated limestone facade. Today Meridian House – as it is known – is an educational and hospitality center for DC's international community.

SHAW & U STREET

Eating p161; Shopping p219

These days U Street and the Shaw are going through a bit of an identity crisis, struggling with their new status as DC's hippest nighttime hot spot. At one time the cultural heart of African American DC, the turf of working-class families, burgeoning rappers, rum-guzzling bums and gun-toting gang-bangers, today it feels like an episode of *Extreme Makeover: Home Edition,* where the mission is gentrification.

Trendy lofts are replacing decaying housing projects. The mom-and-pop grocery on the corner is still the place to catch up on local gossip but, should you wish, you can just as easily chat in the sleek new bar across the street. For now Shaw is the kind of place where both Paris Hilton and the neighborhood boys from the tenement housing on V Street would feel at home bar-hopping. It's got enough glitz to keep the celebutants happy, and enough edge to keep hard-core urbanites from bitching their 'hood has gone to pot – become just another stomping ground for the yuppie-playing-ghetto fabulous crowd.

Even if you're not into partying, we encourage you to journey through Shaw. For a trip around these blocks is a journey through the history of Black Washington. Starting in the 1890s, Shaw became the political and cultural center of African American DC as Black families and opinion makers settled here, driven out of increasingly segregated downtown Washington. Civil rights leaders Archibald and Francis Grimké lived here, as did Calvin Chase, editor of the crusading *Washington Bee.* Black lawyers, doctors and tradesmen opened offices along U St, which blossomed into a separate downtown for those excluded by racism from DC's other shops.

(Continued on page 113)

NATIONAL MALL

The Washington Monument rising above the Capitol and the National Mall (p110)

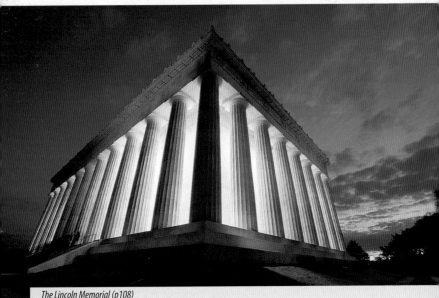
The Lincoln Memorial (p108)

Growing up in the nation's capital, the National Mall has been a constant in my life. My earliest memories of this grand expanse of green grass and larger-than-life ornate marble museums and monuments is a collage of random images spun in five-second old movie clips, still clear enough to hear, smell and taste.

I remember eating a coffee hot-fudge sundae, piled high with whipped cream, topped with a sticky fire-engine-red maraschino cherry so unnatural it made my mother cringe, in the basement of the **National Museum of American History** (p67). A trip to the old fashioned ice-cream parlor was the reward my sister and I were given for following my mother around every art museum in the city.

I remember the first time I made a wish while touching a piece of the moon in the National Air & Space Museum (p66). And the day my sister and I took our grandma to the museum and they happened to be filming an IMAX movie and we all got to be extras in the robot scene and how exciting that was.

The National Mall got me in trouble my sophomore year of high school when I skipped school to attend Bill Clinton's 1992 presidential inauguration. I'll never forget the crowds, and how my friends and I had to elbow our way through a sea of people that stretched for dozens upon dozens of blocks. Somehow we made it all the way to the front, to the VIP section, so close we could see the new president take the oath. I think that was the first time the power of DC hit me full force.

After college the National Mall gave me a first-hand look at democracy in action when I covered the Million Mom March (see Mall of Justice, p32) for a small daily newspaper in Manassas, VA. Interviewing celebrities such as Reese Witherspoon and Rosie O'Donnell was a pretty big rush at the age of 22, but even bigger was getting caught up in the tide of people, from all over America, united together to march on the Capitol with one goal: to ask Congress to hear their voice.

I think it is moments like this that make the National Mall special, the moments when you glimpse past the shiny (often distracting) facade of pretty buildings, the smells of hot dogs and doughy pretzels, and the crunch of red and yellow leaves under your feet while playing Frisbee with the dogs on a gorgeous fall day, and realize that the National Mall's secret weapon is its ability to act as America's front yard.

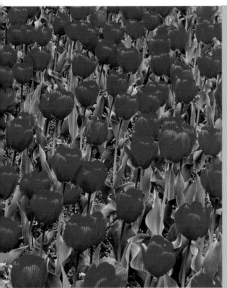
Red tulips at the National Mall

top five
CLASSIC NATIONAL MALL PHOTO OPS

DC is jam-packed with postcard-perfect photo opportunities. Below are a few of our favorites for famous stuff:

- Cherry Blossoms and Tidal Basin from the Thomas Jefferson Memorial – This one is best in late April or early May when the Cherry Blossom trees surrounding the Tidal Basin are in full pink splendor. The Thomas Jefferson Memorial, with its marble curves, makes a great focal point.
- The Capitol from Pennsylvania Ave – Hit this one just after dark. The blur of red and white lights streaming down Pennsylvania Ave juxtaposed against a glowing marble backdrop is a classic DC shot. Extra points if you capture a passing motorcade.
- DC from the steps of the Lincoln Memorial – Climb the steps of the Lincoln Memorial as the sun starts to set and grab a few frames of another classic Washington shot. First you'll need a couple of pictures of the larger-than-life marble Lincoln sitting on his larger-than-life marble chair, but then turn around and point your camera east, across the shimmering Reflecting Pool towards the Capitol in the distance and the fading sun behind.
- Vietnam Veterans Memorial – Don't get up in anyone's face here, but if you shoot from a bit of a distance, this might be your most poignant Washington shot. The somber image of mourners placing flowers by the base of the black marble wall is powerful.
- Protestors on the Mall – At least once a week someone is protesting about something on the grounds near the Capitol. If you happen to be around, snapping photos at a rally, with the Capitol in the background (America's symbol of democracy and freedom of speech and all its other lofty ideals), can create powerful shots. Score extra points if you arrive during a big march and get some celebrity shots in the mix. It's another classic and you just have to snap it. Try standing six or seven blocks back, so you get a feel for the expanse of the Mall.

The national monuments and museums on the Mall serve as America's most treasured history lesson, the physical embodiment of everything that's patriotic (and iconic) about the USA. George Washington commissioned Pierre L'Enfant to design the National Mall as open space and parklands for residents to gather and play. Over the years it has become a center for national expressions of remembrance, protest and observance. The green lawns are lined with 2000 American elms, while 3000 Japanese cherry trees ring the Tidal Basin. For more than half the year the place is filled with color – there are thousands of tulips, pansies and annuals displayed in more than 170 flower beds scattered across the 2 mile expanse of ground stretching from the Lincoln Memorial to the Capitol grounds, while another 35 ornamental pools and fountains, an old time merry-go-round and even a castle round out the grandiose, Euro-style expanse.

CAPITOL Map p304

☎ 202-225-6827; www.aoc.gov; admission free;
🕙 9am-4:30pm; Ⓜ Capitol South

The Capitol is the only building in DC lacking an address – it stands dead center in the city's street plan. It also doesn't have a front or back, but east and west entrances (no one seems to know why). The public enters at the east front while senators and representatives enter from the west. From 1829 to 1977, all the presidents were inaugurated on the east lawn. In 1981 Ronald Reagan was sworn in on the west side and the five inaugurations since have followed the precedent. Up until 1928 Americans could enter the Capitol every day at noon to talk to the president!

The Space and Missile Hall in the National Air & Space Museum (p109)

LINCOLN MEMORIAL Map pp292-3
☎ 202-426-6841; www.nps.gov/linc; ☼ 9.30am-midnight; M Foggy Bottom-GWU

In a stunning location overlooking the loooooonnng Reflecting Pool, this memorial is a favorite location spot for Hollywood block-busters. Owen Wilson and Vince Vaughn discussed girls on the steps in *Wedding Crashers*; Reese Witherspoon's Elle Woods sought Lincoln's advice in *Legally Blonde 2*; and many a romantic kiss has been shot on the marble steps at sunset.

Trivia buffs listen up: Abraham Lincoln is the only US president to have a patent – 'for buoying vessels over shoals.' (In plain and simple English that means he created floatation devices to help large boats pass more easily through shallow water.)

The Capitol (p107)

GETTING THERE
Most museums along the Mall are closest to the Orange Line Smithsonian metro stop, with the exception of the Capitol, which is closed to the Capitol South metro stop. Most monuments are clustered on the west end of the Mall and not near metro stops – it's about 1 mile from the Washington Monument to the cluster of memorials to its west. The closest stop is Foggy Bottom-GWU or Farragut West if you're heading to the west end.

NATIONAL AIR & SPACE
MUSEUM Map pp292-3
☎ 202-357-2700; www.nasm.si.edu; 4th St &
Independence Ave SW; admission free, IMAX or
planetarium adult/senior & child $7.50/6; ⏱ 10am-
5:30pm, tours 10:15am & 1pm; Ⓜ L'Enfant Plaza
Where in the world can you touch the moon
and eat freeze-dried astronauts' ice cream
under the shadow of a nuclear missile left
over from the Cold War? The National Air
& Space Museum, of course. Washington's
favorite museum is filled with some great
exhibits.

NATIONAL MUSEUM OF
NATURAL HISTORY Map pp292-3
☎ 202-357-2700; www.mnh.si.edu; 10th St & Constitution Ave NW; admission free, IMAX adult/senior
& child $7.50/6; ⏱ 10am-5:30pm, to 7:30pm Jun-
Aug, tours 10:30am & 1:30pm; Ⓜ Federal Triangle
You can thank the trigger-happy Theodore Roosevelt for many of the taxidermy
animals on display at the National
Museum of Natural History, one of the
world's most popular museums. The
Smithsonian Institution commissioned the
former president to shoot the animals while
on safari in Africa and to bring them back
for display.

Marching through the streets to the Washington
Monument (p110)

Roosevelt's contribution numbers in the
thousands. However, it is only a miniscule
portion of the museum's natural collection. The museum owns more than 120
million specimens and artifacts including
an enormous African elephant in the entrance hall.

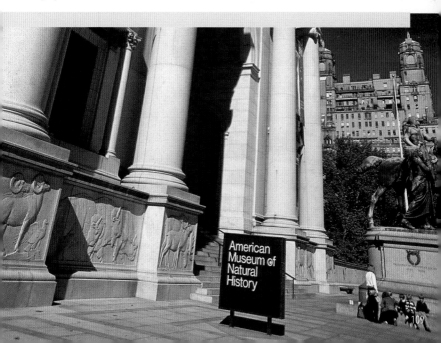

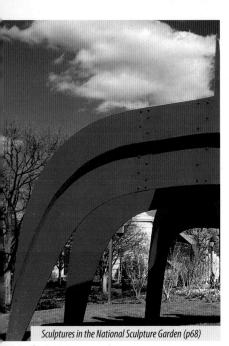

Sculptures in the National Sculpture Garden (p68)

NATIONAL WORLD WAR II MEMORIAL Map pp292-3

☎ 800-639-4992; www.wwiimemorial.com; 900 Ohio Drive SW; Ⓜ Smithsonian

DC's newest memorial is particularly moving at dusk, when the American flags are lowered and the white lights illuminating marble pillars and fountains, reflecting in inky pools, create a picture as haunting as it is beautiful.

WASHINGTON MONUMENT Map pp292-3

☎ 202-619-7222; www.nps.gov/wamo; Constitution Ave & 15th St; admission free, reservations $2; ☙ 9am-5pm, tickets available from 8am; Ⓜ Smithsonian

Strangely, this pale obelisk near the Mall's west end was originally conceived as an equestrian statue to honor George Washington. We guess it grew a little big for its britches. At 555ft, the monument is not only the tallest building in DC, it is also the tallest masonry structure in the world!

When the stock market crashed in 1929, Herbert Hoover once looked out a White House window, and pointing toward the monument said, 'This apparently is the only stable thing in my administration.'

NATIONAL MALL WALKING TOUR

When I was a kid, every time someone came to visit my family in Washington, my mother dragged my father, sister and I along to show our guest the National Mall. Nearly 20 years later, when I return to DC I take visitors on the same tour.

Start on the **Capitol Grounds 1** (p87), designed by famed landscape architect Frederick Law Olmsted. Snap a few pictures of the building itself before heading west for three blocks on Pennsylvania Ave to the **National Gallery of Art 2** (p66). Pop inside the east entrance and check out the famous paintings and impressive Alexander Calder mobiles before leaving through the west exit. From here, cross 7th St and check out 6-acre **National Sculpture**

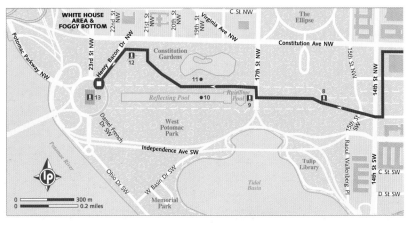

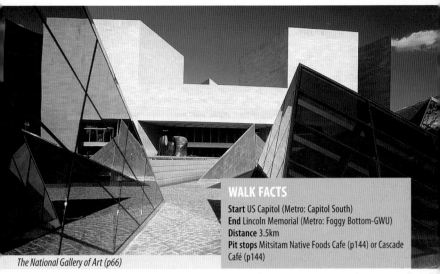

The National Gallery of Art (p66)

WALK FACTS

Start US Capitol (Metro: Capitol South)
End Lincoln Memorial (Metro: Foggy Bottom-GWU)
Distance 3.5km
Pit stops Mitsitam Native Foods Cafe (p144) or Cascade Café (p144)

Garden 3 (p68). It is filled with whimsical sculptures and scattered with fountains and benches. Head at an angle across the grass to the National Air & Space Museum 4 (p66), your next stop. After you've had your fill of flying, walk next door and take a peek at the fabulous layout inside the National Museum of the American Indian 5 (p68). The café here is also worth a stop; it does delicious lunches.

Afterwards, walk west along the Mall then head north, past the impressive red sandstone turrets of the Smithsonian Castle 6 (p68). From here you'll want to continue heading north, then climb the marble steps and enter the National Museum of Natural History 7 (p67).

When you've finished exploring the world of dinosaurs and extinct mammals, set the Washington Monument 8 (p73) in your sight and walk toward the grassy hill it sits upon. From here it's a straight shot across 17th St to the somber, but very impressive, new National WWII Memorial 9 (p71). When you've paid respect, continue west toward the Reflecting Pool 10 (see Capitol Grounds, p87). Walk through Constitution Gardens 11 (p69) on the north side of the pool, making a slight detour to the Vietnam Veterans Memorial 12 (p72) before returning to course and ending your journey on the steps of the Lincoln Memorial 13 (p108).

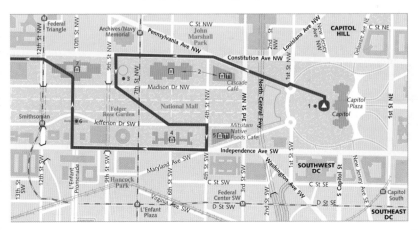

The Three Servicemen Statue at the Vietnam Veterans Memorial (p72)

Civil rights struggles were a constant feature of Shaw life: in the 1950s Washington's Committee for School Desegregation first met at **John Wesley AME Zion Church** (Map pp302–3; 1615 14th St NW). Their work led to the landmark *Brown v Board of Education*, which mandated school desegregation.

In Shaw's theaters and music halls a vibrant arts scene sprang up in the 1920s. This 'Black Broadway' flourished until the 1940s. Duke Ellington grew up on T St; Pearl Bailey waited tables and danced at U St's Republic Gardens (p189); Ella Fitzgerald sang at Bohemian Caverns (p184), the 11th St jazz club; Louis Armstrong played the Dance Hall at V and 9th Sts; and the Lincoln Theatre (p192) and Howard Theatre presented Harlem's and DC's finest to Black audiences. Shaw was a high point on the renowned 'chitlin circuit' of Black entertainment districts.

By the 1950s segregation started to ease. Middle-class Blacks could live elsewhere, so some moved. Shaw entered a decline that became a tailspin in April 1968, when riots exploded after the murder of Dr Martin Luther King, Jr. Centered on 14th and U Sts, the violence destroyed many Black-owned businesses and frightened others away. The neighborhood languished until the late 1980s.

In 1991 the opening of the U Street-Cardozo Metro station started to attract businesses again. The high price of housing in other parts of the city fomented the demand for real estate: young, hip urbanites – especially African Americans – started buying and repairing houses in the surrounding residential streets. Recognizing the historic appeal of the area, bars and clubs opened in the same buildings where the jazz greats used to play. Unlike other parts of DC, it's an area of deep roots and of reawakening history. Shaw is where Black community developed and persevered, and now flourishes in a multicultural setting. And it should come as no surprise that the reawakening has – for accompaniment – the rhythms and melodies of the most vibrant live music scene in DC.

Orientation

Named for Robert Gould Shaw, a Civil War colonel mortally wounded while commanding the famed Black 54th Massachusetts Regiment, Shaw is a rectangular block that sits above the downtown district. It stretches from Thomas Circle and Mt Vernon Sq in the south, to Harvard St in the north; and, for our purposes, from 14th St NW in the west to N Capitol St in the east. The district is bisected by north–south Georgia Ave, which becomes 7th St south of Florida Ave.

Much of Shaw's northeastern corner is consumed by the Howard University campus and McMillan Park and Reservoir. Funky shops and inexpensive restaurants catering to African American students and scholars are clustered along Georgia Ave and near the Shaw-Howard U Metro station at 7th and S Sts NW. East of here, between 2nd and 7th Sts NW, is LeDroit Park, a small subdivision of Victorian homes from the 1870s. Originally a segregated White enclave, the subdivision later attracted Howard's faculty and other Black elite.

Much of Shaw's activity – especially the nightlife – is centered on the 'New U,' along 14th and U Sts NW. Hot clubs and slick boutiques line these streets, illustrating the renaissance in this neighborhood. South of here, at the intersection of Rhode Island and Vermont Aves with 13th and P Sts NW, is Logan Circle, another historic district that is now being rediscovered by yuppies and buppies (Black urban professionals).

AFRICAN AMERICAN CIVIL WAR MEMORIAL Map pp302-3

☎ 202-667-2667; www.afroamcivilwar.org; U St & Vermont Ave NW; Ⓜ U Street-Cardozo
At the center of a granite plaza, the bronze statue of rifle-bearing troops is DC's first major art piece by Black sculptor Ed Hamilton. The sculpture is surrounded

TRANSPORTATION

Metro The Brookland-CUA Metro station is two stops past Union Station on the Red Line.

Parking Outside of Brookland, many places are not accessible by public transport, so you may need to drive. Street parking is easy in most parts of the Northeast quadrant (but watch your two-hour limit).

on three sides by the Wall of Honor, listing the names of 209,145 Black troops who fought in the Union Army, as well as the 7000 White soldiers who served alongside them. Use the directory to locate individual names within the regiments.

AFRICAN AMERICAN CIVIL WAR MUSEUM

Map pp302-3

☎ 202-667-2667; www.afroamcivilwar.org; 1200 U St NW; admission free; ☾ 10am-5pm Mon-Fri, 10am-2pm Sat; Ⓜ U Street-Cardozo

In 1862 Abraham Lincoln sanctioned the participation of fully armed Black regiments in the Union army. Thousands of former slaves and free Blacks, as well as fleeing slaves, enlisted. This one-room museum highlights the participation of over 200,000 Black soldiers who fought for the Union in the Civil War. The permanent exhibit includes photographs and documents, and some audiovisual programs, following African American history from the Civil War through the Civil Rights movement. The Civil War Soldiers and Sailors Project allows visitors to search for ancestors in databases of Black troops, regiments and battles. In the near future the museum is moving to Shaw's historic Masonic Temple, adjacent to the memorial.

BLACK FASHION MUSEUM

Map pp302-3

☎ 202-667-0744; bfmdc.tripod.com/about.htm; 2007 Vermont Ave NW; admission by donation; ☾ by appointment only; Ⓜ U Street-Cardozo

This eclectic little museum showcases the work of Black designers past and present. Here you can see slaves' dresses, the dress Rosa Parks wore during her historic bus ride, and the handiwork of unsung seamstresses who costumed famous figures from Mary Todd Lincoln to Jackie Kennedy.

HOWARD UNIVERSITY

Map pp302-3

☎ 202-806-6100; www.howard.edu; 2400 6th St NW; Ⓜ Shaw-Howard U

Anchoring the neighborhood is Howard University, which was founded in 1867. Distinguished alumni include the late Supreme Court Justice Thurgood Marshall (who enrolled after he was turned away from the University of Maryland's then all-White law school), Ralph Bunche, Nobel laureate Toni Morrison and former New York City mayor David Dinkins. Today it has over 12,000 students in 18 schools. There are campus tours (☎ 202-806-2900). The Welcome Center is at 1739 7th St NW.

Founders' Library, a handsome Georgian building with a gold spire and giant clock, is the campus' architectural centerpiece. It houses the Moorland-Spingarn Research Center (☎ 202-806-4237), which boasts the nation's largest collection of African American literature. Also worth visiting is the Howard University Gallery of Art (☎ 202-806-7070; Childers Hall), which has an impressive collection of work by African and African American artists, as well as other notable pieces. Both are open 9:30am to 4:30pm Monday to Friday and are free of charge.

LOGAN CIRCLE

Map pp292-3

Ⓜ Shaw-Howard University

Not so long ago this was seedy, crime-ridden turf of no interest to most residents and visitors. Today, Logan Circle is DC's *it* multicolor neighborhood, home to the trendiest of yuppies and buppies. It's been restored to its original Victorian splendor: last century's crack houses are today's boutiques and fusion restaurants. Logan Circle is especially fabulous to wander around on an autumn day, when the urban landscape glows yellow with falling leaves and October sunshine.

NORTHEAST DC

Eating p162

It was not long ago that most of DC's Upper Northeast district was considered off-limits for casual visitors. Students made a beeline from the Brookland Metro stop back to their dorms on Catholic University or Trinity College campuses. Drivers admired the greenery of the National Arboretum from their cars as they drove by on New York Ave, but nobody bothered to stop.

As in many parts of DC, however, times are changing. The Brookland area is one of DC's hottest real-estate markets, as buyers – driven out of the desirable Northwest quadrant by the now-impossible prices – grab up the large houses with leafy yards. The area around 12th St NE is becoming its own little college town, drawing local residents and students from the nearby campuses. You won't confuse Brookland with Georgetown, by any means. But this is a place in the city where real people can afford to buy homes and hang out at the local pub, all just two Metro stops from Union Station.

The incongruous features of this neighborhood – which are a reminder that Brookland is not Collegetown, USA – are the spectacular National Shrine of Immaculate Conception and the little known Franciscan Monastery. Exquisite landmarks in their own right, they add a touch of spiritual significance to the neighborhood. Not many college towns attract a steady stream of pilgrims outside of football season!

Orientation

DC's Northeast quadrant is a huge area of mostly peaceful residential streets and green college campuses, but rudely interrupted by noisy traffic on unfriendly highways. Bladensburg Rd and Rhode Island Ave (Rte 1), further north, both cut across the quadrant from southeast to northwest, while New York Ave (Rte 50) roars by east to west. For our purposes, the neighborhood includes areas east of N Capitol St and north of L St NE. Its eastern boundary is the Anacostia River, and it stretches north to the Maryland line.

Northwest of Rhode Island Ave, the increasingly popular Brookland neighborhood is bursting up around the campuses of Catholic University and Trinity College. There is a little downtown Brookland center along 12th St NE between Monroe and Perry Sts. The shady, green Franciscan Monastery is amid the residential streets a few blocks northeast of here.

Further south, Gallaudet University is squeezed in between New York Ave and Bladensburg Rd. It is flanked on either side by Brentwood Park and Mt Olivet Cemetery, which offer a protective barrier to the roar. And, tucked into an unlikely spot in the southeast corner of the quadrant, the pristine US National Arboretum occupies almost all the space between Bladensburg Rd, New York Ave and the Anacostia River.

HENRY ADAMS' GRIEF

In Rock Creek Cemetery on Rock Creek Church Rd NW, just west of Catholic University, off New Hampshire Ave, is one of Washington's most poignant monuments: the Adams Memorial, or *Grief*. Sculpted by Augustus Saint-Gaudens, the shrouded figure was commissioned in 1890 by the historian and novelist Henry Adams after the suicide of his wife, Marian (who killed herself by drinking photographic chemicals). Often, you'll see solitary visitors sitting on the bench across from it, studying its exhausted yet strangely peaceful face. Adams never remarried and when he died, in 1918, he was buried here next to Marian.

BASILICA OF THE NATIONAL SHRINE OF THE IMMACULATE CONCEPTION

Map pp302-3

☎ 202-526-8300; www.nationalshrine.com; 400 Michigan Ave NE; ⏱ 7am-7pm, Mass 9am, 10:30am, noon, 1:30pm (Spanish), 4:30pm Sun; Ⓜ Brookland-CUA

The largest Catholic church in the Western Hemisphere (and some say the Catholic answer to the Washington National Cathedral), this huge church accommodates 6000 worshipers. In addition to its unearthly size, the Marian shrine sports an eclectic mix of Romanesque and Byzantine motifs, from classical towers to a mosque-like dome, all anchored by a 329ft minaret-shaped campanile. Downstairs, the original Eastern-style crypt church has low, mosaic-covered vaulted ceilings lit by votives and chandeliers. Upstairs, the main sanctuary is lined with elaborate saints' chapels, lit by rose windows and fronted by a dazzling mosaic of a stern Christ. A large gift shop sells religious literature, rosaries and statues.

FRANCISCAN MONASTERY

Map pp292-3

☎ 202-526-6800; www.myfranciscan.com; 1400 Quincy St NE; admission by donation; ⏱ hourly tours 9am-4pm Mon-Sat, 1-4pm Sun

The Franciscan Monastery is set amid 44 beautifully landscaped acres of gardens that, in spring, explode into a riot of color as tulips, dogwoods, cherry trees and roses bloom. This place isn't just about flowers, however. The Order of St Francis is charged with guardianship of the Holy Land's sacred sites. The monastery has interpreted that task in a unique way, constructing replicas of those sites for the faithful who are unable to visit the Holy Land. Among the glorious blooms are life-size fake-granite reproductions of the Tomb of Mary, the Grotto at Lourdes and other subterranean sacred places. More oddities await inside Mt St Sepulchre itself, including reproductions of the Roman Catacombs under the sanctuary floor. These dark, narrow passages wind past fake tombs and the actual remains of Sts Innocent and Benignus. It's all very creepy and fascinating, like a holy Disneyland.

GALLAUDET UNIVERSITY
Map p304
☎ 202-651-5505, TDD 651-5359; www .gallaudet.edu; 800 Florida Ave NE
Established in 1864, Gallaudet University is the world's only accredited liberal-arts school for the hearing-impaired. The college's first hearing-impaired president was appointed after student protests in 1989. Few sports fans know that, in 1894, Gallaudet football players invented the American football huddle to prevent their opponents from reading the sign language used to call the plays. Tours of the campus are available by reservation. No Metro station is nearby, so you'll need to drive.

KENILWORTH AQUATIC GARDENS
Map pp290-1
☎ 202-426-6905; www.nps.gov/kepa; 1550 Anacostia Ave NE; admission free; ⏰ 8am-4pm; Ⓜ Deanwood
The only national park devoted to water plants is across the Anacostia River from the National Arboretum, in Anacostia Park. The aquatic gardens were begun as the hobby of a Civil War veteran and operated for 56 years as a commercial water garden, until the federal government purchased them in 1938. Highlights include the lovely water lilies, which are the star of an annual festival every July. To reach the park follow the Douglas Street signs out of the Deanwood metro (you'll cross over a pedestrian overpass), then make a right on Anacostia Ave. If you are driving you'll want to take New York Ave (Rte 50) east to Kenilworth Ave south (I-295). From here

TRANSPORTATION

Metro From Dupont Circle, the Red Line runs through Upper Northwest DC, first following Connecticut Ave through Woodley Park-Zoo/Adams Morgan, Cleveland Park and Van Ness-UDC, then continuing along Wisconsin Ave through Tenleytown-AU and Friendship Heights.

Bus Buses 30, 32, 34 and 36 run up and down Wisconsin Ave between Friendship Heights and Georgetown.

Parking Street parking is not as difficult in this mostly residential neighborhood, but keep in mind that you are still limited to two hours Monday to Saturday.

you'll make a right on Douglas St and then another right on Anacostia Ave.

POPE JOHN PAUL II CULTURAL CENTER
Map pp302-3
☎ 202-635-5400; www.jp2cc.org; 3900 Harwood Rd NE; admission by donation adult $5, senior & student $4; ⏰ 10am-5pm Tue-Sat, noon-5pm Sun; Ⓜ Brookland-CUA
This impressive modern building is an unexpected setting for an interactive museum of the Catholic Church. Five galleries explore the history of the Church, personal faith, and its relation to science, community and social service. The excellent Gallery of Imagination allows visitors to participate in a carillon-ringing ensemble or to design an electronic stained-glass window.

UNITED STATES NATIONAL ARBORETUM
Map pp290-1
☎ 202-245-2726; www.usna.usda.gov; 3501 New York Ave NE; admission free, tram tour adult/ child/student $4/2/3; ⏰ 8am-5pm, tram tours Sat, Sun & holidays Apr-Oct
Way out in Northeast DC are 446 acres of blooming trees, ornamental plants and lovely verdant meadows. But because it's hard to access the national gardens – they're in a gritty area far from the Metro – they remain among DC's most hidden treasures and are a wonderful place to stroll and flower-peep in peace.

Stop at the **Administration Building** near the R St gate for a map and information. Highlights include the **Bonsai & Penjing Museum** (🕙 10am to 3:30pm), east of the Administration Building, and the **Capitol Columns Garden**, south along Ellipse Rd. The latter is studded with Corinthian pillars removed from the Capitol in the 1950s.

The best times to visit are spring (March to May, when the azaleas bloom) and fall (September to November, for colorful autumn leaves). No direct buses serve the gardens and it's hard to negotiate them on foot, so drive or bike.

UPPER NORTHWEST DC

Eating p163; Shopping p221; Sleeping p238

Wealthy folks have been showing Upper Northwest the love for a couple of centuries now. And how can you blame them? With gentle hills and winding roads, safe neighborhoods offering big leafy lots, good schools and miles of bucolic parkland, Upper Northwest is a suburban oasis in the urban jungle and a damn good place to raise a family to boot. In the age before air-conditioning, Washington's political elite built summer retreats here in an effort to escape the stifling heat (we're pretty sure that was just an excuse to live in the woods: the hills here aren't exactly mountains…).

The stucco-covered manor house **Woodley** (Map pp300–1; 3000 Cathedral Ave) was a summer home for Presidents Van Buren, Tyler and Buchanan. In 1881 President Grover Cleveland bought a country house (he hoped anonymously) on Newark St, thus inspiring the naming of the neighborhood Cleveland Park (so much for anonymity).

The neighborhood didn't really take off as a year-round spot until the early 1900s, when trolley cars crossing Rock Creek Park began running, and people discovered just how pleasant a place it was to live. Lawyers, bureaucrats and journalists bought up big parcels of property, building spacious houses with wraparound porches and white picket fences and shading it all with elms.

The Upper Northwest today is a clear product of this development; in fact, some may wonder how much has changed. Highly educated and well-regarded residents (many of them lawyers, bureaucrats

and journalists) reside in the same comfortable homes on these shady streets, enjoying suburban amenities, while the city has grown up around them. Indeed, the suburban amenities are among the attractions that may draw you up here: shopping strips with a selection of stores to rival the suburban mall; classy old-style movie theaters showing artsy and second-run films; miles of rambling, forested parks and paved bike trails and some of the city's top dining venues.

Orientation

The vast Upper Northwest stretches from W St – just north of Georgetown and Shaw – all the way to the Maryland line, which is marked by the diagonal southwest–northeast Western Ave. Luscious, green Rock Creek Park runs north–south down the center of the quadrant (although there are few attractions east of the park this far north).

West of the park is mostly affluent residential neighborhoods filled with large homes on quiet, tree-lined streets, with major pockets of development along Connecticut and Wisconsin Aves. Heading up Wisconsin Ave, just north of Georgetown, is Glover Archbold Park (named for the park that dominates the neighborhood), a very quaint community of brownstones housing graduate students and young families. Further north is Tenleytown and American University.

Just north of Dupont Circle, Woodley Park and Cleveland Park are upscale communities, which occupy the shady streets between Connecticut and Wisconsin Aves. The Washington National Cathedral is tucked in here off Wisconsin Ave. The zoo is nestled in between Connecticut Ave and Rock Creek Park. In DC's far northwestern corner, swanky Friendship Heights borders Chevy Chase, Maryland.

BATTERY KEMBLE PARK & GLOVER ARCHBOLD PARK

Map pp290-1

🚌 D1 from Dupont Circle to Glover Park, D3 or D6 from Dupont Circle to Battery Kemble Park

Glover is a sinuous, winding park, extending from Van Ness St NW in the Tenleytown area down to the western border of Georgetown University. Its 180 tree-

MEET TAI SHAN

DC's most famous celebrity is more popular than any president or politician and he isn't even human. He's Tai Shan, a black-and-white ball of fluff, otherwise known as a giant panda cub. Born in the summer of 2005 at the National Zoo, Tai Shan made his public debut in December 2005. He was a smash before his fans even met him – 13,000 free tickets to see him were snapped up online in two hours; thousands more admirers braved subzero temps for weeks to line up at the zoo's ticket booth hours before it opened in hopes of scoring one of the 60 tickets handed out each day. And more than 200,000 people across the nation voted on the cub's name, Tai Shan (tie-SHON), which means peaceful mountain. A rambunctious bundle of fur, Tai Shan is also the star of his own show. Millions check out his 'panda cam' each day. Go to www.nationalzoo.si.edu/Animals/GiantPandas to see for yourself.

Tai Shan is definitely a popular little guy, but he's also pretty special. He is the zoo's first surviving panda cub, born to resident zoo pandas Mai Mei Xiang and Tian Tian, and only the fourth born nationwide (there has been at least one more since).

'(He) is the culmination of a decade of collaborative research between the United States and China,' David Wildt, chairman of the Zoo's Reproductive Sciences Dept, told *Smithsonian Magazine.*

covered acres follow the course of little Foundry Branch Creek, along which runs a pretty nature trail. Another good place to access this trail is Reservoir Rd, which crosses the park just north of the university. Further west, skinny Battery Kemble Park, about a mile long but less than a quarter-mile wide, separates the wealthy Foxhall and Palisades neighborhoods of far northwestern DC. Managed by the National Park Service, the park preserves the site of a little two-gun battery that helped defend western DC against Confederate troops during the Civil War.

FORT STEVENS PARK

Map pp290-1
www.nps.gov/rocr/ftcircle/stevens.htm; 13th & Quackenbos Sts NW; E2, E3 or E4 from Friendship Heights or bus 71 or 72 from Gallery Pl-Chinatown

In a daring raid on July 11, 1864, Confederate General Jubal Early attacked Fort Stevens, the northernmost of the defensive ramparts ringing the city. A small but fierce battle raged until Early's men were forced back across the Potomac. Abraham Lincoln himself was drawn into the shooting: the president, observing the battle from Fort Stevens' parapet, popped his head up so many times that Oliver Wendell Holmes, Jr, then a Union captain, yelled: 'Get down, you damn fool, before you get shot!' The fort has been partially restored. Forty-one Union men who died in the Fort Stevens' defense were buried at tiny **Battleground National Cemetery** (6625 Georgia Ave), a half-mile north of the fort. The fort – which was

dedicated by Lincoln – has been partially restored. You can wander around in daylight hours to see the markers and plaques honoring DC's defenders.

HILLWOOD MUSEUM & GARDENS

Map pp290-1
☎ 202-686-8500; www.hillwoodmuseum.org; 4155 Linnean Ave NW; adult/child/senior $12/7/10; ☉ 9:30am-5pm Tue-Sat, closed Jan; Ⓜ Van Ness-UDC or Cleveland Park

Housing the biggest collection of Russian imperial art outside Russia itself, Hillwood is the former estate of heiress Marjorie Merriweather Post (of Post cereal fame), who was married to the ambassador to the USSR in the 1930s. By all accounts a formidable woman, Post convinced Stalin and the Soviets to sell her lots of Czarist swag, and her collection includes furniture, paintings, exquisite Fabergé eggs and jewelry. The 25-acre estate features lovely gardens with notable azalea and orchid collections (as well as Post's dog cemetery), a greenhouse and a museum shop. A café serves Russian treats (borscht, blintzes) and afternoon tea. Reservations are required to visit.

KAHLIL GIBRAN MEMORIAL GARDEN

Map pp300-1
3100 Massachusetts Ave NW; Ⓜ Dupont Circle

In the midst of the wooded ravine known as Normanstone Park, the Kahlil Gibran garden memorializes the arch-deity of soupy spiritual poetry. Its centerpieces are a moody bust of the Lebanese mystic

BEASTIES ON THE BUTTRESSES: THE NATIONAL CATHEDRAL GARGOYLES

Gargoyles serve a practical function: they're rainwater spouts – their name derives from the French *gargouille*, to gargle. They also serve numerous spiritual functions: they warn churchgoers of hell's terrors, ward off the devil's assaults on the holy and represent pagan deities long ago assimilated by Christian monotheism. They reached their apotheosis on European churches like Notre Dame, but the National Cathedral has raised the gargoyle tradition to comical new heights. On its southern facade perch dogs and cats, boars and donkeys, and beasts wholly imaginary (including a dragon skeleton with a snake lunging from its eye socket). On the western side loom the god Pan, a feasting glutton and a reading elephant. Elsewhere are Darth Vader, a stonemason leering at the Cathedral school girls, a placard-toting hippie, a sobbing tortoise, and caricatures of craftspeople and clergy associated with the cathedral. Like everything else in the National Cathedral, each gargoyle is a handcrafted original, and many were 'donated' by individual supporters of the century-long cathedral-building project. The cathedral hands out three flyers that guide you around its gargoyles and grotesques. Binoculars help. Should you feel the urge to adopt a beast, go to the cathedral's downstairs gift shop for miniature replicas of its critters, plus stuffed gargoyles (for your baby goth), garden gargoyles (to eat the squirrels), blow-up life-size gargoyles, gargoyle jewelry, gargoyle lollipops ($4) and carve-your-own-gargoyle kits ($23).

and a star-shaped fountain surrounded by flowers, hedges and limestone benches engraved with various Gibranisms: 'We live only to discover beauty. All else is a form of waiting.' From a trailhead just north of the garden, you can hop onto trails that link to both Rock Creek Park and Glover Archbold Park.

NATIONAL MUSEUM OF HEALTH & MEDICINE Map pp290-1
☎ 202-782-2200; http://nmhm.washingtondc.museum; 6825 16th St NW, Walter Reed Army Medical Center Bldg 54; admission free; ⏰ 10am-5:30pm; Ⓜ Takoma
Forensics junkies love this 'Library of Congress of the dead,' as described by science writer Gina Kolata, which contains both straightforward scientific exhibits and freakish medical oddities. Visitors can see

TEA FOR TOURS
Do you take your tea with lemon and sugar, or with a fabulous city view? Two afternoons a week, the National Cathedral's Tour & Tea Program (☎ 202-537-8993; adult/child $22/14; ⏰ 1:30pm Tue & Wed) opens up the high West Tower for high tea, following an informative tour of the cathedral and grounds. The tour provides an in-depth look at the cathedral's art, architecture and history. Afterwards, enjoy tea and scones in the beautiful, wood-paneled St Paul Room. Located in the Pilgrim Observation Gallery, it provides magnificent views on a clear day. Reservations are required.

antique microscopes and surgical instruments, as well as exhibits on renowned scientists and research initiatives. What you come here for, though, is much more thrilling: cannonball-shredded leg bones removed from Civil War soldiers, the bullet that killed Lincoln and fragments of his shattered skull, President Garfield's spinal column, and many other preserved body parts.

The temporary exhibits are eclectic, sometimes downright bizarre, but never dull. Recent shows included an exhibition commemorating the 125th anniversary of the assassination of James Garfield, the nation's 20th (and rather obscure) president.

NATIONAL ZOOLOGICAL PARK
Map pp300-1
☎ 202-673-4800; www.nationalzoo.si.edu; 3001 Connecticut Ave NW; admission free; ⏰ grounds 6am-8pm May-Sep, 6am-6pm Oct-Apr, buildings 10am-6pm May-Sep, 10am-4:30pm Oct-Apr; Ⓜ Woodley Park-Zoo/Adams Morgan
The latest effort in the National Zoo's modernization plan, the Asia Trail, opened in September 2006. The centerpiece of the area is the newly renovated Fuji-film–sponsored Giant Panda Habitat. The enlarged habitat nearly doubles the outdoor playground for pandas Mei Xiang, Tian Tian and cute cub Tai Shan. It attempts to mimic the panda's natural Chinese habitat with cooling rocks and fog machine.

Among the best recognized but rarest animals in the world, giant pandas have come to symbolize endangered species and conservation efforts. Only about 1000 individuals survive in the mountain forests of central China. They specialize in eating bamboo, so they are suffering from the destruction of the temperate bamboo forest in the mountains of central China. Another 120 are in Chinese breeding facilities and zoos, and about 20 live in zoos outside China.

The Smithsonian Institution zoo was founded in 1889 and beautifully planned by Frederick Law Olmsted, designer of New York's Central Park. The zoo's 130 acres follow the natural contours of its woodland-canyon setting. It is intensively involved in worldwide ecological study and species-preservation work, and its exhibits are noted for natural-habitat settings. Tamarins scamper uncaged through the treetops, piranhas hunt in a simulated Amazon and tigers snooze on terraced grass hillsides.

The zoo's higher path, the Olmsted Walk, passes the American prairie exhibit, panda house, and the elephant and giraffe, primate and reptile houses. Nearby is **Think Tank**, a wonderful collection of interactive exhibits on animal intelligence and social structure aimed at the six-to-12 set.

Down the trail a bit are open-air lion and tiger enclosures and the dark **Bat Cave**, a perennial kids' favorite. Big cat fans will love the cheetahs' display, What's for Dinner?, where overly honest scales inform you who would like to feast on you. ('100lb to 150lb – you're a female warthog. A pack of lions could finish you off in an hour.')

The lower Valley Trail passes the bird house, seal tanks and wetlands displays. At its eastern end is **Amazonia**, a mini-ecosystem complete with aquariums and a conservatory. Piranhas and magnificent fish swim in the water, and the trees are filled with epiphytes, ferns, birds and monkeys.

To beat the zoo crowds, visit early morning on a cloudy, cool, even slightly rainy day. Such weather not only keeps human herds at bay, it encourages heat-sensitive or shy animals to venture outside their dens.

US NAVAL OBSERVATORY

Map pp300-1

☎ 202-762-1438; www.usno.navy.mil; 3450 Massachusetts Ave NW; admission free; ☯ tours by reservation 8:30pm Mon

Its entrance framed by a pair of stately white ship's anchors, the US Naval Observatory was created in the 1800s 'to determine the positions and motions of celestial objects, provide astronomical data, measure the Earth's rotation, and maintain the Master Clock for the US.' Modern DC's light pollution prevents important observational work these days, but its cesium-beam atomic clock is still the source of all standard time in the US. Tours let you peek through telescopes, yak with astronomers and learn about the Master Clock. They fill up weeks in advance, may be cancelled at any time and are only offered on select Mondays at 8:30pm, so reserve early – check the website or phone. At other times the observatory's closed to the public. On observatory grounds above Massachusetts Ave is the official **Vice President's Residence** (Admiral's House), which is closed to the public. Driving is the best way to reach the observatory.

WASHINGTON DOLLS' HOUSE & TOY MUSEUM Map pp290-1

☎ 202-244-0024, 202-363-6400; www.dollshouse museum.com; 5236 44th St NW; adult/child/senior $4/2/3; ☯ 10am-5pm Tue-Sat, noon-5pm Sun; Ⓜ Friendship Heights

This quirky museum is based on the belief that dolls' houses provide a history of architecture and decorative arts, while antique toys reflect social history. It displays a marvelous collection of antique Victorian dolls' houses and toys: a tiny Capitol; mansions complete with tiny china and linens; and amazingly detailed castles. The museum's miniatures shop sells dolls, accessories and kits so that you can build your own dolls' house.

WASHINGTON NATIONAL CATHEDRAL Map pp300-1

☎ 202-537-6200; www.nationalcathedral.org; Massachusetts & Wisconsin Aves NW; admission by donation, audio tour per person $5; ☯ 10am-5:30pm Mon-Fri, to 8pm May-Sep, 10am-4:30pm Sat, 8am-6:30pm Sun, tours 10am-3:15pm Mon-Sat, 12:45-2:30pm Sun, main service 11am Sun; Ⓜ Tenleytown or bus 30, 32, 34 or 36

A national cathedral in a country premised upon the separation of church and state is an unusual idea. So, by definition, the National Cathedral, run by the Episcopal

TRANSPORTATION

Metro Arlington is well served by Metro, including Orange Line stops (Rosslyn, Courthouse, Clarendon, Virginia Sq and Ballston) and Blue Line stops (Rosslyn, Arlington Cemetery, Pentagon, Pentagon City, Crystal City and Ronald Reagan Washington National Airport).

Parking Street parking is easier in Arlington than in DC, but still not a given. There is a cheap garage at Pentagon City mall.

diocese but paying tribute to many faiths and peoples, is an unusual place.

Teddy Roosevelt laid the cornerstone of this majestic Gothic cathedral in 1908, and construction didn't stop until 1990. Its pale limestone walls, flying buttresses, intricate carving and exquisite stained glass (all intended to rival Europe's great cathedrals) have won for the cathedral, in many critics' eyes, the title of the country's most beautiful church. Martin Luther King, Jr gave his last Sunday sermon here; now it's the standard place for state funerals and other high-profile events.

Take the elevator to the **tower overlook** for expansive city views; posted maps explain what you see. Downstairs in the main sanctuary, chapels honor the Apollo astronauts, MLK, Abe Lincoln, and abstract ideas like peace and justice. The endearing **Children's Chapel** is filled with images of real and imaginary animals. Downstairs in the crypt, famous folks like Helen Keller and Woodrow Wilson are buried. Outside, walk through the charming **Bishop's Garden**, a small English-style garden with winding paths that lend a mood of solitude.

The 11am Sunday service features lovely choral music and a 10-bell peal of the carillon afterwards. Cathedral choristers sing Evensong at 5:30pm Tuesday to Thursday during the school year.

ROCK CREEK PARK

Map pp290-1

☎ 202-282-1063; www.nps.gov/rocr; Ⓜ Cleveland Park or Woodley Park-Zoo/Adams Morgan

Dropping a slice of wilderness into urban DC, Rock Creek Park begins at the Potomac's east bank near Georgetown and extends to and beyond the northern city boundaries. Narrow in its southern

stretches, where it hews to the winding course of Rock Creek, it broadens into wide, peaceful parklands in Upper Northwest DC. Terrific trails extend along its entire length. Its boundaries enclose Civil War forts and dense forest, recreational facilities (including even a theater) and wildflower-strewn fields. Established in 1890, Rock Creek Park is one of the country's finest urban parks, and as you walk in its midst you may forget you're in a city altogether.

A great first stop is the **Nature Center & Planetarium** (Map pp290–1; ☎ 202-426-6829; off Military Rd; ◷ 9am-5pm Wed-Sun Sep-May, daily Jun-Aug). Besides informative exhibits on park flora, fauna and history, it has two little nature trails and tons of information on the park, plus maps and field guides to the city. A fun 'touch table' is set up for small children, and rangers lead child-oriented nature walks featuring cool activities like poking around in the mud for salamanders.

A bit north of here, on the west side of Beach Dr, is the **Joaquin Miller Cabin**, a little log house that once sheltered the famed nature poet. Miller built the cabin, originally located in Arlington, in 1883 to serve as his writer's retreat.

Further south, the park's western **Soapstone Valley Park** extension, off Connecticut Ave at Albemarle St NW, preserves quarries where the area's original Algonquin Indian residents dug soapstone for shaping their cookware.

Alongside the creek, the 1820 **Pierce Mill** (Map pp290–1; ☎ 202-426-6908; Tilden St; ◷ 9am-5pm Wed-Sun Sep-May, daily Jun-Aug) is a small, beautiful fieldstone building that was once a water-driven gristmill. Next door, local artists display work in a 19th-century carriage house known as the **Rock Creek Gallery** (☎ 202-244-2482; 2401 Tilden St; ◷ 11am-4:30pm Thu-Sun). The gallery holds poetry readings and art classes, and sells handmade jewelry and crafts.

In summer, pick up an events calendar at the **Carter Barron Amphitheater** (Map pp290–1; ☎ 202-426-6837; www.nps.gov/rocr/cbarron; 16th & Kennedy Sts NW). It's a wonderful 4000-seat outdoor theater where concerts and plays, many of which are free, are held on summer evenings. See also Entertainment (p192).

Sights

UPPER NORTHWEST DC

REMEMBERING AMERICA'S FALLEN HEROES – VISITING ARLINGTON NATIONAL CEMETERY

The 612 acres and 245,000 graves of **Arlington National Cemetery** (Map pp306–7; ☎ 703-607-8052, Tourmobile 888-868-7707; www.arlingtoncemetery.net; admission free, Tourmobile adult/child $6/3; ☷ 8am-5pm Oct-Mar, 8am-7pm Apr-Oct; Ⓜ Arlington Cemetery) are a somber counterpoint to the soaring monuments to US history just across the Potomac. It's the burial ground for military personnel and their families, the dead of every war the US has fought since the Revolution, and American leaders, such as JFK, Oliver Wendell Holmes and Medgar Evers.

At the end of Memorial Dr, the first site you'll see is the **Women in Military Service for America Memorial**, honoring women who have served in the armed forces in times of war and peace, from the Revolution onward. The memorial includes an education center and theater.

On the slopes above are the **Kennedy gravesites**. Near the eternal flame that marks the grave of John F Kennedy lie gravestones for Jacqueline Kennedy Onassis and their two children who died in infancy, and Robert Kennedy. The site is one that JFK admired just days before his assassination.

The **Tomb of the Unknowns** holds unidentified bodies from WWI, WWII and the Korean War. Soldiers march before it 24 hours a day, performing an impressive ceremonial changing of the guard every hour (every half-hour mid-March to September). For several years after the Vietnam War, the US government had no 'unknown' Vietnam War soldier to inter here. All recovered remains were identified, albeit slowly, via new forensic techniques. Finally, in 1984, an appropriately anonymous set of remains was located, and Defense Secretary Caspar Weinberger approved their burial in the tomb.

But in 1998, the family of Michael J Blassie, an Air Force lieutenant shot down near An Loc in 1972, discovered via DNA testing that the corpse was that of their lost relative. Blassie was removed in the first-ever Unknowns disinterment and reburied in Missouri. The Vietnam crypt at Arlington, meanwhile, stands permanently empty.

Other memorials include the **Confederate Monument**, the tomb of **Pierre L'Enfant**, the **mast of the battleship USS Maine**, the **Challenger memorial** and the **Nurses' Memorial**. The **Iwo Jima Memorial**, dedicated to the Marine Corps, is on the cemetery's northern fringes. You can also check out the graves of boxer **Joe Louis**, explorer **Rear-Admiral Richard Byrd Jr** and **President William Taft**. Funerals are held here daily.

The remains of Civil War forts are among the park's most fascinating sites. During the war, Washington was, essentially, a massive urban armory and supply house for the Union Army. Its position near the Confederate lines made it vulnerable to attack, so forts were hastily erected on the city's high points. By spring 1865, 68 forts and 93 batteries bristled on hilltops around DC.

Fort DeRussy is one of the best preserved forts, with its moat and rammed-earth parapet still apparent. Reach the fort by following the trail from Military Rd and Oregon Ave NW. The remains of other forts – Battery Kemble near the Potomac, Fort Reno, Fort Stevens and on to Fort Bunker Hill in Northeast DC – are also administered by Rock Creek Park, and some earthworks remain visible.

Overlooking Rock Creek in Cleveland Park is the **Klingle Mansion** (Map pp300–1; ☎ 202-282-1063; 3545 Williamsburg Lane; ☷ 7:45am-4:15pm Mon-Fri). Built in 1823 by Joshua Pierce, the 10-room Pennsylvania Dutch fieldstone house is now park headquarters, and is open for information and permits for special events.

ARLINGTON

Eating p164; Sleeping p238

Just a hop, skip and a jump across the Potomac from Georgetown, Arlington has always been popular with young professionals wanting the kind of spacious house and lawn one cannot find in the city without sacrificing proximity to the hedonistic pleasures of DC at night. The ever-changing city can be a fun place, with a slew of old favorites and an assortment of newbie restaurants, bars and billiard halls.

Arlington absorbs the spillover from the capital: it is home to federal agencies that expanded beyond the walls of their downtown buildings; government contractors who aim to be near their clients (or 'Beltway bandits' as they are commonly known); bureaucrats who work in the city but don't want to live there; even ethnic enclaves that settled in Washington, but dispersed as they assimilated. Arlington's environment is the same suburban sprawl that one finds throughout the United States, but with a sense of national importance and political awareness that might not exist elsewhere.

Orientation

Arlington's neighborhoods are clustered around Metro stops just across the Potomac River from Northwest DC.

Rosslyn is a bureaucratic, steel and glass district in the north of town, directly across the Francis Scott Key Bridge from Georgetown. From here, Metro's Orange Line heads west, with stops at Courthouse, Clarendon, Virginia Sq and Ballston: all blossoming neighborhoods with diverse populations and small but lively food and drink scenes.

Metro's Blue Line turns south from Rosslyn and follows the Potomac River.

In addition to Arlington Cemetery and Pentagon, Blue Line stops at Pentagon City and Crystal City: both corporate areas with hotels, high-rises and shopping malls (lots of conveniences but not much character).

Ronald Reagan Washington National Airport is in the southern corner of Arlington on the Potomac River.

Drivers can reach Arlington by crossing the Francis Scott Key Bridge from Georgetown, as well as the Theodore Roosevelt, Arlington Memorial and 14th St (I-395) Bridges further south.

ARLINGTON HOUSE

Map pp306-7

☎ 703-557-0613; www.arlingtoncemetery.net /arlhouse; admission free; ☽ 9:30am-4:30pm; Ⓜ Arlington Cemetery

Robert E Lee resided in this gracious home set high on the hills overlooking the Potomac River. His home and part of his 1100-acre property were confiscated after he left to command the Confederate Army of Virginia, and Union dead were buried around the house to spite him. After the war, the family sued the federal government for reimbursement: the government paid off the Lees, and Arlington Cemetery was born on their old lands. The historic house has been open since 1817 for public tours, and serves as a tribute to the general who earned the respect of Northerners and Southerners alike.

DEA MUSEUM

Map pp306-7

United States Drug Enforcement Agency Museum; ☎ 202-307-3463; www.deamuseum.org; 7200 Army Navy Drive; admission free; ☽ 10am-4pm Mon-Fri; Ⓜ Pentagon City

Those interested in (or disgusted by) the never-ending US War on Drugs might enjoy a visit to the United States Drug Enforcement Agency (DEA) Museum (the latter group will only appreciate it in a twisted way for its full frontal propaganda). Exhibits range from Target America, which tries badly to link terrorism and drugs together, to the slightly more thoughtful, and quite elaborate, timeline display on the history of drugs in America, but the overall theme is pretty damn clear: drugs are bad and you should want to send users and pushers to prison for long periods of time. In the museum's defense, this is the only place in official Washington where you can see a variety of drug paraphernalia – from old rolling papers to pipes – on display, which can be fun. Kids will like the gift shop, where they can purchase 'official' DEA badges and other law enforcement gear.

FREEDOM PARK

Map p299

1101 Wilson Blvd; Ⓜ Rosslyn

Paying tribute to a free press, Freedom Park features a memorial honoring journalists killed on the job. Icons from political struggles around the world are on display, including chunks of the Berlin Wall.

GEORGE WASHINGTON MEMORIAL PARKWAY Map pp306-7

☎ 703-289-2500; www.nps.gov/gwmp; Ⓜ Rosslyn

The 25-mile Virginia portion of this highway honors the first US president. It winds past recreation areas and memorials all the way south to his old estate at Mt Vernon. A national parkland, it's lined with remnants of Washington's life and works, such as his old Patowmack Company

---

TRANSPORTATION

Metro The Yellow Line goes to Braddock Rd and King St further south. Both are several blocks west of most of the Alexandria destinations, including Old Town.

Bus On weekends, a free shuttle bus runs between King St Metro station and Old Town Market Sq (☽ 7pm-midnight Fri, 10am-midnight Sat, 11am-10pm Sun)

Parking Street parking is not impossible but be sure to watch the two-hour time limit (even if you are not at a meter).

canal (in Great Falls National Park) and parks that were once part of his farmlands (Riverside Park, Fort Hunt Park). The road is a pleasant alternative to the traffic-choked highway arteries further away from the river.

The 18.5 mile **Mt Vernon Trail** parallels the parkway from Francis Scott Key Bridge to Mount Vernon – it's paved and perfect for biking. Along the way, **Lady Bird Johnson Park** remembers the First Lady who tried to beautify the capital via greenery-planting campaigns and includes a memorial grove dedicated to her husband. Just north of Ronald Reagan Washington National Airport, **Gravelly Point** provides a vantage point for watching the planes take off and land; or check out the natural airborne creatures at the **Roaches Run Waterfowl Sanctuary**.

NATIONAL AIR FORCE MEMORIAL

Map pp306-7

www.airforcememorial.org; ☽ 24hr; Ⓜ Arlington Cemetery

Overlooking the Pentagon and adjacent to Arlington National Cemetery, this new memorial opened in time to celebrate the 60th birthday of the United States Air Force. It pays tribute to the millions of men and women who served in the air force and its predecessor organizations.

PENTAGON Map pp306-7

☎ 703-695-1776; www.pentagon.gov; ☽ closed to public; Ⓜ Pentagon

The US Department of Defense is housed in what may be the world's biggest office building, the Pentagon. This massive building was constructed in just 16 months during WWII and was completed on January 15, 1943. About 25,000 people work in this massive polygon, which has more than a dozen miles of corridors and five sides surrounding a 5-acre courtyard. This formidable edifice appears impenetrable, an impression that was proven wrong on September 11, 2001, when American Airlines flight 77 crashed into the side of the building. Between the passengers on the airplane and workers in the building, 184 people were killed in this shocking tragedy. Since then the Pentagon building is open only for pre-arranged group tours (be sure to call at least several weeks in advance). Virtual tours are online at www.defenselink.mil/pubs/pentagon.

PENTAGON MEMORIAL

Map pp306-7

☎ 703-695-1776; http://memorial.pentagon.mil; admission free; Ⓜ Pentagon

In the fall of 2005 the Pentagon unveiled a new memorial to the victims of the attack on the Pentagon on September 11, 2001. The poignant memorial plaza occupies almost 2 acres on the west side of the Pentagon building, representing each of the 184 victims with a pool of light and an inscription. The memorial design is symbolic down to the details: for example, memorials representing victims who were in the Pentagon are situated so a visitor sees the engraved name in the same view as the building; memorials to victims who were on flight 77 face an alternative direction, so the background is only sky. The Age Wall on the plaza's western edge grows in proportion to the ages of the victims, who ranged from three to 71.

THEODORE ROOSEVELT ISLAND

Map p299

☎ 703-289-2500; www.nps.gov/this; admission free; ☽ dawn-dusk; Ⓜ Rosslyn

This 91-acre wooded island, in the Potomac off Rosslyn, is a wilderness preserve honoring the conservation-minded 26th US president. A large memorial plaza and statue of Teddy dominate the island's center, and trails and boardwalks snake around the shorelines. The island's swampy fringes shelter birds, raccoons and other small animals. A fine place for a hike, it offers great views of the Kennedy Center and Georgetown University across the river. The island is accessible from the Mt Vernon Trail and is a convenient stop on a long bike ride or jog. Note that bikes aren't permitted on the island itself; lock them up in the parking lot.

WASHINGTON & OLD DOMINION TRAIL

W&OD; ☎ 703-729-0596; www.nvrpa.org/wod; admission free; ☽ dawn-dusk; Ⓜ East Falls Church

Despite its dense suburbs, northern Virginia is laced with hiking and biking trails. The 45-mile paved Washington & Old Dominion Trail follows an old railway bed from Shirlington, in southern Arlington, to Purcellville, in Virginia's Alleghany foothills. (For the truly ambitious, it's a short jump from here to the 2000 miles of Appalachian Trail going south to Georgia and north to Maine.) The scenic, well-maintained trail allows horseback riding between Vienna and Purcellville. Exit right from the East Falls Church Metro station.

ALEXANDRIA

Eating p166; Shopping p221; Sleeping p238

Alexandria is buzzing these days. Everyone in DC is talking about its restaurants, and Washingtonians are making the trek out to dine at some of the hottest spots around. They find its laid-back charm so alluring they usually return the following weekend. Partake in an afternoon of antique shopping in Old Town, stay for dinner, then linger over cocktails at a swank new lounge well into the night.

Founded in 1699 (pre-dating DC), Alexandria was once a very bustling port city that rivaled New York and Boston; now it plays up its colonial roots for all its worth. The restored Old Town district retains its pre-Revolutionary charm, and many 18th-century houses and colonial sights are open to the public for touring. Old buildings and port warehouses hold upscale restaurants, pubs, shops and hostelries. Just up the street from George Washington's Mt Vernon Estate (p246), this is one of the DC area's most established, and storied, satellite communities, rich in history and charisma.

Head to the 100 block of Prince St, called Captain's Row, one of two remaining cobblestone streets in Alexandria. The cobblestones served as the ballast of English ships and were possibly laid by Hessian prisoners of war. It's lined with lovely private homes, many built for sea captains.

Gentry Row, the 200 block of Prince St, is named after the number of imposing private dwellings. The Athenaeum (Map p311; ☎ 703-548-0035; www.alexandria-athenaeum.org; 201 Prince St; ☷ 11am-3pm Wed-Fri, 1-3pm Sat & Sun Mar-Oct) was home to the Bank of the Old Dominion. Now the Greek-revival building is an art gallery.

Orientation

Alexandria is south of Arlington along the Potomac River. The main streets dividing Alexandria are north–south Washington St

(George Washington Memorial Parkway) and east–west King St. Addresses are numbered by the 100s (eg Cameron to Queen is the 200 block north).

The historic area, Old Town, is a square bounded by the King St Metro to the west, Slaters Lane to the north, the Potomac River to the east and the Beltway to the south. You will discover that most historic sights lie between Washington St and the river.

ALEXANDRIA BLACK HISTORY RESOURCE CENTER

Map p311

☎ 703-838-4356; www.alexblackhistory.org; 638 N Alfred St; admission free; ☷ 10am-4pm Tue-Sat, 1-5pm Sun; Ⓜ Braddock Rd

Paintings, photographs, books and other memorabilia documenting the Black experience in Alexandria are on display at this small resource center (enter from Wythe St). Pick up a brochure for self-guided walking tours of important Alexandria Black-history sites. In the next-door annex, the **Watson Reading Room** has a wealth of books and documents on African American topics. Operated by the museum, the **African American Heritage Park** (Holland Lane) is worth a stop to see headstones from a 19th-century Black cemetery.

CHRIST CHURCH

Map p311

☎ 703-549-1450; www.historicchristchurch .org; 118 N Washington St; admission by donation; ☷ 9am-4pm Mon-Sat, 2-4pm Sun; 🚐 Old Town shuttle from King St Metro

Since 1773, this red-brick Georgian-style church has welcomed worshipers, including George Washington and Robert E Lee. The interesting churchyard cemetery contains the mass grave of Confederate soldiers.

FORT WARD MUSEUM & HISTORIC SITE

☎ 703-838-4848; www.fortward.org; 4301 W Braddock Rd; admission free; ☺ 9am-dusk, museum 9am-4pm Tue-Sat, noon-5pm Sun; 🚌 Old Town shuttle from King St Metro

Fort Ward, northwest of Old Town along Braddock Rd, is the best-restored of the 162 Civil War forts known as the Defenses of Washington. The Northwest Bastion of the fort has been completely restored, and the remaining earthwork walls give a good sense of the defenses' original appearance. The on-site museum features exhibits on Civil War topics.

FRIENDSHIP FIREHOUSE MUSEUM

Map p311

☎ 703-838-3891; www.friendshipfirehouse.org; 107 S Alfred St; admission free; ☺ 10am-4pm Fri & Sat, 1-4pm Sun; 🚌 Old Town shuttle from King St Metro

This 1855 Italianate firehouse displays historic firefighting gear – a great draw for kids. Local legend has it that George Washington helped found this volunteer fire company, served as its captain and even paid for a new fire engine.

GADSBY'S TAVERN MUSEUM

Map p311

☎ 703-838-4242; www.gadsbystavern.org; 134 N Royal St; adult/child $4/2; ☺ 10am-5pm Tue-Sat, 1-5pm Sun & Mon Apr-Oct, 11am-4pm Wed-Sat, 1-4pm Sun Nov-Mar; 🚌 Old Town shuttle from King St Metro

Once a real tavern (operated by John Gadsby from 1796 to 1808), this building now houses a museum demonstrating the prominent role of the tavern in 18th-century Alexandria. As the center of local political, business and social life, the tavern was frequented by anybody who was anybody, including George Washington, Thomas Jefferson and the Marquis de Lafayette. The rooms are restored to their 18th-century appearance.

GEORGE WASHINGTON MASONIC NATIONAL MEMORIAL Map p311

☎ 703-683-2007; www.gwmemorial.org; 101 Callahan Dr at King St; admission free; ☺ 9am-5pm, tours on the hour; Ⓜ King St

Alexandria's most prominent landmark features a fine view from its 333ft tower, where you can see the Capitol, Mount Vernon and the Potomac River. It is modeled after the lighthouse in Alexandria, and honors the first president (who was initiated into the Masons in Fredericksburg in 1752 and later became Worshipful Master of Alexandria Lodge No 22). Artifacts of Washington's life and a striking bronze statue do the job.

LEE-FENDALL HOUSE

Map p311

☎ 703-548-1789; www.leefendallhouse.org; 614 Oronoco St; adult/child $4/2; ☺ 10am-4pm Tue-Sat, 1-4pm Sun, tours on the hour; Ⓜ Braddock Rd

Between 1785 and 1903 generations of the Lee family lived in this architecturally impressive house. Guided tours show the restored house as it probably was in the 1850s and 1860s, showcasing Lee family heirlooms and personal effects, and period furniture. The Georgian-style town house across the street (607 Oronoco St; ☺ closed to public) was Robert E Lee's childhood home from 1810.

STABLER-LEADBEATER APOTHECARY MUSEUM

Map p311

☎ 703-836-3713; www.apothecary.org; 105-107 S Fairfax St; adult/child $4/2; ☺ 10am-4pm Mon-Sat, Sun 1-5pm; 🚌 Old Town shuttle from King St Metro

In 1792 Edward Stabler opened his apothecary – a family business that would operate for 141 years. In 1933 the Depression forced the shop to close; the doors were simply locked, shutting history inside. Over 8000 medical objects and fixtures remained in place. Now the shop is a museum, its shelves lined with 900 beautiful hand-blown apothecary bottles and strange old items like Martha Washington's Scouring Compound.

TORPEDO FACTORY ART CENTER

Map p311

☎ 703-838-4565; www.torpedofactory.org; 105 N Union St; admission free; ☺ 10am-5pm; 🚌 Old Town shuttle from King St Metro

Built during WWI to manufacture torpedoes, this complex today manufactures art. At the center of a revamped waterfront with a lively marina, shops and residences, it houses nearly 200 artists and craftspeople who sell their creations directly from their studios.

The **Alexandria Archaeology Museum** is also housed here. This is the laboratory where archaeologists clean up and catalog the artifacts they have unearthed at local digs. First-hand observation of the work, excavation exhibits and hands-on discovery kits allow visitors to witness and participate in the reconstruction of Alexandria's history.

US PATENT & TRADEMARK OFFICE MUSEUM Map p311

☎ 571-272-0095; 600 Dulany St, Madison Bldg; admission free; 🕙 9am-5pm Mon-Fri, noon-5pm Sat; 🚌 Old Town shuttle from King St Metro

This nearly new museum tells the history of the United States patent. Step inside to see where the story started in 1917 in Memphis, TN. That's when a wholesale grocer named Clarence Saunders invented and patented what he called 'Self-Servicing' stores, now commonly known as supermarkets. Incidentally, he went from rags to riches and almost back to rags again, but you'll have to visit the museum to get the rest of the story, along with displays depicting the world's other most famous and influential patents.

BETHESDA

Eating p167; Shopping p222

Beguiling Bethesda personifies Pleasantville, USA, that quintessential American dream suburb where the streets are safe, the schools are good and the neighbors are all friends. There's no question Bethesda, Maryland is a wealthy enclave: that's evident from the sprawling estates where elegant homes are tucked neatly away behind white picket fences and manicured hedges, but Bethesda is far from snobby. College kids, yuppies, bartenders and young professionals with two kids, a BMW and a shaggy dog all co-exist in one of DC's favorite satellite communities.

If you're looking to eat, sleep or shop outside of the city for a few nights, Bethesda is a great option. With a Metro stop right in town and more restaurants than you could possibly imagine, plus more plentiful parking and a small town vibe to its trendy boutique lined streets, you have the nearly perfect package.

Orientation

Old Georgetown Rd and Wisconsin Ave are the two major thoroughfares through Bethesda. Downtown Bethesda refers to the west end of town, especially around Woodmont Triangle and Bethesda Row. Cordell Ave is also home to many restaurants and bars.

BETHESDA ROW & WOODMONT TRIANGLE

Map p310

Bethesda & Woodmont Aves; Ⓜ Bethesda

It's not exactly a triangle, but the intersection of Woodmont and Bethesda Aves, anchored by a giant Barnes & Noble bookstore, is happening. Bethesda Row (as Bethesda Ave is affectionately dubbed) is filled with unique boutiques and galleries selling everything from handcrafted knobby wood tables to designer children's apparel. Head north on Woodmont Ave and you'll discover **Bethesda Row Cinema** (p195), a wonderful art-house movie theater, and hundreds of restaurants hailing from every corner of the globe. At night the place buzzes with young revelers flocking from Irish pub to sports bar, to all-American breweries. A free trolley circles through this part of Bethesda until 2am on weekends, making barhopping easy even when it's cold out.

CAPITAL CRESCENT TRAIL

Map p299 & Map p310

www.cctrail.org; Ⓜ Bethesda

Running between Bethesda and Georgetown, the constantly evolving Capital Crescent Trail is a fabulous (and very popular) jogging and biking route. Built on an abandoned railroad bed, the 11-mile trail is paved and is a great leisurely day trip through woody parkland – it links up with the C&O Canal Towpath (p82) and paths through Rock Creek Park (p121). In Bethesda the trail begins at the Wisconsin Ave Tunnel, on Wisconsin Ave just south of Old Georgetown Rd (it is clearly marked).

Walking & Biking Tours

Walking & Biking Tours

Washington, DC, is unusual for its large amounts of green space, its lack of towering buildings and its miles and miles of off-road walking and biking trails. Its small size and planned layout make it easy to navigate by your own leg power: by foot and by bicycle are the best ways to get around many of the neighborhoods.

This chapter provides some ideal and unusual ways to see Washington's most talked-about sites. The White House Walk examines the presidential palace from every angle, but does not skim over the historic homes, pretty parks and notable museums in the area. The Monumental Bike Ride provides a spectacular view of Washington's most famous monuments, plus a few you might have missed if you were in your car.

The other walking tours dive deeper into the neighborhoods that may not be on every visitor's itinerary, but that constitute DC's heart. Strolling along Embassy Row allows an appreciation for the architecture and atmosphere of DC's diplomatic center. The Georgetown Walk-Around explores the storied neighborhood's historical roots, which range from urban Black to upper class. The Night Crawl gives visitors a chance to taste the best of DC nightlife, with drinking, dancing and dining venues to suit all tastes. And the Shaw Shuffle dives deep into the heart and soul of DC's African American history.

So lace up your walking shoes and hit the road.

EMBASSY ROW

Flags of every shape and color fly above the stately mansions along Massachusetts Ave's Embassy Row. It's an area that is unique in the nation for its combination of distinctive architecture and international flavor. Here tongues of 100 nations are heard, streets are crowded with sleek sedans sporting embassy plates, and diplomats and dignitaries congregate in hotel bars. The elegant buildings that house the embassies were once mainly private residences dating from the turn of the century – a time when industrialists and financiers were spending their lavish wealth for all to see.

Start at the bottom of Embassy Row, where Massachusetts Ave meets Dupont on the circle's west side. The ominous **Blaine Mansion** (1; 2000 Massachusetts Ave) was built in 1881 by Republican Party founder 'Slippery Jim' Blaine. It is not actually a diplomatic building, but it ranks as the oldest surviving mansion in the Dupont Circle area.

The Walsh-McLean House (2020 Massachusetts Ave) houses the **Indonesian embassy 2**. The gold-mining magnate Thomas Walsh commissioned this lavish home in 1903, when it was said to be the costliest house in the city (not surprising, considering the gold-flecked marble pillars). To honor his fortune, Walsh embedded in the foundation a gold nugget, which has never been found.

Continue up Massachusetts Ave to the grand **Anderson House** (3; 2118 Massachusetts Ave). Note the military-themed ornamentation above the entrance and the fancy egg-and-dart molding along the roofline. Across the street, a simple **statue of Mahatma Gandhi 4** – a gift from the people of India – sits in front of the Indian embassy.

The rich mansion at 2121 Massachusetts Ave – designed to resemble Petit Trianon at Versailles – has been the headquarters for the **Cosmos Club 5** since 1952. The building is a befitting home for the most prominent social club of DC's intellectual elite: from the rich, wood-paneled library to the sculpted lion overlooking the blooming gardens, it oozes culture and learning.

Back on the south side of Massachusetts Ave, a bronze statue honors **Tomas Masaryk 6**, a leading advocate for Czech independence after WWI and the first president of the new state of Czechoslovakia (1918–35). Nearby is the **Luxembourg embassy** (7; 2200 Massachusetts Ave).

Now you are approaching Sheridan Circle, wreathed in lavish embassies and centered on Gutzon Borglum's equestrian statue of Civil War General Philip Sheridan. (Borglum later sculpted Mt Rushmore.) The nearby **plaque 8** remembers the 1976 car-bomb assassination of pro-Allende Chilean exile Orlando Letelier; agents of the Pinochet dictatorship were later connected to the murder.

Edward Everett, who made his million inventing the grooved bottle cap, commissioned the **Turkish embassy** (9; 16606 23rd St) in 1914. Architect George Oakley Totten had just returned from a stint in Turkey, which inspired many of the building's features, such as the 3rd-story balcony. That Mr Everett's widow later sold the property to the Turkish government for its embassy is a happy coincidence.

The **Haitian embassy** (10; 2311 Massachusetts Ave) is a little beaux-arts jewel from 1909. Next door, the 1908 Moran House is now the **Pakistani embassy** (11; 2315 Massachusetts Ave), another Totten masterpiece.

You are going to turn right on Decatur Pl, but first look a little further up Massachusetts Ave. The **Cameroon embassy** (12; 2349 Massachusetts Ave) is also the work of Totten. He designed this castle-like mansion for Norwegian diplomat Christian Hauge, who died in a snowshoe accident before its completion. At No 2343, a cross-legged sculpture of St Jerome dreams over his book before the **Croatian embassy 13**.

Now take a detour east on Decatur Pl to 23rd St. The rise up to S St here was deemed too steep for the road, so city planners constructed a delightful pedestrian staircase, which has been dubbed the '**Spanish Steps**' 14 for its resemblance to Rome's Piazza di Spagna. Climb the steps and return to Massachusetts Ave via S St. As you continue north on Massachusetts Ave you will pass the **Zambian embassy 15** at No 2419 and the **Venezuelan embassy 16** at No 2443.

The **Japanese embassy** (17; 2516 Massachusetts Ave) cleverly blends Georgian and Asian architectural styles. The beautifully

WALK FACTS

Start Massachusetts Ave and 20th St NW
(Metro: Dupont Circle)
End Connecticut Ave and Kalorama Rd NW
(Metro: Woodley Park-Zoo/Adams Morgan)
Distance 2.5km
Pit stops Lebanese Taverna (p163) or Petits Plats (p164)

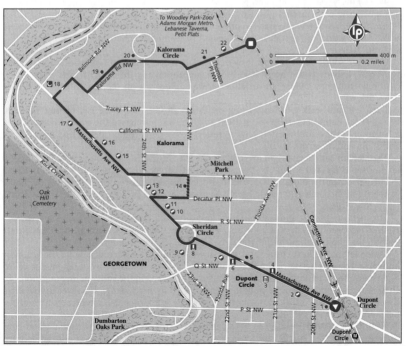

landscaped grounds hold a reconstruction of an antique teahouse, which was brought from Japan in 1960. Its name, Ippakutei, means 'one hundred virtues,' or 'hundredth anniversary,' referring to the US–Japan Treaty of Amity and Friendship it commemorates.

You will turn right up Belmont Rd, but not before admiring the strikingly ethereal Islamic Center (18; p101; 2551 Massachusetts Ave). Now head northeast on Belmont Rd into the interior of Kalorama, where the tree-lined streets and stately homes are among the loveliest in DC.

For this reason – and for its proximity to Embassy Row – many ambassadors' homes are in this neck of the woods. Turn right on Tracey Pl and left on Kalorama Pl to find the Icelandic ambassador's residence (19; 2443 Kalorama Rd). This half-timbered brick mansion looks built to survive an Arctic winter. DC's oldest extant building is the Lindens (20; 2401 Kalorama Rd). The Georgian-style mansion was built in Massachusetts in 1754 and shipped to DC in 1934. The magnificent Tudor mansion at 2222 Kalorama Rd is the French ambassador's residence 21.

Continue east on Kalorama Rd to Connecticut Ave. Your tour ends here, in front of the Portuguese embassy (22; 2125 Kalorama Rd). A left on Connecticut will take you across the bridge to the Woodley Park-Zoo/Adams Morgan Metro station. If Embassy Row's international flavor has made you yearn for a further taste of international flavors, check out the restaurants and cafés clustered around the Woodley Park-Zoo/Adams Morgan Metro stop.

GEORGETOWN WALK-AROUND

The Georgetown Walk-Around starts, quite appropriately, at Georgetown University (1; p83), the founding of which, in 1789, capped the good fortune of this already prospering neighborhood.

Enter the campus through the iron gates at 37th and O Sts NW to admire the Gothic spires of the Healy Building and the concrete towers of its modern counterpart, Lauinger Library.

From the gates, walk one block east on O St and turn right on 36th St. Dating from 1794, Holy Trinity Church (2; 36th and N Sts NW) was the first Roman Catholic Church in the area. The original church – now housing the convent – is the smaller building at 3525 N St. In the 19th century, this was the only place in Georgetown where Black Catholics were welcome to worship; they sat in a designated section of the choir loft, entering through a separate stairway.

Continue south on 36th St to Prospect St. The loooooong flight of stairs leading down to M St is known as the Exorcist Stairs 3 for its appearance in the horrific film. These stairs continue to torment Georgetown athletes, who often run up them with coaches yelling from below.

Turn left and walk two blocks east on Prospect St. The private Halcyon House (4; 3400 Prospect St) dates back to 1786; in 1900 an eccentric purchased the property and added a ballroom, chapel and theater, plus countless mysterious rooms, doors leading nowhere and stairs ending in solid walls.

Turn left on 34th St and right on N St. On the left, the five Federal houses Nos 3327 to 3339 are known as Cox's Row 5, built by the fashionable Georgetown mayor (1823–45) John Cox.

Further down the block, the formal, red-brick Marbury House (6; 3307 N St) was the home of John and Jacqueline Kennedy before Kennedy became president and they moved into the White House.

Turn left on 33rd St and walk up two- and-a-half blocks to the little house at No 1524. Back in Georgetown's days as a bustling port, this building was known as the Yellow Tavern 7 (private), a popular stopover for travelers, including Thomas Jefferson.

Take a left at the next corner and walk down Volta Pl to a narrow lane on the left, now known as Pomander Walk 8. In the first half of the century, it was a row of tenements called Bell Court, home to domestics, mostly Black, who worked in the surrounding mansions. In 1950, the city condemned the buildings and evicted their residents. However unfortunate this history, the row today is a colorful and well-kept corner that's representative of the neighborhood's restoration.

Head back east on Volta Pl to Wisconsin Ave. Cross this busy thoroughfare and continue east on Q St to 31st St, and turn left. Tucked into five acres of beautifully landscaped

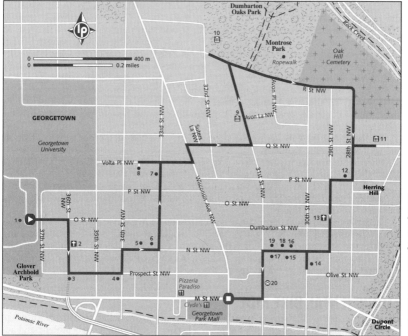

grounds, **Tudor Place** (9; p84; 1644 31st St) is the gracious urban estate of the prominent Custis Peter clan (descendants of George Washington). Continue further up 31st St to the intersection with R St. Before you is one of Georgetown's hidden highlights, the eclectic museum and gorgeous gardens of **Dumbarton Oaks** 10 (p83).

Turn right and walk east on R St. The intimate and somehow incongruous cobblestone trail on the left was years ago dubbed Lovers' Lane. It leads down into lovely, lush overgrown Dumbarton Oaks Park. Further along R St, tamer Montrose Park hosts the

WALK-AROUND FACTS

Start Georgetown University, 37th and O Sts NW (Georgetown shuttle from Foggy Bottom-GWU or Rosslyn Metro)
End Wisconsin Ave and M St NW (Georgetown shuttle from Foggy Bottom-GWU or Rosslyn Metro)
Distance 4km
Pit stops Clyde's (p149) or Pizzeria Paradiso (p148)

requisite dogs chasing balls, and kids on swings. The park's unique feature is the celebrated 'ropewalk,' remaining from the days when this property was used for rope manufacturing. Workers walked up and down the long, straight stretch when fashioning hemp into rope. Adjoining Montrose Park is Oak Hill Cemetery (p84), set on the slopes dropping down to Rock Creek Park.

Continue on R St to its terminus, and turn right to head south on 28th St. Take a quick detour left on Q St to historic **Dumbarton House** (11; p82) at No 2715. Built in 1797, the Federal mansion is one of Georgetown's oldest. Back on 28th St, continue south to P St. The three houses at the corner (2803–11 P St) are protected by **Daw's Fence** 12. Reuben Daw built the storied fence with Mexican War muskets he found at a pawnshop.

Walk one block west on P St, then turn left to continue heading south on 29th St. This area between 29th St and Rock Creek Park, especially north of P St, is known as Herring Hill. In the early 19th century, it was home to a flourishing free Black community. Churches in the area such as **Mt Zion United Methodist Church** (13; p83; 1334 29th St) served as stops on the

Underground Railroad and defied the neighborhood's reputation as a Confederate bastion during the Civil War.

Continue several more blocks south on 29th St, and turn right on N St to walk west. At 30th St, near the corner on the left-hand side, is a house with a most dubious claim to fame as Georgetown's narrowest house. (It is 11ft wide, in case you are wondering what it takes.)

The little row house at 1239 30th St has been dubbed **Spite House 14**, as it was supposedly built to cut off the neighbor's light.

The block of N St between 30th and 31st Sts holds some of Georgetown's most exemplary 18th-century architecture. **Laird-Dunlop House 15**, the red-brick Georgian at No 3014, is now the home of Benjamin Bradlee, the editor who directed the *Washington Post* through the Watergate scandal.

The **Thomas-Beall House 16**, across the street at 3017, has had such prominent residents as the widow Jacqueline Kennedy.

Other architectural gems: the Federal **Riggs-Riley House 17** at No 3038; the 1780 brick **Beall Mansion 18** at 3033 N St; and the Victorian town houses of **Wheatley Row** (19; 3041–45 N St).

Turn south on 31st St and descend to bustling M St. Don't overlook the elegant facade of the **post office** (20; 1215 31st St). When Georgetown was an affluent port, this building served as a lucrative customs house.

The walk-around ends at the intersection of Wisconsin Ave and M St, the heart of Georgetown's commercial activity. We have seen the neighborhood's historical landmarks and architectural masterpieces, but this is the place to experience the buzz of modern Georgetown: shopping, eating and drinking. Pick a spot at a friendly bar or a sidewalk café, and end your walk-around with a sit down.

MONUMENTAL BIKE RIDE

Washington, DC, is blessed with fresh air and green space uncharacteristic of an urban setting, as well as hundreds of miles of off-road trails. For the moderately athletic and adventurous, there is no better way to see the city than with two wheels and a pair of pedals. In DC, the Metro makes it easy, allowing bicycles on the trains except during rush hour, and equipping buses with racks to transport bikes.

The bike ride starts at the **Thompson Boat Center** (1; p203), where you can rent a bicycle if you need to. Exit the boathouse over the small bridge to Rock Creek & Potomac Parkway, and turn right on the parkway trail that runs between the road and the river.

Pedaling along the Potomac, you immediately pass the gargantuan **Watergate Complex** (2; p80) and ride under the overhang of the **Kennedy Center** (3; p79). The trail leads underneath the Theodore Roosevelt Bridge and up a slight incline. Cries of 'Bump, set, spike!' may drift across from the sand **volleyball courts 4**, crowded on weekends with shirtless guys, tanned and buff.

Stop at the top of the hill for a breath and to take in the view (of the environs, not of the guys). Two bronze statues representing the **Arts of Peace 5** flank the road. Look for Aspiration and Literature on the left, Music and Harvest on the right. The wild patch of green across the river is actually Theodore Roosevelt Island (p124), accessible from Arlington. And looming in front of you is the marble-columned **Lincoln Memorial** (6; p70).

Cross the street to your left and follow the pedestrian signs to the front of the memorial. Here it will be difficult to ride, with tourists posing for pictures in your path. You can either lock your bike or take it with you as you explore the surrounding memorials on foot. (Either way, be grateful you don't have to find a parking space.) Facing the reflecting pool, the **Vietnam Veterans Memorial** (7; p72) is to your left and the **Korean War Veterans Memorial** (8; p70) is to your right.

After shedding a tear at the granite wall and locating the spot where MLK, Jr spoke his famous words, hop back on your bike and ride around to the east side of the Lincoln Memorial. Pick up the path that will take you over Arlington Memorial Bridge on the left side of the road. Before you cross, you will notice the bronze **Arts of War 9**, the counterparts to the Arts of Peace you saw earlier: Valor on the left and Service on the right.

Directly ahead of you, Virginia's rolling hills are covered with the white headstones of Arlington National Cemetery. The mansion on the crest of the hill in the middle of the burial ground is **Arlington House** (10; p123), once owned by Robert E Lee. Once on the Virginia side of the Potomac, turn left to pick up the Mount Vernon Trail (see Biking, p200) heading south. This lovely ride will provide fabulous views of the DC skyline across the river.

The path takes you through Lady Bird Johnson Park, dedicated to the first lady whose efforts beautified many nooks and crannies of the city, including this one. The **LBJ Memorial Grove** 11 pays tribute to her husband.

Just before the Rochambeau Memorial Bridge (commonly known as the 14th St Bridge) the bike path forks; stay left and continue straight under the bridge. Now you are approaching Ronald Reagan Washington National Airport, which will be apparent from the constant roar of airplanes overhead. The park between the bridge and the airport is known as **Gravelly Point** 12, an ideal (if noisy) spot to take a break and pull out your picnic, if you thought to bring one. Flocks of geese and other feathered friends often find their way over from the Roaches Run Waterfowl Sanctuary across

BIKE RIDE FACTS

Start & End Thompson Boat Center, Rock Creek & Potomac Parkway and I St NW (Metro: Foggy Bottom-GWU)
Distance 10km
Pit stops Bring a picnic! Otherwise, try Sequoia (p150) or A La Lucia (p166)

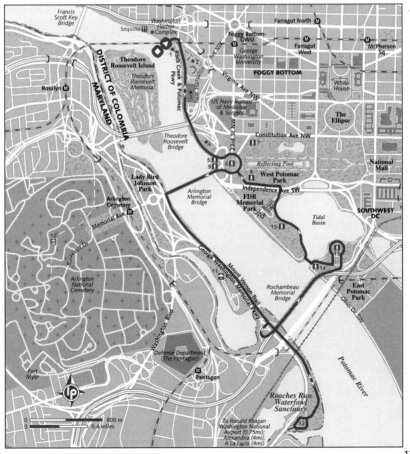

the George Washington Memorial Parkway (p123); even more awesome is watching the iron birds take flight, à la *Bill & Ted's Excellent Adventure*.

If you did not bring a picnic, you might consider continuing south here for a few miles to the heart of Old Town in Alexandria (p125) and a host of lunching options. Otherwise, this is the turn-around point. When your buns are ready, get them back on that bike seat and head from whence you came.

After passing back under the 14th St Bridge, look again for the fork in the path. This time, turn off the path and loop back to the left and over the bridge. Pedal around the domed **Thomas Jefferson Memorial** (13; p71) on the banks of the peaceful Tidal Basin across the street. Exiting the memorial, turn right onto Ohio Dr. There is no separate bike path here, so be very careful of cars and pedestrians. Duck down the path on the left-hand side of the road before crossing the small inlet bridge to discover the hidden **George Mason Memorial** (14; p70).

Cross the inlet bridge and follow the pedestrian signs to the **Franklin Delano Roosevelt Memorial** (15; p69). You must walk your bike through this maze of open-air rooms paying tribute to different eras of the great president's life. Exit the memorial on the northwest side of the Tidal Basin and turn right onto W Basin Dr. The park to your left – FDR Memorial Park – is often the site of polo matches or helicopter landings or other excitement.

Cross Independence Ave and go left on the paved walkway along West Potomac Park, back to the Lincoln Memorial. To return to Thompson Boat Center pass between the Lincoln Memorial and the Reflecting Pool to retrace your pedals on the Rock Creek Parkway bike path. After such a ride, you'll need nothing more than to rest your bones and replenish your fluids. Fortunately, the Washington Harbor Complex, just steps from Thompson Boat Center, has a few options to enjoy the breeze off the river and do just that.

NIGHT CRAWL

So many choices, how to decide? Well, here is a sampler plate for night crawlers just itching to get a taste of all that DC's after-dark scene has to offer. The tour starts in DC's hottest new nightspot, Shaw, before heading down to ever-hip Dupont Circle, then dives into the heart of DC's most established nightspot, Adams-Morgan. Stops along the way range from swank to dive, from artsy to sporty, from ethnic to American. Keep in mind that, the city that never sleeps, Washington is not (most of these places close at 2am weekdays, 3am Friday and Saturday). Get an early start to take advantage of happy-hour specials and to take it all in.

Start at the corner of 14th and U Sts NW, two blocks west of the U Street-Cardozo Metro stop. These streets have attracted night crawlers since the 1920s, when music lovers came from all corners of the city to hear the sweet sounds of jazz that emanated from the many nightclubs in the area. One block south of here, the intersection of 14th and T Sts NW was the site of the magical Club Bali, which hosted greats like Louis Armstrong and Sarah Vaughn. Today, the area is enjoying a renaissance as a venue for music, arts and nightlife.

Step into **Tabaq Bistro** (1; p178; 1336 U St) for a drink with a view. The glass-enclosed retractable rooftop restaurant also does a lively bar trade. Suck down flamboyant $10 cocktails with stellar views then backtrack a few doors down to **Café Nema** (2; p185; 1334 U St). This is one of the coolest joints in the city to listen to live music, everything from chill jazz to beat-busting hip-hop are in store. If you arrive early and just want to chill, head to the top floor lounge.

Walk three blocks west on U St to the intersection of New Hampshire Ave and 16th St NW, a neighborhood – literally and figuratively – on the edge. These northeastern reaches of Dupont Circle sport some of its trendiest spots, such as the **Chi-Cha Lounge** (3; p176; 1624 U St). Is it sinking into a plush velvet sofa or smoking a fruity-flavored hookah that makes everybody here so chill? In any case, sit back with a signature *chi-cha* (some South American concoction), pass around the Ecuadorian tapas, and enjoy this eclectic mix of East and West.

When your lungs can't take it any more, continue west on U St and then north on 18th St and Florida Ave. Pop into the **Common Share** (4; p176; 2003 18th St) to stock up on some

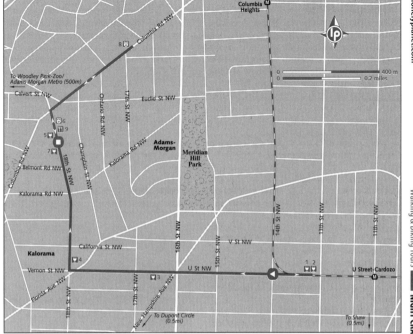

of the city's all-night budget drinks – \$3
for a cup of booze and soda or juice. It's a
perennial favorite with the young, fabulous
but still broke crowd, along with plenty of
college kids. Expect to be elbow-deep in
people here most nights, but you're only
here to pick up some fuel before your trek
north on 18th St.

CRAWL FACTS

Start 14th and U Sts NW (Metro: U Street-Cardozo)
End 18th St NW (U Link shuttle to Woodley Park-Zoo/
Adams Morgan or U Street-Cardozo Metro)
Distance 2km

The dense strip nestled between Kalor-
ama and Columbia Rds is the epicenter of
Adams-Morgan and, arguably, of all nightlife in Washington, DC. Your first stop is **Bukom
Café** (5; p185; 2442 18th St), where live juju and other West African beats rock the house.
If world music's not your thing, head across the street to No 2461 for live blues at **Madam's
Organ** (6; p184).

Don't get too comfortable, though – just south of Bukom Café is the **Left Bank** (7; p177;
2424 18th St). A new edition to Adams-Morgan, the Left Bank is a hip, modern lounge
with stark white walls and orphanage chairs and booths. It's the perfect place to rest your
feet and slurp down a martini while chilling out to mellow DJ vibes with a sophisticated,
international crowd.

When you think you can't take any more sitting and chilling, hit the streets again.
Turn right on Columbia Rd and head up a few blocks to **Chief Ike's Mambo Room** (8; p187;
1725 Columbia Rd), between 17th and 18th Sts. The venue is three clubs in one, so you
are bound to find something you like, be it live bands playing rock or reggae or DJs
spinning discs. The catch is that everybody is dancing, so make sure you get out there
and shake that thang.

By now you must be exhausted and – more urgent – starving. So double back onto 18th
St and settle into a comfy booth at the **Diner** (9; p160; 2453 18th St) for a cheesy Western
omelette or a juicy burger.

SHAW SHUFFLE

'Before Harlem, there was Shaw,' locals boast about the vibrant African American community that thrived in this part of DC for the first half of the 20th century. Centered on U St NW, the area was home to hundreds of Black businesses, churches, schools and civic organizations, not to mention a prominent Black university and a magical live music scene.

Start your shuffle through Shaw at the corner of 12th and U Sts NW, just outside the U Street-Cardozo Metro station. Back in its heyday, the True Reformer Building (1200 U St) was the setting for many of the business meetings and social gatherings that kept this community ticking. The grand 1903 Italianate building was designed, built, financed, and ultimately utilized and appreciated by African Americans. Today it houses the **African American Civil War Museum** (1; p114).

Walk south on 12th St past the corner of T St to the **Thurgood Marshall Center** (2; 1816 12th St). This community center was built in 1908 to house the nation's first African American YMCA, an institution that nurtured the likes of Langston Hughes, Joe Louis and Georgetown University basketball coach John Thompson.

Head west on T St and stroll past **Duke Ellington's childhood home** (3; 1212 T St). The elegant **Whitelaw Hotel** (4; 1839 T St) was a luxurious, first-class hotel – the first in segregated DC to welcome Black travelers.

Now turn right on 13th St and make your way back to U St, the central artery of Shaw. At the corner of 13th and U Sts, Duke Ellington belts out his blue notes from the colorful **mural 5**, painted by DC artists and students, on the exterior wall of the Metro station.

Turn right and head east on U St passing the historic **Lincoln Theatre** (6; p193; 1215 U St),

SHUFFLE FACTS

Start 12th and U Sts NW (Metro: U Street-Cardozo)
End Vermont Ave NW (Metro: McPherson Sq)
Distance 2.5km
Pit stops Ben's Chili Bowl (p161) or Coppi's Organic (p162)

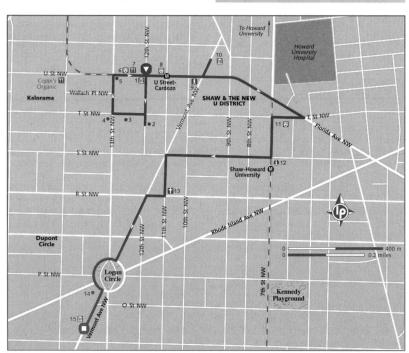

one of three first-run movie theaters that were clustered here back in its day. Its neighbor, **Ben's Chili Bowl** (7; p161; 1213 U St NW), has been a gathering place for DC's Black politicos and community leaders since opening in 1958.

One block further at the corner of 11th St, the sax-shaped sign and keyboard trim leave no doubt about what goes on inside **Bohemian Caverns** (8; p184). This hip venue for live jazz and soul music is the reincarnation of the fashionable Club Cavern, which occupied the basement here from 1926, and attracted big names from Duke Ellington and Pearl Bailey to Aretha Franklin and the Supremes.

At U St and Vermont Ave, just outside the Metro station's east entrance, is the steel-sculptured **African American Civil War Memorial** (9; p113), honoring the Black soldiers who fought in the Union Army.

Turn north to see the eclectic **Black Fashion Museum** (10; p114; 2007 Vermont Ave NW), showcasing the work of Black designers past and present. Entry is by appointment only.

Return to U St, walk one block east and turn right down Florida Ave. The blocks northeast of here constitute the campus of Howard University (p114), alma mater of notables like Thurgood Marshall and Toni Morrison. Later in the tour, we will pass the Howard University welcome center several blocks south of here.

Continue down Florida Ave to the intersection with T St, then take a sharp turn right. A key fixture on 'Black Broadway' was the **Howard Theatre** (11; 620 T St), which still stands but is unused and in disrepair (although efforts to restore it are occasionally launched). Ella Fitzgerald, Billie Holiday and Lena Horne sang here, followed later by James Brown and Motown bands.

Take a left on 7th St, passing the **Howard University welcome center** (12; 1739 7th St). Walk four blocks west on S St and one block south on 11th St.

At the corner of 11th and R Sts, **Lincoln Memorial Church** 13 is one of several churches that have sustained this community since the Civil War – by providing spiritual nourishment, but also by organizing its members socially and politically. Black religious institutions were at the forefront of the civil rights movement.

Return to Vermont Ave and walk three blocks south to reach Logan Circle, a historic district of well-preserved Victorian homes. The ornate cream-colored manse at **1 & 2 Logan Circle** 14 (private) was built in 1877 by Ulysses S Grant Jr.

One block further down at 1318 Vermont Ave, the National Council of Negro Women has its headquarters at the **Bethune Council House** (15; p98), the former home of the great Black educator, Mary McLeod Bethune.

WHITE HOUSE WALK

Our stroll through this neighborhood begins where the nightly network news always seems to begin: on the north side of the White House in Lafayette Sq. In the 19th century Lafayette Sq (named after the Marquis de Lafayette, the Revolutionary War hero) was an orchard lined with the mansions of the rich and powerful. Writer Henry Adams, who lived in a mansion on its northern edge, described it thus: 'Lafayette Square was society...Beyond the square, the country began.'

Among the square's remaining Victorian homes is **Decatur House** (1; p75; 748 Jackson Pl). Around the corner at 1 Lafayette Sq, the **Hay-Adams Hotel** (2; p76) is an exclusive, luxurious hostelry that was built on the site of Henry Adams' old mansion.

Across the street, **St John's Church** (3; p77) has a pew permanently reserved for presidential families.

Circle around to Pennsylvania Ave NW, which runs between Lafayette Sq and the White House. Until recently, it was a central thoroughfare, but after two threatening incidents in 1994 (a stolen airplane crashed into White House grounds, and a man fired a semiautomatic at the mansion), the portion in front of the White House was closed to car traffic. Now concrete blockades and a heightened security presence add an imposing imperial air to the White House, but they also make the area a more pleasant pedestrian walkway.

Pass in front of the White House, which is almost dwarfed by the wonderfully baroque Old Executive Office Building (p77), where White House staff work. Across the street, the national crafts museum, the **Renwick Gallery** (4; p77), is housed in a historic mansion at the corner of 17th St NW.

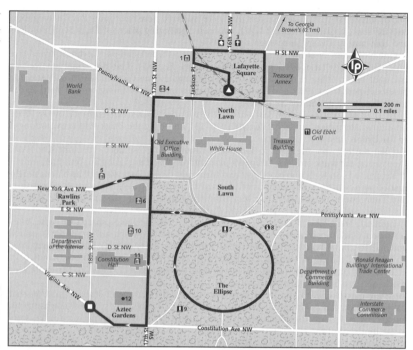

Turn left on 17th St and walk three blocks to New York Ave. Walk west on New York Ave to the oddly shaped but appropriately named **Octagon Museum** (5; p79). Across the street, blooming magnolias and gurgling goldfish ponds decorate Rawlins Park – a remarkably peaceful place considering it's named after US Grant's Secretary of War.

Back on 17th St, the beautiful beaux-arts building at No 500 is the **Corcoran Gallery of Art** (6; p75), a magnificent collection of American and European art.

The Ellipse (p76) is the expansive park across the street. Its northernmost point provides you the classic photo opportunity: the White House facade, in dignified remove across its private South Lawn. Walk around the elliptical road that circles the park.

At the north edge, the **Zero Milestone 7** is the stone marker from which all US highway distances are measured (in case you ever wondered). In December, the National Christmas Tree is illuminated here. Information is available at the **National Park Service Ellipse Visitor Pavilion 8**. Along the southern edge, you cannot miss the **Second Division Memorial 9** with its giant golden hand thrusting forth a flaming sword.

Make your way around the Ellipse and back to 17th St NW. Head south to admire the rest of the monumental buildings along this row: the pillared, marble mansion that serves as the headquarters and museum of the **Red Cross (10**; 1730 E St NW); the stately Memorial Continental Building housing the **Daughters of the American Revolution (11**; 1776 D St); and the **Organization of American States (12**; OAS; p77), in the marble palazzo at the corner of Constitution Ave. All have exhibits open to the public, so you can end your tour with a stroll through art galleries and historic rooms. Or kick back in the sculpture-studded Aztec Gardens skirting the OAS.

WALK FACTS

Start Lafayette Sq (Metro: McPherson Sq)
End Aztec Gardens (Metro: Farragut West)
Distance 4km
Pit stops Georgia Brown's (p145) or Old Ebbit Grill (p145)

Eating

Eating

Washingtonians love to dine out. From the martini lunch at the venerated Old Ebbitt Grille to the family dinner at the boisterous Rio Grande Café, Washington is one of the nation's culinary wonders offering an especially dizzying array of dining options considering its smallish size. Washington is an ethnically diverse city and this is reflected in its cooking. There's the usual international array of Ethiopian, Japanese, French, Asian-Fusion style restaurants, but there are also hundreds of places serving lesser-known specialties – Senegalese delicacies, Venezuelan tapas, Vietnamese so authentic you could be in Hanoi. The only cuisine that Washington seems to be lacking in copious quantities is true Mexican. It has loads of great Tex-Mex places along with lots of Central American joints, but if you're looking for authentic south-of-the-border cuisine, there are only a handful of options.

PRICE GUIDE

$	under $15
$$	$15 to $30
$$$	more than $30

With pleasant weather eight months a year, DC has plenty of opportunities for alfresco dining, including sidewalk cafés (fabulous for people-watching) and roof-deck restaurants (fabulous views). Trendy theme restaurants with funky interiors have also become a hot commodity. And DC is undoubtedly the number-one spot in the country for sighting political celebrities out on the town. Between its creative cuisine, delightful decors and powerful patrons, DC dining is a stimulating sensory experience.

Opening Hours

Most restaurants are open for lunch and dinner daily, although there are exceptions. Restaurants that depend on weekday business-lunch trade (such as in the White House Area) may be open for dinner only on weekends, or not at all. Other restaurants – especially family-owned joints – may close on Sunday or Monday. DC also has its share of breakfast joints (most top-end hotel restaurants serve breakfast) and 24-hour diners (for more on these, see p151).

Unless noted otherwise, restaurants in this chapter are open daily from 11:30am to 2:30pm for lunch, 5:30pm to 10:30pm for dinner and later (until 11pm or midnight) on Friday and Saturday.

How Much?

Travelers in Washington can expect to spend a fair amount of their budgets on eating out. For travelers on a budget, food courts and takeout, where large portions are inexpensive, are handy options. Otherwise, a restaurant dinner with a drink usually starts at $30 and the price goes up as high as you are willing. Lunch costs around $20, although many restaurants offer lunch specials and buffets, which can be a thrifty way to enjoy a nice meal.

Booking Tables

While most restaurants do not require bookings, it is recommended on weekends, especially at upscale restaurants. Normally, a phone call in the afternoon is sufficient, although some of the hottest, new restaurants require reservations several days or a week in advance.

Takeout & To Go

Having a picnic on the National Mall or on the banks of the Potomac is among the most pleasant dining experiences in DC. Grabbing a 'take-out' meal is quite common in the States, with even some of the fancier restaurants offering this service. It can be a good way to save money and still eat well – phone in your order, pick it up and bring it back to your hotel room. You won't have to worry about tipping staff or paying for over-priced drinks (stop at the local liquor store and buy that same bottle of Italian red for a fraction of the restaurant price), which could cut your bill nearly in half! Besides the inspirational setting, DC's farmers markets (below) and gourmet stores offer a wonderful selection of fresh produce and exotic eats to pack in your picnic basket or chow in front of the TV.

If you are feeling lazy, **Takeout Taxi Washington** (☎ in Virginia 703-578-3663, in DC 202-986-0111 for DC; www.takeouttaxi .com) delivers food from numerous DC restaurants straight to your room for a service fee of between $5 and $10 (you'll also be expected to tip the delivery person around 15% on top of this).

FARMERS MARKETS

In addition to Eastern Market (the granddaddy of DC open-air markets, see p151), numerous local farmers markets offer fresh produce, meats, seafood, flowers, locally made baked goods, jewelry, crafts and even clothing. Try the following:

- Adams-Morgan Farmers Market (Columbia Rd & 18th St NW, Crestar Bank Plaza; ⏰ 8am-1pm Sat May-Dec; 🚌 U Link Shuttle from Woodley Park-Zoo/Adams Morgan or U Street-Cardozo)
- DC Open-Air Farmers Market (Map pp290–1; RFK Stadium parking lot, Oklahoma Ave & Benning Rd NE; ⏰ 7am-5pm Thu & Sat plus Tue Jun-Sep; Ⓜ Stadium-Armory)
- Historic Brookland Farmers Market (10th & Otis Sts NE; ⏰ 4-7pm Tue, 10am-2pm Sun Jun-Oct; Ⓜ CUA-Brookland)
- Fresh Farm Market (Map pp292–3; 8th & E Sts NW, ⏰ 3-7pm Thu; Ⓜ Gallery Pl-Chinatown)
- Old Town Farmers Market (Map p311; 301 King St, Old Town, Alexandria; ⏰ 9am-2pm Sat; 🚌 Old Town shuttle from King St Metro)

EATING WITH KIDS

DC is a family-friendly city, and all the museum cafés make great lunch spots with the kiddies (or do it picnic style, pick up a hotdog at a vendor and eat on the National Mall). Below are our top picks if you're dining with the young ones.

- Zoo Bar (p163) – It's on the way out of the zoo, has an unprecedented cheap kids' menu, patient waitstaff and loads of animals on the walls to keep the kids entertained.
- Generous George's Positive Pizza & Pasta Place (p166) – Crowded, chaotic and a little crazy, this is one of the best places around the city to eat with the tots.
- America (p151) – Menus shaped like maps and fun American trivia mean there's plenty to keep the kids occupied here.
- Rio Grande Café (p167) – The place is loud enough for it not to matter if your kids make lots of noise. Plus it has a popular children's menu and special spill-proof cups for young ones.
- Hard Times Café (p165) – A cheap kids' menu that includes Frito Pie and hot-dogs, your little one will be in heaven.

Tipping

Tipping is an important part of restaurant culture in the US: servers make less than minimum wage and rely on tips to earn their living. Tipping 15% of the total bill is the accepted minimum. If service is good, 20% is a decent average tip, while it is appropriate to tip more if service is exceptional.

NATIONAL MALL & MONUMENTS

Most of the museums have overpriced restaurants with mediocre menus; however, there are a few exceptions, which we have listed below.

ICE CREAM PARLOR
Map pp292-3   Desserts $

National Museum of American History, 14th St & Constitution Av NW; dessert from $4; ⏰ 11am-5pm Mar-Oct; Ⓜ Smithsonian

When the American History museum re-opens in 2008, make sure you stop in at this traditional ice-cream parlor for a spot of dessert. Thick milkshakes, hot-fudge sundaes and the mountainous Star-Spangled Banner Split taste fantastic in this quaint Victorian-era setting.

MITSITAM NATIVE FOODS
CAFE Map pp292-3   Café $

☎ 202-633-1000; National Museum of the American Indian, 4th St & Independence Ave SW; mains $8-14; ⓨ 11:30am-3pm Mon-Sat, noon-6:30pm Sun; Ⓜ Smithsonian

As much a sensory experience as the exhibits themselves, this is a fabulous cafeteria tucked away in the National Museum of the American Indian. An airy joint, with booths as modern and curvy as the museum it resides in, it features five food stations each focusing on a different Native American region and its indigenous ingredients. Menus rotate daily, and with the crowds of tourists it can be hard to figure out what is what. Usually, you can't go wrong with the South American station near the entrance.

PAVILION CAFÉ
Map pp292-3   Café $

☎ 202-289-3660; National Sculpture Garden, 7th St & Constitution Ave NW; mains from $8; ⓨ 11am-3:30pm Mon-Fri, 5-8pm Fri, 11am-4pm Sat, 11am-5:30pm Sun; Ⓜ Smithsonian

Boasting a panoramic view of the **National Sculpture Garden** (p68), the Pavilion Café offers specialty pizzas, sandwiches, salads, desserts and assorted beverages, as well as a children's menu. The café also offers a seasonal tapas-style menu on Friday nights in summer, when DC-area jazz musicians put on free concerts.

CASCADE CAFÉ
Map pp292-3   Café $

☎ 202-216-2480; East Bldg, National Gallery of Art, 4th St & Constitution Ave NW; mains from $10; ⓨ 10am-3pm Mon-Sat, 11am-4pm Sun; Ⓜ Archives-Navy Memorial

Oh what a lovely place for a bowl of stuffed tortellini or a croissant sandwich. You can dine in the shadow of IM Pei's waterfall at our pick for museum dining on the Mall. Located in the East Building of the National Gallery, it offers a range of American cuisine along with specialty menus that complement current exhibits (eg regional African American dishes in honor of the Art of Romare Beardon).

FULL CIRCLE CAFÉ
Map pp292-3   Café $

☎ 202-633-4674; Hirshhorn Museum, 7th & Independence Ave SW; mains from $12; ⓨ 11am-4:30pm Mon-Fri, to 8pm Thu summer; Ⓜ Smithsonian

Linger on the breezy patio and people-watch while downing a pint or two. The menu is loaded with soups, salads and sandwiches.

WHITE HOUSE AREA & FOGGY BOTTOM

Stomping ground of lobbyists and executive-branch power brokers, this area is replete with fancy digs. The restaurants around the White House are among the top spots for spying on politicians while they dine.

MARVELOUS MARKET
Map pp292-3   Self-catering $

☎ 202-828-0944; 1800 K St NW; sandwiches from $6, mains from $8; ⓨ 7am-7pm Mon-Fri; Ⓜ Farragut West

Besides gourmet grocery-store items, this chain also carries fresh bread, pastries and sandwiches, making it a good bet for stocking up on picnic items or healthy cheap dinners to eat back at the hotel. There are other branches scattered around the city.

BREADLINE
Map pp292-3   Bakery/Deli $

☎ 202-822-8900; 1751 Pennsylvania Ave NW; sandwiches from $6; ⓨ 7am-5pm Mon-Fri; Ⓜ Farragut West

'Food is ammunition – don't waste it!' commands a WWII-era poster on the wall of this polished bakery and sandwich shop. Chef and local food celebrity Mark Furstenberg uses his ammunition to create fresh and filling sandwiches and to-die-for sweet treats.

TEAISM
Map pp292-3   Teahouse $

☎ 202-835-2233; 800 Connecticut Ave NW; mains from $8; ⓨ 7am-5pm Mon-Fri; Ⓜ Farragut West

This teahouse is unique in the area for its very affordable lunch options – hot noodle dishes and fresh bento boxes – and its pleasantly relaxing atmosphere. The entrance is on H St between 17th and Connecticut – near Lafayette Sq and the Farragut West Metro Stop. There is also a branch Downtown, as well as one located near Dupont Circle.

KAZ SUSHI BISTRO

Map pp292-3   Japanese $$

☎ 202-530-5500; 1915 I St NW; lunch specials $10, mains $10-20; ⏱ lunch & dinner Mon-Fri, dinner Sat; Ⓜ Farragut West

Fusing East and West, chef Kaz Okochi presents his own invention, 'free-style Japanese cuisine.' The sushi on its own is fresh and flavorful and good enough. Many clever combinations, however, add a certain *je ne sais quoi* to the traditional tastes.

CIRCLE BISTRO

Map pp292-3   French $$

☎ 202-293-5390; One Washington Circle NW; mains $10-22; ⏱ lunch & dinner Mon-Fri, dinner Sat; Ⓜ Farragut West

For romantic dining and delectable French cuisine at reasonable prices, you can't beat Circle Bistro (it's one of the few places in the city where you can impress a date on less than $100), a respectable hotel restaurant tucked into a quiet part of town. Try the juicy roast chicken bursting with smoky flavor or the gooey leek-and-goat cheese tart. On the downside, the menu won't satisfy picky eaters – it's not big on variety.

LEGAL SEAFOODS

Map pp292-3   Seafood $$

☎ 202-496-1111, 2020 K St NW; mains $10-30; ⏱ lunch & dinner Mon-Fri, dinner Sat; Ⓜ Farragut North

A beloved Boston export, this place serves some of the freshest seafood in town. The menu features New England favorites like creamy white clam chowder and lobster plates, but also focuses on the local specialties – the Maryland jumbo lump crab cakes are delicious. There are a few locations scattered across the metro area, including at Ronald Reagan Washington National Airport. It has a sedate and polished steakhouse atmosphere; service is fast and professional.

BOMBAY CLUB

Map pp292-3   Indian $$

☎ 202-659-3727; 815 Connecticut Ave NW; mains $15-25; ⏱ lunch & dinner Sun-Fri, dinner Sat; Ⓜ Farragut West

Lauded as one of DC's top Indian restaurants, this place is popular with movie stars, such as Harrison Ford and Bruce Willis. It features cuisine inspired by the subcontinent's diverse cultures and an award-winning wine list. House specialties draw on the best of these, adding the chef's modern touch: spicy seafood curry, succulent chicken tikka masala and hot, hot, hot green chili chicken. The Bombay Club's elegant setting and indulgent service allow guests to experience the life of a maharaja, if only for a few hours.

OLD EBBITT GRILL

Map pp292-3   American $$

☎ 202-347-4801; 675 15th St NW; mains $15-25; Ⓜ Metro Center

This all-American saloon has been a venerable favorite with Washington's good ol' boys club since it opened its doors around 1846. Serving local choices like Maryland rockfish, crab cakes, steak and burgers, the brass and wood lends a powerful atmosphere and the place is always popular with DC's power-broking crowd. Don't miss the delightful Sunday brunch.

DC COAST

Map pp292-3   Seafood $$

☎ 202-216-5988; 1401 K St NW; mains $15-30; ⏱ lunch & dinner Mon-Fri, dinner Sat; Ⓜ McPherson Sq

Although the Art Deco space is rich, the scrumptious seafood is the reason to come to this perennial DC favorite. Who can pass up a 'Tower of Crab' with spicy, citrusy Tabasco butter? It does a serious lawyer-and-lobby lunch trade; the dull roar can be intrusive or exciting depending on your mood.

GEORGIA BROWN'S

Map pp292-3   Southern $$

☎ 202-393-4499; 1 McPherson Sq (15th & K Sts NW); mains $16-24; ⏱ 10:30am-2:15pm Mon-Fri, brunch Sun; Ⓜ McPherson Sq

Sunday brunch at Georgia Brown's has become a veritable DC institution ever since it was rumored to be Bill Clinton's favorite place to get food like down home. Serious Southern cooking with an emphasis on savory Low Country dishes combines seafood from the Carolina coast with flavors from West Indian plantations. Georgia's is popular with the K St lobbying crowd, Black urban professionals and anyone else who wants a good plate of grits.

OLIVES

Map pp292-3   Mediterranean $$

☎ 202-452-1866; 1600 K St NW; mains from $20; ☾ lunch & dinner Mon-Fri, dinner Sat; Ⓜ Farragut North

Just north of the White House, Boston-based chef Todd English operates this stylish, two-story hotspot. The kitchen-side bar upstairs is a prime seat, especially for solo diners: you can watch the sous-chefs chop and stir, and then order whatever whets your appetite. Handmade pastas are a good bet, if you can resist the aroma of the juicy, wood-grilled steaks and veal.

GALILEO

Map pp292-3   Italian $$

☎ 202-293-7191; 1110 21st St NW; mains $20; ☾ lunch & dinner Mon-Fri, dinner Sat & Sun; Ⓜ Foggy Bottom-GWU

Galileo tops many DC foodies' lists for its wonderful array of pastas, risottos and grilled meats. Owned by DC's Italian-cuisine wonder kid, Roberto Donna, Galileo is a favorite power-dinner spot for the times when you need to impress. For extra-special occasions, book the Laboratorio, where 10 to 12 guests dine in a private space and observe the preparation of their custom meal.

KINKEADS

Map pp292-3   Seafood $$

☎ 202-296-7700; 2000 Pennsylvania Ave NW; mains $20; Ⓜ Foggy Bottom-GWU

The seafood here arrives so fresh you can taste the sea, and it is always artfully combined with inventive spices and sauces. Acclaimed chef Robert Kinkead's imaginative specialties include pepita-crusted salmon, roasted cod with crab imperial, or – as an appetizer – tuna carpaccio. Even if you can't stay for dinner, a half-dozen oysters and a stiff whiskey here are the antidote to your midwinter blues.

LE TARBOUCHE

Map pp292-3   Mediterranean $$

☎ 202-331-5551; 1801 K St NW; meze $5-11, mains $20-30; ☾ lunch & dinner Mon-Fri, dinner Sat; Ⓜ Farragut West

With its lovely, rich decor of saffron-colored walls accented by ultramarine glassware, Le Tarbouche – meaning 'fez' – serves refined Lebanese-French cuisine with innovative spice-and-ingredient combinations. Candlelight and lots of nooks and crannies make this a prime spot for romancing. The internationals come out late on Saturday nights to dance to world-beat Latin and Middle Eastern music.

OCCIDENTAL GRILL

Map pp292-3   Steakhouse $$$

☎ 202-783-1475; 1475 Pennsylvania Ave NW; mains $20-30; Ⓜ Metro Center

This DC institution is practically wall-papered with mug shots of congressmen and other political celebs who have dined here throughout the years. Although the Occidental isn't the nerve center it once was, plenty of bigwigs still roll up their pinstripes to dive into hamburgers, chops and steaks.

MAXIM

Map pp292-3   Russian $$$

☎ 202-962-0280; 1725 F St NW; mains $25-35; Ⓜ Farragut North

Russian and Georgian specialties, regional wines and vodka, and international panache will take you to the Motherland for dinner. And we're not talking sad-looking Soviet salads here. Thick, rich soups, spicy Georgian treats, like *shashlyk* (shish kebabs) and *khachapuri* (cheesy bread) and – if you can afford it – *bliny* (Russian crepes) with caviar, reveal this Old World cuisine as it was meant to be. Euros get their groove on Friday and Saturday nights, making this *the* place to meet Russian speakers in the DC area.

JEFFREY'S AT THE WATERGATE

Map pp292-3   Tex-Mex $$$

☎ 202-298-4455; 2650 Virginia Ave, Swissôtel Watergate; mains $25-30; Ⓜ Foggy Bottom

Rumored to be a favorite of President and Mrs Bush, Jeffrey's delivers contemporary Texas cuisine with a spectacular view of the Potomac River. The menu features the culinary specialties of chef David Garrido: favorites like crispy Texas Gulf Coast oysters, yucca root chips with habanero honey aioli, and Texas beef tenderloin with Roquefort mashed potatoes and caramelized onions. This is a top spot for pre- or post-theater dining.

PRIME RIB
Map pp292-3   Steakhouse $$$

☎ 202-466-8811; 2020 K St NW; mains from $30; ☼ lunch & dinner Mon-Fri, dinner Sat; Ⓜ Farragut North

It seems like this place has always been synonymous with DC's most important movers-and-shakers, a notion that only becomes more apparent once stepping into its time-warp-inducing interior. Tuxedoed waiters serve suit-bedecked patrons (mandatory attire) prime aged steak and some of the city's top crab cakes. Few things at this institution ever change (which can be both good and bad – progressive it is not), and you'll be treated like a VIP regardless of your social status (as long as you dress the part).

MARCEL'S
Map pp292-3   French $$$

☎ 202-296-1166; 2401 Pennsylvania Ave NW; mains $30-40; ☼ dinner; Ⓜ Foggy Bottom

Located on the edge of Georgetown and the West End, this gem offers French fare with Flemish flair. That translates into fresh fish, farm-raised produce and high-quality ingredients whipped up into dishes like roasted rack of lamb with polenta and goat cheese garlic confit, or pan-seared salmon dusted in coriander and fennel seeds in citrus sauce. One classy touch: Marcel's offers a complimentary limousine service to the Kennedy Center and a prix-fixe menu ($48), so this is an ideal spot for pre-theater dining.

GEORGETOWN

Over one hundred eateries line M St and Wisconsin Ave and the surrounding blocks. From fancy French to Viet *pho*, and from pub grub to fine wine, Georgetown will feed just about any hungry body.

You'll find the cheap-eat options at the Georgetown Park food court, on the lower level of the mall at M St and Wisconsin Ave.

FIVE FOR FOODIES

DC's has many great restaurants to choose from, but true-blue foodies will really dig into these. The following places boast hot decor, fun scenes and a reputation for a unique gourmet dining experience. These are the kind of restaurants to hit when you really want your dinner to invigorate all the senses.

- Citronelle (p150) – One of DC's most acclaimed restaurants, anything wrapped in pastry is phenomenal. A favorite with DC celebrities, from talking heads to presidents.
- Komi (p159) – This eclectic endeavor offers an array of gourmet fusion cuisine that has foodies running towards its Venetian fairytale setting.
- Minibar at Café Atlantico (p156) – Adventurous foodies flock to this microscopic restaurant for a pre-set menu of 30 salacious morsels.
- Nora (p159) – The long reigning queen of the DC foodie scene, this restaurant has a reputation for serving organic food straight from local farmers and ranchers. It's in a quaint carriage house in Dupont.
- Obelisk (p160) – A set three-course Italian feast lovingly prepared with first-rate ingredients is served inside a dining room intimate enough to make you feel like a real somebody.

FIVE GUYS
Map p299   Burgers $

☎ 202-337-0400; 1335 Wisconsin Ave; burgers from $3.50; ☼ 11am-11pm Mon-Fri, 11am-4am Sat & Sun; 🚌 Georgetown shuttle from Rosslyn or Foggy Bottom-GWU Metro

DC's fastest-growing hometown burger chain, Five Guys just opened another restaurant in Georgetown and it's already become a favorite lunch joint with the retail crowd. A few years ago Five Guys had just three locations, now there are more than 20 flung across the city – we guess they are doing something right. The burgers and fries are done perfectly (mouthwateringly juicy with just the right amount of grease and a dizzying choice of condiments) and are what to order. Sit at the long bar and fill up on peanuts while your food's being fried. No booze.

BOOEYMONGER
Map p299   Sandwiches $

☎ 202-333-4810; 3265 Prospect St NW; sandwiches from $4; ☼ 8am-10pm; 🚌 Georgetown shuttle from Rosslyn or Foggy Bottom-GWU Metro

Create your own sandwich or choose one from the big board. Ingredients are fresh and service is quick, which explains why this local institution is often packed at lunchtime.

MOBY DICK HOUSE OF KABOB

Map p299   Middle Eastern $

☎ 202-333-4400; 1070 31st St; sandwiches from $4, platters from $6; ☽ 11am-10pm Sun-Thu, 11am-4am Fri & Sat; 🚌 Georgetown shuttle from Rosslyn or Foggy Bottom-GWU Metro

Why it's called Moby Dick is a mystery, but this is another hole-in-the wall joint serving tasty Persian food into the wee hours. The highlight is the pita bread, fresh and warm from the clay oven. Daily lunch specials are $6.25.

GEORGETOWN CAFÉ

Map pp300-1   American $

☎ 202-333-0215; 1623 Wisconsin Ave; mains from $5; ☽ 24hr; 🚌 Georgetown shuttle from Rosslyn or Foggy Bottom-GWU Metro

The place claims to stay open 24 hours, although it's been known to shut early on slow nights. Greasy-spoon American fare, steaming mugs of coffee and bleary-eyed partiers greet you late night.

DEAN & DELUCA

Map p299   Café, Self-catering $

☎ 202-342-2500; 3276 M St; lunch $8, coffees $5; 🚌 Georgetown shuttle from Rosslyn or Foggy Bottom-GWU Metro

The sunny café is enclosed in glass when weather demands it, but is otherwise open-air. Sandwiches and snacks are served cafeteria style, but they're fresh and delicious.

The gourmet market is worth a visit just for the pleasure of wandering among the potent cheeses, juicy fruits, fresh-baked breads, smooth mousse spreads and spicy sausages (many of which are available to sample).

CHING CHING CHA

Map p299   Asian $

☎ 202-333-8288; 1063 Wisconsin Ave NW; appetizers $2-5, mains $10; ☽ lunch & dinner Tue-Sat, to 7pm Sun; 🚌 Georgetown shuttle from Rosslyn or Foggy Bottom-GWU Metro

A serene interior takes you far away from the Georgetown traffic outside the front

door. This Asian teahouse is filled with plush red pillows that encourage lotus-style lingering. There are more than 48 different teas to choose from, along with lots of small appetizer plates (meant for nibbling over pots of smoky tea) and healthy mains. The place is most vibrant at lunch.

PIZZERIA PARADISO

Map p299   Italian $

☎ 202-337-1245; 3282 M St NW; mains from $10; 🚌 Georgetown Shuttle from Rosslyn or Foggy Bottom-GWU Metro

This casual restaurant serves wood-oven Neapolitan-style pizzas with scrumptious toppings to crowds of starving patrons with rave results. The pizza crust is perfect – light, crisp and a little flaky. Great people-watching from the big plate-glass windows, popular happy hours, and a hand-picked beer and ale selection heighten the appeal. There's a second location in Dupont Circle.

MARTIN'S TAVERN

Map p299   American $

☎ 202-333-7370; 1264 Wisconsin Ave NW; mains $10-25; 🚌 Georgetown shuttle from Foggy Bottom-GWU Metro

John F Kennedy proposed to Jackie in booth number three at Georgetown's oldest saloon, and if you're thinking of popping the question there today the attentive waitstaff keep the champagne chilled for that very reason. With an old-English country scene, including the requisite fox-and-hound hunting prints on the wall, this DC institution serves a mean burger and icy cold pints of beer to college students and senators alike.

CAFÉ LA RUCHE

Map p299   French $

☎ 202-965-2684; 1039 31st St; mains from $10, brunch $12; ☽ lunch & dinner, brunch 9am-2:30pm Sat & Sun; 🚌 Georgetown shuttle from Rosslyn or Foggy Bottom-GWU Metro

Set on a quiet lane away from the crowds and near the canal, La Ruche bills itself as Georgetown's oldest French bistro. This quintessential café has a dining room packed with tiled tables and a garden draped in vines, making it an appealing date spot. The menu is straightforward, featuring classic items like steamy, spicy, garlic *moules* (mussels) or fresh, tangy salad Niçoise. On weekends, come for brunch and a complimentary Mimosa.

BANGKOK BISTRO

Map p299   Thai $$

☎ 202-337-2424; 3251 Prospect St NW; mains $10-20; ☺ lunch & dinner; 🚍 Georgetown shuttle from Rosslyn or Foggy Bottom-GWU Metro

Locals love this joint on their birthdays – the birthday person eats free. Actually this modern Thai restaurant with a lively sidewalk café does a fast trade most nights of the week. Serving a long line-up of Thai favorites, it doesn't try anything too adventurous (true lovers of Thai cuisine might argue it's too Americanized) with its cooking, but dishes are consistently good and can be spiced accordingly. We always like the drunken noodles and green-curry mains.

PAOLO'S

Map p299   Italian $$

☎ 202-333-7353; 1303 Wisconsin Ave; mains $10-20; ☺ lunch & dinner; 🚍 Georgetown shuttle from Rosslyn or Foggy Bottom-GWU Metro

Pop into this Italian bistro at night when the vibe is rowdy and crowds waiting for a table (try to score a coveted spot on the outdoor patio or by the big street-side windows) spill onto Wisconsin. Brick-oven baked pizzas, grilled meats and pastas complement the award-winning wine list, and with the white tablecloths and lots of ambient noise, it makes an easy-going first date spot.

Visit late at night to score $10 pizza specials, perfect if you're woozy from a night of drinking.

CLYDE'S

Map p299   American $$

☎ 202-333-9180; 3236 M St NW; mains $10-20; ☺ 11:30am-midnight Mon-Thu, 11:30-1am Fri, 10-1am Sat, 9am-midnight Sun; 🚍 Georgetown shuttle from Foggy Bottom-GWU

A true Georgetown institution, Clyde's has been around for almost 40 years. It's a comfortable yet classy tavern best known for its fantastic Sunday brunch. The American dishes are pretty basic – don't expect any super-fancy twists – but they usually come out tasting fresh and fulfilling.

Clyde's has five other DC locations, each themed differently, including a new multi-million-dollar property in the Verizon Center.

VIETNAM GEORGETOWN

Map p299   Vietnamese $$

☎ 202-337-5588; 2928 M St NW; lunch buffet $6.45, dinner mains from $12; 🚍 Georgetown shuttle from Rosslyn or Foggy Bottom-GWU Metro

A pioneer of Vietnamese cooking in the neighborhood, this restaurant serves steaming bowls of noodles and deep-fried crispy rolls: spicy and satisfying. The lunch buffet is particularly good value. The setting and staff are charming, if somewhat frazzled. The garden out back is decked with colorful lights and is especially attractive on a summer evening. (Minus the garden, this place is nearly interchangeable with its next-door neighbor, the Saigon Inn.)

HANKS OYSTER BAR

Map pp300-1   Seafood $$

☎ 202-462 4265; 1624 Q St NW; mains $13-22; ☺ dinner Wed-Mon , brunch Sat & Sun

It's hard not to fall in love with this tiny oyster bar, where the daily half-shell specials are scribbled on a blackboard and pen-and-ink portraits of fish adorn the walls. There are always at least four varieties of oysters, along with a menu that mixes fresh grilled fish with buttermilk onion rings and cheddar-and-gouda mac 'n' cheese. Quarters are cramped, and you'll have to wait for a table. Kick back with a couple shots of sake and a calamari appetizer and wait it out like everyone else.

ZED'S ETHIOPIAN CUISINE

Map pp292-3   African $$

☎ 202-333-4710; 1201 28th St NW; mains $15-25; ☺ lunch & dinner; 🚍 Georgetown shuttle from Foggy Bottom-GWU

Of the dozens of Ethiopian restaurants scattered around the district, Zed's has the distinction of being the Ethiopian embassy's host for official dinners. In a classic two-story Georgetown townhouse on a quiet side street, this restaurant serves hearty, spicy dishes that you eat with your fingers or dip with spongy flat bread.

SEQUOIA

Map p299   American $$

☎ 202-944-4200; Georgetown Harbor, 3000 K St; mains $15-30; ☽ 11:30am-midnight Mon-Thu, 11:30-1am Fri & Sat, 10:30am-midnight Sun; 🚌 Georgetown shuttle from Foggy Bottom-GWU

With views to die for and mouthwatering seafood, this classic Georgetown restaurant pleases all your senses. Overlooking the Potomac River, try the more casual outdoor patio where the menu is a little cheaper and the sunsets spectacular. Inside it's all white linen and china and suits. Inside or out, the food is creative and elegant and the service excellent. At night Sequoia is a popular drinking spot with Washington's preppy pretty people. You'll pay royally to drink your Corona at the packed outside bar, but it's quite a social experience.

J PAUL'S

Map p299   American $$

☎ 202-333-3450; 3218 M Street; mains $15-30; ☽ 11:30-2am Mon-Thu, 11:30-3am Fri & Sat, 10:30-2am Sun; 🚌 Georgetown shuttle from Rosslyn or Foggy Bottom-GWU Metro

J Paul's house favorite, the jumbo lump crab cakes, is what you should order. Skip the appetizer sliders, which have too much bun and not enough meat, and stick to the mains instead. An atmospheric old dining saloon with lots of heavy wood, it features a popular raw bar (where live shellfish are shucked and served) and does a busy happy-hour trade. If you're just in the mood for booze and munchies, try the cheesy crab-and-shrimp dip ($11) and a perfect martini.

CAFÉ MILANO

Map p299   Italian $$$

☎ 202-333-6183; 3251 Prospect St; mains $20-30; ☽ 11:30am-midnight Sun-Wed, 11:30-2am Thu-Sat; 🚌 Georgetown shuttle from Rosslyn or Foggy Bottom-GWU Metro

DC's most famous people-watching spot, it draws everyone from high-class call girls to diplomats and White House insiders for Italian food like you find in Italy, but more importantly the opportunity to see and be seen. Followers of mode and mafia fight for prime tables and service can be snotty. If you want to be treated like royalty, you'd better dress the part.

1789

Map p299   American $$$

☎ 202-965-1789; 1226 36th St; mains $20-40; ☽ dinner; 🚌 Georgetown shuttle from Rosslyn or Foggy Bottom-GWU Metro

Set in a welcoming Federal row house, 1789 is well known to Georgetown students as *the* place to take your visiting parents (or rather, have them take you). Chef Ris Lacoste uses local, seasonal produce and game to create new twists on American classics, such as rabbit and sweetbreads and soft-shell crabs with corn pudding. You won't pass up dessert if you catch a glimpse of the pastry chefs working in the front window next door. Upstairs you will find the students' favorite drinking spot, **Tombs** (p172).

MIE N YU

Map p299   Fusion $$$

☎ 202-333-6122; 3125 M St; mains from $25; ☽ lunch & dinner Mon-Fri, dinner Sat & Sun; 🚌 Georgetown shuttle from Rosslyn or Foggy Bottom-GWU Metro

It's been around for more than a few years now, but Mie N Yu shows no signs of losing its coolness. Featuring an eclectic menu and exotic decor, it's the coolest lounge-restaurant in Georgetown. The seven different rooms represent the world's exotic wonders – from the suspended birdcage room in the back to the opium-den colonial Silk Rd bar.

Depending where you are seated, you might dine in a Bedouin camp or in the sultan's harem, but rest assured colorful pillows will surround you and you'll be waited on hand and foot – although you'll pay through the nose for all this coolness, cocktails and even house wines average around $14! The menu is nouveau Asian with lots of salads and other non-fatty dishes. Don't leave without checking out the fancy, unisex toilet in the basement. Reservations recommended.

CITRONELLE

Map p299   French $$$

☎ 202-625-2150; 3000 M St NW, Latham Hotel; dinner from $100; ☽ dinner Sat & Sun; 🚌 Georgetown shuttle from Rosslyn or Foggy Bottom-GWU Metro

Tucked away inside the **Latham Hotel** (p228), this elegant, bi-level restaurant is one of

EATING 24/7

It's not New York, but DC is good for late-night dining if you know where to go.

- Afterwords Café & Kramerbooks (p158) – Coffee, books and café fare all night long (how very Dupont).
- Annie's Paramount Steakhouse (p158) – One of DC's hottest gay spots after 3am.
- Georgetown Café (p148) – Greasy spoon food 24/7.
- Diner (p160) – Classic post-clubbing cuisine at any hour.
- Pizza Mart (p160) – Grab a jumbo slice to go.

DC's most acclaimed. Chef Michel Richard began his career as a pastry chef, so you can't go wrong with menu items such as shrimp wrapped in filo or, well, dessert. Reserve your table in advance and dress up for the occasion.

CAPITOL HILL

Capitol Hill offers a mixed bag of dining options: old-boy, cigars-and-gin steakhouses where senators conspire; free-chips-and-cheap-booze eateries where their underpaid staffers drown their sorrows; and the friendliest open-air farmers market in town.

EASTERN MARKET

Map p304   Self-catering $

www.easternmarket.net; 7th St & North Carolina Ave SE; ☾ 10am-6pm Tue-Fri, 8am-4pm Sat & Sun; Ⓜ Eastern Market

Fresh meats and cheese, colorful produce and sweet-smelling baked goods fill the cases at Eastern Market. Particularly lively on weekends, it's a treat anytime to buy fresh ingredients straight from their source. See also Sights (p87).

JIMMY T'S

Map p304   American $

☎ 202-546-3646; 501 E Capitol St; breakfast & lunch from $6; ☾ 7am-3pm Tue-Sun; Ⓜ Eastern Market

The ultimate in neighborhood joints, this tiny corner diner is jammed on weekends with locals swilling coffee and reading

the *Post* at the little counter and in the scuffed-up booths. Breakfast is served all day along with short-order sandwiches and burgers.

MARKET LUNCH

Map p304   Seafood $

☎ 202-546-2698; 225 7th St SE; lunch $8; ☾ 8am-3pm Tue-Sat, 11am-3pm Sun; Ⓜ Eastern Market

Inside historic Eastern Market alongside the butchers and bakers and candlestick makers, this unassuming take-out counter serves some of DC's freshest, tastiest seafood. Crab-cake platters, soft-shell crabs and fried oyster sandwiches don't get much better than this. Saturday and Sunday morning brunch features equally delicious butter-and-syrup-soaked pancakes (blueberry, buckwheat or blue-bucks).

SONOMA RESTAURANT & WINE BAR

Map p304   American $$

☎ 202-544-8088; 223 Pennsylvania Ave SE; small plates $7-17 ☾ lunch & dinner; Ⓜ Eastern Market

A relative newcomer to the Pennsylvania Ave scene, this fancy wine bar was packed with suity hill types around 6pm on a Tuesday so it must be doing something right (plus it made *Washingtonian* magazine's 100 Best Bargains barely a year after opening). Two floors provide plenty of space for classy tables. The menu features lots of small plates (although a few like the sumptuous Linguine alla Vongole are big enough to be mains) and fresh cheeses, as well as a very reasonably priced tasting menu. Loosen your tie and dig in.

AMERICA

Map p304   American $$

☎ 202-682-9555; 50 Massachusetts Ave, Union Station; mains $10-18; Ⓜ Union Station

Claiming to be DC's 'only 50-star restaurant,' this place takes the theme as far as it goes, with menus shaped like maps and mains from every state in the Union (from New York steak to grilled mahimahi and don't forget Boston cream pie for dessert). The varied menu draws Hill-rats during the week and tourists on weekends. It's a good place to bring the family; couples might find the mall atmosphere a little unromantic.

2 QUAIL

Map p304   Continental $$

☎ 202-543-8030; 320 Massachusetts Ave; lunch
from $10, dinner from $20; ☯ lunch & dinner;
Ⓜ Union Station

Tucked away in an unassuming brick row
house, this gem of a restaurant is truly a
Washington landmark. Frilly, romantic and
cluttered with chintz and velvet, it looks
like a cross between grandma's attic and an
elegant parlor and makes all the romantic-
dining shortlists. The food seems to take a
back seat to the fancy decor, but nobody is
complaining about the fine mains, such as
roasted duck, seafood pasta or the signa-
ture quail.

There are great lunch and happy-hour
specials, including $12 bottles of wine on
the patio and the $10 'Senator's Lunch',
which includes a chef's pick of main, soup
and salad. If you're interested in learning
how to taste wine, ask your waiter about
the seminars run by the restaurant.

TORTILLA COAST

Map p304   Tex-Mex $

☎ 202-546-6768; 400 First St SE; mains $12-20;
Ⓜ Capitol South

Hillies have been flocking to this old
stand-by joint on the House side for
decades now for lunch and après-work
cocktails. Tortilla Coast serves great chips
and salsa – the chips are neither too heavy
nor greasy – along with unique margaritas
and the usual fajitas and enchiladas
(although we have to say people come
more for the congenial gossipy ambiance
than for divine cuisine).

BISTRO BIS

Map p304   French $$

☎ 202-661-2700; 15 E St NW, Hotel George; mains
$15-30; ☯ breakfast, lunch & dinner; Ⓜ Union
Station

La favorite among DC's real and wannabe
power brokers, this oh-so-chic bistro
inside the Hotel George (p230) features nouveau versions of French classics: succulent
duck confit with garlic and thyme; seared
sea scallops served with roasted eggplant;
and steak frite with tarragon hollandaise
(but with the mandatory pommes frites).

Bistro Bis is open for breakfast, one of
the few restaurants in its class to do so,
making it the perfect spot to squeeze in

a gourmet omelette and glass of freshly
squeezed juice before dashing off to
explore the city.

B SMITH'S

Map p304   Southern $$

☎ 202-289-6188; 50 Massachusetts Ave, Union
Station; mains $16-30; Ⓜ Union Station

With its spectacular vaulted ceilings, mar-
ble floors and Ionic columns, you can't
beat B Smith's location in the former Presi-
dential Waiting Hall at Union Station. It is
a remarkable contrast to the down-home
Southern fare that's served here by former
model Barbara Smith (whose unclouded
complexion once graced Oil of Olay ads).
Which is not to say the food is not deli-
cious: it is. She upgrades Southern classics
like fried chicken and blackened shrimp
to sophisticated oeuvres (eg jumbo black-
ened shrimp served over crisp mesclun
greens with a tangy soy-lime vinaigrette).

The restaurant attracts an affluent
African American crowd, and is as popular
for après-work drinks as it is for dinner. The
ambiance is soul soothing with mellow
lights and music, muted colors and mod
art on the walls.

MONOCLE

Map p304   American $$

☎ 202-546-4488; 107 D St NE; mains from $20;
☯ lunch & dinner Mon-Fri; Ⓜ Union Station

The best place to spot your senator off-
duty and glass-in-hand is this good ol'
boys' club just behind the Capitol. The
dark bar only helps to boost the haughty
atmosphere. Check out the walls festooned
with politicians' quotes ('If you want a
friend in Washington, get a dog'). The
food – surf-and-turf American classics like
salmon and rib-eye steak – is less appetiz-
ing than the people-watching.

MONTMARTRE

Map p304   French $$$

☎ 202-544-1244; 327 7th St SE; mains $25-40;
Ⓜ Eastern Market

You may mistake Capitol Hill for Paris if
you dine on the patio at the city's best
French bistro. Apparently the building
used to be a post office, but you wouldn't
know it now for its pretty dining room
and clean-lined bar. The place is chaoti-
cally cozy and perfect for lingering over

a bottle of red. Culinary masterpieces include delicious chilled soups in summer, fresh fish seared to perfection and tender, juicy steaks.

CHARLIE PALMER STEAK

Map p304   American $$$

☎ 202-547-8100; 101 Constitution Ave NW; mains from $35; Ⓜ Capitol South

In the shadow of the Capitol (you can see the marble dome through the plate-glass windows in the dining room), this place simply oozes power. And while it has the requisite swirling cigar smoke and old boys-club feel, it's also got a muted blue and orange color scheme and bold, award-winning modern menu with an all-American wine list. The downside? Prices at celebrity chef-owner Charlie Palmer's restaurant are appallingly high.

SOUTHEAST & SOUTHWEST DC

Dining in this neighborhood takes place entirely in the Southwest quadrant (we're just not going to send you to the streets of Anacostia for lunch, it's not safe and there isn't anything to eat). The cuisine of choice along the Waterfront is seafood. Whether seasoned with hot peppers or fruity flavors or nothing at all, it was not too long ago that your dinner was swimming around in the ocean somewhere. This area's lovely views of the Potomac – especially superb at sunset – are a welcome feature of this otherwise drab setting.

FISH WHARF

Map pp308-9   Seafood $

Waterfront, Washington Channel; meals from $6; ⏱ 7:30am-8:30pm Sun-Thu, to 9:30pm Jun-Aug, 7:30am-9pm Fri & Sat, to 10pm Jun-Aug; Ⓜ L'Enfant Plaza

Just south of the I-395 bridge are barges and stalls selling seafood so fresh that some of it is still moving. Stalls are packed with huge barrels of blue crabs and silver fish. With all the tentacles, smells and flying shells, it's a sensory spectacle even if you're not hungry. The fishmongers will cook for you, too: soft-shell crab sandwiches, oysters on the half-shell and crab cakes are the specialties. Alas, there are no tables, so take

BEST FOR BRUNCH

Washingtonians love nothing more than lingering over the paper and bloody marys at Sunday brunch. The meal is a city institution, and some of the best spreads are found in the posh hotels. These are a favorite with interns and young Hillies as they let them get the power feeling of eating at a power hotel with less-steep prices. The following are our favorite non-hotel joints.

- Clyde's (p149) – A Georgetown institution known for its classy environs, jumbo lump crab cakes and Sunday brunch.
- Kinkeads (p146) – Oysters and Mimosas, how much more stylish can you get?
- Tabard Inn (p159) – Chocolate-almond pancakes in the garden, need we say more?
- Perry's (p161) – The drag-queen brunch is where to be on Sunday morning, even if you're not queer.
- Georgia Brown's (p145) – Sunday brunch at Georgia Brown's has become a veritable DC institution ever since it was rumored to be Bill Clinton's favorite place to get food like down-home.

your meal south along the channel-side walkway where there is bench seating.

BANANA CAFÉ & PIANO BAR

Map pp308-9   Caribbean $$

☎ 202-543-5906; 500 8th St SE; lunch from $10, dinner from $16; Ⓜ Eastern Market

Amid all the activity on 8th St SE, this funky, colorful café mixes it up with traditional Cuban and Puerto Rican dishes and a few Tex-Mex favorites thrown in for good measure. The house specialty 'Cuban' is a Dagwood sandwich with Caribbean flair – juicy roast pork, honey-baked ham and Swiss cheese with all the fixings. Veggies will love the sweet plantain timbales stuffed with picadillo (pepper and potato hash) and topped with sharp cheddar cheese. On Tuesday to Saturday nights, jazz filters down from the fun piano bar upstairs.

ZANZIBAR

Map pp308-9   Afro-Caribbean $$

☎ 202-554-9100; 700 Water St SW; mains $16-24; ⏱ lunch & dinner Tue-Sun; Ⓜ Waterfront

Seafood here has an Afro-Caribbean twist: spicy sauces, fruit garnishes and rum drinks characterize the creative menu. The bold, colorful decor complements the African theme. Upstairs there is a large dance floor, often frequented by very elegant-looking African American couples. See Entertainment (p190).

H20

Map pp308-9   Surf & Turf $$
☎ 202-484-6300; 800 Water St SW; mains $16-24;
Ⓜ Waterfront
River views and an appeasing assortment of steak, crab cakes and pasta mains make this one of the best choices on the Waterfront. It's also pretty swanky, with a remodeled interior and an attached glam lounge and club. The Captain's Platter is a bargain if split. It offers a heaping portion of seafood favorites for $35.

DOWNTOWN

During the boom years of the 1990s, the neighborhoods north of the Mall transformed themselves. Once this area was a ghost town after dark, but now you can find established restaurant districts in Chinatown, along 7th and 8th Sts NW and close to the White House. For cheap eats you can't beat the Old Post Office Pavilion's food court at lunch.

CAPITAL Q BBQ

Map pp292-3   BBQ $
☎ 202-347-8396; 707 H St NW, dishes $4.50;
Ⓜ Gallery Place-Chinatown
A must for Texas-style BBQ lovers, with piled-high portions of smoked meat and plenty o' slaw on the side; try the brisket sandwich. A very casual eating environment, usually packed at lunch with journalists, office workers and other city folk.

FULL KEE

Map pp292-3   Chinese $
☎ 202-371-2233; 509 H St NW; mains from $6;
🕑 11-1am Sun-Thu, 11-3am Fri & Sat; Ⓜ Gallery Pl-Chinatown
At the very best dive in Chinatown, fill yourself for next to nothing with a simple noodle dish or gorge on a wondrous stir-fry. Better still, go for one of the rich savory casseroles you won't find at other places, like eggplant and short ribs or

pork and bean curd. Full Kee does not accept credit cards. No alcohol.

WOK & ROLL

Map pp292-3   Chinese & Japanese $
☎ 202-347-4656; 604 H St NW; mains from $8;
🕑 lunch & dinner Mon-Sun, to 3am Fri & Sat;
Ⓜ Gallery Pl-Chinatown
At this inauspicious address, Lincoln's assassins plotted their scheme (they were later hanged for it). These days, much happier plotting takes place here, such as deciding whether to order light, fresh sushi or steaming, spicy noodles for lunch. The selection of teas – black, green, hot or cold – is impressive; try one of the delicious and healthy milk teas.

TONY CHENG'S SEAFOOD RESTAURANT

Map pp292-3   Chinese $
☎ 202-371-8669; 619 H St NW; dim sum items from $3, mains $10-25; 🕑 lunch & dinner;
Ⓜ Gallery Pl-Chinatown
Skip the Mongolian barbeque on the ground floor – everything tastes pretty much the same, and head upstairs to the seafood restaurant instead. The place looks a little dingy, but it has one of Chinatown's best kitchens. The fare is mostly Cantonese and seafood is what to order (you can watch your dinner swimming about in tanks).

On weekends Tony Cheng's attracts droves of Chinese Americans for the traditional Hong Kong dim sum – you can still order during the week, but the choices are less varied, coming off a menu and not a rolling cart.

ZAYTINYA

Map pp292-3   Mediterranean $$
☎ 202-333-4710; 701 9th St NW; meze $4-8, lunch mains $12, dinner mains $20; Ⓜ Gallery Pl-Chinatown
Earth tones, high ceilings and clean lines characterize this elegant bi-level. After stints at Café Atlantico and Jaleo, chef Jose Andres applies his expertise to the fare of Greece, Lebanon and Turkey. The extensive menu of hot and cold meze – 'little dishes' – reflects the rich, regional diversity of these cuisines. Reservations recommended for lunch. If you come for dinner, be prepared

to wait: reservations are not accepted and this place is all the rage.

JALEO

Map pp292-3   Spanish $

☎ 202-628-7949; 480 7th St NW; tapas $4-8, mains $15; Ⓜ Archives-Navy Memorial

Although 'Jaleo' can refer to a popular Andalusian dance, in this case the alternative definition is more appropriate: revelry and merrymaking.

Dominated by a large semicircular bar (where you should not pass on a pitcher of sangria), the place is decorated with Andalusian pottery and warm Mediterranean colors. Dinner can be paella or a few other *platos fuertes* (main dishes), but the star of the menu is the selection of over 40 tapas.

Reservations are highly recommended for dinner.

ANDALE

Map pp292-3   Mexican $$

☎ 202-783-3133; 401 7th St NW; mains from $15; Ⓨ lunch & dinner Mon-Sat; Ⓜ Archives-Navy Memorial

The executive chef spent the summer in Mexico and was so inspired that she revamped her restaurant – formerly the Mark – into this innovative, contemporary, south-of-the-border gem. It's been more than five years now, but Andale is still a local favorite serving a solid lineup of complex Mexican dishes. Everything here reflects thoughtful effort, from the original artwork and Mexican lanterns adorning the dining room, to the *caldo de mariscos* (spicy seafood stew).

RED SAGE

Map pp292-3   Tex-Mex $$

☎ 202-638-4444; 605 14th St NW; mains $15-20; Ⓨ lunch & dinner Mon-Fri, dinner Sat & Sun; Ⓜ Metro Center

Georgia O'Keeffe probably inspired these cave-like, rose-stucco, subterranean rooms with wood-beam ceilings and fancy ironwork. It's a fine setting to enjoy chef Morou Ouattara's Southwestern-inflected American cuisine (apparently Bill Clinton used to). These are not your typical fajitas and margaritas; chef specialties include red-chili pecan-crusted chicken, grilled diver scallops with saffron, acorn squash

risotto, and smoked antelope, bison and ostrich.

ROSA MEXICANO

Map pp292-3   Mexican $$

☎ 202-783-5522; 575 7th St NW; mains $15-30; Ⓜ Archives-Navy Memorial

With house specialties like made-at-your-table guacamole and pomegranate margaritas, it's no wonder this visual masterpiece across from the MCI Center is usually packed. With a shockingly pink dining room and a blue-tiled waterfall filling an entire wall, the place is anything but subtle and draws a mixed crowd, from tourists coming from the Spy Museum to locals grabbing an early drink and enchilada. The menu is sophisticated Nouveau Mexican, although with the exception of the guacamole, the food can be hit and miss – ask your server for a recommendation.

TENPENH

Map pp292-3   Asian $$

☎ 202-393-4500; 1001 Pennsylvania Ave; mains $20-25; Ⓨ lunch & dinner Mon-Fri, dinner Sat; Ⓜ Federal Triangle

Jewel-toned walls and shimmering lights, an abstract painting of an Asian warrior, a 17th-century black Buddha statue: such stylistic touches set the tone for this ultra-hip Asian-fusion masterpiece. The food is by no means secondary, however. Jeff Tunks – of DC Coast fame – adds ingredients and spices from China, Thailand and Vietnam to his well-honed traditional techniques, resulting in eclectic but exceptional culinary experiences for his guests.

ZOLA

Map pp292-3   American $$

☎ 202-654-0999; International Spy Museum, 800 F St; mains $20-30; Ⓨ lunch & dinner Mon-Fri, dinner Sat & Sun; Ⓜ Gallery Pl-Chinatown

A subtle but playful theme of espionage runs through this hip restaurant, named for French author Emile Zola, who championed the case of Alfred Dreyfus when he was falsely accused of being a spy. Located inside the International Spy Museum, it is only appropriate that guests should be able to monitor the kitchen through discreet one-way mirrors in the booths, or slip off to the restroom through a hidden door. Black-and-white photographs and projections of coded text further add to the mysterious air. In the midst of this secrecy, Zola's cuisine is surprisingly straightforward. Upscale versions of American classics include veal and mushroom meat loaf wrapped in bacon for dinner, or baked ham and smoked gouda grilled sandwiches for lunch (not exactly like Mom used to make, but we're not complaining).

POSTE

Map pp292-3   New American $$$

☎ 202-783-6060; 555 8th St NW; mains $25-30; ⏰ 7am-11pm; Ⓜ Gallery Pl-Chinatown

This restaurant was named for its previous incarnation as the mail sorting room for the City Post Office. Many of the brasserie's restored architectural features had a practical purpose back in their day – cast-iron ceilings to protect the mail from fire, skylights and a picture window to provide light to sort by, and a portal entry (which now leads to the patio seating) large enough for a horse-drawn carriage. The space is now a fantastic place for a drink (try a 'Skyy Love Letter') or a delightful, French-influenced meal.

INDEBLEU

Map pp292-3   Indian-French Fusion $$$

☎ 202-333-2538; 707 G St NW; mains $25-35; Ⓜ Gallery Pl-Chinatown

This dramatic-looking space is an oasis of hipness in the heart of Downtown. Reach the muted beige-and-cream dining room on the 2nd floor via a futuristic catwalk to join Washington's beautiful people in an exotic explosion of Indian-influenced French grub. Attentive service and delicious food are plusses, although the pulsating house-track din drifting up from the lounge makes conversation hard. If you'd rather just grab a cocktail, join the Euro crowd at the orange-hued mod bar downstairs.

MINIBAR AT CAFÉ ATLANTICO

Map pp292-3   Modern American $$$

☎ 202-393-0821; 405 8th St NW; micro-meals from $10; Ⓜ Archives/Navy Memorial

Minibar takes dining to the microscopic (and oh so trendy) level at this restaurant within a restaurant. Located in a corner of Café Atlantico, adventurous foodies flock

here for a completely different dining experience. The pre-set menu of 30 tasty morsels – ranging from cotton candy – slicked foie gras to a whisky sour frothed up in a shot glass – is whisked up by well-known local chef José Andres in front of your very eyes. Many of the creations are delightful and its definitely the place to be seen. On the down side, however, you don't get to choose what you're eating and it sometimes seems the chef is more interested in creating something that sounds truly bizarre than worrying about its taste.

DUPONT CIRCLE & KALORAMA

Dupont Circle demonstrates the best of DC's dining scene. Classy nouveau cuisine and upscale ethnic eateries cater to the flocks of diplomats and businesspeople, and casual cafés cater to the more bohemian.

COSI

Map pp296-7   Café $

☎ 202-296-9341; 1350 Connecticut Ave NW; mains $6-8; ⏰ 6.30am-midnight Mon-Thu, to 1am Fri, 8-1am Sat, 8am-11pm Sun; Ⓜ Dupont Circle

Get your coffee straight up in the morning, and with a few shots of booze in the evening, at this friendly café where the mood is all about mellow lingering. Fresh salads and ciabatta sandwiches keep your stomach happy as you toil away on your laptop or devour the morning's *Washington Post*. After 4pm the place serves liquor – choose from alcoholic coffee cocktails and a range of wine, spirits and beer. There are numerous locations around the city.

THAIPHOON

Map pp296-7   Thai $

☎ 202-667-3505; 2011 S St NW; lunch from $6, dinner from $10; Ⓜ Dupont Circle

The quality of the food does not always match the sleek decor, which features a wall of windows, a colorful interior and a funky bar. But Thaiphoon's seafood and veggie dishes are good enough to draw crowds, giving the place a buzz to match the tingle of Thai spices.

LAURIOL PLAZA

Map pp296-7   Tex-Mex $

☎ 202-387-0035; 1835 18th St NW; lunch specials
$7, dinner from $10; Ⓜ Dupont Circle
This lively spot is popular for its pitchers
of margaritas, its huge rooftop terrace and
its gentrified Tex-Mex dishes. Grilled marinated quail and pork roasted in Seville's
bitter oranges are among the fancier items
on the menu. But never fear, there are
enchiladas and fajitas here, too.

WELL-DRESSED BURRITO

Map pp296-7 Tex-Mex $

☎ 202-293-0515; 1220 19th St NW (enter through
the alley); mains $8; Ⓨ 11:45am-2:15pm;
Ⓜ Dupont Circle
Brought to you by CF Folks, across the
street, this hidden culinary gem is arguably
the best Tex-Mex in the neighborhood. The
gigantic 16oz El Gordo burrito – stuffed
with marinated beef, chicken or vegeta-
bles, plus beans and cheese – receives rave
reviews from office folk working in the
'hood.

ZORBA'S CAFÉ

Map pp296-7   Greek $

☎ 202-387-8555; 1612 20th St NW; mains $8-12;
Ⓜ Dupont Circle
Generous portions of moussaka and souv-
laki, as well as pitchers of Rolling Rock,
make this Greek diner one of DC's best bargain haunts. Contrary to the menu's promise, you will probably not confuse yourself
for being in the Greek Isles (despite the
bouzouki music). But the fresh food and
quick service make this family-run place a
good option.

CITY LIGHTS OF CHINA

Map pp296-7   Chinese $

☎ 202-265-6688; 1731 Connecticut Ave; mains
$8-15; Ⓜ Dupont Circle
It's not much to look at, but City Lights
is actually one of the better inexpensive
Chinese restaurants in DC. The house
specialty is Peking duck, but all the old
favorites are here. For the more health
conscious, the menu now offers some
of the old favorites, like General Tsao's
chicken, with sautéed white meat instead
of deep-fried batter and served with
steamed broccoli and brown rice.

RAKU

Map pp296-7   Asian $

☎ 202-265-7258; 1900 Q St; tapas from $4, mains
from $9; Ⓨ lunch & dinner Tue-Sun; Ⓜ Dupont
Circle
We absolutely love the chicken-curry
udon noodles at this place. We love them
so much we often dream about them
while we're away. Our obsession with
the noodles at Raku may be unique, but
everyone else seems to be obsessed with
the restaurant itself these days. Where else
can you get such a delicious assortment
of fabulous fresh Asian-fusion delights at
such reasonable prices? Other Raku menu
musts include 'Pan-Asian tapas' (treats
such as mussels sautéed in a ginger black-
bean sauce, or shrimp and crab dump-
lings in a Thai chili sauce) and the wide
selection of sushi, sashimi, salads, fish
and meat. The Asian-fusion concept even
extends to the drinks menu. How about
a green-tea martini? There's a second
branch in Bethesda.

AQUA ARDIENTE

Map pp296-7   Spanish $$

☎ 202-833-8500; 1250 24th St NW; mains $10-30;
Ⓜ Dupont Circle
Sshhh, don't tell anyone, Washingtonian's
would rather keep this neighborhood
Spanish place a secret. The vibe is tribal
trendy meets spiritual, with a Madonna
shrine, Indian masks and silky rouge
curtains. The menu is billed as Nouveau
Latino, and offers a slew of ceviches and
an extensive wine list.

UNI

Map pp296-7   Sushi $$

☎ 202-833-8038; 2122 P St NW; mains $11-20;
Ⓨ lunch & dinner Mon-Sat, dinner Sun;
Ⓜ Dupont Circle
The decor is a little outdated at this
friendly sushi bar (think Hello Kitty and
bamboo), but Uni gets good marks for its
sushi and innovative 'small dishes' ranging from pickles and tofu to mussels and
calamari. Looking down on P St from a
2nd-floor perch, jazz plays from the speakers and diners can even take advantage of
high-speed wireless access should they be
carrying a laptop. Monday through Friday,
enjoy Sake-tini happy hour, featuring $1
sushi and $3.50 sake martinis.

AFTERWORDS CAFÉ & KRAMERBOOKS

Map pp296-7   American $$

☎ 202-387-1462; 1517 Connecticut Ave; mains from $12; ☾ 8:30-1:30am Sun-Thu, 24hr Fri & Sat; Ⓜ Dupont Circle

Some locals would claim this independent bookstore with café attached is the center of the DC universe. The café changes its moods throughout the day: in the morning, people schmooze over lazy cups of coffee and muffins; in the afternoon and early evening, readers dally over newspapers and new-bought novels; at night, it's a bar scene with live music. The food is good, if slightly overpriced. But the real treat here is to see and be seen.

LA TOMATE

Map pp296-7   Italian $$

☎ 202-667-5505; 1701 Connecticut Ave NW; mains $13-20; ☾ lunch & dinner; Ⓜ Dupont Circle

A favorite for years now with folks working and living in the neighborhood, La Tomate has a prime people-watching location on the corner, which it makes the best of with long glass windows and tables clad with starched white linens pushed up against them. The ambiance is reminiscent of an Italian bistro, and there are daily pasta and salad specials.

BISTROT DU COIN

Map pp296-7   French $$

☎ 202-234-6969; 1738 Connecticut Ave; mains from $15; Ⓜ Dupont Circle

Ou est Phillipe? At this happening bistro, no doubt. This raucous room looks like the real thing, the waiters gargle their Rs, and the food on the plate smells and tastes just as it should. The dishes are heavy on rich sauces, with perfect frites and greens on the side.

MOURAYO

Map pp296-7   Greek-Med $$

☎ 202-667-2100; 1732 Connecticut Ave NW; lunch $15, dinner $20-25; ☾ lunch & dinner; Ⓜ Dupont Circle

Art Deco meets seafaring at this Greek restaurant that's known for its low-key, yet intimate, dining experience. The seafood dishes are delicately prepared and full of robust flavors. There is a lengthy ouzo list

as well as a long list of reasonably priced Greek wines. Make sure you save room for the desserts, which are as simple and appealing as the ambiance.

JOHNNY'S HALF SHELL

Map pp296-7   Seafood $$

☎ 202-296-2021; 2002 P St NW; mains $15-25; ☾ lunch & dinner; Ⓜ Dupont Circle

Happening Johnny's Half Shell is the place to come for local specialties: Maryland crab cakes; fried oyster po'boys; and sautéed soft-shell crabs. The barbecued shrimp with asiago cheese grits are 'better than my mother's,' according to one Southern patron. The friendly bar always seems to be hopping and boasts strong drinks, but don't come here without sampling the seafood.

ANNIE'S PARAMOUNT STEAKHOUSE

Map pp296-7   Steakhouse $$

☎ 202-32-0395; 1609 17th St NW; meals $16-30; ☾ 11:30am-11:30pm Mon-Thu, 24hr Fri-Sun; Ⓜ Dupont Circle

This neighborhood steakhouse attracts a predominately gay clientele, which says more about its location than anything else. After hours on weekends the place is at its best, hopping with clubbers grabbing a burger or breakfast on their way home. Waitstaff are friendly, making this one of the best places to meet and greet the gay community.

FIREFLY

Map pp296-7   New American $$

☎ 202-861-1310; 1310 New Hampshire Ave NW, Hotel Madera; mains $20; ☾ 8am-10pm; Ⓜ Dupont Circle

This happening bistro inside the Hotel Madera draws consistent crowds coming to taste the creations of chef John Wabeck, who's known for his use of fresh, seasonal ingredients. Although you wouldn't expect it from the trendy menu, the best thing to order here is actually the big juicy burger done up in gourmet style. Low lights and earth tones lend an intimate atmosphere indoors, while the sunny terrace is perfect for warm summer nights. The adjacent cocktail lounge packs a glam crowd.

SESTO SENSO

Map pp296-7   Italian $$

☎ 202-785-9525; 1214 18th St NW; mains from $20; ⏰ lunch & dinner, plus 11pm-2am Fri & Sat dancing; Ⓜ Dupont Circle

Early in the evening, this restaurant is ideal for a business lunch or a romantic dinner. The Northern Italian menu is authentic and affordable, featuring delicious, lightly fried calamari, fresh vegetarian pastas and thin, crispy pizzas. After hours, the Euros show up in all their finery to dance the night away.

TABARD INN

Map pp296-7   New American $$

☎ 202-331-8528; 1739 N St NW; mains from $20; Ⓜ Dupont Circle

This delightful oasis consists of a warm, dark bar inside or a sun-dappled, walled garden outside. Eclectic mains include fish stew, pastas and chops for dinner, which you might enjoy on a rainy night next to the roaring fire in the lounge. Or come for beignets with vanilla whipped cream or chocolate-almond pancakes for brunch in the garden. Life is sweet.

KOMI

Map pp296-7   Fusion $$$

☎ 202-332-9200; 1509 17th St NW; mains from $20, tasting menu $60; ⏰ dinner Mon-Sat; Ⓜ Dupont Circle

A favorite with DC's foodie crowd, this eclectic new endeavor offers a delectable array of gourmet fusion cuisine (although sometimes chef Johnny Monis takes his ambitious cooking a little too far out of the ballpark). The setting is Venetian fairytale romance with plaster walls and antique candle sconces. The five-course tasting menu is the way to go – DC's best deal for fine dining in fact, though if you want to spend a bit less there is always the constantly changing à la carte menu (that way you can still people-watch amid Washington's fashionable crowd without killing your wallet in the process).

PALM

Map pp296-7   American $$$

☎ 202-293-9091; 1225 19th St NW; mains $20-40; ⏰ lunch & dinner Mon-Fri, dinner Sat & Sun; Ⓜ Dupont Circle

Fun for people-watching as well as meat-eating, this classic American steakhouse is a media and political-celebrity magnet (Larry King likes to hang out here). Everyone's lunch seems to consist of sirloin, straight-gin martinis and cigar smoke. Its waitstaff are renowned for giving their customers a hard time.

MIMI'S

Map pp296-7   American & Middle Eastern $$$

☎ 202-464-6464; 2120 P St NW; lunch $20, dinner $30; Ⓜ Dupont Circle

Mimi's calls itself an 'American bistro' but the menu and decor argue otherwise: the walls are elegantly draped with Persian rugs; the menu includes merguez (grilled North African sausage) and an appetizer for sharing, called the 'Peace Meal,' which features hummus and baba ganouj (eggplant dip); and the last Sunday of the month Mimi's hosts an Arab-Jewish dialogue for anyone that wishes to participate. The novelty at Mimi's, however, is the waitstaff, who are all starving musicians. They occasionally break from waiting tables to sing opera or play jazz piano.

PESCE

Map pp296-7   Seafood $$$

☎ 202-466-3474; 2016 P St NW; mains from $25; Ⓜ Dupont Circle

The colorful fish decor gives away the menu at this consistently delicious award-winning Dupont restaurant featuring all things with fins – bluefish, salmon and grouper – all perfectly fresh and simply prepared. The dishes at this crowded café have a Mediterranean twist: seafood pastas, Provençal fish soup, grilled sardines and scallop ceviche are among the specialties.

NORA

Map pp296-7   New American $$$

☎ 202-462-5143; 2132 Florida Ave; mains from $25; ⏰ dinner; Ⓜ Dupont Circle

Nora is the queen of the Washington food scene. She has made her reputation serving food from local farmers and ranchers, usually organic and always fresh, and she creatively combines ingredients in innovative ways. All this happens in a quaint carriage house on one of Dupont's loveliest corners.

OBELISK

Map pp296-7   Italian $$$

☎ 202-223-1245; 2029 P St NW; prix-fixe $60;
☾ dinner; Ⓜ Dupont Circle

Oh the pleasure of dining at Obelisk. You need only do it once, but you need to do it. The small and narrow dining room feels almost like eating at someone's kitchen table, and the three-course Italian feast is lovingly prepared with first-rate ingredients. The menu changes daily, but doesn't give you much selection (picky eaters should call ahead).

ADAMS-MORGAN

Adams-Morgan is Washington's international smorgasbord. Here you can dine on *mee goreng* (Indonesian noodle dish), shish kebabs, *yebeg alicha* (Ethiopian lamb stew), calzones, jerk chicken, ceviche, *pupusas* (Salvadoran meat-stuffed pastry) and, of course, Happy Meals.

PIZZA MART

Map pp296-7   Italian $

☎ 202-234-9700; 2435 18th St; pizza from $4;
☾ 11-3am Sun-Thu, 11-4am Fri & Sat; Ⓜ Woodley
Park-Zoo/Adams Morgan

Any place that sells 'jumbo' slices (and we mean jumbo) until the wee hours in the middle of bar-hopping central is bound to be a hit; believe it or not, this pizza is actually pretty good, at least after enough beers.

DINER

Map pp296-7   American $

☎ 202-232-8800; 2453 18th St NW; breakfast from $5, sandwiches from $6; ☾ 24hr; Ⓜ Woodley
Park-Zoo/Adams Morgan

Late-night breakfast and satisfying comfort food hit the spot around the clock. Crowds of bar-hoppers agree, as they flock to this retro diner for refueling. Cartoons on the big screen are a nice touch.

MAMA AYESHA'S

Map pp296-7   Middle Eastern $

☎ 202-232-5431; 1967 Calvert St NW; mains $5-10; Ⓜ Woodley Park-Zoo/Adams Morgan

This neighborhood institution has changed little since it opened 50 years ago, neither prices nor decor. Mama's specializes in

Syrian takes on hummus, kebabs and other Levantine classics.

ANZU

Map pp296-7   Mediterranean $

☎ 202-462-8844; 2436 18th St NW; tapas from $5, pizzas from $8; ☾ dinner daily, brunch Sat & Sun;
Ⓜ Woodley Park-Zoo/Adams Morgan

The best thing about this sophisticated wine bar is nothing on the menu costs more than $11. Plus the modern European fare – thin-crust pizzas, homemade ravio-lis, seared seafood and seasonal veggie tapas – is far from shabby. Order several items and pass them around the table.

EL TAMARINDO

Map pp296-7   Salvadoran $

☎ 202-328-3660; 1785 Florida Ave NW; mains $6-15; Ⓜ Woodley Park-Zoo/Adams Morgan

The waitstaff arrive with water and chips and spicy homemade salsa as soon as you sit down at this friendly, family-run Salva-doran restaurant. Young urbanites flock here early to fill-up on inexpensive taco dishes before heading out to the clubs. The food is cheap; the margaritas or pitchers of Sangria, strong and tasty.

PASTA MIA

Map pp296-7   Italian $

☎ 202-328-9114; 1790 Columbia Rd NW; mains $10-15; ☾ dinner Mon-Sat; Ⓜ Woodley Park-Zoo/
Adams Morgan

People line up on the sidewalk for gener-ous servings of 20-some kinds of pasta made the way your mother does (if she is an Italian gourmand). The heaps of deli-cious pasta are worth the long waits and brusque treatment, which are all part of the experience.

MESKEREM

Map pp296-7   Ethiopian $$

☎ 202-462-4100; 2434 18th St NW; mains from $10; ☾ noon-midnight Sun-Fri, noon-1am Sat;
Ⓜ Woodley Park-Zoo/Adams Morgan

To many folks, Adams-Morgan means just one thing: Ethiopian food. You can eat it at several restaurants, but the leading place is Meskerem, named for the first month of the Ethiopian calendar. This place goes for an exotic atmosphere, with traditional woven straw-basket tables and camel-leather hassocks. Use your hands to sample beef, poultry, lamb, seafood and vegetarian dishes, which are served on whole-wheat *injera* (pancake-like bread).

RUMBA CAFÉ

Map pp296-7 Brazilian $$

☎ 202-588-5501; 2443 18th St NW; tapas $5-8, mains $15-20; ✆ 5:30pm-2am; Ⓜ Woodley Park-Zoo/Adams Morgan

Sit outside on the sidewalk and watch life pass you by while sipping some of the most minty mojitos in the city and munching on mouth-watering morsels from spicy South America. This tiny, eclectic restaurant's menu is mainly Brazilian, although it also includes famous dishes from other parts of the continent. We love the empanadas and anything steak based is usually delicious. After dinner it hosts live Latin bands in its shabby-chic red-and-mirror clad interior. Be warned: in colder months when everyone is packed inside it can feel claustrophobic.

PERRY'S

Map pp296-7 Asian $$

☎ 202-234-6218; 1811 Columbia Rd NW; mains $15-30; Ⓜ Woodley Park-Zoo/Adams Morgan

You can do sushi at Perry's, but the creative fusion fare really deserves your tongue's attention. The only problem is deciding whether to dine in the funky lounge or under the stars. For the very adventurous, the Sunday drag-queen brunch is a hoot. This place can be hard to spot because there's no real sign – the doorway canopy uses rebus symbols (like a pear) to spell out the name.

LOCAL 16

Map pp296-7 New American $$

☎ 202-265-2828; 1602 U St NW; mains from $20; ✆ dinner daily, to 2am Fri & Sat; Ⓜ U Street-Cardozo

Voted best pick-up spot by *Washington Post* readers in 2006, this trendy restaurant-lounge serves mouthwatering concoctions like balsamic filet mignon and pan-seared salmon with a healthy side of pheromones. Ruby-colored walls, clean lines and jazz music strike the mood for dining, and the place is filled with the young and beautiful on the prowl. The lounge upstairs and the roof deck are where to head after dinner for the hottest drinking experience on the block.

CASHION'S EAT PLACE

Map pp296-7 New American $$

☎ 202-797-1819; 1819 Columbia Rd NW; mains $20-30; ✆ dinner Tue-Sun, brunch Sun; Ⓜ Woodley Park-Zoo/Adams Morgan

Restaurateur and chef Ann Cashion is somewhat of a local celebrity for the original menu and inviting decor she has invented at this little bistro, lauded as one of the city's very best. Cashion's serves food that can be light and rich at the same time (or just rich and rich, as in duck breast served with foie gras). The mismatched furniture and flower boxes create an unpretentious setting to enjoy her work.

SHAW & U STREET

New restaurants are popping up in this district every week (thank you gentrification), and although it's still not exactly a culinary center, there are now quite a few great choices for noshing before catching a live show. From down-home soul to yuppie organic, Shaw and U St's eating options are as diverse as the 'hood itself.

BEN'S CHILI BOWL

Map pp302-3 American $

☎ 202-667-0909; www.benschilibowl.com; 1213 U St; dogs from $4; ✆ lunch & dinner daily, to 4am Fri & Sat; Ⓜ U Street-Cardozo

Newlyweds Ben and Virginia Ali launched this neighborhood institution in 1958. It became a lunch staple for all the locals, including the stars playing at the neighborhood clubs. Everyone from Redd Foxx to Duke Ellington to Bill Cosby has eaten at Ben's. Despite radical changes in the neighborhood, Ben's Formica counters and bright booths still look pretty much the same. And the spicy dogs ('Our chili will make a hot dog bark!') are always drawing crowds at lunchtime.

FLORIDA AVENUE GRILL

Map pp302-3 Southern $

☎ 202-265-1586; 1100 Florida Ave NW; mains from $8; ✆ lunch & dinner Tue-Sat; Ⓜ U Street-Cardozo

Eating

SHAW & U STREET

A Washington institution that has been around for almost 60 years, this place has a loyal clientele that swears by its down-home grits, meatloaf and barbecued ribs. It's a greasy spoon in the truest sense and that's part of the charm. Its walls are lined with signed photos of singers, actors and politicos who have enjoyed its soul food, as well as Southern memorabilia and kitsch.

OOHH'S & AAHH'S
Map pp302-3 American $
☎ 202-667-7142; 1005 U St NW; mains $8-25; ☺ 4-11pm; Ⓜ U Street-Cardozo
DC's best soul food is on offer at this barebones U St joint popular with every-one from the homeless to sports super-stars. The down-home southern cooking comes in plentiful portions and remains affordable for the residents living on this still-edgy block of town. A plate of three heaping side portions costs just $8, while for $13 you can score meat or fish plus two sides. The ambiance is as unfussy as the food – this is a spot meant for eating not socializing.

ISLANDER CARIBBEAN
Map pp302-3 Caribbean $
☎ 202-234-4971; 1201 U St NW; mains from $10; Ⓜ U Street-Cardozo
Spicy cuisine and tropical drinks will whisk you to the islands – a perfect spot to be on a humid, DC August evening. Service is decidedly laid-back, but it's worth the wait for grilled fish, fried plantains and rum smoothies, all set to a Caribbean beat.

AL CROSTINO
Map pp302-3 Italian $$
☎ 202-797-0523; 1324 U St NW; mains $10-20; ☺ dinner; Ⓜ U Street-Cardozo
Al Crosinto's cuisine isn't the best food in the city, but for the price it's pretty damn tasty. The menu offers a range of tradi-tional Italian dishes, such as beef carpac-cio, pasta, chicken, and steak; the simple, hearty food is served in reasonable por-tions. The pastas are probably your best bet, although the steaks can be an equally good choice. In summary, Al Crostino is a welcoming trattoria, where the chef is known to check on patrons and the service is refreshingly attentive.

COPPI'S ORGANIC
Map pp302-3 Italian $$
☎ 202-319-7773; 1414 U St NW; pizza from $13, mains from $18; ☺ dinner; Ⓜ U Street-Cardozo
An old-school U St restaurant that fires up the wood-burning oven nightly to serve perfectly crusted, crispy pizzas along with other seasonal and traditional Italian deli-cacies. The owner is crazy about bicycles and the cozy restaurant is jammed with bikes and bicycling memorabilia. It gets packed on weekends when locals flock in to partake in generally tasty Italian dishes and good cheap wines. The only downer is that non-pizza mains can feel a bit over-priced.

NORTHEAST DC
The edgy northeast quadrant still does not have too many eating options, but if you are in the area exploring Catholic Univer-sity and checking out the Basilica, you will have no trouble sating your appetite at one of these friendly choices.

DELI CITY
Map pp290-1 American $
☎ 202-526-1800; 2200 Bladensburg Rd NE; sandwiches $2.25-6.50, mains $8-10
Deli City sees no class or color. No, this faded orange building in a faded Northeast neighborhood attracts everyone from the haggard to the haughty craving the per-fect over-stuffed sandwich south of New York. Eat in or takeout, this no-frills place also does solid soul food like gravy smoth-ered pork chops and fried fish at bargain prices. There is no nearby Metro station, you'll need to drive.

COLONEL BROOKS' TAVERN & ISLAND JIM'S CRAB SHACK
Map pp302-3 Southern/Seafood $
☎ 202-529-4002; 901 Monroe St NE; mains $10-15; Ⓜ Brookland-CU
This friendly bar fills with regulars at lunchtime and happy hour. In the wood-paneled dining room, it serves pub grub and Southern fare. Live jazz bands play in the evenings. If you are feeling tropical, head to the tiki bar next door. Romp in a palm tree-shaded sandpit or sip umbrella drinks on the outdoor deck. Try the 'Kick Ass Margarita – hot and spicy, cold and icy.'

Boogie down to live music on Wednesday evenings. Life is good, mon.

UPPER NORTHWEST DC

Despite its distance from the city center, Upper Northwest DC has its fair share of excellent eateries. Most are clustered around the Metro stops in Cleveland Park, Tenleytown and Woodley Park, although several are in Glover Park, just north of Georgetown.

ROCKLANDS BARBECUE

Map pp300-1   Southern $

☎ 202-333-2558; 2418 Wisconsin Ave; mains $5-10; 🚌 30, 32, 34, 36 from Tenleytown-AU or Foggy Bottom-GWU Metro

Order up some spicy ribs and choose your favorite side dish from Southern classics like potato salad or collard greens. While you wait for your order, check out the huge selection of hot sauces ('From the Depths of Hell'). Then take a seat at the wooden counter in the window and watch the passers-by drool.

ZOO BAR

Map pp300-1   American $

☎ 202-232-4225; 3000 Connecticut Ave; kids' menu $3.50, sandwiches from $6; Ⓜ Woodley Park-Zoo/Adams Morgan

This neighborhood pub is really more of a drinking establishment than an eatery, but the zoo theme and value-minded menu make it an ideal lunch spot on your way out of the zoo. This place welcomes children, which is apparent by the animals on the walls, the patient waitstaff and the cheap kids' menu.

BRICKS TAVERN

Map pp300-1   Italian $

☎ 202-362-8440; 3421 Connecticut Ave; mains from $9; Ⓜ Cleveland Park

'Bricks' means the ovens in which the gourmet pizzas are baked and topped with the freshest of toppings: grilled chicken with sun-dried tomato and lemon-dressed arugula; roasted eggplant with sweet peppers and goat cheese; and classics like tomato, basil and fresh mozzarella. Salads, sandwiches and pastas round out the menu beautifully. You can enjoy your

meal at the long, friendly bar or upstairs on the rooftop.

2AMYS

Map pp300-1   Italian $

☎ 202-885-5700; 3715 Macomb St NW; pizza $8-13; 🕑 lunch & dinner; Ⓜ Cleveland Park

This neighborhood pizzeria is a little out of the way, but it's worth hoofing it there if you're in the mood for some of the best gourmet pizza in the city. The margarita pizza is truly an orgasm for the senses, made with freshly ripped basil, sweet tomatoes, smoky mozzarella and high-quality sea-salt and olive oil. Order it naked or adorned with delicious Italian ham or sausage. Environs are simple, black-and-white checkered floors and yellow walls, as if the proprietors didn't want the ambiance to detract patrons from the food. If you're not in the mood for pizza, 2Amys offers delicious small plates and creamy desserts.

LEBANESE TAVERNA

Map pp296-7   Middle Eastern $

☎ 202-265-8681; 2641 Connecticut Ave; meze from $5, mains from $10; Ⓜ Woodley Park-Zoo/Adams Morgan

This family-run Middle Eastern joint ranks among our favorite DC restaurants. Make a whole meal out of meze, like creamy *labneh* (yogurt cheese), tangy grape leaves, *kibbeh* (beef-stuffed pasta) and garlicky *foole m'damas* (fava-bean dip), which please both vegetarians and meat eaters. An outdoor patio makes this a fine summertime choice.

HERITAGE INDIA

                                               Indian $$

☎ 202-331-1414; 1337 Connecticut Ave; mains $10-20; Ⓜ Glover Park

Some of Washington's best Indian cuisine is served at this 2nd-story elegant restaurant in Glover Park, where photographs of long-forgotten Indian princes grace pumpkin-hued walls. Although the chefs certainly know how to spice things up when the time is right, Heritage India has become a favorite in Washington because its food doesn't kill your taste buds. Most of the dishes on the menu are mild enough to really enjoy their complex, earthy flavors.

NAM VIET

Map pp300-1   Vietnamese $$

☎ 202-237-1015; 3419 Connecticut Ave NW; mains
$10-25; ☺ lunch & dinner; Ⓜ Cleveland Park
Serving consistently good Vietnamese food,
this homey place features uncomplicated
cooking including especially rich and tasty
pho (beef noodle soup). Digs are a bit unim-
aginative, although there are a few creative
pieces of art gracing the walls. The quality
of the food compensates for any lack of
ambiance, however. This place has scored
numerous awards for taste and is a bargain.

ARDEO'S

Map pp300-1   New American $$

☎ 202-244-6750; 3311 Connecticut Ave NW; mains
$15; Ⓜ Cleveland Park
Prices in this slick joint are quite reasonable, considering the posh decor and the
sophisticated menu. The latter features a
few rich pastas, lots of fresh fish and juicy
meat selections, plus a few salads and
sandwiches. Try a local specialty like succulent, pan-roasted rockfish served with
a ragout of prosciutto, sweet corn and
plantains. There's also a giant wine list. For
a sample, check out three tasters of new
stock for $14; the wines change seasonally.

BUCK'S FISHING & CAMPING

Map pp290-1   Modern American $$

☎ 202-364-0777; 5031 Connecticut Ave; mains
$15-30; ☺ dinner Tue-Sun; Ⓜ Tenley Town
Resembling a lakeside fishing camp, com-
plete with canoes, this place has become a
neighborhood haunt that has pundits and
politicos making the trek to the 'hood to
see what all the fuss is about. The food is
American comfort cooking at its best, and
the restaurant does everything from chicken
livers on toast to lobster and sirloin. The no-
reservations policy means you'll be waiting
ages for a seat on weekend evenings, but
when you do score one of the chairs at the
communal tables you could be sharing it
with your state's senator and the guy selling
books at the coffee shop across the street.

PETITS PLATS

Map pp300-1   French $$

☎ 202-518-0018; 2653 Connecticut Ave; mains
from $25, 3-course early-bird special $23;
☺ dinner; Ⓜ Woodley Park-Zoo/Adams Morgan

This petite French bistro fits a warm, welcoming atmosphere into its little rooms.
The traditional French menu gets high
marks for delicious appetizers, salads,
seafood and desserts. But this place is so
charming you might not care what you eat,
so long as the waiter continues to pour
your wine. The artichoke soup with scallops is a winner, as is the seafood-packed
bouillabaisse with its smooth, garlicky
punch.

NEW HEIGHTS

Map pp300-1   New American $$$

☎ 202-234-4110; 2317 Calvert St NW; mains
$25-35; ☺ dinner daily, brunch Sun; Ⓜ Woodley
Park-Zoo/Adams Morgan
This airy 2nd-floor restaurant, winner of
the American Institute of Architects (AIA)
design award, has a prime perch overlook-
ing Rock Creek Park. Here, acclaimed chef
Arthur Rivaldo serves up delicious new
American dishes with Asian and Mediter-
ranean influences and complementary
wines. Specialties range from local jumbo
lump crab cakes (and they do mean
jumbo) to the exotic Opaka-Paka Hawaiian
red snapper grilled with black trumpets
and grapefruit. The signature appetizer,
black-bean and goat cheese pâté, is a rich,
creamy delicacy.

SUSHI-KO

Map pp300-1   Sushi $$$

☎ 202-333-4187; 2309 Wisconsin Ave; dinner $35;
☺ lunch & dinner Tue-Fri, dinner Sat-Mon; 🚌 30,
32, 34, 36 from Tenleytown-AU or Foggy Bottom-
GWU Metro
DC's first sushi bar, this stripped-down,
modern place is still beloved for impecca-
bly fresh fish. The kitchen serves the basics
(tuna belly, California roll) and the exotic
(raw-trout napoleons). It's as popular with
tourists as it is with university students,
Gucci-clad glam girls and fashion conscious diplomats.

ARLINGTON

Consider Arlington as an eating alternative, even if you're staying inside the city.
Just across Key Bridge from Georgetown,
the neighborhood has a lively culinary
scene where the emphasis is on Asia and
Latin America. It's a great place for visitors

because most restaurants are clustered around Metro stops. If you're driving, parking is easier here (some places even have lots, others comp for parking in a paid area) and driving is less of a hassle.

EL POLLO RICO

Map pp306-7   Latin American $
☎ 703-522-3220; 2917 N Washington Blvd; chicken with sides $4-12; ⊙ 11am-10pm; Ⓜ Clarendon

Drooling locals have flocked to this Peruvian chicken joint for decades now in search of tender, juicy, flavor-packed birds served with succulent (highly addictive) dipping sauces, crunchy fries and sloppy 'slaw – lines form outside the door come dinnertime. You can eat at rather unappealing plastic tables inside (this author was once taken here on a first date – needless to say she is no longer with the man), or do the recommended thing and take the precious stuff back to your hotel room to chow to the noise of HBO dramas and taste of icy mini-fridge beer.

HARD TIMES CAFÉ

Map pp306-7   American $
☎ 703-528-2233; 3028 Wilson Blvd, Arlington; chili from $5, kids' menu $3; Ⓜ Clarendon

This menu features four distinct chilies: traditional Texas; hot and sweet Cincinnati (traditionally served over spaghetti); hearty vegetarian; and the house original Terlingua Red, a tribute to the ghost town that hosted the first chili cook-off. Experimental types may want to try chili on a dog, in a tortilla, or even over a bowl of Frito's, known as 1940s Frito Pie. Monday to Friday happy hours feature half-price draughts.

KABOB BAZAAR

Map pp306-7   Middle Eastern $
☎ 703-522-8999; 3133 Wilson Blvd; mains from $6; Ⓜ Clarendon

That this place is often crowded with swarthy men and Middle Eastern families is proof that the spicy meat skewers and fresh veggie salads are top-notch. Cool green walls and faux marble columns add to the exotic atmosphere, not to mention the open kitchen, which allows guests to catch a glimpse – and a whiff – of the juicy meats roasting over the flame.

RED HOT & BLUE

Map p299   American $
☎ 703-276-7427; 1600 Wilson Blvd; sandwiches from $6, ½-slab ribs $12; Ⓜ Rosslyn

The logo featuring pigs in sunglasses jamming on guitars says it all: Memphis-style barbecue. And this Memphis-born author says the place is almost worthy of that title. The traditional spicy dry ribs are undeniably the best, but you can also get them smothered in sauce. In any case, they are smoked over hickory wood for hours and hours, and served with beans, coleslaw or other classic Southern side dishes.

PHO 75

Map p299   Vietnamese $
☎ 703-525-7355; 1721 Wilson Blvd; small/large pho $6/7; ⊙ 9am-8pm; Ⓜ Clarendon

The name means soup, but this local chain is so much more than a beef noodle soup shop. For a cultural experience visit on a Sunday, when fathers teach their first-generation American daughters how to slurp slippery white noodles simmering in richly flavorful broth. For a no-frills dining experiment offering only one item: *pho*, the place is amazingly successful. Hordes of tourists, locals and Vietnamese pack communal tables each slurping their own unique variation of the soup – some add brisket or tripe, meatballs or flank steaks; others douse with lime, hot sauce and Asian basil. Whatever you're choice, odds are it will be delicious.

BANGKOK 54 RESTAURANT & BAR

Map pp306-7   Thai $
☎ 703-521-4070; 2919 Columbia Pike; mains $7-20; Ⓜ Clarendon

From generic to exotic, this award-winning restaurant serves up Thai cuisine that's often fiery and always flavorful. And you don't have to compromise aesthetics for good food, Bangkok 54 looks as good as it tastes. The modern decor mixes granite with bright reds for a sleek finish.

LEBANESE VILLAGE

Map pp306-7   Middle Eastern $
☎ 703-271-9194; 549 S 23rd St; mains from $10; Ⓜ Crystal City

This family-run Middle Eastern joint represents the best of Crystal City's restaurant row: friendly service and top-notch food at prices that are bargains by DC standards. Charcoal-grilled kebabs and rotisserie-roasted shawarma are highlights of the menu; or one could easily fill up on classic meze, like *baba ganouj,* hummus and *fattoush* (salad).

ALEXANDRIA

Washingtonians have discovered that sleepy Alexandria is the perfect tonic when they tire of dining in the big city. As a result Alexandria is brimming with restaurants, many featuring gourmet cooking as good as any you'll find in DC. The city also has loads of hot ethnic places.

KABUL KABOB HOUSE

Map p311   Afghan $
☎ 703-751-1833; 514-A Van Dorn St; mains $4-12; 🚐 Old Town shuttle from King St Metro

Don't let the depressing set-up deter you; Kabul Kabob is one of Alexandria's best cheap eats. Once the food arrives you'll forget about the TV blaring American sitcoms, the solitary, sad-looking diners sipping tea, their heads buried in the paper, the way the waiter slapped the menu on the table and passed on few pleasantries. Kebabs are cooked to order (they take around 20 minutes to prepare) and are filled with sublimely succulent chicken or tender, juicy lamb. The Afghan cooking here is some of DC's best, and the menu is quite large for such a tiny place. The price is excellent, and dishes like the house pilaf are big enough to feed a small family.

KING STREET BLUES

Map p311   Southern $
☎ 703-836-8800; 112 N Saint Asaph St; early bird special $7, mains from $10; 🚐 Old Town shuttle from King St

King Street Blues is a crazy Southern 'roadhouse' diner that serves really good baked meat loaf, country fried steak, Southern fried catfish and other diner favorites. It is strewn with colorful papier-mâché figures floating across its three levels, while shiny chrome furniture and multicolored tablecloths lend it an attractive retro air. Live blues is played on Thursday nights.

A LA LUCIA

Map p311   Italian $$
☎ 703-836-5123; 315 Madison St; mains $11-26; 🚐 Old Town shuttle from King St Metro

Dishing up a winning concoction of uncomplicated Italian meals at affordable prices inside a vibrant dining hall, this newbie restaurant has already made a name for itself. Plates are of the generous grandma's kitchen variety – heaping portions of spaghetti bolognaise, rich lasagna, and veal masala. The ambiance is refined in the back, all-white tablecloths and low lighting and a stunning wine bar. In the front room it's all about color; walls are bright and decked with original pieces.

GENEROUS GEORGE'S POSITIVE PIZZA & PASTA PLACE   Italian $
☎ 703-370-4303; 3006 Duke St; pizzas from $12; Ⓜ King St

Positively the very best place in the DC area for kids, Generous George will fill them up with his big, crispy-crusted pies. If you can't decide between pizza and pasta, never fear; oddly enough, pasta is also served on pizza crust. It's crowded, chaotic and a little crazy. You will find it about 3 miles west of Old Town Alexandria.

100 KING RESTAURANT

Map p311   Lebanese $$
☎ 703-299-0076; 100 King St; mains $15; 🚐 Old Town shuttle from King St Metro

Washingtonians are trekking to the 'burbs to dine at Alexandria's hippest taverna. The restaurant specializes in small plates from the Middle East and Mediterranean, with mostly favorable results. Hit the happening bar before and after dinner.

ELYSIUM DINING ROOM

Map p311   New American $$$
☎ 703-838-8000; 116 S Alfred St, Morrison House; mains from $25; 🚐 Old Town shuttle from King St Metro

Inside the posh hotel **Morrison House** (p239), the highlight of the Elysium is its one-of-a-kind Chef of Your Own experience. Chef Ulrich visits with each Elysium guest before preparing a custom-made meal, designed to fulfill each guest's desires. Suggested wines complement his creations. It's quite a dining adventure.

GADSBY'S TAVERN RESTAURANT

Map p311   American $$$

☎ 703-548-1288; 138 N Royal St; mains from $25;
🚌 Old Town shuttle from King St Metro

Set in the building of an 18th-century tavern, Gadsby's is named after the English-man who operated the tavern from 1796 to 1808 (it was then the center of Alexandria's social life). This place tries hard to emulate an 18th-century hostelry. The overall effect is rather kitsch, but it's all good, clean and historical fun. Besides, who wouldn't be curious to try 'George Washington's Favorite,' duck stuffed with tart fruit and topped with sweet Madeira gravy?

MAJESTIC CAFÉ

Map p311   New American $$$

☎ 703-837-9117; 911 King St; mains from $30;
🚌 Old Town Shuttle from King St Metro

It's hard to say what's more appealing, the Majestic's modernized diner setting, or its mouthwatering modern diner menu. The American Institute of Architects (AIA) has recognized this Art-Deco café for the extremely slick renovation of its historic building. But the menu is no afterthought: it changes regularly, depending on what is fresh and seasonal, but it is always perfectly divine.

Sautéed soft-shell crabs are a perennial favorite, as are the desserts.

BETHESDA

Just over the line in Maryland, Bethesda has enough restaurants to keep you eating (and eating well) for months to come. Easily accessible by Metro, it's a fun place to wander and has a less-chaotic air than much of the city. Check out the area around Woodmont and Bethesda Aves, dubbed 'restaurant row.'

TASTEE DINER

Map p310   American $

☎ 301-652-3970; 7731 Woodmont Ave; mains $3.50-8; Ⓜ Bethesda

Maryland's favorite greasy spoon, this is the place to get eggs at midnight after some heavy drinking down the street. The kind of restaurant that's been around long enough (since 1935, in fact) to be considered an establishment – the waitress with the Mimi from *The Drew Carey Show* blue eye shadow and authentic beehive has been there for at least two decades. In a ramshackle tin and brick building, this is an authentic old-school diner, complete with long bar and Formica tables touting personal jukeboxes. Local high-school kids pack the place on weekend nights, settling in for cups of coffee and plates of fries and grilled cheese.

PENANG

Map p310   Malaysian $

☎ 301-657-2878; 4933 Bethesda Ave; dishes from $7; Ⓜ Bethesda

You can eat like a king at this authentic Malaysian restaurant when cheap meal deals are offered, 11:30am–3pm Monday to Friday. For $8 you get soup, salad, appetizer, drink and noodle dish. Otherwise portions are large, delicious and almost all can be made vegetarian. Try the Kari Mee noodle soup ($7). Don't let the outside discourage you, inside the place is intimate Asian chic.

TEL AVIV CAFÉ

Map p310   Israeli $

☎ 301-718-9068; 4869 Cordell Ave; mains $10-20; Ⓜ Bethesda

This 'sceny' restaurant is a perennial favorite with Maryland's hip Israeli and Jewish crowd (although the place is equally attractive to cool cats of all religions and penguin-costumed servers from the ritzy French restaurant down the road). There are many falafel dishes on the menu, which also offers popular Israeli and Mediterranean cuisine. Grab the sidewalk seating on a summer night. With the exotic-looking patrons smoking cigarettes and talking on their microscopic cell phones mixed up with random street noise, you'll think you really are in a café in Tel Aviv.

RIO GRANDE CAFÉ

Map p310   Tex-Mex $$

☎ 301-656-2981; 4780 Bethesda Ave; lunch menu $8-11, mains $15-25; Ⓜ Bethesda

One of the city's top spots for Tex-Mex. Start with a bowl of melted *queso* (cheese); ask for some fresh-flour tortillas on the side. The fajitas are some of the best in the business and what to order (skip the only so-so tacos and enchiladas).

Our lunch menu favorite is *camerones a la parilla* (spicy bite-size, mesquite-grilled shrimp done up fajita style). Order a margarita or the signature 'swirl' (frozen margarita and sangria) – both pack enough booze to get you tipsy. Portions are large, and appetizers double as meals, especially if you fill up on the free chips (delectably light, crispy and perfectly salted) and salsa (delicious mixed with the *queso*) first.

This is a loud, crazy place where the service is top-notch and kids are made quite welcome. The restaurant boasts super, fast service, but sometimes it feels too fast; it's not somewhere to linger over a meal.

Drinking

Drinking

In the nation's capital it's all about the party. And we're not just talking partisan lines – DC is a city that knows how to play. Young, vibrant and cosmopolitan, there's an exotic sauciness (okay we agree it's mixed with stale smoke) in the air here, especially in summer when temperatures soar and college interns filter in for a taste of power. Work hard, play harder seems to be the motto of the young and restless. And when the sun sinks low over the Potomac, seemingly straight-laced congressional aides, lobbyists and lawyers trade Capitol Hill deal brokering for dingy bars and happy-hour martinis (although the talk at the table can stay political well into the night), then shift into the heat of things at a trendy new lounge or roof-top café.

The drinking age in DC – as in the rest of the US – is 21. Bars don't let anyone under that age through the door (except in some places if they are accompanied by a parent). The best place to find out what's happening is the free weekly *Washington City Paper* (issued Thursday) or the monthly *On Tap*, both available in heaps at the entrances of stores and clubs. A more mainstream resource is the Weekend section of the Friday *Washington Post*. The free *Washington Blade*, available at stores and clubs, gives the scoop on gay and lesbian happenings.

To check things out online visit the *Washington Post's* website www.washingtonpost .com and click on the city-guide link. From here you can browse reviews of nearly every bar in the city.

Considering the city's small size, the number of bars and pubs in DC is staggering; and they may leave you staggering, too.

WHITE HOUSE AREA & FOGGY BOTTOM

College kids, doctors and journalists co-exist in this neighborhood. For the most part the vibe is sort of White-yuppie-meets-college-scruffy at the local pub.

BOTTOM LINE Map pp292-3

☎ 202-298-8488; 1716 I St NW; 🕑 11:30-1:30am Mon-Thu, 11:30-2:30am Fri & Sat; Ⓜ Farragut West

This long, dark and friendly basement bar draws prosperous patrons for lunchtime and happy hour. It's more grown-up than most pubs in the area and many folk appear to be conducting business-related tête-à-têtes.

FROGGY BOTTOM PUB Map pp292-3

☎ 202-338-3000; 2141 Pennsylvania Ave NW; 🕑 11:30-1:30am Mon-Thu, 11:30-2:30am Fri & Sat; Ⓜ Foggy Bottom-GWU

This popular GWU hangout attracts students with its grub-and-pub specials, like Saturday's $10 all-you-can-eat-and-drink. Happy-hour specials run 5pm to midnight.

It's also a good place to try local brews and shoot a few games of pool.

MACKEY'S PUBLIC HOUSE Map pp292-3

☎ 202-331-7667; 1823 L St NW; 🕑 11:30-2am Mon-Fri, noon-2am Sat; Ⓜ Farragut North

The fireplace and easy chairs recall an Irish country pub – one where the whole town puts on suits and comes to drink every afternoon around 5pm. Mackey's is welcoming and comfortable, especially when the bartenders are drawing you pints of Guinness, Harp and Caffrey.

GEORGETOWN

Georgetown is one of DC's most revered drinking zones. M St is lined with all sorts of bars and pubs, many of which are close clones – British-style pubs with lots of heavy wood and dark nooks. Home to Georgetown University, this neighborhood attracts a largely stylish young crowd with money to burn (drinks can be amazingly expensive). Luckily a few of those college kids must be poor, because Georgetown also boasts some of the city's best happy

HAPPIEST HOURS

Happy hour seems to be a federally mandated institution in DC, catering to the plethora of poor students and interns. But we can all benefit from this social safety net: on any given weeknight, there is no need to pay full price for booze or snacks if you know what's up.

Capitol Lounge (p173) A perennial favorite with Hillies and interns. It offers $2 beers, $3 well drinks, plus cheap appetizers like 10¢ wings or 25¢ tacos, from 4pm to 7pm.

Front Page (p176) DC's number-one happy hour on Thursday nights, when a free taco bar complements cheap beer and the entire city stops. Happy hour runs 4pm to 7pm nightly. Specials include half-price appetizers, $2 beers, wine and well drinks.

Lucky Bar (p176) We love this happy hour for the simple fact that it runs for longer than most places – from 3pm to 8pm Monday through Friday. Nightly specials include $2.50 pints and $3.50 well drinks; Wednesday is half-price burger night. Bike messengers, restaurant servers and soccer enthusiasts are all fans.

Mr Smith's (p172) Half-price rail drinks and appetizers, $2.50 beer-of-the-month, from 4pm to 7pm. Mr Smith's has been running this happy-hour combo for decades now and the success has yet to wane – the bar is always packed during these hours.

Tapatinis (p174) At the time of research Tapatinis was offering the best deal in town on Thursday night: free booze. Each week after 9pm a different major liquor distributor gives away its product free while bottles last. Ask the bartender for the free drink: it could be anything from Remy Martin cognac to Belvedere vodka. Otherwise, happy hour runs from 5pm to 8pm Monday through Friday and offers specials like $4 Absolut drinks on Monday, $5 top-shelf cocktails on Thursday and $2 wine for women on Tuesday.

---

hours. If the weather is nice, make sure to head to the Potomac Waterfront. Here you'll find a slew of alfresco sidewalk cafés lining the riverfront. The happening (and gigantic) Sequoia (p172) anchors the eastern edge of the strip. Nearby, **Tony & Joes Seafood Place** (☎ 202-965-1789; Georgetown Waterfront; ☒ lunch-late; ◼ shuttle from Foggy Bottom-GWU) is another popular option. It has alfresco tables on the sidewalk near the water and serves good seafood.

BIERRERIA PARADISO Map p299
☎ 202-337-1245; 3282 M St NW;
◼ Georgetown shuttle from Foggy Bottom-GWU
In 2005 the unused basement of popular Pizzeria Paradiso (p148) was given a slick makeover. It's now Birreria Paradiso, Washington's coolest new beer bar. Despite its low-level environs, the place gets lots of sunlight and has a warm Mediterranean vibe. The reason to come, however, is for the beer. There are 16 different types on draft and 80 bottles offered. The selection covers much of the world.

BLUE GIN Map p299
☎ 202-965-4005; 1206 Wisconsin Ave NW;
◼ Georgetown shuttle from Foggy Bottom-GWU
When it opened a few years back it attracted the likes of Owen Wilson and

Vince Vaughn (in town to shoot the popular movie *The Wedding Crashers*), which instantly placed this trendy cocktail lounge at the top of Washington's hot list. Its residential location, however, means it has to operate under pretty strict conditions liquor-wise and no one under 25 is allowed through the door. As a result the crowd here is more mellow and less worried about the scene than at some of DC's other hip spots.

This doesn't mean Blue Gin isn't a good place for singles; it is. There are two levels. We like upstairs best – it has lots of good-for-sinking couches, plenty of funky sculptures and two bars. If it's crowded, however, getting past bouncers and the velvet ropes to actually reach the 2nd floor can be difficult. Dress to impress and arrive early. Downstairs isn't shabby either. It's minimalist and dimly lit, and there's sometimes dancing.

CLYDE'S Map p299
☎ 202-333-9180; 3236 M St NW; ◼ Georgetown shuttle from Foggy Bottom-GWU
A true Georgetown warhorse, Clyde's has been around for almost 40 years. Back in the day, it used to cater mainly to Georgetown students, but Clyde's has gone upscale in recent years; now yuppies are

more likely than students to drink in this classy saloon. The **Railroad Bar**, salvaged from a Baltimore station and tucked into the back of the bar, is the best spot in the house. It's famous for its half-price burgers at happy hour.

DEGREES BAR & LOUNGE

Map p299

☎ 202-912-4100; 3100 South St NW, Ritz-Carlton Hotel; 🚌 Georgetown shuttle from Foggy Bottom-GWU

In the lobby of the swanky **Ritz-Carlton** (p228), this classy place captures the history of the incinerator with exposed brick walls and black slate floors. The lounge is all the rage among the businesspeople who work in the area and come here to sip the signature Zentini, which replaces sake with vodka in a martini.

GARRETT'S Map p299

☎ 202-333-8282; 3003 M St NW; ⏰ 11:30-1:30am Mon-Thu, noon-2:30am Fri & Sat, noon-1:30am Sun; 🚌 Georgetown shuttle from Foggy Bottom-GWU

An old standby, Garrett's is one of Georgetown's most-established (and popular) watering holes. Packed with suity types and college kids any night of the week, the mood at this English-style pub always feels welcoming, and there's an outdoor patio. It also serves decent, and quite cheap, grub.

MR SMITH'S Map p299

☎ 202-333-3104; 3104 M St NW; ⏰ 11-2am; 🚌 Georgetown shuttle from Foggy Bottom-GWU

Dark and welcoming, Mr Smith's is really an old-timers' bar, although daily specials like half-price burgers and all-you-can-eat fish-and-chips draw students, too. The crowded, friendly front bar (you'll rub bodies with at least two strangers while drinking) hides a more spacious rear seating area with a fireplace and open patio with a sort of greenhouse feel – there are lots of plants.

SEQUOIA Map p299

☎ 202-944-4200; Georgetown Harbor, 3000 K St; 🚌 Georgetown shuttle from Foggy Bottom-GWU

On a steamy summer night, Sequoia's patio is the spot to be. Plop down on a plastic chair on its cascading terrace overlooking the Potomac and check out

the rich people messing around in boats. Or fight your way through the throng at the bar, grab an overpriced Corona, then start flirting and talking politics with the hottie of your choice. This bar attracts all types – from pretty gays to trustafarian college kids to 30-something lawyers – although it has a reputation as a pick-up spot.

TOMBS Map p299

☎ 202-337-6668; 1226 36th St NW; ⏰ 11:30-2am Mon-Thu, 11:30-3am Fri, 11-3am Sat, 9:30-2am Sun; 🚌 Georgetown shuttle from Rosslyn or Foggy Bottom-GWU

Georgetown University's most-revered drinking spot is filled with students, professors and even the occasional Jesuit priest. They flock to this dive nightly to indulge in cheap pitchers and better-than-average pub grub priced for college pockets. The square bar is illuminated by dim lighting and there are plenty of grubby wood tables to share (and scope the competition out). Walls are decked with sports junk and, oddly, WWI-era posters.

CAPITOL HILL & SOUTHWEST DC

Power drinking is the name of the game in Capitol Hill (that and swapping as many business cards as possible). The domain of Hillies (folks who live or work on the Hill), Pennsylvania Ave SE between 2nd and 8th Sts, is the main bar-hopping street behind the capital. The TVs here are likely tuned to CNN, and the crowd generally sports suits and ties. Happy hours are huge (a good thing considering how low government salaries can be), and so is picking up – some of DC's raunchiest action gets started at Hill bars and finishes in the lobby of some Senator's office (everyone here has a revered ID card, and rumor has it guards often let young aides and staffers in well after dark).

The area around Union Station also has its share of bars, including a few good Irish ones. Another option is the Waterfront in Southwest, which has an assortment of restaurants (see p153) that boast bars with Washington Channel views.

18TH AMENDMENT Map p304

☎ 202-543-3522; 613 Pennsylvania Ave SE;
Ⓜ Eastern Market

Still in its infancy when we visited, this place embraces a speakeasy theme – hence the name. Gangsters and bootleggers should head directly to the basement, where the furniture is made from beer barrels and whiskey crates and pool tables on which to fight your duel. Upstairs there's a late 1920s art deco air, reminiscent of prohibition-era Chicago. It has ample seating and eight beers on tap.

BULLFEATHERS Map p304

☎ 202-543-5005; 410 First St SE; Ⓜ Capitol South

Clubby and cozy, this is one of Capitol Hill's long-time favorites and political paparazzi may just get lucky and catch your senator walking out the door. Named after Teddy Roosevelt's euphemism of choice for BS, it serves affordable beers in graceful old environs.

CANTINA MARINA Map pp308-9

☎ 202-554-8396; 600 Water St SW;
Ⓜ Waterfront

When the summer heat becomes unbearable head to Cantina Marina's patio to cool down and forget the temperature with frozen margaritas and fresh Potomac breezes. This Tex-Mex joint, built right over the Washington Channel, is packed on hot summer evenings, when its outdoor seating in the midst of the marina and live music on weekends draws hordes of festive diners and dancers. The food is only so-so, but most folks just come for a little vacation from the city.

CAPITOL LOUNGE

Map p304

☎ 202-547-2098; 229-31 Pennsylvania Ave SE;
Ⓜ Eastern Market

A year after it was severely damaged by a fire in August 2005, Capitol Lounge is back in full swing with hardly a scar marring its pretty face. More upscale than other divey neighborhood pubs, this is a Hillie hotspot that serves cigars and martinis along with 10¢ wings. Pool tables, sports on TV and familiar faces draw the staffers in droves. They come to flirt and network and just talk smack about work.

HAWK & DOVE Map p304

☎ 202-543-3300; 329 Pennsylvania Ave SE;
Ⓜ Eastern Market

Reputed to be a Republican hangout, the Hawk & Dove has been a Capitol Hill institution since the 1960s. It's not really a partisan place, though. Everybody eventually finds their way here, including congressional staffers and even some of the younger representatives of all parties. Friday nights are particularly lively: pick up a date or just a game of pool and enjoy the happy-hour specials.

KELLY'S IRISH TIMES Map p304

☎ 202-543-5433; 14 F St NW; Ⓜ Union Station

Kelly's implores: 'Give me your tired, your hungry, your befuddled masses,' and the masses respond. Fans of the on-tap Guinness and Wednesday to Saturday live music tend to be younger than the patrons next door at the Dubliner – students and staffers and other suds-drinkers.

LOUNGE 201 Map p304

☎ 202-544-5201; 201 Massachusetts Ave NE;
🕑 6pm-2am Tue-Sat; Ⓜ Union Station

Decidedly retro decor and brightly colored martinis go hand-in-hand at this swanky, new cocktail lounge. The menu claims that 'To drink is human, to lounge is divine' and you will certainly believe it after spending an evening here sipping martinis and munching on gourmet finger food.

PENN AVE POUR HOUSE Map p304

☎ 202-546-1001; 319 Pennsylvania Ave SE;
Ⓜ Eastern Market

This very popular bar pays tribute to the Keystone state (Pennsylvania) on its 1st floor. Here you'll find Penn State pennants gracing scarred walls. The menu features sausage sandwiches and Iron City beer on tap. Regardless of your Pennsylvania obsession level, this is a fun place to hang out that's usually packed to the gills with interns and congressional aides. Upstairs you'll find a plush lounge.

PHASE ONE Map pp308-9

☎ 202-544-6831; 525 8th St SE; 🕑 7pm-2am Thu-Sun; Ⓜ Eastern Market

The city's only bar dedicated exclusively to lesbians is a cozy neighborhood joint that's been serving booze for more than 30 years.

DRINKS WITH A BREEZE – BEST PATIO BARS

Despite heat and humidity, Washingtonians will tell you that, come 5pm, there is no better summer tonic than partaking of a cold cocktail from an alfresco rooftop bar or windy patio with killer views. We've listed our top five choices below.

Beacon Martini Sky-Bar (opposite) Take the express elevator to the roof and enjoy some of DC's top skyline views from the breezy outdoor patio at this swank bar perched atop the new Beacon Hotel & Corporate Quarters.

Caddies on Cordell (p180) Casually clad servers, grad students and young professionals like to mingle on Caddie's giant rooftop deck. Flirting is the focal point, although the breezes that stir the humid summer air are another key attraction.

Cantina Marina (p173) Hanging over the Washington Channel, Cantina Marina boasts fabulous watery views from its deck. This is the escape of choice for a drink with a breeze on days when the humidity is just too stifling.

Local 16 (p177) Washington's beautiful (but not necessarily rich) people flock to Local 16's rooftop for steamy summer drinks and a down-to-earth U St view.

Sky Terrace (opposite) Enjoy spectacular views of the entire city from this hotel bar's rooftop.

It attracts single women and couples in search of a good time (and possibly more). It also caters to just-out-of-the-closet girls (it's the kind of place that makes you feel accepted). Come early to mingle in peace and quiet, or late to shake your booty on the packed dance floor. Line dancing lessons and a pool tournament take place on Sundays.

TAPATINIS Map pp308-9
☎ 202-546-8272; 711 Eighth St SE;
Ⓜ Eastern Market
This hot joint, located a little further into the heart of Southeast, runs all sorts of promotional specials that will have you drinking cheaply. At the time of research Thursday night was when to visit – sponsors passed out free samples of their product from 8pm until the booze ran out. On Friday lines form for an all-night $20 open bar, and there are nightly martini happy hours. Martinis are what to order here, by the way. There is a long list of perfectly mixed concoctions to choose from. If you're feeling a little tipsy from all the free alcohol, order a few plates of Mediterranean tapas, which come in huge portions.

DOWNTOWN

Downtown used to be the dumps, totally deserted after dark. Now it's pretty damn hot, known especially for its VIP club scene, but there are plenty of bars and lounges to chill before the dancing starts.

The Penn Quarter and Chinatown are both good nightlife bets. Sports fans will love the streets surrounding the MCI Center, as they are home to DC's biggest sports bars. This area also has some of DC's best microbreweries.

DA'S RFD WASHINGTON Map pp292-3
☎ 202-289-2030; 810 7th St NW; Ⓜ Gallery Pl-Chinatown
One of DC's top-two bets for serious beer geeks (the other is the **Brickskeller**, opposite) it offers a dizzying 40 local and international beers on tap along with 300 bottles. This is definitely a good choice if you want to sample a microbrew; plus it's centrally located near the MCI Center if you're in the neighborhood to catch a game.

DISTRICT CHOPHOUSE & BREWERY
Map pp292-3
☎ 202-347-3434; 509 7th St NW;
Ⓜ Gallery Pl-Chinatown
Jazzing up the Penn Quarter, this stylish place in a stunningly converted old bank building oozes attitude. It also serves up around eight of its own microbrews, ranging from lager to stout. The place offers food, but it's just so-so, which means most guests stick to drinking in the busy bar.

ESPN ZONE Map pp292-3
☎ 202-783-3776; 555 12th St NW;
Ⓜ Metro Center
This three-floor, 200-TV emporium features the **Sports Grill**, a massive screening room

with speakers in its chairs and a 16ft TV that looks like a war-room missile monitor. Next door, the **Sports Arena** is packed with video games, air hockey and other table games. This is a happening place to watch a game (any game), but it's often crowded with tourists.

FADÓ IRISH PUB & RESTAURANT

Map pp292-3

☎ 202-789-0066; 808 7th St NW; ⏰ 11:30-2:30am; Ⓜ Gallery Pl-Chinatown

This place sticks out in Chinatown like James Joyce in Shanghai. Somehow the Chinese restaurants are not so conducive to drinking, so Fadó packs in the thirsty, especially after games at the nearby MCI Center. Every room in this Disney-esque pub is decked out in its own unique Celtic style – country library, medieval castle etc. The place is old school; it has a following that remembers when this was still considered in the 'hood.

GREEN LANTERN & TOOL SHED

Map pp292-3

☎ 202-347-4533; 1335 Green Ct NW; ⏰ 9pm-2am Wed-Thu, 9pm-3am Fri & Sat, 6pm-2am Sun; Ⓜ McPherson Sq

The gay Green Lantern is downstairs, with leather-lovers' Tool Shed on the 2nd floor. This bi-level place attracts a slightly older crowd. Shirtless men get free beer on Thursday night.

SKY TERRACE Map pp292-3

☎ 202-638-5900; Hotel Washington, 515 15th St NW; ⏰ May-Oct; Ⓜ Metro Center

This is the best spot to watch the sunset on a hot summer night. From the rooftop the entire city stretches out in front of you, and the panoramic view is nothing short of spectacular. It's a perfect spot to go on a date or impress your mother. Expect a wait for a table when the weather is nice.

DUPONT CIRCLE & KALORAMA

DC's gay and lesbian nightlife Mecca, this neighborhood is packed with bars ranging from raunchy to ritzy. Regardless of your sexual orientation, there's something to keep you drinking around the circle.

Chill coffee houses, super sleek lounges and ramshackle joints known for cheap happy hours abound. Check out the area around 18th and Connecticut Aves.

BEACON MARTINI SKY-BAR

Map pp296-7

☎ 202-296-2100; Beacon Hotel & Corporate Quarters, 1615 Rhode Island Ave NW; ⏰ May-Oct; Ⓜ Dupont Circle

On top of the swank new **Beacon Hotel** (p234), this patio on the roof offers ample sky-high city views and an opportunity to mingle with new friends over signature martinis. If you're hungry, order from the light-fare menu.

BIG HUNT Map pp296-7

☎ 202-785-2333; 1345 Connecticut Ave NW; Ⓜ Dupont Circle

Yes, the name is played for all the puns it is worth: the bar advertises itself as the 'happy hunting ground for humans in pursuit of a mate, food and drink.' But it's not actually that cruisey. Most patrons focus on the 27 on-tap beers and bar-eats deals, amid cheesy Hemingway decor: animal-print upholstery and mosquito nets. Coin-operated pool tables are on the 2nd floor.

BRICKSKELLER INN Map pp296-7

☎ 202-293-1885; 1523 22nd St NW; Ⓜ Dupont Circle

This underground beer paradise has 900 varieties, listed on a menu heavy enough to cause trouble after the fifth pint or so. Shandies, stouts, darks, lights, lagers and creams – it claims the world's largest selection. Its subterranean red-brick warren is usually choked with college-age folks arrayed around big circular tables. Most bottles cost around $4, but true exotics can cost up to $15. It also offers accommodations (p232).

BUFFALO BILLIARDS Map pp296-7

☎ 202-331-7665; 1330 19th St; ⏰ 4pm-2am Mon-Thu, 4pm-3am Fri, 1pm-3am Sat, 1pm-1am Sun; Ⓜ Dupont Circle

The 30 pool and snooker tables pull college kids and yuppies into this bright, below-street-level cave. There is usually a wait for a table – pull up a lounge chair and play Score Four while you are waiting.

FRONT PAGE Map pp296-7

☎ 202-296-6500; 1333 New Hampshire Ave NW;
Ⓜ Dupont Circle

Making Thursday-night happy hour at the Front Page is mandatory for many downtown office types. The mixed, oft boisterous, crowd flocks in after 5pm on this night for a free taco bar along with cheap beer and plenty of pick-up options amid heavy wood and brick environs. Other nights, happy hour offers half-price appetizers and some $2 beer, wine and well drinks.

JR'S Map pp296-7

☎ 202-328-0090; 1519 17th St NW; ⏱ 2pm-2am Mon-Thu, 2pm-3am Fri, noon-3am Sat, noon-2am Sun; Ⓜ Dupont Circle

At JR's weekday happy hour you might think you've stepped into a living Banana Republic ad: chinos and button-downs are de rigueur at this popular gay hangout frequented by the 20- and 30-something, work-hard and play-hard set. Some DC residents claim that the crowd at JR's epitomizes the conservative nature of the capital's gay scene; but even if you love to hate it, as many do, JR's is the happy-hour spot in town and is packed more often than not.

LUCKY BAR Map pp296-7

☎ 202-331-3733; 1221 Connecticut Ave NW;
Ⓜ Dupont Circle

Catering to the city's young and poor, this rambling three-story dive-like place runs its happy hour from 3pm to 8pm weekdays and has a rotating list of specials – half-price burgers on Wednesdays, 25¢ wings on Tuesdays – along with $2.50 pints and $3.50 well drinks.

The crowd is a soup of bike messengers, restaurant servers and K St lawyers. A DJ spins a mix of hip-hop house and Britpop on weekends, when Lucky gets really packed. It's popular during the day with soccer fans who watch English, Spanish and American-league games on the giant projection screen.

SIGN OF THE WHALE Map pp296-7

☎ 202-785-1110; 1825 M St; ⏱ 11:30-1am;
Ⓜ Dupont Circle

Next to DC's most notorious gentleman's club, Camelot, Sign of the Whale is a shotgun-style Brit pub with a big fireplace, high ceilings and a long wooden bar, with boars'

heads overlooking the scene. It's popular for happy-hour specials and a weekend brunch that features unlimited Mimosas for $9 or a Bloody Mary bar for $10.

ADAMS-MORGAN

Adams-Morgan is the epicenter of DC's nightlife scene. Simply put, the city rocks to its multicultural beat. The range of bars is as diverse as the neighborhood itself. Columbia Rd and 18th St are the two bar-hopping strips. You'll find most of the Latino bars and clubs on Columbia Rd, while 18th St has more cultural variety. Both only run a few blocks, so make a loop.

CHI-CHA LOUNGE Map pp296-7

☎ 202-234-8400; 1624 U St NW; ⏱ 5:30pm-2am Sun-Thu, 5:30pm-3am Fri & Sat;
Ⓜ U Street-Cardozo

On first thought, Arabic *arguilehs* (hookahs) and Andean food don't seem a felicitous combination, but Chi-Cha makes it work. Curl into velvet settees, nibble Ecuadorian tapas and order a pipe of Bahrainian fruit-and-honey-cured tobacco. Ah, East and West do combine beautifully. Hookahs are available weekdays only.

COMMON SHARE Map pp296-7

☎ 202-588-7180; 2003 18th St NW; ⏱ 5:30pm-2am Sun-Thu, 5:30pm-3am Fri & Sat; Ⓜ Woodley Park-Zoo/Adams Morgan

This is DC's cheapest bar that doesn't involve brown paper bags, a place that commendably considers the buzz a basic human right. It sells every beer (even nice ones like Guinness) and mixed drinks for just $2 to $3. Beaten-up curbside freebies furnish the place, but at these prices, who's complaining?

FELIX Map pp296-7

☎ 202-483-3549; 2406 18th St; Ⓜ Woodley Park-Zoo/Adams Morgan

Lines form early on weekend nights when the beautiful people flock to this beautiful lounge to down beautiful sorrows in beautifully constructed martinis. Yes, Felix is a swank place where the attitude has attitude and the bouncer behind the plush velvet ropes can be a little too selective in his entrance policy for some people's patience. Plate-glass windows, neon letters and super-sleek decor give it serious character. Live jazz and funk banks set up on a stage pushed against the front windows on Friday and Saturday night.

LEFT BANK Map pp296-7
☎ 202-328-2100; 2424 18th St NW; Ⓜ Woodley Park-Zoo/Adams Morgan

A new edition to Adams-Morgan, the Left Bank is a hip, modern lounge with stark white walls and orange chairs and booths. It's the perfect dark cave in which to escape a hot summer afternoon's mounting heat. The prime location, smack in the middle of 18th St, is perfect for people-watching from open windows if the place is quiet. Left Bank attracts a sophisticated, international crowd that comes to sip martinis and listen to DJs spin mellow vibes. There's a menu, but the food is only okay.

LOCAL 16 Map pp296-7
☎ 202-265-2828; 1602 U St NW; Ⓜ U Street-Cardozo

Voted best pick-up spot by *Washington Post* readers in 2006, this trendy restaurant-bar is filled with the young and beautiful on the prowl. The rooftop bar is brilliant in summer; when its cold the scene moves to the upstairs lounge. It also serves food.

MILLIE & AL'S Map pp296-7
☎ 202-387-8131; 2440 18th St NW; ⏰ 4pm-2am Mon-Thu, 4pm-3am Fri & Sat; Ⓜ Woodley Park-Zoo/Adams Morgan

This comfortably worn dive is an Adams-Morgan institution, famous for its $2 drafts, Jell-O shots and hit-the-spot pizza (best consumed in that order). Two TVs show a constant stream of sports. It has always been, and probably will always be, a yup-pie bar with a frat-house flavor. The kind of place where you can be expected to be hit on and have beer spilled on you in the same night.

PHARMACY BAR Map pp296-7
☎ 202-483-1200; 2337 18th St NW; ⏰ 5pm-1:30am Mon-Thu, 5pm-2:30am Fri & Sat; Ⓜ Woodley Park-Zoo/Adams Morgan

As tribute to this building's previous in-carnation as a drugstore, this cool bar is decorated with old medicine jars on the walls and pills embedded in the tabletops.

A quiet contrast to the wild Adams-Morgan scene, it's an ideal spot for a late-night snack or a nightcap.

SPY LOUNGE Map pp296-7
☎ 202-483-3549; 2406 18th St NW; Ⓜ Woodley Park-Zoo/Adams Morgan

The Spy Lounge has been one of the hottest spots in Adams-Morgan for a while now, very cleverly playing on everyone's secret desire to be suave, sneaky and – well – more like James Bond. Espionage is in; conven-iently, so are martinis: both are on tap at this swanky lounge, next door to funky Felix (opposite).

STETSON'S FAMOUS BAR & RESTAURANT Map pp296-7
☎ 202-667-6295; 1610 U St NW; ⏰ 5pm-1am; Ⓜ U Street-Cardozo

'Famous' might be a bit of a stretch, but Stetson's can lay claim to fame as *the* neighborhood bar in the U St area. It is basic – the ratty pool table and the jukebox are the primary amenities – and comfort-able, with good and tasty burgers and cheap happy-hour specials.

TRYST Map pp296-7
☎ 202-232-5500; 2459 18th St NW; ⏰ 6:30-2am Mon-Thu, 6:30-3am Fri & Sat, 8-12:30am Sun; Ⓜ Woodley Park-Zoo/Adams Morgan

This Greenwich Village–style place is probably the best coffeehouse in DC. The couches, armchairs and bookshelves scat-tered about, and the light flooding through street-side windows, lure patrons so faithful they probably should pay rent. Sweet alco-holic concoctions flow along with caffeine (sometimes in the same glass), nice com-plements to the menu of waffles, muffins and cake. It's a great place to meet up with old friends or make new ones.

SHAW & U STREET

This is DC's new wannabe hot nightlife district right now – one of those neighbor-hoods in the process of turning trendy, but hasn't become so cool it's lost its edge. You'll find a mixture of long-established neigh-borhood dives next to brand-new lounges with velvet ropes and dressed-to-impress crowds outside the bouncer-guarded gates. You'll either love it or hate it. Most of the action happens on U St between 8th and 14th Sts, with new bars also opening on 14th St (formerly famous for its hookers). This area can still be a little dangerous after dark, so keep an eye on your surroundings and take a cab if you're worried.

CAFÉ SAINT-EX Map pp302-3
☎ 202-265-7839; 1847 14th St NW; ☾ 5:30pm-1am Sun-Wed, 5:30pm-2am Thu-Sat; Ⓜ U Street-Cardozo

Reminiscent of the Parisian Latin Quarter, Saint-Ex attracts a mix of ages, ethnicities and orientations. Different DJs spin tunes every night and there is no cover charge. A bar salvaged from a 1930s Philadelphia pub, seats from an old movie theater and classic movies running on the TVs all lend a nostalgic air. The downstairs lounge, **Gate 54**, plays up the aeronautic theme with a wooden propeller from the owner's grandfather's WWI fighter plane (author Antoine de Saint-Exupéry was also a pilot).

CUE BAR Map pp302-3
☎ 202-332-7665; 1115 U St NW; Ⓜ U Street-Cardozo

This new U St establishment is making ping-pong cool, and a mixed-race crowd is lining up to play. A basement-level joint that vaguely resembles a community rec room, Cue Bar offers a couple of pool tables, a lounge area full of furniture, TVs with sport and the ever-popular ping-pong table ($10 per hour). On Sundays an 8-ball tournament starts at 7pm.

POLLY'S CAFÉ Map pp302-3
☎ 202-265-8385; 1342 U St NW; ☾ 6pm-2am Mon-Thu, 6pm-3am Fri, 10-3am Sat, 10-1am Sun; Ⓜ U Street-Cardozo

This friendly, no-attitude, basement-level bar was a U St pioneer: it has been around for more than a decade. Exposed brick walls and fireplace coziness make Polly's Café a fine place to rendezvous with friends before or after a night of music. Polly serves reasonably priced pints and a menu of basic eats, such as salads and burgers. Polly's does a great brunch on Saturdays and Sundays. It is a quiet spot to nurse your hangover with Bloody Marys or Mimosas served by the pitcher (only $8.25). Sop it up with one of eight varieties of eggs benedict.

SALOON Map pp302-3
☎ 202-462-2640; 1207 U St NW; Ⓜ U Street-Cardozo

The Saloon is made for chatting – there's no TV to distract you, no loud music to clog your ears. It's a comfortable place to go for a drink even if you're solo as seating is communal (to encourage conversation) with lengthy tables stretched out across the brick-lined room. There is a solid beer selection at the J-shaped bar, and light jazz plays in the background.

TABAQ BISTRO Map pp302-3
☎ 202-265-0965; 1336 U St NW; Ⓜ U Street-Cardozo

You can't beat the view from this fabulous retractable-rooftop restaurant and bar. In winter you can gaze at the snow falling on the glass ceiling; in summer the enclosure is opened up and the sounds and smells of U St drift up from four stories below. If you're hungry, the food is not bad – Tabaq Bistro has a selection of Turkish and Middle Eastern cuisine – and the setting is urban romantic (think lots of elbow-to-elbow tables perfect for low conversation and cocktails). Come at sunset, order something flamboyant from the drink menu and toast the beginning of your night out.

TITAN Map pp302-3
☎ 202-232-7010; 1337 14th St NW; ☾ 5pm-2am; Ⓜ U Street-Cardozo

This upstairs bar (look for it above Dakota Cowgirl Restaurant) at this crazy place hosts gay Family Feud, which is wildly popular among the Dupont set. State Department and World Bank types – officially Gays & Lesbians in Foreign Affairs – meet here for happy hour every month (third Thursday). There are nightly happy hours.

UPPER NORTHWEST DC

This area is not particularly known for its nightlife, and most places tend to be the quiet neighborhood pub variety where upper middle–class couples linger over bottles of vintage Chardonnay.

The area exception is a cluster of rowdy Irish bars around Connecticut Ave in Cleveland Park, near the Uptown movie theater. This is probably Upper

Drinking

UPPER NORTHWEST DC

Northwest's most concentrated nightlife strip, and the crowd here is young, international and determined to party.

AROMA COMPANY
Map pp300-1
☎ 202-244-7995; 3417 Connecticut Ave NW; ⏱ 5:30pm-1am; Ⓜ Cleveland Park
There's a pronounced fascination with the 1950s at this sleek retro bar: it's filled with those kidney-shaped coffee tables and old sofas; the tiled bar serves up the Scotch and ciggies. Live jazz plays here on Friday nights.

IRELAND'S FOUR PROVINCES
Map pp300-1
☎ 202-244-0860; 3412 Connecticut Ave NW; ⏱ 5pm-1am Sun-Thu, 4pm-2am Fri, 5pm-2am Sat; Ⓜ Cleveland Park
This landmark Irish bar offers live Celtic and folk music, 21 beers on tap, relentless emerald-shamrock decor, and a friendly scene of late-20s neighborhood professionals cruising and schmoozing. Come on a hot summer night to sit on the streetside patio, or during weekday happy hour, when you can get a 20oz Guinness for $4.

NANNY O'BRIEN'S IRISH PUB
Map pp300-1
☎ 202-686-9189; 3319 Connecticut Ave NW; Ⓜ Cleveland Park
Washington's most authentic Irish pub, Nanny O'Brien's has been a favorite with real and wannabe Irish people for decades. You won't find any cheesy shamrock schlock or shameless promotions here; no, this bar would rather concentrate on serving stiff drinks along with fantastic music. The place is packed and rowdy most nights.

ARLINGTON
It's often cheaper to sleep in Arlington than in the city, and if you do, you won't have to travel far to find a bar. The city has always had a lively nightlife scene. Head to Wilson and Clarendon Blvds for good bar-hopping. Young professionals and workers from the food-service industry are the major demographic here.

CONTINENTAL
Map p299
☎ 703-465-7675; 1911 N Fort Myer Dr; Ⓜ Rosslyn
A stone's throw from many Rosslyn hotels, this posh new pool hall isn't your average billiards club. There's no stale-beer-and-cigarette stink about this place where spaghetti lights form constellations on the ceiling and the patterned columns are painted like palm trees. Tiki heads and bars painted with silver glitter complete the picture. The owner says Disneyland was the inspiration for his style faux pas that somehow manages to epitomize cool.

IRELAND'S FOUR COURTS
Map pp306-7
☎ 703-525-3600; 2051 Wilson Blvd, Arlington; ⏱ 11-2am Mon-Sat, 10-2am Sun; Ⓜ Courthouse
Buckets of Guinness lubricate the O'Connors and McDonoughs at Arlington's favorite Irish pub. The sidewalk seating draws a lunchtime crowd for shepherd's pie and fish and chips, while the verdant Irish grass-green interior attracts an evening crowd for cold drafts and live tunes.

WHITLOW'S ON WILSON
Map pp306-7
☎ 703-276-9693; 2854 Wilson Blvd, Arlington; ⏱ 11:30-2am Mon-Fri, 9-2am Sat & Sun; Ⓜ Clarendon
Occupying almost an entire block just east of Clarendon Metro, Whitlow's has something for everyone: burgers, brunch and comfort food on the menu; happening happy hours and positive pick-up potential; plus 12 brews on tap, a pool table, jukebox, live music and an easygoing atmosphere. It's a favorite with singles.

ALEXANDRIA
With its growing popularity as a dining destination, Alexandria's nightlife scene is starting to take off as well, and the city has quite a few good places to drink. The scene is a slightly older (and more professional) crowd than you would find on Capitol Hill. Brew pubs are popular here. Explore the cobbled streets of Old Town until you find somewhere you like.

CAFÉ SALSA–BAR

Map p311

☎ 703-684-4100; 808 King St; 🚌 Old Town shuttle from King Street Metro

Old Town's best happy hour is offered from 4pm to 7pm – all drinks and appetizers are half-price – at the 2nd-floor bar, which is of course packed during these hours. The drink selection is varied – Latin American beers to match the Nuevo Latin menu served in its downstairs restaurant, delicious Mojitos and a fabulous Caribbean rum cooler, which blends four different rums with pineapple and orange juices.

FOUNDERS' BREWING CO

Map p311

☎ 703-684-5397; 607 King St; 🚌 Old Town shuttle from King St Metro

Founders' four brews (and counting) play off themes of local Alexandria history (such as Smoot's Stout, named for a 19th-century mayor). The beers are smooth and refreshing, a mix of American stouts and pale ales and German-style Kolsch and altbier. The place serves a full American menu.

UNION STREET PUBLIC HOUSE

Map p311

☎ 703-548-1785; 121 S Union St; 🕒 11:30-1am Mon-Sat, 11-1am Sun; 🚌 Old Town shuttle from King St Metro

Gas lamps out front welcome tourists and locals into this spacious taproom for frosty brews, raw-bar delights and nightly dinner specials. Inside, the atmosphere is equally inviting: a wide bar, heavy wooden furniture and exposed brick hark back to Alexandria's days as a bustling Colonial port.

BETHESDA

Bethesda is filled with restaurants, and after they close its hordes of service staff need somewhere to let off a little steam (and burn some of the evening's tips), which is perhaps the reason Bethesda has so many happening bars. The scene here usually kicks off around 9pm or 10pm, although many places also garner a pre-dinner happy-hour crowd. Check out the Woodmont Triangle area (anchored by a giant Barnes & Noble), which positively buzzes at night.

CADDIES ON CORDELL Map p310

☎ 301-215-7730; 4922 Cordell Ave; Ⓜ Bethesda

You'll find a giant rooftop deck here, where everyone gathers for sunset shots then lingers over beers late into the night. Caddies is a down-to-earth place where the crowd is a mix of graduate students and restaurant servers and the vibe is as low-key and refreshing as the breeze sweeping across the patio. Inside there is a golf theme, tons of TVs broadcasting sport and a golden-tee video game that's ridiculously popular. The place also serves a full menu.

UNION JACK'S Map p310

☎ 301-652-2561; 4915 St Elmo Ave; Ⓜ Bethesda

A staple of the Bethesda nightlife scene since it opened in 2005, Union Jack's tries to re-create jolly old England in the 'burbs. There's a restaurant that resembles the pub in the *Harry Potter* movies and a front room that's trying to be all of downtown London, with many street lamps and a replica of Big Ben. Way in the back is a marvelous saloon with pool tables, darts and welcoming leather chairs to sink your tired bum. The entire thing sounds ridiculous, but somehow works.

Entertainment

Entertainment

When it comes to entertainment, DC delivers a lot of bang for your buck. Okay, so the city doesn't boast a Broadway theater district like New York or a club scene like Los Angeles, but what it lacks in fame it more than makes up for in sophisticated oomph. This is a city that takes performing arts seriously. From the sparkling-white Kennedy Center, with its dizzying red-carpeted halls and magnificently high ceilings, to the Shaw neighborhood's old-time jazz joints, where the chairs are faded, the walls are grubby and the gin has been flowing for more than half a century, Washington offers a tempting buffet of charismatic night-time attractions.

Jazz, rock and punk history all have roots in DC, and the city is famous for its own brand of music – go-go (see p187). Its clubs are big on variety – from the dark and smoky to the swank and snotty. You'll find the usual red-velvet ropes, glam girls, PR hawkers and beefy bouncers, but you'll also find basement joints where anyone is welcome and the Reggae pumping in the background is a mix from Ghana and Alpha Blondie, c early '90s. It's cool enough for rockers to take interest – long-time favorite DC haunt the Black Cat is part owned by Dave Grohl of the Foo Fighters.

DC has a thriving theater scene. The district, anchored in the Penn Quarter, is small, but the stately beaux-art theaters put on world-class performances of favorite Broadway musicals and cutting-edge plays. Scattered around the city are numerous smaller venues, from black box to high-school auditorium, where budding actors and actresses get their start and less mainstream, more multicultural, subject matter is explored.

The drinking age in DC – as in the rest of the US – is 21. Although bars don't let anyone under that age through the door, DC is one of the few places in America where many clubs have 'over-18' policies that let you enter to dance or see shows, but don't give you the hand-stamp that lets you buy alcohol. Bring a photo ID to prove your age: a driver's license is the usual kind.

Tickets

Most venues sell discounted tickets on the day of the performance, either for standing room or obstructed-view spots. Call the box office for details. Discounted tickets are also available at Ticketplace (Map pp292–3; ☎ 202-842-5387; www.cultural-alliance.org/tickets; 1100 Pennsylvania Ave NW, Old Post Office Pavilion; ☺ 11am-6pm Tue-Sat; Ⓜ Federal Triangle), which sells day-of-performance tickets to citywide concerts and shows for half-price plus 10%. Available tickets are listed on a board hanging in the office. Ticketmaster (Map pp292–3; ☎ 202-432-7328; www.ticketmaster.com; 2000 Pennsylvania Ave NW, Tower Records; ☺ 9am-midnight Mon-Sat, 10am-10pm Sun; Ⓜ Foggy Bottom-GWU) has information on, and sells full-price tickets to, citywide events.

Festivals

DC's most venerable music festival, the WHFStival, began as a grunge fest in the early 1990s. Although the original Washington radio station, 99.1 WHFS, is no longer on the air (the Baltimore partner station is still going, though), the festival continues, held over two days on the last weekend in May. In 2006 the line-up featured Kanye West, Counting Crows, The Strokes and local success Jimmie's Chicken Shack.

The Merriweather Post Pavilion in Columbia, MD, and the Nissan Pavilion near Manassas, VA, host outdoor concerts seven months of the year.

DC hosts a number of film festivals during the year. FilmFest DC (☎ 202-628-3456; www .filmfestdc.org), in late April, is an international festival; past features included topics like Politics in Film. The best of new gay, lesbian, bisexual and transgender films the world over can be viewed at the Reel Affirmations (☎ 202-986-1119; www.reelaffirmations.org)

FREE FUN

In DC, it's easy to entertain yourself for next-to-nothing (or for nothing, for that matter). As well as offering free admission to all its museums and collections, the **Smithsonian** (☎ 202-357-2020) sponsors evening lectures, films, concerts and other performances that are often free. In summer the city becomes one giant outdoor venue for free concerts and fun. Here are five options for culture vultures with empty pockets.

Art Gallery Openings (p191) Free wine and cheese and a chance to meet the artist. Most galleries hold these on the first Friday of the month.

Carter Barron Amphitheater (p192) Shakespeare in the Park or music after dark.

Mary Pickford Theater (p196) Historical and artsy films, Tuesday, Thursday and Friday at 7pm.

Millennium Stage (p192) Live jazz, blues, folk, world-beat or classical music at the Kennedy Center – every night at 6pm.

Screen on the Green (☎ 877-262-5866) On Mondays at sundown between mid-July and mid-August head to the National Mall (between 4th and 7th Sts) for a free screening of a Hollywood classic.

in mid-October. The festival also runs late-night camp films, lively parties and a women's filmmaker brunch. The **Washington Jewish Film Festival** (☎ 202-777-3248; www.wjff.org), in late November-early December, explores and celebrates contemporary Jewish-American themes.

In summer, one of DC's favorite traditions is the **Screen on the Green** movie festival. Held Monday nights at sundown between mid-July and mid-August, it features a different Hollywood classic each week on the National Mall (between 4th and 7th Sts).

LIVE MUSIC

Washingtonians have long had a love affair with jazz and blues, but in this most international of American cities you'll also find abundant places to groove to reggae, salsa, African beats and world-music fusion. The scene is constantly evolving – 10 years ago it was Fugazi, now it's Jimmie's Chicken Shack for rock and the Young Lions for jazz. Many of the bigger venues bring in nationally known acts on weekends, although you can often catch up-and-coming local performers at these same clubs on less-popular nights of the week or as openers.

Rock, Hip-Hop & Indie

Many venues incorporate all three genres into their line-ups, featuring hip-hop one night and modern rock the next. DC has a progressive alternative rock and punk scene. Two of the city's top rock venues are found in the Shaw neighborhood.

9:30 CLUB

Map pp302-3
☎ 202-3-930-930; www.930.com; 815 V St NW; admission $10-35; ⏲ from 7:30pm Sun-Thu; Ⓜ U Street-Cardozo

In 1996 DC's premier live rock venue moved from its small downtown digs to this spanking new warehouse, which holds 1200 patrons and has two levels and four bars. (If you've been in DC a while, you'll recognize the basement bar, salvaged from 9:30's old home.) The calendar is packed with the most random assortment of big names – Justin Timberlake, The Violent Femmes, George Clinton and The Black Crowes. Concerts usually include around three acts, with the headlining band taking the stage between 10:30pm and 11:30pm.

BLACK CAT

Map pp302-3
☎ 202-667-7960; www.blackcatdc.com; 1811 14th St NW; admission $8-15; ⏲ box office 8pm-midnight; Ⓜ U Street-Cardozo

Co-owned by Foo Fighter Dave Grohl, the Black Cat is head kitty of DC's indie-rock clubs. Set in a beat-up old warehouse, the Black Cat draws fans of grunge and industrial rock. The venue's cover charge varies with the band, but there's no cover in the Red Room bar, where there's a good selection of Belgian beer, pool tables and a jukebox.

MADAM'S ORGAN

Map pp296-7

☎ 202-667-5370; www.madamsorgan.com; 2461 18th St NW; admission $1-10; ☿ shows 9:30pm Mon-Thu, 10pm Fri & Sat; Ⓜ Woodley Park-Zoo/ Adams Morgan

'Where the beautiful people go to get ugly,' according to the T-shirt. It's not far off the mark – this is the kind of perfect dive where you'll see a beautiful girl shaking her ass on the bar one minute and puking in the bathroom the next.

An enigmatic ramshackle place that's been around forever, Madam's Organ was once named one of *Playboy* magazine's favorite bars in America. The live jazz, blues and bluegrass can be downright riot inducing. There is a roving magician, raunchy bar-dancing scene, and funky decor with stuffed animals and bizarre paintings on the 1st floor. On Wednesdays there's a fine bluegrass jam with much whoopin' and stompin'. Who says DC's don't have soul?

VELVET LOUNGE

Map pp302-3

☎ 202-462-3213; www.velvetloungedc.com; 915 U St NW; admission $5; ☿ 8pm-2am; Ⓜ U Street-Cardozo

DC bands on their way up continue to play at this tiny club with a big dedication to local talent. Emerging grungy acts play to alt-rock fans in the Velvet's upstairs hall; downstairs is a dark little pit of a bar.

Jazz & Blues

U St has been synonymous with good jazz since the days when Duke Ellington called it home in the early 1900s.

BASIN STREET LOUNGE

Map p311

☎ 703-549-1141; 219 King St, Alexandria; admission Fri & Sat $5; ☿ shows 8pm Tue-Thu, 9pm Fri & Sat; ⊜ Old Town shuttle from King St Metro

Wire-rimmed glasses and black turtlenecks may be the uniform at this sophisticated jazz venue. The downstairs lounge boasts quaint French Quarter Victorian decor, which is appropriate for the swinging piano, saxophone and bluesy jazz performances.

BLUES ALLEY

Map p299

☎ 202-337-4141; www.bluesalley.com; 1073 Rear Wisconsin Ave; admission $15-45; ☿ shows 8pm & 10pm; ⊜ Georgetown shuttle from Foggy Bottom-GWU

The city's pre-eminent jazz and blues club is tucked into a dark alley off Wisconsin Ave in the heart of Georgetown. Inside, this elegant candlelit supper club has attracted such artists as Ahmad Jamal and the late Dizzy Gillespie. Current performers include Mose Allison Trio, Ann Hampton Callaway and the Marcus Johnson Project. The Creole specialties are delicious. The crowd is largely professional.

BOHEMIAN CAVERNS

Map pp302-3

☎ 202-299-0801; www.bohemiancaverns.com; 2001 11th St NW; admission from $15 ☿ 6pm-2am Wed-Sat; Ⓜ U Street-Cardozo

This legendary jazz club – where Miles Davis, John Coltrane, Ella Fitzgerald and Duke Ellington once played – reopened in 2000, after 32 years of decline and decay since the 1968 riots. The new club maintains the mysterious cave-like decor in the basement lounge and features weekly open-mic nights, poetry readings, and live jazz and blues Wednesday to Saturday.

COLUMBIA STATION

Map pp296-7

☎ 202-462-6040; 2325 18th St NW; admission free; ⊜ shuttle from Woodley Park-Zoo

Columbia Station is an intimate spot to listen to nightly jazz and blues. If you're on a budget it's especially appealing – it doesn't have a cover charge. The quality of music varies; it's mostly local acts. The vibe is unpretentious and you can order Creole and American specialties to go with your music.

SALOUN

Map p299

☎ 202-965-4900; 3239 M St NW; admission $5; ☿ 5:30pm-2am Sun-Thu, 5:30pm-3am Fri & Sat; ⊜ Georgetown shuttle from Foggy Bottom-GWU

More casual and cheaper than the better-known Georgetown venue **Blues Alley** (above), the Saloun attracts patrons who are younger, less polished, but more fun. The mostly local acts play jazz during the week and blues and Motown on weekends. There are 18 beers on tap and Cajun food to soak up all the liquor swirling inside your tummy.

Folk & World

During the summer lots of folk acts play at the outdoors Wolf Trap Center (see Mega Venues, p186). Otherwise, Alexandria and Arlington have a proportionally high number of folk/country venues. Adams-Morgan and Shaw both have world-class world music.

BIRCHMERE

☎ 703-549-7500; www.birchmere.com; 3701 Mt Vernon Ave, Alexandria, VA; admission $15-35; ⊗ box office 5-9pm, shows 7:30pm; 🚌 10A from Pentagon City

Known as 'America's Legendary Music Hall,' this is the DC area's premier venue for folk, country, Celtic and bluegrass music. Mary Chapin Carpenter, Lyle Lovett, Shawn Colvin and Aimee Mann are some of the musicians who have performed here. It is located north of Old Town Alexandria off Glebe Rd. Unlike other venues, there is no standing room or dancing; seating is general admission (unallocated).

BOSSA

Map pp296-7

☎ 202-667-0088; 2463 18th St NW; admission free-$10; ⊗ 6pm-1am Sun-Thu, 6pm-2am Fri & Sat; Ⓜ Woodley Park-Zoo/Adams Morgan

Latin jazz, flamenco and bossa nova are on the music menu at this Adams-Morgan watering hole. The music is upstairs in the dark, candle-lit lounge, but the 1st-floor dining room – with high ceilings and art-canvassed walls – is also worth a visit. Come drink Mojitos and martinis, and taste the delectable tapas during happy hour.

BUKOM CAFÉ

Map pp296-7

☎ 202-265-4600; 2442 18th St NW; admission free; ⊗ shows 9pm Mon-Thu, 10pm Fri & Sat; Ⓜ Woodley Park-Zoo/Adams Morgan

Adams-Morgan is known for East African establishments, but Bukom taps the other side of the continent. It draws a stylishly dressed crowd of West Africans and African Americans to share its excellent cuisine and sexy late-night club scene, where bands play African and Caribbean music: reggae, highlife, funky jazz. There's hardly any room to dance, so everyone kind of stands in place, bounces to the music and rubs against their neighbors.

CAFÉ NEMA

Map pp302-3

☎ 202-667-3215; 1334 U St NW; admission varies; Ⓜ U Street-Cardozo

Café Nema is one of the coolest places in the city to listen to music. Once as a hole-in-the-wall basement joint owned by a Somali immigrant who let a group of boys from Howard University play jazz in a corner some nights, today Nema covers three floors. The Young Lions are playing in the colorful basement (think abstract paintings and old photos of jazz pioneers), while upstairs local hip-hop star Asheru is holding a young crowd's captive court with his monthly Guerilla Lounge, a showcase for emerging, underground MCs. The place also features DJs and open mics; the top-floor lounge had slouchy couches for quiet chats.

CLARENDON BALLROOM

Map pp306-7

☎ 703-469-2244; 3185 Wilson Blvd; cover varies; Ⓜ Clarendon

A gorgeous ballroom done up to look like a Big Band–era dance hall, it attracts throngs of young professionals coming to hear emerging local rock bands or artists on national tours. On the nights when there isn't music, you can try your hand at swing dancing or jive to what the DJ's spinning. The upstairs deck is open Wednesday through Friday nights and is perfect for lingering over a sunset cosmopolitan.

DC9

Map pp302-3

☎ 202-483-5000; 1940 9th St NW; admission $12; ⊗ 5pm-2am Thu-Sat; Ⓜ U Street-Cardozo

Accommodating up to 250 people, DC9 offers music lovers a live experience in a smaller venue. Up-and-coming local bands, with an emphasis on indie rockers, play most nights of the week; when the live music finishes (often around 11pm)

CLUBBING

MEGA VENUES

Many of metro DC's larger concert venues are outside the city in the suburbs of Maryland and Virginia.

MCI Center (Map pp292-3; ☎ 202-628-3200; www.mcicenter.com; 601 F St NW; Ⓜ Gallery Pl-Chinatown) The giant 20,000-seat sports and concert venue in downtown DC.

Merriweather Post Pavilion (☎ 301-596-0660; www.mppconcerts.com; 10475 Little Patuxent Parkway, Columbia, MD) An outdoor venue in suburban Maryland with pavilion and lawn seating.

Nissan Pavilion (☎ 703-754-6400; www.nissan pavilion.com; 7800 Cellar Door Dr, Bristow, VA) A huge outdoor venue with lawn and pavilion seating.

Wolf Trap Center (☎ 703-255-1860; www .wolf-trap.org; 1645 Trap Rd, Vienna, VA) A beautifully landscaped 4000-seat outdoor venue.

CLUBBING

Clubbing in DC can be a wide-ranging experience. Head to Dupont and the Penn Quarter for velvet-rope glamour – the clubs around here are the closest you'll get to the New York or LA circuit (although, surprisingly, most lack the snobby attitude and turn-away policies of their big-city counterparts). This is also the heart of the gay club scene. In Adams-Morgan and U St the scene is definitely more mixed, as regards race, music and style, with everything from salsa to rap on tap. Georgetown and Foggy Bottom attract the preppy college crowd, along with a lot of young professionals and Hillies. Pretty much all genres of music are played at DC clubs, although we have to say the city is lacking in country-and-western dance halls.

DJs keep the place spinning until about 3am. On the 2nd floor zodiac murals and diner booths set the mellow vibe; downstairs you'll find a narrow shotgun bar and a digital jukebox offering more than 130,000 songs.

IOTA Map pp306-7

☎ 703-522-8340; www.iotaclubandcafe.com; 2832 Wilson Blvd, Arlington; tickets $8-15; Ⓨ 11-2am; Ⓜ Clarendon

With shows almost every night of the week, Iota is the best venue for live music in Clarendon's music strip. Tickets are available at the door only (no advance sales) and this place packs 'em in (the seating is first come, first served). Iota also hosts poetry readings every second Sunday and open-mic night every Wednesday.

STATE THEATRE

☎ 703-237-0300; www.thestatetheatre.com; 220 N Washington St, Falls Church; admission from $15; Ⓜ East Falls Church

It's a bit of a drive, but this stylish suburban venue is worth it. Country, blues and folk groups perform regularly, and the lighting and acoustics in the stylishly remodeled movie house are quite good. Dancing, food and a well-thought-out seating plan add to the revelry. You'll need to grab a cab from the metro to get here.

18TH STREET LOUNGE

Map pp296-7

☎ 202-466-3922; 1212 18th St NW; admission free-$20; Ⓨ 9:30pm-2am Tue-Wed, 5:30pm-2am Thu, 5:30pm-3am Fri, 9:30pm-3am Sat; Ⓜ Dupont Circle

The lack of a sign on the door proclaims the exclusivity of this swanky yet cozy club. In a beautiful mansion that once housed Teddy Roosevelt, its sleek dancefloors are ruled by hip-hop and dub. The decor ranges from gold upholstered couches and candelabras to blue walls, gilded mirrors, marble tables and flickering candles. The club is famed for bouncers leaving lesser patrons waiting in the cold. Girls, wear your spikiest Manolos and skimpiest Gucci skirt to avoid any problems. Boys, dress it up with slacks and a Ben Sherman button down. Leave the denim and sneakers behind.

APEX

Map pp296-7

☎ 202-296-0505; 1415 22nd St NW; admission $10; Ⓨ 9pm-2am Tue & Thu-Sun; Ⓜ Dupont Circle

Crown jewel of the gay P-St dance-club scene, Apex brings out the college kids and buff boys in droves, especially on Friday. Don't come here to cruise, though; everybody is far too busy getting his groove on to be bothered. This is a popular spot for after-hours dancing on Friday and Saturday.

THE GODFATHER OF GO-GO

When you mention go-go to someone outside the DC area, they're more likely to think of scantily clad women in knee-high boots dancing in cages than a percussion-driven style of music. But in Washington, go-go dancing translates to moving to the groove.

Go-go is a unique brand of dance music with both its funky boots planted squarely in DC's Black neighborhoods. Go-go is defined by complex, continuous, heavy rhythm arrangements performed on multiple congas, tombadoras, cowbell parts and drums, punctuated by crowd participation and sometimes a swing rhythm.

The go-go scene hit its peak in the mid-'80s and never gained a national following, but fame and recorded tracks aren't really the point with go-go – the essence is the live jam and the dance party. African-derived rhythms, loud brass and bass drums and audience call-and-response ('Are you ready to go? Hell, no!') keep the floor moving at go-go shows.

The musicians trace their influences back to the pre-1970s de facto segregation of DC. White clubs wouldn't admit Black patrons, so they flocked to neighborhood dance halls and Black-run venues like the Howard Theatre and Northeast Gardens, which gave rise to a vibrant new soul music played by bands such as the Young Senators and Black Heat.

Chuck Brown (b 1934) is regarded as the driving force behind the creation of go-go-music. An African American jazz guitarist and singer, he is affectionately known as the Godfather of Go-Go. Brown's musical career started in the 1960s, but the 62-year-old artist still performs in the city today. He lives in Waldorf, MD.

Although go-go only gained limited degrees of national and international success, in DC it is still going strong. Brown served as a mentor for the next generation of go-go artists, including The Junk Yard Band and Rare Essence. The Junk Yard Band started as a rag-tag group of kids, as young as nine years old, performing a hodge-podge of music on discarded pieces of metal and string they'd fashioned into musical instruments. They quickly gained popularity in the underground scene and even signed and toured with famed Def Jam Records. Their 12-inch single, 'The Word,' was a hit around Washington and the mid-Atlantic.

Go-go has always been street music, and it's always performed live at nightclubs and parties – which is perhaps the reason for its lack of popularity in the digital world. If you aren't around it, you're not likely to hear it. Experiencing a concert can be a phenomenal, high-octane experience. Finding a club playing go-go today can be quite a task. Following a well-publicized murder and other sundry events at Club U in 2005 (it is now closed, but used to stand at the corner of 14th and U Sts NW), some club owners ran scared. Many DC clubs are not permitted to play the music and those that do are often located in shady neighborhoods.

Check the *City Paper* if you are looking for a show and be prepared to head to the suburbs. Much of the scene (along with the folks that helped create it) has moved to the suburbs. Prince George's County, MD, was where to go when we visited.

Go-go influenced music is also hitting mainstream radio with a vengeance. Its success can be mostly attributed to Rich Harrison, a DC-born producer who has infused the genre with his own personal sound. In 2003, Harrison worked with Beyoncé Knowles, of Destiny's Child fame, to produce the single 'Crazy in Love,' which featured samples of 'Are You My Woman?' by popular go-go band the Chi-Lites. The song went on to become a massive international success and helped introduce the world to DC's own brand of music. Knowles' 2006 album, *B'Day*, also features plenty of go-go influenced tunes.

BRAVO BRAVO

Map pp292-3

☎ 202-223-5330; 1001 Connecticut Ave NW; admission $5; 10pm-4am Wed-Sat; Ⓜ Farragut North

The mood at Bravo Bravo is flirty, the dancers are polished, and both men and women wear their best clothes to this salsa and Latin dance club popular with the under-30 set. Set in an enormous basement club, Bravo Bravo gets going after midnight on Friday and Saturday nights and doesn't slow down until after 4am. Thursday night features live go-go music.

CHIEF IKE'S MAMBO ROOM

Map pp296-7

☎ 202-332-2211; 1725 Columbia Rd NW; admission downstairs/upstairs $4/8; ☿ 9pm-2am; Ⓜ Woodley Park-Zoo/Adams Morgan

Despite the mixed crowd of young students and older professionals, ain't nobody getting dressed up here. The decor is *Day of the Dead* meets *Night of the Living Dead:* blinking lights, monster comics laminated onto the tables and voodoo critters on the walls. Dance on weekends and drink all week. Two additional clubs are upstairs: punk **Chaos** (not to be confused with **Club Chaos**, p188) and hip-hop **Cosmo Lounge**.

CLUB CHAOS

Map pp296-7

☎ 202-232-4141; www.chaosdc.com; 1603 17th St NW; admission free; ⌚ 5pm-2am Mon-Fri, 5pm-3am Sat & Sun; Ⓜ Dupont Circle

A must-visit on the DC gay club circuit, this place offers everything from bawdy drag brunches to country-and-western dance nights. Thursday's Latin night packs the gay boys and draws a fair number of women into this steamy basement for dancing to salsa and meringue. Saturday night is also popular. Early evenings mid-week, live comedy and drag shows attract a more mature crowd.

COBALT & 30 DEGREES

Map pp296-7

☎ 202-462-6569; www.foodbardc.com; 1639 R St NW; admission Sun-Thu free, Fri & Sat $5; ⌚ 5pm-2am; Ⓜ Dupont Circle

The latest, greatest addition to the 17th-St gay scene is a reincarnation of a club that burned down in 1998. Reopened and renovated, the 1st floor now has **Food Bar** (it's menu gets mixed reviews). The 2nd-floor lounge, **30 Degrees**, has been dubbed the 'Pottery Barn' for its oh-so-tasteful decor. Cobalt is the disco ballroom where pretty boys get down and let loose.

DC SANCTUARY

Map p304

☎ 202-399-4033; www.dcsanctuary.com; 1355 H St NE; admission $10-20; ⌚ 11pm-5am Fri & Sat

Check your attitude at the door, DC Sanctuary welcomes everyone – Black and White, straight and gay – so long as they have an appreciation for soul-soothing house and garage, blue lights, disco balls and a mellow vibe – this is not a pick-up joint. Couches, paintings and a big dance-floor fill the minimalist-looking space. The club is in a transitional neighborhood, far from any Metro stop, so you'll need to drive or take a cab.

FIVE

Map pp296-7

☎ 202-331-7223; www.fivedc.com; 1214B 18th St NW; admission from $10; ⌚ 9pm-2am Wed-Sat; Ⓜ Dupont Circle

One of the city's hottest clubs, Five keeps its patrons happy by (1) letting them inside (you won't find those super-snotty bouncers here); and (2) offering a smorgasbord of house, reggae and hip-hop, and sometimes drum & bass spun by well-known local and international DJs. Spanning three floors, Five has a popular Caribbean-inspired rooftop deck. The bars are where to flirt. Coupons (check the local papers) grant free entry until midnight.

HABANA VILLAGE

Map pp296-7

☎ 202-462-6310; 1834 Columbia Rd NW; admission Fri & Sat men only $5, lesson $10; ⌚ 7pm-1am Wed-Thu, 7pm-2am Fri & Sat, lesson 7-9pm Wed; Ⓜ Woodley Park-Zoo/Adams Morgan

DC's best Latin club is in an old town-house with a cosmopolitan bar and romantic back room where you can sip Mojitos and nibble tapas in front of the fireplace. After 10:30pm the scene on the upstairs dancefloor explodes, as DJs spin salsa, meringue, mambo, tango and bossa nova to a mixed Latin and White crowd.

HEAVEN & HELL

Map pp296-7

☎ 202-667-4355; 2327 18th St NW; Heaven/Hell $5/free; ⌚ Hell 7:30pm-2am Sun-Thu, 7:30pm-3am Fri & Sat, Heaven 7:30pm-2am Tue-Thu, 7:30pm-3am Fri & Sat; Ⓜ Woodley Park-Zoo/Adams Morgan

A perennial favorite with the college crowd, this hot spot hosts **Heaven** (upstairs), with thematic dance parties to flashing disco lights, and Hell (downstairs), which is grittier and attracts hard drinkers. The large outdoor patio in **Heaven** overlooks the 18th St strip and is popular on steamy nights.

HOME Map pp292-3

☎ 202-638-4663; 911 F St NW; admission $10-20; ⌚ Thu 6pm-2am, Fri & Sat 10pm-3am; Ⓜ Gallery Place-Chinatown

Smaller, more intimate and, as clichéd as it sounds, more like home, this plush place is a must-go when doing the DC club circuit. It features armless couches for lounging, multiple dancefloors and the requisite VIP rooms, but the whole atmosphere just feels more casual than other velvet-rope nightclubs. Sweeping 30ft carved plaster ceilings and decorative marble panels up the swank appeal.

LOVE

Map pp290-1

☎ 202-636-9030; www.lovetheclub.com; 1350 Okie St NE; admission $10-20; ☽ 9pm-4am Thu, 6pm-4am Fri, 9pm-4am Sat; 🚌 D3 or D4 from Union Station

Love books big names – Beyoncé and the Roots have both played here. As Washington's biggest and most popular spot, Love (formerly known as Dream) has four floors, each beautifully designed, with its own theme and style of music. Make sure to check out the tropical-themed deck. Dress to impress (the code is strict, no sneakers or baggy jeans allowed) as this club attracts thousands and lines form out the door. Friday nights see a predominately hip-hop–heavy menu and African American crowd. Saturdays are more diverse, with international electronica pumped through the speakers and a mixed crowd. On Thursdays the place opens up to the 18-plus crowd.

MCCXXIII

Map pp296-7

☎ 202-822-1800; 1223 Connecticut Ave NW; admission $5-25; ☽ 4pm-2am Tue-Thu, 4pm-3am Fri, 6pm-3am Sat; 🇲 Farragut North

This is the place in DC where you're most likely to see an Icelandic beauty tangoing with a suave Pakistani diplomat. DC's internationalistas, many of them Embassy Row residents, congregate in this beautifully designed club (the name is the street address in Roman numerals). Patrons sip martinis while waiting for DJs to start at 11pm to play world-beat and techno so they can shimmy onto the dancefloor. Sunday night is a popular gay night.

PLATINUM

Map pp292-3

☎ 202-393-3555; www.platinumclubdc.com; 915 F St NW; admission $10; ☽ 10pm-3am Thu-Sun; 🇲 Metro Center

Beautiful people all dressed up dance to the usual mélange of world and electronic music at this well-established hotspot housed in a grand former bank. Theme nights include College and Latin, but check the website in advance as the schedule changes. Sign up beforehand to get on the guest list, in which case there is no cover charge before 11pm.

PLAY LOUNGE

Map pp296-7

☎ 202-466-7529; 1219 Connecticut Ave NW; admission $5-20; ☽ 10pm-3am Thu-Sun; 🇲 Dupont Circle

How can you resist a place with a motto of 'no rules and everyone has a good time?' Especially when such place has a stripper pole on which to play (when we visited there was a line of girls waiting to show off their moves). This club, smack in the middle of the city's after-dark zone, consists of one very packed room, vaguely reminiscent of a kick-ass college party – no space and tons of sweaty, thriving bodies. If you're in the right mood (and can get past the burly bouncer), it can be a very fun place to just kick loose and play.

REPUBLIC GARDENS

Map pp302-3

☎ 202-232-2710; www.republicgardens.com; 1355 U St NW; ☽ 5:30-11:30pm Tue, 5:30pm-2am Wed-Thu, 5:30pm-2:30am Fri, 6:30pm-2:30am Sat; 🇲 U Street-Cardozo

This historic club (where Pearl Bailey waited tables in the 1940s) still looks fabulous three years after its major overhaul. Exposed brick walls, shiny wood floors and modern leather furniture give it a look of slick sophistication. The program was still being developed at the time of research, so keep your eye on the website.

RHINO BAR & PUMP HOUSE

Map p299

☎ 202-333-3150; 3295 M St NW; admission free; ☽ 4pm-2am; 🚌 Georgetown shuttle from Foggy Bottom-GWU Metro

The previous bar on this site, Winston's, was legendary for its dance-and-grope scene. The Rhino Bar has sanitized the premises a bit, but the college-age crowd still checks its inhibitions at the door. DJs play dance music Thursday to Saturday. There are great happy-hour specials – if you can call 9pm to midnight happy hour – including 10¢ wings on Monday and half-price burgers and beers on Friday.

SAKI Map pp296-7

☎ 202-232-5005; www.sakidc.com; 2477 18th St NW; admission $5; ☽ 5pm-2am Thu, to 3am Fri & Sat; 🇲 Woodley Park-Zoo/Adams Morgan

GAY & LESBIAN DC

Home to more than 30 national gay and lesbian organizations and more than 300 social, athletic, religious and political support groups, DC is one of the most gay-friendly cities in the USA and is often the scene of huge gay-rights marches; gay pride is an integral part of DC's character.

Dupont Circle is by far the city's most gay-friendly neighborhood, with numerous gay-owned businesses and the bulk of the city's nightlife options clustered on 17th NW between P and R Sts NW and along P St west of the circle. Another hot spot is the club and bar scene on Pennsylvania Ave and around Capitol Hill. You'll find popular male strip clubs – one of the few places in the US where full nudity is legal – in Southeast DC near the Navy Yard Metro station. Take a cab here after dark.

Lambda Rising (p217) is the landmark bi-gay bookstore in Dupont Circle, and has free flyers on local entertainment. It serves as a popular community gathering place. Pick up a copy of the *Washington Blade* (www.washblade.com) for news, listings and classified ads. If you are looking purely for entertainment, check out the *Metro Weekly*, which is a great gay nightlife guide and gives the scoop on special events, happy hours and DJs (all accompanied by a map – very handy).

Various gay and lesbian festivals are held throughout the year. Big-time events include **Cherry** (www.cherryfund.com), held in April. A weekend dance party with top DJs, it benefits various gay and AIDS organizations. **Capital Pride** (www.capitalpride.org) in early June has been running strong for more than 30 years now. It features political, cultural and community events, including films, a parade, pageants and a street festival along Pennsylvania Ave.

Our top after-dark choices:

Apex (p186) The hottest, most happening gay dancefloor in the city.

Club Chaos (p188) With everything from bawdy drag brunches to country-and-western dance nights, it's popular with the girls and boys.

Cobalt & 30 Degrees (p188) Three levels of chic, shapely boys – eating, drinking and getting down.

JR's (p176) It might have a rep as the spot for gay republicans to schmooze, but regardless of your political orientation, no one can deny JR's has a happening happy-hour scene. Come to scope out the cute boys in suits.

Phase One (p173) This long-time favorite lesbian bar on the Hill has been going strong for 30-plus years now.

At first Saki's basement lounge gives the impression of being a little like a psychiatric institution: low white ceilings, white walls, white floor and tables. But after a while your eyes adjust and you realize that creatively placed rectangular panels are bouncing constantly changing rainbows of light around the room, bathing the trendy couples sipping cocktails at the corner table in a wash of fire-engine red and dusty orange. Light shows aside, Saki is best known for its DJs. The space is small, but locals recommend it for the music, especially on Fridays when you get a mix of old-school funk and electro house. On other nights the DJ music ranges from acid rock to broken beat and hip-hop. This spot is very in with the crowd in Washington obsessed with being in – you know who you are.

THIRD EDITION
Map p299

☎ 202-333-3700; 1218 Wisconsin Ave NW; admission $5; ☽ 5pm-1am Mon-Thu, 5pm-2am Fri,

11:30-2am Sat & Sun; 🚌 Georgetown shuttle from Foggy Bottom-GWU Metro

For a cinematic college-bar experience, visit this place, which was featured in the 1985 film *St Elmo's Fire*. This is a serious singles' scene: people are listening more closely to pick-up lines than to the music. When you get tired of the crowded dancefloor, relax out on the back patio at the tiki bar. Nearly everyone who graduates from Georgetown has some comic or tragic story about this place.

ZANZIBAR
Map pp308-9

☎ 202-554-9100; 700 Water St SW; admission $10; ☽ 5pm-1am Wed-Thu, 5pm-4am Fri, 9pm-4am Sat, 6pm-1am Sun; Ⓜ Waterfront

This elegant waterfront dance club draws a well-dressed, primarily Black clientele. On the large dancefloor upstairs, groove the night away to live bands or DJ spins, depending on the night of the week. Wednesday night is among the most popular Latin nights in Washington; other nights feature music ranging from techno and zouk to Caribbean and world-beat. The seafood, too, has an Afro-Caribbean touch (see p153).

ART GALLERIES

Attending a Friday evening gallery opening in DC is a great way to experience the city's creative face in a more fun, less museum-structured environment. There are more than 30 galleries in Dupont Circle alone, and many hold openings between 6pm and 8pm on the first Friday of each month. Gallery openings are festive occasions, and Washingtonians use them as excuses to dress up and socialize. Drinks (often wine or champagne) and some kind of cheese-and-cracker snack are served and the artist whose work is showcased is on hand for ego stoking and Q&A sessions. If you like what you see, this is a good time to buy – although you'll have to be satisfied with a sales receipt and letting the painting stay on the wall for the duration of the exhibit. Head to the area around R St between 20th and 22nd Sts (P St is also a good choice) in Dupont and see if any of the quirky galleries catch your eye. A complete list is available in the *Guide to the Galleries of Dupont Circle*, found free at most DC galleries.

The *Washington Post's* Weekend section lists current shows. Also check out www .artlineplus.com/gallerymagazine.

FOUNDRY GALLERY

Map pp296-7

☎ 202-387-0203; www.foundry-gallery.org; 9 Hillyer Ct NW; ☽ 11am-5pm Tue-Sat, 1-5pm Sun; Ⓜ Dupont Circle

A nonprofit member-run organization, this gallery features a diverse range of super contemporary art made in the last decade – mediums include painting, sculpture and drawings – all created by local artists. Openings are held the first Friday of the month.

KATHLEEN EWING GALLERY

Map pp296-7

☎ 202-328-0955; www.kathleenewinggallery .com; 1609 Connecticut Ave NW; Ⓜ Dupont Circle

Photography is the focus at this gallery, which is renowned for its collection of 19th- and 20th-century photos. It also offers more contemporary pictures and multimedia works. Openings are held the first Friday of the month.

STUDIO GALLERY

Map pp296-7

☎ 202-232-8734; 2108 R St NW; ☽ 11am-5pm Wed-Sat, 1-5pm Sun; Ⓜ Dupont Circle

A 30-artist cooperative featuring canvases and sculpture, it is the longest running artist-owned gallery in the area. There are both solo and group exhibits in all mediums. Openings are held the first Friday of the month.

ENTERTAINING THE KIDDIES

Unlike so many towns that shut down after dark as far as kids go, DC stays awake. No matter what time of year, there is always something to do with the kids outside the hotel room. We've listed a few of our favorites here, but for more ideas check out the Best Bets section of the *Washington Post's* Weekend section, along with listings in the back for story hours, carnivals and other child-friendly events.

Folger Shakespeare Library & Theatre (p192) Runs a kiddy program throughout the year, making it a great place to bring the young ones.

Discovery Theatre (p193) Delightful productions for children, including puppet shows.

Kennedy Center (p192) There is always something kid-oriented going on at DC's most magnificent performing-arts venue. The center also puts on many G-rated musicals or African drum and dance shows that, while not specifically tailored for young children, have hordes of kids in the audience, especially during matinees.

Olsson's Books & Records (p195) Story hours are held at this favorite independent DC bookstore.

Arlington Cinema 'N' Drafthouse (p195) You wouldn't guess from the name, but this brew-house-come-movie-theatre actually runs quite a few children's programs on various weekends throughout the month. Check the website www.arlingtondrafthouse.com.

TROYER GALLERY
Map pp296-7

☎ 202-328-7189; 1710 Connecticut Ave NW;
🕑 11am-5pm Tue-Sat; Ⓜ Dupont Circle
Among DC's better-known galleries, especially for emerging artists, it features a lot of home-grown paintings and sculptures, along with a large photography collection. Openings are held the first Friday of the month.

THEATER
The Washington, DC, theater scene is divided into three distinct camps: the renowned Kennedy Center, presenting world-famous companies and productions; a second string of well-established theaters, which often host Broadway national runs; and a third group of adventurous small stages, presenting cutting-edge works whose quality ranges from totally fabulous to sophomoric.

ARENA STAGE
Map pp308-9

☎ 202-488-3300; www.arenastage.org; 1101 6th St SW; tickets from $35; Ⓜ Waterfront
The three theaters at Arena Stage (including a theater-in-the-round) are top venues for traditional and experimental theatrical works, especially American classics, premieres of new plays and contemporary stories. Arena Stage was the city's first racially integrated theater and has continued its progressive tradition through performances addressing African American history.

CARTER BARRON AMPHITHEATER
Map pp290-1

☎ 202-426-0486; www.nps.gov/rocr/cbarron; 16th & Colorado Ave NW, Rock Creek Park; tickets free or $18; 🕑 box office noon-9pm show days; 🚌 S2 or S4 from McPherson Sq
The outdoor amphitheater in Rock Creek Park is the venue for Shakespeare Free for All, a free series staged by the Shakespeare Theatre. It is also host to music festivals and concerts throughout the summer. For free shows, tickets are distributed from 4pm on the day of the performance. For more information about Rock Creek Park, see p121.

FOLGER SHAKESPEARE LIBRARY & THEATRE
Map p304

☎ 202-544-7077; www.folger.edu; 210 E Capitol St SE; tickets from $30; Ⓜ Capitol South
The magnificent Globe-style theater attached to the Folger Shakespeare Library stages classic and modern interpretations of the Bard's plays. Exhibitions, poetry readings and great programs for kids are all part of the repertoire, in addition to world-class Shakespearean theater.

FORD'S THEATRE
Map pp292-3

☎ 202-218-6500, 800-955-5566; www.fords theatre.org; 511 10th St NW; tickets $25-40; 🕑 box office 10am-6pm Mon-Fri; Ⓜ Gallery Pl-Chinatown
The historical theater – where John Wilkes Booth killed Abraham Lincoln – has staged world-premier musicals, mostly about Lincoln's life and times. It also hosts a series on American Originals: influential individuals who have played significant cultural roles. For more information, see Sights (p94).

KENNEDY CENTER
Map pp292-3

☎ 202-467-4600; www.kennedy-center.org; 2700 F St NW; Ⓜ Foggy Bottom-GWU
Washington's main cultural jewel is given credit for transforming DC from a cultural backwater to an artistic contender in the late 20th century. The stately white-marble building overlooking the Potomac River opened to the public in 1971. It holds two big theaters, a theater lab (where new or experimental theater is staged), cinema, opera house and concert hall (and the fine Roof Terrace Restaurant to boot). It is home to the National Symphony Orchestra and the Washington Chamber Symphony (p194), both directed by Leonard Slatkin, the Washington Opera (p194), directed by Placido Domingo, and the Washington Ballet (p194). Film festivals and cultural events are frequent highlights. About 3000 performances are held here annually.

Orchestra seats cost about $40 for concerts, $60 for theater, $140 for opera. On the day of the performance, reduced-rate tickets are sometimes available for students and for obstructed-view seats. Order tickets by phone or purchase them at the box office.

The Kennedy Center also hosts the **Millennium Stage**, a series of first-rate music and dance performances that take place every day at 6pm in the Grand Foyer and cost absolutely nothing. Pick up a schedule at the Kennedy Center, or check the website for details.

A free shuttle bus runs between Foggy Bottom-GWU Metro station and the Kennedy Center every 15 minutes from 9:45am to midnight Monday to Saturday, noon to 8pm Sunday. There's also paid parking underneath the Kennedy Center. See also Sights (p79).

NATIONAL THEATRE

Map pp292-3

☎ 202-628-6161, 800-447-7400; www.national theatre.org; 1321 Pennsylvania Ave NW; ⏰ box office 10am-9pm Mon-Sat, noon-8pm Sun; Ⓜ Federal Triangle

Established in 1835 and renovated in 1984, the National is Washington's oldest continually operating theater. This is where you would catch *Les Misérables* and *Rent*. Half-price tickets are available for students and seniors. Monday nights at the National are good value as they feature free performances at 6pm and 7:30pm.

SHAKESPEARE THEATRE

Map pp292-3

☎ 202-547-1122; www.shakespearetheatre.org; 450 7th St NW; tickets $16-60; ⏰ box office 10am-6pm Mon-Sat, noon-6pm Sun; Ⓜ Archives-Navy Memorial

Under artistic director Michael Kahn, this little theater on Gallery Row has been called 'one of the world's three great Shakespearean theaters' by the *Economist*. Its home company stages a half-dozen works annually, plus a free summer Shakespeare series in Rock Creek Park (see **Carter Barron Amphitheater**, opposite).

WARNER THEATRE

Map pp292-3

☎ 202-783-4000; www.warnertheatre.org; 1299 Pennsylvania Ave NW; tickets $25-55; ⏰ box office 10am-4pm Mon-Fri, noon-3pm Sat; Ⓜ Federal Triangle

The beautifully restored 1924 art-deco theater was originally built for vaudeville and silent films, but it now stages headliner concerts, comedians and national runs of Broadway musicals.

Smaller venues and troupes:

Asian Stories in America (☎ 703-979-0875; www .asianstoriesinamerica.com) Performing primarily at venues in Arlington, highlights the work of playwrights from Asia and the Pacific Rim.

Catalyst Theater (Map pp308-9; ☎ 202-547-6839; 545 7th St SE; Ⓜ Eastern Market) Part of the Capitol Hill Arts Workshop, which stages theater, cinema and musical events.

DCAC (Map pp296-7; ☎ 202-462-7833; www.dcart scenter.org; 2438 18th St NW; Ⓜ Woodley Park-Zoo/ Adams Morgan) A 50-seat black-box theater hosting the improvisational interactive Playback.

Discovery Theatre (Map pp292-3; ☎ 202-357-1500; www.discoverytheatre.si.edu; Smithsonian Arts & Industries Bldg; Ⓜ Smithsonian) Stages delightful productions for kids, such as puppet shows.

Gala Hispanic Theatre (Map pp300-1; ☎ 202-234-7174; www.galatheatre.org; 1625 Park Rd NW; Ⓜ Columbia Heights) Maintains a 25-year tradition of four annual Spanish-language productions.

Lincoln Theatre (Map pp302-3; ☎ 202-328-9177, 328-6000; 1215 U St NW; Ⓜ U Street-Cardozo) Historic cinema recently renovated to host music and theater.

Source Theatre Company (Map pp302-3; ☎ 202-462-1073; www.sourcetheatre.com; 1835 14th St NW; Ⓜ U Street-Cardozo) In the heart of the new U district, hosts the Annual Washington Theatre Festival.

Stanislavsky Theatre (Map pp296-7; ☎ 800-494-8497; www.sts-online.org; 1742 Church St NW; Ⓜ Dupont Circle) The best of world theater, especially Russian, with a twist.

Studio Theatre (Map pp292-3; ☎ 202-332-3300; www .studiotheatre.org; 1333 P St NW; 🚌 G2 from Dupont Circle) Twenty-five years of producing Pulitzer Prize–winning and premiere plays.

Theater J (Map pp296-7; ☎ 202-777-3229; www.dcjcc .org/theaterj.htm; 1529 16th St NW; Ⓜ Dupont Circle) Addresses urban American Jewish experience.

West End Dinner Theatre (☎ 703-370-2500; www .wedt.com; 4615 Duke St, Alexandria; tickets $30-35; ⏰ dinner 6pm Tue-Sun, show 8pm) The area's largest dinner-theater stage, featuring Broadway musicals and comedies. The theater is on Duke St west of Old Town Alexandria.

Woolly Mammoth Theatre Co (Map pp292-3; ☎ 202-393-3939; www.woollymammoth.net; 641 D St; Ⓜ Archives-Navy Memorial) The edgiest of the experimental groups.

CLASSICAL MUSIC, OPERA & DANCE

The Kennedy Center is the premier venue for classical music and opera, but performances also take place at venues around town, including the National Gallery of Art, National Building Museum, Corcoran Gallery and Library of Congress, as well as at local universities and churches.

Performance dance in Washington, DC, is surprisingly limited. The premier dance venue is the Kennedy Center, home of the Washington Ballet, but the lesser-known, and oddly located, Dance Place experiments with some more daring choreography.

DANCE PLACE Map pp302-3

☎ 202-269-1600; www.danceplace.org; 3225 8th St NE; tickets $18; Ⓜ Brookland
The only truly cutting-edge dance space in the capital is quite hidden in a rather obscure neighborhood in Northeast DC. It's run by five resident modern-dance companies offering a year-round calendar of new work, which includes festivals featuring African dance, tap dancing and other genres. It also hosts the work of top-notch national companies, such as the Joe Goode Performance Group.

NATIONAL SYMPHONY ORCHESTRA & WASHINGTON CHAMBER SYMPHONY

Map pp292-3

☎ 202-467-4600, 800-444-1324; www.kennedy -center.org; 2700 F St NW; Ⓜ Foggy Bottom
Both directed by Leonard Slatkin, these classic instrumental ensembles perform at the Kennedy Center (p192) and at Wolf Trap Center (see Mega Venues, p186) in summer.

WASHINGTON BALLET

Map pp292-3

☎ 202-467-4600, 800-444-1324; www.kennedy -center.org; 2700 F St NW; Ⓜ Foggy Bottom
Housed at the Kennedy Center (p192), the Washington Ballet hasn't been known for any groundbreaking productions, although its reputation is beginning to change as it explores the work of younger choreographers. The center also hosts fine visiting groups like Merce Cunningham and Alvin Ailey.

WASHINGTON OPERA

Map pp292-3

☎ 202-295-2400, 800-876-7372; www.dc-opera .org; www.kennedy-center.org; 2700 F St NW; Ⓜ Foggy Bottom
The Washington Opera is housed at the Kennedy Center (p192) and puts on a varied showcase throughout the year. Previous choices have included *La Traviata* and *A Streetcar Named Desire*.

COMEDY

Washington, DC, is not exactly Comedy Central, but the follies of the federal government provide fodder for some serious fun.

CAPITOL STEPS POLITICAL SATIRE

Map pp292-3

☎ 202-312-1427; www.capsteps.com; Ronald Reagan Bldg & International Trade Center Amphitheater; tickets $31.50; ☷ shows 7:30pm Fri & Sat; Ⓜ Federal Triangle
This troupe claims to be the only group in America that tries to be funnier than Congress. It's actually composed of current and former congressional staffers, so they know their stuff. The best of political comedy, this DC tradition pokes satirical bipartisan fun at both sides of the spectrum.

IMPROV

Map pp296-7

☎ 202-296-7008; www.dcimprov.com; 1140 Connecticut Ave; tickets Sun-Thu $15, Fri & Sat $17; ☷ shows 8:30pm Tue-Thu, 8pm & 10:30pm Fri & Sat, 8pm Sun; Ⓜ Farragut North
This is comedy in the more traditional sense, featuring stand-up by comics from Comedy Central, Mad TV and HBO, among others. The Improv also offers workshops for those of us who think we're pretty funny. Six two-hour weekly workshop sessions costs $180.

READINGS & LECTURES

Check the *City Paper* and the *Washington Post* Weekend section for upcoming readings by local, national and international authors, lectures, poetry slams and open-mic nights. DC has hundreds of these things, held everywhere from brightly colored bookstores to dingy church basements. This type of event is hot with Washington singles, especially those who consider finding a match over shots at the local dive an appalling concept.

OLSSON'S BOOKS & RECORDS
Map pp296-7

☎ 202-78501133; 1307 9th St NW;
Ⓜ Dupont Circle

One of DC's oldest independent chains, the Dupont location is right at the entrance to the Metro stop. International and local authors frequently give readings in this intimate shop (it's smaller than other Olsson's stores, which makes it perfect for a stimulating reading and subsequent discussion).

POLITICS & PROSE BOOKSTORE
Map pp290-1

☎ 202-364-1919; 5015 Connecticut Ave NW;
Ⓜ Van Ness-UDC

Tucked away in a quiet corner of Northwest, Politics & Prose is famous with the literary set. Selling thousands of titles along with steaming mugs of chai, this independent bookstore is known for hosting brain-food readings and discussions on a regular basis. Best-selling authors Nora Ephron and Brad Meltzer (whose latest thriller is set partially in DC) were recent speakers.

CINEMA
Washington offers a few excellent opportunities for film buffs to see some unusual work. The Smithsonian, the Library of Congress and other museums round out the programming by offering a great variety of international, historical and educational films. Of course, Hollywood's finest are on view here, too.

AMC 9 THEATRES Map p304

☎ 202, 703-998-4AMC; www.amctheatres.com;
50 Massachusetts Ave; adult/child/senior matinee
$5.50/6.50/6.50, evening $8.50/5.50/6.50;
Ⓜ Union Station

This giant theatre shows the latest and greatest from Hollywood from romantic comedy to action-adventure. You can enter the cinema from inside Union Station.

ARLINGTON CINEMA & DRAFTHOUSE
Map p304

☎ 703-486-2345; www.arlingtondrafthouse
.com; 2903 Columbia Pike; admission from $5.50;
Ⓜ Clarendon

Ice-cold beers and second-run films at bargain-basement prices? Who could resist? Not many. Washington Post readers voted Arlington Cinema 'N' Draft the best movie theater in DC in 2006 and we concur – this place rocks. You need to be 21 to enter (or with a parent), but once inside you will find comfy chairs for flick-viewing, a menu of sandwiches, pizzas and, of course, popcorn, as well as a selection of alcoholic drinks (this is one of the few places in DC where you can drink and catch a movie). At the time of writing, smoking was still permitted in designated areas – extremely rare for the metro area. Some nights the theater skips the movies and hosts stand-up comedy instead. Check the website. There are also family-oriented programs some weekends.

BETHESDA ROW CINEMA
Map p310

☎ 301-652-7273; 7235 Woodmont Ave; adult/child $9.50/6.75, matinee all tickets $6.75;
Ⓜ Bethesda

In the heart of bustling downtown Bethesda, this first-rate art-house theater is the best in DC. With eight screens and stadium seats, it's slick and modern, and serves gourmet treats like espresso and locally baked pastries. It showcases a wide variety of independent films, from the obscure to Cannes and Sundance winners.

CINEPLEX ODEON

☎ 333-FILM; www.cineplex.com; matinee $7, adult $10, child & senior $7

This chain operates several cinemas that show a mixture of popular and art-house movies. Branches include: Uptown (Map pp300–1; 3426 Connecticut Ave NW; Ⓜ Cleveland Park); Janus (Map pp296–7; 1660 Connecticut Ave NW; Ⓜ Dupont Circle); and Outer Circle (Map pp290–1; 4849 Wisconsin Ave NW; Ⓜ Tenleytown-AU). The Uptown is by far the best: with a giant screen, intermissions and two levels of seating, it is DC's favorite date theatre. It's also the last of a species, with only one screen.

You'll need to buy tickets well in advance on opening weekends of big shows.

LOEWS CINEPLEX Map p299

☎ 202-342-6441; www.enjoytheshow.com; Wisconsin Ave & K St NW; matinee $7.50, evening adult $10, child & senior $7.50; 🚌 Georgetown shuttle from Foggy Bottom-GWU

Housed in a refurbished old industrial building on the waterfront, this modern, comfortable cinema has 10 theaters offering Hollywood's finest.

MARY PICKFORD THEATER

Map p304

☎ 202-707-5677; www.loc.gov/rr/mopic/pickford; 101 Independence Ave SE, 3rd fl, Madison Bldg; admission free; 🕑 shows 7pm Tue, Thu & Fri; Ⓜ Capitol South

The Mary Pickford Theater at the Library of Congress screens films on historical or cultural themes, relevant to current events. Seating is limited to only 64 people, but reservations can be made by telephone up to one week in advance.

Activities ■

Activities

Taking into consideration DC's youthful populace and expansive parkland, it comes as little surprise to see urban outdoor types jogging up the Capitol steps, biking around the Jefferson Memorial and in-line-skating down the National Mall.

Fast-paced Ultimate games in front of the Smithsonian Castle, competitive two-on-two volleyball near the Lincoln Memorial and league softball on the Mall all take place on any given sunny weekend in DC. Where else in the world can you pant, perspire and groan in the shadow of such monumental surroundings?

If you are a person who needs to be outdoors, and don't find the marble and memorials interesting enough, the Potomac River, Rock Creek Park, and the C&O Canal Towpath are some really fantastic venues for hiking, biking and kayaking – escape the city, right in the city.

All of this is happening while the face-painters and big-foam-finger-wavers sit focused on their TVs, watching the Redskins. When it comes to armchair athletics, DC has Southern roots: this is football country and the 'Skins still reign supreme among Washington teams.

The Wizards and the Hoyas have their fans as well (especially during a strong season). The most loyal fans are urban youth, who – when they are not watching hoops – are playing hoops. Washington's NHL team, the Capitals, are cultivating a decent following now.

'Sports' can imply numerous things to different people and DC is no exception. Being a city with inhabitants so diverse, the choices of activities naturally follow suit. The happy result is every sportsperson finding something to enjoy.

WATCHING SPORT

Offensive choreography, defensive policy and stiff competition: politics and sports have a lot in common. Watching sport in Washington, DC, may come second to following politics, but it is still a popular pastime. Professional baseball, football, basketball, hockey and soccer teams, as well as competitive college basketball, keep DC sports fans active year-round.

FOOTBALL

The Washington Redskins are a populist religion in DC, no matter whether they are winning or losing. 'Skins games empty the city, drawing streams of people into sports bars and living rooms to cheer on the tackles, turnover and touchdowns.

The Redskins play September through January at **FedEx Field** (☎ 301-276-6050; www.redskins .com; 1600 Raljon Rd, Landover, MD; tickets $50-100), but rare is the opportunity to actually see them play here.

There is a miles-long waiting list to buy season tickets, so there are never tickets left for individual games. The only exception is when some are returned to the box office by the opposing team, which you can find out about by calling the stadium two or three days before the game. If you have your heart set on seeing the 'Skins in person, many on-line agents will be pleased to sell you tickets with a hefty markup. Try **DreamTix** (☎ 703-931-0916; www.dreamtix .com;), **StubHub!** (☎ 1-866-788-2482; www.stubhub.com), **TicketMonster.com** (☎ 301-669-9659, 800-637-3719; www.ticketmonster.org) and **StageFront Tickets** (☎ 301 953-1163, 800-528-4257; www.tickets-redskins.com).

If you do manage to secure tickets, you can drive to FedEx Field by taking the Central Ave exit from I-495, or take the $5 shuttle from the Landover or Addison Rd Metro station. Otherwise, enjoy the game from a bar stool at ESPN Zone (p174).

BASKETBALL

All of DC's basketball teams – including the National Basketball Association (NBA), Washington Wizards, the women's team (WNBA) Washington Mystics, and the Georgetown University Hoyas – play at the **MCI Center** (Map pp292–3; ☎ 202-628-3200; www.mcicenter.com; 601 F St NW; ☯ box office 10am-5:30pm Mon-Sat; Ⓜ Gallery Pl-Chinatown).

The Washington Wizards play November through April. Tickets are as cheap as $10 for the nosebleed section; $50 for decent seats in the upper concourse; $80 to $90 for the club concourse; and higher and higher.

The Washington Mystics play May through September and ticket prices are cheaper ($8 to $50). The Georgetown Hoyas are part of the National College Athletic Association (NCAA), which plays during the same season as the NBA, ending with the NCAA tournament in March.

Tickets to regular season games are $5 to $35, but they can be hard to come by for the games against the Hoya's toughest rivals, like Syracuse and Boston College. Tickets for all teams are available at the MCI Center box office, or through **Ticketmaster** (☎ 202-397-7328; www.ticketmaster.com), for which you will have to pay a service charge.

Also in the NCAA, the University of Maryland Terrapins has a consistently strong basketball team. Season-ticket holders buy up all the seats at the sleek, new **Comcast Center** (☎ 301-314-7070; Terrapin Tri, College Park, MD) on campus at the University of Maryland. If students don't pick up their entire allotment, single-game tickets may go on sale about two weeks before the game, but it is advisable to phone the ticket office to find out for sure.

BASEBALL

Alas, Major League Baseball (MLB) has returned to DC in the form of the former Montreal Expos, now the Washington Nationals. The end to their 36-year hiatus in the national pastime is something for capital residents to be excited about. For now, they play at **RFK Stadium** (Map pp290–1; ☎ 703-478-6600; East Capitol St; Ⓜ Stadium-Armory), but a new home is in the works. On the other hand, fans of the de facto favorite, the Orioles, must trek up to Baltimore, unless they're playing in DC. For MLB fans it's a win–win situation. **Oriole Park Camden Yards** (☎ 410-685-9800, 888-848-BIRD; www.theorioles.com; 333 W Camden St, Baltimore; ☯ box office 10am-5pm Mon-Sat, noon-5pm Sun).

During the regular season (April to September), tickets are readily available at the box office or through **Ticketmaster** (☎ 410-547-7328, 800-527-6384; www.ticketmaster.com) for a service charge. If you don't have a car, you can get to Camden Yards by MARC or Amtrak trains from Union Station, or take a $9 bus ride from the Greenbelt Metro station.

HOCKEY

The **MCI Center** (Map pp292–3; ☎ 202-628-3200; www.mcicenter.com; 601 F St NW; ☯ box office 10am-5:30pm Mon-Sat; Ⓜ Gallery Pl-Chinatown) turns to ice when DC's National Hockey League team, the Washington Capitals, are playing. From October to May, tickets are $25/40/55 and up for the upper-upper/upper/club concourse. Again, they are available from the box office or through **Ticketmaster** (☎ 202-397-7328; www.ticketmaster.com) for an inconvenient 'convenience' charge.

SOCCER

Multiple-time Major League Soccer champions DC United play April through October at **RFK Stadium** (Map pp290–1; ☎ 703-478-6600; East Capitol St; Ⓜ Stadium-Armory). Tickets are $18 to $40, but the only way to get them is by purchasing a season-long package (tickets to six/nine games $60/144) or by paying the service charge and going through **Ticketmaster** (☎ 202-397-7328; www.ticketmaster.com).

The women's team, Washington Freedom, whose roster has included US national team stars such as Mia Hamm and Abby Wambach plans to return to the disbanded Womens United Soccer Association (WUSA) when the women's professional league is relaunched.

OUTDOOR ACTIVITIES

Washington, DC, has an ideal climate for outdoor activities, although it can be humidly muggy or may rain often in the

SEVEN ON THE LINE – ULTIMATE IN DC

Looking for a fast-paced sport that challenges you both physically and mentally, requires minimal equipment, and is one of the fastest-growing non-ball team sports in the country? Then try Ultimate Frisbee. The game, usually referred to as just 'Ultimate' (the word Frisbee is copyright protected), by the participants, combines elements of soccer, football and basketball. It has become quite popular in the nation's capital in the last few years, with numerous clubs and growing still.

Unlike other competitive sports, the players are responsible for ensuring that a high level of competition is sustained, but not at the expense of fouling a fellow player to gain an advantage. The result is rivalry in its rawest form. The player who reaches the disc, for instance, without pushing, shoving or elbowing another player out of the way, relies on pure athleticism to win, not on inhibiting the other's right to make a play on the disc. Teamwork, smart decisions, unselfishness and etiquette are all essential.

A team of seven players advances a 175g plastic disc (Frisbee) down a rectangular field measuring roughly 70yd by 40yd, with 25yd end zones at each end, by passing (throwing) the disc to another player on their team until it is caught by a receiver inside the end zone, resulting in a goal for the team on the offense.

There are a few ways to accomplish this. A good thrower-receiver combo can traverse the field and score with just one pass and some fast footwork but, mostly, teamwork is the preferred method for reaching the end zone. Of course, the opposing team is constantly playing defense to try to intercept the disc or cause a turnover by applying pressure, guarding or 'marking' the thrower by trying to block the disc as it's released. Here is where it is a little different from other sports and 'Spirit of the Game' is implemented – Ultimate is a noncontact sport of self-officiating players. That's right: no referees. Competitors themselves are responsible for calling fouls, such as pushing, setting picks and bodily contact.

Contact most often occurs when a defensive player tries to block the thrower's pass and incidentally hits their hand or arm instead of plastic, or when two players jump to receive a pass and there is a midair collision. Did we mention that the thrower has only till a count of 10 seconds (counted aloud by the defender) to release the disc, or a turnover occurs?

This sport relies on hand-eye coordination, cardiovascular stamina, quick decision-making skills and good spirit, which are all reasons why it has become so popular in the last decade. Once an obscure fringe sport invented by a group of high-school students in Maplewood, NJ, in 1968, the games of today are played around the world with levels of competition mirroring that of any professional sport out there.

With its wide-open spaces and pristine green lawns, DC's National Mall makes a picture-perfect field of play. Arrive on a summer evening or weekend morning, and you are likely to see the fields packed with hordes of quick-moving players yelling out 'ultimate' – which signals the kick-off or start of play.

For general area info, specifics on league games and times, visit the website of the **Washington Area Frisbee Club** (www.wafc.org) or call the hotline (☎ 301-588-2629). Other good Ultimate resources include www.ultimatefrisbee .meetup.com and www.upa.org. If you want to watch or join a game of pick-up, show up on the National Mall in the afternoon or on weekend mornings – check the websites for times as these vary with the seasons. Games take place on the polo fields by the FDR memorial (p69), in front of the Smithsonian Castle (p68) and on the Ellipse (p76) near the White House.

warmer months. The city's geography, focused around the Potomac River, covered with parks and green space, allows plenty of opportunities to take advantage of the outdoors. Whether your thing is hiking, biking, running, sunning, canoeing, kayaking, equestrian outings or rock climbing, you will find a place to do it in DC.

BIKING

Acres of parkland along the Potomac and around the National Mall and a relatively flat landscape make for great bike touring around DC. The kicker is the miles and miles of off-road bike trails, many of which became a part of Rails to Trails. Now that Metro allows bicycles on trains and buses, there is almost no place in DC that cannot be reached by bike.

In Rock Creek Park (p121) Beach Drive, between Military and Broad Branch Rds, closes to traffic on weekends. South of Broad Branch, a paved trail parallels the parkway past the zoo and all the way to the Potomac. The trail is narrow in spots and gets crowded on weekends, but it's an easy way to traverse the city by bike. Access the trail at 27th and P Sts NW, or at Connecticut Ave and Calvert St NW.

From Georgetown, take the 10-mile Capital Crescent Trail (Map p299; www.cctrail .org) along the Potomac and into downtown Bethesda, Maryland. This paved trail is one of the best maintained in the city. It has some beautiful lookouts over the river, and winds through woodsy areas and upscale neighborhoods. The southern trailhead is at the east end of K St (called Water St here) under the Francis Scott Key Bridge. From downtown Bethesda, the trail continues for another 2 miles to northern Rock Creek Park, but it is not paved. For maps, call the **Coalition for the Capital Crescent Trail** (☎ 202-234-4874).

The C&O Canal & Towpath (p82) starts in Georgetown and stretches 184 miles northwest to Cumberland, Maryland. This wide dusty path parallels the Capital Crescent Trail for a few miles. The latter turns west, while the towpath continues 14 miles north to Great Falls (p245) and beyond. Note that the towpath is not paved, so all-terrain tires are an asset.

Ohio Dr starts at the Tidal Basin and circumnavigates the peninsula that contains East Potomac Park (p91). A wide, paved sidewalk runs parallel for cyclists who are not at ease sharing the road with cars. The 5-mile loop runs along the Washington Channel on one side and the Potomac River on the other.

Across the Potomac, the Mt Vernon Trail (Map pp306–7) is a beautiful paved riverside path that is a favorite with local cyclists. From the Francis Scott Key Bridge, it follows the river south past Roosevelt Island, Arlington Cemetery and National Airport, through Old Town Alexandria, all the way to Mount Vernon (18 miles). The course is mostly flat, except the long climb up the hill to George Washington's house at the end. The scenery is magnificent – DC skylines and all – and the historical component is certainly unique. Old Town Alexandria provides a much-appreciated opportunity to take a break for a drink or a snack.

Also in Virginia, the **Washington & Old Dominion Trail** (W&OD; www.wodfriends.org) starts in southern Arlington and follows the old railway bed through historic Leesburg and on to Purcellville, in the Allegheny foothills. Its 45 miles are paved and spacious, winding their way through the Virginia suburbs. The easiest place to pick up the trail is outside the East Falls Church Metro station: exit right and turn right again onto Tuckahoe St, then follow the signs. Vienna and Leesburg are pleasant places to stop along the way.

If you prefer to ride, the Custis Trail (Map p299) connects the W&OD to the Mount Vernon Trail or to Washington DC via the Francis Scott Key Bridge.

The Monumental Bike Ride (p134) is the best way for cyclists to take in Washington's memorial sights.

If you would like a guide, **Bike the Sites** (Map pp292–3; ☎ 202-842-2453; www.bikethesites.com; 1100 Pennsylvania Ave, Old Post Office Pavilion; adult/child $40/30; ☉ tours 9am & 1pm; Ⓜ Federal Triangle) offers professionally guided tours of the Capital, the monuments, and even a Sites @ Nite tour. The price includes bike, equipment, bottled water and a snack. For more information, pick up *25 Bicycle Tours in and Around Washington D.C.: From the Capitol Steps to Country Roads,* by Anne H Oman, or *ADC's Washington Area Bike Map.*

The **Washington Area Bicyclists' Association** (WABA; ☎ 202-518-0524; www.waba.org) offers information on bike advocacy, education, bike maps and group rides.

See p263 for a list of bike-rental outlets.

HIKING & RUNNING

Besides the trails mentioned under Biking (opposite), many miles of unpaved trails provide walkers and runners a softer terrain and uninterrupted time on their feet. Rock Creek Park (p121) has 15 miles of unpaved trails. On the west side of Rock Creek, the 4.5-mile green-blazed Western Ridge Trail winds through the forest; pick it up at Beach Dr near the intersection with Porter St NW (Ⓜ Cleveland Park). On the east side, the 5.5-mile blue-blazed Valley Creek Trail runs closer to the creek; pick it up at Park Rd near the **tennis courts** (Ⓜ Cleveland Park). The trails are lightly trafficked and clearly blazed. Maps are available at the **Nature Center & Planetarium** (Map pp290–1; ☎ 202-426-6829; off Military Rd; ☉ 9am-5pm Wed-Sun Sep-May, daily Jun-Aug). There is also a 1.5-mile exercise trail behind the **Omni Shoreham Hotel** (2500 Calvert St NW; Ⓜ Woodley Park-Zoo/Adams Morgan), with 18 exercise station stops.

Extensive trail networks connect Rock Creek Park to the other northwestern DC parks – Normanstone, Montrose, Dumbarton Oaks, Whitehaven, Glover Archbold and Battery Kemble – so you can take a terrific cross-city parkland ramble. A good map is *Trails in the Rock Creek Park Area,*

TOP FIVE NONPOLITICAL RACES

- Subpoena yourself to Washington Harbour at Georgetown for the **Lawyers Have Heart 10K** fun race (p16), which has raised more than $3.7 million for the American Heart Association. Miles 1–2: present your case; miles 2–4: seek advice from council. Then conduct closing arguments on the last two if you are in good enough shape.

- Motorcycle-straddling Vietnam Veterans descend on the National Mall to promote POW-MIA concerns in the **Rolling Thunder Ride for Freedom** (p16) . More than 30 years after the Vietnam War, the unofficial number of Americans still missing is around 1800.

- Dash through Dupont in high heels in the **High Heel Drag Race** (p17), a never-dull Halloween extravaganza that's DC's most gender-bendingly outrageous.

- Run 26 gung-ho miles from the Monument of Iwo Jima around DC and back again in the **Marine Corps Marathon** (p17).

- Lace-up and celebrate a founding father's birthday by participating in the **Alexandria George Washington Classic 10K** (☎ 703-683-5561; www.washingtonbirthday.net), an annual President's Day race through scenic Eisenhower Valley and Alexandria Parklands.

published by the Potomac Appalachian Trail Club.

Other good books include *60 Hikes within 60 Miles: Washington DC,* by Paul Elliot, and the *Washington, DC, Running Guide,* by Don Carter. For organized road races, check out www.runwashington.com or www.dcfrontrunners.org.

IN-LINE SKATING

The 1995 closure of Pennsylvania Ave to car traffic opened an unprecedented opportunity: an expanse of flat, smooth pavement – a parking lot without the cars – right in front of DC's most prime of prime real estate. It did not take long for in-line skaters to discover this outdoor roller rink.

Nowadays Pennsylvania Ave is a meeting place for bladers of all types. The **Washington Area Roadskaters** (www.skatedc.org) is a loose organization of avid skaters that leads group skates, ranging from the beginners' monument loop to an advanced night skate. Their goal is to promote conscious riding, but they also have a great time skating and

socializing together, often wrapping up the skating outings with beers at the Froggy Bottom Pub (p170). They meet in front of the White House on Wednesday and Friday at 7pm and Sunday at 11am from April to October. The White House also hosts informal roller-hockey pick-up games, often on Thursday evenings and on weekends.

In-line skates are available for rental from the **Ski Center** (Map pp290–1; ☎ 202-966-4474; www.skicenter.com; 4300 Fordham Rd NW; per day $15; ☺ from 10am Sat, from noon Sun; Ⓜ Tenleytown-AU) and the **Ski Chalet of Arlington** (☎ 703-521-1700; www.skichalet.com; 2704 Columbia Pike; per hr/day $5/15; ☺ from 10am Sat, from noon Sun; 🚌 16 from Pentagon Metro), southwest of Arlington Cemetery.

KAYAKING & CANOEING

Kayaks and canoes can cruise on the waters of both the Potomac River and the C&O Canal. The canal is ideal for canoeing between Georgetown and Violettes Lock (Mile 22); canoeists must portage around each lock. The Potomac is for the more adventurous, but it is a great vantage point from which to admire the city skyline. North of Georgetown, white-water areas can be dangerous, especially between Great Falls and Chain Bridge.

ATLANTIC KAYAK Map pp308-9
☎ 301-292-6455; www.atlantickayak.com; 600 Water St, Gangplank Marina; 2hr tour $32; ☺ 10am-8:30pm; Ⓜ Waterfront
Atlantic Kayak offers beginners' kayaking classes, as well as tours of the Washington Channel, Anacostia River and Potomac River. Romantic moonlight tours are offered every month. Atlantic's main facility is in Alexandria, VA (Map p311; ☎ 703-838-9072, 800-297-0066; 1201 N Royal St, Alexandria).

FLETCHER'S BOATHOUSE
☎ 202-244-0461; www.fletchersboathouse.com; 4940 Canal Rd NW; canoe per hr/day $12/23; ☺ 9am-7:30pm Mar-Nov; 🚌 D5 from Foggy Bottom-GWU Metro.
This boathouse is a few miles upriver from Georgetown (accessible by bike from the C&O Canal Towpath or by car from Canal Rd). Canoes, rowboats and bicycles are available.

POTOMAC PADDLESPORTS Map pp292-3

☎ 301-831-8270, 877-529-2542; www
.potomacpaddlesports.com; Potomac, MD
White-water- and sea-kayaking lessons are
the focus here, but there are also flat-water
trips, such as fall foliage tours, moonlight
tours of the Potomac and nature-lovers'
tours through a wildlife refuge ($95 each).

THOMPSON BOAT CENTER Map pp292-3

☎ 202-333-9543; www.thompsonboatcenter.com;
2900 Virginia Ave NW; watercraft per hr $8-13, per
day $22-30; ⏰ 6am-8pm; M Foggy Bottom-GWU
Just across the street from the Kennedy
Center, Thompson Boat Center rents canoes
and kayaks, and offers rowing classes. This
is also a convenient place to rent bicycles.

GOLF

DC's three public golf courses are all fine
places to enjoy a few rounds in the city.

EAST POTOMAC PARK Map pp308-9

☎ 202-554-7660; Ohio Dr SW; 18 holes weekday/
weekend $20/25, 9 holes $12/16; ⏰ dawn-dusk;
M Smithsonian
This busy place is a bit scrubby. But where
else can you golf in sight of the Jefferson
Memorial and the Washington Monument complete with jet airliners flying
just overhead? The downside is it can be
loud (thanks to aircraft) and windy. There
are three courses: the par-72 18-hole Blue;
nine-hole White; and 12-hole Red, which is
in the best condition.

LANGSTON Map pp290-1

☎ 202-397-8638; 26th St NE & Benning Rd NE; 18
holes weekday/weekend $15/19; ⏰ dawn-dusk;
🚌 X1, X2 or X3 from Union Station
Considered by many to be DC's best public
course, Langston opened in 1939 as a course
for African American golfers and is still predominantly played by Black golfers. Fairways
are flat, with lots of trees on the back nine.

ROCK CREEK PARK Map pp290-1

☎ 202-882-7332; 1600 Rittenhouse St NW; 18
holes weekday/weekend $20/25, 9 holes $15/18;
⏰ 6am-9pm Apr-Oct, 7am-5:30pm Nov-Mar;
🚌 S1, S2, S4
This 18-hole course does not get great
reviews for the upkeep of its tee boxes or

fairways. However, this 'citadel of working
person's golf' offers convenience and value.
Hilly and narrow fairways with large eleva-
tion changes provide a bit of a risk/reward
scenario – dense woods on either side
replace water hazards to make things more
challenging.

HORSE RIDING

Thirteen miles of wide dirt trails crisscross
the northern part of Rock Creek Park, with
an Equitation Field (Map pp290–1) nearby.
The **Rock Creek Horse Center** (Map pp290–1;
☎ 202-362-0117; 5100 Glover Rd NW; per
hr $25; ⏰ 3pm Tue-Thu, noon, 1:30 & 3pm
Sat & Sun) offers guided trail rides, lessons
and pony rides. Reservations required.

If you are interested in longer-term options than the casual riding lesson, head
out on River Rd towards and then past
Potomac, MD. There are numerous horse
farms out here offering everything from lessons to full board. Check out a couple until
you find one you like.

ROCK CLIMBING

In DC, climbers head for Rock Creek Park
(p121). The bouldering area underneath the
bridge at Massachusetts Ave and Whitehaven
Rd is 20ft high and 50ft wide, large enough
for four defined routes and the potential for
more. Other climbing spots are at Carderock
Recreation Area on the C&O Canal Towpath
(p82) and Great Falls (p245). Indoor climbing walls are at the National Capital YMCA
(p204) and Results the Gym (p204).

TENNIS

The city maintains over 50 free public
courts, including Montrose Park at 31st
and R Sts NW and Rock Creek Park at
24th and N Sts NW. Call the **DC Dept of Parks
and Recreation** (☎ 202-673-7647; http://dpr
.dc.gov; ⏰ 8am-6pm Mon-Fri) for information, schedule and calendar of events.

ROCK CREEK PARK Map pp290-1

☎ 202-722-5949; 16th & Kennedy Sts NW; courts
per hr from $4; ⏰ 7am-11pm; 🚌 S1, S2 or S4
Both hard- and soft-surface courts (25 in
total) are open to the public, but they must
be reserved from April to October. For more
about the park, see p121.

HEALTH & FITNESS

When in DC, there is no need to forego your regular routine of running or reflexology. The city has plenty of fitness centers and health spas to meet the calisthenics and chill-out needs of any visitor.

SWIMMING POOLS

When air-conditioning is not enough, get relief from the summer heat at one of these facilities.

Capitol East Natatorium (Map p304; ☎ 202-724-4495; 635 N Carolina Ave SE; adult/child $7/4; ☻ 6:30am-9pm Mon-Fri, 10am-5pm Sat & Sun; Ⓜ Eastern Market) Indoor 25m facility.

Francis Pool (Map pp292-3; ☎ 202-727-3285; 2500 N St NW; adult/child $7/4; ☻ 1-8pm Mon & Wed-Fri, noon-6pm Sat & Sun; Ⓜ Dupont Circle) Outdoor pool open June to August.

Georgetown Pool (Map p299; ☎ 202-282-2366; 3400 Volta Pl; adult/child $7/4; ☻ 1-8pm Tue-Fri, noon-6pm Sat & Sun; 🚌 Georgetown shuttle from Foggy Bottom-GWU Metro) Outdoor pool open June to August and crowded with kids.

GYMS & FITNESS CENTERS

In the dead of winter or the humid heat of summer, DC gyms are packed with type-As. The good news is that you can join them. DC has so many visitors and transient residents that most gyms allow for short-term (as short as one-day) memberships.

Fitness First (Map pp292-3; ☎ 202-659-1900; www.fitnessfirstclubs.com; 1075 19th St NW; day/month pass $10/75; ☻ 5am-11pm Mon-Thu, 5am-10pm Fri, 8am-8pm Sat & Sun; Ⓜ Farragut North) All the weight machines and cardiovascular equipment you could hope for, plus free weights; kickboxing, aerobics, spinning, Pilates and yoga classes; sauna and steam room.

National Capital YMCA (Map pp296-7; ☎ 202-862-9622; www.nationalcapitalymca.com; 1711 Rhode Island Ave; day pass/steam room $15/20; ☻ 5:30am-10:30pm Mon-Fri, 8am-6:30pm Sat, 9am-5:30pm Sun; Ⓜ Farragut North) Seven floors of fitness and fun, including squash courts, basketball courts, indoor track, rock-climbing wall, free weights, cardio machines and classes.

Results the Gym: Capitol Hill (Map pp308-9; ☎ 202-234-5678; www.resultsthegym.com; 315 G St SE; day pass $18; ☻ 5am-11pm Mon-Fri, 8am-9pm Sat & Sun; Ⓜ Capitol South) Light-filled cardio room; rotating climbing wall; specialty classes for abdominals, as well as varying levels of yoga and urban funk.

Results the Gym: Dupont Circle (Map pp296-7; ☎ 202-518-0001; 1612 U St NW; ☻ 5am-11pm Mon-Fri, 7am-9pm Sat & Sun; Ⓜ U Street-Cardozo)

Spiral Flight (Map pp300-1; ☎ 202-965-1645; www.spiralflightyoga.com; 1726 Wisconsin Ave NW; class 60/90min $16/18; ☻ classes vary seasonally; 🚌 Georgetown shuttle from Foggy Bottom-GWU Metro) Center for yoga and tai chi, in art-gallery setting.

YWCA (Map pp292-3; ☎ 202-626-0710; www.ywcanca.org; 624 9th St NW; day pass $12; ☻ 6:30am-9pm Mon-Fri, 8:30am-4:30pm Sat, 10am-4:30pm Sun; Ⓜ Gallery Pl-Chinatown) Free weights, machines and a 25m lap pool; women and men welcome.

MASSAGE & DAY SPAS

Every now and then, everyone needs to indulge. Hair gets frizzy, feet get sore, minds grow weary and nothing but a little pricey self-indulgence can fix matters. Here's a list of good day spas where you can spoil yourself:

Andre Chreky Salon (Map pp292-3; ☎ 202-293-9393; 1604 K St NW; ☻ 8:30am-8pm Mon, 7am-8pm Tues-Fri, 7am-7pm Sat, 9am-5pm Sun; Ⓜ McPherson Sq) A sleek business-district spa fixing up skin, hair and nails. It has a coffee bar to keep you awake while you're fussed over.

Aveda Georgetown (Map p299; ☎ 202-965-1325; 1325 Wisconsin Ave NW; ☻ 10am-7pm; 🚌 Georgetown shuttle from Foggy Bottom-GWU Metro) Does nice herbal things to skin, body and hair.

EFX/Blue Mercury (Map p299; ☎ 202-965-1300; 3059 M St NW; ☻ 10am-8pm Mon-Sat, noon-5pm Sun; 🚌 Georgetown shuttle from Rosslyn or Foggy Bottom-GWU Metro) A small Georgetown spa drawing a hip young clientele, EFX/Blue Mercury has facials, massages, waxing, friendly low-key staff and better-than-average piped-in music.

Four Seasons Fitness Club/Spa (Map pp292-3; ☎ 202-944-2022; 2800 Pennsylvania Ave NW; 🚌 Georgetown shuttle from Foggy Bottom-GWU Metro) Part of the luxurious Four Seasons Hotel. You can't use the gym itself unless you stay overnight, but exercise classes and spa treatments are available to nonguests.

Jolie Four Seasons Fitness Club/Spa (☎ 301-986-9293; 7200 Wisconsin Ave NW, Bethesda; Ⓜ Bethesda) One of the area's better-known spas. It's pretty affordable, despite its expensively frilly decor, and offers all the services: massage, vitamin facial wraps and pedicures. It's close to Bethesda Metro.

Tara Salon (Map pp292-3; ☎ 202-333-8099; 2715 M St NW; Ⓜ Foggy Bottom-GWU) Offers all sorts of skin and hair stuff, from basic leg waxes to massage and electrolysis.

Shopping

Shopping

No one actually visits Washington, DC, just to shop (or at least we would hope no one does), but when it comes to retail therapy the nation's capital is an absolute paradise for souvenir lovers. From rubber Nixon masks to stars-and-stripes underpants, Washington shops sell the ultimate in kitsch and memorabilia. And there are the classic souvenirs in Washington, too: stuffed pandas from the National Zoological Park, shredded money from the Bureau of Printing & Engraving, and balsa-wood airplanes from the National Air & Space Museum.

Museum shops (of which there are many in Washington, DC,) are packed full of unique gifts. They offer something for everyone, including books, jewelry, crafts, art and souvenirs from across the US. Imported goods, such as textiles and art, are also available at museum and import shops throughout the city. World-music buffs will find plenty of stores offering a varied selection of music from around the planet.

Secondhand shops, clothing boutiques, bookstores and art galleries keep browsers busy for hours in Georgetown and Dupont Circle. Unlike New York and San Francisco, however, surprisingly Washington doesn't have a strip of haute couture shops downtown. So if you're looking for Louis Vuitton or Gucci in their own home stores, you'll have to visit the malls in the 'burbs (see p220).

Shopping Areas

Georgetown is DC's number-one shopping strip. Stores are lined up along M St and Wisconsin Ave and the neighborhood features a giant indoor mall. Adams-Morgan, along 18th St, is where to go for ethnic goodies and a couple of unique boutiques – although this is historically more of a nightlife area than a shopping strip. The same story is true in the Shaw, which has a cluster of hipster boutiques along 14th St, but not much else. Dupont Circle is another major shopping area, with stores lined up along Connecticut Ave and the streets running off the circle. Here you'll find the latest boutiques carrying fashions, plenty of bookstores, vintage shops and art galleries. The Smithsonian museums each have their own souvenir stores – some better than others. Downtown you'll find plenty of stores selling kitschy DC souvenirs, T-shirts and political schlock, but check out the area around 7th St in Chinatown for up-and-coming galleries and department stores. Further out, Bethesda and Alexandria both have heaps of interesting retailers, many specializing in antiques, high-end clothing and fair-trade crafts.

TOP FIVE SHOPPING STRIPS

These top shopping locales are good for souvenirs, galleries, bookstores and specialty shops. Serious consumers, however, should head to the suburban malls (see p220) where you will find huge selections of clothing, electronics, books and furniture stores.

- Chinatown area – Peruse the bargain bins at department stores like Hecht's. Use your savings to shop for art at the galleries clustered along the 400 block of 7th St.
- Connecticut Ave & around, Dupont Circle – DC's best collection of art galleries and import shops.
- M St NW, Georgetown – Art galleries, boutiques and bookstores galore.
- Union Station – Hundreds of stores selling Americana-themed souvenirs and gifts (and regular stuff you might need, too).
- Woodmont Triangle, Bethesda – Fair-trade arts and crafts, creative furnishings and hip boutiques all in a small, safe and easily accessible circumference.

Opening Hours

Generally, stores in DC are open 10am to 7pm Monday to Saturday and noon to 5pm Sunday, although some stores close on Sunday. Smaller shops may close at 5pm every day, or stay open until 7pm one night a week, eg Thursday. Museum shops are open according to museum hours.

Sales Taxes & Refunds

Sales tax is 5.75% in DC, 4.5% in Virginia and 5% in Maryland. For more info, see p272.

NATIONAL MALL & MONUMENTS

DC souvenir shopping at its finest is found in this area. Most of the shops are located in the museums and galleries – nearly every establishment has one, some better than others. If you are looking for a unique present for a hard-to-shop-for dad or limited-edition prints for your dining room, this is where to go. Don't miss the souvenir stands scattered around the edges of the National Mall. The regular deal for decades now has been three DC T-shirts (saying everything from FBI to political jargon) for $10.

ARTHUR M SACKLER GALLERY

Map pp292-3   Museum Shop
☎ 202-633-4800; www.asia.si.edu; 1050 Independence Ave SW; ☉ 10am-5:30pm, to 8pm Thu Jul & Aug; Ⓜ Smithsonian

Asian art posters and limited-edition prints, jewelry and world crafts are found in this gallery shop. It also sells loads of books and educational materials.

FREER GALLERY OF ART

Map pp292-3   Museum Shop
☎ 202-633-4800; www.asia.si.edu; 1050 Independence Ave SW; ☉ 10am-5:30pm, to 8pm Thu Jul & Aug; Ⓜ Smithsonian

As well as prints, posters, jewelry and crafts, world-music enthusiasts will find an extensive selection of traditional and contemporary music from Asian countries. Fun kits for kids teach them about brush painting, origami and haiku.

HIRSHHORN MUSEUM

Map pp292-3   Museum Shop
☎ 202-357-2700; 7th St & Independence Ave SW; ☉ 10am-5:30pm; Ⓜ Smithsonian

Grab one of the exhibition catalogs for your coffee table – they make great souvenirs and are a terrific way to share your experience in DC with visitors. The museum gift shop is small, but has an excellent collection of books on modern art.

NATIONAL AIR & SPACE MUSEUM

Map pp292-3   Museum Shop
☎ 202-357-2700; 6th St & Independence Ave SW; ☉ 10am-5:30pm; Ⓜ Smithsonian

This gift shop is more like a gift mall: it's a three-floor emporium offering books, toys,

CLOTHING SIZES

Measurements approximate only, try before you buy.

Women's Clothing

Aus/UK	8	10	12	14	16	18
Europe	36	38	40	42	44	46
Japan	5	7	9	11	13	15
USA	6	8	10	12	14	16

Women's Shoes

Aus/USA	5	6	7	8	9	10
Europe	35	36	37	38	39	40
France	35	36	38	39	40	42
Japan	22	23	24	25	26	27
UK	3½	4½	5½	6½	7½	8½

Men's Clothing

Aus	92	96	100	104	108	112
Europe	46	48	50	52	54	56
Japan	S		M	M		L
UK/USA	35	36	37	38	39	40

Men's Shirts (Collar Sizes)

Aus/Japan	38	39	40	41	42	43
Europe	38	39	40	41	42	43
UK/USA	15	15½	16	16½	17	17½

Men's Shoes

Aus/UK	7	8	9	10	11	12
Europe	41	42	43	44½	46	47
Japan	26	27	27½	28	29	30
USA	7½	8½	9½	10½	11½	12½

GET THE POOP

The zoo's animals collectively produce hundreds of pounds of manure every day. Most is trucked off to the dump, but some is made into DC's most unusual souvenir: ZooDoo fertilizer. Composted animal dung (only from plant-eating beasties) is mixed with wood chips, straw and leaves, and sold in buckets decorated with little drawings of animal butts. Buy ZooDoo at any zoo information booth, or order it from **Friends of the National Zoological Park** (☎ 673-4989); a 1lb bucket costs about $5. The zoo uses ZooDoo on its own beautiful grounds, so you can see how well it works – and you'll probably be the only person on your block with genuine zebra poop in your zinnias.

posters, model aircraft and such iconic DC souvenirs as freeze-dried Astronaut Ice Cream (tasting like cotton candy squished by a steamroller). It has an incomparable selection of books on all aspects of aviation – it would be hard to find such a collection in any other US bookstore. All kinds of kites roost here, too, from classic diamond shapes to neon butterflies.

NATIONAL GALLERY OF ART

Map pp292-3   Museum Shop
☎ 202-737-4215; www.nga.gov; 4th St & Constitution Ave NW; ⏰ 10am-5pm Mon-Sat, 11am-6pm Sun; Ⓜ Archives-Navy Memorial
If you're in the market for art reproductions of any kind, browse the elongated shops lining the underground corridors linking the East and West Buildings (you can enter from either building). The collection here is quite extensive, with framed and unframed reproductions of the museum's best-known works, greeting cards, jewelry and loads of books. A good children's section has crafty kits to encourage your kid's creative tendencies.

NATIONAL MUSEUM OF AFRICAN ART

Map pp292-3   Museum Shop
☎ 202-357-2700; 950 Independence Ave SW; ⏰ 10am-5:30pm; Ⓜ Smithsonian
Almost as good as a trip to the 'Dark Continent.' African art collectors will relish the incredible selection here. Textiles, baskets, musical instruments, dolls and other wares come from Angola, Zimbabwe and everywhere African in between.

NATIONAL MUSEUM OF AMERICAN HISTORY

Map pp292-3   Museum Shop
☎ 202-357-2700; 14th St & Constitution Ave NW; ⏰ 10am-5:30pm; Ⓜ Smithsonian
It will be closed until the museum finishes renovations, but once it reopens (in 2008) it's bound to be even more dazzling than before. In the spirit of consumerist America, this place offers four (and counting) venues for your wallet to 'celebrate' American history. The main museum shop has reproductions of old war posters and newspapers with newsworthy headlines from the 20th century. There is an excellent selection of crafts, including Navajo pottery and Inuit statues. Other stores in the museum focus specifically on presidents, music and – in keeping with the museum's latest exhibit – transportation. The museum also has the Smithsonian's largest collection of books and videos on all aspects of American culture and history.

NATIONAL MUSEUM OF NATURAL HISTORY

Map pp292-3   Museum Shop
☎ 202-357-2700; 10th St & Constitution Ave NW; ⏰ 10am-5:30pm; Ⓜ Smithsonian
This museum is another gift emporium. It has four different specialty shops, including the main store on the ground floor. The Tricera Shop is entirely devoted to dinosaur merchandise (now that is specialized). The glittering Gem Store – outside the Geology Hall – has an extensive selection of fine and costume jewelry, including stunningly beautiful amber samples that are millions of years old. The newest Mammals Museum Store, which is designed to represent four continents (Asia, Australia, North and South America), carries toys, crafts, posters and books focusing on mammals and evolution.

NATIONAL MUSEUM OF THE AMERICAN INDIAN

Map pp292-3   Museum Shop
☎ 202-287-2020; www.americanindian.si.edu; 4th St & Independence Ave SW; ⏰ 10am-5:30pm, to 7:30pm Jun-Aug; Ⓜ Smithsonian
Not only is this gift shop aesthetically pleasing – the shelves are inlaid with

purple and white quahog shell tiles – it is also packed with a range of perfect stocking stuffers. It has a large collection of Native American books, everything from children's lore to adult-oriented history, along with an extensive jewelry and crafts section.

WHITE HOUSE AREA & FOGGY BOTTOM

You'll find many of the same tourist-aimed souvenir shops repeated throughout these neighborhoods. Amid all the junky places, however, are some gems, including bookstores specializing in travel or the White House and a boutique selling espionage essentials.

ABC MAP & TRAVEL CENTER
Map pp292-3   Maps
☎ 202-628-2608; 1636 I St NW; ⊗ 9am-6:30pm Mon-Thu, 9am-5:30pm Fri, 9am-5pm Sat; Ⓜ Farragut West
This wee downtown storefront is packed with everything from DC activity guides to bus-route maps to huge foldout sheet maps of the district.

AMERICAN INSTITUTE OF ARCHITECTS BOOKSTORE
Map pp292-3   Books
☎ 202-626-7475; 1735 New York Ave NW; Ⓜ Foggy Bottom
Architecture buffs are in heaven in this sleek (and rather unusual) specialty shop, which stocks the latest architecture and design titles and periodicals. If you need a present for a hard-to-shop for architect, it also has a collection of unusual architectural-focused gifts.

CHAPTERS
Map pp292-3   Books
☎ 202-347-5495; 1512 K St NW; ⊗ 10am-6:30pm Mon-Fri, 11am-5pm Sat; Ⓜ McPherson Sq
The best bookstore in this area is dedicated almost exclusively to literary fiction; it has one of the liveliest reading calendars in town and an active book club that meets monthly. Blocks from the White House, it is a favorite of white-collars, as well as tourists.

INDIAN CRAFT SHOP
Map pp292-3   Art
☎ 202-208-4056; 1849 C St NW, No 1023 Dept of Interior; Mon-Fri; Ⓜ Farragut West
This crowded one-room shop sells gorgeous but costly basketry, weavings and jewelry made by Native Americans. Show photo ID to enter the building.

RENWICK GALLERY
Map pp292-3   Museum Shop
☎ 202-357-2700; 17th St & Pennsylvania Ave NW; Ⓜ Farragut West
In one of DC's best museum shops handmade textiles and hand-dyed silks are available, as is glasswork, woodwork and unique jewelry, much of it quite affordable (a pair of hand-blown ruby-glass earrings costs $12). Its excellent choice of books includes how-to manuals on jewelry- and fabric-making, ceramics, glassblowing and cabinetry, many appropriate for kids. In this store you can learn as well as buy; it feels like an organic extension of the crafts museum upstairs.

SECURITY INTELLIGENCE TECHNOLOGIES
Map pp292-3   Espionage Essentials
☎ 202-887-1717; 1001 Connecticut Ave NW, No 530; ⊗ 9am-6pm Mon-Fri by appointment; Ⓜ Farragut North
Wannabe G-men won't find a better place to pick up surveillance and countersurveillance gear. Some patrons seem to be here for a laugh, but others are very serious indeed. Check out the Predator VI night-vision goggles, Air Tasers, line-bug detection devices – everything your paranoid little heart desires.

WHITE HOUSE HISTORICAL ASSOCIATION GIFT SHOP
Map pp292-3   Souvenirs
☎ 202-737-8292; 740 Jackson Pl NW, Lafayette Sq; ⊗ 9am-4pm Mon-Fri; Ⓜ Farragut West
Peruse a wide selection of books, videos, gifts, posters, Christmas ornaments, jewelry, postcards and educational materials, all on the theme of the big house across the square. This is the place to buy your dad a White House necktie. There is a similarly stocked store in the White House Visitors Center.

WORLD BANK INFOSHOP

Map pp292-3   Books

☎ 202-458-5454; www.worldbank.org/infoshop;
1818 H St NW, No J1-060; ⏱ 9am-5pm Mon-Fri;
Ⓜ Farragut West

The controversial multilateral lender runs the excellent World Bank InfoShop, which sells a vast collection of books and documents on all aspects of development and economics.

GEORGETOWN

Far-and-away Washington's most popular shopping strip, historic Georgetown offers something for everyone in the pretty shop fronts of brick buildings lining the cobbled streets. Depending on your budget, you can drop big money on designer labels in the very swanky Georgetown Park Mall, which occupies a big strip on the center of M St, or search for fire-engine-red hair dye in one of the punky shops on Wisconsin Ave. The district stretches along M St between 27th and 35th Sts and on Wisconsin Ave between M and S Sts.

BUYING FAKE: THE DRIVE-BY BAG BUY

Georgetown has some great stands to buy designer knock-off bags and wallets – copies of Louis Vuitton, Gucci, Prada and Kate Spade are all big sellers. The products are usually of quite high quality and do a good job of mimicking the real thing (although if you know your designers, you'll be able to tell these bags are fake). There are two good stands, one on the corner of N St and Wisconsin Ave and the other in front of the High Fashion shop, one block south of N St on Wisconsin Ave. Bags cost between $25 and $40. Prices start higher, but you should barter – it's one of the few opportunities to do so in DC.

Other good spots to look for bags include the K St corridor just south of Georgetown and occasionally at vendors scattered around Metro stops (Rosslyn has a few). As a rule, though, those who buy fakes say the Georgetown stalls are the best – you won't find anything saying 'Prata.'

Oh, and if you're short of time, or can't be bothered with parking, it's not unheard of to drive up, honk, shout what you want and five minutes later drive away with your product.

APPALACHIAN SPRING

Map p299   Art

☎ 202-337-5780; 1415 Wisconsin Ave NW;
🚌 Georgetown shuttle from Rosslyn Metro

Touting its motto, 'celebrating American craft,' this local chain features fine hand-made pottery, woodcarvings, quilts and jewelry. It's good for wedding gifts – we like the carved wooden boxes and hand-blown glass bowls.

BETSEY JOHNSON

Map p299   Designer Boutique

☎ 202-338-4090; 1319 Wisconsin Ave NW;
🚌 Georgetown shuttle from Rosslyn Metro

Perennially trendy designer Betsey Johnson serves up her latest creations, always featuring lots of gauze, velvet and lace, in her dishy pink boutique. The designer has girly yet punk flair, using many vibrant pinks against black lace. Check the sale rack: Betsey Johnson on sale is very affordable.

BETTER BOTANICALS

Map p299   Ayurvedic Goods

☎ 888-224-3727; 3066 M St NW; ⏱ 9am-6pm
Mon-Fri; 🚌 Georgetown shuttle from Foggy
Bottom-GWU Metro

Feeling stressed by your travels? This unique reader-recommended shop prepares custom-made Ayurvedic herbal products. Choose your scent and have the staff personalize your soaps, oils, lotions and shampoos.

BEYOND COMICS 2

Map p299   Books & Toys

☎ 202-333-8651; 3060 M St; 🚌 Georgetown
shuttle from Rosslyn

Teens love this small shop, crowded with scores of new and secondhand comic books. Trading cards and heaps of action figurines from TV, movies and animation are also for sale.

COMMANDER SALAMANDER

Map p299   Funky Clothing & Accessories

☎ 202-337-2265; 1420 Wisconsin Ave NW;
⏱ 10am-9pm Mon-Thu, 10am-10pm Fri & Sat,
11am-7pm Sun; 🚌 Georgetown shuttle from Rosslyn

This Georgetown institution has been a friend to street punks and wannabes for decades. (Thirty-somethings remember it fondly from the days when Friday night in Georgetown meant seeing *The Rocky Horror Picture Show* at the now-defunct Key Theatre, and this was the place everyone stopped on the way for black lipstick and handcuffs.) It now sells funky makeup, all colors of hair dye, Goth-wear, and baggy clothes from such brands as Moschino and Hook-Ups.

COWBOY WESTERN WEAR

Map p299   Western Wear

☎ 202-298-8299; 3147 Dumbarton Ave NW; 🚍 Georgetown shuttle from Foggy Bottom-GWU Metro

This great little Western shop will guarantee you are dressed to the nines for that night out two-steppin'. Even if you don't know how to 'swing your partner,' it has a very good selection of boots and other Western wear.

DEAN & DELUCA

Map p299   Gourmet Food

☎ 202-342-2500; 3276 M St NW; 🕙 10am-8pm Sun-Thu, 10am-9pm Fri & Sat; 🚍 Georgetown shuttle from Foggy Bottom-GWU Metro

The New York gourmet chain has an overwhelming and mouthwatering selection of produce, meat and baked goods in this revamped brick warehouse (all costly; this is a place for Black Angus beef and caviar). Outside is a lovely canopied dining area for noshing on its ready-made sandwiches and pastries.

DEJA BLUE

Map p299   Jeans

☎ 202-337-7100; 3005 M St NW; 🕙 10am-7pm Mon-Sat, noon-5pm Sun; 🚍 Georgetown shuttle from Foggy Bottom-GWU Metro

Looking for vintage jeans? This place has stacks of them, plus salespeople who can take one glance at you and throw you several pairs that will fit like they were tailored for your booty alone. They usually run between $30 and $40, but they're worth it.

DREAM DRESSER

Map p299   Adult Clothing

☎ 202-625-0373; 1042 Wisconsin Ave NW; 🚍 Georgetown shuttle from Foggy Bottom-GWU Metro

The girls come here to purchase bachelorette gifts, or so they say… This racy exotica boutique has been around long enough to be considered legendary in Washington, and it has all you'll ever need in the leather and lace department. There's a bunch of whips, plus giant dildos, a selection of strap-ons and all sorts of toys for nights behind closed bedroom doors.

FIRE & ICE OF GEORGETOWN

Map p299   Jewelry

☎ 202-338-0024; 3222 M St NW, Georgetown Park Mall; 🚍 Georgetown shuttle from Foggy Bottom-GWU Metro

The eye-catchers at this unique jewelry boutique are the creative pieces crafted from silver and semiprecious stones, but you'll also find smaller trinkets, like polished fossils perfect for your daughter to purchase with her allowance.

GEORGETOWN PARK MALL

Map p299   Mall

☎ 202-298-5577; Wisconsin Ave & M St NW; 🕙 9am-9pm Mon-Sat, noon-6pm Sun; 🚍 Georgetown shuttle from Foggy Bottom-GWU Metro

This elegantly designed upscale mall is on the north bank of the C&O Canal. It has a nice downstairs food court (with splashing fountains) and more than 100 shops, including FAO Schwarz, J Crew and Victoria's Secret. Here, too, is 250-year-old Caswell-Massey, an apothecary that once sold soaps and toiletries to George Washington.

HATS IN THE BELFRY

Map p299   Millinery

☎ 202-342-2006; 1250 Wisconsin Ave NW; 🕙 10am-9pm Mon-Thu, 10am-midnight Fri & Sat, 10am-8pm Sun; 🚍 Georgetown shuttle from Foggy Bottom-GWU Metro

From fashionable (but affordable) bonnets to costume caps, this shop has been topping off Georgetown's heads for years. The place has many mirrors and you are welcome to try on the goods.

INGA'S ONCE IS NOT ENOUGH

Map pp290-1   Secondhand Clothing & Accessories

☎ 202-337-3072; 4830 Macarthur Blvd NW; 🕙 Mon-Sat; 🚍 D5 from Foggy Bottom-GWU Metro

Known as the first lady of retail couture, Inga has all the big names – Chanel, Gucci,

Prada, Marc Jacobs – for sale at her fine consignment shop. Inga herself, who is a fashion consultant for the local Fox channel, takes her customers firmly in hand, showing them what they really want to buy in her very crowded shop, which is thick with designer labels. It's easiest to drive here. There is street parking, although it can take a while to nab a spot. Try cruising down N or Prospect Sts to the north of Wisconsin Ave (around 36th Street).

KIEHL'S

Map p299   Face, Hair & Body Products

☎ 202-333-5101; 3310 M St NW; 🚌 Georgetown shuttle from Foggy Bottom-GWU Metro

Favorites of movie stars, Kiehl's products are well known for their exceptional quality. This neat brick shop with attentive salespeople is filled with all the Kiehl's goodies you could ever want – divine shampoos and conditioners, rich and creamy body lotions, energizing facial scrubs and a wonderful self-tanner (it doesn't turn you orange) are just some of the offerings. The prices are a little high, but the effectiveness of the products makes the cost worth it.

MOVIE MADNESS

Map p299   Movie Posters

☎ 202-337-7064; 1083 Thomas Jefferson St NW; 🚌 Georgetown shuttle from Foggy Bottom-GWU Metro

A trip to Movie Madness has become a rite of passage for Washington teenagers redecorating their bedrooms before the start of high school. Thousands of modern and classic movie posters, along with celebrity pictures, political memorabilia and old-fashioned advertisements, are for sale here.

PARISH GALLERY

Map p299   Art

☎ 202-944-2310; 1054 31st St NW; 🕑 noon-6pm Tue-Sat; 🚌 Georgetown shuttle from Foggy Bottom-GWU Metro

This is among conservative Georgetown's more contemporary galleries, featuring the work of African Americans and other minority artists. The works of many local artists are represented.

PATAGONIA

Map p299   Men's & Women's Active Apparel

☎ 202-333-1776; 1048 Wisconsin Ave NW; 🕑 11am-7pm Mon-Fri, 10am-7pm Sat, 11am-5pm Sun; 🚌 Georgetown shuttle from Foggy Bottom-GWU Metro

Staffed with knowledgeable sales clerks and stocked with everything you need for a trip to the great outdoors, this tri-level shop has a giant collection of Patagonia's trusted gear, including trendy garb for women and men along with camping supplies, down jackets, and hiking shoes and shorts.

SECONDHAND ROSE

Map p299   Quality Secondhand Clothing

☎ 202-337-3378; 1516 Wisconsin Ave NW; 🕑 Mon-Sat; 🚌 Georgetown shuttle from Foggy Bottom-GWU Metro

Somewhat pricey for a secondhand shop, Rose offers consignment women's clothing that's no more than two years old. This isn't a place for bargain hunters – no $10 dresses here – but this Georgetown store has a fast turnover and all items are in good condition.

SMASH!

Map p299   Punk Clothing & Records

☎ 202-337-6274; 3285 1/2 M St NW; 🚌 Georgetown shuttle from Foggy Bottom-GWU Metro

When this author was young, she remembers sneaking down to Smash! to buy striped tights and magenta hair dye. It used to make her feel so grown up; so punk. Today, punky teenagers flock to this misfit looking shop on a street of fresh-scrubbed storefronts for studded belts, secondhand jackets and a collection of punk classics on vinyl.

STEVE MADDEN

Map p299   Shoes

☎ 202-342-6195; 3109 M St NW; 🚌 Georgetown shuttle from Foggy Bottom-GWU Metro

The flagship Steve Madden store in DC has a giant selection of the designer's footwear. From spiky heels to trendy sneakers, you're likely to find something here. Plus shopping in this airy space is pretty damn fun. Don't forget to check out the sale rack in the back – there are usually shoes going for 50% off.

CAPITOL HILL

You can shop the world on Capitol Hill, home to two DC shopping institutions – Union Station and Eastern Market. Although they're only physically separated by mere blocks, the two feel continents apart. Union Station is a model of the aesthetically perfect corporate indoor shopping experience, while bohemian Eastern Market feels more like a gypsy camp plopped down in the South. The Hill is also home to vintage-clothing shops and plenty of stores selling political mementos.

BACKSTAGE

Map pp308-9   Fancy Dress

☎ 202-544-5744; 545 8th St SE; ☸ 11am-7pm Mon-Sat; Ⓜ Eastern Market

This costume and theatrical store caters to both the drag crowd and government types in search of fancy dress for parties. It rents outfits, and you can buy funky face paints, wigs and masks.

CLOTHES ENCOUNTERS OF A SECOND KIND

Map p304   Secondhand Clothing

☎ 202-546-4004; 202 7th St SE; Ⓜ Eastern Market

If it's not in style this season, you won't find it at this high-end consignment shop. Each item is carefully selected and you can find some designer classics discarded by Washington's upper crust at reasonable – although definitely not bargain-basement – prices.

EASTERN MARKET

Map p304   Food & Beverages, Art, Antiques

☎ 202-546-2698; www.easternmarket.net; 225 7th St SE; ☸ 10am-6pm Tue-Fri, 8am-4pm Sat & Sun; Ⓜ Eastern Market

Eastern Market's **South Hall** is the closest DC gets to foodie heaven: in its friendly confines are a bakery, dairy, fish counter, poultry counter, butcher, produce vendors and flower stands. Foodies can put together a real Southern feast here – the Southern Maryland Seafood Company serves up the blue crabs and shrimp; over at Union Meat Company are fresh chitterlings, pigs' trotters, and all kinds of sausage and steak. To get it all blessed, stop by Calomiris, the Greek produce stand. It

sells Orthodox icons among its cucumbers and oranges.

Next door, **Market 5 Gallery** is a space used by local artists to exhibit visual and performing arts. On weekends, both the artists and the farmers markets spill out onto the sidewalks. Besides fresh produce, you can pick up handmade scarves, prints, smelly soaps and candles, colorful pottery, painted ceramics and unusual jewelry. Across the street at the weekend **flea market**, vendors hawk cool refinished (or not) furniture.

GOVERNMENT PRINTING OFFICE & BOOKSTORE

Map p304   Books

☎ 202-512-0132; 710 N Capitol St; ☸ 8am-4pm Mon-Fri; Ⓜ Union Station

Perhaps you needed to pick up a title published by the US government. (You never know…there are 15,000 of them.) Here, you can peruse blockbusters like *Selling to the Military* and *Nest Boxes for Wood Ducks* (among many others).

NATIONAL POSTAL MUSEUM

Map p304   Museum Shop

☎ 202-357-2991; www.postalmuseum.si.edu; 2 Massachusetts Ave NW; Ⓜ Union Station

It's pretty much a no-brainer. Philatelists should head to the National Postal Museum shop for current US stamps and poster-size blow-ups of unique historical stamps.

TROVER SHOP

Map p304   Books

☎ 202-547-2665; 221 Pennsylvania Ave SE; Ⓜ Eastern Market

This two-level goldmine is a DC institution for books, cards and gifts. It also has a wide selection of books on tape, which are rentable. Unsurprisingly, its section on politics is primo.

UNION STATION

Map p304   Mall

☎ 202-289-1908; www.unionstationdc.com; 50 Massachusetts Ave NE; ☸ 10am-9pm Mon-Sat, noon-6pm Sun; Ⓜ Union Station

Not only an architectural landmark and a train depot, Union Station is also a good-sized mall, complete with multiscreen cinema, food court, restaurants and hundreds of shops. The mall's shops include your standard mall chains, but there is also a great selection of boutiques selling toys, jewelry and DC souvenirs. Highlights include the National Zoo Store, Appalachian Spring for arts and crafts, Discovery Store, the Great Train Store (selling train memorabilia and toys) and the Best of DC souvenir shop. Two-hour validated parking is available for shoppers. For more on Union Station, see p89.

DOWNTOWN

Downtown has two malls, but with the exception of the Old Post Office Pavilion's exceptional architecture, neither is particularly memorable. Stick to the smaller shops sprinkled around the Penn Quarter and Chinatown. You'll find quite a few good museum shops here. The area around 7th St is an up-and-coming art district – check out the group of galleries clustered along the 400 block.

ARTIFACTORY

Map pp290-1   Eclectic Gifts & Home Furnishings
☎ 202-393-2727; 641 Indiana Ave NW;
Ⓜ Archives-Navy Memorial

Some of the pieces at this African and Asian gallery-store are worthy of museum displays – and priced to match. Others are less precious and reasonably marked. Inside one of the city's oldest buildings, Artifactory procures sculptures, masks and clothing from both continents.

BEAD MUSEUM

Map pp292-3   Jewelry & Accessories
☎ 202-624-4500; www.beadmuseumdc.org; 400 7th St NW; Ⓨ 11am-4pm Wed-Sat, 1-4pm Sun;
Ⓜ Archives-Navy Memorial

The shop reflects the museum's educational mission by offering one-of-a-kind contemporary and ethnic beaded jewelry, books, posters and videos that relate to the exhibits.

CELADON

Map pp292-3   Beauty Products
202-347-3333; 1180 F St NW; Ⓨ 9am-7pm Mon-Fri, 8am-4pm Sat; Ⓜ Metro Center

Washingtonians come to this rather luxurious spa for a day of pampering – from

perfect pedicures to Swedish massages – but check out the store in front for a very impressive array of beauty products by such upscale designers as Peter Thomas Roth and Jack Black.

CHANEL BOUTIQUE AT THE WILLARD COLLECTION

Map pp292-3   Designer Boutique
☎ 202-638-5055; 1455 Pennsylvania Ave NW;
Ⓜ Metro Center

One of the world's largest Chanel boutiques, this shop inside the classy DC hotel offers the classic designer's signature line of shoes, suits, purses and sunglasses. It's also one of the few major designers to have a shop downtown.

CITY MUSEUM OF WASHINGTON, DC

Map pp292-3   Books
☎ 202-785-2068; 800 Mt Vernon Sq; Ⓨ 10am-5pm Tue-Sun, to 9pm 3rd Thu of month;
Ⓜ Mt Vernon Sq/7th St-Convention Center or Gallery Pl-Chinatown

The museum's unique bookstore has an extensive selection of books on all aspects of DC history, including specific neighborhoods, ethnic groups and historical periods.

FILENE'S BASEMENT

Map pp292-3   Discount Clothing
☎ 202-363-3466; 529 14th St NW; Ⓨ 9am-10pm Mon-Sat, 10am-7pm Sun; Ⓜ Metro Center

If you aren't from the east coast, you probably haven't ever had the privilege of shopping at Boston-based Filene's Basement. This discount store is a bargain-hunter's paradise devoted to men's and women's clothing, shoes and accessories. Unlike discount stores like Ross Dress for Less and TJ Maxx, designer clothes are the norm rather than the exception at Filene's Basement. If you take the time to look hard enough, you can score anything here from Prada to Armani at rock-bottom prices.

INTERNATIONAL SPY MUSEUM

Map pp292-3   Museum Shop
☎ 202-393-7798, 866-SPYMUSEUM; 800 F St NW; Ⓨ 10am-8pm Apr-Oct, 10am-6pm Nov-Mar;
Ⓜ Gallery Pl-Chinatown

Let's face it, every so often everyone needs a pair of reverse-mirrored sunglasses, whether you are being followed or you just want to check out the hottie behind you in the elevator. Now you know where to get them, and piles of other nifty spy gadgets you may need some day. The store claims that such spy paraphernalia is 'bound to make your life, well, more cool,' and who could possibly argue with that? Other Bond-gear that might come in handy includes concealed video and listening devices, disguise kits, micro cameras and recorder pens.

NATIONAL BUILDING MUSEUM

Map pp292-3   Museum Shop

☎ 202-272-2448; www.nbm.org; 401 F St NW; ☽ 10am-5pm Mon-Sat, 11am-5pm Sun; Ⓜ Judiciary Sq

This museum shop is an amateur architect's dream, with small pieces of furniture, rich coffee-table books, paper models of famed buildings, and a collection of books on American and international architecture.

NATIONAL MUSEUM OF WOMEN IN THE ARTS

Map pp292-3   Museum Shop

☎ 202-222-7270; www.nmwa.org; 1250 New York Ave NW; ☽ 10am-5pm Mon-Sat, noon-5pm Sun; Ⓜ Metro Center

This unique institution dedicated to women artists has an equally unique shop. A small room left of the museum entrance, it holds books, prints, posters, jewelry and handicrafts – all created by women.

NATIONAL PLACE

Map pp292-3   Mall

☎ 202-662-1250; 14th & F Sts; ☽ 10am-7pm Mon-Sat, noon-5pm Sun; Ⓜ Metro Center

This little mall has a handful of boutiques and a decent food court. It's not worth a special trip, but it is useful to fulfill some basic needs (eg birthday card, watch band, button-down shirt) if you happen to be in the neighborhood.

OLD POST OFFICE PAVILION

Map pp292-3   Mall

☎ 202-289-4224; 12th St & Pennsylvania Ave NW; Ⓜ Federal Triangle

It's not exactly a shopping center, but it does have a tourist-crowded food court,

as well as souvenir shops, newsstands and stores. It's worth a visit just for a look around the gorgeous central atrium. For more details, see p96.

POLITICAL AMERICANA

Map pp292-3   Political Souvenirs

☎ 800-333-4555; 1331 Pennsylvania Ave NW; Ⓜ Federal Triangle

You'll have to dig a bit, but hidden amid the bland heaps of token Americana trinkets are one-of-a-kind political souvenirs – signed documents by famous statesmen, single-print historical photos and old videos of important moments in American history.

PUA NATURALLY

Map pp292-3   Boutique Clothing

☎ 202-347-4543; 444 7th St NW; Ⓜ Gallery Pl-Chinatown

On the revitalized 7th St gallery strip, Pua Naturally provides a refreshing retreat from staring at art. Instead, women head here to splurge on high-end ethnic clothing, like long flowing skirts and hand-woven jackets from southern Asia.

TOUCHSTONE GALLERY

Map pp292-3   Art

☎ 202-347-2787; www.touchstonegallery.com; 406 7th St NW; ☽ 11am-5pm Wed-Fri, noon-5pm Sat & Sun; Ⓜ Archives-Navy Memorial

One location encompasses several galleries, including the spacious, artist-owned Touchstone Gallery, which exhibits modern art created by its 40 members. Works cover multiple mediums, including cartoonish paintings and brightly colored sculptures.

ZENITH GALLERY

Map pp292-3   Art

☎ 202-783-0050; www.zenithgallery.com; 419 7th St NW; ☽ 11am-4pm Mon, 11am-6pm Tue-Fri, noon-7pm Sat, noon-5pm Sun; Ⓜ Archives-Navy Memorial

Margery Eleme Goldberg's gallery has been an anchor of the DC art scene for several decades, showcasing new and established local and national (and some international) artists. She hosts exhibits of interesting paintings and sculpture, as well as three-dimensional mixed media works – unusual

215

tapestries, fine crafts and furniture, and wearable art.

DUPONT CIRCLE

Dupont is one of DC's most dazzling shopping strips. Most of the action lies along Connecticut Ave, which offers everything from gay bookstores to retro jewelry shops to some of the best vintage boutiques in the city. When the weather is nice, browsing Dupont's varied and eclectic shops can make for a day's activity. When you get tired, pop into one of the myriad coffee shops and bars for a pick-me-up or consolatory martini after maxing out the credit card on designer shoes.

BEADAZZLED

Map pp296-7   Jewelry
☎ 202-265-2323; 1507 Connecticut Ave NW;
Ⓜ Dupont Circle

Crafty types and jewelry lovers should not miss this specialty shop, which carries all things small and stringable. The selection from around the world ranges from 5¢ clay doohickeys to expensive pearls. Helpful staff will tell you how to put them together, and classes are offered on weekends.

BEST CELLARS

Map pp296-7   Wine
☎ 202-387-3146; 1643 Connecticut Ave NW;
Ⓨ 10am-9pm Mon-Thu, 10am-10pm Fri & Sat;
Ⓜ Dupont Circle

For a libation to complete your gourmet feast, go to this elegantly designed vintner's shop. Arranged by taste categories (sweet, fruity, bold) rather than by type, it is helpful for vino novices, particularly since many bottles are under $15. The shelves display fun little wine facts, too, like a Renaissance pope's desire to have his corpse washed in Orvieto.

BETSY FISHER

Map pp296-7   Clothing & Accessories
☎ 202-785-1975; 1224 Connecticut Ave NW;
Ⓜ Dupont Circle

The sales team at this classy women's boutique makes you feel like a queen while trying on fantastic pieces by mid-price designers, such as Diane von Furstenberg

and Max Studio. The best part about this boutique is the effort it makes to include all body types – carrying sizes up to 18.

CANDEY HARDWARE

Map pp296-7   Hardware
☎ 202-659-5650; 1210 18th St NW; Ⓨ 8:30am-6:30pm Mon-Fri; Ⓜ Dupont Circle

This family-owned hardware shop – around since 1891 – is like something out of small-town USA. It survives in transient DC by offering friendly service and everything the locals need around their homes.

CLAUDE TAYLOR PHOTOGRAPHY

Map pp296-7   Art Gallery
☎ 202-518-4000; www.travelphotography.net;
1627 Connecticut Ave NW; Ⓜ Dupont Circle

Claude Taylor's travel photographs are quite good quality, featuring people and landscapes from around the world, and this gallery houses hundreds of his photographs. The photographer has a keen eye for color and composition, and the prints (which come in all shapes and sizes) start at about $100.

DESIGNER ART & CRAFT USA, INC

Map pp296-7   Imported Goods
☎ 202-462-5489; 1709 Connecticut Ave NW;
Ⓨ 10am-10pm; Ⓜ Dupont Circle

Why 'USA' is included in the name of this shop is unclear, as it carries clothing, textiles and jewelry from everywhere else. The selection of pashmina shawls and woven kilims is huge.

DJ HUT

Map pp296-7   Records & CDs
☎ 202-659-2010; 2010 P St NW; Ⓜ Dupont Circle

If you're looking for hard-to-find breakbeat or jungle in vinyl, try this shop. DJ Hut caters to DJs working the turntables, and has a large collection of obscure secondhand and new records, including many funk and hip-hop choices.

EVERETT HALL DESIGNS

Map pp296-7   Men's Designer Clothing
☎ 202-467-0003; 1230 Connecticut Ave NW;
Ⓜ Dupont Circle

Celebs, NBA and NFL stars, and other wealthy types hit Everett Hall's boutique when they're in town. This big-name DC designer does beautiful hand-tailored Italian suits for men, often in bright colors, as well as cutting-edge sportswear and shoes.

GINZA

Map pp296-7   Japanese Homewares
☎ 202-331-7991; 1721 Connecticut Ave NW;
Ⓜ Dupont Circle
Japan is the theme at Ginza. There is a nice selection of beautiful (looking and sounding) indoor fountains, scented candles and other interesting elements of Asian decor.

GUITAR SHOP

Map pp296-7   Musical Instruments
☎ 202-331-7333; 1216 Connecticut Ave NW;
Ⓣ noon-7pm Mon-Fri, 11am-6pm Sat;
Ⓜ Dupont Circle
Although it's the size of a phone booth, this is DC's most impressive instrument retailer and repairer. Around since 1922, this store has serviced Springsteen and Dylan. The dedicated staff is quite helpful in assisting musicians – novice or star – to find what they really need. And you will need help, as the incredibly dense collection ranges from top-of-the-line Martins to off-brand cheapies.

HIMALAYAN HOUSE

Map pp296-7   Imported Goods
☎ 202-223-3366; www.himalayanhouse.com;
Ⓣ 9am-9pm Mon-Sat, noon-8pm Sun; 1319 Connecticut Ave NW; Ⓜ Dupont Circle
This place oozes positive karma, probably because the handicrafts, jewelry and clothing all come straight from Nepal and Tibet. The Tibetan ritual crafts are fun to investigate even if you are not buying.

KRAMERBOOKS

Map pp296-7   Books
☎ 202-387-1400; 1517 Connecticut Ave NW;
Ⓣ 8:30am-1:30am Sun-Thu, 24hr Fri & Sat;
Ⓜ Dupont Circle
With the Afterwords café and bar behind the shop, this round-the-clock bookstore is as much a spot for schmoozing as for shopping. You can listen to live bands, drink a pint, check email for free on the public terminal, and nosh and flirt with

comely strangers (the store is a fabled pick-up spot for straights and gays). This flagship independent – which leapt into First Amendment history when it firmly refused to release Lewinsky's book-buying list to Starr's snoops – features fine current literature, travel and politics sections.

LAMBDA RISING

Map pp296-7   Books
☎ 202-462-6969; 1625 Connecticut Ave NW;
Ⓣ 10am-10pm Sun-Thu, 10am-midnight Fri & Sat; Ⓜ Dupont Circle
This landmark in gay and lesbian DC sells CDs and videos, as well as books. The flyers and free giveaways near its door are a good way to learn about happenings in gay DC.

LAMMAS

Map pp296-7   Women's Books
☎ 202-775-8218; 1607 17th St NW; Ⓣ 10am-6pm Mon-Sat; Ⓜ Dupont Circle
This women's bookstore offers a good stock of lesbian, feminist and spiritual titles.

OLSSON'S BOOKS & RECORDS

Map pp296-7   Books & Music
☎ 202-785-1133; 1307 19th St NW; Ⓣ 10am-10pm Mon-Wed, 10am-10:30pm Thu-Sat, noon-8pm Sun; Ⓜ Dupont Circle
A local chain, Olsson's sells both books and music. Its indie mood is invigorated by a small army of book-obsessed employees ready to offer you great recommendations and opinions.

PHILLIPS COLLECTION

Map pp296-7   Museum Shop
☎ 202-387-2151; 1600 21st St NW; Ⓣ 10am-5pm Tue-Sat, noon-7pm Sun; Ⓜ Dupont Circle
The museum shop has a good collection of posters, pop and scholarly art books, and knickknacks imprinted with famous paintings, such as umbrellas sporting Renoir's *Luncheon of the Boating Party* and Monet water-lily mugs.

PROPER TOPPER

Map pp296-7   Millinery
☎ 202-842-3055; 1350 Connecticut Ave NW;
Ⓜ Dupont Circle
Fedoras, floppy-brimmed picture hats, berets – they're all for sale at the fun

Shopping

DUPONT CIRCLE

Proper Topper, along with wallets, umbrellas, passport holders, cigarette books and a select selection of women's clothing.

SECOND STORY

Map pp296-7   Secondhand Books & Music

☎ 202-659-8884; 2000 P St NW; ⊙ 10am-10pm; Ⓜ Dupont Circle

Up to its eyeballs in dusty secondhand tomes, this Dupont Circle fixture also offers secondhand LPs and CDs, and a small stock of Asian antiques. It's a good place to stop on your way to the local cafés, and an impromptu pick-up scene flourishes among its shelves. It's such a beloved DC institution that Defense Secretary William Cohen wrote a cheesy poem in its honor ('Hieroglyphics heaped/in deep layers of ink…').

SECONDI

Map pp296-7   Secondhand Clothing

☎ 202-667-1122; 1702 Connecticut Ave NW; Ⓜ Dupont Circle

This is our favorite vintage shop in Washington for serious designer retail therapy at rates poor travel writers can afford. Up a narrow row of stairs, Secondi is filled with beautiful Marc Jacobs jackets and slightly loved, but still fabulous, Manolo Blahniks. It's not the cheapest shop in the city, but it has the densest collection of big-name designers. The trick is shopping for killer stuff that's somehow been overlooked – pieces that have been on the rack for more than a month come with reduced price tags.

UNIVERSAL GEAR

Map pp296-7   Men's Clothing

☎ 202-319-0136; 1601 17th St NW; Ⓜ Dupont Circle

Gay men flock here for this season's fashion trends, from hipster athletic-inspired T-shirts designed to show of those rippling abs to dark-wash Diesels perfect for clubbing.

WRITTEN WORD

Map pp296-7   Unique Gifts

☎ 202-223-1400; 1365 Connecticut Ave NW; Ⓜ Dupont Circle

Pick up something special for the writer in your family here. The store sells beautiful

handmade paper sheets, unique journals and greeting cards, along with custom-designed stationery and old-fashioned fountain pens.

ADAMS-MORGAN

Adams-Morgan is much better known for its nightlife than as a shopping area, but if you happen to arrive in the neighborhood a few hours early there are still some stores to distract you. The predominant shopping theme here seems to be funky boutiques, antique shops and stores selling ethnic knickknacks (much of which is pretty junky).

ALL ABOUT JANE

Map pp296-7   Women's Clothing

☎ 202-797-9710; 2438 18th St NW; ⊙ noon-9pm Mon-Sat, noon-7pm Sun; Ⓜ Woodley Park-Zoo/ Adams Morgan

For chic fashion, this popular women's boutique is a great stop. The prices are reasonable and the designs are truly unique – something that's increasingly hard to come by these days. The only downer is that the selection is rather limited.

BRASS KNOB

Map pp296-7   Antiques & Hardware

☎ 202-332-3370; 2311 18th St NW; Ⓜ Woodley Park-Zoo/Adams Morgan

This unique two-floor hardware shop sells 'rescues' from old buildings: fixtures, lamps, tiles, stained glass, mantelpieces, key plates and mirrors. This place is an absolute fantasyland for anybody renovating (or even just living in) an old house or apartment. Staff can help you find whatever you need.

DAISY

Map pp300-1   Women's Clothing

☎ 202-797-1777; 1814 Adams Mill Rd NW; Ⓜ Woodley Park-Zoo/Adams Morgan

This flirty California-style boutique sells jeans to fit every kind of booty. The store stocks designer baby tees and sunglasses from names like Billy Blues and Diane von Furstenberg – designers that are affordable to people collecting less than triple-figure salaries.

FLEET FEET

Map pp296-7   Sports Footwear

☎ 202-387-3888; 1841 Columbia Rd NW;
Ⓜ Woodley Park-Zoo/Adams Morgan

Shoes for every sporting activity are on sale here; service is personalized and staff tries to match customers' feet with their activity of choice.

IDLE TIME BOOKS

Map pp296-7   Secondhand Books

☎ 202-232-4774; 2467 18th St NW; ⏱ 10am-10pm; Ⓜ Woodley Park-Zoo/Adams Morgan

Three creaky wooden floors are stuffed with secondhand literature and nonfiction, including the best secondhand political and history collection in the city. Its sci-fi, sports and humor sections are top-notch, and there's a good newsstand in its front window. A sweet-tempered old cat patrols the upper floors.

KOBOS

Map pp296-7   African Clothier

☎ 202-332-9580; 2444 18th St NW; ⏱ Mon-Sat;
Ⓜ Woodley Park-Zoo/Adams Morgan

Not at all your average clothing shop, Kobos is an African clothier. The Afro boutique carries a good selection of kente cloth, as well as cool tapestries and African music.

OYA MINI BAZAAR

Map pp296-7   Imported Goods & Souvenirs

☎ 202-667-9853; 2420 18th St NW; ⏱ noon-11pm; Ⓜ Woodley Park-Zoo/Adams Morgan

African art and curios are sold at prices only slightly higher than you'd pay on the continent itself. There is a massive collection of West African masks, along with mainstream curios like Washington DC T-shirts.

SHAKE YOUR BOOTY

Map pp296-7   Women's Shoes

☎ 202-518-8205; 2324 18th St NW; Ⓜ Woodley Park-Zoo/Adams Morgan

'Booty' here means boots…and pumps and sandals and any other accessories you might need to hit the town (and then shake your other booty). The footwear here is trendy and fun, but it's only for women.

SKYNEAR & CO

Map pp296-7   Home Furnishings

☎ 202-797-7160; 1800 Wyoming Ave NW;
Ⓜ Woodley Park-Zoo/Adams Morgan

Explore four (count 'em, four!) levels of rooms crowded with 'stressed' armoires, funky sofas and kitschy coffee tables. The stuff is unique and prices are reasonable.

YAWA BOOKS & GIFTS

Map pp296-7   African American Books

☎ 202-483-6805; 2206 18th St NW; ⏱ 11am-7pm Mon-Fri, 11am-9pm Sat; Ⓜ Woodley Park-Zoo/ Adams Morgan

The focus here is on the books – lots of 'em – addressing African American political, social and cultural issues. Sports, spirituality, sex…absolutely nothing is overlooked. There is also a good selection of fiction by African American writers.

SHAW & U STREET

Once a shopping wasteland, this still edgy 'hood is growing hipper by the day. Just five years ago 14th St was known mainly for its streetwalkers, but today the neighborhood houses a whole variety of funky shops selling political schmuck and upscale gag gifts along with a growing number of art galleries and cool secondhand clothing stores.

ANDRE CHREKY

Map pp292-3   Bath & Beauty

☎ 202-293-9293; 1604 K St NW; Ⓜ Mt Vernon Sq/7th St-Convention Center

South of U St, this chic salon is creating a lot of talk among Washington's beautiful crowd. Its stylists and color technicians are versed in this minute's hair trends. You can also indulge in luxurious spa pampering, with a treatment menu that varies seasonally.

GO MAMA GO!

Map pp302-3   Art

☎ 202-299-0850; www.gomamago.com; 1809 14th St NW; Ⓜ U Street-Cardozo

These 'moms with an attitude' offer pottery and art handcrafted by Asian and African artisans. The unique dinnerware is green, blue, cobalt – all clear, strong colors with very simple shapes.

HOME RULE

Map pp302-3   Homewares

☎ 202-797-5544; 1807 14th St NW;
Ⓜ U Street-Cardozo

Tired of Pottery Barn homogeneity around
your house? Check out Home Rule's amus-
ingly original stock: frog-shaped tooth-
brush holders, brightly colored martini
glasses, animal-shaped salt-and-pepper
sets, and rugs and linens, too. The mosaic
decorating the front counter symbolizes
the U St district's revitalization – it's made
with smashed glass from the 1968 riots.

MEEPS FASHIONETTE

Map pp296-7   Vintage Clothier

☎ 202-265-6546; 1520 U St NW; ☺ 4-7pm Tue-
Thu, noon-8pm Fri, 1-6pm Sun;
Ⓜ U Street-Cardozo

This vintage clothier appeals to both boy
and girl denizens of the New U club district with its 1950s and '60s swinger-style
clothes: puffy skirts for dancing, suede-
lapelled blazers, and such accessories as
funky hats and beaded purses. Items are
moderately priced (dresses around $30)
and in decent shape.

PULP

Map pp302-3   Gifts

☎ 202-462-PULP; 1803 14th St NW;
Ⓜ U Street-Cardozo

This quirky, kitschy gift shop has all kinds
of things you were not looking for – funky
frames, funny cards, silly toys, smelly candles, retro art and tons of political gag gifts.
It's a good place to come looking for a gift
(as long as you don't know what you are
looking for).

SHOP POP

Map pp302-3   Clothing & Accessories

☎ 202-332-3312; 1803 14th St NW; ☺ 11am-7pm
Mon-Sat, noon-6pm Sun; Ⓜ U Street-Cardozo

This boutique for women and men features
designers like Ben Sherman and Tipton
Charles. Prices can be high, so check the
sale rack.

UP AGAINST THE WALL

Map pp302-3   Hip-Hop Clothing

☎ 202-234-4153; 2301 Georgia Ave;
Ⓜ Shaw-Howard U

The music-blaring boutique is one of DC's
top funky fashion spots for the hip-hop

SHOPPIN' IN THE SUBURBS: LOCAL MALLS

Several big malls on DC's outskirts draw shoppers in search of chain stores and bargains.

Mazza Gallerie (Map pp290–1; ☎ 202-966-6114; 5300 Wisconsin Ave NW; ☺ 10am-8pm Mon-Fri, 10am-
7pm Sat, noon-5pm Sun; Ⓜ Friendship Heights) This upscale mall is on the Red Line at the Maryland border at
Bethesda. Anchored by Neiman-Marcus and patronized by matrons in search of the perfect cocktail dress, it has
a variety of costly boutiques focusing on women's fashion and jewelry, plus a Williams-Sonoma. Downstairs is a
seven-screen movie theater, but there's no food court. There's a Hecht's department store just across Western Ave
from the mall.

Pentagon City (☎ 703-415-2400; 1100 S Hayes St, Arlington; ☺ 10am-10pm Mon-Sat, 10am-8pm Sun;
Ⓜ Pentagon City) Houses 160 shops, including Macy's, Nordstrom, Gap, a cinema and a food court. It's not
distinguished by anything, but this was where Monica Lewinsky got busted by Ken Starr's troopers back in '98.

Potomac Mills (☎ 703-490-5948; Woodbridge, VA; ☺ 10am-9:30pm Mon-Sat, 11am-7pm Sun) A fire-breath-
ing monster of mid-Atlantic outlet malls, just a half-hour drive south of DC, it features about 250 discount shops,
including Ikea, Saks, Marshall's and Spiegel. This place now draws more tourists (about 24 million per year) and
tour buses than Williamsburg or Virginia's other historic sites, which might say something about Americans'
priorities. Take Exit 158-B off I-95.

Tysons Corner (☎ 703-893-9400; 1961 Chain Bridge Rd, McLean; ☺ 10am-9:30pm Mon-Thu, 10am-10pm Fri &
Sat, 10am-8pm Sun) Further north in Virginia and just west of the Beltway is this gigantic shopping complex that
has, over the years, metastasized into its own strange, sidewalkless suburban Edge City. With about 250 stores,
there are few human needs Tysons can't fill: it has over 20 restaurants, big department stores from Bloomie's to
Nordstrom, and smaller shops from Abercrombie & Fitch to Georgetown Tobacco. The adjacent, swanker complex
has Louis Vuitton, Gucci, Fendi, Chanel and Hermés. You'll need to drive here.

set. It sells baggy jeans, sports jerseys and all the other bling you need to dress like a rapper.

UPPER NORTHWEST DC

Shops are strung out across this corner of the city, although you'll find major clusters near Metro stations on both Wisconsin and Connecticut Aves. The area around the Cineplex Odeon Uptown movie theater (see p195) is a good starting point. Further north, near the Maryland line, Friendship Heights is home to Mazza Gallerie (see Shoppin' in the Suburbs, opposite), a ritzy shopping mall with lots of designer labels and swank decorating. Around here you'll also find branches of discount stores like Filene's Basement (p214).

KRÖN CHOCOLATIER

Map pp290-1   Edible Treats
☎ 202-966-4946; Mazza Gallerie, 5300 Wisconsin Ave NW; Ⓜ Friendship Heights
This shop is known for hand-dipped truffles and amusing novelties, like edible chocolate baskets, milk-chocolate telephones and cars.

NATIONAL ZOOLOGICAL PARK

Map pp300-1   Museum Shop
☎ 202-673-4800; 3001 Connecticut Ave NW; Ⓜ Woodley Park-Zoo/Adams Morgan
The National Zoological Park has several shops on its grounds that sell toys and products featuring all manner of charismatic fauna: ostriches, seals, tigers, wolves, elephants and the inevitable pandas. (Bring home a plastic hyena for less-beloved relatives.) It also has the Zoo Bookstore, in the Education Building on the Connecticut Ave NW side, which has a decent natural-history and field-guide section.

POLITICS & PROSE BOOKSTORE

Map pp290-1   Books
☎ 202-364-1919; 5015 Connecticut Ave NW; ⏱ 9am-10pm Mon-Thu, 9am-11pm Fri & Sat, 10am-8pm Sun; 🚇 L1 or L2
Way up in Northwest DC is a key literary nexus and coffeehouse. This active independent has an excellent selection of literary fiction and nonfiction – it's fiercely

supportive of local authors – plus dedicated staff, high-profile readings and 15 active book clubs.

SULLIVAN'S TOY STORE

Map pp300-1   Toys
☎ 202-362-1343; 3412 Wisconsin Ave NW; 🚇 30, 32, 34 or 36
This independent toy store specializes in European and educational toys that are a nice antidote to the video-game fare of many children's toy stores.

WAKE UP LITTLE SUZIE

Map pp300-1   Gifts
☎ 202-244-0700; 3409 Connecticut Ave NW; Ⓜ Cleveland Park
This funny and original gift shop sells stuff like neon clocks, bright chunky metal-and-ceramic jewelry, polka-dotted pottery, cards and T-shirts. If you have a need for an *Invasion of the Monster Women* lunch box or boxing-rabbi windup doll, Suzie's your woman.

ALEXANDRIA

Alexandria's pretty, cobbled Old Town streets are full of charming shops, heavy on unique jewelry and imported goods.

OLD TOWNE SCHOOL FOR DOGS

Map p311   Pets & Toys
☎ 703-836-7643; 529 Oronoco St; 🚌 Old Town shuttle from King St Metro
Grab a gift for the pooch you left behind at this popular Old Town shop selling everything from organic treats to plush toys. If your puppy is in town, he's welcome inside as well, of course.

TEN THOUSAND VILLAGES

Map p311   Imported Goods
☎ 703-684-1435; 824 King St; 🚌 Old Town shuttle from King St Metro
A unique nonprofit store, Ten Thousand Villages imports handcrafts from developing countries for a fair price, so you won't find any incredible bargains here. On the other hand, the furniture, pottery and textiles are high quality, and you can rest easy knowing your purchase helps to pay for food, education, health care or housing for somebody who needs it.

TORPEDO FACTORY ART CENTER

Map p311   Gallery Shop

☎ 703-838-4565; www.torpedofactory.org; 105 N Union St; 🚌 Old Town shuttle from King St Metro

Built during WWI to manufacture torpedoes, this complex today manufactures art. At the center of a revamped waterfront with a marina, shops, parks, walkways, residences, offices and restaurants, it houses nearly 200 artists and craftspeople who sell their creations directly from their studios.

BETHESDA

Bethesda has quite a few upmarket women's boutiques and eclectic shops selling everything from scarves knitted by Peruvian Indians (with profits going back to the women doing the knitting) to unique wooden furniture and gag gifts. Check out the area around Woodmont Triangle. Bethesda and Woodmont Aves both have loads of stores. If you're lost, look for the giant Barnes & Noble and head out in either direction from there.

MUSTARD SEED

Map p310   Secondhand Clothing

☎ 301-907-4699; 7349 Wisconsin Ave; Ⓜ Bethesda

A Bethesda stalwart, this secondhand clothes shop has been around for decades. Skip the overpriced new clothes displayed up front of the shop and head straight for the better deals in the middle. You have to dig a bit, but you can come up with designer finds.

SANSAR

Map p310   Art

☎ 301-652-8676; 4805 Bethesda Ave; Ⓜ Bethesda

This unique gallery specializes in fine-crafted wooden pieces that are gorgeous and functional – think knotted coffee tables and intricately carved boxes. It also sells objects made from other mediums, many of which are priced to buy for gifts. Even if you're not buying, it's worth browsing.

Sleeping

Sleeping

Tourism is Washington's bread and butter, and the city offers the complete range of accommodations, from dormitory-hostels to historic five-star hotels.

Most DC hotels, particularly upscale chains, have no set rates. Instead, prices vary from week to week and even day to day, depending on season and availability. Hotel rates are generally lower on weekends (Friday and Saturday) than on weekdays. Rates often vary seasonally as well, with peak seasons being late March through mid-July and September through October. Discounts are often available for seniors, children and just about anybody if business is slow, so don't be shy about asking.

Keep in mind that calling the hotel is rarely the best way to find the cheapest rate. When quoting prices, hotels will often offer their rack rate, which is a base rate with no discount or special criteria applied. No smart traveler should ever pay rack rates, however. Better rates are undoubtedly available via hotel websites, and bidding and discount websites (below).

Most of the following sleeping places offer parking. However, it's rarely free. Expect to pay from $15 to $25 per day to keep your car in the city.

BIDDING FOR TRAVEL

In recent years, the internet has revolutionized many aspects of travel, not the least of which is finding and booking hotel rooms. Savvy surfers visit bid-for-booking sites and discount hotel sites before they travel, guaranteeing a significantly reduced hotel room rate. These sites can be used for hotels all over the country – if not the world – so anybody who is online has access to the hotels' cheapest rates. Here are the sites we recommend, and how they work.

www.biddingfortravel.com The goal of this website is to promote informed bidding when using the services of www.priceline.com (see below). Visitors are invited to post their successful bidding history on specific hotels so that others learn the lowest acceptable prices. An administrator monitors the site and can give answers and advice to subscribers who want to bid.

www.hoteldiscounts.com Enter your destination and dates and the website will provide information and prices for hotels with rooms available. You can book through the website at the discounted rate offered.

www.kayak.com This website is rather unique in that it gathers thousands of rates from other discount websites and lets you comparison-shop for the best rates. You don't actually book over the site: instead, if you see something you like you are directed to the host site's booking page. The downside is it can be a bit overwhelming and sometimes prices don't really seem that discounted.

www.orbitz.com Owned by the major American airline carriers. We've been pleased with Orbitz's rates for hotels lately – we used them ourselves when researching this book. If you don't like what you see on Orbitz, other comparable sights are www.travelocity.com, www.hotels.com and www.expedia.com.

www.priceline.com Choose your desired neighborhood, star-rating and price; enter dates and credit card info. If www.priceline.com finds something that meets your criteria, your reservation is automatically booked and you learn the hotel specifics afterwards. There's nothing to stop you from starting very low and gradually increasing your bid so you get the best price possible. We've scored some major deals here in the past, although if you are searching for a hotel in DC in the middle of the week or the summer, you're unlikely to get anything too amazing. Try weekends for the best deals and use the site in conjunction with biddingfortravel.com to find the best rates.

B&Bs

DC has its fair share of B&Bs from the simple room in a private home to private homes turned exclusively into eccentric guesthouses (try the **Mansion on O Street** – p237 – our personal favorite). Many are clustered around Dupont Circle and Adams-Morgan as well as in Upper Northwest.

The following B&B agencies offer rooms in small inns, private homes or apartments starting from around $75 per night. Prices at the luxury guesthouses, however, can be as high as $300. **Bed & Breakfast Accommodations Ltd** (☎ 877-893-3233; www.bedandbreakfast.com) is a good starting point, or try **Capitol Reservations** (☎ 202-452-1270, 800-847-4832; www .capitolreservations.com).

Long-Term Stays

If you're in DC for a while and need a roof over your head, your first option is, of course, the *Post* or *City Paper* classifieds, but you also might try **Roommates Preferred** (Map pp300–1; ☎ 202-965-4004; Ste 136, 3000 Connecticut Ave NW; Ⓜ Woodley Park-Zoo/Adams Morgan) or **Spectrum Apartment Search** (Map p310; ☎ 800-480-3733; www.apartmentsearch.com; 7629 Old Georgetown Rd, Bethesda, MD; Ⓜ Bethesda).

Private Apartments

Rent swapping is another option if you are looking to stay in DC for a week or two and have a place of your own to swap. Check **Craig's List** (www.craigslist.com) to see if there are any apartment or house swaps available. The site lets you search by city and post ads of your own. Another option is **Vacation Rentals by Owner** (www.vrbo.com), which lets you list and search for vacation homes by state and country.

WHITE HOUSE AREA & FOGGY BOTTOM

Sleeping in the president's 'hood has lots of perks even if the areas themselves don't have much 'neighborhood' feeling. The White House Area and Foggy Bottom are full of luxurious, often historic, hotels that usually cater to visiting dignitaries, movie stars and high-profile politicians. If you can afford it, this is a great place to lay your head, as the central location means it's just minutes from some of DC's most popular attractions. Foggy Bottom is slightly cheaper than the White House Area, and has some fun boutique options.

White House Area
HOTEL WASHINGTON

Map pp292-3   Independent $$
☎ 202-638-5900, 800-424-9540; www.hotel washington.com; 15th & Pennsylvania Ave; r from $175; Ⓜ McPherson Sq; Ⓟ ☒ ☒ ☐ ☖
DC's oldest continuously operating hotel has sat just around the corner from the White House since about 1918, and retains the elegance and refinement with which it was built. Newly restored rooms are adorned with marble bathrooms, mahogany furniture, and historic print fabrics and wallpaper (the latter lending a distinctly old-fashioned feel). This family-friendly hotel is most famous for its fabulous view from the rooftop Sky Terrace Lounge. Check the website for seasonal specials.

SOFITEL LAFAYETTE SQUARE

Map pp292-3   Business $$$
☎ 202-730-8800, 800-763-4835; www.sofitel.com; 806 15th St NW; r from $385; Ⓜ McPherson Sq; Ⓟ ☒ ☒ ☐ ☖
In a fabulous corner location with lots of windows, the Sofitel's airy rooms let in loads of natural sunlight (try to reserve one of the 2nd- or 3rd-floor rooms facing 15th or H Sts, they are the brightest). The historic building, erected in 1880, contains 220 modern rooms with plush down comforters and practical perks like high-speed internet access. The hotel theme is French. One child stays free with parents and so do pets! Downstairs are a refined French restaurant and a rather spiffy fitness center.

SCANDALOUS SLEEPS

Scandal never goes out of style, and for some reason it seems to be drawn towards hotels in the same devious fashion that tornadoes always seem to devour trailer parks. The comparison stops here, however. There's nothing even slightly poor about some of these hotels. No, they're the poshest in town. In DC, at least, scandal equals business (there's something inherently sexy about sleeping amid history's most notorious ghosts). These are a few of the best.

Hay-Adams Hotel (below) Ollie North's venue for wooing contributors to illegal contras.

Jefferson Hotel (p237) Where Clinton aide Dick Morris was caught (and photographed) trysting with a prostitute and sharing secrets.

St Regis Washington (below) Ken Starr's investigators got Monica Lewinsky to divulge the story of her presidential tryst here.

Swissôtel Watergate (opposite) Scandal central – from Nixon to Monica.

Wyndham Washington (p235) Where Marion Barry muttered his famous last words, 'Bitch set me up,' after being busted for cocaine.

ST REGIS WASHINGTON

Map pp292-3   Business $$$

☎ 202-638-2626, 800-562-5661; www
.starwoodhotels.com; 923 16th St NW; r from $385;
Ⓜ McPherson Sq; Ⓟ ⊠ ⊠ ▭ ⊕

With crystal chandeliers hanging from the coffered ceilings and Oriental rugs on the parquet floor, the lobby of the St Regis Washington reflects the grandeur of a Renaissance palace. Its 200 rooms and suites have every provision imaginable, from dataports to marble bathrooms, and there's even a butler on each floor. Room No 1012 is famed for being the place where Monica Lewinsky spilled details of her now infamous shenanigans with President Clinton to Ken Starr's investigators. The hotel offers babysitting services and has a fitness center.

HAY-ADAMS HOTEL

Map pp292-3   Business $$$

☎ 202-638-6600, 800-853-6807; www.hayadams
.com; 1 Lafayette Sq; rack rates r from $600;
Ⓜ McPherson Sq; Ⓟ ⊠ ⊠ ▭

This landmark hotel, where 'nothing is overlooked but the White House,' was named for two mansions that once stood on the site (owned by Secretary of State John Hay and historian Henry Adams). In their day, they hosted the political and intellectual elite at Washington's leading salons. Today, it has 145 subtly luxurious rooms, a palazzo-style lobby and a tasteful soupçon of Washington scandal: back in the 1980s, this hotel was a site where Oliver North wooed contributors to his illegal contra-funding scheme.

Foggy Bottom

RIVER INN

Map pp292-3   Boutique $$

☎ 202-337-7600, 800-424-2741; www.theriverinn
.com; 924 25th St NW; r from $150;
Ⓜ Foggy Bottom-GWU; Ⓟ ⊠ ⊠ ▭

On a quiet residential street (despite the name, it's not on the river) a block from the Kennedy Center, this generic-looking brick facility has 126 stylish suites inside. They all have sleek-lined ebony furniture, black-and-white photographs, entertainment centers with Nintendo and video/CD libraries, workstations with dataports, and full kitchens with marble floors. The new American restaurant, DISH, is already popular with the theater crowd. A fitness center and laundry are available. Check the website for special packages.

GEORGE WASHINGTON UNIVERSITY INN

Map pp292-3   Family $$

☎ 202-337-6620, 800-426-4455; www.gwuinn
.com; 824 New Hampshire Ave NW; r from $150;
Ⓜ Foggy Bottom-GWU; Ⓟ ⊠ ⊠ ▭

Set on a quiet tree-lined street, this boutique hotel has guest rooms and suites featuring colonial-style furniture and two-line phones with dataports. While some suites have full kitchens, all rooms include refrigerators, microwaves and coffeemakers. The GW Inn is only a block away from the Foggy Bottom Metro stop, but its immediate vicinity is residential and academic, offering a pleasant retreat from the city. Rates vary widely. When the place is empty, rooms can go for as little as $100, on busy nights expect to pay more than $200.

HOTEL LOMBARDY

Map pp292-3   Boutique $$

☎ 202-828-2600, 800-424-5486; www .hotellombardy; 2019 I St NW; r from $175; Ⓜ Foggy Bottom-GWU; Ⓟ ⊠ 📵 🖳

Done up in funky Venetian decor (shuttered doors, warm gold walls), and beloved by World Bank and State Department types, this European boutique hotel has a multilingual staff and an international mood – you hear French and Spanish as often as English in its halls. Many of the 125 rooms have original artwork, Chinese and European antiques, as well as kitchens and dining areas. On-site are the well-reviewed **Café Lombardy** and the decadent **Venetian Room Lounge** (with a fireplace, tasseled hassocks and velvet banquettes). Fitness buffs will like the workout room.

ONE WASHINGTON CIRCLE

Map pp292-3   Suites $$

☎ 202-872-1680, 800-424-9671; www .onewashingtoncirclehotel.com; 1 Washington Circle; ste from $175; Ⓜ Foggy Bottom-GWU; Ⓟ ⊠ 📵 🖳 📺

At its eponymous address, this sleek, modern all-suite hotel has always attracted high-profile guests; for example, Nixon maintained offices here after the Watergate scandal totaled his presidency. Some of the features of these suites (besides the expected kitchen) are entertainment centers with CD player and Nintendo, and walk-out balconies with views of Washington Circle. Facilities like the sophisticated Circle Bistro and the outdoor pool are also welcome.

MELROSE HOTEL

Map pp292-3   Boutique $$

☎ 202-955-6400, 800-MELROSE; www .melrosehotelwashingtondc.com; 2430 Pennsylvania Ave NW; r from $200; Ⓜ Foggy Bottom-GWU; Ⓟ ⊠ 📵 🖳

A few blocks from the Metro, steps from Rock Creek Park and just over the bridge from Georgetown, this luxury hotel sits on one of Pennsylvania's nicest stretches. The revamped 14-story building has 400 fancy rooms with original artwork, terry

bathrobes, dataports and wireless access. Off the elegant lobby is a bar – the warm, wood-paneled Library – and restaurant, as well as a fine fitness center.

DOUBLETREE GUEST SUITES WASHINGTON DC

Map pp292-3   Suites $$

☎ 202-785-2000; www.doubletree.com; 801 New Hampshire Ave NW; ste from $245; Ⓜ Foggy Bottom-GWU; Ⓟ ⊠ 📵 🖳 📺

This all-suites hotel is a good choice for families or small groups – the one- and two-bedroom digs are large and come with separate sitting rooms, sofa beds and fully equipped kitchen. It gets good reviews for value, and the quiet residential neighborhood is another plus. Pets are allowed.

SWISSÔTEL WATERGATE

Map pp292-3   Legendary $$$

☎ 202-965-2300; www.watergatehotel.com; 2650 Virginia Ave NW; r from $250; Ⓜ Foggy Bottom-GWU; Ⓟ ⊠ 📵 🖳 📺

Here you can lodge in the company of political scandal. Nixon's operatives tried to bug Democratic National Committee headquarters here back in 1972 and famed residents have included Bob Dole and Monica Lewinsky. The hotel is luxurious but, apart from its notoriety, unremarkable. If you are an amenity hound, however, you'll be wowed by the bonuses: a gym with a spectacular indoor swimming pool, great Potomac views and a fine location just downriver from Georgetown. A self-enclosed village of swank – couture shops, the restaurant **Jeffrey's at the Watergate** (p146) – is here, too.

WILLARD INTER-CONTINENTAL HOTEL

Map pp292-3   Legendary $$$

☎ 202-628-9100; www.washington .intercontinental.com; 1401 Pennsylvania Ave NW; r from $250; Ⓜ Federal Triangle

Here, in DC's most history-laden hotel, MLK wrote his 'I Have a Dream' speech; the term 'lobbyist' was coined (by President Grant to describe political wranglers trolling the lobby); and Lincoln, Coolidge and Harding all stayed. Nathaniel Hawthorne observed that it could 'much more justly [be] called the center of Washington…than either the Capitol, the White House, or the State Department.'

Today the very luxuriously restored 1904 beaux-arts hotel – the third to be built on this site – is still favored by powerbrokers, and its chandelier-hung hallways are still thick with lobbyists and corporate aristocrats buffing their loafers on the dense carpets. It offers a gym, business center, concierge, airline and car-rental desks, upscale shops, the Willard Room restaurant and the marvelous Round Robin Bar, which claims to be the birthplace of the mint julep.

GEORGETOWN

Georgetown is one of DC's loveliest neighborhoods and its accommodations options match its character: elegant and expensive. Keep in mind that staying in Georgetown is not convenient to visiting other parts of the city, as the Metro is not close.

LATHAM HOTEL

Map p299   Boutique $$
☎ 202-726-5000; www.thelatham.com; 3000 M St NW; r from $175; 🚍 Georgetown shuttle from Foggy Bottom-GWU Metro; Ⓟ ☒ ☒ ▣ ▣
Hot with visiting celebrities and European jet setters, this chic red-brick boutique hotel in the midst of the M St scene exudes European charm. It has 142 rooms, including two-story Carriage House suites, as well as one of DC's finest restaurants, Citronelle (p150). Chill out on the rooftop sundeck by the pool.

GEORGETOWN INN

Map p299   Romantic $$
☎ 202-333-8900, 800-424-2979; www .georgetowninn.com; 1310 Wisconsin Ave NW; d $175-255; 🚍 Georgetown shuttle from Rosslyn Metro; Ⓟ ☒ ☒ ▣
The blue-blooded Georgetown Inn with a Revolutionary war–period look (think old Europe meets American colonial) is a gorgeous property favored by Georgetown University alumni and parents on college weekends. The inn spreads 95 rooms through a collection of restored 18th-century townhouses and its stately decor (four-post beds, furniture with feet) is matched by stately service.

GEORGETOWN SUITES

Map p299   Suites $$
☎ 202-298-7800; www.georgetownsuites.com; 1111 30th St NW; ste from $175; 🚍 Georgetown shuttle from Foggy Bottom-GWU Metro; Ⓟ ☒ ☒
Although rather soulless, this is a convenient choice for families or longer-term visitors, who will appreciate a private kitchen and studio, and one- and two-bedroom suites. The location, near the C&O Canal, provides a quiet retreat from city congestion.

HOTEL MONTICELLO

Map p299   Boutique $$
☎ 202-337-0900, 800-388-2410; www .monticellohotel.com; 1075 Thomas Jefferson St NW; r $200; 🚍 Georgetown shuttle from Foggy Bottom-GWU Metro; Ⓟ ☒ ☒
An attractive boutique hotel popular with European visitors, Hotel Monticello is just off M St near the C&O Canal. Each of its stylish 47 suites has a fully equipped kitchen, brass-and-crystal chandeliers, Colonial-reproduction furniture and tasteful flower arrangements. A continental breakfast is included in the price of the room, as is parking (a real find in Georgetown).

RITZ-CARLTON GEORGETOWN

Map p299   Luxury $$$
☎ 202-835-0500; www.ritzcarlton.com; 3100 South St NW; r from $350; 🚍 Georgetown shuttle from Foggy Bottom-GWU Metro; Ⓟ ☒ ☒ ▣
Discreetly tucked into the revitalized waterfront of the harbor, the Ritz-Carlton reeks of swankness. Its slick design incorporates the surrounding industrial buildings, including a towering incinerator smokestack and several historic houses: the result is a modern, luxurious but understated setting. Rooms feature feather duvets, goose-down pillows and oversized marble bathrooms; many also offer fabulous views of the Potomac. The hotel bar, Degrees, crawls with white-collars from area offices during happy hour.

FOUR SEASONS HOTEL

Map pp292-3   Boutique $$$
☎ 202-342-0444; www.fourseasons.com; 2800 Pennsylvania Ave NW; r from $375; 🚍 Georgetown shuttle from Foggy Bottom-GWU Metro; Ⓟ ☒ ☒ ▣ ♿

HOT BOUTIQUE & B&B BEDS

No need to stay in a cold, charmless chain hotel, when brilliant boutiques and fabulously original B&Bs are busting out all over DC.

Hotel Helix (p234) The free champagne served every evening may help you swallow the more kitsch elements of this fun pop-art paradise.

Hotel Monaco (p232) Rich architectural details are combined with bright colors, modern furniture, hi-tech facilities and funky artwork in this pet-friendly place.

Jefferson Hotel (p237) Mix with visiting diplomats in this stylish and luxurious place, which also offers the latest hi-tech facilities and friendly staff.

Mansion on O Street (p237) With a different theme for every room and playing host to celebrity functions, this 19th-century mansion is one of DC's most eccentric B&Bs. It also has wheelchair access.

Palomar (p234) Free wine for you and gourmet treats for fido during the complimentary happy hour. In the boldly stylish rooms you'll feel like you're sleeping in your own private art gallery.

Topping most 'best hotels in Washington' lists, the ultra-luxurious Four Seasons Hotel is perched atop Rock Creek Park's south end. This five-star property looks boxy and plain on the outside (it has none of the architectural charms of, say, the Willard or the Sofitel). But inside, the 260 spacious rooms and suites are strewn with antiques; a full-service gym keeps you toned while the day spa pampers with some of Washington's most exotic treatments. The staff is extraordinarily attentive; kids' activities and babysitting provided.

CAPITOL HILL

Capitol Hill can be easily divided into two accommodations areas. The northwest side of the Capitol, bordering Downtown, is an area in which the accommodations options are mainly upscale hotels – most of them are large chain hotels with hundreds of rooms. These places cater mainly to lawyers and lobbyists who have business at the Capitol. By contrast, Capitol Hill itself (east of the Capitol building) is a residential area where accommodations options include many gorgeous Victorian mansions that house B&Bs.

WILLIAM PENN HOUSE

Map p304   Hostel $

☎ 202-543-5560; www.quaker.org/penn-house; 515 E Capitol St SE; r per person $35; Ⓜ Capitol South or Eastern Market; Ⓟ ✗

No drugs or booze allowed, and there is a religious theme throughout, but this is not only one of the cheapest places to stay in the city (and in a prime location at that), it's also clean, and breakfast is included. Family rooms (up to four people) are available for $100 per night. The Quaker-run facility doesn't require religious observance, but there is a religious theme throughout. It also prefers guests be active in progressive causes.

EAST CAPITOL STREET GUESTHOUSE

Map p304   Budget $

☎ 202-328-3210; cnr 6th & E Capitol St SE; r from $60; Ⓜ Eastern Market

In a restored Victorian townhouse this place is nothing fancy, but offers cheap and comfortable rooms with fridge, microwave and coffeemaker. There are six rooms, two of which share bathrooms. Crystal chandeliers and an electric fireplace in the entrance foyer create a lived-in vibe.

CAPITOL HILL SUITES

Map p304   Suites $$

☎ 202-543-6000; www.capitolhillsuites.com; 200 C St SE; ste incl breakfast from $150; Ⓜ Capitol South; Ⓟ ✗ ✗

This 152-room, all-suite property is ideally located in the heart of Hill legislative action. It's the only hotel that is actually *on* the Hill and heavily favored by congressional interns (even a few congressmen and senators rent suites). And no wonder: the place is good value, especially since weekly and monthly rates are available. Rooms are newly renovated and quite chic. All have a kitchen or kitchenette; laundry facilities are on-site. Rates include passes to a nearby gym.

PHOENIX PARK HOTEL

Map p304   Business $$

☎ 202-638-6900, 800-824-5419; www.phoenixparkhotel.com; 520 N Capitol St; r from $150; Ⓜ Union Station; Ⓟ ✗ ✗ 🖥 🕭

If you are not a fan of the American corporate hotel, check out this 'Center of

Irish Hospitality' upstairs from the Dubliner pub. Although it's set in the midst of hotel row, it is homier than the other behemoth options on the block. It has also been a home away from home for visiting Irish politicians like Gerry Adams. The hotel's 150 rooms feature period furnishings, Irish linens, cable TV and computer hookups. Other facilities include a small business center, a gym and laundry. Kids under 16 stay free.

HOTEL GEORGE

Map p304   Boutique $$
☎ 202-347-4200; www.hotelgeorge.com; 15 E St NW; r from $175; Ⓜ Union Station; Ⓟ ☒ ☒ ⌨
George was really the first DC hotel to take the term 'boutique' to a daring, ultramodern new level. The stylish interior features clean lines, chrome-and-glass furniture, and modern art. The 139 rooms have all the niceties, including high-speed internet access, cotton duvets, leather chairs, marble bathrooms and terry bathrobes. Grab a massage in your room or hit the 24-hour gym sauna and steam rooms. It's pet friendly.

HYATT REGENCY WASHINGTON ON CAPITOL HILL

Map p304   Luxury $$
☎ 202-737-1234; http://washingtonregency.hyatt.com; 400 New Jersey Ave NW; r from $220; Ⓜ Union Station; Ⓟ ☒ ☒ ⌨ ⓡ
Previous guests give the Hyatt high marks for friendly service, great location and fair prices. The 834 rooms feature masculine, earthy tones meant for relaxing, although some are starting to show their age. The fitness center and indoor swimming pool have recently been renovated and are quite cool, but you'll be charged an extra $14 per day to use them.

SOUTHWEST & NORTHEAST DC

It may not be DC's most exciting neighborhood, but staying in Southwest has its advantages. Although isolated by highways and waterways, it is remarkably close to the National Mall and the Tidal Basin, which makes for easy access to the major sights. The livelier nightlife is across town, but the waterfront area does boast a few restaurants, the Arena Stage, the colorful seafood market and a pleasant waterfront park.

Northeast DC is pretty far off the beaten track. Parts of it feel like a quiet town in middle America rather than a neighborhood of the nation's capital, other parts are rather dangerous and not recommended for tourists (we haven't listed any places in these areas). The advantages of staying out here are noteworthy: besides the obvious (cheap, cheap, cheap), Northeast also has a friendly local feel that does not exist in many parts of DC. Furthermore, these places are just a few Metro stops past Union Station, a quick easy commute to the center of it all.

HILLTOP HOSTEL

Map pp290-1   Hostel $
☎ 202-291-9591; www.hosteldc.com; 300 Carroll St; dm/d $22/50; Ⓜ Takoma; Ⓟ ☒ ☒ ⌨
Laid-back and super-friendly, this hostel is in the bohemian, politically leftist neighborhood of Takoma Park, in far northeast DC. Set in a century-old Victorian mansion, the hostel is frequented by crowds of backpackers from all over the world. The backyard BBQ and hammock inspire frequent impromptu parties. Nine dorm rooms have four or six bunks and shared bathrooms. Facilities include lockers, laundry, an old-fashioned kitchen, a lounge with TV and free high-speed internet access.

Don't be frightened off by the hostel's distance from downtown: it's across the street from the Metro, which gets you to Capitol Hill in about 15 minutes. Besides, Takoma has its own strip of antique shops and vegetarian restaurants to explore.

THOMPSON-MARKWARD HALL

Map p304   Long-term $
☎ 202-546-3255; www.ywch.org; 235 2nd St NE; r $800 per month; Ⓜ Union Station; ☒
Young women visiting the city on long stays might consider this communal option, which is open to women 18 to 34 who are working or studying in Washington. (In summertime, 90% of its guests are Hill interns.) The minimum stay is two weeks; rates include two meals a day plus Sunday brunch. That's good value, considering the average price of a sublet apart-

ment in Washington, so reserve at least two or three months in advance. All rooms are small, furnished singles with phones, computer hookups and shared bathroom. The mood is like that of an upscale dorm, with a spacious courtyard, sundeck, pretty dining room and sitting areas. Coin laundry is available.

Drawbacks: you can't drink, smoke or bring male guests above lobby level. (Thompson-Markward's second name is The Young Woman's Christian Home but, apart from these rules, you'd never know it.) If you start missing the Y-chromosome set, the Capitol Hill bar scene is just a couple of blocks away.

CHANNEL INN

Map pp308-9   Family $

☎ 800-368-5668; www.channelinn.com; 650 Water St SW; r from $125; Ⓜ Waterfront; Ⓟ ⊠ ⚎ ⚌ ⚐

Overlooking the Washington Channel, this modern hotel features many rooms with balconies facing the water, offering fabulous sunset views. It also has a restaurant and swimming pool. The lively marina, tour-boat operators and giant seafood restaurants drawing tour-bus crowds are all nearby. There is nothing particularly special about the Channel Inn's decor, but the low prices and just-off-the-Mall locale make it a popular choice, especially with families – many rooms come with two queen beds.

DOWNTOWN

With the revitalization of the Penn Quarter and its trendy bars and restaurants, Downtown is becoming a hip sleeping option. The construction of the Convention Center also means it has become hotel central for business travelers. The obvious result is that accommodations are expensive in this area, although there is certainly no shortage of choice.

HOSTELLING INTERNATIONAL – WASHINGTON DC

Map pp292-3   Hostel $

☎ 202-737-2333, 800-909-4776; www .hiwashingtondc.org; 1009 11th St NW; dm incl breakfast members/nonmembers from $32/36; Ⓜ Metro Center; ⊠ ⚎ ⚐

Well organized and centrally located, this HI-AYH hostel has 250 beds (linen provided) in various-sized rooms. Although this neighborhood is not as exciting as, say, Adams-Morgan, it is closer to the action during the day and is convenient to many transportation options. Well-kept facilities include modern bathrooms and kitchen, dining and lounge rooms with big-screen TV, coin laundry, storage lockers and free internet access. A programming office organizes often free and always unique outings: night tours of the monuments, political panel discussions, concerts at the Kennedy Center and the like. The on-site travel office is also helpful and convenient. Reservations highly recommended March to October.

HOTEL HARRINGTON

Map pp292-3   Family $

☎ 202-628-8140, 800-424-8532; www.hotel -harrington.com; 436 11th St NW; r from $115, shared bathroom s/d from $89/99; Ⓜ Federal Triangle; Ⓟ ⊠ ⚎ ⚐

As one of the most affordable options near the Mall, this hotel is popular among school groups, families and international guests. All rooms have cable TV, and there are several restaurants and laundry facilities on-site. The place is not particularly attractive, but it is serviceable and friendly, and good value for the budget-minded.

SWISS INN

Map pp292-3   Family $

☎ 202-371-1816, 800-955-7947; www .theswissinn.com; 1204 Massachusetts Ave NW; r from $115; Ⓜ Metro Center; ⚐

This restored brownstone houses a delightful family-run budget inn. The rooms, which can sleep one to four people, all have a kitchenette, TV, telephone and private bathroom. They are nothing fancy, but they are all crisply clean with sparkling tiles, and new carpeting and windows. One of DC's friendliest, it draws lots of internationals and travelers. Pets and kids are welcome.

HAMILTON CROWNE PLAZA

Map pp292-3   Business $$

☎ 202-682-0111; www.crowneplaza.com; 1001 14th St NW; r $150-250; Ⓜ McPherson Sq; Ⓟ ⊠ ⚎ ⚐

This newly restored 1920s building looks lovely and the rooms inside are nothing to scoff at. They woo guests with 'seven-layer beds,' soft duvets and fluffy feather comforters. Marble bathrooms and royal-blue bathrobes add to the luxury. For practical matters, the rooms have high-speed internet access and CD players. The 24-hour fitness center also has a sauna. Off its lobby, the new restaurant serves contemporary Italian fare and has a pretty patio overlooking Franklin Sq.

HENLEY PARK HOTEL

Map pp292-3   Boutique $$

☎ 202-638-5200; 800-222-8474; www
.henleypark.com; 926 Massachusetts Ave; r $150-
300; Ⓜ Mt Vernon Sq/7th St-Convention Center;
Ⓟ ⊠ ⊠ 🖳

A beautiful Tudor building with gargoyles and stained glass makes a fine setting for this historic hotel. The rooms – decked in flowery prints and brass furniture – are as elegant as the edifice. They are all up-to-date, featuring dataports and dual phone lines, coffeemakers and minibars.

MORRISON-CLARK INN

Map pp292-3   Boutique $$

☎ 202-898-1200, 800-332-7898; www
.morrisonclark.com; 1015 L St NW; r incl breakfast
$150-300; Ⓜ Mt Vernon Sq/7th St-Convention
Center; Ⓟ ⊠ ⊠ 🖳

Conjuring the spirit of the South, this inn is listed in the National Register of Historic Places and often shows up on lists of DC's best hotels. Combining two 1864 Victorian residences, the boutique hotel has 54 rooms and suites furnished with fine antiques, lace, chintz, marble fireplaces, polished wood floors and all modern conveniences. Outside are two shady verandas; inside, the Morrison-Clark Restaurant serves highly praised Southern cuisine.

HOTEL MONACO

Map pp292-3   Boutique $$

☎ 877-202-5411; www.monaco-dc.com; 700 F
St NW; r from $225; Ⓜ Gallery Pl-Chinatown;
Ⓟ ⊠ ⊠ 🖳

The Kimpton Group's Hotel Monaco artfully combines modern and historic in the grand Corinthian-columned, all-marble 1839 Tariff Building. Bold, colorful artwork

and modern furniture blend masterfully in the wood-paneled lobby; funky prints and jewel tones add new life to the arched ceilings and wood molding in the guestrooms. Each room is equipped with a cordless speakerphone, high-speed internet access, luxurious bathrobes and, in case you need company, a resident goldfish. (The hotel is otherwise pet-friendly, by the way, stocking dog-walking maps and offering room service for pets.) The on-site restaurant Poste (p156) is one of DC's hottest.

DUPONT CIRCLE & KALORAMA

Convenient transportation, lively nightlife and endless options make Dupont Circle the ideal destination for sleeping in DC. Shops, restaurants, museums and galleries are all at the doorstep of most hotels and B&Bs in this vicinity. The Metro, too, is easily accessible, as there are several stations in the neighborhood. Kalorama is not quite as convenient, as it lies in the northern part of the neighborhood and further from the Dupont Circle Metro.

BRAXTON HOTEL

Map pp296-7   Family $

☎ 202-232-7800; www.braxtonhotel.com; 1440
Rhode Island Ave NW; r $75-300; Ⓜ McPherson Sq;
Ⓟ ⊠ ⊠ 🖳

Rates vary wildly at this hotel. They're based almost entirely on occupancy, if it's empty you'll get a good room with fluffy white duvets and fresh paint for cheap, if it's full you'll pay more than $100 for one of the small, college dorm-like ones with a depressing hue about them. The Braxton is in a fast growing neighborhood between downtown and Dupont Circle proper and used to look more forlorn. It is under new management now and renovations are ongoing.

BRICKSKELLER INN

Map pp296-7   Guesthouse $

☎ 202-293-1885; brickskl@aol.com; 1523 22nd St
NW; s/d $97/$112, d with shared bathroom $97;
Ⓜ Dupont Circle

Located above the famous saloon by the same name (p175), which carries over 1000 brands of beer from all over the world, the

Brickskeller Inn is a convenient place to retire after imbibing. Rooms are showing their age and are very basic, but on the upside they are clean! All have TV, plus there are coin-operated laundry facilities on the 2nd floor. Still for the location you can't beat the price of less than $100 for a private room (and a great bar downstairs).

INTERNATIONAL STUDENT HOUSE

Map pp296-7   Long-term $

☎ 202-387-6445; www.ishdc.org; 1825 R St NW; dm incl breakfast & dinner from $850 per month; Ⓜ Dupont Circle

This spectacular mansion houses a vibrantly multicultural residence for 100 guests. Residents sign up for at least three or four months of an in-depth experience in international living, but many stay for a year or even longer. Americans as well as international visitors are welcome; most guests are students or interns. Rates include 13 meals weekly (higher rates for single rooms, private bathrooms, parking etc).

Shared facilities include a laundry, a large-screen TV with cable and DVD player, a computer lab with high-speed internet access, a gorgeous library with Tudor accents, plus a lovely walled courtyard.

BED & BREAKFAST ON U STREET

Map pp296-7   B&B $

☎ 413-582-9888; www.washingtonlodging .worldweb.com/BedBreakfasts; cnr 17th & U Sts NW; r $110-250; Ⓜ Dupont Circle; Ⓟ ⊠ 🐾 🖳

With hardwood floors, carved-wood trim, decorative fireplaces and high ceilings, this Victorian-era B&B is comfortable and just minutes' walk from Dupont Circle (it's just north of it, but despite being on U St it is not in the U St neighborhood). The 2nd-floor suite, with a sleeper sofa and sitting room, is a good choice for families – mom and dad even get their own space. The cheapest rooms share bathrooms.

TABARD INN

Map pp296-7   Boutique $

☎ 202-785-1277; www.tabardinn.com; 1739 N St NW; s/d incl breakfast from $150/165, with shared bathroom from $105/120; Ⓜ Dupont Circle; Ⓟ ⊠ 🐾

Named for the inn in *Canterbury Tales,* this delightful, historic hotel is set in a trio of Victorian-era row houses. Its 40 rooms are furnished with vintage quirks, like iron bedsteads, overstuffed flowery sofas and wing-backed armchairs. Down stairs the parlor, beautiful courtyard **restaurant** (p159) and bar have low ceilings and are filled with funky old furniture, highly conducive to curling up with a vintage port and the *Sunday Post.* The Wife of Bath never had it so good.

INN AT DUPONT CIRCLE

Map pp296-7   B&B $

☎ 202-467-6777; www.theinnatdupontcircle.com; 1312 19th St NW; r incl breakfast $110-230; Ⓜ Dupont Circle; Ⓟ ⊠ 🐾 🖳

Once owned by astrologer-to-the-stars Jeanne Dixon, this 19th-century Victorian townhouse is now a friendly and reasonably priced B&B. Rooms have phones, cable TV and fireplaces. The inn's luxuries include a solarium overlooking the garden and a Steinway concert grand piano in the salon. Continental breakfast is included in the price and served in the sunny dining room. A two-night stay is required on weekends. The cheapest rooms share bathrooms.

WINDSOR INN

Map pp296-7   Family $

☎ 202-667-0300, 800-423-9111; www .windsorembassyinns.com; 1842 16th St NW; r from $115; Ⓜ Dupont Circle; Ⓟ ⊠ 🐾

Operated by the same management as the **Embassy Inn** up the street, this pleasant inn has an art-deco lobby, and original 1920s moldings and floor tiles. Its 46 small but very tastefully decorated rooms have private bathrooms, cable TV and phones. In the European tradition, guests receive continental breakfast, and evening snacks and sherry are included.

EMBASSY INN

Map pp296-7   Family $

☎ 202-234-7800, 800-423-9111; www .windsorembassyinns.com; 1627 16th St NW; r from $115; Ⓜ Dupont Circle; Ⓟ ⊠ 🐾

This 38-room place, a couple of blocks east of Dupont Circle, is very solid value with the feel of a small European hotel. The furniture is mostly tasteful reproductions, but the mosaic at the entrance and the marble stairway are originals from 1910. Rooms are pleasantly furnished and have cable TV, phones and private bathrooms. Continental breakfast and an evening sherry are included in the rates.

CARLYLE SUITES

Map pp296-7   Suites $

☎ 202-234-3200, 800-944-5377; www
.carlylesuites.com; 1731 New Hampshire Ave NW;
r from $129; Ⓜ Dupont Circle; Ⓟ ☒ ❌ 🖳 ⬆
The art-deco decor lends a retro air to this
all-suite hotel, but its facilities are modern.
All 170 suites were custom-designed by
a local artist and have full kitchens, TVs,
phones and brightly colored furnishings.
Laundry and health-club facilities are
on the premises. This is a great place for
families: kids under 18 stay free. Head to
the bar to check email (free) and have
a martini (definitely not free but damn
delicious). Book online.

HOTEL PALOMAR

Map pp296-7   Boutique $$

☎ 202-448-1800; www.hotelpalomar-dc.com;
r $130-400; Ⓜ Dupont Circle; Ⓟ ☒ ❌ 🖳 🕮
The newest property in the eclectic Kimpton
stable, Palomar has an 'art in motion' theme
inspired by the 1930s French Modern design-
ers. The rooms look like multi-media galler-
ies, with furniture that resembles modern
art and geometric marble floors. Colors are
bold, objets d'art grace the walls.

We just love how pet-friendly every
Kimpton is. Not only does your pooch get
pampered each night with gourmet treats
at turndown, he can also get a doggie mas-
sage. If he wants to socialize, head to the
Bark Bar, a three-tiered water bar for thirsty
pets just outside the hotel. Humans will dig
the complimentary evening wine recep-
tion in the hotel living room, but there's no
reason to leave Fido upstairs. Drop him off
at the Dish, the hotel's pet lounging area.

BEACON HOTEL & CORPORATE QUARTERS

Map pp296-7   Business $$

☎ 202-296-2100; www.beaconhotelwdc.com; 1615
Rhode Island Ave NW; r $135-300; Ⓜ Farragut
North; Ⓟ ☒ ❌ 🖳
Steve Biko, the concierge at the new
Beacon Hotel and Corporate Quarters,

always recommends room 209 to his
guests. He says you don't get the wet-bar
and kitchen, but what is lost in dining
amenities is made up for in spades by
the floor space – this room is huge with a
separate sitting area. Walk-in rates can be
ridiculously low if the place is empty, so
it's worth passing by.

Spotless rooms are masculine, with
striped bedspreads, muted walls, flat-
screen TVs and a neutral brown-and-tan
color scheme. The martini bar on the roof
is fabulous – there are great city views. If
it's too cold for the rooftop, the cozy bar
in the lobby area is perfect for pints and
watching sport. There is a 24-hour fitness
center.

TOPAZ HOTEL

Map pp296-7   Boutique $$

☎ 202-393-3000, 800-424-2950; www.topazhotel
.com; 1733 N St NW; r from $140; Ⓜ Dupont Circle;
Ⓟ ☒ ❌ 🖳
This Kimpton hotel provides a Zen experi-
ence for its guests – special features range
from the morning power hour (serving
energy drinks) to complimentary daily
horoscopes, to an in-room teapot with
herbal teas. Check out the special Energy
Rooms, private rooms equipped with
treadmills and Stairmasters, or try out the
private Yoga Rooms.

HOTEL HELIX

Map pp292-3   Boutique $$

☎ 202-462-9001, 866-508-0658; www.hotelhelix
.com; 1430 Rhode Island Ave NW; r from $150;
Ⓜ McPherson Sq; Ⓟ ☒ ❌ 🖳
Washington's most fashionable hotel is
as intoxicating as the free champagne
poured during the evening 'bubbly hour.'
A pop-art masterpiece from Kimpton, this
Hollywood-style boutique joint is the kind
of place you'll either love or hate. From
the pink neon lights and sliding doors at
the entrance, to the sign in the gym commanding 'Burn, baby, burn,' to the orange
Barbie-doll throw pillows decorating the
rooms, Hotel Helix is at once playful and
kitschy. Specialty rooms include Bunk
(that's right, bunk beds) and the more
enticing Zone, which features lounge seating and a loaded entertainment center.
Beautifully aromatic Aveda products grace
the bathrooms.

HOTEL MADERA

Map pp296-7   Boutique $$

☎ 202-296-7600, 800-368-5691; www
.hotelmadera.com; 1310 New Hampshire Ave NW; r
from $150; Ⓜ Dupont Circle; Ⓟ ⊠ 📵 💻

Cozy yet cosmopolitan, this boutique hotel
is one of five that Kimpton has opened
in DC in recent years. Besides the usual
amenities, guests can enjoy satin and terry
bathrobes and freshly brewed Starbucks
coffee. The restaurant downstairs, **Firefly**
(p158), is one of Dupont's hottest spots for
dinner or cocktails.

ROUGE HOTEL

Map pp296-7   Boutique $$

☎ 202-939-6421; www.rougehotel.com; 1315
16th St NW; r from $150; Ⓜ McPherson Sq;
Ⓟ ⊠ 📵 💻

Rouge is perhaps the most playful of
Kimpton's DC boutique hotels. Appropriately, the decor is definitively red, with bold
designs, funky furniture and hip posters decorating the rooms. Specialty rooms include,
Chat Rooms with Pentium computers Chow
Rooms with kitchenettes, and Chill Rooms
with Sony Play Stations and DVD players. As
funky as the hotel, **Bar Rouge** attracts a regular
stream of locals, especially for its Thursday
happy hours.

SWANN HOUSE

Map pp296-7   B&B $$

☎ 202-265-4414; www.swannhouse.com; 1808
New Hampshire Ave NW; r incl breakfast $150-305;
Ⓜ Dupont Circle

Set in an exquisite 1883 Romanesque
mansion, Swann House has nine plush
rooms, all with luxurious private bath-
rooms, goose-down pillows, plush bath-
robes, cable TV/VCR, and high-speed and
wireless internet access. The grandest of
them may have a fireplace or a Jacuzzi,
too. In any case, you can sit on the deeply
set brick porch and watch the Dupont
scene, or retire to the privacy of the back
garden with outdoor pool. Afternoon
snacks are included. A two-night stay is
required on weekends.

WYNDHAM WASHINGTON

Map pp292-3   Business $$

☎ 202-429-1700; www.wyndham.com; 1400 M St
NW; r $150-225; Ⓜ McPherson Sq; Ⓟ ⊠ 📵 💻

You gotta feel a little sorry for this place
near Thomas Circle: in its former incarnation as the Vista Hotel, it was where the
FBI busted former Mayor Marion Barry for
smoking crack with an ex-girlfriend. It's
a perfectly decent business hotel despite
that stigma, with high-speed internet access in its 12 floors of generic rooms.

TAFT BRIDGE INN

Map pp296-7   B&B $$

☎ 202-387-2007; www.taftbridgeinn.com; 2007
Wyoming Ave NW; s incl breakfast $150-170, d
$166-186, with shared bathroom s $80-95, d $96-
111; Ⓜ Dupont Circle; Ⓟ ⊠ 📵

Named for the bridge that leaps over Rock
Creek Park just to the north, this beautiful
19th-century Georgian mansion is an easy
walk to Adams-Morgan or Dupont Circle.
The inn has a paneled drawing room,
classy antiques, six fireplaces and a gar-
den. Parking (per day $15) and laundry are
on the premises.

DUPONT AT THE CIRCLE

Map pp296-7   B&B $$

☎ 202-332-5251, 888-412-0100; www
.dupontatthecircle.com; 1604 19th St NW; r incl
breakfast $165-265, ste incl breakfast from $265;
Ⓜ Dupont Circle

This upscale inn is housed in a stately
brick Victorian row house, one block north
of the circle. Its seven fully equipped
guestrooms and two suites are furnished
differently with tasteful antiques from
varying periods – room two is named after
Lincoln, another after Cuba – but all have
private bathrooms with claw-foot tubs
or Jacuzzis. Breakfasts are modest affairs:
muffins, granola and fruit. Check out the
Pinnacle for a special romantic evening:
the inn's newest and poshest suite boasts
22ft ceilings, a stained-glass window,
a giant Jacuzzi for two and flat-screen
plasma TV on a private floor perched at
the very top of the Inn.

MADISON

Map pp296-7   Luxury $$

☎ 202-862-1600; www.loewshotels.com; 1177
15th St NW; r $175-350; Ⓜ Farragut North;
Ⓟ ⊠ 📵 💻

The recent recipient of a $40-million up-
grade, the Madison is looking great these

days. And if you snag the low internet rate, it's quite reasonable. Having hosted every US president since JFK, this is a luxury hotel trying to be a family home – fresh fruit and bottled water is always available; there's a whole floor dedicated to folks traveling with pets (and no deposit or size limit either). Beds sleep firm, too firmly some argue, and come with Frette duvets. As a side note, the Madison is supposedly the first hotel in the world to have introduced the minibar!

WASHINGTON HILTON & TOWERS

Map pp296-7   Business $$

☎ 202-483-3000; www.hilton.com; 1919 Connecticut Ave NW; weekend r from $175; Ⓜ Dupont Circle; Ⓟ Ⓧ Ⓧ Ⓛ

This 1960s-style semicircular structure is a giant hotel with all the amenities you would expect from a Hilton. It is famed as the site of John Hinckley's attempt to assassinate President Ronald Reagan, on March 30, 1981. Hoping to impress the actress Jodie Foster, the disturbed young man shot Reagan, his press secretary and an FBI agent near the T St NW entrance. Hinkley was declared insane at the trial and is now housed at St Elizabeth's psychiatric hospital in Southeast DC. In 2006 he was granted unsupervised weekend visits with his parents. The hotel has since constructed a big protective entryway.

HILTON WASHINGTON EMBASSY ROW

Map pp296-7   Business $$

☎ 202-265-1600; www.hiltonembassyrow.com; 2015 Massachusetts Ave NW; r from $200; Ⓜ Dupont Circle; Ⓟ Ⓧ Ⓧ Ⓛ Ⓡ

Diplomatic visitors favor this luxurious yet reasonably priced hotel, set amid the stately mansions on Embassy Row. Although it is big (193 rooms, 11 floors), it blends modestly into its elegant surroundings. Its rooms have niceties like two phones (one in the bathroom), and there's a rooftop pool with an outdoor bar. Staff members speak six languages.

JURY'S WASHINGTON

Map pp296-7   Business $$

☎ 202-483-6000; www.jurysdoyle.com; 150 New Hampshire Ave NW; r from $200; Ⓜ Dupont Circle; Ⓟ Ⓧ Ⓧ Ⓛ

Smack dab in the center of Dupont Circle, this newly renovated hotel features 314 rooms, a fitness center, valet parking and the excellent Dupont Grill. Rooms have all the expected amenities, including dataports.

PARK HYATT

Map pp296-7   Business $$

☎ 202-789-1234, 800-233-1234; www .parkwashington.hyatt.com; 1201 24th St NW; r from $200; Ⓜ Foggy Bottom-GWU; Ⓟ Ⓧ Ⓧ Ⓛ Ⓡ

Occupying almost the entire 1200-block of 24th St midway between Dupont Circle and Foggy Bottom, this massive hotel has lots of quiet lounge space and hundreds of luxurious rooms. So crisply fresh that they smell like new cars, the rooms offer every amenity (even TVs in the bathrooms). A full gym and swimming pool are on-site. Downstairs, Melrose is among DC's best hotel restaurants.

RENAISSANCE MAYFLOWER HOTEL

Map pp292-3   Luxury $$

☎ 202-347-3000; www.renaissancehotels.com; 1127 Connecticut Ave NW; r from $200; Ⓜ Farragut North; Ⓟ Ⓧ Ⓧ Ⓛ Ⓡ

J Edgar Hoover dined here; Richard Nixon resided here; and there are rumors that John F Kennedy sampled the charms of the fairer sex here. Although not the exclusive enclave it once was, this hotel remains regal with lots of frills and marble, and a beautiful grand ballroom. Plus it just completed a $10-million renovation, which means the rooms at this historic landmark are looking more modern and classy than ever. High tea in the lounge-like hotel restaurant is great.

WESTIN EMBASSY ROW

Map pp296-7   Business $$

☎ 202-293-2100, 888-625-5144; www.westin.com; 2100 Massachusetts Ave NW; r from $205; Ⓜ Dupont Circle; Ⓟ Ⓧ Ⓧ Ⓛ

Appropriate to its name and locale, this international-looking hotel has a majestic, flag-draped, Georgian entrance. Interior decor retains suave touches of the 1920s, when the hotel was built, and the 200 rooms have both lovely old-fashioned elements (cozy down pillows, overstuffed furniture) and modern ones (dataports, cable TV, honor bars).

JEFFERSON HOTEL

Map pp296-7   Boutique $$

☎ 866-270-8118; www.thejeffersonwashingtondc .com; 1200 16th St NW; r from $250; Ⓜ Farragut North; Ⓟ ⊠ ⌘ ⌷

Travel & Leisure magazine just rated this luxury boutique one of the best 500 hotels in the world. An elegant, two-winged 1923 mansion, it has an ornate porte cochere, beaux-arts architecture, and a luxurious interior full of crystal and velvet. Favored by diplomatic visitors, its 100 antique-furnished rooms have dual-line speakerphones, CD players, VCRs, computer hookups, faxes and black-marble bathrooms. Despite all the glitz, the staff is friendly and helpful.

MANSION ON O STREET

Map pp296-7   B&B $$

☎ 202-496-2020; www.omansion.com; 2020 O St NW; r incl breakfast from $250; Ⓜ Dupont Circle; ⊠ ⌘ ♿

It doesn't advertise. It doesn't even have a sign or a brochure. But this place has quite a reputation anyway – it's just about the most flamboyant, original B&B around. Housed in a 100-room 1892 mansion (a remnant of the days when Dupont was a millionaires' neighborhood), it is part inn, part gallery-performance space and part private club. In this latter incarnation, the Mansion has hosted Hollywood celebrities and Chelsea Clinton's sweet-16 party. Its owner, grande dame HH Leonards, has done the place up like a wedding at Castle Dracula: swags of velvet drapery, ornate chandeliers and lampshades, candelabras and concealed doorways. No two rooms, from the Russian Tea Room to the Log Cabin to the Billiards Suite, are alike, and everything from the bedstead to the pictures is for sale. This is one of the few inns in the area offering wheelchair-accessible rooms.

FAIRMONT WASHINGTON DC

Map pp296-7   Luxury $$$

☎ 202-429-2400; www.fairmont.com; 2401 M St NW; r from $300; Ⓜ Foggy Bottom-GWU; Ⓟ ⊠ ⌘ ⌷ ⌘

This West End option is one of the best luxury bets in Washington, and it gets high accolades from past guests for its prime location – it's just a short stroll from Georgetown's shops. The spacious rooms are light and airy, but the bathrooms, featuring Botticino marble, deluxe toiletries and orchid sprigs, really stand out. So does the aesthetically pleasing courtyard filled with flowers. The full health club features a lap pool and ball courts.

RITZ-CARLTON

Map pp296-7   Luxury $$$

☎ 800-241-3333; www.ritzcarlton.com; 1150 22nd St NW; r incl breakfast from $350; Ⓜ Farragut North; Ⓟ ⊠ ⌘ ⌷ ⌘

Defining standards of luxury, DC's first Ritz-Carlton offers its guests 300 spacious rooms with lots of little perks: goose-down pillows, marble bathrooms, dataports with high-speed internet access, and portable phones. The hotel allows access to the Sports Club/LA, a huge spa and fitness center. Special weekend packages throw in treats such as rental of a Mercedes-Benz.

ADAMS-MORGAN & SHAW

This colorful neighborhood offers its temporary residents an endless array of nightlife options, including restaurants and bars, music and dancing.

Since the area is primarily residential, accommodations are all B&Bs, and they are set on quiet tree-lined streets with friendly neighbors.

The disadvantage is the lack of public transport – it's a 15-minute walk to the nearest Metro.

WASHINGTON INTERNATIONAL STUDENT CENTER

Map pp296-7   Hostel $

☎ 202-667-7681, 800-567-4150; www .washingtondchostel.com; 2451 18th St NW; dm/s incl breakfast $23/56; Ⓜ Woodley Park-Zoo/Adams Morgan

This place was closed following a fire when we stopped by, so check the website to see if it's up and running again. In the past it was the spot for young travelers who want to be right in the midst of 18th St's swarming entertainment strip. We bet it will be again soon.

KALORAMA GUEST HOUSE

Map pp296-7   B&B $

☎ 202-667-6369; 1854 Mintwood Place NW; s/d incl breakfast from $75/105, with shared bathroom from $60/70; Ⓜ Woodley Park-Zoo/Adams Morgan; ⊠ ⊠

This Victorian townhouse is a couple of blocks west of 18th St and was among Washington's first B&Bs. Its 31 rooms have Oriental rugs, down comforters and turn-of-the-century art. The friendly atmosphere encourages a devoted band of return guests. Continental breakfast and an afternoon sherry are served in the parlor.

ADAM'S INN

Map pp296-7   B&B $

☎ 202-745-3600, 800-578-6807; www.adamsinn .com; 1744 Lanier Place NW; r incl breakfast $113; Ⓜ Woodley Park-Zoo/Adams Morgan; ⊠ ⊠

Recommended by the popular *Today* show in 2006 as one of the city's best-value sleeping bets, this place is seeing plenty of business these days. The owner (and yes, his name really is Adam) converted two adjacent townhouses and a carriage house on a shady residential street into an inviting and homey guesthouse.

The 25 walk-up rooms are comfortably furnished. The pleasant common areas include a nice garden patio with picnic table, a living room with a TV, a computer room with free high-speed internet access, and laundry and kitchen facilities.

UPPER NORTHWEST DC

The accommodations options in Upper Northwest DC are clustered around Woodley Park. This area offers easy access to transport. There are also many restaurants, as well as some good nightlife, in the immediate vicinity.

KALORAMA GUEST HOUSE AT WOODLEY PARK

Map pp300-1   B&B $

☎ 202-328-0860; 2700 Cathedral Ave NW; r incl breakfast $75-135, with shared bathroom $60; Ⓜ Woodley Park-Zoo/Adams Morgan; ⊠ ⊠

This sister to the Kalorama Guest House (above) in Adams-Morgan is a cozy 1910 Victorian row house with 19 antique-furnished rooms. Additional facilities are in another

property down the street. In winter guests are served sherry in the evenings; in summer fresh lemonade is poured throughout the day. Laundry and kitchen facilities are on-site.

WOODLEY PARK GUEST HOUSE

Map pp300-1   B&B $

☎ 202-667-0218, 866-667-0218; www .woodleyparkguesthouse.com; 2647 Woodley Rd NW; r incl breakfast $165-205, with shared bathroom $100; Ⓜ Woodley Park-Zoo/Adams Morgan; Ⓟ ⊠ ⊠

This elegant 1920s-era home is a beautiful, historic B&B that is excellent value. Seventeen sunny rooms have antique furniture, hardwood floors and white coverlets. The very wide and welcoming front porch is a wonderful place to sit out a hot summer afternoon. The owners are friendly and it sees many return guests.

ARLINGTON & ALEXANDRIA

A comfortable bed in Virginia costs less than one in DC. Loads of chain hotels are clustered around Ballston, Crystal City and National Airport. Pick one near a Metro and it's almost as convenient as staying in the city. This is especially true if you have your car – parking in the city costs upwards of $30 per day at hotels, while most in Arlington offer it for free.

Old Town Alexandria offers a trade-off: Metro is not in the immediate vicinity and prices are higher, but the charming neighborhood makes it worth it. Virginia room tax is about 10%.

Arlington

DAYS INN CRYSTAL CITY   Family $

☎ 703-920-8600; www.daysinn.com; 2000 Jefferson Davis Hwy; r incl breakfast from $80; Ⓜ Crystal City; Ⓟ ⊠ ⊠ ▯ ▣

Just a mile from Ronald Reagan Washington National Airport, Days Inn is an affordable accommodations option if you need to be near the airport. The traditionally decorated rooms are very spacious and comfortable. The hotel's facilities include a fitness center and outdoor swimming pool, as well as free parking. Book through an online consolidator for the cheapest rates.

KEY BRIDGE MARRIOTT

Map p299   Business $

☎ 703-524-6400; www.marriott.com; 1401 Lee Hwy; r from $80; Ⓜ Rosslyn; Ⓟ ⊠ 🏢
Located on the banks of the Potomac, this place is almost as good as staying right in Georgetown – the difference is you are closer to the Metro and you can enjoy a lovely view of the university campus from your room. Georgetown is a 20-minute walk across the Francis Scott Key Bridge. The immediate area around the hotel is a bit sterile, but you can't beat the easy access to the George Washington Memorial Parkway and public transportation. Book online for the best rates – try www.orbitz.com.

RITZ-CARLTON PENTAGON CITY

Business $

☎ 703-415-5000; www.ritz-carlton.com; 1250 S Hayes St; r from $125; Ⓜ Pentagon City; Ⓟ ⊠ 🏢 💻 📷
Staying at the Ritz in Pentagon City is almost better than staying in DC proper, because the rooms allow you to look out your window and enjoy fabulous views of the city, which you certainly can't do if you are in the middle of it. You will also appreciate cordless phones, plush terry bathrobes and comfy feather beds. The state-of-the-art fitness facility includes a heated lap pool, steam room and sauna, and massage therapy. Oh, and the rates are much, much lower, too!

Alexandria

ALEXANDRIA TRAVEL LODGE

Map p311   Motel $

☎ 703-836-5100; 702 N Washington St, Alexandria; r $60-100; 🚐 Old Town shuttle from King St Metro; Ⓟ ⊠ 🏢
This motel – on a busy section of Washington St – is about a mile north of Old Town's historic district. It is a good bet for budget travelers who have their own car; parking is free. Basic clean rooms have TVs, telephones and full bathrooms. Amenities are otherwise limited, but you can't beat the price.

HOLIDAY INN SELECT OLD TOWN

Map p311   Family $

☎ 703-549-6080; www.holiday-inn.com; 480 King St; r from $85; 🚐 Old Town shuttle from King St Metro; Ⓟ ⊠ 🏢 💻 📷 🏊
The reliable, universal standards of Holiday Inn do not disappoint here, at the most affordable option in Old Town Alexandria. Enjoy an indoor and outdoor pool and a nice fitness facility with a Jacuzzi. Rooms feature high-speed internet access and some have a balcony overlooking a lovely central courtyard. Pets and kids are welcome!

MORRISON HOUSE

Map p311   Boutique $$

☎ 703-838-8000; www.morrisonhouse.com; 116 S Alfred St; r from $165; 🚐 Old Town shuttle from King St Metro; Ⓟ ⊠ 🏢
In the heart of Old Town Alexandria, Morrison House captures the neighborhood's charm in its Georgian-style building and the Federal-style reproduction furniture.

This boutique hotel offers the service and amenities of a luxury hotel: terry bathrobes and high-speed internet access for every room. Rooms are beautifully decorated, especially the elegant library, where afternoon tea is served.

The kicker here is the service of a butler to cater to your every whim, any time of day or night. The on-site restaurant is well respected.

Excursions

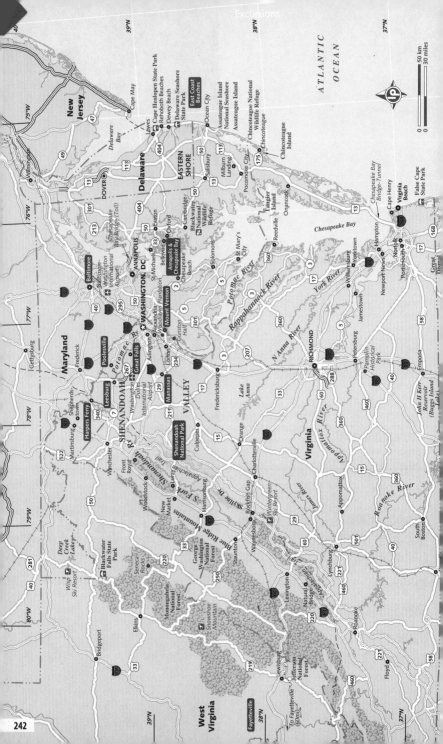

Excursions

If you picture the Capital Region as a giant artichoke, then Washington, DC, would surely be the heart. But even though the nation's capital yields the greatest chunk of meat, the rest of the region still packs in plenty of flavor.

Beyond DC limitless adventures await. Maryland is a snapshot of America and all its treasures. Blue collar-Baltimore offers boundless partying, while the Chesapeake Bay has loads of cherished maritime heritage explorations. There's swimming in the warm waters of the Atlantic beaches, wild-pony watching on windswept islands and fistfuls of famous Maryland blue crabs to eat. The world-renowned sailing center of Annapolis and numerous fishing communities along the bay's fringe are other must-sees.

Virginia's Blue Ridge Mountains offer hikes through lush green forests and over rolling blue hills. Here you'll find the beautiful Shenandoah Valley along with charming small towns such as Manassas and Leesburg and important Civil War battlefield historic sites.

AMERICAN HISTORY

The outskirts of DC have no shortage of historic sites in the near vicinity. George Washington's magnificent estate at **Mount Vernon** (p246) is an easy half-day trip from the city, as is **Manassas** (p247), the site of the first major Civil War battle and a shining example of old-fashioned America. The Colonial town of **Leesburg** (p247) is one of the oldest settlements in the area – the old town is still an easy charmer, but avoid it during rush hour when the roads are clogged with miles upon miles of commuters. The towns on the **Chesapeake** (p255) – such as Annapolis and St Michaels – are less touristy and preserve their maritime history with harbors that have been bustling for hundreds of years, and with old mansions overlooking the bay.

LOCAL SECRET: POOLESVILLE IN OCTOBER

When the leaves turn in October, it's time to head to the country. Our favorite escape is around Poolesville, MD. Shouting distance from DC, it's horse country. Home to acres of fields interspersed by tidy white barns and thick groves of trees.

Homestead Farm (☎ 301-926-6999; www.homesteadfarm.com; 156000 Sugarland Rd; ✹ 8am-6pm late-May-Oct 31), about 20 minutes west of DC off River Rd, is a perfect first stop. The family-run farm opens in late May, just in time for the summer fruit picking season – everything is available for self-picking, and the farm market sells a big selection of jams, pickles, local honey and, in autumn, delicious caramel apples. The place really shines in October, though, when you can take a hayride out to the pumpkin patch to pick your own giant orange squash or crunchy red apples.

The farm is set on 230 acres along Seneca Creek, on which the Allnut family has been homesteading since 1763.

After the sun sets, embark upon Washington's other favorite fall activity: getting scared witless in the middle of nowhere. **Markoff's Haunted Forest** (☎ 301-216-1248; 19222 Martinsburg Rd, Dickerson, MD; admission $15; ✹ dusk-9pm Mon-Thu & Sun, to 10:30pm Fri & Sat Oct 13-31) is the perfect place to get into the Halloween spirit (this is the area where the late-1990s cult thriller the *Blair Witch Project* was filmed), and Washingtonians have been making the trek out to the woods since the early 1990s.

Named for its founder, Adam Markoff, the annual scare-fest attracts people from all over the metropolitan area. They come to wander around a dark forest for 25 minutes while a host of professional spookers scare the living daylights out of them – expect everything from headless horsemen to chainsaw-wielding crazies with enough fake blood to drown DC. The event is aimed more at teenagers and adults than small children, who will probably find it slightly too terrifying.

Both Homestead Farm and the Haunted Forest can be reached from DC by taking River Rd north until it ends. Make a left when River Rd dead-ends and follow the signs for Homestead Farm. To reach the Haunted Forest, turn right on Partnership Rd from Seneca Rd and follow it through Poolesville until you reach Martinsburg Rd, where you should turn right (everything is clearly marked).

BEACHES

Nothing relieves the hellish heat and humidity of DC summers like a trip to the beach. Fortunately, the Atlantic coast of Virginia, Maryland and Delaware offers a wide variety of options. Pristine **Assateague Island** is protected by the National Park Service and is void of any development. It is accessible from two towns that are complete opposites in character: quiet **Chincoteague** in the south and party town **Ocean City** in the north. Delaware's beach resorts fall somewhere in the middle of this spectrum. **Rehoboth** and **Dewey** are fun family towns with a lively bar and club scene and a built-up beach. Rehoboth is also the local gay beach. The protected **Delaware Seashore State Park** is also nearby. See East Coast Beaches (p257) for more information.

PARKS & WILDLIFE

Your choice here will be determined by the time you have available. If you can only spare a few hours, **Great Falls** (opposite) is a wonderful waterside getaway, less than 20 miles northwest of the city. It stretches across both sides of the Potomac, but on the Maryland side the falls are part of **C&O Canal National Historical Park**, which is fabulous for easy hiking and bicycling. If you have a day or more, head west to the wonderful forested hills of **Shenandoah National Park** (p252) with its curvaceous mountains of purple and blue, making sure to linger along the fantastic

---

WEEKEND GETAWAY: A DIFFERENT KIND OF APPALACHIAN ADVENTURE

Adventure addicts pack your bags and hit the road, 'cause we're taking you on a trip. You'll need three days (two nights) for this excursion – more if you really want to get into the thick of things – but if you're craving more than the generic walk in the park, you won't be disappointed.

The destination is **Fayetteville**, WV, in the southern portion of the state, about five hours (300 miles) from DC. The fastest route is I-66 West to I-81 South. Turn off at I-64 West and follow it to I-60 West. We'd suggest getting off the highway at some point, however, and taking some time to drift down long-forgotten byways that meander through the heart of the state. Often the brunt of city-dwellers' jokes, the people of West Virginia's Appalachia have seen hard times since the coal-mining industry collapsed almost a century ago. Poor and rugged towns feature peeling paint and sagging porches, but plenty of character. Don't judge a place on a first drive through; get out and wander around. In quintessential small-town America you'll discover kind-hearted folks, hear strains of dulcimer and fiddle in the air, and discover run-down bars ready to quench your thirst and hunger with cold beer and a burger.

Once a sleepy blue-collar town, Fayetteville is the new adrenaline-junkie hotspot deep in the heart of Appalachia, and a mecca for white-water rafting (not to mention hiking, mountain biking and cross-country skiing). It's here you will find the New and Gauley Rivers, which offer some of the best Class V rafting in the country – the Gauley is ranked one of the top 10 rivers in the world. On the Lower New (the best stretch of the New for adventurous types) you'll encounter the first rapid just after put-in, and they'll keep coming for the next three hours. At one point the river drops 32ft in less than a quarter mile.

The best of the Gauley is rafted on select dates in September and October, which also means you will get some visuals in the form of red and orange foliage. During this time an immense amount of water is released from Summersville Dam to create stomach-churning world-class white-water. Trips fill up fast, so booking ahead is advised. It's cheaper to raft the New during the week when trips cost $50. The Gauley starts at $70.

Among the many state-licensed rafting outfitters in the area, **USA Raft** (☎ 800-872-7232; www.usaraft.com; Appalachian Dr, Fayetteville; trips from $50) stands out.

For sleeping try **Hawk's Nest State Park** (☎ 304-658-5212; Hwy 60; r from $70), northwest of Fayetteville. It offers views from its rim-top lodge; in summer it operates an aerial tram down to the river, where you can catch a cruising boat ride (tram closed Monday). **Elliot's Whitewater Grill** (☎ 304-574-3443; Laurel Crescent & Rte 19; dishes $9) is a good place to replenish and relax after rafting.

Between Hinton and Fayetteville you'll find 63,000 acres of stunning landscape protected at the **New River Gorge National River**. The 1000ft-deep gorge is the dramatic setting for the rafting on the New River. At one point the river falls 750ft in 50 miles, creating the New's best sets of rapids. The crowning manmade attraction is the gorge bridge. It's the second highest bridge in the US and the longest single-arch steel bridge in the world. The **Canyon Rim Visitors Center** (☎ 304-574-2115; US Rte 19 at Fayetteville) is the best place to view the bridge. Rim and gorge trails offer beautiful views. There are four free basic camping areas; for more info on camping, head to the visitors center.

Skyline Dr. Further afield, in West Virginia, there are outdoor adventures to be had in **Harpers Ferry** (p254) and some kick-your-ass-down-the-river whitewater near **Fayetteville** (opposite).

GREAT FALLS

Fourteen miles upriver from DC's Georgetown, where the central Piedmont meets the coastal plain, the normally placid Potomac cascades 77ft down a series of beautiful, treacherous rapids known as Great Falls. The Chesapeake & Ohio (C&O) Canal was constructed to allow barges to bypass the falls. Today there are parks on both sides of the river providing glorious views of the falls, as well as hiking, bicycling and picnicking spots. (The entry fee is good for three days at both parks.) The Maryland side hooks up to Georgetown via the **C&O Canal Towpath** (p82), which is an excellent route for a bicycling trip (it's not paved).

On the Virginia side, the falls lie in the 800-acre **Great Falls National Park**, in the northern part of the George Washington Memorial Parkway in McLean. Several miles of trails wind through the woods and along the falls. In 1785 George Washington's Patowmack Company built a canal here to circumvent the falls – a 0.75-mile stretch of it remains, and you can explore what's left on foot. You can also hike among the ruins of Matildaville, a trading town that died in the 1820s as canal business declined.

On the Maryland side, the falls are part of **C&O Canal National Historical Park**, the entrance of which is in the sprawling, wealthy suburb of Potomac. **Great Falls Tavern**, built in 1828, holds the park visitors center, which features exhibits on how the canal locks work. The *Clipper,* a mule-drawn barge, cruises the canal, departing from here several times a day.

From the tavern, a half-mile walk down the towpath and across a series of bridges to **Olmstead Island** leads to the falls overlook, which offers a beautiful view of rugged rock and roaring rapids. (The whitewater is dangerous, so keep kids close.) For serious scramblers, the 2-mile **Billy Goat Trail** traverses mountainous rock crags, and the towpath provides an easy loop back. Other easy loop trails lead through the woods past the remains of gold-mine diggings, prospector's trenches and overgrown Civil War earthworks.

Three miles further up the river, **Swains Lock** was operated by the Swain family for generations. Jesse Swain was lock-tender from 1907 until the lock closed in 1924. Today his grandson Fred runs **Swains Boathouse**, which rents out bicycles, canoes, kayaks and boats. He also sells fishing tackle and bait, and oversees a hiker/cyclist campground for towpath through-travelers.

The Great Falls area is ideal for day trips (there aren't any accommodations options in the area).

TRANSPORTATION

Distance from Washington, DC 14 miles.

Direction North.

Travel time 20 minutes.

Bicycle Pick up the C&O canal path anywhere in Georgetown and head north.

Car To reach the C&O National Historic Park on the Maryland side, take Canal Rd out of Georgetown, then MacArthur Blvd to its end. For Great Falls National Park in Virginia, from I-495 take exit 13 to Georgetown Pike. Drive 4 miles to Old Dominion Dr and turn right to enter the park.

DETOUR

Twenty miles upriver from Great Falls, **White's Ferry** (☎ 301-349-5200; 24801 Whites Ferry Rd, Dickerson, MD; cars one way/round-trip $4/6, bikes 50¢; ⏰ 5am-11pm) is the last of the many ferries that once plied the Potomac. It's a nice way to hop from the Maryland to the Virginia shore, particularly if you're headed for historic Leesburg, which is just 4 miles west of here. A general store on the premises rents out canoes (call for prices) and there are shady, grassy picnic places by the Potomac. The river here is safe for swimming; however, the current can be quite strong, so don't venture out too far. While we were crossing with the ferry two swimmers got too close and were sucked under – they were fine, but you need to be careful.

Sights & Information

Great Falls National Park (VA) (☎ 703-285-2966; www
.nps.gov/gwmp/grfa; car/walker $5/3; ☒ park 7am-dusk,
visitors center 10am-5pm Jun-Aug, 10am-4pm Sep-May)

**Great Falls Tavern (C&O Canal National Park Great Falls
Visitors Center)** (☎ 301-767-3714; www.nps.gov/choh;
11710 MacArthur Blvd, Potomac, MD; car $5, walker & cyclist
$3, barge ride adult/child/senior $8/5/6; ☒ 9am-5pm)

Swains Boathouse (☎ 301-299-9006; canoes & kayaks
per hr/day $8.50/20, bike rental per hr/day $5.50/12.75;
☒ 10am-6pm May-Sep, 10am-4pm Fri-Sun Oct-Nov & Apr)

Eating

L'Auberge Chez Francois (☎ 703-759-3800; 332
Springvale Rd, Great Falls, VA; dinner $50 ☒ 5:30-
9:30pm Tue-Sat, 5:30-8pm Sun) One of the Washington
area's best restaurants. French-Alsation cuisine is served.
Reservations required.

Old Angler's Inn (☎ 301-365-2425; 10801 MacArthur
Blvd, MD; dinner $40-50; ☒ noon-2:30pm & 6-9:30pm)
This longtime local first choice in the southern tip of the
park has been feeding hungry hikers since 1860.
Reservations recommended.

MOUNT VERNON

A visit to George Washington's Virginia
home, **Mount Vernon**, is an easy escape from
the city – one that the president himself
enjoyed. It's also a journey through history: the country estate of this quintessential gentleman has been meticulously
restored and affords a glimpse of rural
gentility from a time long gone. On the
Potomac banks, the 19-room mansion displays George and Martha's Colonial tastes,
while the outbuildings and slave quarters
show what was needed for the function-
ing of the estate. George and Martha are
both buried here, as requested by the first
president in his will.

In the town of Mount Vernon, **Woodlawn
Plantation** features two very different houses
that are both splendid examples of their
architectural times. The plantation home
itself once belonged to Eleanor 'Nelly' Custis, granddaughter of Martha Washington,
and her husband, Major Lawrence Lewis,
George Washington's nephew. The house
contains period antiques and a stunning
rose garden.

Also on the grounds, architect Frank
Lloyd Wright's **Pope-Leighey House** is a 1940s
Usonian dwelling of cypress, brick and
glass. Originally intended as low-cost

TRANSPORTATION

Distance from Washington, DC Mount Vernon 18
miles; Woodlawn Plantation 18 miles; Gunston Hall
23 miles.

Direction South.

Travel Time 30 minutes.

Bicycle From the Key Bridge or Arlington Cemetery,
take the George Washington Memorial Parkway
trail south.

Boat The cruise ship **Potomac Spirit** (☎ 866-211-
3811; www.cruisetomountvernon.com; Ⓜ Waterfront) departs for Mount Vernon from Pier 4, at 6th
& Water Sts SW.

Car Drive south on the George Washington Memor-
ial Parkway to Mount Vernon. At the traffic circle at
Mount Vernon, head south on Rte 235. Woodlawn
is at the intersection of Rte 235 with Rte 1. To reach
Gunston Hall, turn left on Rte 1 and left on Gunston
Rd (Rte 242).

Metro Take a Yellow Line to Huntington, then board
Fairfax Connector (☎ 703-339-7200) bus 101 to
Mount Vernon.

housing for the middle class, Wright's Usonian dwellings featured aesthetically elegant
designs yet used durable, inexpensive materials. It was moved to Woodlawn in 1964 from
Falls Church to rescue it from destruction. Furnished with Wright pieces, the house is
utilitarian in structure, but quite beautiful.

The new **Ford Orientation Center** is a must-see on the grounds. It features a 20-minute film
that re-enacts Washington's life, including his pivotal crossing of the Delaware River
(the crowning moment of the Revolutionary War). The center also hosts a timeline of
Washington's major milestones and an impressive stained-glass window depicting important scenes from his life.

Also new is the **Donald W Reynolds Museum and Education Center**. Home to galleries and theaters, it gives even more insight into Washington's life using interactive displays, short
films (produced by the cable TV History Channel) and three life-size models of old

George himself. The museum also features period furnishings, china, clothing, silver and jewelry.

Southwest of Mount Vernon, on a bend in the Potomac River, is the 1775 brick mansion **Gunston Hall**, which belonged to a statesman and contemporary of George Washington, George Mason. Mason penned the lines 'all men are by nature equally free and independent, and have certain inherent rights' – words adapted by Thomas Jefferson for the Declaration of Independence. Dating from 1755, the mansion is an architectural masterpiece, with elegantly carved wooden interiors and meticulously kept formal gardens.

Sights & Information

Gunston Hall (☎ 703-550-9220; www.gunstonhall .org; 10709 Gunston Rd, Mason Neck, VA; admission & tour adult/child $5/1.50; ☼ 9:30am-5pm)

Mount Vernon (☎ 703-780-2000; www.mountvernon .org; 3200 George Washington Memorial Parkway; admission adult/child $11/5, audio tour $4; ☼ 9am-4pm Nov-Feb, 9am-5pm Mar, Sep & Oct, 8am-5pm Apr-Aug)

Pope-Leighey House (www.nationaltrust.org /national _trust_sites/pope_leighey.html; 9000 Richmond Hwy, Mount Vernon; Woodlawn combo pass adult/child $13/5; ☼ 10am-5pm Mar-Dec)

Woodlawn Plantation (☎ 703-780-4000; www .woodlawn1805.org; 9000 Richmond Hwy, Mount Vernon; adult/child $7.50/3; ☼ 10am-5pm Mar-Dec)

Eating

The ubiquitous food court is in the visitors center.

Mount Vernon Inn (☎ 703-780-0011; 3200 George Washington Memorial Parkway; lunch $10, dinner $16-24; ☼ lunch & dinner Mon-Sat) A Colonial-style restaurant on the grounds of Mount Vernon serving traditional lunches and candle-lit dinners.

Sleeping

Comfort Inn Gunston Corner (☎ 703-643-3100; www .cigunston.com; 8180 Silverbrook Rd, Lorton, VA; r incl continental breakfast from $115; P ✕ ✕ ✕) A comfortable suburban hotel with an outdoor pool and exercise facility; provides convenient shuttle to Metro. Lorton is about 5 miles southeast of Mount Vernon (from Rte1 turn right on Lorton Rd and right on Silverbrook Rd).

MANASSAS & LEESBURG CIVIL WAR TRAIL

A visit to the **Manassas National Battlefield Park** is a must for enthusiastic historians and Civil War buffs. The battles that took place at Manassas (known as Bull Run in the north) were not the most significant, but the grassy hills tell a dramatic tale of two unexpected Confederate victories. Manassas I, the war's first major battle, shocked soldiers and spectators alike by its bloody outcome – see the boxed text, p248. Start at the visitors center, which has a small exhibit and an excellent film about the battles. You can also pick up a pamphlet, which outlines several walking and driving tours around the points of interest in the battlefields. In August, reenactments of the two Civil War battles are staged.

The town of Manassas lies 5 miles south

TRANSPORTATION

Distance from Washington, DC 26 miles.

Direction West.

Travel Time 40 minutes.

Car Take Rte 66 to Rte 234 exit 47: the battlefield is half a mile north; the town of Manassas is 5 miles south.

Train A commuter service runs between Washington, DC's Union Station and downtown Manassas on weekdays. Unfortunately, once in Manassas there is no way to reach the battlefield without a car.

---

of the battlefield along Rte 234. Don't be fooled by the heavily trafficked, strip-mall lined highway: the old center of town is a quaint area with antique shops and galleries, and a keen sense of history. The **Manassas Railroad Depot**, built in 1914, also houses the visitors center. Across the tracks, the **Manassas Museum** emphasizes Civil War history, but also displays photographs, artifacts and videos about the community. The **Center for the Arts at the Candy Factory** is a spacious, light-filled gallery housed in a reconverted candy factory that offers theatrical performances throughout the year and free summer concerts on alternate Saturday evenings (call for specifics).

THE BATTLES OF MANASSAS (1861 & 1862)

Not long after the first shots were fired at Fort Sumter, SC, on April 12, 1861, sizable armies of both Union and Confederate troops began to gather around the capitals of Richmond and Washington, DC.

The first significant battle of the Civil War occurred after Confederate soldiers, commanded by PGT Beauregard, camped near the rail junction of Manassas, perilously close to the national capital. The battle that Northerners hoped would end the war, Manassas I (Bull Run), started with an air of ebullience. Under orders from Abraham Lincoln, Brigadier General Irvin McDowell roused his 32,000 poorly trained troops on the afternoon of July 16 and marched to Centreville, 20 miles west of DC. McDowell's men skirmished and scouted near Bull Run, gathering scanty intelligence and, on July 21, the general committed two divisions, including cavalry and artillery, against the Confederate lines.

McDowell's first assault on the right flank was checked by Stonewall Jackson's soldiers and driven back. Then, what was meant to be an organized retreat turned into a rout. The Union troops knew tactical drilling techniques well enough, but they had not been taught the essentials of withdrawal under fire.

On the supposedly 'safe' side of Bull Run, there had been a macabre picnic in progress, with civilians from Washington, DC, coming down to witness the fray. As the soldiers fled in panic, they intermingled with this now-befuddled crowd of onlookers, and there was a melee, especially when a strategic bridge across Cub Run collapsed. When the counting ended, the Confederates, who incurred about 2000 casualties as opposed to McDowell's 3000, could claim victory. Both groups were so ill trained at this early stage of the war, however, that any advantage could not be followed up.

More than a year later, the war returned to Manassas. Following McClellan's Peninsula Campaign and the Seven Days Battles, Union troops had withdrawn to the safety of DC, and many of McClellan's soldiers were handed over to a new commander, John Pope. By the time Pope was ordered to move against Richmond, Robert E Lee was in command of the Confederates.

Pope advanced south toward the Rappahannock River, and Lee advanced north to confront Pope's troops before they could be reinforced by McClellan. Lee brilliantly split his force and consigned an attack on Pope's supply base at Manassas to Stonewall Jackson's men. Jackson's force came up against a numerically inferior force commanded by Nathaniel Banks at Cedar Mountain and, after a seesawing battle, the Union troops were forced back with heavy losses.

Pope's main body came up the next day, and Manassas II (Bull Run) commenced on August 29, with Pope making heavy but futile attacks on Jackson's troops, who were in defense behind the bed of an unfinished railroad.

The following day, Lee unexpectedly arrived in force with the 30,000-strong force of James Longstreet, which in a devastating flank assault on the Union's left (combined with Jackson's attacks on the other flank) caused a repeat of Manassas I, with the Northerners fleeing back across Bull Run to the security of Washington, DC. At this stage, almost all of Virginia had been returned to the hands of the Confederates.

Pope lost his job when it was revealed that he had lost about a quarter of his force of 70,000 (the remainder of which was then incorporated into the Army of the Potomac), while Lee had lost only 10,000 of his 60,000.

Other Civil War sights are in the area. The **Ben Lomond Manor House** is famous for its use as a hospital for Union and Confederate soldiers during the war. **Signal Hill** was an integral Confederate observation post during the Civil War (and you'll understand why when you see the view it provides). It directly contributed to the Confederate victory at the first Battle of Bull Run. Signal Hill is located just off Signal Hill Road across from the entrance to Signal Hill Park. Ask at the Manassas Museum or Manassas National Battlefield Park for specific directions to the site.

If you're starving after touring the battlefields, pop into the **City Tavern** for a meal. With 1940s pin-up girls and military recruiting posters gracing its historic walls, the tavern has long been the center of the Manassas social world, and even doubled as a crime scene once. Few long-time residents, including this author, will forget the shoot-out back in '99. Think of City Tavern as the kind of place where the mayor lunches with the police chief and the local journalist over cheap beer and even cheaper steaks. Yes, ladies and gentleman, this is the home of the $9 steak. It even comes with sides. The rest of the menu is other American pub schlop. There are even cheaper happy-hour specials.

Leesburg is one of Northern Virginia's oldest towns and is jam-packed with Colonial-era buildings, antique shops and nearby plantations. Unfortunately it's also jam-packed with highways and cars – loads of people commute from here to work in the city, and an outlet mall on the outskirts draws more people in. Try to avoid the place at rush hour. Otherwise, old town Leesburg is a delightful little place to explore, boasting a rich military and political history that's palpable on its quaint streets. Leesburg sits along the **Washington & Old Dominion Trail** (see Biking, p200), and makes an excellent bicycling destination.

The pleasure of **Leesburg** is wandering its streets, poking into antique shops and galleries, and soaking up the small-town atmosphere. For historical sights, start at the **Loudoun Museum**, which narrates the history of northern Virginia from the first Native American settlements to present day. It's of interest to non-Virginian visitors because of its attention to the Civil War and slavery. This is also the starting place for **First Friday Gallery Walks**, which occur every month from 6pm to 9pm, and other walking tours. For more info on the walks contact the **Loudoun Arts Council** (☎ 703-777-7838; www.leesburg firstfriday.com).

Located 1 mile outside Leesburg, **Morven Park** is a 1500-acre historic property that was once the home of Virginia Governor Westmoreland Davis. The Greek Revival mansion, with its manicured boxwood gardens, resembles a transplanted White House, and its antique carriage museum includes more than 100 horse-drawn vehicles.

Six miles south of Leesburg, **Oatlands Plantation** was established in 1803 by a great-grandson of Robert 'King' Carter, a wealthy pre-Revolutionary planter. The carefully restored Greek Revival mansion is surrounded by 4 acres of formal gardens and connecting terraces.

TRANSPORTATION LEESBURG

Distance from Washington, DC 35 miles.

Direction Northwest.

Travel Time 40 minutes.

Bicycle Pick up the Washington & Old Dominion Trail just outside the East Falls Church Metro in Arlington and head west.

Car Take I-495 or Rte 66 to the Dulles Toll Rd exit (Rte 267). When it turns into the Dulles Greenway, continue 13 miles to the end. Exit left and take the first right exit to Leesburg Business. Follow King St to Loudon St, the center of historic Leesburg. Morven Park is west of Leesburg off Rte 7 (Market St). Turn north onto Fairview St, go 1 mile to the dead end and turn left on Old Waterford Rd. Oatlands is located off Rte 267 at exit 1A, then take the second right on South Warrenton.

Sights & Information

Ben Lomond Manor House (☎ 703-367-7872; www .benlomondmanorhouse.org; 10311 Sudley Manor Dr; admission free; ☷ 10am-5pm Sat)

Center for the Arts at the Candy Factory (☎ 703-330-ARTS; www.center-for-the-arts.com; 9419 Battle St; admission by donation; ☷ 10am-4pm)

Leesburg Tourist Office (☎ 703-777-2420; www .leesburgva.org; 108-D South St, Market Station, Leesburg; ☷ 9am-5pm)

Loudoun Museum (☎ 703-777-7427; www .loudounmuseum.org; 16 Loudoun St, Leesburg; admission free, guided city tours adult/student/senior $4/2/2; ☷ 10am-5pm Mon-Sat, 1-5pm Sun)

Manassas Museum (☎ 703-368-1873; www .manassasmuseum.org; 9101 Prince William St; adult/child $3/2; ☷ 10am-5pm Tue-Sun)

Manassas National Battlefield Park (☎ 703-361-1339; www.nps.gov/mana; 12521 Lee Hwy; adult/child $2/free, film $3; ☷ 8:30am-5pm, tours 11:15am, 12:15pm, 2:15pm Jun-Aug)

Manassas Railroad Depot (Visitors Center ☎ 703-361-6599; 9431 West Street; ☷ 9am-5pm)

Morven Park (☎ 703-777-2414; www.morvenpark.org; 17263 Southern Planter Lane, Leesburg; adult/child/student/senior $7/1/6/6; ☷ 11am-4pm Fri-Mon)

Oatlands Plantation (☎ 703-777-3174; 20850 Oatlands Plantation Lane, Leesburg; adult/child/student/senior $10/7/9/9; ☷ 10am-5pm Mon-Sat, 1-5pm Sun Apr-Dec)

Eating

City Tavern (☎ 703-330-0076; 9405 Main St; mains $5-15; ☷ lunch & dinner) Serves American pub grub, and is known for its $9 steaks.

Lightfoot (☎ 703-771-2233; 11 N King St, Leesburg; lunch from $20, dinner from $30; ☷ 11:30am-9pm, to 10pm Fri & Sat) A progressive American bistro with an à la carte seasonal menu.

Okra's Louisiana Bistro (☎ 703-330-2729; 9413 cnr Battle & Center Sts; dishes $8-16; ☷ 11am-midnight Mon-Fri, 11am-2pm Sat & Sun) Delectable Cajun cooking in Southern country kitchen environs. There's a big selection of soups and vegetarian dishes.

Philadelphia Tavern (☎ 703-393-1776; 9413 Main St; dishes $8-15; ☷ 11:30am-10pm, to midnight Fri & Sat) Cheese steaks and other Philly specialties are on the menu at this old-school Manassas joint attracting noon-time punters then families at dinner.

Tuscarora Mill (☎ 703-771-9300; 203 Harrison St, Leesburg; lunch $15; ☷ lunch) Hunker down for a hearty lunch in a restored 19th-century mill.

Excursions

MANASSAS & LEESBURG CIVIL WAR TRAIL

DETOUR: TARARA VINEYARD

Virginia vineyards have gained some degree of attention in recent years, and Leesburg is one place to check them out. Ten miles north of the historic center, nestled in alongside the Potomac, is the **Tarara Vineyard** (☎ 703-771-7100; www.tarara.com; 13648 Tarara Lane, Leesburg; ☺ 11am-5pm). The 475-acre farm produces a wide variety of delicious reds, whites and blushes. The winery, located in a 6000 sq ft cave, is open year-round for tasting; there is also a romantic B&B here. Head north from Leesburg on Rte 15 to Lucketts and turn right on Rte 662.

For the last 11 years the vineyard has hosting a wine festival at the end of September. Grape-stomping competitions, craft vendors, tasting, food, music and plenty of kiddy activities are all on tap – it's a lively experience.

If you are in town during the summer, Tarara runs an alfresco summer concert series from a stage suspended above a lake on Saturday evenings. The performances take place on Saturday evenings from July through September and include all genres of music, from jazz to blues, '80s rock, country and modern pop. Check the website for schedule and prices.

Sleeping

Bennett House (☎ 703-368-6121; www.virginia-bennett house.com; 9252 Bennett Dr; r $85-125) A genteel Victorian inn that offers a full Virginia-style country breakfast.

Laurel Brigade Inn (☎ 703-777-1010; 20 W Market St, Leesburg; d $75-100) Founded in 1766, this bargain features lovely gardens and a pleasant restaurant.

Norris House Inn (☎ 703-777-1806; www.norrishouse .com; 108 Loudoun St SW, Leesburg; d $115-150) A renovated 1760 red-brick Colonial; tea is served in the lovely Stone House Tearoom. The rate is for weekends; weekday rates are cheaper.

Old Towne Inn (☎ 703-368-9191; 9403 Main St; r from $60) A motel in the center of town, rumored to be haunted.

BALTIMORE

Baltimore's dramatic and continuing redevelopment has transformed the gritty city into an exciting historical and modern destination. The Inner Harbor's waterfront promenade and distinct neighborhoods bursting with personality are the main draws. The city's undeniable importance in shaping American history – from the birthplace of the national anthem to Underground Railroad hideaways – is highlighted in numerous attractions, and there's plenty of nightlife if you're looking to stay up late. It's a great hardworking, ball-playing, no-nonsense US city where blood largely runs blue, and citizens are eager to welcome visitors with a friendly 'Hey Hon.'

Thanks to major revitalization projects, the Inner Harbor is packed with renovated attractions and is a great place to spend the afternoon. The area is dominated by **Harborplace**, two complexes that house restaurants, shops and the **Inner Harbors Tourist Center.**

TRANSPORTATION

Distance from Washington, DC 45 miles.

Direction North.

Travel Time 45 to 60 minutes.

Car Take I-95 or I-295 (Baltimore-Washington Parkway) north to Russell St, which terminates west of the Inner Harbor. Or take I-95 north to I-395, which spills out downtown as Howard St. Beware of this drive during rush hour.

Train Both **Amtrak** (☎ 800-872-7245; www .amtrak.com) and the **Maryland Rail Commuter** (MARC; ☎ 800-325-7245; www.mtamaryland .com; ☺ 5am-midnight Mon-Fri) travel between Washington, DC's Union Station and Baltimore's Penn Station. MARC is cheaper but it runs only on weekdays. Buses 3 and 11 travel up Charles St past Penn Station at 1515 N Charles St.

The **National Aquarium in Baltimore** put the city on the map as a tourist destination when it opened in 1981. Stretching seven stories high over two piers, its tanks house more than 10,000 marine animals, including sharks, rays and porpoises, plus dolphins in the Marine Mammal Pavilion.

One of the most distinctive museums around here is the **American Visionary Art Museum**, on the south side of the harbor. This avant-garde gallery showcases the raw genius of 'outsider' artists: broken mirror collages, a maniacally embroidered last will, a giant model ship constructed from toothpicks…you get the idea.

Baltimore boasts two top stops for kids, both within a few blocks of the Inner Harbor. The **Maryland Science Center** sits at the harbor's southeast corner. The excellent rotating exhibits and IMAX films are the highlight. Two blocks north, **Port Discovery** is a converted fish market, which has a playhouse, laboratory, TV studio and even Pharaoh's tomb. Wear your kids out here.

The Orioles' baseball park, **Camden Yards**, occupies an entire city block west of the Inner Harbor. It was the first 'retro' ball park, which reconciled Major League Baseball's need for more space with fans' nostalgia. Painted baseballs on the sidewalk lead two blocks northwest to the birthplace of a baseball legend; it's now the **Babe Ruth Museum**, a must for baseball fans, paying homage to the Sultan of Swat.

Four blocks north of Camden Yards is **Lexington Market**. A city market has thrived on this site since 1782. More than 140 merchants hawk everything from homemade kielbasa to Korean barbecue. Around the corner, Edgar Allan Poe is buried in **Westminster Cemetery**. If you are here around his birthday, January 19, you may see roses and cognac decorating the gravesite.

Behind the power plant is the delightful Little Italy neighborhood, packed with exquisite restaurants and a bocce ball court and a giant brick wall that doubles as an outdoor movie screen in summer. For a dose of American nostalgia head to the **Star-Spangled Banner Flag House & 1812 Museum**. It opens the home where Mary Pickersgill sewed the flag that inspired Francis Scott Key's *Star-Spangled Banner* poem. On Mt Vernon Sq you'll find **Walters Art Museum**, the city's finest museum. Its art collection spans 55 centuries, from ancient to contemporary, with excellent displays of Asian treasures, rare and ornate manuscripts and books, and a comprehensive collection of French paintings; there's also a great atrium café.

The **Fort McHenry National Monument & Historic Shrine** is one of the most-visited sites in Baltimore, and was instrumental in saving the city from the British attack during the War of 1812.

Cobblestones fill Market Sq between the **Broadway Market** and the harbor in the historic maritime neighborhood of **Fells Point**. Here, you'll find the **Fells Point Maritime Museum**, which tells the story of Baltimore's seafaring history as an important port city. A number of 18th-century homes now house restaurants, bars and shops that range from funky to upscale. Further east, the slightly more sophisticated streets of **Canton** fan out around a grassy square surrounded by more great restaurants and bars.

The 'Hon' expression of affection, an often imitated but never quite duplicated Baltimorese peculiarity, was born from **Hampden**, an urban neighborhood just reaching its pinnacle of hipness. Spend a long afternoon browsing kitsch, antiques and eclectic clothing along the avenue (aka 36th St).

Sights & Information

American Visionary Art Museum (☎ 410-244-1900; www.avam.org; 800 Key Hwy; adult/child/student/senior $9/6/6/6; ☼ 10am-6pm Tue-Sun)

Babe Ruth Museum (☎ 410-727-1539; www.baberuthmuseum.com; 216 Emory St; adult/child/senior $6/3/4; ☼ 10am-5pm Apr-Oct, to 7pm on Orioles' game days, 10am-4pm Nov-Mar)

Camden Yards (☎ 410-685-9800, 888-848-BIRD; www.theorioles.com; 333 W Camden St, Baltimore; tickets from $20; ☼ box office 10am-5pm Mon-Sat, noon-5pm Sun)

Fells Point Maritime Museum (☎ 410-732-0278; www.mdhs.org; 1724 Thames St; adult/child $4/3; ☼ 10am-5pm Thu-Mon)

Fort McHenry National Monument & Historic Shrine (☎ 410-962-4290; 1 E Fort Ave; admission $5; ☼ fort & grounds 8am-7:45pm summer, to 4:45pm rest of yr)

Maryland Science Center (☎ 410-685-5225; www.mdsci.org; 601 Light St; ☼ 10am-5pm Tue-Fri, 10am-6pm Sat, noon-5pm Sun; adult/child/senior $12/8/11, IMAX $7.50)

National Aquarium in Baltimore (☎ 410-576-3800; www.aqua.org; Piers 3-4, 501 E Pratt St; adult/child/senior $15.50/7.50/12.50; ☼ 10am-7pm Sat-Thu, 10am-10pm Fri Sep-Jun, 9am-8pm Sun-Thu, 9am-10pm Fri & Sat Jul & Aug) Enter two hours before closing time.

Port Discovery (☎ 410-727-8120; www.portdiscovery.org; 35 Market Place; adult/child/senior $11/8.50/10; ☼ 9:30am-4:30pm Tue-Fri, 10am-5pm Sat, noon-5pm Sun)

Star-Spangled Banner Flag House & 1812 Museum (☎ 410-837-1793; 844 E Pratt St; admission $5; ☼ 10am-4pm Tue-Sat)

Walters Art Museum (☎ 410-547-9000; www.thewalters.org; 600 N Charles St; adult/child/student/

young adult under 25yrs/senior/ $8/free/5/6; 10am-5pm Tue-Sun)

Eating

Bertha's (410-327-0426; 734 S Broadway; mussels $9, meals from $12; 11:30am-11pm Sun-Thu, 11:30am-midnight Fri & Sat) A Baltimore institution famous for Bloody Marys ('bloodies'), mussels, and live blues and jazz. You'll spot 'Eat Bertha's Mussels' bumper stickers around town.

Harborplace (410-332-4191, 800-HARBOR1; www.harborplace.com; cnr Pratt & Light Sts; 10am-9pm Mon-Sat, 11am-7pm Sun) Two pavilions contain a giant food court, and many popular national and local chain restaurants. Some bars and restaurants stay open later. Prices range from inexpensive fast food to fancy sit-down fare.

Joy America Cafe (410-244-6500; 800 Key Hwy; lunch $10-20, dinner $30-50; 11am-10pm Tue-Sat, 11am-4pm Sun brunch) The food version of the American Visionary Art Museum: radical. Feed the soul with organic ingredients and gorgeous views.

La Scala (410-783-9209; 1012 Eastern Ave; dishes $14-30; 5:30-10pm) Oh so worth the price for Little Italy's best. Here you'll find creamy risotto, penne and gnocchi

dishes that melt on the tongue, and a wine list that'd make even the Godfather cry.

Sleeping

Admiral Fell Inn (410-522-7377, 800-292-4667; www.admiralfell.com; 888 S Broadway; r $150-200) An old Fells Point sailors' hotel that has been converted into a lovely inn with Federal-style furniture and four-post beds.

Harbor Court Hotel (410-234-0550; 550 Light St; r from $199) The city's premier hotel, featuring heavenly harbor views.

Mount Vernon Hotel (410-727-2000; www.bic.edu/mtvernon.asp; 24 W Franklin St; r from $95;) Located in a swank neighborhood, this place offers nine floors of functional rooms and has free shuttle buses into town.

Mr Mole B&B (410-728-1179; www.mrmolebb.com; 1601 Bolton St; r from $119;) This beautifully restored town house in the upscale Bolton Hill area is a good choice for those wanting to explore the city's cultural arts district. Garage parking makes this B&B's price a steal. Gay-friendly.

SHENANDOAH NATIONAL PARK

Shenandoah National Park is easy on the eyes, set against a backdrop of the dreamy Blue Ridge Mountains, ancient granite and metamorphic formations that are more than one billion years old. The park itself is almost 70 years old, founded in 1935 as a retreat for East Coast urban populations. It is an accessible day-trip destination from DC, but stay longer if you can. The 500 miles of hiking trails, 75 scenic overlooks, 30 fishing streams, seven picnic areas and four campgrounds are sure to keep you entertained.

Skyline Dr is the breathtaking road that follows the main ridge of the Blue Ridge Mountains and winds 105 miles through the center of the park. It begins in Front Royal near the western end of I-66, and ends in the southern part of the range near Rockfish Gap near I-64. Mile markers at the side of the road provide a reference.

Your first stop should be the **Dickey Ridge Visitors Center** at Mile 4.6, close to the northern end of Skyline Dr, or **Byrd Visitors Center** at Mile 50. Both places have exhibits on flora and fauna, as well as maps and information about hiking trails and activities. Miles and miles of blazed trails wander through the park. Some choices for hiking:

Compton Peak Mile 10.4, 2.4 miles, easy to moderate.

Traces Mile 22.2, 1.7 miles, easy.

Overall Run Mile 22.2, 6 miles, moderate.

White Oak Canyon Mile 42.6, 4.6 miles, strenuous.

Hawksbill Mountain Summit Mile 46.7, 2.1 miles, moderate. This is the park's highest peak.

TRANSPORTATION

Distance from Washington, DC Front Royal 70 miles; Luray 90 miles.

Direction West.

Travel Time 90 minutes to the northern entrance at Front Royal.

Car From Washington, DC, take I-66 west to Rte 340. Front Royal is 3 miles south; Luray is 27 miles south.

Excursions

SHENANDOAH NATIONAL PARK

DETOUR

If you're already in the park and have a few extra days on hand, take a drive down the **Blue Ridge Parkway** (www .blueridgeparkway.org). One of the prettiest drives in the region, it traverses the southern Appalachian ridge from Shenandoah National Park at Mile 0 to North Carolina's Great Smoky Mountains National Park at Mile 469. Wildflowers bloom in spring, and fall colors are spectacular on the windy country road. In winter, snow can cause the parkway to close at times. High-quality NPS campgrounds and visitors centers are open May to October. To break up the scenery, detour often.

A stop well worth making for gritty, Friday-night bluegrass jamborees is the tiny town of **Floyd** (Mile 154) and the famous **Floyd's Country Store** (206 S Locust St; jamboree admission per adult $2). Further south, **Mabry Mill** (☎ 540-952-2947), at Meadows of Dan, is one of the most photogenic objects in the state.

The parkway has nine **campgrounds** (☎ 800-933-7275; campsites $9), four in Virginia:

Otter Creek (Mile 61) Year-round.

Peaks of Otter (Mile 86) Seasonal.

Roanoke Mountain (Mile 120) Seasonal.

Rocky Knob (Mile 167) Seasonal, plus full-facility cabins.

The **HI Blue Ridge Country** (☎ 540-236-4962; Mile 214.5; dm $15) offers dorm lodging with fantastic views.

To drive the entire parkway would take at least a few days. If you just want to explore a portion of it, allocate at least three hours.

Horseback riding is allowed on designated trails: pick up your pony at **Skyland Stables**, near Mile 41.7. Bicycling is allowed on Skyline Dr only – not off-road. Backcountry camping is allowed but requires a permit, which you can pick up at the visitors centers.

The town of **Front Royal**, at the northern end of Skyline Dr, is a convenient jumping-off point for the park. It's a good place to pack your picnic before heading into the wilderness. If you have some free time here, visit the **Oasis Winery**, known internationally for its sparkling wines. The town is also home to the **Skyline Caverns**, whose interiors are decked with unusual anthodites ('cave flowers'). Unlike stalactites and stalagmites, these spiky nodes defy gravity and grow in all directions, one inch every 7000 years.

The small town of **Luray** sits snug between Massanutten Mountain, in George Washington National Forest, and Shenandoah National Park. The eastern US's largest and most popular caves, **Luray Caverns**, are 9 miles west of here on Rte 211.

Sights & Information

Byrd Visitors Center (☎ 540-999-3283; Skyline Dr, Mile 50; ☾ 9am-5pm Apr-Nov)

Dickey Ridge Visitors Center (☎ 540-635-3566; Skyline Dr, Mile 4.6; ☾ 9am-5pm Apr-Nov)

Luray Caverns (☎ 540-743-6551; www.luraycaverns .com; Rte 211; admission and/or tour adult/child/senior $17/8/15; ☾ 9am-7pm Jun-Aug, 9am-6pm Sep-Nov & Apr-May, 9am-4pm Mon-Fri Dec-Mar)

Oasis Winery (☎ 540-635-7627; www.oasiswine.com; 14141 Hume Rd; wine tasting from $5; ☾ 10am-5pm) Off Rte 635 near Front Royal.

Shenandoah National Park (☎ 540-999-3500; www .nps.gov/shen; 3655 US 211 E, Luray; 7-day entry car $10, walker & cyclist $5)

Skyland Stables (☎ 540-999-2210; guided group rides per hr $22; ☾ 9am-5pm May-Oct)

Skyline Caverns ☾ 800-296-4545; www.skylinecaverns

.com; entrance to Skyline Dr; adult/child $14/7; ☾ 9am-6:30pm Jun-Aug, 9am-4pm Nov-Mar, 9am-5pm Mon-Fri, 9am-6pm Sat & Sun Sep, Oct, Apr & May)

Eating

Elkwallow Wayside (☎ 540-999-2253; Skyline Dr, Mile 24.1; ☾ Apr-Oct) Camp store with supplies and ice.

Fox Diner (☎ 540-635-3325; 20 South St, Front Royal) Nothing fancy, just honest, old-fashioned cookin'.

Panorama (☎ 540-999-2265; Skyline Dr, Mile 31.5; sandwiches from $5, mains from $10; ☾ 9am-5:30pm Apr-Nov) Traditional Virginia country fare and hearty sandwiches.

Parkhurst Restaurant (☎ 540-743-6009; Rte 211W; sandwiches $5-6, mains $8-15; ☾ 11:30am-9pm Sun-Thu, 11:30am-10pm Fri & Sat) American continental fare served on a veranda with great views. West of Luray Caverns.

Sleeping

Lewis Mountain Campground (☎ 800-365-CAMP; www.nps.gov/shen; Skyline Dr, Mile 57.6; campsite $16; ⊙ Apr-Oct) A park-service campground with a store, laundry and showers. Lewis Mountain has several suitably rustic cabins that feature private baths in which you can rejuvenate your weary body after a hard day's hiking.

Potomac Appalachian Trail Club Cabins (☎ 703-242-0693; www.patc.net; per person weekday/weekend $18/28) Six cabins with bunk beds, water and stoves in beautiful backcountry areas. Reservations mandatory.

Skyland Lodge (☎ 540-743-5108, 800-999-4714; Skyline Dr, Mile 41.7; cabins $80-150; ⊙ Mar-Dec) Rustic cabins with magnificent views.

HARPERS FERRY

Rich history and wild recreation are packed onto a scenic spit of land where the Shenandoah and Potomac Rivers meet to form the boundaries of three states in Harpers Ferry. The federal armory here was the target of abolitionist John Brown's raid in 1859 and, though Brown's ambition to arm slaves and spark a national rebellion against slavery died once he was caught and hanged, the incident incited slaveholders' worst fears and helped precipitate the Civil War. Union and Confederate forces soon fought for control of the armory and town.

TRANSPORTATION

Distance from Washington, DC 66 miles.

Direction Northwest.

Travel Time 90 minutes.

Car From Washington take I-495 north to the I-270 north. I-270 turns into I-70. Merge onto US-340 west and follow the signs for downtown Harpers Ferry.

The most fun to be had in Harpers Ferry takes place on foot, bicycle and boat. The 2160-mile Appalachian Trail (AT) not only passes through town, it has headquarters at the **Appalachian Trail Conference**, which is a tremendous resource for local hikers as well as backpackers. Day hikers can scale the Maryland Heights Trail past Civil War fortifications or the Loudoun Heights Trail for scenic river views.

River Riders is a one-stop shop for adventure sports, and rental bikes (half-day $27) to explore the **C&O Canal Towpath** (also see p82). The scenic path follows the Potomac River. It's not exactly technical mountain biking stuff, but it's a beautiful ride. Or take a raft or kayak trip down the Shenandoah River (Class I–III). The rafting costs $49, the kayaking $59. Try the kayaking if you're looking for more of an adrenaline rush. A cheaper (and equally fun) option is tubing. For $24 the company will give you a tube, life jacket and shuttle transport to and from the Potomac River. You're then on your own to negotiate the Class I–III rapids.

Sights & Information

Appalachian Trail Conference (☎ 304-535-6331; www.atconf.org; cnr Washington & Jackson Sts; ⊙ Apr-Oct) A nonprofit organization devoted to protecting and maintaining the Appalachian Trail. Visit the website for info on how you can help clean up this legendary hiking route.

River Riders (☎ 800-326-7238; www.riverriders.com; 408 Alstadts Hill Rd)

Visitors Center (☎ 304-535-2482; off Hwy 340; passes for vehicle/pedestrian $5/3)

Eating

Anvil (☎ 304-535-2582; 1270 Washington St; dishes $11-23; ⊙ lunch & dinner) Seafood, steak and fun happy hours, can you ask for more?

Mountain House Cafe (☎ 304-525-2339; 179 High St; dishes $5; ⊙ lunch & dinner) Serves up fresh salads and sandwiches in the backyard rose garden.

Sleeping

Harpers Ferry KOA (☎ 304-535-6895; campsite/cabin $26/42; ⊙ year-round; ⊠) Two miles southwest on Hwy 340, Harpers Ferry KOA is a good camping option that offers rustic cabins as well as campsites. The heated Olympic-sized swimming pool is an added bonus for travelers year-round.

HI Harpers Ferry Lodge (☎ 301-834-7652; www.harpersferryhostel.org; 19123 Sandy Hook Rd; dm members/nonmembers $15/17; ⊙ closed Nov–mid-Mar) Located 2.5 miles from the train station in Knoxville, MD. It has the usual hostel amenities, as well as an outdoor campfire and a bike and inner tube that hostel guests can borrow.

Last Resort Inn (☎ 304-535-2812; www.bbonline.com/wv/lastresort; 280 Clay St; weekdays/weekends r $80/90; ⊠) It boasts magnificent views of three states and two rivers from its sweeping porch.

ANNAPOLIS & CHESAPEAKE BAY

Sailors and seafood-lovers will relish exploring the coves and waterways of the Chesapeake Bay. A day trip to endearing Annapolis is the easiest way to get a dose of both treats, but if you have time to spare check out the Eastern Shore. Here you'll find ancestral farms, working waterways and small towns to explore by bike or boat.

Boasting some of the tastiest seafood in the region, Maryland's capital city, Annapolis, is a tribute to the Colonial era. The historic landmark is a perfectly preserved tableau of narrow lanes, brick houses and original 18th-century architecture (one of the largest concentrations of such buildings in the country).

TRANSPORTATION

Distance from Washington, DC Annapolis 35 miles; Easton 73 miles; St Michaels 79 miles; Oxford 79 miles.

Direction East.

Travel Time Annapolis 50 minutes; Easton, St Michaels & Oxford 90 minutes.

Car Rte 50 east goes straight into downtown Annapolis. To Easton, continue east over the Chesapeake Bay Bridge and stay on Rte 50 (east) to Rte 33 west.

Home of the US Naval Academy since 1845, Annapolis Harbor and its connecting tidal creeks shelter dozens of marinas where thousands of cruising and racing sailboats tie up, earning the city the title 'Sailing Capital' – it has 17 miles of waterfront and there are more than 2500 craft docked here.

The lovely Navy Campus is northwest of the Annapolis historic district; enter via Gate 1 (at the intersection of King George, East and Randall Sts) and head to the US Naval Academy Armel Leftwich Visitors Center, which features a film, some exhibits and guided tours. Preble Hall contains the US Naval Academy Museum with lots of artifacts, including remnants of the famed battleship USS Maine.

Annapolis' lively harbor, City Dock, is the center of its nightlife and – obviously – its nautical life. There are many opportunities to experience it firsthand. Take one of the regularly scheduled cruises that leave from City Dock, or sign up for a sailing class or rental from Annapolis Sailing School or Womanship. Note the Kunta Kinte-Alex Haley Memorial, which marks the spot where the enslaved African arrived in the USA, as told by Alex Haley's novel Roots.

The heart of Annapolis is the Maryland State House. A dignified domed building built in 1792, it served as the first capitol of the fledgling United States and as a meeting place for the Continental Congress from 1783 to 1784. The period artwork and furnishings are worth a peek around; guided tours are also available.

The collection of historic homes and buildings clustered on Cornhill and Fleet Sts between the State House and the harbor is extraordinary. Guided walking and bus tours abound, or you can pick up a free brochure at the Annapolis & Anne Arundel County Conference & Visitors Bureau. Some of the highlights that are open to the public include the jewel Hammond Harwood House and the William Paca House & Garden.

On the Eastern Shore of the Chesapeake Bay, Easton is known more as a gateway to the nearby town of St Michaels, but it is also the commercial and cultural center of surrounding Talbot County. Travelers will discover a town with an 18th-century center that has all the tradition and charm of Annapolis. Stop by the Talbot County Chamber of Commerce for information about the Eastern Shore.

The Historical Society of Talbot County runs a local history museum in its 19th-century headquarters and offers guided tours of three historic houses. Other old buildings that are open to the public include the 1794 Talbot County Courthouse and the 1682 Third Haven Meeting House. The Academy Art Museum houses a good collection of 19th- and 20th-century art in an 1820s schoolhouse.

Bay Hundred Peninsula thrusts into the Chesapeake near Easton. Along the shores lie the sweeping manors and productive fishing ports that have typified Chesapeake life for three centuries. The highlight is St Michaels, a gem of a Colonial town with red-brick Georgian

DETOUR: BLACKWATER NATIONAL WILDLIFE REFUGE

This 17,000-acre refuge, 20 miles south of Easton, contains tidal marshes protected for migrating waterfowl. It has large populations of bald eagles, snow geese, peregrine falcons, blue herons, ospreys and 20 species of duck. Mid-October to mid-March is prime bird-watching time. You may also spot woodland creatures like red foxes, fox squirrels and white-tailed deer.

A 5-mile nature drive cuts through the refuge. This is also a great spot for cyclists and kayakers to explore: paddling maps are available at the **Blackwater Refuge Visitors Center** (☎ 410-228-2677; www.friendsofblackwater.org; 2145 Key Wallace Dr, Cambridge; refuge admission per car $3, walker & cyclist $1; ☒ 8am-4pm Mon-Fri, 9am-5pm Sat & Sun) Take Rte 50 south to Cambridge, then Rte 16 south to State Rd 335. Take a left at Key Wallace Dr.

buildings, flowering gardens and historic watercraft tied at the wharf. It is a popular tourist spot and the harbor is packed with visiting yachts. Despite its tourist allure, the place manages to retain traces of its not-so-distant maritime past, when many citizens earned a living harvesting the bay's oysters in winter and blue crabs in summer.

Overlooking the harbor from Navy Point, the 1879 Hooper Strait octagonal lighthouse has become the image most people associate with Chesapeake Bay. It is the focal point for the **Chesapeake Bay Maritime Museum**, a collection of historic buildings that surround the lighthouse on the 18-acre grounds.

St Michaels is packed with shops and galleries, and a few historic houses. But the real reason to come here is to explore the maze of coves by boat, or to cycle around and admire the stately manor houses. Rent bikes and boats at **St Michaels Harbour Inn & Marina** or **St Michaels Marina**.

Travelers come to **Oxford** to ride the village's historic **Oxford–Bellevue Ferry**, which has been operating since 1683. The car ferry crosses the Tred Avon River from Oxford to Bellevue in 10 minutes; from Bellevue you can drive or cycle 7 miles to St Michaels. There is always a cooling breeze and a lovely view of the pastoral peace surrounding Oxford.

Sights & Information

Academy Art Museum (☎ 410-822-2787; www
.art-academy.org; 106 South St, Easton; admission free;
☒ 10am-4pm Mon-Sat, to 9pm Wed)

**Annapolis & Anne Arundel County Conference &
Visitors Bureau** (☎ 410-263-9591; 26 West St,
Annapolis; ☒ 9am-5pm)

Annapolis Sailing School (☎ 410-267-7205; www
.annapolissailing.com; 601 6th St, Annapolis)

Chesapeake Bay Maritime Museum (☎ 410-745-2916;
www.cbmm.org; St Michaels; adult/senior/child $9/8/4;
☒ 9am-4pm Nov-Feb, 9am-5pm Oct & Mar-May, 9am-
6pm Jun-Sep)

Hammond Harwood House (☎ 410-263-4683; www
.hammondharwoodhouse.org; 19 Maryland Ave, Annapolis;
adult/child/student $6/4/5.50; ☒ noon-5pm Wed-Sun
Apr-Oct)

Historical Society of Talbot County (☎ 410-822-0773;
www.hstc.org; 25 S Washington St; admission free;
☒ 10am-4pm Mon-Sat)

Maryland State House (☎ 410-974-3400; 91 State
Circle, Annapolis; admission free; ☒ 9am-5pm Mon-Fri,
10am-4pm Sat & Sun, tours 11am & 3pm)

Oxford–Bellevue Ferry (☎ 410-745-9023; www
.oxfordbellevueferry.com; Oxford; passenger/bicycle/car

$1/2.50/6; ☒ 7am-dusk Mon-Fri, 9am-dusk Sat & Sun,
closed Dec-Feb)

St Michaels Marina (☎ 410-745-2400; www.stmichaels
marina.com; 305 Mulberry St, St Michaels; bike rental per
hr/day $4/16; ☒ May-Oct)

Talbot County Chamber of Commerce (☎ 410-822-
4653; www.talbotchamber.org; 210 Marlboro Rd, Easton;
☒ 8:30am-5pm Mon-Fri)

Talbot County Courthouse (☎ 410-822-2401; 11 N
Washington St, Easton; ☒ 9am-5pm Mon-Fri)

Third Haven Meeting House (☎ 410-822-0293; 405 S
Washington St, Easton; admission free; ☒ 9am-5pm)

US Naval Academy Armel Leftwich Visitors Center
(☎ 410-263-6933; www.usna.edu; tours adult/stu-
dent/senior $6.50/4.50/5.50; ☒ 9am-5pm Mar-Dec,
9am-4pm Jan & Feb, tours 10am-3pm Mon-Sat, 12:30-
3pm Sun)

US Naval Academy Museum (☎ 410-293-2108; www
.usna.edu/Museum; 118 Maryland Ave, Annapolis; admission free; ☒ 9am-5pm Mon-Sat, 11am-5pm Sun)

William Paca House & Garden (☎ 410-267-7619; www
.annapolis.org; 186 Prince George St, Annapolis; house
or garden adult/child/senior $5/3/4, combo $8/5/7;
☒ 10am-5pm Mon-Sat, noon-5pm Sun Apr-Dec, 10am-
4pm Sat, noon-5pm Sun Jan-Mar)

Womanship (☎ 410-267-6661; www.womanship.com; 137 Conduit St, Annapolis; 2-day courses $495; ☼ Apr-Oct) A sailing school tailored to women – its website proclaims Womanship is 'designed by women for women.'

Eating

49 West Cafe (☎ 410-626-9796; 49 West St; dishes $2-12) Grab one of the books or newspapers scattered around this casual café that encourages lingering. Food is light gourmet and there is live classical and jazz music Tuesday to Saturday nights. The giant appetizers make a meal, or try the slippery $1 oyster shooters and platefuls of other catches-of-the-day in this historic waterfront tavern.

Carpenter St Saloon (☎ 410-745-5111; 113 S Talbot St, St Michaels; mains $10-16; ☼ 11:30am-9pm) Atmospheric corner bar for oysters and beers, with an airy dining room for families next door.

Chick & Ruth's Delly (☎ 410-268-5665; 165 Main St, Annapolis; light meals $5-10, dinner $8-14; ☼ 6:30am-10pm Sun-Thu, to 11:30pm Fri & Sat) A second-generation Annapolis institution serving up burgers, milkshakes, crab cakes and breakfast goodies all with a smile.

Hunter's Tavern (☎ 410-822-1300; 101 E Dover St, Easton; breakfast & lunch $12-16, dinner $30; ☼ breakfast, lunch & dinner) A comfortable restaurant inside Tidewater Inn serving civilized breakfast and lunch and fancy dinners.

Riordan's Saloon (☎ 410-263-5449; 26 Market Space, Annapolis; sandwiches $7-10, dinners $15-20; ☼ 11am-midnight Sun-Thu, 11am-1am Fri & Sat) Steamed shrimp and microbrews or bloodies and brunch overlooking the lively Annapolis City Dock.

Sleeping

Historic Inns of Annapolis (☎ 410-263-2641; www.annapolisinns.com; 58 State Circle, Annapolis; r from $150) Three historic properties with period furnishings and modern conveniences.

Kemp House Inn (☎ 410-745-2243; www.kemphouseinn.com; 412 S Talbot St, St Michaels; r from $120) A fine 1807 Georgian house with period furnishings and working fireplaces. Robert E Lee spent two nights here (in the subsequently named 'Lee Room').

ScotLaur Inn (☎ 410-268-5665; www.scotlaurinn.com; 165 Main St; r from $75) Ten simple newly furnished B&B rooms in the heart of the historic district are found at this good value inn.

St Michaels Harbour Inn & Marina (☎ 410-745-9110; www.harbourinn.com; 101 N Harbor Rd, St Michaels; r from $200) Deluxe waterfront hotel overlooking the harbor. Also offers bike rental (per hour/day $5/20), canoes and kayaks (per hour/day $10/35).

Tidewater Inn (☎ 410-822-1300, 800-237-8775; 101 E Dover St, Easton; r from $160) Queen Anne replica with modern rooms and traditional mahogany furniture.

EAST COAST BEACHES

When the temperature soars, do as the locals do and hit the beach. From Virginia through Maryland and up to Delaware, the Atlantic coast is a string of protected marshland and preserved beaches, interspersed with resort towns. Chincoteague, Ocean City, Rehoboth and Dewey all offer a most welcome – even necessary – respite from the heat and humidity of Washington summers. These places are all too far for a day trip from DC: you will want the weekend to get your fill of boogie-boarding and all-you-can-eat crabs.

With no contest, the loveliest of the group is Chincoteague, VA. It's also the furthest from DC. The small beach town (population 1600) sits across an inlet from Assateague Island, which contains Chincoteague National Wildlife Refuge. Famous from the 1940s novel *Misty of Chincoteague*, the island is still home to wild ponies, but they are not really that wild. In July they are herded across the channel in an annual celebratory festival.

Besides miles of pristine sandy beaches, the refuge contains marshland that attracts migrating waterfowl – a bird-watchers' paradise. Paved trails and roads provide various tours for walkers, cyclists and drivers to try to spot birds, ponies and other wildlife. Bicycling or kayaking is definitely the way to explore this place. Rent the gear at the **Piney Island Country Store** or **Tidewater Expeditions.** In town, there is not much to keep you occupied in case of rain, only the **Oyster & Maritime Museum,** which has exhibits on the history of the area, marine life and seafood.

Long before Fox TV introduced America to *The OC* (Orange County, California), Washingtonians had their own OC. **Ocean City,** MD, that is. The mammoth Atlantic coast resort swells in summer when Coppertone-slicked beachgoers crowd the boardwalk corn-dog stands and Skee-Ball arcades, and cruise the Coastal Hwy, which is lined with budget motels. Slightly sleazy, ultra-cheesy and very American, OC is both a party and a family destination and Washingtonians of all ages flock here by the thousands on the weekends.

Excursions

EAST COAST BEACHES

For most of its length it's barely three blocks wide, yet it sprawls southward from the Delaware border along 10 miles of barrier beach lined with side-by-side hotels and motels. It's a sunscreen-scented town of bikini contests, water slides, saltwater taffy, airbrushed T-shirts, go-carts and mini golf. Pick up information on all this fun at the **Ocean City Convention & Visitors Bureau**.

The town originated at the southern tip of the Strand, now called the Inlet, which retains a tiny hint of Victorian flavor. Here, a 2½-mile boardwalk provides a pedestrian promenade that is the heart of the Ocean City experience.

Across the Inlet is **Assateague Island**. This beautiful 37-mile-long barrier island preserves a rare stretch of undeveloped seashore, one of the most pristine and picture-perfect spots on the mid-Atlantic coast. As an undeveloped barrier island, it provides a sharp contrast to the overdeveloped beach resorts that dominate the coast. Besides its natural appeal, the island is home to a legendary herd of wild ponies, whose dramatic silhouettes race across the dunes.

The National Park Service manages most of the protected national seashore; the southern end of the island is **Chincoteague National Wildlife Refuge**. A bridge accesses the northern portion of the island, but roads do not go further. To drive from the northern end near Ocean City to the southern end at Chincoteague requires a circuitous inland detour.

The island is a sanctuary where you can get away from the crowds of Ocean City and swim, bicycle, hike, fish canoe, kayak or camp, with nothing but the sound of the surf and the whir of the wind as your companions. Drive south on Rte 611 from Ocean City Drive to visit the **Barrier Island Visitors Center**. Flat, paved pathways along the island are ideal for bicycling; the protected marshland shores make for adventurous canoeing; and conditions are ideal for swimming, hiking and watching birds. Rent bikes and boats at the recreation outpost beyond the Bayside Campground. If you're searching for serenity, backcountry camping is the answer – inquire about regulations at the visitors center.

Further north up Rte 1, the **Delaware Seashore State Park** is a 10-mile long, half-mile wide peninsula with a long, straight, clean beach. Stop at the **park office** to pick up information about pontoon boat tours, hiking trails and guarded swimming areas. The **Indian River Inlet Marina** is west of the park office – this is where you can charter fishing boats.

Long known as a fashionable gay resort, Rehoboth, DE also provides a sort-of happy medium between family-friendly Chincoteague and kid-crazy Ocean City. It's a vibrant old seaside town tucked behind a very tacky stretch of Hwy 1 (follow signs to the resort area). Beach houses trimmed in clapboard and cedar shingles sit among tree-lined streets and picturesque lagoons. Modern oceanfront resort motels and hotels spoil the magic a bit as you approach the waterfront.

Poodle beach, at the southern tip of the boardwalk, is primarily gay, while lesbians congregate at **North Shores** beach at the south end of **Cape Henlopen State Park**. Straight folks shouldn't feel excluded – the beach attracts all types.

The main drag, Rehoboth Ave, is lined with restaurants, food stalls and souvenir shops, from the easy-to-miss **Rehoboth Chamber of Commerce & Visitors Center** (look for it just across the canal bridge in the restored 1879 railway station) to the mile-long beach boardwalk.

TRANSPORTATION

Distance from Washington, DC Chincoteague and Assateague 160 miles; Ocean City 130 miles; Rehoboth and Dewey 115 miles.

Direction East.

Travel Time Four hours to Chincoteague; three hours to Ocean City, Rehoboth and Lewes.

Boat The **Cape May-Lewes ferry** (☎ 800-643-3779) travels year-round between Lewes and Cape May, the southern tip of the New Jersey shore. The ferry takes 70 minutes to transport cars and bikes across the open mouth of the Delaware Bay. On weekends, make reservations in advance. Reach Dewy Beach from Rehoboth on the **Jolly Trolley** (☎ 302-227-1197; fare $1.50; ✆ late May–late Aug). It departs at the boardwalk and Rehoboth Ave in Rehoboth Beach.

Car Take Rte 50 south to Rte 13 in Salisbury, MD. To Chincoteague, take Rte 13 south to Rte 175, about 5 miles past Pocomoke City, MD. Travel east on Rte 175 to Chincoteague Island, then east on Maddox Blvd. To reach Ocean City, stay on Rte 50, which leads right to the inlet. For Rehoboth and Lewes, take Rte 50 to Rte 404 east. To Rehoboth, go south on Rte 1; to Lewes, head east on Rte 9.

Travel further south along Hwy 1 and you'll reach **Dewey Beach**. Rehoboth's wild little sister, Dewey is best known for its frantic nightlife. When the sun goes down throngs of under-30s swarm the streets and quickly forget their sunburn after downing a couple at the numerous watering holes.

Sights & Information

Assateague State Park (☎ 410-641-2120; 7307 Stephen Decatur Hwy;campsites $20) The park is 8 miles south of Ocean City, MD, and can be reached via Maryland Rte 50 or Rte 611.

Barrier Island Visitors Center (☎ 410-641-1441; Rte 11 near Verrazzano Bridge; per bike/car $3/10; ☽ 9am-5pm)

Cape Henlopen State Park (☎ 302-645-6852; www .destateparks.com; 42 Cape Henlopen Dr, Lewes, DE; per in-state/out-of-state car $2.50/5; ☽ park dawn-dusk, visitors center 8am-5pm)

Chincoteague National Wildlife Refuge (☎ 757-336-6122; http://chinco.fws.gov; Chincoteague, VA; 1-week car pass $10, walker & cyclist free; ☽ 5am-10pm May-Oct, 6am-6pm Dec-Mar, 6am-8pm Apr & Nov)

Delaware Seashore State Park Office (☎ 302-227-2800; www.destateparks.com; Rte 1, south of Dewey, DE; per car Jun-Oct & weekends $5; ☽ 8am-4:30pm)

Indian River Inlet Marina (☎ 302-227-3071; www .irimarina.com; Rte 1, DE) North of Indian River Inlet Bridge. Charter fishing boats here.

Ocean City Convention & Visitors Bureau (☎ 410-289-8181, 800-626-2326; www.ococean.com; 40th St & Coastal Hwy, Convention Center, Ocean City, MD; ☽ 9am-5pm Mon-Fri)

Oyster & Maritime Museum (☎ 757-336-6117; www .chincoteague.com/omm; 7125 Maddox Blvd, Chincoteague; adult/child/senior $4/2/2; ☽ 10am-5pm Jun-Aug, 10am-5pm Sat & Sun Apr, May, Sep & Oct)

Piney Island Country Store (☎ 757-336-5511; 785 Maddox Blvd, Chincoteague, VA) Rents out bicycles and sells a variety of gear – from walking shorts to ski parkas.

Rehoboth Chamber of Commerce & Visitors Center (☎ 302-227-2233, 800-441-1329; www.beach-fun.com; 501 Rehoboth Ave, Rehoboth, DE; ☽ 9am-5pm Mon-Fri year-round, 9am-2pm Sat, 9am-1pm Sun summer)

Tidewater Expeditions (☎ 757-336-3159; 7729 East Side Dr, Chincoteague, VA) Rents out bicycles and sells adventure gear – from jackets to hiking shoes and shorts.

Eating & Drinking

Bottle & Cork (☎ 302-227-8545; Dagsworthy St, Dewey) Get ready to party at this gigantic joint, which rocks especially royally when live acts (past performers include Dave Matthews Band and Joan Jett) take the stage. Rowdy!

Buxy's Salty Dog Saloon (☎ 410-289-0973; cnr 28th St & Bayside, Ocean City, MD; dishes from $6) The casual (and often boisterous) Salty Dog delivers inexpensive burgers. It has a daily happy hour and lunch specials.

Corner Cupboard (☎ 302-227-8553; 50 Park Ave, Rehoboth; dishes $10) Standout for its tucked-away location and Eastern Shore cookin'.

Crabbers' Cove (☎ 302-227-4888; Dickenson St, Dewey; dishes from $10) This open-air seafood restaurant features all-you-can-eat specials, and various other seafood dishes.

Dogfish Head Brewing & Eats (☎ 302-226-2739; 320 Rehoboth Ave, Rehoboth, DE; pizzas $12, mains $16-20; ☽ 4-11pm Mon-Thu, 4pm-1am Fri, noon-1am Sat, noon-11pm Sun) A popular, family-friendly microbrewery and restaurant with a great menu of pizza and main meals. It also has live music.

Obie's by the Sea (☎ 302-227-6261; cnr Virginia & Olive Aves, Dewey; dishes from $5) Eat on the beach or overlooking it from the inside dining area. The menu features sandwiches, burgers, ribs and salads. On weekends a DJ spins and revelers dance.

Phillip's Restaurant at 21st Street (☎ 410-289-6821; 2004 Philadelphia Ave, Ocean City, MD; dishes from $10) Though now synonymous with crabs in the DC region (Phillip's operates restaurants throughout the capital region), it all started in Ocean City. The restaurant is a casual place, with white paper on the tables and a huge menu emphasizing crabs, which is what you should order.

Rusty Rudder (☎ 302-227-3888; 113 Dickenson St, Dewey) One of the most popular nightspots in town, it holds nightly deck parties overlooking the bay.

Seacrets (☎ 410-524-4900; 117 W 49th St, Ocean City, MD) A Jamaican-themed bar and club straight out of MTV's *Spring Break*, Seacrets has beach parties, spring-loaded indoor dance floors, and watery areas where you can drift in an inner tube while sipping your drinks.

Scandals Night Club & Sports Bar (☎ 410-723-0500; 44th St Shopping Center, Ocean City, MD) Catering to 20-somethings looking to drink, Scandals has fish bowl draft beers, a packed dance floor and a sports bar.

Steamers (☎ 757-336-6236; 6251 Maddox Blvd, Chincoteague, VA; ☽ noon-10pm Apr-Oct, 5-10pm Thu-Sat Nov-Mar) A fun family place – get messy with all-you-can-eat crabs.

Sydney's Blues & Jazz (☎ 302-227-1339; 25 Christian St, Rehoboth; dishes from $13) Black-and-white photos of Hollywood royalty grace the walls, and gold and silver mobiles are suspended from the ceiling at this eclectic place that serves tasty Creole dishes and nightly jazz and blues.

Sleeping

Assateague Inn (☎ 757-336-3738; www.assateague -inn.com; Maddox Blvd & Chicken City Rd, Chincoteague, VA; r from $85) Reasonable rooms with balconies overlooking the saltwater marsh.

Dunes Manor Hotel (☎ 410-289-1100; www .dunesmanor.com; 28th St & Baltimore Ave, Ocean City, MD; r from $145) A huge high-rise with a touch of class and nice ocean views.

King Charles Hotel (☎ 410-289-6141; www .kingcharleshotel.com; 1209 Baltimore Ave, Ocean City MD; r weekdays/weekends from $83/101;) This place feels like a summer cottage and is an outstanding deal for the high season. It's centrally located half a block from the beach in the heart of the boardwalk action.

Rehoboth Guest House (☎ 302-227-4117; www .guesthse.com/reho; 40 Maryland Ave; r with shared bathroom from $70;) Gay-owned and -operated, this cool guesthouse is wildly popular for its afternoon wine-and-cheese parties, private sunbathing decks and immaculate rooms, not to mention its five-minute walk to the boardwalk. Reservations are highly recommended.

Royal Rose Inn B&B (☎ 302-226-2535; www .royalroseinn.com; 41 Baltimore Ave; r from $115;) This place is a great bang for your buck, with a rooftop hot tub, screened porch and sundeck. It's just a block from the boardwalk.

Summer Place Hotel (☎ 302-226-0766; www .rehobothsummerplace.com; 30 Olive Ave, Rehoboth; r weekday/weekend $80/120;) You'll find the best budget option here, with a choice between spacious condos and comfy hotel-style rooms with refrigerators, microwaves and TV.

Surf Villa (☎ 410-289-9434, 888-333-7873; www .surfvilla.com; 705 N Baltimore Ave, Ocean City, MD; r weekdays/weekends from $79/99;) A comfy hotel boasting rocking chairs, ocean-view rooms, and shower and changing facilities on checkout days.

Directory ■

Directory

TRANSPORTATION

Flights, tours and rail tickets can be booked online at www.lonelyplanet.com/travel _services.

AIR

Following the September 11 terrorist attacks, air travel in the United States changed drastically. Heightened security means only ticketed passengers are allowed through the security screening and into the gate area, and some items are no longer allowed to be carried on board. What is allowed in your carry-on seems to change daily, but lighters, knifes and box cutters are always prohibited. Make sure you arrive at the airport two hours before your flight as sometimes security checkpoint lines are very long at Washington's airports. When flying into Ronald Reagan Washington National Airport passengers are not allowed to leave their seats (or even stand up) for the last half hour before the plane lands – the flight crew will warn you well in advance, but make sure to use the bathroom if you need to. This extra security measure was put in place following September 11 because the flight path into National Airport crosses over many of DC's most important buildings.

Airlines

Most major airlines offer service to DC. Here's a nonexhaustive list of those with toll-free telephone numbers (free within the US).

Air Canada	☎ 888-247-2262
Air France	☎ 800-237-2747
Air New Zealand	☎ 800-262-1234
All Nippon Airways	☎ 800-235-9262
American Airlines	☎ 800-433-7300
British Airways	☎ 800-247-9297
Canadian Airlines	☎ 800-426-7000
Continental Airlines	☎ 800-525-0280
Delta Air Lines (& shuttle)	☎ 800-221-1212
Ethiopian Airlines	☎ 877-389-6753
KLM Royal Dutch Airlines	☎ 800-374-7747
Korean Air	☎ 800-438-5000
Lufthansa	☎ 800-645-3880
Mexicana	☎ 800-531-7921
Northwest Airlines	☎ 800-225-2525
Qantas Airways	☎ 800-227-4500

CLIMATE CHANGE & TRAVEL

Climate change is a serious threat to the ecosystems that humans rely upon, and air travel is the fastest-growing contributor to the problem. Lonely Planet regards travel, overall, as a global benefit, but believes we all have a responsibility to limit our personal impact on global warming.

Flying & Climate Change

Pretty much every form of motorized travel generates CO_2 (the main cause of human-induced climate change) but planes are far and away the worst offenders, not just because of the sheer distances they allow us to travel, but because they release greenhouse gases high into the atmosphere. The statistics are frightening: two people taking a return flight between Europe and the US will contribute as much to climate change as an average household's gas and electricity consumption over a whole year.

Carbon Offset Schemes

Climatecare.org and other websites use 'carbon calculators' that allow travelers to offset the level of greenhouse gases they are responsible for with financial contributions to sustainable travel schemes that reduce global warming – including projects in India, Honduras, Kazakhstan and Uganda.

Lonely Planet, together with Rough Guides and other concerned partners in the travel industry, support the carbon offset scheme run by climatecare.org. Lonely Planet offsets all of its staff and author travel. For more information, check out our website at www.lonelyplanet.com.

Southwest Airlines	☎ 800-435-9792
Spanair	☎ 888-545-5757
TACA	☎ 800-535-8780
United Airlines	☎ 800-241-6522
US Airways (& shuttle)	☎ 800-428-4322
Virgin Atlantic	☎ 800-862-8621

Airports

Three major airports serve DC.

Ronald Reagan Washington National Airport (Map pp306–7; ☎ 703-417-8000; www .metwashairports.com), across the river in Arlington, VA, handles domestic service plus some flights to Canada. After a huge renovation a few years back, National was renamed and now contains two fancy terminals (B and C) of shops and restaurants in addition to the original Terminal A. It is easily accessible by Metro (Yellow or Blue Line).

Washington Dulles International Airport (☎ 703-572-2700; www.metwashairports.com), designed by Eero Saarinen, looms like a space-age castle in the Virginia suburbs 26 miles west of DC. Take I-66 west to the Dulles Toll Rd. Both domestic and international flights (to Asia, Europe, South America, the Middle East and Africa) depart from here. Dulles is not on a Metro line, although **Washington Flyer** (☎ 888-927-4359; www.washfly.com; round-trip/one way $16/9; ⏰ 6am-11pm Mon-Fri, 8am-11pm Sat & Sun) operates a shuttle from West Falls Church Metro station. Average length of shuttle trip is 20 to 30 minutes.

Baltimore-Washington International Airport (BWI; ☎ 800-435-9294; www.bwiairport.com) is 30 miles, or about 45 minutes' drive, northeast of DC in Maryland. Get onto the Baltimore–Washington Parkway via New York Ave NE, follow the parkway until you see the I-195/BWI exit. Often you will find that cheaper fares are available to/from BWI than to either National or Dulles; so despite its geographic inconvenience, this is a handy airport for those on a budget. Both Maryland Rail Commuter (MARC; weekends only) and Amtrak trains travel between DC's Union Station and a terminal near BWI.

BICYCLE

Cycling is one of the best ways to get around DC. In recent years, Metro has taken new measures to encourage bicycle commuting.

GETTING INTO TOWN

If you fly into Ronald Reagan Washington National Airport, you can catch the Metro directly into the city. From Washington Dulles or BWI the options are more limited. The cheapest way is the **SuperShuttle** (☎ 800-258-3826; www.supershuttle.com; National/Dulles $12/25; ⏰ 5:30am-12:30am), which provides door-to-door service to/from the airports in a shared van.

Riders can take their bikes free of charge on trains, except during rush hour (7am to 10am and 4pm to 7pm Monday to Friday) and on busy holidays, like July 4. Bikes are not permitted to use the center door of trains or the escalator. All buses are now equipped with bike racks, so riders can transport their bikes by bus, too. Here are some options for rental:

Better Bikes Inc (☎ 202-293-2080; per 24hr $38) Delivers and picks up bikes anywhere in the DC area. Price includes helmets, locks and assistance.

Big Wheel Bikes (Map p299; ☎ 202-337-0254; 1034 33rd St NW; per hr/day $7/35; Ⓜ Rosslyn) In Georgetown, just up the hill from the end of the Capital Crescent Trail. Just below M Street, look for the bright-yellow building with a huge bicycle on it. There's a three-hour minimum with rentals.

Bike the Sites (Map pp292–3; ☎ 202-842-2453; 1100 Pennsylvania Ave, Old Post Office Pavilion; per hr/day $7/35; Ⓜ Federal Triangle) Weekly rentals, plus guided tours also available.

Blazing Saddles (Map pp292–3; ☎ 202-544-0055; 445 11th St NW; Ⓜ Metro Center) Provides maps of favorite biking routes.

Thompson Boat Center (Map pp292–3; ☎ 202-333-9543; 2900 Virginia Ave; bikes per hr/day $8/25; Ⓜ Foggy Bottom-GWU) Easy access to Rock Creek Park and the Capital Crescent Trail. As well as hiring out all types of watercraft and offering rowing classes (p203), Thompson Boat Center rents bicycles to suit every rider.

BUS

DC's bus system (technically called 'Metrobus') is operated by the Washington Metropolitan Transit Authority, or Metro. It provides a clean and efficient bus service throughout the city and to outlying suburbs. Stops are marked by red, white and blue signposts. The fare is $1.25 ($3 on express routes), or 35¢ with a Metrorail transfer. Kids under four ride free. Automatic fare machines accept paper dollars, but you must have exact change. Useful bus routes include:

30, 32, 34, 36, Wisconsin Ave Runs from Friendship Heights down Wisconsin Ave (through Georgetown) to Foggy Bottom-GWU.

98 (the Link) Traverses Adams Morgan from Woodley Park-Zoo to U Street-Cardozo Metro stations.

L2, 18th St NW Connects Woodley Park-Zoo to Foggy Bottom-GWU via Adams Morgan.

D2, P St NW Connects Georgetown to Dupont Circle.

Intercity bus service in the US is relatively cheap, but not the most pleasant – although it's useful if you're on a tight budget.

The main bus company is **Greyhound** (Map p304; ☎ fares & schedules 800-229-9424, customer service 202-289-5101; www .greyhound.com; 1005 1st St NE), which provides nationwide service.

Peter Pan Trailways (☎ 800-343-9999), which travels to northeastern US, uses a terminal just opposite Greyhound's. This run-down neighborhood is deserted after dark, and the nearest Metro station is several blocks south (via 1st St NE) at Union Station. Cabs are usually available at the bus station, and you should use one; don't walk across town from the bus station at night.

Your cheapest option to New York is the Chinatown buses by **New Century Travel** (☎ 202-789-8222; 513 H Street NW), which only charges $20 (one way) to get to the Big Apple. The buses are generally clean, and very popular.

CAR & MOTORCYCLE
Driving

Many visitors are surprised to learn that DC has some of the nation's worst traffic congestion. The Washington area has the third-worst problem with traffic in the nation, behind Los Angeles and San Francisco. The worst bottlenecks are in the suburbs, where the Capital Beltway (I-495) meets Maryland's I-270 and I-95, and Virginia's I-66 and I-95. Avoid the Beltway during early-morning and late-afternoon rush hours (about 6am to 9am and 3pm to 6pm). Clogged rush-hour streets in DC include the main access arteries from the suburbs: Massachusetts, Wisconsin, Connecticut and Georgia Aves NW, among others.

Certain lanes of some major traffic arteries (such as Connecticut Ave NW) change direction during rush hour, and some two-way streets become one way. Signs indicate hours of these changes, so keep your eyes peeled. Except where otherwise posted, the speed limit on DC surface streets is 25mph (15mph in alleys and school zones). You must wear your seat belt and restrain kids under three years in child-safety seats.

For emergency road service and towing, members can call the **American Automobile Association** (☎ 800-222-4357). It has a branch: **AAA travel agency** (Map pp292–3; ☎ 202-331-3000; 701 15th St NW, Ste No 100; ☺ 9am-5.30pm Mon-Fri).

Parking

Finding street parking is difficult in popular neighborhoods (Georgetown and Adams-Morgan are particularly limited), but it's reasonably easy in less-congested districts. Note that residential areas often have a two-hour limit on street parking. This limit is enforced, even if it is not metered (parking police monitor the comings and goings of cars by chalking tires). You must park at least 3ft from other cars, 5ft from private driveways and alleys, 10ft from fire hydrants and 25ft from the corner of one-way streets. You can leave a car on the street for only 72 hours before you need to move it. Parking garages in the city normally cost about $6 an hour or $25 a day.

Rental

All the major car-rental agencies and many small local ones are represented in DC, especially at the airports. Many big agencies maintain offices downtown and at Union Station. Airport rates are often better than those at downtown offices. Car-rental rates do fluctuate radically, but weekly rates are often the best deal. An economy-sized car typically costs $120 to $150 per week. Expect to pay more during peak visitor times, such as the Cherry Blossom Festival, and when big conventions and political demonstrations are in town. Add 5.75% sales tax in DC (up to 8% at the airports). The cost of petrol, at an all time high and currently showing no likely future decrease, is shockingly pricey in the city. Your best bet for cheaper fuel is to fill up further out of town.

Basic liability insurance, required by US law, is generally included in the rental price, but check the contract carefully. You can also purchase Loss/Damage Waiver (LDW) insurance, usually about $8 to $13 per day. Your personal auto-insurance policy may also cover car-rental insurance (if so, bring along a photocopy of your policy). If a rate seems too cheap, it may be because you'll get a mileage charge. Make sure you ask if the rate is for unlimited miles. Return the car with a full tank of gas. Booking well in advance of your visit usually yields the best rate.

Unfortunately for young drivers, most major agencies in DC won't rent to anyone under 25. Some local companies rent to drivers over 21 who have a major credit card, but their rates generally aren't competitive. Agencies in DC include the following:

Alamo (☎ 800-327-9633, 703-260-0182; Dulles airport)

Avis (Map pp296–7; ☎ 800-331-1212, 202-467-6585; 1722 M St NW); National airport (☎ 703-419-5815); Dulles airport (☎ 703-661-3505)

Budget (Map p304; ☎ 800-527-0700, 202-289-5373; Union Station); National airport (☎ 703-920-3360)

Dollar National airport (☎ 800-800-4000, 703-519-8700); Dulles airport (☎ 703-661-6630)

Enterprise (Map pp292–3; ☎ 800-325-8007, 202-393-0900; 1029 Vermont Ave NW); National airport (☎ 703-553-7744); Dulles airport (☎ 703-661-8800)

Hertz (Map pp292–3; ☎ 800-654-3131, 202-628-6174; 901 11th St NW); National airport (☎ 703-979-6300); Dulles airport (☎ 703-471-6020)

National (Map p304; ☎ 800-328-4567, 202-842-7454; Union Station); National airport (☎ 202-783-1590); Dulles airport (☎ 703-471-5278)

Thrifty (Map pp292–3; ☎ 800-367-2277, 202-783-0400; 1001 12th St NW); National airport (☎ 703-658-2200); Dulles airport (☎ 703-481-3599)

METRO

DC's sleek modern subway network is the Metrorail, commonly called **Metro** (☎ 202-637-7000; www.wmata.com; fares from $1.35; ☽ 5am-midnight Sun-Thu, 5am-3am Fri, 7am-3am Sat, 7am-midnight Sun). It is managed by DC, Maryland, Virginia and the federal government. Thanks to ample federal funding, its trains and stations are well marked, well maintained, well lit, climate controlled, reasonably priced, decently staffed, reliable and safe. Parking is available at certain outlying stations.

To ride Metro, buy a computerized farecard from the self-service machines inside the station entrance. The minimum fare is $1.35, although it increases for longer distances and during rush hour. The posted station-to-station chart provides exact fares for each route. You must use the farecard to enter *and* exit station turnstiles. Upon exit, the turnstile deducts the fare and returns the card. If the value of the card is insufficient, you need to use an 'Addfare' machine to add money. Other machines inside the gates dispense free bus transfers that enable you to pay just 35¢ on connecting bus routes.

A variety of passes are available, including a one-day pass ($6.50) or a weekly pass ($32.50). Special passes are available from the **Sales & Information office** (Metro Center station, 12th & F Sts NW), from the website, and from Safeway and Giant grocery stores.

TAXI

Taxicabs are plentiful in central DC; hail them with a wave of the hand. **Diamond** (☎ 202-387-4011), **Yellow** (☎ 202-546-7900) and **Capitol** (☎ 202-545-8900) are three major companies. The fare structure works on a complicated zone system rather than by the traditional metered system. DC consists of eight concentric zones (zone maps are posted in taxis), and rates are determined by how many zones you cross, the number of passengers and time of day (there's a $1 rush-hour surcharge). You pay a base fare of $5 to travel within one zone. Each additional zone costs $1.50. Each additional passenger costs $1.50. More fees are added for extra services (large bags, ordering a taxi by phone, traveling during snow emergencies). Taxis in the Virginia and Maryland suburbs use the usual metering method. Taxi drivers are usually tipped about 10%.

TRAIN

In addition to the Metro, two commuter train systems serve downtown DC from the Maryland and Virginia suburbs. Remember they're *commuter* lines: most trains run weekdays only, with the most regular service during rush hour.

Maryland Rail Commuter (MARC; ☎ 800-325-7245; www.mtamaryland.com; ⊙ 5am-midnight Mon-Fri) is a 40-station, 187-mile system connecting DC, the northern Maryland suburbs, Baltimore and eastern West Virginia. It has three lines, one of which stops at BWI airport. A fare from Baltimore to DC would cost about $7. The MARC train's only DC stop is Union Station.

From downtown DC, Virginia Railway Express (VRE; ☎ 703-684-1001, 800-RIDE-VRE; www.vre.org) serves northern Virginia's suburbs with lines to Manassas (stops include Fairfax and Alexandria) and Fredericksburg (stops include Quantico, Franconia/Springfield and Crystal City). VRE has only two stops in DC itself: Union Station and L'Enfant Plaza.

The center of train travel to/from DC is the magnificent, beaux-arts Union Station (Map p304; ☎ 202-371-9441; www.unionstationdc.com; 50 Massachusetts Ave NE; Ⓜ Union Station). It is the flagship terminal of the national train company, Amtrak (☎ 800-872-7245; www.amtrak.com), which is located on the ground floor.

Most trains departing Union Station are bound for other East Coast destinations. The station is the southern terminus of the northeast rail corridor, which stops at Baltimore, Philadelphia, New York, New Haven (Connecticut), Boston and intermediate points. There is usually at least one departure per hour throughout the day. Regular (unreserved) trains are cheapest, but pokey. Express Metroliners (reserved) to New York are faster; fastest of all are the fewer-stop Acela trains that zing to New York and on to Boston at speeds in excess of 150mph.

Trains also depart for Virginia destinations (Richmond, Williamsburg, Virginia Beach), and southern destinations, including Florida, New Orleans, Montréal and Amtrak's national hub, Chicago, where you can connect to Midwest- and West Coast-bound trains. MARC and VRE commuter trains connect Union Station to Virginia and Maryland.

Fares vary according to type of seating (coach seats or sleeping compartments) and season. Amtrak also offers a variety of all-inclusive holiday tour packages along with regional rail passes and frequent specials.

PRACTICALITIES
ACCOMMODATIONS

Accommodations options are listed in the Sleeping chapter according to neighborhood. They are organized by budget, with the cheapest rooms listed first. Accommodations prices in Washington, DC, fluctuate widely according to season and availability. Peak seasons are spring (April to June) and autumn (September to October). Hotels that cater mainly to business and government travelers drop their prices significantly – by as much as 25% – on weekends. The best rates are usually available by reserving on the Internet or through a booking agent. Many small B&B options do not advertise or book rooms *except* through a booking agent. See p224 for more information on web-based hotel deals. Check-in/check-out time is normally 3pm/noon. Many places will allow early check-in as long as the room is available, or will provide temporary luggage storage if it is not.

To make your life simpler, we've included DC's 14.5% room tax in all rates in this book.

Boutique hotels are hot in DC and there seems to be a new one opening every day. Calling ahead is rarely the best way to score a room. Instead, try an Internet booking agent, which purchases blocks of rooms at a discounted rate and then passes a portion of this discount on to the consumer. We like:

www.expedia.com

www.hoteldiscounts.com

www.hotels.com

www.lonelyplanet.com

www.orbitz.com

www.placestostay.com

Booking Services

Bed & Breakfast Accommodations Ltd (☎ 413-582-9888, 877-893-3233; www.bnbaccom.com) Specializing in private-home B&Bs and long-term accommodations in the Washington, DC, area.

Capitol Reservations (☎ 800-847-4832; www.capitolreservations.com)

Washington, DC, Accommodations (☎ 703-875-8711; www.dchotels.com)

BUSINESS

Most offices and government agencies in Washington are open 9am to 5pm Monday to Friday. Most shops are open 10am to 7pm Monday to Saturday, noon to 5pm Sunday. Smaller shops may be closed Sunday or Monday or both days. Restaurants are usually open 11:30am to 2:30pm for lunch and 5:30pm to 10pm for dinner Monday to Friday. Most restaurants tend to stay open later (until 11pm or midnight) on Friday and Saturday nights. Bars are open until 1am or 2am during the week and 3am on weekends. Banks, schools and offices are closed on all public holidays; most shops, museums and restaurants stay open on public holidays, except July 4, Thanksgiving, Christmas and New Year's Day.

CHILDREN

Washington may be the best big city in the US to travel with children: all the major museums are oriented (in part or in total) toward kids; the monuments and historical sites are child friendly; and there's plenty of parkland and green space where kids can romp. Furthermore, a vacation to Washington is usually educational. Best of all, most attractions here are absolutely free.

The *Washington Post* Weekend section, published each Friday, features 'Saturday's Child,' which details upcoming family- and kid-oriented activities, exhibits and cultural events. See also the great website **Our Kids** (www.our-kids.com) for event listings and local kid-related news. Helpful books include *Going Places with Children in Washington, DC* by Pamela McDermott and *Travel with Children* published by Lonely Planet.

Baby-sitting

Many hotels offer baby-sitting services on-site. If your lodge does not have a relationship with a childcare provider, a reputable organization is **Mothers' Aides** (☎ 703-250-0700, 800-526-2669; www.mothersaides.com), which will send a caregiver to a hotel for a minimum of four hours. Rates are generally $17 to $25 per hour depending on the number of children and the time of year.

CLIMATE

The best time to visit DC is spring (April to May) or autumn (September to October). Summer is a busy tourist season, but weather can be extremely hot and humid, especially in July and August. Plan your travel for the cooler mornings and late afternoons (advance planning can also reduce your time in queues); aim to be inside in air-conditioning during the midday heat; carry water; and wear hats, sunblock and loose, light clothing. Winters are generally mild, with temperatures hovering around freezing. The city has been known to shut down due to snow storms, especially in January. For weather conditions and forecasts, go to www.washingtonpost.com and click on 'Weather.'

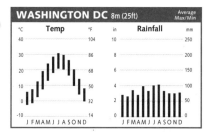

CUSTOMS

Everyone entering the US is required to fill out a customs declaration form. Visitors over 21 can bring in 200 cigarettes and 1L of alcohol. US citizens are allowed a $400 duty-free exemption; non-US citizens are allowed $100. Strict rules apply to fruit, flowers, meats and animals. There's no limit on the amount of cash, traveler's checks etc that you can bring in, but you must declare any amount over $10,000.

DISABLED TRAVELERS

DC is an excellent destination for disabled visitors. Most museums and major sights are wheelchair accessible, as are most large hotels and restaurants. The **Smithsonian** (☎ 202-633-1000, TTY 202-357-1729) and many other museums arrange special tours for people with visual, auditory or other impairments.

All Metro trains and most buses are wheelchair accessible. All Metro stations have elevators, and guide dogs are allowed on trains and buses. Disabled people who can't use public transit can use **MetroAccess** (☎ 301-562-5361), a door-to-door transport provider. Many large hotels have suites for disabled guests, but call the hotel itself – not the chain's 800 number – to check before you reserve. Larger car-rental agencies offer hand-controlled models at no extra charge. All major airlines, Greyhound buses and Amtrak trains allow service animals on board and frequently sell two-for-one packages if you need an attendant to accompany you.

Out of doors, hindrances to wheelchair users include buckled-brick sidewalks in the historic blocks of Georgetown and Capitol Hill, but sidewalks in most other parts of DC are in good shape and have dropped curbs. Unfortunately, only a handful of crosswalks, mostly near the Mall, have audible crossing signals.

The **Washington, DC, Convention & Visitors Association** (Map pp292–3; ☎ 202-789-7000; www.washington.org; 901 7th St NW; Ⓜ Gallery Pl-Chinatown) provides a fact sheet with details regarding accessibility at local attractions, lodgings and restaurants.

Hearing-impaired visitors should check out **Gallaudet University** (p116) in Northeast DC, which hosts lectures and cultural events especially for the deaf.

DISCOUNT CARDS

There are not many discount-card options, as most of the city's cultural attractions are free. The International Student Identity Card (ISIC) is recognized at some hostels, restaurants and bars in DC. Buy it at **STA Travel** (Map p299; ☎ 202-337-6464, www.statravel.com; 3301 M St NW) for $22 (you have to be a university student).

ELECTRICITY

Electric current in the USA is 110V to 115V, 60Hz AC. Outlets may accept flat two-prong or three-prong grounded plugs. Adapters are readily available at drugstores and anywhere that sells hardware.

EMBASSIES

Nearly every country in the world has an embassy in DC, making this one of the US's most vibrant multinational cities.

The handy **Electronic Embassy** (www.embassy.org) offers links to all DC embassy homepages. The hours listed represent the visa office.

Australia (Map pp296–7; ☎ 202-797-3000; 1601 Massachusetts Ave NW; Ⓨ 8:30am-2:30pm; Ⓜ Dupont Circle)

Canada (Map pp292–3; ☎ 202-682-1740; 501 Pennsylvania Ave NW; Ⓨ 9am-noon; Ⓜ Archives-Navy Memorial)

China (Map pp296–7; ☎ 202-328-2500; 2300 Connecticut Ave NW; Ⓜ Woodley Park-Zoo/Adams Morgan); visa office (Map pp300–1; ☎ 202-338-6688; 2201 Wisconsin Ave NW, Ste 110; Ⓨ 10am-12:30pm & 1-3pm; Ⓑ 30, 32, 34 or 36 from Tenleytown station)

France (Map pp300–1; ☎ 202-944-6000; 4101 Reservoir Rd NW; Ⓨ 8:45am-12:45pm; Ⓑ D6 from K St NW downtown)

Germany (Map pp290–1; ☎ 202-298-4000; 4645 Reservoir Rd NW; Ⓨ 8:30-11:30am; Ⓑ D6)

India (Map pp296–7; ☎ 202-939-7000; 2107 Massachusetts Ave NW); visa office (2536 Massachusetts Ave NW; Ⓨ 9:30am-12:30pm; Ⓜ Dupont Circle)

Ireland (Map pp296–7; ☎ 202-462-3939; 2234 Massachusetts Ave NW; Ⓨ 9am-1pm & 2-4pm; Ⓜ Dupont Circle)

Israel (Map pp290–1; ☎ 202-364-5500; 3514 International Drive NW; Ⓨ 9:30am-1pm; Ⓜ Van Ness-UDC)

Japan (Map pp300–1; ☎ 202-238-6700; 2520 Massachusetts Ave NW; Ⓨ 10am-noon & 2-4pm; Ⓜ Dupont Circle)

Mexico (Map pp292–3; ☎ 202-728-1600; 1911 Pennsylvania Ave NW; Ⓨ 8am-1pm; Ⓜ Farragut West)

Netherlands (Map pp290–1; ☎ 202-244-5300; 4200 Linnean Ave NW; Ⓨ 10am-noon; Ⓜ Van Ness-UDC)

New Zealand (Map pp300–1; ☎ 202-328-4800; 37 Observatory Circle; Ⓨ 9am-5pm; Ⓑ N6 from Farragut Sq downtown)

Romania (☎ 202-332-4846; 1607 23rd St, NW); visa office (2641 Tunlaw Rd NW, behind main office; Ⓨ 9am-12:15pm; Ⓑ 30, 32, 34 or 36)

Russia (Map pp300–1; ☎ 202-298-5700; 2650 Wisconsin Ave NW); visa office (2641 Tunlaw Rd NW, behind main office; Ⓨ 9am-12:15pm; Ⓑ 30, 32, 34 or 36)

South Africa (Map pp300–1; ☎ 202-232-4400; 3051 Massachusetts Ave NW; Ⓨ 9am-12:30pm; Ⓑ N6)

Spain (Map pp292–3; ☎ 202-452-0100; 2375 Pennsylvania Ave NW; Ⓨ 9am-12:30pm; Ⓜ Foggy Bottom-GWU)

UK (Map pp300–1; ☎ 202-588-6500; 3100 Massachusetts Ave NW); visa office (19 Observatory Circle NW; Ⓨ 8-11:30am; Ⓑ N6) The embassy is around the corner from the visa office.

EMERGENCY

Ambulance/police/fire	☎ 911
DC Rape Crisis Center	☎ 202-333-7273
Poison Control	☎ 202-362-3867
Travelers' Aid Society	☎ 202-546-3120

GAY & LESBIAN TRAVELERS

Home to more than 30 national gay and lesbian organizations and more than 300 social, athletic, religious and political support groups, DC is one of the most gay-friendly cities in the US. The community is most visible in the Dupont Circle and Capitol Hill neighborhoods, where there are many gay-friendly businesses, including the landmark bookstore **Lambda Rising** (p217). The *Washington Blade* (www.washingtonblade.com), a gay and lesbian weekly newspaper, offers coverage of politics, information about community resources, and lots and lots of nightlife and meeting-place listings. Other good sources include *WOMO* (www.womo.com), a monthly publication with information about a slew of women's organizations in the Washington area, from the DC Lesbian Avengers to Older, Wiser Lesbians (OWLS). You can also check out the Washington, DC, Convention & Visitors Association's free *Gay & Lesbian Guide to Washington, DC,* available at the organization's website (www.washington.org).

AIDS Hotline (☎ 800-342-2437) 24-hour help line.

Bi Women's Cultural Alliance (☎ 202-828-3065) Organizes casual get-togethers for lesbians and bisexual women.

Gay & Lesbian Hotline (☎ 202-833-3234) Phone counseling and referrals.

Whitman-Walker Clinic (Map pp302–3; ☎ 202-797-3500; www.wwc.org; 1407 S St NW; Ⓜ U Street-Cardozo) General health care and HIV/AIDS care.

Women in the Life (Map pp296–7; ☎ 202-483-9818; www.womeninthelife.com; 1611 Connecticut Ave NW; Ⓜ Dupont Circle) An advocacy group for lesbians. Sponsors a variety of events during the summer.

HOLIDAYS

Much of Washington, DC, shuts down over Christmas and New Year, but other holidays are bustling. The busiest times are in the spring, especially during the Cherry Blossom Festival (p15) and Easter week, early summer, and the week of Independence Day and Thanksgiving weekend. At these times, expect museums to be packed and prices to be high. Alternatively, during the month of August, and from mid-December to mid-January when Congress is not in session, crowds disappear and bargains abound. For a listing of public holidays, see p16.

INTERNET ACCESS

For travelers without a computer, the cheapest place to access the internet is at any branch of the DC public library. Fifteen-minute-limit terminals are available free to the public. If you wish to use the internet for longer than 15 minutes, you must sign up for a user's card, which is also free and allows access to computers at any DC public library:

Public Library – Cleveland Park Branch (Map pp300–1; ☎ 202-282-3080; 3310 Connecticut Ave at Macomb St NW; Ⓜ Cleveland Park)

Martin Luther King Jr Memorial Library (Map pp292–3; ☎ 202-727-1126; 901 G St NW; Ⓜ Metro Center)

Public Library – Tenley-Friendship Branch (Map pp290–1; ☎ 202-282-3090; 4450 Wisconsin Ave at Albemarle St NW; Ⓜ Tenleytown)

West End Branch (Map pp292–3; ☎ 202-724-8707; 1101 24th St at L St NW; Ⓜ Foggy Bottom-GWU)

Other commercial ventures that offer internet access:

Atomic Grounds (Map p299; ☎ 703-524-2157; 1555 Wilson Blvd; Ⓜ Rosslyn)

CyberStop Café (Map pp296–7; ☎ 202-234-2470; 1513 17th St NW; Ⓜ Dupont Circle)

Kinko's Georgetown (Map p299; ☎ 202-965-1414; 3329 M St NW; Ⓜ Rosslyn)

Kinko's White House Area (Map pp292–3; ☎ 202-466-3777; 1612 K St NW; Ⓜ Farragut North)

Kramerbooks & Afterwords Café (Map pp296–7; ☎ 202-387-1400; 1517 Connecticut Ave NW; Ⓜ Dupont Circle)

WI-FI IN DC

Many coffee shops around the city offer wi-fi with the purchase of a beverage – look for the sticker on the door announcing the place has wireless internet access. Most of the mid- to top-end hotels also offer wi-fi to guests with their own computers, although there is often a charge for this service.

LEGAL MATTERS

You must be 21 to buy or drink alcohol in DC. Club and bar bouncers are generally fastidious about seeing photo ID for proof of age, especially in university districts like Georgetown. Stiff fines, jail time and loss of your driver's license are the usual penalties for driving while intoxicated.

If you are arrested, you have the right to remain silent and the right to a lawyer. There is no legal reason to speak to a police officer if you don't want to, but never walk away from an officer until given permission. If you're arrested, you are legally allowed one phone call. If you don't have a lawyer or a relative to help you, call your embassy. The police will give you the phone number upon request.

MAPS

Lonely Planet's *Washington, DC* street map is a laminated pocket-size guide that shows all major DC attractions. ADC's *Washington, DC* street atlas is a folio-size book that shows all city streets in detail. The best place to buy maps is the **ABC Map & Travel Center** (Map pp292–3; ☎ 202-628-2608; 1636 I St NW; Ⓜ Farragut West), a wee downtown storefront packed with everything from DC activity guides to bus-route maps to huge foldout sheet maps of DC.

MEASUREMENTS

Like the rest of the country, DC is afraid of the metric system and uses the US measurement system instead. Distances are in feet, yards and miles; weights are in ounces and pounds. There's a conversion chart inside the front cover of this book.

MEDICAL SERVICES

Washington, DC, has no unexpected health dangers and excellent medical facilities; the only real concern is that a collision with the US medical system might injure your wallet. Remember to buy health insurance before you travel. Recommended medical facilities:

DC General Hospital (Map pp290–1; ☎ 202-675-5000; 1900 Massachusetts Ave SE; Ⓜ Stadium-Armory) Most noninsured emergency patients are brought here.

George Washington University Hospital (Map pp292–3; ☎ 202-715-4000; 900 23rd St NW; Ⓜ Foggy Bottom-GWU) Major teaching hospital with 24-hour emergency.

Institute of International Medicine (Map pp292–3; ☎ 202-715-5100; Ⓜ Foggy Bottom-GWU) Offers immunizations and health advice for travelers going anywhere on the planet; it's housed inside GWU.

MONEY

Most DC businesses accept cash, credit and/or debit cards and traveler's checks; for security and convenience, it is useful to have all three. A credit card may be required for renting a car or making reservations at some hotels.

ATMs

Most banks have 24-hour ATMs affiliated with various networks, including Exchange, Accel, Plus and Cirrus. If you use a credit card, however, you probably will be charged a small fee and incur interest on the withdrawal until you pay it back. Furthermore, if you use an ATM that doesn't belong to your own bank, you'll be charged $2 per withdrawal.

Changing Money

Although the airports have exchange bureaus, better rates can usually be obtained at banks in the city.

American Express (Map pp296–7; ☎ 202-457-1300; 1150 Connecticut Ave NW; Ⓜ Farragut North)

Thomas Cook (Map pp292–3; ☎ 202-237-2229; 5335 Wisconsin Ave NW; Ⓜ Friendship Heights)

Credit Cards

Carry copies of your credit-card numbers separately from the cards. If you lose a card or it's stolen, contact the company. Following are the main companies' toll-free numbers:

American Express	☎ 800-528-4800
Diners Club	☎ 800-234-6377
Discover	☎ 800-347-2683
MasterCard	☎ 800-826-2181
Visa	☎ 800-336-8472

Currency & Exchange Rates

The only currency accepted in DC is the US dollar ($), consisting of 100 cents (¢). Coins are the penny (1¢), nickel (5¢), dime (10¢), quarter (25¢), half-dollar and dollar (the gold-colored 'Sacajawea' coin). Lately, the United States Treasury has been introducing more color into paper bills in an effort to thwart counterfeits. So don't be surprised when you see red-, blue-, yellow-, and even copper-colored ink along with the original green. Keep a stash of quarters for use in vending machines, parking meters and laundromats. US bills can confuse the foreign visitor – they're all the same size – and exist in denominations of $1, $2 (rare), $5, $10, $20 (the only bills dispensed by ATMs), $50 and $100. For exchange rates, see the inside front cover of this guide.

Traveler's Checks
Traveler's checks are generally as good as cash in the US. Their major advantage is that they are replaceable if stolen. American Express and Thomas Cook (see office locations, opposite) have efficient replacement policies. A record of the check numbers is vital should you need to replace them – note them carefully and keep the record separate from the checks themselves. Buy checks in US dollars and in large denominations to avoid excessive service fees.

NEWSPAPERS & MAGAZINES
The *Washington Post* (www.washingtonpost.com) is among the nation's top newspapers. Its competitor is the conservative and less-respected *Washington Times* (www.washingtontimes.com). The *Washington Afro-American* is the city's African American newspaper. The *Washington City Paper* (www.washingtoncitypaper.com) is an alternative weekly, distributed free throughout the city. It scrutinizes DC politics and has great entertainment coverage. *On Tap* is another freebie, providing the scoop on local watering holes. Most DC neighborhoods have their own papers, such as the *Georgetown Independent* and the *Hill Rag*. The *Washingtonian* is a gossipy lifestyle magazine. The *Smithsonian* has articles about the institution – an enjoyable, less-slick *National Geographic*.

PHARMACIES
The most prominent pharmacy chain is CVS, with locations all around the city. These convenient branches are open 24 hours:

CVS Dupont Circle (Map pp296–7; ☎ 202-833-5704; 6-7 Dupont Circle; Ⓜ Dupont Circle)

CVS Thomas Circle (Map pp292–3; ☎ 202-628-0720; 1199 Vermont Ave NW; Ⓜ McPherson Sq)

PHOTOGRAPHY
There are hundreds of stores throughout the district that sell both film and digital cameras along with supplies. CVS pharmacy and Ritz Camera are just two of many chain that transfer digital images to CD or make prints from either digital or film.

You can photograph anything outdoors in DC, although video and still camera use is generally restricted in airports and other high-security areas. Depending on the terrorist-threat level in the United States at the time of your visit, photography and video use may be restricted in other public areas as well.

If you are interested in photography, check out Lonely Planet's *Travel Photography* book.

POST
The most convenient post offices are located in the Old Post Office Pavilion (Map pp292–3) and the National Postal Museum (Map p304). Branch post offices (☎ 800-275-8777) are found throughout the city.

The main post office (Map pp302–3; ☎ 202-635-5300; 900 Brentwood Rd NE; ⏰ 8am-6pm Mon-Fri, 7:30am-4pm Sat; Ⓜ Rhode Island Ave) is where you will receive poste restante. All poste restante items should be addressed to you c/o General Delivery, Main Post Office, 900 Brentwood Rd NE, Washington, DC, 20066, with 'Hold for Arrival' written on the front of the envelope. Mail is usually held for 10 days; a picture ID is required for collection of poste restante items. American Express (opposite), Thomas Cook (opposite) and Mailboxes, Etc (Map pp292–3; ☎ 202-986-4900; 17th & M Sts NW; Ⓜ Farragut North) all provide mail services for their customers.

Priority & express mail service (www.usps.com) is available. You can buy stamps at post offices and ATMs around the city. If you have the correct postage, you can drop mail into any blue street mailbox. If your items require packaging, you might call on a local packaging service, such as

Mailboxes, Etc, which provides shipping services and sells packaging materials.

Item	Postal Rates
1st-class mail within the USA	37¢ for letters up to 1oz, 22¢ each additional ounce
postcards within the USA	20¢
letters to Canada and Mexico	60¢ per ½oz
international airmail rates	80¢ per ½oz letter, 70¢ per postcard

RADIO

National Public Radio programs and classical music are on WETA-FM 90.9; more NPR and talk shows are on WAMU-FM 88.5. Alternative plays on WHFS-FM 99.1, and album-oriented dinosaur rock is on the menu at WWDC-FM 101.1. News junkies like WTOP-FM 107.7 for round-the-clock local and national political coverage. Radio heads will enjoy tours of DC-based **National Public Radio** (p21).

SAFETY

Washington, DC, has a reputation for violent crimes, but it is worth noting that the homicide rate has dropped considerably from where it was in the late '90s. For better or for worse, the violence is still very localized, and visitors do not need to worry too much about being victims themselves. Dupont Circle, Adams-Morgan, Georgetown, Foggy Bottom and most of downtown are quite safe.

Visitors should be cautious in particularly poverty-stricken areas: all of Anacostia, Southeast and Northeast DC east of about 15th Sts SE and NE, and the southeastern waterfront near the Navy Yard. These areas have attractions of their own, but use extra caution when visiting them. You should take a cab if you visit at night. Other normally safe districts may have some dodgy areas on their fringes. If you visit at night, be very aware around Shaw, especially east of 13th St NW, and in Adams-Morgan east of Columbia Rd and 16th St.

TAXES

Some tax is charged on nearly everything you buy in the USA. It may be included in the price or added onto advertised prices. When inquiring about lodging rates, always ask whether taxes are included. Unless otherwise stated, prices given in this book don't include taxes. Airport departure taxes ($6 for foreign-bound passengers) are usually included in the price of tickets bought in the US, but they may not be included with tickets bought abroad. A US$6.50 North American Free Trade Agreement tax is charged to foreigners entering the US from abroad. Both fees are essentially 'hidden' taxes added to the purchase price of your ticket.

Tax	%
DC sales tax	5.75
DC restaurants, bars, rental cars, liquor tax	10
DC room tax	14.5 (plus an additional $1.50 per-night surcharge)
Maryland sales tax	5
Maryland room tax	10
Virginia sales tax	4.5
Virginia restaurant/bar tax	8
Virginia room tax	10

TELEPHONE

Pay phones are generally coin operated and cost 50¢ to make a local call. Prepaid phone cards are sold at newsstands and pharmacies around town. Fax services are available at Kinko's (p269), Mailboxes, Etc (p271) and many upscale hotel business centers. When calling DC from abroad, first dial the US country code (1). To place an international call from DC, dial ☎ 011 + country code + area code (dropping the leading 0) + number.

Useful Numbers

DC area code	☎ 202
Directory assistance for toll-free numbers	☎ 800-555-1212
Directory assistance outside DC	☎ 1+area code+555-1212
Directory assistance within DC	☎ 411
International operator	☎ 00
Maryland suburbs area code	☎ 301
Operator	☎ 0
Toll-free prefixes	☎ 800, 888
US country code	☎ 1
Virginia suburbs area code	☎ 703, 571

TELEVISION

All of the national networks are represented on the DC dial: NBC is on Channel 4, Fox on Channel 5, ABC on Channel 7 and CBS on Channel 9. Each of these channels has its own Sunday morning political talk show based in Washington and focuses on national events: *Meet the Press* on NBC, *Face the Nation* on CBS and *This Week* on ABC. The federally supported Public Broadcasting System, based in DC, is on WETA Channel 26. C-SPAN broadcasts live from the floor of Congress (aired in offices and bars across Capitol Hill).

TIME

DC is on Eastern Standard Time, five hours behind Greenwich Mean Time. Daylight Saving Time is observed between April and October. When it's noon in DC, it's 5pm in London, 6am the next day in Sydney and 8am the next day in Auckland.

TIPPING

Gratuities are not optional in the US. Wait staff, hotel-room attendants, valet parkers and bellhops receive the minimum wage or less and depend on tips for their livelihoods. Service has to be pretty dreadful before you should consider *not* tipping. In restaurants tipping 15% of the total bill is the accepted minimum. If service is good, 20% is a decent average tip, while it is appropriate to tip more if service is exceptional. Hotel-room attendants should get $1 per guest per day, eg $10 for two people who have stayed five days. Tip taxi drivers about 10% of your fare. Airport baggage handlers get about $1 per bag. Hairdressers usually get tips, too (20%), as do coat-check staff ($1).

TOURIST INFORMATION

Washington, DC, operates several information centers in the city to help travelers arrange accommodation and develop itineraries.

DC Chamber of Commerce Visitor Information Center (Map pp292–3; ☎ 202-328-4748; www.dcchamber.org; 1300 Pennsylvania Ave NW, Ronald Reagan Bldg; ⏰ 8am-6pm Mon-Sat; Ⓜ Federal Triangle) Offers tours, maps, lodging brochures and events listings, and sells film, tickets and souvenirs.

International Visitors Information Service (☎ 703-572-2536; International Arrivals Bldg, Washington Dulles International airport; ⏰ 6:30am-10:30pm) Free brochures, maps and information.

NPS Ellipse Visitor Pavilion (Map pp292–3) Situated at the northeast corner of the Ellipse, south of the White House.

NPS Information Office (Map pp292–3; ☎ 202-208-4747, Dial-a-Park 202-619-7275; Interior Department, C St NW; ⏰ 9am-3pm Mon-Fri) Supplies pamphlets on most NPS-managed DC sites and US national parks.

Smithsonian Visitors Center (Map pp292–3; ☎ 202-357-2700, TTY 357-1729; www.smithsonian.org; 1000 Jefferson Dr SW, Smithsonian Institution Bldg – The Castle; ⏰ 9am-4pm Mon-Sat; Ⓜ Smithsonian) Everything you ever wanted to know about the museum programs.

Washington, DC, Convention & Visitors Association (Map pp292–3; ☎ 202-789-7000; www.washington .org; 901 7th St, 4th fl; ⏰ 9am-5pm Mon-Fri; Ⓜ Gallery Pl-Chinatown, Metro Center) Distributes information on lodgings, restaurants and attractions by mail, or you can pick them up at its office.

Other useful websites:

www.culturaltourismdc.org An extensive calendar of events, tours and information.

www.dc.gov The website of the local government.

www.dcmusicnet.com An extensive database of Washington, DC, area bands.

www.dcpages.com Information and links on everything from A-arts to Z-zoos.

www.dcregistry.com Extensive listings and links to DC-area businesses.

TRAVEL AGENTS

Two convenient agencies specializing in low-budget and student-oriented travel are **STA Travel** (Map p299; ☎ 202-337-6464; www.statravel.com; 3301 M St NW) and **American Youth Hostel Travel Center** (Map pp292–3; ☎ 202-737-2333, 800-909-4776; 1009 11th St NW; ⏰ 10am-7pm Mon-Sat) downtown on the 1st floor of the Hostelling International-Washington, DC, hostel. They help find airfare discounts and sell Eurail passes; the Travel Center hosts travel seminars, and maintains a small library and bookstore as well.

Online travel agencies and bid-for-tickets internet sites often offer the best deals on airfares (or at least a basis for comparison if you prefer to deal with a human travel agent). Check out www.cheaptickets.com, www.expedia.com or www.priceline.com.

Directory

PRACTICALITIES

VISAS

With the exception of Canadians, who need only proper proof of Canadian citizenship, all foreign visitors to the USA must have a valid passport, and most must also have a US visa. Check current regulations with the US embassy in your home country before you depart. Keep photocopies of these documents, too; if stolen, they'll be easier to replace. Your passport should be valid for at least six months longer than your intended stay in the USA. Documents of financial stability and/or guarantees from a US resident are sometimes required.

The reciprocal Visa Waiver Pilot Program allows citizens of certain countries to enter the USA for stays of 90 days or less without a visa. They must have a nonrefundable round-trip ticket and a passport valid for six months past their scheduled departure date. Currently, these countries are Andorra, Austria, Australia, Belgium, Brunei, Denmark, Finland, France, Germany, Iceland, Ireland, Italy, Japan, Liechtenstein, Luxembourg, Monaco, the Netherlands, New Zealand, Norway, Portugal, San Marino, Singapore, Slovenia, Spain, Sweden, Switzerland and the UK. For an updated list, see www.uscis.gov. Other travelers must obtain a visa from a US consulate or embassy. Contact your local US consulate for requirements, or see Lonely Planet's website at www.lonelyplanet.com.

Visa Extensions

Tourist visitors are usually granted a six-month stay on first arrival. If you try to extend that time, immigration authorities' first assumption is that you're working illegally – so hang on to evidence that shows you've been a model tourist (like receipts to demonstrate that you've spent money in the USA or ticket stubs to show that you've traveled extensively). You must apply for an extension *before* the six months have expired. Visitors admitted under the Visa Waiver Pilot Program cannot apply for extensions. To extend your stay, you must file Form I-539, obtained from the **Bureau of Citizenship & Immigration Service** (☎ 800-870-3676; www.uscis.gov; Washington District Office, 4420 N Fairfax Dr, Arlington,

Virginia 22203; ⏰ 8am-2:30pm Mon-Fri; Ⓜ Ballston).

VOLUNTEERING

If you want to volunteer in the DC metro area, check out www.volunteermatch.org, which offers hundreds of ways you can make a difference in the District.

WOMEN TRAVELERS

Washington is a safe and fascinating destination for women travelers: innumerable monuments and historic sites remember women's key roles in the nation and the city, including the **National Museum of Women in the Arts** (p96), the **Women in Military Service for America Memorial** (p122), and the **Mary McLeod Bethune Council House** (p98).

Women traveling alone might appreciate the all-woman hostel **Thompson-Markward Hall** (p229) on Capitol Hill. Other useful organizations:

Columbia Hospital for Women (Map pp292–3; ☎ 202-293-6500; 2425 L St NW; Ⓜ Foggy Bottom-GWU) Provides a range of health-care services.

Lammas (Map pp296–7; ☎ 202-775-8218; 1607 17th St NW; Ⓜ Dupont Circle) The city woman's bookstore: a place to find out about women-oriented groups and events.

Planned Parenthood (Map pp292–3; ☎ 202-347-8512; 1108 16th St NW; Ⓜ Farragut North) Offers obstetric, gynecological and counseling services.

Washington Women Outdoors (☎ 301-864-3070; www.washingtonwomenoutdoors.org; 19450 Caravan Dr, Germantown, Maryland 20874) About 30 miles northwest of DC. A full calendar of hikes, climbs and biking trips that are a great way to befriend local women.

WORK

Foreign visitors are not legally allowed to work in the USA without the appropriate working visa. But US citizens, especially young ones, flock here in summer to take up internships on Capitol Hill, at federal agencies and in think tanks. If you want an internship, it's important to start looking early – the fall of the preceding year is a good time to start. Find your congressional representatives' office addresses via the **Capitol switchboard** (☎ 202-224-3121).

Behind the Scenes

THE LONELY PLANET STORY

The story begins with a classic travel adventure: Tony and Maureen Wheeler's 1972 journey across Europe and Asia to Australia. There was no useful information about the overland trail then, so Tony and Maureen published the first Lonely Planet guidebook to meet a growing need.

From a kitchen table, Lonely Planet has grown to become the largest independent travel publisher in the world, with offices in Melbourne (Australia), Oakland (USA) and London (UK). Today Lonely Planet guidebooks cover the globe. There is an ever-growing list of books and information in a variety of media. Some things haven't changed. The main aim is still to make it possible for adventurous travellers to get out there – to explore and better understand the world.

At Lonely Planet we believe travellers can make a positive contribution to the countries they visit – if they respect their host communities and spend their money wisely. Every year 5% of company profit is donated to charities around the world.

THIS BOOK

This 3rd edition of Washington DC was written by Becca Blond and Aaron Anderson. Adam Karlin contributed the Politics chapter. Previous editions were written by Mara Vorhees and Laura Harger. This edition was commissioned in Lonely Planet's Oakland office and produced by the following:

Commissioning Editor Jay Cooke

Coordinating Editor Louise Clarke

Coordinating Cartographer James Ellis, Jolyon Philcox

Coordinating Layout Designer Clara Monitto

Managing Editor Melanie Dankel

Managing Cartographer Alison Lyall, David Connolly

Assisting Editors Janice Bird, Tom Smallman, Kristin Odijk, Joanne Newell

Assisting Cartographers Julie Dodkins, Joshua Geoghegan, Corey Hutchison, Herman So

Assisting Layout Designers Wibowo Rusli, Cara Smith

Cover Designer Jane Hart

Project Manager Fabrice Rocher

Thanks to Holly Alexander, Sally Darmody, Nancy Ianni, Wayne Murphy, Raphael Richards, Celia Wood

Cover photographs An illuminated statue of the 'Great Emancipator', Abraham Lincoln, casts his eye through the Doric columns of the Lincoln Memorial, Washington, DC, Dennis Johnson/Lonely Planet Images (top); Flags Around the Washington Monument at dusk, Photosforme (bottom). High school footballers, Jeff Hutchens/Getty Images (back).

Internal photographs by Dan Herrick/Lonely Planet Images, except for the following: p2, p105, p106, p107, p110, p111, p112 Richard Cummins/Lonely Planet Images; p109 (top)

Rick Gerharter/Lonely Planet Images; p5 (#3) Jeff Hutchens/Getty Images; p4 (#1), p5 (#1) Dennis Johnson/Lonely Planet Images; p109 (bottom) Allan Montaine/Lonely Planet Images; p3, p7 (#3), p8, p108 (top) John Neubauer/Lonely Planet Images; p4 (#1) Brent Winebrenner/Lonely Planet Images.

All images are copyright of the photographer unless otherwise indicated. Many of the images in this guide are available for licensing from Lonely Planet Images: www.lonelyplanetimages.com.

THANKS

BECCA BLOND & AARON ANDERSON

First off we (Aaron & Becca) owe a huge debt to Jesi Smith & Andrew Drake, in Lake Jackson, VA, for allowing us to dump Duke ('da Dog) on them for three weeks while we were at a conference in Australia, and then letting us crash at their awesome pad for a few more weeks. We are also ingratiated to Bill and Carol Holland in Poolesville, MD, for babysitting Duke while we were traipsing around the city, and allowing us to crash in Carol's massage room. To Grandma Jennie and John it was so special getting to spend time with you guys,

LONELY PLANET AUTHORS

Why is our travel information the best in the world? It's simple: our authors are independent, dedicated travellers. They don't research using just the internet or phone, and they don't take freebies in exchange for positive coverage. They travel widely, to all the popular spots and off the beaten track. They personally visit thousands of hotels, restaurants, cafés, bars, galleries, palaces, museums and more – and they take pride in getting all the details right, and telling it how it is. For more, see the authors section on **www.lonelyplanet.com**.

we both love you so much. Also, Pansy, the blue Toyota, we couldn't have gotten through the monsoons without you.

Other thanks from Becca go to all my DC crew (especially you crazy Washingtonians) for all their vocal opinions, and Colorado best pals (and VA natives) Natalie Swetye and Mike Pugh for more advice. To my girls Tami Pruitt, Shari Fischer, Heather Dickson and Danielle Martien, thanks for always being around for girl talk. To my boy Ovidio, congrats on finally tying the knot but don't ever forget the rock stars. Matt F, you are my advice guru, I couldn't have gotten through the write-up with your crack-me-up emails. To my family, you are used to this by now, but David, Patricia, Jessica, Vera, Janette, Steve, Dennis, Regina, Eric, Matt, Lily, Joe, Ted, Barbara, Lee, Spanky the Dishwasher, Brittany and Daisy, you're all the best. Finally, Aaron, you are the only MSB for me. I love you and thanks for such great teamwork.

Aaron would like to thank his Grandma Pauline, his Uncle Joe and his mom Joyce-Ann. He also wants to thank his friends Bryan C & family, Brian D, Charlene, Jon, Mark and Paul, Russell, Adam, Chris, his Austrian dad John Bacher and family, and finally the readers of the guides for their feedback and letters which showed him that considering different points of view when visiting places is essential.

OUR READERS

Many thanks to the travelers who used the last edition and wrote to us with helpful hints, useful advice and interesting anecdotes:

Helen Battleson, Lesli Bell, Anne-Trine Benjaminsen, Jo Ann Berlin, Andrzej Blachowicz, Leah Bloomfield, John Borg, Michael Borger, Christian Bosselmann, Clare & Peter Braithwaite, Jennifer Brewer, Marianne Busch, Michael Campilia, Amelie Cherlin, James Collier, Danyl Cook, Adam Crain, Marie Danch, Jeri Dansky, Mark Davey, Nuala Ui Dhuill, Tony Dragon, Mary Duffy, Laura Erion, Denise Evangelista, Rebecca Feldman, Annette Ferguson, Margo Freistadt, Erith French, Dan Frownfelter, Sean Geiger, Ross Geraghty, Yvonne Green, Deb Grupenhoff, Kristin Haltinner, Murray Hassan, Lisa Hatle, Carmen Hernandez, Annette Hilton, Krisztian Hincz, Susan Hodge, Mindy Hohman, Pat & Brian Holbrook, Kelly Holmes, Leo Hornak, Tom Hunter, Louise Joergensen, Erica Johnston, Leah Kaplan, Mirjam Knapp, Michael La Place, Zippy Larson, Yuli Law, Carl Long, Don Lotze, Marc Lutz, John Lynch, Janna Marks, Erik Marr, James Marshall, Eileen & Ted Matthew, Caitlin McCullough, Claire McKenzie, Rob McMeekin, Heather Monell, Deb Moore-Marchant, Dominique Morrow, Ron Myers, Robin Nahum, Drew Nielsen, Chris Offutt, Allan Parker, Linda Perry, Tony & Jill Porco, Wade Price, Ian Randall, Thomas Reiser, Thomas J Reiser, M Riphagen, David Roland, Liz Rose, Tyson Sackett, Norman Sadler, Arne Scheehl, Carol Schwartz, Elizabeth Sercombe, Kerri Shimshock, John Sietsema, Adam Simmons, Peter Smith, Sandy Smith, Jennie So, Martin Sobek, Christopher Springate, Carl Sprute, Ian C Story, Katie Sweetman, Julie Tambrini, Jettie van Caenegem, Rob van den Brand, Joan Walsh, Peter Wehmeier, Linda Wilson, Laura Winton, John Witten, M'Leah Woodard, Cathy Wright, Alex Young, Andrew Young

ACKNOWLEDGMENTS

Many thanks to Washington Metropolitan Area Transit Authority (WMATA) for the use of their Metro map.

SEND US YOUR FEEDBACK

We love to hear from travelers – your comments keep us on our toes and help make our books better. Our well-traveled team reads every word on what you loved or loathed about this book. Although we cannot reply individually to postal submissions, we always guarantee that your feedback goes straight to the appropriate authors, in time for the next edition. Each person who sends us information is thanked in the next edition – and the most useful submissions are rewarded with a free book.

To send us your updates – and find out about Lonely Planet events, newsletters and travel news – visit our award-winning website: www.lonelyplanet.com /contact.

Note: We may edit, reproduce and incorporate your comments in Lonely Planet products such as guidebooks, websites and digital products, so let us know if you don't want your comments reproduced or your name acknowledged. For a copy of our privacy policy visit www.lonelyplanet.com/privacy.

Notes

Notes

Notes

Index

See also separate indexes for Eating (p286), Drinking (p287), Entertainment (p287), Shopping (p287) and Sleeping (p288).

000 map pages
000 photographs

000 map pages
000 photographs

Index

MAP LEGEND

ROUTES

Tollway	One-Way Street
Freeway	Mall/Steps
Primary Road	Tunnel
Secondary Road	Walking Tour
Tertiary Road	Walking Tour Detour
Lane	Walking Trail
Under Construction	Walking Path
Track	Pedestrian Overpass
Unsealed Road	

TRANSPORT

Ferry	Rail
Metro	Rail (Underground)
Monorail	Tram
Bus Route	Cable Car, Funicular

HYDROGRAPHY

River, Creek	Canal
Intermittent River	Water

BOUNDARIES

International	Regional, Suburb
State, Provincial	Ancient Wall

AREA FEATURES

Airport	Forest
Area of Interest	Land
Building, Featured	Mall
Building, Information	Park
Building, Other	Reservation
Building, Transport	Rocks
Cemetery, Christian	Sports
Cemetery, Other	Urban

POPULATION

CAPITAL (NATIONAL)	CAPITAL (STATE)
Large City	Medium City
Small City	Town, Village

SYMBOLS

Sights/Activities
- Castle, Fortress
- Christian
- Jewish
- Monument
- Museum, Gallery
- Other Site
- Ruin
- Swimming Pool
- Zoo, Bird Sanctuary

Eating
- Eating

Drinking
- Drinking
- Café

Entertainment
- Entertainment

Shopping
- Shopping

Sleeping
- Sleeping
- Camping

Transport
- Airport, Airfield
- Bus Station
- General Transport
- Parking Area
- Taxi Rank

Information
- Bank, ATM
- Embassy/Consulate
- Hospital, Medical
- Information
- Internet Facilities
- Police Station
- Post Office, GPO
- Telephone
- Toilets
- Wheelchair Access

Geographic
- Lookout
- Mountain, Volcano
- National Park
- River Flow

Maps

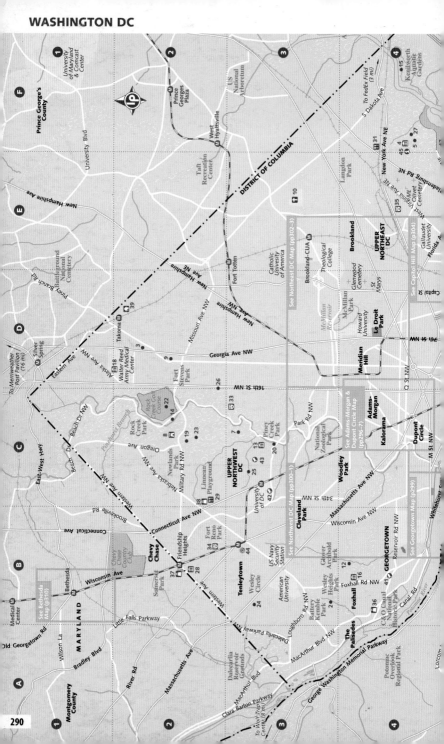

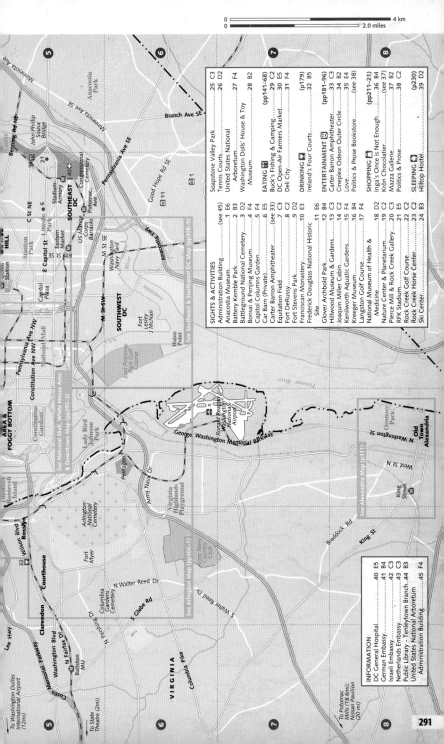

0 — 4 km
0 — 2.0 miles

See Northwest DC Map (pp300–1)

A B C D

1

Dumbarton
Oaks
Park

P St NW

29th St NW
28th St NW
Poplar St NW
27th St NW

40

Dumbarton Ave NW

30th St NW

O St NW

26

N St NW

Olive St NW

126 75

161

Pennsylvania Ave NW

27

25th St NW

23rd St NW

22nd St NW
21st St NW

Twining Ct NW
Hopkins St NW

Newport Rd NW

Ward Pl NW

New Hampshire Ave NW

19th St NW

18th St NW

Dupont
Circle

Sunderland Pl NW

Jefferson Pl NW

17th St NW
16th St NW

P St NW
O St NW

Dupont
Circle

N St NW

Scott
Circle

Massachusetts Ave NW

Rhode Island Ave NW

197

202

De Sales St NW

175

L St NW

See Adams-Morgan & Dupont Circle Map (pp296–7)

2

Juarez
Circle

191

109

172

204

174

26th St NW

24th St NW

Washington
Circle

Queen Annes La NW

176

132

M St NW

L St NW

101

195

K St NW

108

116

169

105

143

198

106

134

25

121

107

110

134

135

Farragut
North

Farragut
West

115

146

93

164

120

127

196

2

15

17

72

Connecticut Ave NW

Farragut Square

16th St NW

3

76

180

Virginia Ave NW

162

H St NW

160

87

73

George
Washington
University

I St NW

30

194

G St NW

F St NW

WHITE HOUSE
AREA &
FOGGY BOTTOM

World
Bank

Pennsylvania Ave NW

94

158

112

63

147

15

69

9 36

157

64

88

17

Lafayette
Square

South
Lawn

Foggy
Bottom / GWU

See Georgetown Map (p299)

4

34

Potomac Parkway NW

New Hampshire Ave NW

US Navy Bureau
of Medicine
& Surgery

23rd St NW

74

42

C St NW

23

1

21st St NW

20th St NW

Rawlins
Park

New York Ave NW

E St NW

18

201

D St NW

16

66

3

6

91

20

The
Ellipse

70

See Arlington Map (pp306–7)

5

Potomac River

37

Henry Bacon Dr NW

82

89

Daniel French Dr SW

35

Constitution Gardens

71

14

Reflecting Pool   68

West
Potomac
Park

10

17th St NW

Rainbow
Pool

60

19

84

Independence Ave SW

6

Lady Bird
Johnson
Park

W Basin Dr SW

83

Memorial
Park

Ohio Dr SW

Tidal
Basin

0 _____ 500 m
0 _____ 0.3 miles

Q St NW
Church St NW
Q St NW
Q St NW
E
F
G
H
142
Kingman Pl
Logan
Circle
Franklin St
NW
Bates St NW
4th St NW
1
Rhode Island Ave NW
39
168
P St NW
Kennedy Playground
O St NW
10th St NW
9th St NW
8th St NW
15th St NW
Morgan
St NW
N St NW
6th St NW
Emmanuel Ct
Pierce St NW
New Jersey Ave NW
2
M St NW
Thomas
Circle
182
12th St NW
New
Convention
Center
Mt Vernon
Square / 7th St
Convention
Centre
M St NW
New York Ave NW
133
Green Ct
NW
192
173
L St NW
Massachusetts Ave NE
179
184
98
163
166
165
Mt 13
Vernon
Square
11th St NW
186
K St NW
K St NW
102
McPherson
Square
Franklin Square
185
Vermont Ave NW
58
5th St NW
McPherson
Square
I St NW
New York Ave NW
Washington
Convention
Center
205
I St NW
1st St NW
2nd St NW
Massachusetts Ave NE
Zei Alley
NW
177
H St NW
57
8th St NW
131
128
97
123
100
H St NW
North Central Fwy
13th St NW
187
188
G St NW
Metro
Center
29
124
111
114
F St NW
38
125
103
Gallery Place/
Chinatown
138
G St NW
46
3rd St NW
F St NW
78
117
149
90
33
53
118
See Capitol Hill Map (p304)
171
113
181
152
154
139
144
130
67
10th St NW
136
137
170
129
199
41
50
Judiciary
Square
51
150
155
167
183
99
104
141
Judiciary
Square
206
Ronald Reagan
Building /
International
Trade Centre
193
22
140
156
159
8
92
145
148
15th St NW
44
65
Federal
Triangle
Pennsylvania Ave NW
95
61
24
Indiana Ave NW
96
C St NW
North Central Fwy
Louisiana Ave NW
45
Archives/Navy
Memorial
189
John
Marshall
Park
Constitution Ave NW
Constitution Ave NW
1st St NW
54
55
49
153
48
11
79
5
14th St NW
12th St NW
7th St NW
59
Madison Dr NW
National Mall
80
190
85
203
12
32
31
43
56
Maryland Ave SW
15th St SW
Smithsonian
Jefferson Dr SW
28
4
21
52
5
Independence Ave SW
7
Washington Ave SW
Department
of
Agriculture
SOUTHWEST
DC
81
Raoul Wallenberg Pl
47
62
C St SW
Hancock
Park
Federal
Center SW
14th St SW
13th St SW
12th St SW
L'Enfant Promenade
Virginia Ave SW
D St SW
2nd St SW
1st St SW
6
77
L'Enfant
Plaza
9th St SW
8th St SW
L'Enfant
Plaza
School St SW

University Pl NW
Clifton St NW
Chapin St NW
Belmont St NW
Florida Ave NW
W St NW
U St NW
15th St NW
Caroline St NW
16
111
Euclid St NW
Malcolm X Park
16th St NW
35
13 67
58
New Hampshire Ave NW
124
Fuller St NW
Meridian Hill
Mozart Pl NW
Cres Pl NW
17th St NW
17th St NW
7
V St NW
Seaton Pl NW
T St NW
72
157
Kalorama Rd NW
Ontario Rd NW
Champlain St NW
Florida Ave NW
U St NW
Willard Pl NW
59
33
88
Lanier Pl NW
Columbia Rd NW
151
Euclid St NW
65
81
76
96
143
147
128
106
46
18
117
121
118
California St NW
Vernon St NW
122
87
370
84
107
37
71
77
48
22
63
113
60
3
NW
98
Wyoming Ave NW
Ontario Pl NW
44
Adams Mill Rd NW
25
102
Adams-Morgan
Biltmore St NW
Calvert St NW
Mintwood Pl
137
Kalorama Park
Belmont Rd NW
19th St NW
Columbia Rd NW
36
20th St NW
Allen Pl NW
Ashmead Pl NW
Connecticut Ave NW
Kalorama
144
146
Wyoming Ave NW
Leroy Pl NW
UPPER NORTHWEST DC
Woodley Pl NW
Waterside Dr NW
Thornton Pl NW
Phelps Pl NW
California St NW
34
154
Calvert St NW
Shoreham Dr NW
Rock Creek Parkway NW
Wyoming Ave NW
Tracey Pl NW
24th St NW
24th St NW
Kalorama Circle

0 ─────── 500 m
0 ─────── 0.3 miles

See Northwest DC Map (pp300–1)

Q St NW
Volta Pl NW
P St NW
Georgetown University
GEORGETOWN
N St NW
Dumbarton St NW
Prospect St NW
Foxhall Rd NW
C & O Canal National Historic Park
Potomac River
Grace St NW
Whitehurst Fwy
Bank Al
M St NW
South St NW
Thomas Jefferson St NW
Pennsy Circle
George Washington Memorial Pkwy
Custis Memorial Pkwy
Colonial Terrace
Colonial Ct
N Key Blvd
22nd St N
21st Rd N
N Rolfe St
18th St N
19th St N
N Fort Myer Dr
N Moore St
Lynn St
N Kent St
N Arlington Ridge Rd
Rosslyn
Courthouse
Wilson Blvd
Clarendon Blvd
Rhodes St
N Cuinn
N Queen
16th Rd N
See Arlington Map (pp306–7)
Theodore Roosevelt Island
Theodore Roosevelt Bridge
Lady Bird Johnson Park

SIGHTS & ACTIVITIES
Aveda Georgetown	1	D1
C&O Canal	2	B2
C&O Canal Towpath	3	A2
Capital Crescent Trail (Start)	4	C2
Custis Trail (Start)	5	C3
Dalghren Chapel	(see 11)	
EFX/Blue Mercury	6	D2
Exorcist Stairs	7	D1
Freedom Park	8	C4
Georgetown Park Mall	(see 47)	
Georgetown Pool	9	C1
Georgetown University	10	B1
Healy Building	11	B1
Old Stone House	12	D2
Theodore Roosevelt Island	13	D3

EATING
	(pp147–51)	
1789	14	C1
Bangkok Bistro	15	D1
Booeymonger	16	D1
Café La Ruche	17	D2
Café Milano	18	D1
Ching Ching Cha	19	D2
Citronelle	(see 60)	
Clyde's	(see 47)	
Dean & DeLuca	20	C2

Five Guys	21	D1
J Paul's	(see 47)	
Martin's Tavern	22	D1
Mie N Yu	23	D2
Moby Dick House of Kabob	24	D2
Paolo's	25	D1
Pho 75	26	A4
Pizzeria Paradiso	27	D2
Red Hot & Blue	28	B4
Sequoia	29	D2
Vietnam Georgetown	30	D2

DRINKING
	(pp170–2)	
Bierreria Paradiso	(see 27)	
Blue Gin	31	D2
Clyde's	(see 47)	
Continental	32	B3
Degrees Bar & Lounge	(see 61)	
Garrett's	33	D2
Mr Smith's	34	D2
Sequoia	(see 29)	
Tombs	(see 14)	
Tony & Joe's	(see 29)	

ENTERTAINMENT
	(pp181–96)	
Blues Alley	35	D2
Loews Cineplex	36	D2

Rhino Bar & Pump House	37	C2
Saloun	38	D2
Third Edition	39	D2

SHOPPING
	(pp210–13)	
Appalachian Spring	40	D1
Betsey Johnson	41	D1
Better Botanicals	42	D2
Beyond Comics 2	(see 42)	
Commander Salamander	43	D1
Cowboy Western Wear	44	D1
Creighton-Davis Gallery	(see 47)	
Dean & DeLuca	(see 20)	
Deja Blue	45	D2
Dream Dresser	46	D2
Fire & Ice of Georgetown	(see 47)	
Georgetown Park Mall	47	D2
Hats in the Belfry	48	D2
Kiehl's	49	C2
Movie Madness	50	D2
Parish Gallery	51	D2
Patagonia	52	D2
Secondhand Rose	53	D1
Smash!	54	D2
Steve Madden	55	D2

SLEEPING
	(pp228–9)	
Georgetown Inn	56	D1
Georgetown Suites	57	D2
Hotel Monticello	58	D2
Key Bridge Marriot	59	B3
Latham Hotel	60	D2
Ritz-Carlton Georgetown	61	D2

TRANSPORT
	(p263)	
Big Wheel Bikes	62	C2

INFORMATION
Atomic Grounds	63	B4
C&O Canal Visitors Center	64	D2
Kinko's Georgetown	65	D2
Riggs Bank	66	D2
STA Travel	67	C2

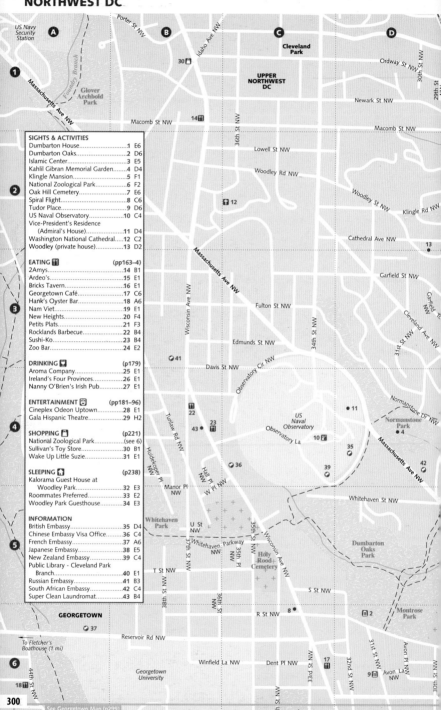

See Georgetown Map (p299)

SIGHTS & ACTIVITIES	(pp114–117)
African American Civil War Memorial	1 B5
African-American Civil War Museum	2 B5
Basilica of the National Shrine of the Immaculate Conception	3 F2
Black Fashion Museum	4 B5
Founders' Library	5 C4
Howard University	6 C4
Howard University Gallery of Art	(see 6)
John Wesley AME Zion Church	7 A6
Moorland-Spingarn Research Center	8 C4
Pope John Paul II Cultural Center	9 F1

EATING	(pp162–3)
Al Crostino	10 B5
Ben's Chili Bowl	11 B5
Colonel Brooks' Tavern & Island Jim's Crab Shack	12 H2
Coppi's Organic	13 A5
Florida Avenue Grill	14 B4
Historic Brookland Farmers Market	15 H1
Islander Caribbean	16 B5
Oohh's & Aahh's	17 B5

DRINKING	(p178)
Café Saint-Ex	18 A5
Cue Bar	19 B5

Polly's Cafe	20 A5
Saloon	21 B5
Titan	22 A5

ENTERTAINMENT	(pp181–96)
9:30 Club	23 C5
Black Cat	24 A5
Bohemian Caverns	25 B5
Café Nema	26 B5
Dance Place	27 G2
DC9	28 C5
Lincoln Theatre	29 B5
Republic Gardens	30 A5
Source Theatre Company	31 A5
Velvet Lounge	32 B5

SHOPPING	(pp219–20)
Go Mama Go!	(see 33)
Home Rule	(see 33)
Pulp	33 A6
Shop Pop	(see 33)
Up Against the Wall	34 C5

INFORMATION	
Children's National Medical Center	35 D3
Howard University Hospital	36 C5
Howard University Welcome Center	37 C6
Main Post Office	38 G5
Whitman-Walker Clinic	39 A6

E   **F**   **G**   **H**

0   500 m
0   0.3 miles

Randolph St NE

Upper Hospital Rd

Scale Gate Rd NW

Scale Gate Rd NE

John McCormack Rd

9th St NE

Perry Pl NE

Michigan Ave NE

Quincy St NE

1

Old Dr

Lower Hospital Rd NW

Hospital

Harwood Rd

9 🏛

Catholic
Univesity
of America

Perry St NE

🕆 3

Otis St NE

15

CUA/Brookland **M**

Bunker Hill Rd NE

Newton St NE

Monroe St NE

7th St NE

🏛 12

10th St NE

Lawrence St NE

2

Kearney St NE

4th St NE

Theological
College

27

Jackson St NE

9th St NE

Irving St NE

Gentain Ct NE

Hawthorne Dr NE

Michigan Ave NE

Trinity
College

8th St NE

Hamlin St NE

3

13th St NE

Girard St NE

12th St NE

Girard St NE

Lincoln Rd NE

Franklin St NE

Evarts St NE

Edgewood St NE

Brookland

Douglas St NW

Glenwood
Cemetery

Douglas St NE

10th St NE

Channing St NW

Cromwell Tce
NE

Channing St NE

4

Saratoga Ave NE

Bryant St NW

4th St NE

Bryant St NE

13th St NE

dams St NW

Ascot Pl
NE

N Capitol St

W St NW

Prospect

St
Marys

Rhode Island Ave NE

Rhode Island
Ave

M

W St NE

V St NW

V St NE

5th St NE

Brentwood Rd NE

W St NE

U St NW

Lincoln Rd NE

Summit Pl NE

2nd St NE

U St NE

38

V St NE

**UPPER
NORTHEAST
DC**

5

Todd Pl NE

T St NW

T St NE

4th St NE

T St NE

9th St NE

Seaton Pl NW

Seaton Pl NE

3rd St NE

andolph Pl NW

Randolph Pl NE

R St NE

N Capitol St

Quincy Pl NE

1st St NE

New York Ave NE

Mount Olivet Rd NE

**Brentwood
Park**

Gallaudet
University

6

See Capitol Hill Map (p304)

0   500 m
0   0.3 miles

Q St NW   **A**   Q St NE   **B**   **C**   See Northeast DC Map (pp302–3)   **D**

Bates St NW

Florida Ave NW   Porter St   New York Ave NE

P St NE   Brentwood Parkway   Gallaudet University

Eckington Pl NE   Brentwood Park   **UPPER NORTHEAST DC**

1   O St NW   O St NE   Neal Pl NE   Lincoln Cir W   Switzer Dr NE

Hanover Pl NW   Morse St NE   Queen St

New York Ave NW   N St NE   Faculty Row   • 6   Penn St

Patterson St NE   Owen Pl NE

M St NW   M St NE   Oates St NE

2   Pierce St NE   Abbey Pl NE   5th St NE   Orleans Pl NE   Florida Ave NE   Neal St NE   West Virginia Ave NE   Morse St NE   Montello Ave NE

L St NW   L St NE   Morton Pl NE   L St NE

Fenton Pl NE   🚇 49   Callan St NE   Kent Pl NE

K St NW   K St NE

I St NW   N Capitol St   I St NE   Wylie St NE

H St NW   H St NE   H St NE

3   🏛 40   G Pl NE   Ⓜ Union Station   3rd St NE   6th St NE   7th St NE   Linden Pl NE   36

G St NW   G St NE   G St NE   12th St NE

🏛 13   🍴 20   4 •   Union Station   Morris Pl NE   8th St NE   9th St NE

🍴 21   🚇 35

F St NW   32 🚇 🚇 46   F St NE   F St NE   E St NE   13th St NE

E St NW   🚇 44   E St NE   • 18   Acker St NE   E St NE   Duncan Pl NE

45   33   Lexington Pl NE   10th St NE

4   🚇   Louisiana Ave NE   Massachusetts Ave NE   Maryland Ave NE

New Jersey Ave NW   17 •   Delaware Ave NE   Union Station Plaza   D St NE   🍴 19   D St NE

24 🚇

C St NW   C St NE   🚇 47   Stanton Park   C St NE

22 🍴   🏛 15

Constitution Ave NW   Constitution Ave NE

• 7   Maryland Ave NE   3rd St NE   A St NE   Park St NE   12th Pl NE

5   • 3   • 1   Capitol Plaza   16 •   2nd St NE   5th St NE   43   11th St NE   Tennessee Ave NE

1st St NE   23 🚇 🏛   E Capitol St   **Lincoln Park**   11 •   🚇 5   🚇 12

48

9 •   2nd St SE   • 8   5th St SE   A St SE   7th St SE   North Carolina Ave SE   Kentucky Ave SE   Massachusetts Ave SE

Independence Ave SW   Independence Ave SE   🏛 14

SOUTHWEST DC   S Capitol St   41 🚇   Pennsylvania Ave SE   • 2   🚇 38   8th St SE   9th St SE   10th St SE   11th St SE   12th St SE   13th St SE

10 •   26   30   🚇 39   **Flea Market**

New Jersey Ave SE   34 🚇   31   Seward Square

C St SE   🚇 42   C St SE   C St SE

CAPITOL HILL

6   Ⓜ Capitol South   D St SE   25 🍴   South Carolina Ave SE

🍴 27   🚇 28   Ⓜ Eastern Market

🚇 29   Folger Park   4th St SE   6th St SE

Ivy St SE   North Carolina Ave SE   South Carolina Ave SE

E St SE   D St SE

See Southeast & Southwest DC Map (pp308–9)

SIGHTS & ACTIVITIES

Arlington House	1 D2
Arlington National Cemetery	2 D3
Challenger Memorial	3 D3
Confederate Monument	4 C3
Franklin Delano Roosevelt Memorial	5 G2
George Mason Memorial	6 H3
George Washington Memorial Parkway	7 G3
Iwo Jima Memorial	8 D1
Joe Louis Gravesite	9 D3
Kennedy Gravesites	10 D2
Lady Bird Johnson Park	11 E2
Mast of the Battleship USS Maine	12 C3
Mount Vernon Trail	13 F2
Nurses' Memorial	14 C3
Pentagon & Pentagon Memorial	15 F4
Pierre L'Enfant Gravesite	16 D2
President William Taft Gravesite	17 D2
Rear-Admiral Richard Byrd Jr Gravesite	18 D2
Thomas Jefferson Memorial	19 H2
Tidal Basin	20 H2
Tomb of the Unknowns	21 D3
Women in Military Service for America Memorial	22 D2

EATING 🍴 (pp164–6)

Bangkok 54 Restaurant & Bar	23 B5
El Pollo Rico	24 A2
Hard Times Café	25 A1
Kabob Bazaar	26 A1

DRINKING 🍸 (p179)

Ireland's Four Courts	27 C1
Whitlow's on Wilson	(see 30)

ENTERTAINMENT 🎭 (pp181–96)

Arlington Cinema 'N' Draft	28 B5
Clarendon Ballroom	29 A1
Iota	30 A1

INFORMATION

Visitors Center	31 E2

0 —————— 500 m
0 —————— 0.3 miles

US Navy Bureau
of Medicine
& Surgery

C St NW

The
Ellipse

E

Theodore
Roosevelt
Bridge

F

G

H

Constitution Ave NW

Constitution
Gardens

1

George Washington Memorial Parkway

Arlington
Memorial
Bridge

Reflecting Pool

Rainbow
Pool

West
Potomac
Park

Potomac River

Independence Ave SW

W Basin Dr SW

SOUTHWEST
DC

2

11

Arlington
Cemetery

Lady Bird
Johnson
Park

Memorial Ave

• 20

Tidal
Basin

See National Mall, White House Area & Downtown Map (pp292–3)

• 13

Memorial
Park

19

Halsey Dr

Jefferson Davis Hwy

Ohio Dr SW

• 5

East
Potomac
Park

31

York Dr

Nimitz Dr

Marshall Dr

Inlet
Bridge

• 6

3

Bradley Dr

Washington Blvd

Macarthur Dr

old Dr

Patton Dr

• 7

14th St Bridge

P

P

Boundary Dr

• 15

4

Pentagon

M

Old Jefferson Davis Hwy

See Southeast & Southwest DC Map (pp308–9)

Army Navy Dr

5

S Hayes St

Gravelly
Point

S Fern St

S Ball St

12th St S

Pentagon
City

M

Virginia
Highlands
Playground

15th St S

S Clark Pl

S Clark St

S Eads St

14th Rd S

S Joyce St

Ronald Reagan
Washington
National Airport

th St S

th St S

18th St S

19th St S

S Grant St

S Ives St

M

Crystal
City

Crystal Dr

6

Tidal
Basin

A **B** **C** **D**

L'Enfant
Plaza

Outlet
Bridge

See National Mall, White House Area & Downtown Map (pp292)

E St SW

Dwight D Eisenhower Fwy

Ohio Dr SW

16

Water St SW

Benjamin
Banneker
Park

7th St SW

G St SW

3rd St SW

H St SW

Southeastern
University

I St SW

Wesley
Pl SW

K St SW

Delaware Ave SW

Lansburgh
Park

East
Potomac
Park

Buckeye Dr SW

17 18

Maine Ave SW

Washington Channel

25

22

12

L St SW

2

M St SW

Waterfront/SEU

19

10

4th St SW

SOUTHWEST
DC

6

Canal St SW

N St SW

14

13

1st St SW

Ohio Dr SW

East Potomac
Park Golf
Course

Waterside
Park

11

P St SW

3

Q St

A St

3rd Ave

B St

1st Ave

S St SW

T St SW

4

2nd St SW

C St

Fort
Lesley
J McNair

4th Ave

5th Ave

V St SW

2nd Ave

D St

Buzzards
Point

Potomac River

E St

Ohio Dr SW

Greenleaf
Point

1

Hains
Point

See Arlington Map (pp306–7)

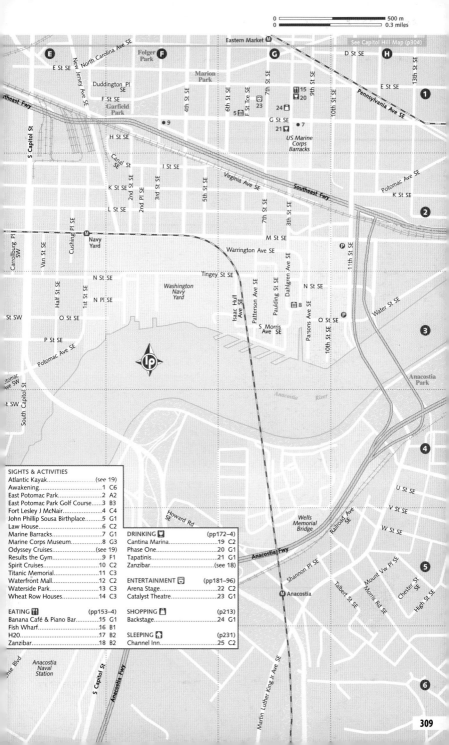

0 — 500 m
0 — 0.3 miles

Eastern Market **M**

E E St SE
New Jersey Ave SE
North Carolina Ave SE

Folger **F** Park

D St SE **H**

13th St SE

Marion Park

G

Pennsylvania Ave SE **1**

Duddington Pl SE

4th St SE
6th St SE
F St Tce SE
7th St SE
9th St SE
10th St SE

E St SE

F St SE
Garfield Park

23
5 ⊞ 15 ⊞ 20
24 ⊞

S Capitol St
Southeast Fwy

H St SE
● 9

G St SE
21 ⊞
● 7

US Marine Corps Barracks

Canal St SE
I St SE

Potomac Ave SE

Virginia Ave SE
Southeast Fwy **2**

K St SE
2nd St SE
3rd St SE
5th St SE
7th St SE
3th St SE

K St SE

2nd Pl SE
2nd Pl SE

L St SE

M St SE

Carrollburg Pl SW
Cushing Pl SE
Van St SE

M Navy Yard

Warrington Ave SE

P **11th St SE**

N St SE
N Pl SE
Half St SE
1st St SE

Washington Navy Yard

Tingey St SE

Patterson Ave SE
Paulding St SE
Dahlgren Ave SE

N St SE

Water St SE

St SW
O St SE

P St SE

Isaac Hull Ave SE
S Morris Ave SE
⊞ 8

Parsons Ave SE
O St SE
10th St SE

P

3

LP

Anacostia Park

Potomac Ave SW
Potomac Ave SE

South Capitol St

Anacostia River

4

U St SE

V St SE

Howard Rd SE

Wells Memorial Bridge

Railroad Ave SE

W St SE

Anacostia Fwy

Shannon Pl SE

5

M Anacostia

Mount Vw Pl SE
Talbert St SE
Morris Rd SE
Chester St SE
High St SE

Blvd
Anacostia Naval Station

S Capitol St
Anacostia Fwy

Martin Luther King Jr Ave SE

6

0   500 m
0   0.3 miles

EATING 🍽	(pp167–8)
Penang	1 A5
Rio Grande Café	2 B5
Tastee Diner	3 B3
Tel Aviv Café	4 B1

DRINKING 🍷	(p180)
Caddies on Cordell	5 A2
Union Jack's	6 B2

ENTERTAINMENT 😃	(p195)
Bethesda Row Cinema	7 B5

SHOPPING 🛍	(p222)
Mustard Seed	8 C4
Sansar	9 B5

SLEEPING 🏠	(p225)
Spectrum Apartment Search	10 B3

Cordell Ave

5

St Elmo Ave   6

Wilson La

Old Georgetown Rd

Woodmont Ave   3

10

East-West Hwy

Arlington Rd

Ⓜ Bethesda

Montgomery Ave

8

7

Barnes
& Noble

Bethesda Ave
9

2

Woodmont Ave

1

Wisconsin Ave

Bradley Blvd

Chevy Chase
Country Club

ALEXANDRIA

SIGHTS & ACTIVITIES (pp125–7)
Alexandria Archaeology Museum....(see 11)
Alexandria Black History Resource
 Center......................................1 D2
Athenaeum.....................................2 E4
Atlantic Kayak................................3 E1
Captain's Row.................................4 E4
Christ Church..................................5 D3
Friendship Firehouse Museum........6 D4
Gadsby's Tavern Museum................7 E4
George Washington Masonic
 National Memorial........................8 B3
Lee-Fendall House...........................9 E3
Stabler-Leadbeater Apothecary
 Museum.....................................10 E4
Torpedo Factory Art Center..........11 E4
US Patent & Trademark Office
 Museum.....................................12 D4
Watson Reading Room.............(see 1)

EATING (pp166–7)
100 King Restaurant.......................13 F4
A la Lucia.......................................14 E3
Elysium Dining Room................(see 27)
Gadsby's Tavern Restaurant.........15 E3
King Street Blues............................16 E3
Majestic Café.................................17 D3
Old Town Farmers Market.............18 E4

DRINKING (p179)
Café Salsa-Bar...............................19 D4
Founders' Brewing Co...................20 E4
Union Street Public House.............21 E4

ENTERTAINMENT (p185)
Basin Street Lounge.......................22 E4

SHOPPING (pp221–2)
Olde Towne School for Dogs........23 E4
Ten Thousand Villages..................24 D3
Torpedo Factory Art Center......(see 11)

SLEEPING (pp238–9)
Alexandria Travel Lodge...............25 E2
Holiday Inn Select Old Town........26 E4
Morrison House..............................27 D4

INFORMATION
Main Post Office............................28 D2
Ramsay House (Convention and
 Visitor Association).....................29 E4

To Fort Ward Museum
& Historic Site (5mi)

To Generous George's
Positive Pizza & Pasta
Place (3mi); West End
Dinner Theatre

To African American
Heritage Park (0.6mi)

To Birchmere
(2.5mi)

Carlisle Dve
Callahan Dve
Sunset Dve
Diagonal Rd
Amtrak
VRE
Station
King
Street
Reinekers La
Dangerfield Rd
Rosemont Ave
Prince St
Duke St
Peyton St
King St
Cameron St
Bagget Pl
West St S
West St N
Princess St
S Payne St
S Fayette St
N Fayette St
Commerce St
S Henry St
N Henry St
S Patrick St
N Patrick St
S Alfred St
N Alfred St
S Columbus St
N Columbus St
S Washington St
N Washington St
Cameron St
Prince St
S Asaph St
King St
Queen St
N Asaph St
Princess St
N St
Oronoco St
Pendleton St
Wythe St
Madison St
1st St
2nd St
Braddock Rd
S Pitt St
N Pitt St
N Royal St
S Royal St
S Fairfax St
N Fairfax St
Gentry Row
Captain's Row
N Lee St
N Union St
Waterfront Park
Founders' Park
Mount Vernon Trail
Oronoco
Park
Wilkes St
Wolfe St
Duke St
Old
Town
Alexandria
3rd St

VIRGINIA
DISTRICT OF COLUMBIA

Potomac River

0   400 m
0   0.2 miles

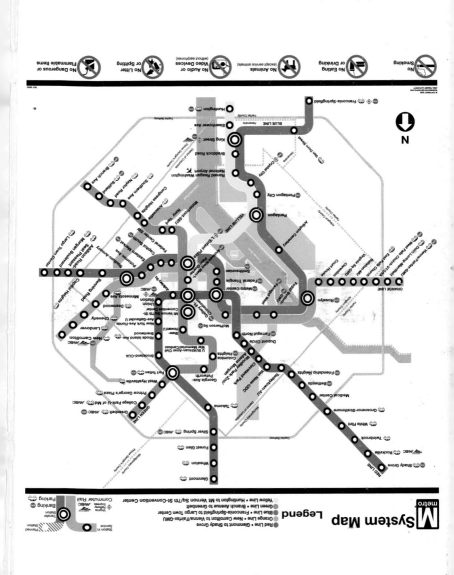

WASHINGTON METRO MAP